MASS
MEDIA IV

MASS MEDIA IV

An Introduction to Modern Communication

Ray Eldon Hiebert
University of Maryland

Donald F. Ungurait
Florida State University

Thomas W. Bohn
Ithaca College

Longman
New York & London

MASS MEDIA IV
An Introduction to Modern Communication

Longman Inc., 1560 Broadway, New York, N.Y. 10036
Associated companies, branches, and representatives
throughout the world.

Developmental Editor: Gordon T. R. Anderson
Editorial and Design Supervisor: Russell H. Till
Interior Designer: Eileen Beirne
Manufacturing Supervisor: Anne Musso
Composition: Maryland Composition Company
Printing and Binding: Alpine Press

Library of Congress Cataloging in Publication Data

Hiebert, Ray Eldon.
    Mass media IV.

    Bibliography: p.
    Includes index.
    1. Mass media. 2. Communication. I. Ungurait,
Donald F. II. Bohn, Thomas W. III. Title.
P90.H479 1984   302.2′3   84-19459
ISBN 0-582-28535-6 (pbk.)

MANUFACTURED IN THE UNITED STATES OF AMERICA
9 8 7 6 5 4 3 2 1   92 91 90 89 88 87 86 85

Contents

Preface

Mass Media IV: An Introduction to Modern Communication, is a consumer-oriented textbook written for education's primary client—the student. Becoming a mass media practitioner or mass communication scholar is a long-range goal of many of this book's readers. The authors believe this work makes an important contribution toward a wide variety of careers because a basic understanding of the theories, elements, media, functions, and effects of mass communication are essential for those seeking entry into communication industries.

Nevertheless, the primary goal of *Mass Media IV* is to assist students in becoming *critical consumers* of the mass media. Too many Americans are either nondiscriminating users or hypercritical abusers of media content. Most citizens can benefit from understanding what the mass media are, how they got that way, and how citizens can have an impact on them. Well-informed audiences can make better decisions as to what they read, listen to, and watch.

Mass Media IV is essentially a toolbox, one that is well stocked with information, ideas, and analysis that can be used to fashion an understanding of mass communication. The master-craftsman faculty member and the apprentice student may not need all the tools herein. You may use one tool considerably more than another. A teacher's specialized knowledge, skills, and goals may emphasize some tools more than others.

But, with thoughtful comparison, *Mass Media IV* contains most of what is needed to construct a basic understanding of the field.

This book was the first introductory text that had the *process* of mass communication as its core. The theories, models, systems, and elements of that process are central to what the mass media are and do. *Mass Media IV* details every phase of the communication process from communicators to media effects.

The *Mass Media IV* toolbox has two sets of power tools: Part Three, "The Media of Mass Communication," and Part Four, "The Uses of Mass Communication." The ordering of the chapters within Part Three does not imply a preference for one medium over another but simply signifies the time of the medium's development. The book came before the newspaper, which developed before the magazine, motion picture, radio, television, or sound recording. The authors also believe that all the uses—functions—roles of the mass media are equally important. We try to avoid making judgments regarding the "morality" of the functions or establishing a hierarchy of values toward these roles. *Mass Media IV* provides a straightforward approach so that the reader can progress through the media's functions and find that all the uses contain entertainment characteristics, which makes media content the art of our time.

The results of studies of mass communication are examined in a number of places in *Mass Media IV*. Chapter 13 reviews the scientific literature as to the effects of mass communication. Chapter 28 assesses the impact of mass communication in terms of observable but not necessarily measurable changes in the fabric of society. Because of growing concerns over the power and policies of the mass media a new Chapter 27 discusses mass media and ethics.

Previous editions of this book had separate chapters on "other media" and "the future of mass media." In *Mass Media IV*, "other media" are covered in the major media chapters. And in mass media terms, "the future is now." Innovations have become everyday tools so rapidly that we have attempted to cover the newest aspect of each medium in the chapter that is specific to the medium. Because of our concern for students and their career opportunities, a revised section on that subject, "Your Future in Mass Communication," appears as Chapter 29. And, as always, we try to suggest and direct independent student study in Chapter 30, "Research Materials."

Some comments may be helpful to instructors as they use *Mass Media IV* and integrate it with lectures and assignments. The book gives equal emphasis to *all* media and *all* media functions. It is more than an introduction to journalism or broadcasting. It is a "foundations" book; it reflects our concern that detailed information be available on all media, intermedia relationships, and media functions. Because of the wealth of detail in *Mass Media IV*, instructors can selectively emphasize particular media or functions and rest assured that the basics outside their personal field of interest are covered in the text. All three authors teach the introductory mass communication course at their respective universities. Frankly, we all use the book differently and emphasize our specialized areas of training and interest. We exercise our academic judgment, as every colleague must. We know there are time constraints in our lectures that limit discussion of certain topics. Nevertheless, we know the basics will be covered in detail in the text.

For students, we have this comment: Since you are among the few who have read this book, spread the word. *Mass Media IV* is written for you and others like you. It is a beginning. It is *An Introduction to Modern Communication*. We hope that it will serve as a guide in your personal journey to become a critical consumer and, perhaps, a media professional. It is a journey all three authors began before you, and we now continue with you.

THE
PROCESS
OF MASS
COMMUNICATION

PART **1**

Mass Media and the Critical Consumer

Consider for a moment the importance of mass communication in our daily lives. For many Americans, the day begins with a wake-up call from a local disc jockey on the clock radio. As we dress, a miniaturized TV set brings us the Cable News Network (CNN) and keeps us "in tune with the world." At breakfast we speed-read the local paper or *USA Today*, the first national, capsule-comment newspaper. If we drive, the tape deck soothes our nerves; if we ride the subway or bus or if we walk, a Sony Walkman sets the pace. On campus the text and the periodical fuel the educational machine. In the workplace high-speed computers process our lifestyles as well as data. At home in the evening it is MTV, HBO, CBN, BET, USA, ESPN, ABC, CBS, and NBC that make up the alphabet soup we consume. Millions of us still curl up with a good book at bedtime. We see a movie or two on the weekend at the cinema draught houses that are springing up across the American landscape, or we watch that same movie on a VHS or Beta tape deck on a large-screen video beam projector, connected to cable or a satellite dish in the back-yard. Or we go to a concert to hear songs the mass media have already taught us to sing.

Mass media consumption and work, school, and sleep are the four activities that dominate our lives, and for the indiscriminate among us it is often hard to tell which of the four is paramount.

The mass media have changed the world. They have changed American political processes. They are revolutionizing the socialization of the young. They are a vibrant part of our lives. Unfortunately, we do not always use them to our best advantage, and there is a lingering suspicion among humanists that it is the mass media that are doing the using.

WHAT ARE THE MASS MEDIA?

The mass media are institutions of public communication. They participate in every political, economic, and cultural aspect of our society. The mass media (a mass *medium* is one of the mass media) are the central focus of this book. Television is a mass medium, as are radio, motion pictures, and sound recording. Aggregated they are the electronic media. Newspapers, magazines, and books, collectively, are the major print media.

Every political state has communication media, but in the United States of America they have been fine tuned into the powerful, industrial art of mass communication. American mass media are primarily privately owned. They are locally, regionally, and nationally based. They are influential because, for the most part, they serve their audiences well and their owners profitably.

One essential characteristic sets our mass media system apart from those of many other nations. In America the mass media are not a part of the government apparatus. Our media are overwhelmingly economically independent. This financial independence, as well as our constitutional tradition of noninterference by elected officials and bureaucrats in media activities, helps guarantee our freedoms.

THE MEDIA MASSAGE

In daily human activities, communicating is our most used conscious action. The mass media bring to the communication process an intensity and complexity that is overwhelming unless examined carefully. Normally, entertainment media content comes under scrutiny in the popular press. Scholarly inquiry tends to focus on the audiences and the effects of mass communication. The viewpoint of *Mass Media IV* is that *every part of the process* is influenced by every other part of the whole. Therefore, this work seeks to be both holistic (to provide an overview) and specific (to isolate each element so as to understand its specific contribution). All elements of the mass communication process are valid areas of scholarship.

Nevertheless, increased emphasis has been placed on the medium itself as an important element in the mass communication process. Indeed, the medium may be the *key component* in the process. Marshall McLuhan, in his book *Understanding Media: The Extensions of Man*, coined the phrase "the medium *is* the message." What this means is that the carrier of communication—whether human voice or printed page, neon sign or electronic impulse—influences the message, the sender, the audience, and the effects of mass communication far more than was previously understood.

McLuhan later rephrased "the medium is the *message*" to "the medium is the *massage*." The use of "massage" rather than "message" emphasizes the carrier rather than the content. McLuhan stated that television itself, not TV programs, massages us. Almost any program content is interchangeable, McLuhan argued, and content is relatively unimportant to the impact that this "electric window" will have on humankind.

Because the mass media affect the message's *content*, the message's *sender*, and the message's *audience*, we suggest that if we do not understand mass media, we cannot understand mass communication. They speak new languages that we must learn.

The electronic media have homogenized America more in the past 30 years than was accomplished by other means in the previous three centuries. And the world is looking more alike all the time. When minuscule groups of terrorists want to emphasize their grievances, they grab us by our international electronic throats. We are all held hostage in this wired starship Earth because we participate mythically with all the other global villagers in their successes and their sorrows.

THE GLOBAL VILLAGE

America is by far the largest producer and consumer of mass communication. Americans use four times as much newsprint as Japan, which is second in the world in newsprint consumption. Almost half of the world's telephones belong to Americans. The ratio of TV sets per person in the United States is far above that of any other country. There are four times more radio sets in America than there are people to use them. America is a mass communication society.

American mass media have a great impact not only on our own society but also on the rest of the world. In Africa, for example, one is more apt to hear American than African music on radio and television, in discos and nightclubs, and on home phonographs. In Asia, American movies are shown more often than Asian movies. In Latin America, the *Reader's Digest* is more popular than any locally produced magazine. A U.S. Information Agency survey found that 15–30% of elite audiences in non-Communist countries read *Time* magazine. More than 200 of the world's leading newspapers subscribe to the *New York Times* or the *Washington Post-Los Angeles Times* news services. And United Press International, one of the two major American wire services (Associated Press is the other), sends its stories to 62 foreign countries in 48 foreign languages.

The world's masses are entertained, and the "information elite" obtain much of what they feel they need to know from our mass media. Make no mistake; American mass communication industries remain in a leadership position and are a critical force in the world today.

In a republic such as ours, the mass media play a vital role. They serve as the central nervous system of the United States—the critical information chain that vibrates without pause. Since a democracy cannot succeed without the support of the people, mass communication networks allow the public and their representatives to interact on a rapid, responsive, representative basis. The government and the governed inform and shape each other using mass communication

Take, for example, the enormously expensive operation that put a man on the moon. Why were American taxpayers willing to put billions of dollars into that venture rather than, say, to clean up the inner cities or build low-cost housing? Part of the answer may be that the space program benefited from compelling mass communication. The officials in NASA (National Aeronautics and Space Administration), the American agency responsible for space exploration, realized early that in order to get suf-

Television provides remarkable pictures of astronaut Bruce McCandless conducting experiments in space.

(Courtesy National Aeronautics and Space Administration)

ficient congressional appropriations of funds to send a man to the moon, they would have to inform the American people of their intentions and persuade people to support the space program.

NASA encouraged full media coverage of the space effort. Television, radio, and the other mass media were there when the first American rocketed into orbit; through the media, millions participated in the event. Mass communication stimulated public interest, allowing NASA to build its case with Congress, the president, and the people. By the time of the Apollo flights that did put a man on the moon, worldwide interest had been captured.

An estimated 528 million people around the world witnessed the moon landing live on television. In nations where home TV sets were not yet common, great crowds gathered in public squares to watch the event on communal television. James Clayton, a *Washington Post* writer, called the *Apollo 11* flight "the most massive publicity effort in the history of the world." He meant that without the tremendous public exposure, NASA would not have been so successful.

The media can also mobilize action against an issue, as in the Vietnam War. In retrospect, it seems clear that the battles in Vietnam were never able to generate much support from the American people. The war in Vietnam was the first war reported live and in color on television, without government censorship. Perhaps seeing the war so intimately, in all its gruesome detail, made the majority of Americans decide against it.

The news media also played an important role in bringing about the resignation of a previous occupant of the White House, Richard M. Nixon. It was the press and not the government—not the FBI, CIA, Secret Service, Justice Department, Congress, or the courts—that made public the wrong-doings of the Nixon administration. The exposure started with the persistent investigations of newspaper reporters Robert Woodward and Carl Bernstein of the *Washington Post*. Soon other newspapers and news magazines were amassing more facts. As this public information stirred Congress into holding hearings on the "Watergate crisis," the radio and TV coverage of those hearings went out to a concerned audience of millions. Richard Nixon was forced to resign his office, the first American president in history to do so.

Presidents Gerald Ford and Jimmy Carter, both bright and good men, failed to kindle enough public support to be reelected. President Ford, was unfairly characterized in the media as physically inept, and he lacked "media magic." Looking back on President Carter, the failure of his administration to solve the Iranian crisis—played out live and in color on television—was undoubtely a major reason for his defeat. President Carter's fall from power was not measured in loss of political clout but from the fact that he disappeared from the front pages and screens of America. The most powerful office in the world was media vacant for the last three months of the Carter administration. Ronald Reagan was already the focus of the news.

(AP/World Wide Photos)

President Ronald Reagan is constantly under the media microscope because the presidency is central in a news environment that is insatiable. Whether one supports this president's policies or not, his media skills are second to none, not even John F. Kennedy, who was the darling of the news establishment. President Reagan is a self-professed ideologue, conservatively committed to doing what he set out to do. He has kept his promises to lower taxes, check domestic spending, reduce inflation, rebuild defense capability, and stand up to the Russians. He ran on these issues, and he has been true to his campaign pronouncements. Ronald Reagan communicates with courtesy, charm, witty self-deprecation, and goodwill. The press and the public have not always agreed with his policies, but it is hard to find fault with his style. That media style has weathered vociferous opposition from a multitude of political action groups. If President Reagan completes a second term in office, he will be the first to do so since Dwight Eisenhower left the presidency a quarter of a century ago.

It is not only presidents who have the ability to harness media power. You and I do it every day with our time and our money. When we buy what the media are selling—when we read, listen to, or watch what the media are saying—we determine in very real terms their ability to survive.

You must also understand that ordinary citizens can and have had their say. Examples abound. The Reverend Martin Luther King, Jr., used television to right a grievous wrong in our society. The efforts of another person removed cigarette advertising from the broadcast media. A group of citizens took on the TV networks and advertisers and changed Saturday morning cartoons and the ads that appeared in those shows.

You can—you must—help harness media power for yourself, for those you love, for the things you believe in, and for the nation. Activists as well as audiences shape mass media and the media policies that affect America.

American public opinion is shaped by the ideas, information, and analysis provided by mass communication. The media play their roles very effectively and therefore are powerful instruments of stability and social progress. The mass media are neither saviors nor destroyers of our society, however. It is the people who gain access to, and make skillful use of, mass media who determine their positive or negative contributions in this country.

It is to an informed public that *Mass Media IV* directs its attention. The more you know about mass communication, the better able you will be to determine for yourself how you want to act and react. *Mass Media IV* wants you to become a critical consumer of mass communication.

FREEDOM OF COMMUNICATION

The purpose of freedom of speech, freedom of assembly, and freedom of the press is to guarantee the citizen's freedom of communication and create the potential for an informed electorate, one that is capable of making educated decisions, to emerge. "Free" speech, assembly, and press are not without costs. Maintaining these freedoms often involves struggle. A free press for example, may step on the toes of members of powerful interest groups. A free press also has responsibilities and must coexist with the other rights Americans enjoy.

Freedom of Information: Inquiry and Disclosure

Our society is information dependent, but there are clouds on the horizon concerning a citizen's rights to inquire about what the government is doing and disclose that information to other citizens. Floyd Abrams, a noted attorney who specializes in constitutional law and represents media clients, summarized a series of disturbing events in 1983 in the *New York Times Magazine*.

> A month ago today, the Reagan administration publicly released a contract that has no precedent in our nation's history. To be signed by all Government officials with access to high-level classified information, it will require these officials, for the rest of their lives, to submit for governmental review newspaper articles or books they write for the general reading public. . . .

The new requirement, warns the American Society of Newspaper Editors, is "peacetime censorship of a scope unparalleled in this country since the adoption of the Bill of Rights in 1791.". . . .

In the two and a half years it has been in power, the Reagan Administration has:

■ Consistently sought to limit the scope of the Freedom of Information Act (F.O.I.A.).

■ Barred the entry into the country of foreign speakers, including Hortensia Allende, widow of Chilean President Salvador Allende, because of concern about what they might say.

■ Inhibited the flow of films into and even out of our borders; neither Canada's Academy Award-winning "If You Love This Planet" nor the acclaimed ABC documentary about toxic waste, "The Killing Ground," escaped Administration disapproval.

■ Rewritten the classification system to assure that *more* rather than less information will be classified.

■ Subjected governmental officials to an unprecedented system of lifetime censorship.

■ Flooded universities with a torrent of threats relating to their right to publish and discuss unclassified information—usually of a scientific or technological nature—on campus.

So far, these efforts to control information have been noticed by those most directly affected, but by few others. The Administration's policies, says the American Civil Liberties Union, have been "quiet, almost stealthy, difficult to see and therefore hard to resist." There is also the feeling among many Americans that the actions of this Administration are less-than-threatening since they are fueled by the deeply felt conservative ideology of Ronald Reagan and not from the anger or meanness of spirit that, many feel, characterized the Nixon Presidency. Furthermore, wrote The Times's columnist Anthony Lewis, these actions "have had little attention from the press, perhaps because the press is not their principal target."[1]

---

[1] Floyd Abrams, "The New Effort to Control Information," *New York Times Magazine*, 25 September 1983, 22–23.

(Reprinted by permission of Newspaper Enterprise Association.)

The ability of citizens to discover the truth depends upon the availability of countervailing opinions. The action the current administration has taken concerning freedom of communication is restrictive at best, if not outright censorship. The administration's actions seriously impede our ability to make informed decisions. Our government must have more faith in "we, the people." What is most distressing in these events is the failure of the press to make us adequately aware of the consequences of these abridgements of our freedom of communication. Most Americans do not even realize they are occurring.

The Government and the Press

There is a natural tension between the press we support and the government we elect. That tension is positive for citizens. If the press and the government ever join forces, we may be in for a bad time.

For example, on 25 October 1983, armed forces of the United States of America invaded Grenada to evacuate American medical students and oust a Marxist, Cuban-backed, Russian-supplied government that had recently murdered its elected leader, Maurice Bishop. American troops were welcomed by both the students and the majority of Grenadians. The troops were "surrounded by friendlies" as they quickly defeated the Grenadian and Cuban forces, who were just as quickly repatriated to Cuba. The UN General Assembly overwhelmingly condemned America's armed intervention, even though some quietly approved of it.

During the invasion the American press corps was "out of action." The press was not informed by the Reagan administration as to the imminence of the invasion and was not allowed into Grenada during the two days of battle. When reporters attempted to enter Grenada by fishing boats, they were turned back by the U.S. Navy.

The press corps fumed. The public yawned, although some chuckled that President Reagan had tweaked the noses of "the fourth estate."

The congressional leadership of both parties fell into line by invoking the War Powers Act. A congressional study group flew to Grenada and determined that indeed the invasion had been justified "under the circumstances."

The rescued students thanked the president. The Grenadians thanked the president. American public opinion thanked the president by giving him the highest ratings of his tenure in office; 63% of those polled said they felt he was doing a good job.

The press corps fumed some more.

Who lost? Certainly not the President—and in the long run, not the news media. We, the people, lost because a serious precedent was set that abridged our freedom of communication.

Why weren't Americans more concerned? Perhaps because we had won quickly and turned out to be the good guys for a change. And perhaps because we have become somewhat less than enamored of the egotistical exercise of power by some reporters, news stars, ambush journalists, and the news apparatus in general.

The press corps has had a "bad press" of late. The TV show "60 Minutes," CBS, and Dan Rather went to court; although they won the case, they lost prestige. Cristine Craft won, then lost, then appealed a sex-discrimination suit against Metromedia. A television news team watched a man set himself on fire before they put the fire out and the networks ran the footage—to the dismay of many groups. Reporters have been caught faking pot parties. A series carried in a respected newspaper, the *Washington Post*, was fabricated by a staff writer.

Astronomical salaries to press "stars" have been demanded, paid, and reported with glee. News has become a "profit center" in local TV stations, "happy talk," not the news itself, is the centerpiece of the show. Newspeople have badgered mothers weeping over the loss of their children. They have trampled and littered the lawns of citizens they deem newsworthy. They have ambushed citizens on their doorstep to discuss allegations of guilt. Too many in the press corps have exhibited unfettered ambition and arrogance. A politician who behaved in a similar manner would be exposed to the most excruciating news coverage.

As in all areas of power brokering, the news corps needs to get its ethics and responsibilities in order. This country can ill afford more incidents like the one involving the press in Grenada—not because of the government's action but because of the people's lack of reaction to it.

The Specter of Censorship

Censorship in time of war is accepted as essential to national survival. The censorship of unpopular views in time of peace endangers the survival of our democratic ideals if not our very democracy. Censorship need not come from Washington. More frequently, the pressure to censor comes from political action groups, and it is often directed at libraries and schools. Unfortunately, it is successful more than 50% of the time.

Let us consider one recent example of an attempt at censorship. On 20 November 1983, ABC's "The Day After" blew the lid off the TV ratings; 48 million homes, or 62% of the viewing audience, were tuned in to the program. Yet this $7 million production had difficulty finding sponsors because (a) it focused on the controversial subject of the aftermath of a nuclear war; and (b) it was threatened with a boycott of advertisers who sponsored the program. The threat came from the Reverend Jerry Falwell and the Moral Majority as part of their campaign against politically sensitive programs. Mr. Falwell's request for equal time was refused by ABC. The network did broadcast a discussion of the issues raised by the film and included nationally recognized authorities with differing viewpoints in the discussion.

Censorship of the program failed, although in some areas the action succeeded. The *Tallahassee Democrat* carried the following story from the Associated Press wire service prior to the airing of the program:

ST. PETERSBURG. Pinellas County School officials have barred a high-school social-studies teacher from showing a taped version of the controversial television movie, "The Day After," to a senior class next week.

Jason Robards and Georgann Johnson console one another surrounded by the aftermath of a fictional nuclear attack in the ABC television movie, "The Day After."

(Photo by Dean Williams. Courtesy American Broadcasting Companies, Inc.)

The movie was to have been videotaped and shown as part of a curriculum on war at Pinellas Park High School.

But Scott Rose, the school superintendent, told teacher Jim Scott and others Thursday not to show the movie because it had not been prescreened and approved under guidelines for teaching controversial issues.

"When the Pentagon makes a make-more-bombs movie, we will be able to show it," Scott said.

The National Education Association has advised that the film not be shown to children under 12, and that parents of children ages 13–16 view it with them.[2]

Pressures that TV networks can withstand with relative impunity are often too strong for a school system to fend off. "The Day After," viewed at home by millions of children, usually with their parents, was unacceptable in the classroom even with parental approval and adult supervision in a course related to the show's subject.

[2] "School Officials Ban Film," *Tallahassee Democrat*, Friday, 18 November 1983.

"The Day After" is not a great work of art, but it had the potential to generate the kind of discussion that is important to a free society. Government representatives have a right to disagree and an obligation to express dissenting points of view. Pressure groups should not have the power to intimidate a school system nor censor expressions of unpopular viewpoints regarding issues of national concern. The real danger in this episode is that it could make other producers too timid to dramatize controversial subjects.

THE HEALTH AND WELL-BEING OF MASS COMMUNICATION

High costs and enormous profits have led to a concentration of media power and information control in the hands of a limited number of sources located in the Northeast. Critics have spoken of an "elite" that controls media content. They have expressed fears that these "media barons" exercise undue influence on the social, economic, and political structure of the United States.

The rise of media giants and corporate conglomerates is an understandable consequence of our economic system, but it is bothersome. It smacks of too much control in the hands of a few, a small minority that is also driven by the profit motive. The alternative seems to be government ownership and control of the media, and this is unacceptable in our society.

Two problems need to be faced:

1. There must be easier access to the media for all segments of society.
2. The media must serve all the functions required of them and not only those that are profitable.

Access and responsibility are the key issues in media today.

The state of the mass media may not be as dire as some people think, however. Cheaper means of publication and production are becoming available. Photo-offset lithography, cold-type composition, and inexpensive paper are bringing down the costs of publishing a newspaper. In many towns and cities in America, new publications, most of them weeklies, are getting established on low budgets through offset printing.

Even the electronic media are becoming less expensive. Hand-held cameras and videotape equipment are being manufactured at prices that many people can afford. This has brought about so-called people's television—neighborhood and inner-city groups that produce closed-circuit telecasting for local viewers.

And in spite of the economic warnings (explored in Chapter 4), mass media in America are more varied in their ownership and ideological commitment than in any other country in the world. One study, undertaken in the greater Washington, D.C., area, found more than 250 discrete information media to be available to the average citizen. These media included daily and weekly newspapers, regularly published local newsletters and magazines, AM and FM radio, and commercial and educational television. The average American can choose among a vast array of media.

Obviously, the media are important to us, or we would not spend the time and money on them that we do. The mass media are not without problems, however, and it is of increasing importance that both average citizen and mass communicator respond to these problems with a sense of responsibility.

In our discussion so far, a basic question remains: If mass media play such an important role in our lives, are we their victims or their masters? That is, are we managed, manipulated, massaged, and brainwashed by the media; or do the media simply reflect us and our wishes, our purchases in the marketplace, our attention, our dial twirling and page turning?

THE CRITICAL CONSUMER

The best answer is probably a combination of both. We still do not know enough about the process to make final judgments. Though we speak of communication science, we have far to go to arrive at answers to some basic questions. One thing does seem clear: The more we know about a subject, the less we can be misled about it.

During the Korean War, when brainwashing in Communist prison camps became a great concern of Americans, a team of psychologists at the University of Illinois undertook an experiment. Two groups were tested to see how their opinions on a topic could be changed. One group was given advance information about the topic; a second, control group was not. Test results showed that the ideas of the group with the advance information were less likely to be changed than were those of the control group. The experimenters concluded that the more information a person had about a topic, the less likely that he or she could be brainwashed.

It seems certain that the mass media will play an ever-increasing role in our lives; therefore, the consumer of mass communication must continue to expand his or her knowledge of the process. Educated people must develop a critical attitude toward mass media. They must be able to make judgments beyond their likes and dislikes. They must know why something is of high quality and when it is not. They must develop a critical awareness about mass media. Universities offer courses on art appreciation, music appreciation, and literary appreciation in which students are taught to be critical of these forms. We need courses in mass media appreciation that will allow students—and all consumers of mass communication—to be critically aware of the problems and processes of mass media.

Uncritical audiences are more likely to believe everything they see in print, hear on radio, or watch on television or at the movies. The power of print has intimidated human beings for hundreds of years, and the power of live-action pictures on television can be even more intimidating. Individuals who believe so completely in what they read in the newspaper or observe on television are apt to become disillusioned when they discover that what they read and see is not always 100% true. They may begin to listen to the voices of suspicion and become easy victims of the prophets of doom. They may settle into a deep-seated suspicion that they are being manipulated and manhandled by those distant puppeteers behind the scenes, by mass media newspeople and Madison Avenue advertisers.

Those who understand the process can achieve a truer perspective. The critical consumer can put what is artificial in mass communication into better balance with the reality of life. The study of mass media is important, then, because it helps the educated person understand one of the critical processes of modern life. Such understanding not only helps the participant in mass communication perform more effectively but can also enable the critical consumer to make more effective use of mass communication.

The Process
of Communication

2

When we complain about *communication problems*, we may mean that we are having *people problems*. Take, for example, the chain-gang warden in the film *Cool Hand Luke* who tells the anti-hero, "What we have here is a failure to communicate." Luke stares back in defiance. There is no communication breakdown; the failure is in the *we*—the characters involved. They choose the conflict. Luke will not bend to the will of the overseer, not because he does not understand, but because he *will not bend*. And he dies for it.

Problems, breakdowns, and conflicts between nations also may be caused by the human beings involved. When this is true, the process of communication can be skillfully used by individuals and their societies to solve these people problems.

Communication is a tool, a means, a process; it is neither good nor bad. Any morality in the act of communicating depends upon the people who generate the action.

Communication is the human cement that glues our society and all other cultures together. Communication links us emotionally and intellectually to other individuals, groups, and institutions. Communication is the cultural imperative that allows societies to exist and flourish.

Luke (Paul Newman)
tacitly refuses to
capitulate to the
arguments of the warden
(Strother Martin) in
Cool Hand Luke.

(Photo: Movie Star News, Courtesy Warner Bros., Inc.)

COMMUNICATION DEFINED

Communication is often defined functionally as "the sharing of experiences" or "the transfer of meaning" or "the transmission of values." Communication is *used* to *do* all these things, but it is more than the sum of those actions. Communication is so diverse and so complex that a single, common definition is difficult, if not impossible, to find. In fact, definitions of communication often limit our understanding of some human interactions. That is why *Mass Media* evaluates communication as a process, as a complex series of cultural actions and reactions that is *always* in motion moving toward changing goals. Communication in our accelerated existence is not a static entity fixed in time and space. It is *the* dynamic of the development of humankind. Our institutions as well as our personal lives would crumble without the process of communication.

COMMUNICATION DESCRIBED

Because satisfactory definitions of communication are difficult to come by, describing the communication process may prove more fruitful. Daily routines involve a myriad of communication experiences. These activities tend to fall into four relatively discrete categories, or levels, of communication:

1. *Intrapersonal communication* describes one person talking to himself or herself. It is the thought process. All of us think things through before we speak or act.

2. *Interpersonal communication* may be dyadic (two persons) or triadic (three people), or it may involve a few individuals communicating with one another in close emotional or physical proximity. The closer the emotional or physical links, the more personal the communication event becomes. Talking on the phone to someone you love may be a more intense experience than sending that person a letter, but both events are usually less involving than the first face-to-face encounter after a separation.

3. *Group communication* covers situations from participating in a business meeting to going to a class to attending a rock concert. As the numbers of people increase, the level of involvement often changes. Some participants are more active than others, listeners drift in and out, and the total experience tends to be less committed than interpersonal communication. Group communication has been institutionalized in the world of work as *organizational communication*, where the memo replaces the personal letter and the conference call preempts travel to a meeting. Work becomes a series of communication events.

4. *Mass communication* involves a communicator (nearly always more than one person) using a mass medium to communicate with very large audiences. It has become the primary leisure industry in America.

The four levels of the process of communication can be visualized along a **V**-shaped continuum with *intrapersonal* experiences at the closed end moving through *interpersonal* and *group* activities (which overlap in many cases) to *mass* communication at the open end of the model.

Four major changes occur as we move to the far right of the model into *the process of mass communication.*

1. *The number of participants increases dramatically.* Obviously, audiences for television, movies, best-selling novels, and urban

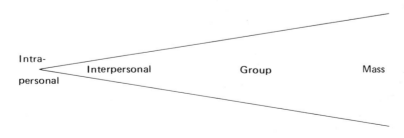

Intra-
personal   Interpersonal   Group   Mass

The V-Shaped Continuum of the Communication Process. (From Gerhart D. Wiebe in *Fundamentals of Social Psychology*, by Eugene L. Hartley and Ruth E. Hartley, New York: Knopf, 1959. Copyright © 1959 by Eugene L. Hartley and Ruth E. Hartley.)

newspapers number in the millions; but what is just as important is that the sender evolves from one person into an organized group with specialized roles.

2. *The message becomes less personal, less specialized, and more general.* This step is necessary if the content is to be understood and accepted by the largest possible portion of the public.

3. *The audience members become physically and emotionally separated in time and space from other audience members and from the mass communicator.* News magazines are read at different times and in different places by people who are usually different from other readers in that they do not care who wrote the content. Emotional commitment to other participants is at a very low level.

4. *A mass medium must always be involved for mass communication to occur.* Complex technologies become involved. "Mass comm" never occurs without a complex organization—a newspaper or record company or publisher or radio station—acting as the channel of communication.

In spite of their differences, intrapersonal, interpersonal, group, and mass communication are basically similar. Variations of the same components contribute to the same basic structure. The most useful way to analyze the common parts of the process of communication is to examine models that visualize how communication works.

BASIC MODELS OF COMMUNICATION

At all levels of communication three basic elements are evident in every model. Someone (*A*) sends something (*m*) to someone else (*B*). Students of communication use a variety of labels for these components, but essentially they are the same three things.

The figure below illustrates that both the sender (*A*) and the receiver (*B*) must act upon the message for interpersonal communication to be successful.

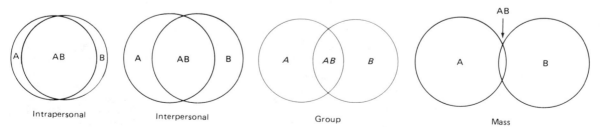

Two Visualizations of the Sender-Message-Receiver Relationship. (From *Men, Messages, and Media* by Wilbur Schramm, p. 43. Copyright © 1973 by Wilbur Schramm. Reprinted by permission of Harper & Row, Publishers, Inc.)

One of the basic concerns of communication scholars has been to emphasize that the message *sent* may not be the message *received*. The model visualizes that in every communication experience, a wide range of factors come into play. Receivers have frames of reference that they use to interpret the sender's message. The sender in turn tries to transmit messages that are easily understood and readily accepted. The more *A*'s frames of reference overlap *B*'s frames of reference, the higher the probability of understanding and eventually accepting what is being communicated.

In intrapersonal communication the circles nearly always overlap, except when we cannot remember something. Depending on the closeness of a relationship or agreement on a subject, interpersonal communication can have considerable overlap and therefore a significant chance of success. The commonality of frames of reference in group communication varies tremendously, based on the purpose of the gathering or the organization's cohesion. (Businesses refer to organizational cohesion as *teamwork*.) By the time we reach mass communication, the two circles in the figure barely touch in some cases, for example in avant-garde foreign films or recordings of Italian operas that are outside our experiences. The greater the overlap of the frames of reference, the better the chance for successful filtering of the communicator's intent by the communicatee.

One of the earliest attempts to model the communication experience was Shannon and Weaver's "mathematical model of communication." This model, developed for the American Telephone and Telegraph Company, identifies a number of elements based on the use of the telephone, which is often referred to as *telecommunication*. The transmitter, signal, signal received, and receiver are part of a system that can have noise anywhere within it. The model emphasizes the movement of a message, using a systems approach to describe the communication process.

The Weaver-Ness model adds further dimensions: codes, which are the symbols used to carry the meaning, and feedback, which is the response of the receiver to the sender. This model emphasizes that interpersonal communication is a circular, response-oriented activity that allows both

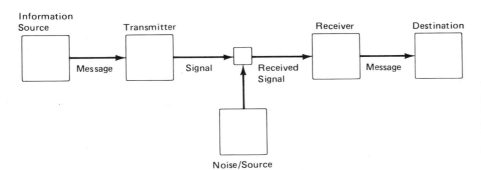

The Shannon–Weaver Schematic Diagram of a General Communication System. (Copyright © 1948, American Telephone and Telegraph Company, reprinted by permission.)

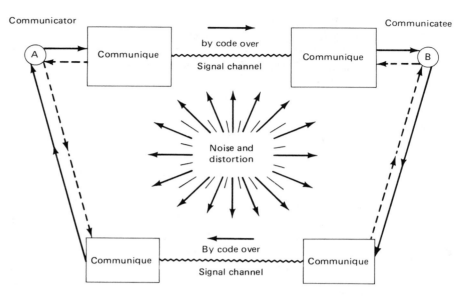

source and destination to react, modify, and clarify the communiqué by using communication pathways, or channels.

In formal, structured organizations—the military, for example—the group becomes stratified; group members refer to "the chain of command" and "going through channels." The vertical nature of this kind of organization sets up layers through which a message must pass for approval or rejection or modification. Each level is a "gate" through which a message must pass, and each gate is "guarded" by the next level of authority, the *gatekeeper.* You can imagine what happens to messages in terms of content modification and time lapse as the private tells the corporal, who tells the sergeant, who tells the lieutenant, and so on up to the general, who responds back through the chain of command—ordering the colonel, who commands the major, who tells the captain, and on down to the troops. It can be a very rigorous process.

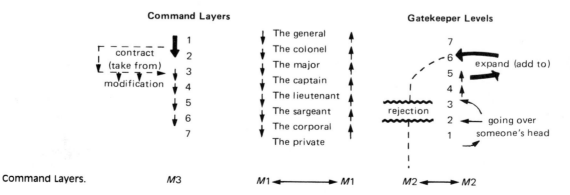

Command Layers.

Combining all the elements in the previous figure, an interpersonal–organizational model emerges. It includes the components that appear later in mass communication, albeit modified. The following figure lays out nine identifiable elements:

(a) An individual acts as the *sender* of

(b) a personal, specialized *message*,

(c) using a *code* of commonly understood symbols

(d) over a *channel* that is a pathway (airwaves or paper and pencil or an amplified microphone),

(e) through one or more members (bosses) acting as *gatekeepers* (if an organization is involed)

(f) to another individual *receiver* or small group,

(g) passing through the receivers' *frames of reference* that interpret the message

(h) so that the *receivers* can react and respond in the form of verbal, nonverbal, or written *feedback* to the sender;

(i) and, of course, *noise* or distortion can occur at any point in the process and needs to be cleaned up by either the sender, the receiver, or both.

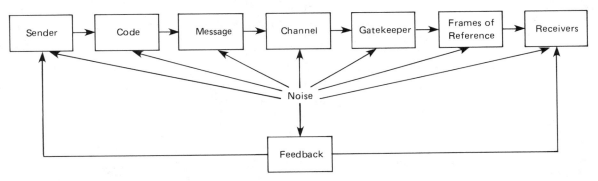

Summary Model of Interpersonal Communication.

Communication, then, is *modular*; and parts can be modified or put on the back burner as needed. Nonetheless, "the more things change, the more they remain the same." As we proceed to mass communication the components take on new variations that make them hybrids of the same aspects of intrapersonal, interpersonal, and group communication models.

Many models have been developed to visualize the changes that differentiate mass communication from other levels of the communication process. Harold Laswell's interpretation of communication as "who says

THE HUB MODEL OF MASS COMMUNICATION

The De Fleur Model of
Mass Communication, *or*
the Component of a
General System for
Achieving Isomorphism of
Meaning. (From *Theories
of Mass Communication*,
Fourth Edition by Melvin
L. De Fleur and Sandra
Ball-Rokeach. Copyright ©
1966, 1970, 1975, and 1982
by Longman Inc.)

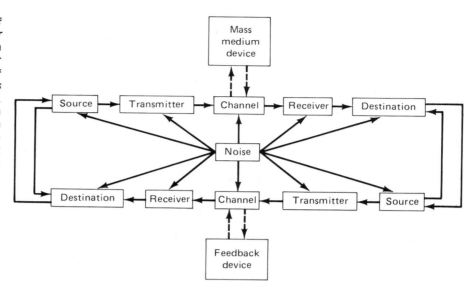

what in which channel to whom with what effect?" adds an impact element to the process; what is the effect? What happens to individuals and
societies as a result of this one communication experience and other communication experiences in combination with it?

Another model, constructed by Melvin DeFleur, outlines a more complete process than we have seen so far. In this model, source and transmitter are shown as different phases of the mass communication act carried out by the originator of the message. The channel becomes a mass
medium through which the information passes. The receiver functions as
an information recipient and decoder, transforming the physical elements
of the information into a message. The destination deciphers messages to
give them a receiver's interpretation. This is a function of the brain. Feedback is the response of the destination to the source. The model reem-
phasizes the fact that noise may interfere at any point in the mass communication process and is not identified solely with the channel or
medium. The major concern of the DeFleur model is to achieve isomorphism, or a commonly shared understanding of the meaning of the message
between source and destination.

The preceding models all contribute valuable insights. For our purposes an alternative model visualizes mass communication more completely as a process, which is a circular, dynamic, ongoing progression.
The HUB Model of Mass Communication is a set of concentric circles that
pulsate as a series of actions and reactions.

The HUB model pictures communication as a process similar to that
of dropping a pebble into a pool. This action causes ripples that expand

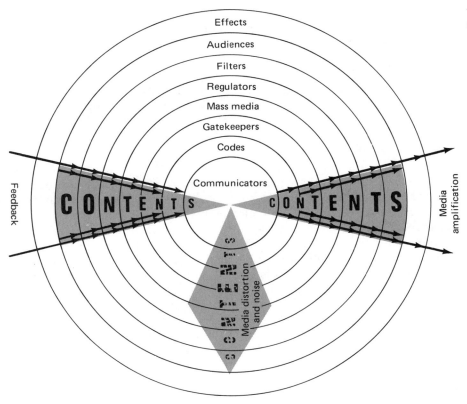

outward until they reach the sides and then a few bounce back toward the center. The content of communication (an idea or an event) is like a pebble dropped into the pool of human affairs. Many factors affect that message as it ripples out to its audience and bounces back. These factors are the components of the total process.

The HUB model's interlocked rings also reflect the physical process of sound conduction and electronic transmission. The goal, of course, is to present mass communication as clearly and completely as possible. Communication is not an uncontrollable, mysterious force. It is the process that makes us human beings.

To help us understand and harness the power of mass communication, as well as to help us manipulate the mass media rather than be manipulated by them, we must analyze this process. To begin, let us try to understand each component that makes up the HUB model and the difference, if any, from the same component at another level of the process of communication.

COMMUNICATORS   In mass communication it is extremely difficult, if not impossible, for an individual to be the sender. The mass communicator is a conglomerate or group of individuals each performing a specialized task. The communicator of "The Tonight Show Starring Johnny Carson" is not simply Johnny Carson but a total organization involving the network, local station, director, and technical staff, as well as the talent appearing on the show. *Time* magazine in the mid-twentieth century developed *group journalism*, in which the style and tone of the magazine required individual talents to blend into a successful format.

The communicators of *USA Today, People Weekly* magazine, or *Mass Media IV* are not only the writers but include reporters, copyeditors, photographers, and many others. Although individual personalities may dominate and become symbols for a television show (David Letterman), a film (George Lucas), a newspaper (Katherine Graham), or a magazine (Hugh Hefner), they are simply one part, albeit an important part, of the conglomerate communicator. An individual can be the dominant creative force, but a team of specialists is at work, and the sum of the team's talents form the conglomerate communicator.

CONTENT   Each mass medium serves a variety of functions or, more correctly, is used by individuals, groups, and society to perform specified roles. In essence, these uses and functions are the *content* of mass communication. There are at least six important tasks or categories of content.

News and Information   The mass media provide timely and important facts that have consequences in our daily lives. They survey events in the society and report them to the publics they serve.

Analysis and Interpretation   The mass media provide us with an evaluation of events, placing them in perspective. In effect, the media take editorial positions and provide insights beyond the single event.

Education and Socialization   The mass media perform educational functions such as socialization, general education, and classroom instruction. The media can serve to reinforce, modify, and replace the cultural heritage of the parent society.

Public Relations and Persuasion   The mass media serve as instruments of propaganda and public persuasion. Governments, business corporations, political action groups, and individuals seek to establish or improve relationships through mass media.

Advertising and Sales   The mass media are part of the marketing and distribution processes of our economic system. Advertising informs the public about new products, convinces them of their value, and persuades them to buy.

The mass media help people relax during their leisure time. The escapist use of media is an overlay function. This means that media entertain as they inform, analyze, persuade, educate, and sell. Entertainment is *the* popular art of our time, but the mass media also contribute to the betterment of our cultural heritage through artistic achievement.

Mass media content is dissimilar to interpersonal messages in four basic areas. Mass communication messages are (*a*) less personal; (*b*) less specialized; (*c*) more rapid; and (*d*) more transient. Obviously, the number of people involved, the distances covered, and the time span are the overriding conditions that create these differences.

Entertainment and Art

In 1983, the *Pioneer 10* spacecraft broke out of the solar system and raced into the universe. When the spacecraft was launched in 1972, scientists persuaded the National Aeronautics and Space Administration to place a plaque on board. The message was coded using a variety of symbols. The earthbound senders assumed that if the message was found by another intelligent life form, the code could be "broken." This code for interbeing communication is not unlike the codes of the mass media, whose messages are cast out and coded in what the sender hopes are understandable patterns.

CODES

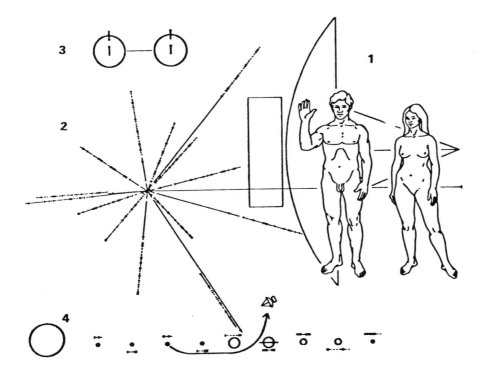

The Plaque on Board the Pioneer 10 Spacecraft, including: 1. A drawing of the life forms who send the spacecraft message with the male's hand raised in greeting. 2. A sketch of our sun radiating pulsars, or sources of cosmic radio energy. 3. The hydrogen atom which can be used as a universal clock. 4. A diagram of our solar system with the path of Pioneer 10 indicated.

Mass communication has modified and expanded the codes (languages and symbol systems) used in communication. For example, in the motion picture, new visual symbol systems often replace verbal language. Camera angles, freeze frames, and editing broaden rather than limit film's communicative capacities. Print media have utilized color printing, computer graphics, and a variety of typefaces to great effect in coding their messages.

GATEKEEPERS

Gatekeepers in mass communication are members of the media organizations that supervise the content. They are in most cases "keepers of the faith," but they also function as censors in "the standards and practices department" where they guard the company from outside legal actions.

Gatekeepers, then, are individuals working in mass media organizations—for example, wire-service editors, TV network continuity personnel, or motion-picture theater managers—who make decisions about what is communicated and how it is communicated. They are not usually originators of content; instead, they function as creative evaluators. In other words, gatekeepers can be positive forces, improving as well as eliminating content. They can delete, insert, emphasize, or deemphasize messages in mass media.

MASS MEDIA

Mass communication *never* occurs without a mass medium, and that medium is more than a mechanical device to send messages. Mass media are societal *institutions* created to perform the tasks the society requires of them. The newspaper, book, magazine, motion picture, radio, television, and sound recording are mass communication media. They are complex industrial organizations.

The devices and products of mass media—printing presses and their output (books, newspapers, and magazines), transmitters and radio and TV programs, cameras and the films shot, and recording equipment and the songs produced—can be used for personal to narrowly organizational purposes to completely mass communication ends. Books or movies are *not* the mass media; neither are computer terminals nor tape decks. The mass media are the *institutions* and *organizations* that use mechanical devices to produce content for use by audiences.

Three characteristics—complex technology, velocity, and amplitude—alter the communication process.

Complex Technology

The mass media use complicated hardware such as transmitters, printing presses, microphones, and motion-picture cameras to serve mass audiences and separate communicators from their audiences. The conglomerate communicator rarely interacts with the audience because feedback is too difficult to achieve. Telephone communication (telecommunication) employs complex technology and is used in phases of mass communication, but the telephone is primarily a medium of interpersonal and organizational communication.

The speed at which mass communication moves has made velocity an essential determinant of each medium's specific functions. Although some media are slower than others, all are faster than communication by nonmedia efforts. Radio, television, newspapers, and weekly news magazines, because of their speed of dissemination, are better vehicles for reporting the news than films, sound recordings, or books. But all are faster than delivering the news to a million homes by personal contact, letter, or telephone.

Velocity

The mass communication process is gigantic compared to interpersonal or group communication. The rock concert at Woodstock, New York, was huge; thousands of people participated. But, mediated into a phonograph album and a film, *Woodstock* reached millions. Amplitude also refers to the vast amounts of high-technology instrumentation necessary to produce, distribute, and exhibit mass communication. The number of employees, for example, are substantial. Mass communication is *big* business. Mass media are the largest leisure-time activities in the world. And the media confer status. The potential to be read, heard, and seen is power. That is amplitude.

Amplitude

The regulators of mass media, such as courts, government commissions, consumers, professional organizations, and public pressure groups, are external in the sense that they function outside the media institution. Regulation consists of laws, rules, restrictions, and informal pressures that control both the content and structure of the media. Regulators of mass media have the ability to close down a theater, delete content, influence news coverage, and revoke TV or radio licenses. Although these powers are not often used, regulators have considerable impact on decisions of the media because no one wants to incur the "wrath of regulators."

REGULATORS

The work of regulators is not unlike that of gatekeepers, but regulators exist outside the media institution and seek to modify their performance to ends that may be in conflict with the goals of mass communication organizations. Information sources, government agencies, advertisers, consumers, and professional media associations all function as regulators.

Filters are the frames of reference through which audiences receive messages. In effect, filters are the eyeglasses through which we view the world. Four kinds of filters—informational, physical, psychological, and cultural—affect an individual's ability to handle content.

FILTERS

Informational Filters

Does the audience understand the symbols or codes being used? If the novice does not understand *FORTRAN* or *COBOL* or other computer languages, computer programming is incomprehensible. Does the receiver have the same linguistic set of symbols in his head as does the sender? *Vietato fumare!* It is forbidden to smoke!

Physical Filters

Is the room too hot? Is the individual receiver running a fever? Is the projector bulb too dim? Is the chair uncomfortable? These physical conditions can affect the message.

Psychological Filters

Is the audience member emotionally committed on the issue? A woman who has been sexually assaulted will respond differently to a television program about rape than a woman who has not had the same experience and therefore has a different psychological set. A man who has been divorced will respond differently to a magazine article on "ingredients for a successful marriage" than a man who stays married or a man who has never wed.

Cultural Filters

Each of us has distinct, shared experiences. A person's cultural heritage, racial experiences, ethnic background, education, work experiences, religion, political history, etc., have an impact on how he or she filters messages culturally. Admittedly, the media are homogenizing American culture, but we still depend on our upbringing and associations and mores and values to help us interpret what the mass media tell us.

AUDIENCES

Audiences are the component of mass communication that is most studied, both by academic scholars and professional research organizations. Their studies are trying to discover who audiences are, what they want, and what happens to them when they get what they want. Mass communication receivers are aggregates that are more heterogeneous than homogeneous, relatively large, anonymous, and physically and emotionally separated from the mass communicator and most other members of the audience. The relationship between sender and receiver is impersonal at best. Audiences are fluid; they change from movie to movie, book to book, record to record. Unlike participants in interpersonal communication, they cannot be measured in time and space. George Orwell's *1984*, written in the Stalinist era, is read today by different audiences with different attitudes. Charlie Chaplin's "little tramp" plays to fresh audiences each generation. Whereas interpersonal communication exists for the moment, the place, and the person, mass communication lives on across time and place wherever it can find a receptive audience.

It is important to deemphasize the negative connotation that has come to be associated with terms like *the masses* or the *mass audience*. Audiences are made up of individuals who remain individual, discriminating human beings when they choose to become part of an audience. The word *mass*, as used in this book, is not a negative term.

In *Triumph of the Will* (1936), director Leni Riefenstal depicts the impressive spectacle of a Nazi rally in Nuremberg using one mass audience to communicate to an even larger mass audience.

(Photo: Museum of Modern Art/Film Stills Archive.)

FEEDBACK

Feedback is the communicated response of audience members to a message sent by the system. In an interpersonal communication situation, feedback is immediate. The sender and the receiver constantly exchange roles, using feedback as a means of interaction. In mass communication, feedback is delayed and diffused. Television ratings are a form of feedback, but even with overnight ratings, TV program producers have no way of knowing if they lost the audience's attention halfway through the program.

Feedback in mass communication is often expressed quantitatively: the number of *U.S. television homes* or a magazine's circulation figures or a film's box-office receipts. A radio station, newspaper, book, or recording company generally succeeds or fails on the basis of its quantitative feedback. Feedback is institutionalized, representative, and indirect when evaluated in mass communication terms.

Distortion and Noise

Mass communication has an increased possibility of media distortion and noise; and noise in the mass communication process can occur at any point, not simply in the medium. Because of its public nature, mass communication allows more interruption on a far broader level than interpersonal communication. Noise can occur in a variety of forms: static on radio or television, a poorly printed newspaper, an out-of-focus motion picture. When the consuming process is in the home, interference from noise is greatly increased and intensified. Competing stimuli from other media, the family, and the outside environment can and do interfere with message reception. Interestingly, noise is more likely to be tolerated in some media than in others. Audiences at a movie object to the same interruptions tolerated by TV audiences at home.

Amplification   The mass media confer status. Appearance in the media amplifies the importance of the individual, the message, and the event. That is why political events are staged for mass media. Every four years the Democratic and Republican conventions are organized for television.

When the news media reported the assassination attempt on Pope John Paul II, the horror of that attack was amplified (made larger than life) by its transmission to millions of homes worldwide. The amplification was psychological and cultural as well as physical. The assailant continues to be a public figure, and mass media conjecture over the involvement of the KGB keep the event alive in the public's eye as evidenced by the 1984 book *Who Shot Pope John Paul?* Watergate, the My Lai massacre, acid rain, the Equal Rights Amendment, the downing of the Korean airliner by the Russians, and other issues and events are given credence by media focus. The mass media seldom, if ever, solve problems; rather, they identify what may need to be done or at least what some who gain access to the media think may need to be done.

EFFECTS   The effects of mass communication can be placed into two overlapping categories: (a) the general *impact* the mass media have on society; and (b) the specific *effects* mass communication content has on specific individuals in the audience. Both issues are of ever-growing importance.

Historically, the media have played an important political role in American society. Freedom of the press remains a central issue. The whole Watergate phenomenon was a media event because the media participated in the political events that led to President Nixon's resignation. The media did have an impact on those events. The coverage of the Iranian hostage crisis was pervasive and contributed to President Carter's failure at the polls against President Reagan in 1980. Civil rights, women's rights, and gay rights organizations have used mass media to raise the public's awareness of these groups and change the social condition. Culturally and politically, mass communication is changing the face of America.

In the areas of specific comprehension, attitude, and behavioral changes, the "negative effects" of the mass media content are being studied concerning violence, erotica, and, especially, children and television. But there are "prosocial" implications as well.

The effects of mass communication are real, but our ability to study them has frankly not kept pace with other aspects of the process. Effects and impacts may well be central issues in the future of mass communication.

In the figure on page 23 then, we show the components of mass communication when we view it as a process. the HUB model pictures communicators, codes, gatekeepers, media, regulators, filters, audiences, and effects as concentric circles through which the content (or the message) must pass. Feedback is the response that comes back through the system to the communicator, whereas noise and amplification can affect the message and feedback as they travel through these steps in the process. If we could present the HUB model *in motion*, you could see that the concentric circles are not rigid but flex, or pulse, to the beat of a complex interaction of all the elements of the process of mass communication.

AN OVERVIEW OF THE HUB MODEL

3 Comparative Media Systems

"**W**hen we come home, the box goes on," Klaus Bohn says. Bohn lives with his wife, Irmtraud, and their two children, Manuela and Marco, in what he calls a "concrete column" on the most densely populated patch of land in West Berlin.

On the other side of Germany, on the outskirts of a small village called Viersen, in a quietly elegant home, a TV set is seldom turned on. Here is where the Fassbenders live.

There are three TV sets at the Fassbender house, counting the one they bought for the camper. But the family insists they are "selective" consumers of Television.

The Fassbenders and the Bohns represent different, but somewhat typical, European TV viewers. In some ways they are strikingly similar to their American counterparts; in other ways they are conspicuously different.

In the Bohns' apartment, it is clear that the TV knob is controlled by Klaus Bohn, the patriarch. "This family watches what Klaus watches," says Irmtraud Bohn, grinning.

Klaus Bohn considers television to be basically entertainment, but he insists that it has provided him with a broad education. He prefers nature and science shows. Irmtraud Bohn and 13-year-old Manuela are devotees of a monthly pop music program called "Hit Parade." Little Marco watches television mostly in the afternoons when he comes home from kindergarten. And in the summer there are special programs for youngsters. On weekends, films for children are more common than cartoons.

Klaus Bohn complains that there are too many boring political talk shows on television. He wishes some of them were replaced by sports programs.

Another thing that bothers the Bohn parents is the $7 or so they have to pay each month for the privilege of watching Germany's two national networks and one regional channel, all of which are publicly owned. They say for that kind of money there should be better films and not so many reruns.

Advertising on German television is limited to 20 minutes each day, or 3.5% of total broadcast time. Commercials can be shown only between 6:00 P.M. and 8:00 P.M. During these hours, German television bears some resemblance to what Americans receive from CBS, ABC, and NBC. There is a short newscast, a block of 5 minutes of advertising, then a short action film or comedy, more advertising, another film or U.S. sitcom, advertising again, then the evening news at 8:00 P.M.

On balance, TV programming in Germany is mostly low voltage, mostly laid back. That makes it possible at times for families like the Fassbenders to enjoy something distinctly European that they call a *Fernsehabend*. The word means "TV evening." It is practically an idiom in Germany, and if you had to use one word to express the difference between the German and the American ways of consuming television, *Fernsehabend* would be it.

"Sometimes Hanna and I get together for a comfortable *Fernsehabend*," Mr. Fassbender says. "We open a bottle of wine, light a couple of candles, sit back on the sofa. . . ."

Because there is a separate word for a TV evening, a word that means more than just the act of watching, one can guess that TV viewing is taken a bit more seriously in Germany than in America. It is a telling sign that TV viewing is a somewhat special event and not merely another part of the daily grind.

"I know television is important for a lot of people," says Mr. Fassbender as he sits with his family in the backyard on a warm summer night. "But this family is just too busy to care about it one way or another."

The Bohns and Fassbenders use mass media, and by doing so they interact with the world. Although the mass media experience is international, each nation has evolved its own mass communication system, based on its unique conditions and problems. The way people use mass media is based, in part, on the kind of media systems they have. The study of how these systems work is called *metacommunication*. If we look at different systems and try to understand why they are different, we will be better able to understand why they are used differently. And by comparing the American system to others, we will come to a fuller understanding of our own use of mass media.

**POLITICAL
PHILOSOPHIES AND
MASS MEDIA
SYSTEMS**

Political philosophies provide an excellent frame of reference for a particular mass media system, and so it is important to look at the major political theories of mass communication.

In a sense, all political philosophies are either libertarian or authoritarian. A libertarian political philosophy basically holds that the individual is most important in society; the state, government, and media exist to serve the needs of the individual. If they are not serving these needs, the individual can change them.

An authoritarian political philosophy basically holds that some higher order has authority over the individual. That higher order may be God, the church, the state, a political leader, a school superintendent, a teacher, or a parent. In an authoritarian society the individual exists to serve the needs of the higher order.

Historically, authoritarian societies have existed longer and have been more prevalent than libertarian ones. Although America came into being as a libertarian society, many of our social institutions, such as the family, the educational system, and much of our religion are still largely authoritarian. Libertarian societies have been prominent only in ancient democratic Greece, in Western Europe and North America since the seventeenth century, and in Japan since the end of World War II.

In an authoritarian system, the press and the other media exist to serve the needs of the state or authority in power. In a libertarian society, mass media exist to serve the needs of the individual. In the former society, the press is controlled by the government to serve its needs; in the latter,

JOEL PETT
*Courtesy Bloomington
Herald–Telephone*

(Copyright © 1984, Joel W. Pett.)

the press is free to provide whatever individuals want from it. But these descriptions are two extremes at either end of a political continuum; in no society is it as simple as either-or. Every nation can be analyzed for degrees of freedom and degrees of control of mass media.

One method used to describe, analyze, and compare different media systems and their political philosophies was outlined in the mid-1950s by Frederick Siebert, Theodore Peterson, and Wilbur Schramm in their book *Four Theories of the Press*. They reasoned that throughout the world, all media systems could be broken down into four basic types: (a) the authoritarian system; (b) the Soviet Communist system, which is a derivative of the authoritarian; (c) the libertarian system; and (d) the social responsibility system, which is a derivative of the libertarian.

The *authoritarian system* is as old as humankind. Throughout history, governments have controlled public expression. As soon as the printing press was developed in fifteenth-century Europe, the powers realized it needed to be controlled. This media philosophy is based on the political assumption that absolute power should rest in the hands of a monarch, a dictator, the ruling church, or the aristocracy.

Authoritarian System

Under this system, the mass media may be privately owned (although the broadcast media are often owned by the state), but they are directly controlled by the government through laws and licenses. Direct criticism of the government by the media is usually forbidden because the media should support the state. Media owners can have their property taken away, and they and their editors and writers can be put in jail, if their products detract from, or compete with, the power of political authority.

Much of the non-Communist world, including many countries in Latin America, Africa, the Middle East, and Asia, still operates under this system. The fascist regimes in Germany and Italy were modern European examples. Adolf Hitler expressed their basic idea when he said:

> Our law concerning the press is such that divergencies of opinion between members of the government are no longer an occasion for public exhibitions, which are not the newspapers' business. We've eliminated that conception of political freedom which holds that everybody has the right to say whatever comes into his head.[1]

The *Soviet Communist system* is simply an extension of the authoritarian. It developed from the application of Marxist-Leninist-Stalinist philosophy to mass communication in the twentieth century. Its basic assumption is that the individual needs to be changed so that he or she will share with and support society as a whole. The purpose of mass communication is to support the Communist party in its efforts to revolutionize society, to make people work for the good of the whole rather than the selfish interests of the individual.

Soviet Communist System

[1] "Hitler's Secret Conversations," from *The Great Quotations*, comp. George Seldes (New York: Lyle Stuart, 1966), 321.

"...WITH LESS THAN ONE PERCENT OF THE VOTE IN, WE ARE PROJECTING COMRADE CHERNENKO THE WINNER... BACK TO YOU, BORIS!...."

(Drawing by Gary Brookins, courtesy the *Richmond Times-Dispatch*.)

Under this system, the mass media are owned by the state, and the media communicators must be loyal party members because they have to interpret all communication from the party's point of view. Owning and operating a private printing press under this kind of system would be as serious a crime as printing counterfeit money would be in the United States. Nicolai Lenin expressed this philosophy when he wrote:

> Why should freedom of speech and freedom of the press be allowed? Why should a government which is doing what it believes to be right allow itself to be criticized? It would not allow opposition by lethal weapons. Ideas are much more fatal things than guns. Why should any man be allowed to buy a printing press and disseminate pernicious opinion calculated to embarrass the government?[2]

The Soviet Communist system prevails not only in the Soviet Union but in all Communist countries. When the Communist revolution succeeded in Cuba, for example, the first act of the new regime was to take over all institutions of communication and education including newspapers, magazine and book publishing, radio and television. The mass media and the schools were reorganized so that they would be owned by the state and run by members of Fidel Castro's Marxist party.

---

[2] Speech in Moscow, 1920. From H. L. Mencken, A *News Dictionary of Quotations on Historical Principles from Ancient and Modern Sources* (New York: Alfred Knopf, 1966), 966.

The *libertarian system* struggled into existence in seventeenth- and eighteenth-century Europe as a revolutionary act against the repressive authoritarianism of the established monarchies. The philosophers of the Enlightenment, men like John Locke and John Milton, gave libertarianism its most eloquent rationale. They argued that the state exists to serve the needs of man, not man to serve the needs of the state. Governments that do not serve the needs of the people can be overthrown. Individuals have the right to seek and know the truth and express their ideas and opinions.

Under such a system, government should not be involved in mass communication. To ensure complete freedom of expression, the media should be privately owned. Indeed, the mass media under a libertarian system should function as watchdogs of government, to make sure government is serving the needs of the people. The only restraints on media should be laws designed to protect the rights of individuals, such as libel laws to protect people's reputations and privacy laws to protect them from the media's invasion of their privacy.

The founding fathers of America—men like Jefferson and Franklin—were imbued with the philosophy of the Enlightenment, libertarianism, and democracy. They wrote the libertarian theory of the press into the First Amendment to the Constitution, which guarantees freedom of speech and of the press. James Madison, signer of the Declaration of Independence, framer of the Constitution, and president of the United States, expressed the essential argument for libertarianism in this manner:

> Nothing could be more irrational than to give the people power and to withhold from them information without which power is abused. A people who mean to be their own governors must arm themselves with power which knowledge gives. A popular government without popular information or the means of acquiring it is but a prologue to a farce or a tragedy, or perhaps both. . . . To the press alone, checkered as it is with abuses, the world is indebted for all the triumphs which have been obtained by reason and humanity over error and oppression.[3]

The libertarian system still prevails in the democracies of Western Europe and North America. But in most of these countries, including the United States, absolute freedom of speech and press has been tempered by the realities of mass societies, political conflict, global wars, economic difficulties, and threats to the security of the nation. So regulation of mass communication, particularly broadcasting, has become more complicated.

The *social responsibility system* of mass media came into existence in some democratic societies in the mid-twentieth century. The realities of mass society have caused many thoughtful people to conclude that absolute freedom for the individual may no longer be possible; too many

---

[3] Quoted from *Speaking of a Free Press* (New York: ANPA Foundation, 1970), 15.

people live close to one another and are dependent on one another for survival. After World War II ushered in the atomic age, a nongovernmental Commission on Freedom of the Press was established in the United States to discuss the relationship between the press and society in a cold-war world. Under the leadership of a Harvard philosophy professor, W. E. Hocking, the commission issued a two-volume report concluding that freedom of the press should be preserved but that it can be maintained only if the mass media accept their responsibility to society as a whole.

Many argue that a free press acts irresponsibly when it serves only its own interest in making money. Publishers and broadcasters can reap great profits by sensationalizing the news. A lurid picture or headline sells many more thousands of copies of a newspaper than a sedate one sells. If two magazines—say, *Time* and *Newsweek*—are placed side by side on the newsstand, and one features a cover picture of the president of the United States and the other a bikini-clad beauty, the magazine with the young woman on the cover usually far outsells the other. Indeed, the annual issue of *Sports Illustrated* devoted to new styles in women's bathing suits sells more newsstand copies than any other issue. Appealing to what some consider to be the lowest common denominator and prurient interests also pays off for radio, television, and movies. "Happy talk" television newscasts, for example, have been the subject of great scorn and concern in recent years.

Is such mass communication in the best interests of society? One could argue that question, depending on one's moral or ethical values. But suppose a publisher decides to publish a magazine article explaining how to build a hydrogen bomb in your basement. Would that be in the best interests of society? In a libertarian system, the freedom to do whatever you want often prevails, and in 1979 the government withdrew its case against a Wisconsin magazine, the *Progressive*, allowing it the legal right to publish an article on how to build a hydrogen bomb. Under the social responsibility theory, such an article would probably not be allowed. The mass media are still privately owned and operated under this theory, but they operate with the sanction of society. If they do not serve the interests of society, or if they threaten the security of society, they can be taken over by the government to ensure public welfare and safety.

The social responsibility theory exists in the United States to some extent in the broadcast media, but not in the print media. Radio and TV stations in the United States are privately owned, but they are licensed by the government. The Supreme Court in the early 1930s ruled that this was constitutional because broadcasters use public property, the airwaves, to communicate. Therefore the public has a right, through its government, to exercise some control over broadcasting. And if the government, through the Federal Communications Commission, finds that a broadcaster is not serving the public interest, the broadcaster's license

The H-bomb secret

To know how
is to ask why

Howard Morland

What you are about to learn is a secret — a secret that the United States and four other nations, the makers of hydrogen weapons, have gone to extraordinary lengths to protect.

The secret is in the coupling mechanism that enables an ordinary fission bomb — the kind that destroyed Hiroshima — to trigger the far deadlier energy of hydrogen fusion.

The physical pressure and heat generated by x- and gamma radiation, moving outward from the trigger at the speed of light, bounces against the weapon's inner wall and is reflected with enormous force into the sides of a carrot-shaped "pencil" which contains the fusion fuel.

That, within the limits of a single sentence, is the essence of a concept that initially eluded the physicists of the United States, the Soviet Union, Britain, France, and China; that they discovered independently and kept tenaciously to themselves, and that may not yet have occurred to the weapon makers of a dozen other nations bent on building the hydrogen bomb.

I discovered it simply by reading and asking questions, without the benefit of security clearance or access to classified materials. There was a missing piece here and there — some parts of the puzzle that eluded my search — but the general accuracy of my descriptions and diagrams has been confirmed by people in a position to know.

Why am I telling you?

It's not because I want to help you build an H-bomb. Have no fear; that would be far beyond your capability — unless you have the resources of at least a medium-sized government.

Nor is it because I want India, or Israel, or Pakistan, or South Africa to get the H-bomb sooner than they otherwise would, even though it is conceivable that the information will be helpful to them.

It isn't so much because the details themselves are helpful to an understanding of the grave public policy

'A complete one-megaton bomb ...would fit under your bed'

questions presented by hydrogen weaponry — though they may well be essential.

I am telling the secret to make a basic point as forcefully as I can: Secrecy itself, especially the power of a few designated "experts" to declare some topics off limits, contributes to a political climate in which the nuclear establishment can conduct business as usual, protecting and perpetuating the production of these horror weapons.

The pernicious effects of hydrogen bomb secrecy are well illustrated by an incident that occurred in Washington five months ago.

On October 24, 1978, Representative Ronald V. Dellums, a member of the House Armed Services Committee, sent a letter asking the Department of Energy to explain publicly why it expects a shortage of plutonium in its nuclear weapons production program.

Would the neutron bomb, which was then going into production, require more plutonium than the standard tactical nuclear weapons it is designed to replace?

Had the shortage been induced by the plutonium requirements of a new generation of multiple-warhead ballistic missiles — the Navy's Trident (successor to Poseidon), and the Air Force's M-X (successor to Minuteman III)?

What were the weapons specifications that had led the Department of Energy to contemplate a massive industrial retooling: the rebuilding of its old plutonium production plant at Hanford, Washington, and the restarting of a standby reactor at Savannah River, South Carolina?

"Each of these options will involve both financial costs and environmental costs," the letter stated. "The American people need to know the reasons for the anticipated plutonium shortage in order to have informed opinions on the cost-benefit aspects of the plutonium shortage issue."

As chairman of the Subcommittee on Fiscal and Government Affairs, and as a Congressman whose California district includes one of the nation's two nuclear weapons laboratories,

THE PROGRESSIVE / 3

The United States government occasionally attempted to prevent the publication of material it considered dangerous to public safety or national security. (Copyright © 1979 by Howard Morland. Courtesy the *Progressive*.)

can be revoked, not renewed, or a fine can be levied. As Chapter 9 indicates, however, deregulation of broadcasting is increasing, and radio and TV stations may soon resemble newspapers and magazines in their freedom from government regulation.

Thus the social responsibility theory exists in the United States to some degree. It exists to an even larger degree in most of the democracies of

Western Europe. In some European countries that consider themselves libertarian and democratic, journalists are licensed and are bound to abide by certain journalistic regulations or they can lose their license. In England, an Official Secrets Act gives the government power over any mass communication that might endanger the security of the nation; in England, the *Progressive* magazine article on building a hydrogen bomb would no doubt have been banned.

The four theories of the press serve as a starting point for the analysis of media systems; however, many countries fail to fit neatly into any of the four groupings. For example, Spain and Portugal seem to be shifting away from their traditional authoritarian systems of control. In terms of the individual media, print media in the English-speaking democracies tend to reflect the libertarian theory, whereas broadcast media in most of these countries reflect the social responsibility philosophy. Censorship of the press, be it under Hitler, Stalin, or Castro, is not significantly different whether it is called totalitarian or Communist. In fact, considerable repressive control of the media is exercised in some democracies during periods of civil strife or under wartime conditions. In other words, there are too many deviant national media systems to rely exclusively on the "four theories" approach to media systems analysis. Other models or theories of mass media include an open–closed model and an ownership-control model.

As the chart below indicates, a media system can be categorized according to how and in what manner both the receiver system and message

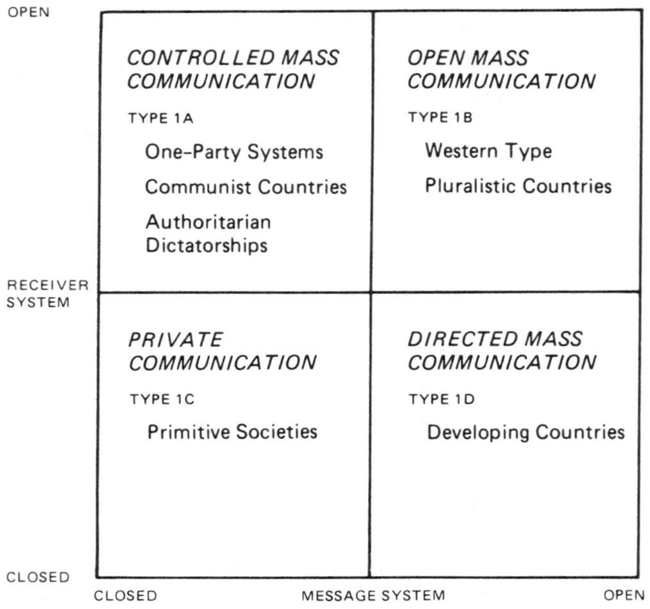

OPEN

	CONTROLLED MASS COMMUNICATION	OPEN MASS COMMUNICATION
	TYPE 1A	TYPE 1B
	One–Party Systems	Western Type
	Communist Countries	Pluralistic Countries
	Authoritarian Dictatorships	

RECEIVER SYSTEM

	PRIVATE COMMUNICATION	DIRECTED MASS COMMUNICATION
	TYPE 1C	TYPE 1D
	Primitive Societies	Developing Countries

CLOSED

Open/Closed Model.   CLOSED   MESSAGE SYSTEM   OPEN system are open or closed. An open mass communication system allows as much audience and message freedom as possible. This would be similar to the libertarian and social responsibility theory of the press. The private system that incorporates such communication as telephone calls and mail is the opposite of the open system. The controlled system exists when the audience is free to receive messages, but the messages are tightly controlled and censored. This system most closely approximates authoritarian and Communist theories. In a directed system the audience is cut off from many messages. Examples of a directed system exist in Asian and Southeast Asian countries where multilingualism prevents portions of the population from receiving the message.

The ownership-control model posits four media systems based on variables of public versus private ownership and decentralized versus centralized control. In the figure of the model, Type 2*a* is best exemplified in western and northern European countries such as France and Denmark where broadcasting companies are publicly owned, but the control system is decentralized so that no one central authority can control the messages. Type 2*b*, the centralized public model, is a typical socialist or Communist model in which the media are owned by society and centrally controlled by the dominant political party. Type 2*c*, the decentralized private model, is typical of the United States and most newspapers in western Europe. Finally, type 2*d*, the centralized private model, is found in many Latin American countries where the media are privately owned and controlled by the countries' rulers.

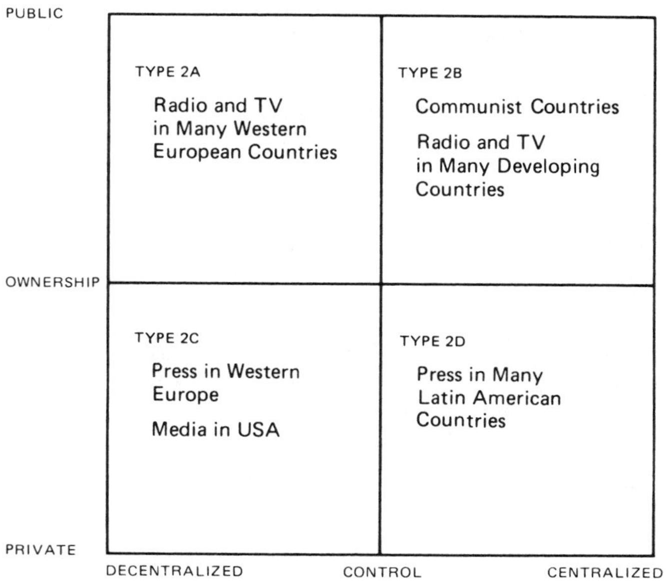

PUBLIC

TYPE 2A Radio and TV in Many Western European Countries	**TYPE 2B** Communist Countries Radio and TV in Many Developing Countries
TYPE 2C Press in Western Europe Media in USA	**TYPE 2D** Press in Many Latin American Countries

OWNERSHIP

PRIVATE

DECENTRALIZED   CONTROL   CENTRALIZED

Decentralized/Centralized Model.

Both the open–closed model and the ownership-control model, like the four theories system, have limitations in that they prescribe rather than describe various media systems. The media systems paradigm, a discussion of which follows, develops an *interactive* model that attempts to capture the dynamic relationship of media and society.

THE MEDIA SYSTEMS PARADIGM

The relationship between media and societies is reciprocal: A country creates a national media system, and this media system in turn modifies that society. Since every nation is different, and media systems vary from nation to nation, the interaction between a given country and its media is unique. Because this relationship is not static, media and societies constantly change each other. For example, the deaths of Mao Zedong and Zhou Enlai were political events of significance. In the People's Republic of China the media and society interacted so that the nation, the people, and the media system were all bound to be changed. Consequently, what may have been a correct observation a short time ago may no longer be accurate.

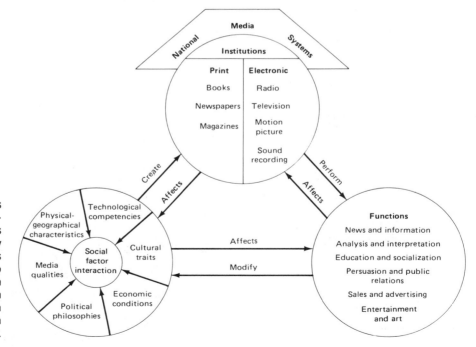

The Media Systems Paradigm. This action-oriented model visualizes the theory that in every country social factors interact in unique ways to create a national media system to perform a variety of functions which eventually participate in reshaping that society.

For our purposes, then, it seems advisable to analyze each national media system as a distinct entity. In order to perform this analysis, we must develop a standard model or paradigm as the basis for comparison. The Media Systems Paradigm is designed to reflect the interplay between media and societies, as well as to help describe similarities and dissimilarities in national media systems. The Media Systems Paradigm is based on the theory that in every country, special factors or social forces interact in unique ways (a) to create a national media system that is used (b) to perform a variety of functions (c) that eventually participate in reshaping that society. This paradigm is action oriented (dynamic vs. static) to emphasize the changing nature and interaction of media and societies.

We can identify six social factors or forces that interact in the development of a media system: (a) physical and geographical characteristics; (b) technological competencies; (c) cultural traits; (d) economic conditions; (e) political philosophies; (f) media qualities. The interaction of these factors, rather than their independent action, is crucial in media systems' evolution. Other factors also affect a country's media system, but the six mentioned here are the most critical.

Every national media system has a variety of individual media institutions. Seven major media merit special consideration: three are print media—the book, the newspaper, and the magazine; and four are electronic media—radio, television, the motion picture, and sound recording.

These media institutions and others are used to perform six basic functions: (a) news and information; (b) analysis and interpretation; (c) education and socialization; (d) persuasion and public relations; (e) sales and advertising; and (f) entertainment and art. As these functions are performed, the media change the societies that created them. The extent and kinds of effects the media have on society are debatable, but it is commonly agreed that the media participate in modifying every society of the world.

FACTORS THAT INFLUENCE THE DEVELOPMENT OF MEDIA SYSTEMS

As we examine each of the six forces that affect media development it is important to reemphasize that these factors seldom operate independently. It is their interaction that stimulates significant differences in media systems. All six are influential to varying degrees in different situations. In fact, it is impractical to designate one factor as the only variable influencing any one aspect of a given media system.

Physical–Geographical Characteristics

A country's climate, geography, and other physical characteristics affect the development of its media system just as they alter population patterns and economic development. For example, many nations have developed frequency modulation (FM) rather than amplitude modulation (AM) radio because the technical characteristics of the FM signal are better suited to mountainous regions. Because film stock tends to deteriorate more rapidly in the tropics than in temperate zones, nations located in tropical areas must take this fact into consideration when setting up film production, distribution, and exhibition facilities. In most regions of the United States winters are less hospitable than summers for outdoor activity. For this reason, audiences available for TV viewing in warmer months are decidedly smaller than in colder months. Climate, audience size, and TV economics interact to require the use of reruns or low-cost replacements during the summer quarter of the television year.

Other factors affect media in other countries. In Tanzania, for example, few trees are available for wood pulp. Because all paper stock must be imported, there are very few newspapers and magazines. Newspapers and magazines are primarily an urban phenomenon, and as a result, a country like the Netherlands with a predominantly urban geographical makeup has many daily newspapers and magazines. The enormous size of the USSR has promoted several layers of regional media and has fostered the use of longwave and shortwave transmission of radio signals. Newspapers in the USSR, and in most other large countries, are published on a regional basis. Indeed, whether to have a national newspaper is primarily determined by a nation's size. Israel's principal papers, for example, are sold nationwide, as are most newspapers in Scandinavian countries. In the United States, only the *Christian Science Monitor*, the *Wall Street Journal*, and *USA Today* can be called national newspapers.

Radio is particularly well suited to the communication needs of countries spread over vast areas, such as China and Russia, or those composed of various scattered elements, such as the Philippine Islands and other nations in the South Pacific.

The location of a country with respect to its proximity to other countries also has an impact on its media system development. This is perhaps nowhere more evident than in Canada. Originally, radio broadcasting in Canada developed along the same lines as it did in the United States. Privately owned commercial stations were licensed to use certain frequencies with few, if any, restrictions. Within a short time, however, Canadian broadcasting became an extension of the American system; most programming was directly "imported," and Canadian radio stations were formally affiliated with American networks. In order to provide motivation for Canadian programming, as well as the development of an east–west network, the Canadian Parliament passed the Broadcasting Act of 1932. This act established the Canadian Radio Broadcasting Commission (CRBC), whose main task was to set up a national service. The Canadian Broadcasting Commission (CBC) soon replaced the CRBC and is today the dominant force in Canadian broadcasting. The Canadian Radio–Television Commission is the equivalent of the FCC in the United States and regulates all electronic communication in Canada. One regulation establishes a quota for Canadian content that all stations must meet. Content quotas are intended to help maintain a Canadian cultural identity in the face of U.S. influence.

In Nicaragua, television has no monopoly on how the local population perceives the world. About half the population watches local television at least one hour a day. But in the border areas, Costa Rican, Honduran, and Salvadoran television can also be received. AM radio broadcasts from Mexico, Cuba, and United States are heard all over the country. And the Spanish-language shortwave broadcasts of the Voice of America and the BBC attract an immense audience.

The porousness of Nicaragua's frontiers, so far as the electronic media are concerned, may be one reason the Sandinistas make no attempt to restrict programming severely. "If we lie, people know we lie," one government official conceded. "If we don't cover their realities, the people will know we're deceiving them and rise up against us."

Other examples abound, but it is clear that physical–geographical conditions influence national media systems.

In order for a mass communication system to evolve in a nation, four technological competencies are needed. First, a society must have a basic scientific capability, as both pure and applied research are necessary to develop media. Early research in electricity was not aimed at creating television, but the results of that research were essential to its application. This ability to apply research findings to improve mass communication is a critical technological competency for media development.

Technological Competencies

Second, a nation needs raw materials to develop mass media or the economic resources to obtain them. In order to have books, magazines, and newspapers, you must have paper, ink, and the machinery to print pages. Paper requires suitable trees, rice, rags, or another source of fibrous material that can be turned into pulp. As we observed in the case of Tanzania, a shortage of trees precluded the development of many newspapers in the system. Ink requires acids, tints, resins, oils, drying agents, and other chemical components. Machines to produce print media need lead for type, aluminum for offset plates, various steels for presses, rubber for belts and rollers, and lubrication oils to keep the presses rolling. Electronic media make similar demands on a nation's natural resources.

Third, a country must have the industrial capability to mass produce media products or the money to buy these finished goods. Mass communication systems cannot operate unless they have sophisticated industrial complexes to support them. A nation must have vast quantities of transistors, cameras, typesetting machines, film stocks, presses, TV sets, inks, vacuum tubes, and other components if its media are to function optimally.

Fourth, trained personnel are needed who can make these complex systems function. A medium cannot function satisfactorily without a technical staff to operate the equipment, a production staff to create content, and a managerial staff to handle the day-to-day operations of the system. This process requires an ongoing program to recruit and train new personnel.

Technical competencies inhibit the development of mass communication systems in many ways. In Pakistan, for example, the national language is Urdu, and until recently, newspapers published in this language depended on handwritten copy prepared by calligraphers. An Urdu paper of 10 pages requires at least 50 calligraphers, and as a result, the work force necessary to produce these papers is enormous. An Urdu keyboard developed in the late 1960s eliminated the need for transcribing by hand, but Pakistani newspapers have been slow to use it. Their readers like the calligraphers' script because it is decorative and easy to read.

In Southeast Asia, radio and TV operations have been greatly limited by a lack of trained production personnel. Because of the personnel shortage (and the high cost of producing programs), many developing countries in Asia and the Pacific import programs whose content is often unrelated to local cultures and values. In addition, the lack of electricity in these countries, and in parts of China, and the developing nations of Africa and South America, has led to a radio-dominated electronic media environment because transistors and batteries allow radio to operate effectively where television cannot. As transistorized and battery-operated television becomes more of a reality it will gain a stronger foothold in these countries' media systems.

Cultural Traits   Every society has unique ways of doing things, of evaluating what is important, and of modifying behavior. There are social laws, taboos, norms, mores, values, and attitudes. All these cultural traits and social characteristics are important in the development of media systems.

In Czechoslovakia, for example, two national groups, the Czechs and the Slovaks, have their own distinct language. Films are made in each of the two national languages to reflect the differences in these two cultures. In Switzerland the government recognizes four national languages. Broadcasts are provided in German, French, Italian, and Romansch.

Danish cultural values have allowed pornographic material to appear in some media. Films, books, and magazines banned as obscene in most countries have been openly available in Denmark. In the United States there is considerable disagreement on the sexual content of the mass media. Recent Supreme Court decisions have not always followed a consistent pattern, and the various media voices have not been unanimous in their thinking. The civil rights and women's movements have changed American cultural attitudes tremendously; the mass media as well as business and industry are hiring minorities and women in senior positions throughout their organizations. Their abilities as journalists aside, Barbara Walters, Max Robinson, Diane Sawyer, Jane Pauley, and Bryant Gumbel can be cited as a reflection of this cultural change.

بغیر کسی سسٹرز

احمد حسین

The Urdu language newspaper, *Akhbar-E-Pakistan* disseminates information in handwritten script. (Courtesy Daud Subhani, editor *Akhbar-E-Pakistan*)

49

A number of cultural or social factors deeply influence media development; these include urbanization, population, sexual taboos, religion, race relations, labor organizations, youth culture, and education. Every mass society is a mixture of stability and change—the resulting conflict deeply involves and affects the development of media systems.

The literacy rate of a population is a critical cultural–social characteristic that determines the growth and diffusion of print media. In Tanzania the literacy rate has only recently reached 60%, and so print media are almost nonexistent. In the Netherlands there is almost a 100% literacy rate, and so print media are very strong. In the Mediterranean states of Spain, Portugal, Italy, Greece and Turkey, where there is poverty as well as illiteracy, especially in the rural areas, broadcast media are more important than print. Even in Italy the number of newspapers per 1000 people is less than one-fifth that of Sweden and Britain, and most Italian newspapers are sold in the industrialized northern third of the country.

As important a factor as illiteracy in many countries is cultural and linguistic diversity. In Africa and the Arab states especially, the number of discrete languages and dialects range from 800 to 2000. Additionally, many of these languages and dialects have no written form or literature. The oral tradition, which dominates in Africa and the Middle East, results in a poorly developed print media system. Electronic media are also affected by the number of languages. In Cameroon, for example, with a population of slightly more than 8 million people, 100 different languages are spoken. Gabon, with only 650,000 people, has 10 discrete languages. Radio broadcasting in Russia is done in 67 languages, and because of the linguistic diversity, radio has developed on regional and local levels rather than as a national system. Multilingualism is also a factor in the development of media systems in Asia and the South Pacific. In New Guinea, for example, broadcasts are made in 33 languages. Daily newspapers exist only in major urban centers in these countries, and the few regional papers are published haphazardly.

Another cultural factor is a country's particular value system. In Sweden, for example, a concern for violence has led to film censorship, especially of films imported from the United States. But censorship of sexual content in film as well as other media is nonexistent. In many ways this attitude is the opposite of the attitude prevailing in the United States; we are more concerned about restricting sexual content than violence. Some people claim that in America, two historical features—a Puritan tradition and the westward expansion—resulted in this strange standard. Puritanism produced sexual constraints, and violence was an accepted part of the move west; our media content reflects this background.

In Thailand, Communist programming is viewed as a national security threat and may prompt the Thai Radio & Television Broadcast Directing Board to end daily, 90-minute TV blackouts, from 6:30 P.M. to 8:00 P.M., which were initiated in 1980 as an energy conservation measure.

In December 1983, a Laotian TV station built by the Soviet Union, Vietnam, and Bulgaria, began transmitting about 30 miles from the Thai border, and many Thais now turn on their sets during the blackout period to watch Russian or Laotian programs.

Members of parliament have called the spillover programs a threat to Thai democracy, and have urged the broadcast directing board to end the blackout period to compete with the Communist programming. Opposition to the move for nonstop Thai evening broadcasts has come from members of the board who think more TV will keep schoolchildren from doing their homework.

Because an end to the 90-minute ban likely will provide more time for commercials, TV advertisers support the move. They have much to gain if anti-Communism wins out over academia.

In Canada, unlike the United States, the power of the "marketplace" in determining and even regulating broadcast content is much weaker. John Meisel, former chairman of the Canadian Radio–Television and Telecommunications Commission, wrote in *Channels* magazine that whatever the merits of the arguments about broadcast regulation, Canada and the United States will unlikely arrive at similar resolutions because they have different cultural traits and characteristics.

For one thing says Meisel, Canadians do not seem to have developed the Americans' finely honed suspicion of government. Why did the forces of law and order—personified in the Royal Canadian Mounted Police— play such a prominent role in the settlement of the Canadian West, while the settlement of the American frontier was much more free-wheeling? Why does Canada's constitution speak of "peace, order, and good government" while America's reveres "life, liberty, and the pursuit of happiness"? Why do Canadian responses to surveys consistently reveal higher levels of trust and confidence in government? A variety of explanations have been suggested—Canada's absence of a revolutionary past; the dispersion of the small Canadian population over vast distances; a sensitivity to society as community.

According to Meisel, Canadian attitudes bespeak more than an absence of distrust. Canadians have used the state as an instrument for common purposes much more often than Americans have. Heavy government involvement in the building of railways was in large part prompted by the need of a vast, sparsely settled country for an effective transportation system. Similarly, broadcasting and telecommunications are considered vitally important in forging and maintaining links among the country's various regions and groups.

The physical devices, content, and personnel that make mass communication systems possible cost vast sums. A country's or an individual's attitude toward a given medium can in part be assessed by the economic commitment made to that medium. A nation's economic

Economic Conditions

philosophy, structure, and conditions determine in great measure the ways and the extent to which media are funded. Capitalist countries are more likely to allow the media to be profit-oriented, while Communist nations are less likely to have advertising in their media.

The economic conditions of a state also determine how the audience gains access to media. Are television sets purchased by individual viewers, or does the state provide communal receivers for group use? If a family buys a receiver, its members tend to exercise somewhat more control over how, when, and where their viewing takes place than those in a communal audience. This makes communal viewing decidedly different from family or individual viewing.

In the United States campus newspapers distributed free of charge have wider circulation than those that students must purchase. Nevertheless, the student press that supports itself is less likely to bend to administrative pressure when sensitive issues arise.

A complex, sophisticated media system cannot thrive in an economically impoverished nation. A poor country with starving people can support only those media that help alleviate immediate problems. In most modern states media survive and prosper because mass communication is a valuable asset to their economic process.

In Tanzania, for example, the average person's income is $136 a year; thus the country has a poorly developed media system. The media contain no advertising, not because of the state's political philosophy, but simply because the people do not earn enough money to buy the goods that would be advertised. In many Third World countries newspapers are an urban—elite form of mass communication. An advertiser support base is possible only in urban centers with a middle- to upper-middle-class audience. In some cases, however, television has developed in spite of economic conditions. Television is seen by many Third World governments as a symbol of prestige and power. Therefore, despite few TV sets and poor production facilities, TV systems are developed in order to enhance the government's prestige in the eyes of its neighbors and the world.

Political Philosophies   A country's political structure and attitudes influence the development of media systems more than any other factor, with the occasional exception of cultural and social traits. The amount and kind of control over mass communication are determined by the nature and structure of the government in power. Political forces establish the laws under which media institutions must operate. Media regulations may be repressive or permissive depending on the political atmosphere of a particular society.

In the People's Republic of China the media system is a political arm of the state used to implement party policy. The system is restricted to party officials in good standing; they alone have access to the media. All mass communication is directly supervised by government officials who are also party members.

During times of severe political stress, such as war, governments tend to exercise greater political control over media systems than in normal times. Both Iraq and Iran exercise censorship over all media content, foreign as well as domestic, during war. During the war in South Vietnam, newspapers that disagreed with political policies of the Thieu government were shut down in the name of national security. After the war, that policy continued, but the papers that were permitted to publish changed. Newspapers that were not a part of the "reunification" effort ceased operation when the North Vietnamese and Viet Cong assumed power.

The events of Watergate led to a major political struggle, which had an impact on and involved the mass media of this country. Significant pressures from a variety of political sources affected the news media during the eclipse of the Nixon administration. The "fairness" tradition of the press was and remained a political force throughout this dark period in American political history.

In many African countries direct censorship is the result of the political heritage of colonialism. This tradition has significantly influenced the new governments' attitudes toward mass media. In Tanzania the government operates the broadcasting system and has "absolute discretion and rights" over content. The government also censors films and stage plays. The president of the country is the editor in chief of both newspapers.

As John C. Merrill notes in his book *Global Journalism*, government pressures on the world's press fall into four basic categories: (a) legal pressures; (b) economic and political pressures; (c) secrecy; and (d) direct censorship. Merrill states further that legal pressures consist of constitutional provisions, security laws, press laws, and penal laws. The critical point of reference for most political systems' interface with the media is the nation's constitution. It defines the freedom *and* the limits of the media system. The Russian constitution speaks of freedom of the press but sets limits on that freedom and in practice controls the media system. The government administers both press and broadcasting through state committees that operate under the Council of Ministers, which is ultimately responsible to and controlled by the Communist party. Even newspaper and magazine circulation and book sales are controlled by the party.

In most socialist governments the media are financed by the government through use taxes or other forms of tax revenue, but the content is basically not controlled. In Norway, for example, both television and motion-picture theaters are run by the state, but no significant censorship results.

The degree and kinds of political controls vary in each country depending on that nation's political philosophies and goals. This aspect may well be the most potent single factor influencing media development because political power is often physical as well as philosophical.

Media Qualities　　　Technical features, media-use patterns, and overall institutional characteristics affect the development of media systems. For example, development of commercial television radically changed radio and motion-picture institutions. The people who ran radio stations and motion-picture companies had to reevaluate and change their roles in the total U.S. media system. This form of media interaction is constantly reshaping the total media system of the United States and every other nation.

Some media are inherently more expensive to operate than others. Television is a more costly medium than radio; high-quality magazines have a higher per-copy production cost than newspapers; it costs less to produce a phonograph record than a motion picture. The unique qualities of each of these media contribute to the per-unit cost, and this cost affects the way the medium is used and its place in the overall system.

As we have seen, print media can be highly effective only in literate societies; electronic media require no more than a speaking knowledge of a given language. Print media are more portable, however, and do not require high-cost playback equipment. Radio is more portable than television, and this fact greatly contributes to its use in countries with large rural populations.

The use of satellites in Western European countries has made it all but impossible to carry on a strictly national broadcasting policy. In Belgium and Holland, for example, TV audiences can now choose from 10 foreign services. As direct satellite-to-home transmission becomes a reality, the concept of a national media system will be altered significantly.

The physical and geographical conditions, the technological competencies, the cultural traits, the economic conditions, the political philosophies, and the quality of the media interact to create unique media systems. The media are then used by the society to perform tasks that are essential to the society including news, analysis, education, persuasion, advertising, and entertainment.

The roles that the media perform in a nation cannot help but modify that nation, and as the parent society changes, the social forces and the uses made of media also change. This interaction of media systems and societies is critical to the development and well-being of the modern industrial state.

THE THIRD WORLD AND A NEW INFORMATION ORDER

One other subject should be discussed while we are examining mass media systems around the world. By and large, the mass media of the main spheres of political power, the capitalist West and the Communist East, dominate world mass communication. But a large and increasingly vocal segment of the world does not want to be dominated by either. This is the so-called Third World, made up primarily of countries in South America, Africa, the Middle East, and Asia.

The countries of the Third World have been growing increasingly restive about the domination of media from East and West. As U.S. media, especially, have grown massive and popular, much of the Third World has come to regard the American media invasion as exploitative and imperialistic. As Herbert Read has written in his book *America's Mass Media Merchants*, "commercial American mass media are permeating human activity on an unprecedented global scale." Mass media have become one of America's biggest exports. Particularly in the Third World, where quality mass media are not readily available, those who want information and entertainment often turn to *Time, Reader's Digest*, American movies, TV programs, and recorded music (especially rock music).

Much of the world's news is reported by American journalists through the news services of the Associated Press and United Press International. These are of course not the only news agencies in the world, but they have the largest staffs, the most equipment, and the most customers. Again, particularly in Third World nations, which do not have well-developed news agencies, people have to depend on agencies in the East and West for news and information even about their own regions.

Resentment in the Third World has been rising against media domination, particularly America's. A Nigerian correspondent writing for the *Nigerian Herald* in 1979 summed up this resentment when he wrote:

> The "free flow of information" tirelessly championed by the heads of Western propaganda services has become a one-way street. The "exchange of ideas" is in fact the ill-camouflaged export of ideas to the developing countries, where sellers employ capitalist marketing techniques and do not stint money on advertising. Western propagandists concentrate on creating in the minds of Africans an idyllic publicity image of capitalism as a society of "equal opportunities," where a person's abilities determine his success or failure. . . . However, despite tremendous efforts by highly skilled propagandists and glossy paper, the ideas exported by the West to Africa are meeting with falling demand.

These problems have been raised by Third World countries in the United Nations, and UNESCO has sponsored several conferences in an effort to find solutions. One result of these conferences has been the call for a "new world information order" that supposedly would help protect the communication integrity of every nation in the world. The more extreme elements of the "information order" clash with traditional tenets of American freedom of the press. The order would give each government authority over who could send reports out of the country, as well as the authority to censor reports coming into the country. Governments could establish regulations for journalists working in their countries and could insist on a "right of reply" to reports filed by journalists, thus giving governments the authority to change the journalists' work. On the positive side, the information order would seek to help Third World and other countries develop their own media systems and would increase educational programs that can provide a trained communication work force, without which mass media are impossible.

4 Economics and Mass Communication

The 1980s have been the best of times for a majority of U.S. citizens. But they have been the worst of times for a growing minority that is unable to enter or remain in the mainstream of the American economic dream.

Over the past 10 years, significant changes occurred in American economic thinking. The 1970s saw the end of the greatest boom in the history of humankind with the United States at the center of economic growth. At the same time the fabric of American life altered radically, and sociopolitical changes made very real demands on the economy. The mass media were the primary catalyst for the development of an American economic attitude that there would always be more of everything. News and entertainment media glorified political change, social progress, consumerism, and hedonism as a part of the American lifestyle.

THE CURRENT STATE OF THE ECONOMY

If we are to understand the strong financial condition of our mass communication industries, we should begin with an overview of the economic facts of life in America today.

1. The industrial base of the United States is changing more rapidly than most people expected; the country is now less a producer of goods and more a provider of services. Information industries

including the mass media have more potential for growth than ever before. Overall, mass communication industries are in amazing health compared to many other sectors of our free enterprise system.

2. America is facing stiff competition from nations it saved from economic ruin after World War II. The improved quality and lower price of foreign goods increases other countries' shares not only of overseas markets but of industries traditionally dominated by U.S.-based companies. American companies are hard-pressed even in the competitive business of making and selling media hardware. Nevertheless, in every country and by any standard, American media content is the unquestioned leader. American movies, music, TV and radio programs, novels, and other services are preeminent.

3. The United States remains central to the international banking system, but our financial institutions are facing increasing difficulties as foreign national debts cannot be repaid but are only *refinanced*. In addition, the federal deficit has grown enormously in the past decade, much of it to support the military, the economies of emerging nations, and domestic social services. Interest rates for borrowers may well be fixed permanently at the double-digit level, and loan availability may remain limited for speculative ventures. Media companies are having as much difficulty borrowing and repaying as everyone else. In addition, major media companies are diversifying into other media and nonmedia businesses. And new economic alliances between media and nonmedia giants are increasing. The breakup of AT&T is a very significant development because of its impact on the communication industry.

4. Most people believe that the American standard of living is declining. In the 1980s some Americans are gradually coming to realize that the next year may not necessarily be better than the last one. The most heretical thought is that young people may well find their future to be less rewarding financially than that of their parents. The salaries of media stars do not reflect the salary levels, job availability, and other realities of media employment. It is tough and competitive in the mass communication job market, even though the market is expanding.

5. Fifty years ago, there were nine workers for each retiree, but by the early twenty-first century it is estimated that there will be only two active workers for each retired person. Beyond the issue of who will support social service systems for the retired is the fact that the population is growing older. This fact has an impact on the mass media, for the available audience is aging. Media content must reflect population changes and the cultural and

political problems inherent in them. More important, delivery systems are emphasizing media consumption in the home environment. We are not going out to the media.

6. By the turn of the next century, perhaps as few as 10% of the country's eligible voters will have school-age children; this compares with 75% in the 1950s. High-technology and information industries depend on a strong educational system. Obviously, better media content must be linked to national and local educational policies. And the focus on "kid-vid" and "youth cult" audiences is going to decline. The precursor of future media content may well be *On Golden Pond*, not *Porky's*. Men's and women's magazines will have older audiences too. And the media will play a large role in what is coming to be called *continuing education*.

7. Unemployment may hover at the 8–10% level in the next quarter-century, not the average of 4% that prevailed throughout most of the century. Social progress has broadened the work force so that traditionally excluded minorities (blacks, Hispanics, and women) now compete vigorously for better-paying jobs. The rules of the media workplace have changed dramatically;

Norman (Henry Fonda) celebrates his 80th birthday with his family in *On Golden Pond* (1981).

(Photo: Museum of Modern Art/Film Stills Archive, Courtesy Universal City Studios, Inc.)

consider the Christine Craft lawsuit against Metromedia because she was demoted from her news anchor position based on what many felt was sex discrimination. Interestingly, Ms. Craft's age was not far short of being an age discrimination factor as well.

8. The two-income family without dependents spends rather than saves; it is the most lucrative target market in the United States. The American lifestyle of owning a home, two cars, complex technological hardware, etc., requires two incomes; and specialized media are rising to the challenge of selling anything this market can afford or is willing to purchase on high-interest credit. Media heroes have come to reflect the consumerist morality of this new target audience.

9. Overconsumption has led to a shortfall in savings, which in turn has decreased the supply of money available for capital investment. And there have been staggering increases in the cost of energy and the goods and services that energy makes possible. Media coverage of political protests against nuclear energy and the environmental problems of coal-fired energy systems have contributed more to the public awareness of the physical danger than to the costs of regulating necessary environmental changes. It is an economic fact of life that overregulation coupled with staggering energy costs have contributed to uncertainty in the value of future capital investments. Long-range capital investments do not justify outlays when they cannot recover initial costs. The media, especially new media ventures, are capital intensive, energy dependent, subject to rapid changes in public taste, in the glare of the regulatory eye, as well as subject to frequent antitrust litigation.

10. Interest groups and corporations plan to keep their hard-won support systems in place, regardless of costs to taxpayers. Although raising taxes *and* cutting military and special-interest spending are essential, elected and appointed decision makers realize that single-issue interest groups do not vote *for* candidates, they vote *against* them. Events are staged for the news media, and politicians are put on the spot and forced to react off the cuff. As a result, hard economic choices are made even more difficult in the legislative halls of America.

This list of observations is not a "gloom and doom, boom or bust" prediction of the decline and fall of the American economic system. Rather, it is a review of the forces that will have an impact on economic conditions in which mass media play a role. A sound economic future for the United States—and for every nation—depends on a number of factors. These factors are increasing in the media eye.

Agricultural
Potential

Food must be grown and marketed worldwide. The profit involved in this undertaking must be worth the risk.

Energy Reserves

Multiple sources of energy must be available. A comprehensive national policy must be developed for energy use.

Raw Materials

Natural resources must be available; these resources must be coupled with the industrial capability to develop them and dispose of the wastes produced. Nevertheless, conservation must be seen as an ever-more-critical issue.

Automated High-
Technology
Industries

High-tech industries are the high-growth profit centers of the future, but they are not currently labor intensive. Most of the employment they produce is at the low end of the salary scale. The ability to retool these industries is also essential.

A Strong, Flexible
Financial System

A solvent economy with the capacity to provide for future capital expansion is essential. This must be integrated with the will to shift away from rampant consumerism and toward saving for the future.

An Educated,
Committed Work
Force

Adversarial relationships and mutual exploitation are much less attractive today than ever before. Successful, competitive industries must have *zero defect* as their standard mode of production. Worker involvement and self-reliance are very real elements in future economic successes.

The media coverage of these six economic factors is expanding. More and more media time is devoted to their analysis, on entertainment as well as news programs. At present, only Australia and North America meet all these criteria. The economic future will be more rugged than the past, and mass media will play a critical role in that future. It is now a question of will.

ECONOMIC THEORY
AND MASS MEDIA

The economic decisions of mass media are based on the same major principles as the rest of America's enterprises in our essentially capitalistic system.

Media Goods and
Services

In popular economic language, there are two kinds of goods: *free goods*, which are supplied by nature; and *economic goods*, those goods to which human effort has added utility. Mass communication industries use free goods to produce economic goods. Trees, a free good, are used to produce newsprint, an economic good. Industrial diamonds are used to make phonograph needles. Within the category of economic goods, there are two classes: *producer goods and services*, which are used in the production of other goods and services; and *consumer goods and services*, which are used directly by the buyer without significant modification. Using the previous examples and extending them, we can say that free goods (e.g, trees and diamonds) are used to make producer goods (e.g., newsprint and phonograph needles), which in turn are used to make consumer goods (e.g., newspapers and record players).

The distinction between media goods and services, at its simplest level, is that media goods are physical things (e.g., TV sets, transistor radios, copies of books and magazines), and media services are the content or activities that supplement or supply goods (e.g., the stories in magazines and books, the programs on radio and television).

The law of supply and demand is always at work in the media marketplace. *Consumer demand* is the desire to use and the ability to pay for goods and services. *Producer supply* refers to the quantity of goods available for purchase at a particular time and at an attractive price. When the consumer demand for color-TV sets exceeds the producer supply, the price tends to increase. When the supply of color-TV receivers exceeds the demand, the price tends to drop. Media people, like any other business people, seek to supply the demand at the most economically rewarding level for themselves (and sometimes even for consumers). Newspapers, magazines, and TV series that consistently misread the media marketplace are headed for economic disaster and oblivion.

Media Supply and Demand

An individual or corporation that buys the goods and services of the newspaper, TV, recording, magazine, radio, motion-picture, or book industry becomes a media consumer. Media consumers use their *time* and *money* to purchase mass communication goods and services. Media consumers can be placed in two distinct categories: audiences and advertisers.

DUAL CONSUMERS OF MASS MEDIA

The audience buys media products so that it can receive and consume media content. Television, radio, and recording audiences use their financial resources to buy the equipment necessary to listen to and view the content. Audiences buy books, newspapers, and magazines in order to read the content.

Audience as Consumer

Short-term and long-term consumption patterns are also realities of the media marketplace; the quicker a given item is consumed, the sooner it must be replaced. Media audiences are willing to invest money and time in short-term consumption of media goods and services. Paperback books and magazines are bought and discarded almost as easily as the daily newspaper. Close to 40% of a TV network's prime-time programming is changed yearly. This rapid turnover is one of the major factors making media businesses viable economic enterprises. The willingness of audiences to spend money and time on short-term media goods and services is one indication of the value they place on them.

The audience as consumer is reflected in microcosm as people line up to purchase magazines and newspapers.

(Photo by Brendan Beirne.)

Advertiser as Consumer

Traditionally, advertisers have been said to be buyers of *time* in the electronic media and *space* in the print media. This labeling process is technically accurate but somewhat misleading as to what is actually being bought. The purchase of a 30-second commercial spot on NBC's "Hill Street Blues" or a full-page advertisement in *USA Today* is a meaningless act—and a poor business decision—unless there are audiences that watch "Hill Street Blues" or read *USA Today*. In reality, advertisers buy *audiences*, not space and time. The estimated audiences for commercial broadcasting stations and most newspapers and magazines are more valuable in the end than the original product—the pages and minutes of content. Although advertisers talk about buying 60-second spots on radio or pages in magazines, their major concern is the audiences that consume these pages and seconds. Advertisers buy people because people consume the products advertised in the media.

CONSUMER LEVELS OF DECISION MAKING

Individual decisions to spend money and time on the media are significant because these decisions determine whether a medium will succeed or fail. The consumer has three basic levels of purchasing power in regard to media consumption.

1. The consumer can choose between media and nonmedia goods and services. A family can spend its money on a new living room sofa, a week's vacation, or a media product.

2. The consumer can choose among various media. The family that decides to spend its money on a media product must determine whether it wants $2000 worth of books or a stereo system or a video beam projector.

3. Once the decision is made to purchase that stereo, the family must then choose among competing brands. Many consumers turn to foreign manufacturers, and many American companies now build their products overseas with components from many nations. In the area of electronic hardware, the *zero defect* work ethic of the Japanese has helped that nation gain a tremendous share of the American market and has silenced jokes of an earlier era about products made in Japan.

There are essentially four kinds of media support systems: (*a*) media supported by audiences; (*b*) media supported by advertisers; (*c*) media supported by advertisers and audiences; and (*d*) media supported by public and private subsidy.

Record companies, the film industry (with the exception of films made expressly for television), pay-cable services, and book publishers derive practically all their revenue from audiences. The audience bears the full brunt of the cost of producing these goods and services. The audience is not resold to advertisers. Commercials can be and occasionally are inserted between chapters of books or cuts on LP records or scenes in motion pictures (as they are when shown on television), but the traditions of our media system have established that the audience pays the entire cost of these three media.

MODELS OF MEDIA SUPPORT

Media Supported by Audiences

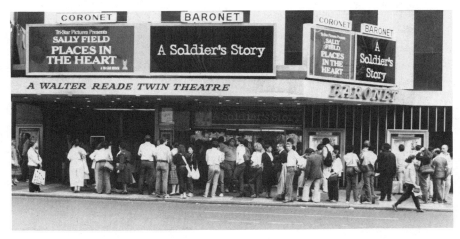

(Photo by Brendan Beirne.)

Motion pictures are supported primarily by audiences such as these lined up to see two recent releases.

Media Supported by Advertisers

Radio and TV stations and some cable services produce programs that they provide "free of charge" to audiences. Stations and networks earn their money by selling these audiences to advertisers, who must recoup their ad costs when they sell their products to the public.

Media Supported by Advertisers and Audiences

Most general-circulation newspapers and magazines derive revenue from both advertisers and audiences. Audiences buy media content directly through subscriptions or newsstand purchases, but advertisers also pay for these audiences. Although the exact amount varies from publication to publication, usually audiences provide only 30% of the total revenue earned by general-circulation newspapers and magazines.

With such a large American market for Japanese products, it makes sense for the advertisers of Toyota to try to buy American audiences. (Copyright © 1984 Toyota Motor Sales, U.S.A., Inc. Used with permission.)

(Photo courtesy WNET-TV.)

Volunteers answer phones at a fund raising event for public television station WNET-TV in New York.

Some media are supported by state and federal agencies, foundations, nonprofit organizations, or private corporations. These media obtain little or no consumer support. Public television and radio, student newspapers, corporate house organs, and subsidized government publishing are supported in this manner. The public pays part of the bill indirectly through local, state, and federal taxes, tuition, or support of those corporations involved with the media. Recently, public radio and TV stations have had to turn more and more to listener–viewer support and use auctions as well as other fund-raising activities. In 1983 National Public Radio (NPR) went begging for dollars when a squabble with the Corporation for Public Broadcasting (CPB) over NPR's alleged mismanagement of funds and deficits seemed likely to lead to a shutdown of NPR's news magazines. A compromise was reached, and programming continues.

Media Supported by Public and Private Groups

THE INDUSTRIAL STRUCTURE OF MASS MEDIA

The mass communication industries have traditionally been described as having three layers: production, distribution, and exhibition.

1. *Production* is the creative development of content.
2. *Distribution* is the moving of product from the producer to the retail outlet.
3. *Exhibition* is the provision of content to the audience by the local retailer.

It is at the distribution level, *the delivery of content*, where the revolution in mass communication is occurring. News and entertainment "product" (actually a media service) are much the same from year to year, although "soft" news has grown.

For example, news is at the edge of a significant change in how users will gain access to information. The time for videotext and teletext displays of information on a TV screen or home printout is near; newspapers, especially the (Chicago) Tribune Company and the Knight-Ridder organization, are very active in this new technology. The newspaper will not disappear, but it will probably be reshaped along the lines of local versions of *USA Today*, which is essentially a headline service. The 24-hour TV news service pioneered by Ted Turner's Cable News Network (CNN) is another radical shift in news distribution. The "superstations" (WTBS, WOR, WGN) are legally local "broadcast" operations, which distribute their programs nationally via satellite, using local cable operators and thus short-circuiting traditional broadcast network and station linkages.

Announcers Lou Dobbs and Marcia Ladendorff anchor CNN's "PRIME NEWS."

(Photo courtesy Cable News Network, Inc.)

Perhaps the most significant change in distribution has occurred in the motion-picture industry. In the past 10 years seven major companies have dominated film distribution: Buena Vista (Disney), Columbia, MGM/UA, Paramount, Twentieth Century-Fox, Universal, and Warner Brothers. They have financed 60 to 70 productions each year and have distributed another 60 to 70 independent productions. They literally have controlled the industry in production and distribution.

Enter the magazine empire of Time Inc., which needed roughly 200 films each year for the Home Box Office (HBO) and Cinemax 24-hour-a-day pay-cable schedule via RCA's *Satcom I* satellite (1975 launch). Obviously, the movie studios controlled the product HBO needed, and they raised pay-cable rental fees of successful theatrical movies to levels nearly equal to total production cost for the films. Home Box Office countered by buying U.S. pay-cable rights from independent producers for roughly 25% of production costs before the producer cut a distribution deal for theatrical release with one of the seven distribution companies. This was the case with hits like *Tootsie* and misses like *Nobody's Perfect*. But, hit or miss, it filled the HBO schedule adequately because HBO does not live by per-pay viewings as do movie theaters. The subscriber's monthly flat fee covers all investments.

To ensure product, Time (HBO) formed Tri-Star Pictures with Columbia (owned by Coca-Cola) and CBS, and they are expected to spend roughly $1 billion for as many as 30 movies and miniseries a year. Columbia can distribute them as movies through traditional international theatrical channels; CBS gets network and, perhaps, syndication rights; and HBO– Cinemax has a year of pay-cable distribution. Antitrust suits are pending. Nevertheless, HBO subscribers are growing by roughly 25% per year, and with flat-rate monthly fees, HBO's income from pay-cable movies is expected to exceed the movie-theater box-office receipts of the combined seven studios and all other sources before 1990.

In effect, the traditional economic associations are breaking down. Media giants are diversifying and are buying into one another's "turf." The shape of things to come for all media is up for grabs, especially in the area of distribution.

THE HIGH COST OF FAILURE: MEDIA EXPENSES

Although the huge dollar amounts used to measure media advertising, sales, rentals, profits, incomes, etc., seem exorbitant, it is important to keep in mind that every medium and every business unit within that medium has extremely high labor and material costs to meet.

The revenue derived from consumers and nonconsumers alike goes to pay media's bills. Media industries incur massive start-up costs. They also incur large operating expenses as they continue to pay for the production costs involved in making media content, the distribution costs incurred in delivering goods and services to the consumer, and the exhibition costs involved in making media products easily available to audiences.

Initial Costs
Some media businesses can start up with relatively little capital investment, whereas others require enormous initial costs. A phonograph record can be produced for whatever a local band can scrape together to rent a studio, cut the necessary tracks, and produce a "demo." Urban monthly magazines can be started with relatively little capital outlay. Books can be produced inexpensively using typed masters, rubber plates, offset printing, and glued binding.

Nevertheless, low initial costs are not the rule in media economics. A textbook such as *Mass Media IV* requires a commitment of over $250,000 on the part of the publisher in terms of total investment in editorial, manufacturing, and promotion costs, as well as the advance payment to the authors. Even bargain-basement films like *Smokey and the Bandit III* cost $3–5 million to make. *Return of the Jedi, Gandhi,* and *Indiana Jones and the Temple of Doom* cost tens of millions. To start a newspaper in a major metropolitan area would require an investment of $10–15 million. Moderately successful TV stations sell for millions of dollars. The impact of these large start-up costs is felt and reflected in the high advertising rates, admission prices, and subscription rates charged by most media.

Operating and
Distributing
Expenses
Most media enterprises involve long-term commitments in the form of operating expenses: supplies, labor overhead, interest, modernization, and expansion. Newspapers alone spend more than $150 million annually to improve their operations. Radio operations purchase music rights, news, and sports information for content because they are relatively inexpensive ways to serve their specialized audiences. Newspapers use newsprint rather than high-quality book paper to cut production costs. All media must distribute their products if they are to survive economically. Distribution costs play a major role in the economic patterns of most mass media. Magazine publishers depend on 750 wholesalers and more than 100,000 retail outlets to help sell their wares. The phonograph industry uses record clubs, distributors, retailers, and rack jobbers to get their records into the hands of the public.

Production Costs
Newspapers must pay a staff of reporters, freelancers, artists, editors, and syndicated services to generate content. Magazines must pay staff costs as well as "job out" articles to nonstaff writers, who are paid well for their work. Radio stations must pay music royalties and local talent costs, as well as cover costs of news and sports programming.

The most publicized costs are those in television. Network prime-time productions run from about $700,000 to $750,000 per hour-long episode; made-for-TV movies average $2–3 million per 2-hour film, and miniseries like "Shogun," "The Thorn Birds," "The Winds of War," and "Chiefs" cost upward of $1.5 million per hour. The three networks spend approximately $5 billion a year on 1500 hours of programming.

The syndication market is still dominated by shows that first appeared on ABC, CBS, and NBC but are owned by syndicators. Of the syndication market, 80% is cornered by product that first appeared on the networks. But shows like "Entertainment Tonight," "Solid Gold," "PM Magazine," and "Family Feud" do well because production costs are lower (approximately $100,000 per hour on the average). The Federal Communications Commission under the Reagan administration is trying to amend the rule that prevents networks from competing in the syndication market.

Programs can be aired live, but because most programs are videotaped or filmed, TV economics has been a primary reason for the death of live programming. High production costs have forced the industry to use reruns, and that means recording programs. Most prime-time TV series produce about 20 new episodes each season, which means it is possible for each show to be run two or three times each year. In theory, this practice cuts production costs for a season by at least 60%.

In prime time (8:00 P.M. to 11:00 P.M. EST) nearly all variety series are videotaped and dramatic series are filmed. In the 1970s situation comedies such as "All in the Family," under impetus from Norman Lear, turned from film to electronic production techniques. Without international markets and the ability to use reruns as syndicated series, few, if any, network prime-time shows would be economically successful. "Star Trek," for example, achieved greater success as a syndicated series than it did on the network.

Television production costs fall into two basic categories:

1. Above-the-line costs cover all items related to creative elements of production including writing, directing, acting, and producing a program.
2. Below-the-line costs relate to physical or technical elements of a program including the production staff, scenery, costumes, location costs, equipment rental, editing, processing, and overhead.

For videotaped variety shows, above-the-line elements account for 50–65% of the total production cost because of high talent costs. Below-the-line items account for 50–65% of film-drama production charges because of high labor, scenery, location, and equipment costs.

The cost of producing a TV program remains the same whether 1000 or 10,000 or 10,000,000 people see it. Network interconnection of local stations by long lines, microwave, and satellites provides an extremely large audience base, thereby achieving a lower unit cost (cost per 1000 viewers).

Program-Distribution Costs

Network time charges are based on the available audience, that percentage of U.S. homes with their TV sets on, not the actual audience

De Forest Kelley, William Shatner, Leonard Nimoy "beam up" on the television series "Star Trek."

(Photo: New York Public Library Photo Collection, Courtesy Paramount Pictures Television.)

turned to a specific program within a specific time slot. The available audience (and therefore network distribution costs) is affected by five variables: (*a*) the number of U.S. homes equipped with TV sets; (*b*) the coverage of the stations affiliated with the network; (*c*) the scope of the available interconnection system; (*d*) the season of the year; and (*e*) the day part (i.e., time segment—daytime, prime time, etc.).

THE BOTTOM LINE

The possibility that a TV program may fail to attract a large audience has led advertisers to the practice of using *scatter plans*, that is, placing ads in a large number of programs. This enables advertisers to hedge their bets with a few winners and some losers. The high costs of production and distribution make it harder and harder to try something new in programming. The high cost of failure has made advertisers very cautious TV consumers. Nevertheless, the recent demand for network TV spots is pushing prices higher, creating long-term commitments, and forcing advertisers to make very early decisions about what they will buy. At the present time the networks are definitely in the driver's seat on commercial prices. All three networks are consistently sold out in nearly all their time periods, regardless of who is winning the current ratings battle. But it is the advertiser who pays a major share of all ad media costs.

Four of the major mass media—newspapers, magazines, radio, and television—depend significantly on advertising revenue. An understanding of the economics of advertising, therefore, is important to understanding why ad media are the way they are.

ADVERTISING ECONOMICS

The value of a magazine, newspaper, radio, or TV advertisement depends on both the size and characteristics of the audience. To an advertiser, the most important audiences are composed of those individuals most likely to buy the product being advertised. These *target audiences* are critical to the ad media because they have real economic value based on the following dimensions:

Value in Advertising

This Revlon ad in *Cosmopolitan* Magazine reflects the sex dimension of targeting an advertiser's audience. (Courtesy Revlon, Inc.)

1. If Mobil Oil does not have many service stations in a given state, it is not worthwhile to advertise there. The *geographical location* of the audience–consumer is critical to the advertiser. It would obviously be foolish for a snowmobile manufacturer to buy time on a Miami TV station.

2. Frequent airline travelers live primarily in metropolitan areas, and so United Airlines advertises mainly in large urban newspapers. *Population density* is an important dimension of the target audience.

3. The Kellogg Company sells most of its presweetened cereals to children. Saturday morning is a good time to advertise its products on television. *Age* is the relevant dimension here. For years, "The Lawrence Welk Show" was sponsored exclusively by Geritol.

4. Women buy Revlon cosmetics, so advertising them in men's magazines would be foolhardy. *Sex* is a dimension of the target audience.

5. Purchases of convenience foods are affected by *family size, income*, and *employment patterns*. Large families eat more and spend a larger portion of the family income for food. Working women use more convenience foods than do women who remain at home.

Research methods are also beginning to report media usage based on *product category*. For example, in Atlanta, Georgia, how many heavy users of coffee read *Family Circle* or watch Cable Network News (CNN)? This kind of information has a significant impact on traditional advertising patterns. One of the major reasons cable's advertiser-supported services have had difficulty selling time is that the TV rating services were not reporting cable audiences. This meant that advertisers could not estimate the economic value of the ESPN or CNN or ARTS or "superstation" advertising campaigns as well as they could more traditional "buys." This problem is now being rectified.

Advertising Efficiency

Advertisers seek the largest possible target audience at the lowest possible price. Advertisers tend to use media vehicles that provide the best cost efficiency. This cost efficiency, or cost per 1000 (CPM) readers or viewers, is determined simply by dividing advertising cost by audience size. Cost efficiency is a means of assigning relative value to media audiences. (See Chapter 11 for a detailed analysis of the concept.)

Advertiser Production Expenses

Besides paying for the costs incurred by the media, advertiser must produce ads to fill their space and time buys. The cost of producing advertising has skyrocketed in the past 10 years. Print ads for major advertisers run as high as $50,000 per layout. Photographing models, retouching photographs, designing paper and setting type, making gravure negatives and screen prints—these are all complicated and time-consuming activities for well-paid technicians using expensive, sophisticated equipment. Radio ad campaigns by recognized talent can run from $25,000 to $50,000 per 60-second spot. The average cost of a 30-second TV spot is $100,000, which is equal to the per-minute cost of a $10 million feature film.

High initial costs and operating expenses have had far-reaching effects on America's mass media. Many people are concerned that not all these changes have been for the better. For example: **EFFECTS OF MEDIA ECONOMICS**

1. Entry into media ownership is becoming increasingly difficult because of the large sums required to start and operate a medium. This is of special concern to minority groups.

2. Groups already involved in media operations are, in general, succeeding at a rapid rate. Successful companies seem to get bigger and bigger with ever-increasing power accruing to them. Because of the economics, media have become "big business" with chain and cross-media ownership dominant. In the most lucrative TV markets, over 70% of the stations are licensed to group owners.

3. Because of the enormous sums risked in the media marketplace, the media in general have become more competitive in trying to capture the largest, most valuable audience available, instead of attempting to meet the special needs of all segments of society. Even public broadcasters now struggle to reach a mass audience in many of their content offerings.

4. Some media business people seem to be sensitive only to the demands of the marketplace. Some media investors refuse to take anything other than mild positions on sensitive issues.

5. Today, over 70% of newspaper circulation comes from papers controlled by fewer than 170 multiple ownerships, and the top 25 chains control more than half the newspapers as well as numerous broadcast stations. Fewer than 50 of America's 1500 cities have more than one newspaper.

6. Networks, syndicates, news services, and other corporate giants operate increasingly within media oligopolies. Only a limited number of powerful competitors exist in every media institution.

7. Financial wealth seems to accrue to limited media groups in major metropolitan areas. Broadcast profits for some stations in the large markets have been reported to return close to 100% on annual tangible investments. Similar profits come to successful record producers, film producers, and publishers.

**Group Ownership
of Media**

Media ownership has a significant impact on what Americans read, hear, and watch; and control of content in the news and entertainment media is in an ever-shrinking number of hands. The chains are getting bigger, and there are fewer and fewer independents. Conglomerates must be of special concern because of the power they now hold and because they are increasingly involved in many media rather than one medium. The marketplace of ideas is shrinking as independent viewpoints are reduced through sales and mergers.

Measured against RCA, most media conglomerates pale by comparison. An anlysis by Ben H. Bagdikian of this prototype conglomerate raises an important concern:

> The RCA Corporation, for example, owns NBC. The parent corporation does more than $7 billion of business a year, of which NBC represents less than 20 percent. It owns the Hertz Corporation. It is a major defense industry, producing military radar, electronic-warfare equipment, laser systems, instruments that guide aerial bombs to targets, hardware that does intelligence processing, guidance for surface-to-air missiles, and it has wholly owned subsidiaries around the world. It controls telecommunications among 200 nation states through its RCA Global Communications, Inc. RCA is also a subcontractor on the Alaska pipeline project, and it has produced guidance systems for Apollo and Skylab spacecraft. One wonders what might have been lost to RCA in its multimillion-dollar Apollo and Skylab space contracts if its wholly owned broadcasting arm, NBC, had produced a convincing documentary against spending all that money on space exploration.[1]

It must be understood that ABC and CBS are also conglomerates: NBC is not alone. But the conglomerates are not limited to parent broadcast companies. Time Inc., for example, publishes magazines (*Time, People Weekly, Fortune, Money,* and *Sports Illustrated*) and in 1978 bought the *Washington Star* for $20 million to add to the 17 weekly newspapers it already controlled. Time Inc., also runs Time-Life Films; Home Box Office; Manhattan Cable Television; a Grand Rapids, Michigan, TV station (WOTV); Time-Life Books; Little, Brown publishers; Book-of-the-Month Club; a paper company; and marketing research companies. Lucrative media operations have become prime targets for big investors not previously involved with public communication systems. The functions of the media may suffer at the hands of individuals whose training is in business rather than in mass communication. Corporate conflicts of interest and the economics of media influence are very real issues in American society. Media people can be resocialized by business people, and vice versa.

---

[1] Ben H. Bagdikian, "Newspaper Mergers—The Final Phase," *Columbia Journalism Review* 15, no. 6 (March–April 1977): 20.

The mass media are the primary sources of passive leisure-time activity in America. We spend enormous amounts of time and money to please ourselves.

DIMENSIONS OF MEDIA ECONOMICS

The tabulation that follows is a complex display of economic data, but careful analysis will give some idea of the financial importance of the mass media. Passive leisure activities account for approximately 2.8% ($82 billion) of the gross national product (GNP); the percentage is about the same as it was in the 1960s. The share of each medium in this financial situation has fluctuated significantly over the past three decades, however.

Television has moved into a leadership position and now accounts for $1 of every $4 spent on leisure (26.3%). The advent of pay and basic cable services has enabled television to move into first place. Television has shown a sizable loss in terms of share of market, however; it is down more than 3% from its 29.4% share in 1970. This medium will be very volatile in the late 1980s as cable and video cassette systems proliferate.

Newspapers remain strong with $19.5 billion spent (23.8% of all leisure dollars spent), but the newspapers' share is down *significantly* from its 32.1% share in 1970 and 37.4% share in 1960. Nevertheless, because many

Economic Ranking of Major Media

1981 Rank Medium	Dollars (in billions) 1981	% of total	Rank	Dollars (in billions) 1970	% of total	Rank	Dollars (in billions) 1960	% of total	Rank	Dollars (in billions) 1950	% of total
1. Television (including cable)	21.6	26.3	2	7.8	29.4	2	2.7	19.4	2	2.1	21.6
2. Newspapers	19.5	23.8	1	8.5	32.1	1	5.2	37.4	1	3.1	32.0
3. Magazines	9.9	12.1	3	2.5	9.4	3	1.6	11.5	5	1.0	10.3
4. Sound Recordings	6.9	8.4	5	2.1	7.9	5	1.0	7.2	6	.4	4.1
5. Video Games (arcade and home)	6.1	7.4									
6. Radio	5.9	7.2	4	2.3	8.7	4	1.3	9.4	4	1.1	11.3
7. Books	4.1	5.0	7	1.0	3.8	7	.4	2.9	8	.2	2.1
8. Movies	3.0	3.7	6	1.1	4.2	5	1.0	7.2	3	1.4	14.4
9. Spectator Sports	2.3	2.8	9	.5	1.9	9	.3	2.2	7	.2	2.1
10. Video Recordings	1.4	1.7									
11. Cultural Events	1.3	1.6	8	.7	2.6	7	.4	2.9	8	.2	2.1
TOTAL	82.0	100.0		26.5	100.0		13.9	100.1[a]		9.7	100.0
2.8 PERCENT OF GNP			2.7			2.7			3.4		

[a] Totals may add to over 100 due to rounding.

newspapers also own TV stations and cable systems, they are quite strong financially. Television and newspapers account for half (50.1%) of all leisure dollars spent in the United States.

Magazines continue to gain strength after rough periods in the late 1950s and early 1960s. Periodicals now command a 12.1% share (nearly $10 billion per year) of all leisure dollars. Special-interest magazines are very solid and have helped this medium maintain its position and show a very strong increase of nearly 3% in share of the leisure market since 1970.

Sound recording, despite slowed growth in software sales, has moved up one notch to fourth place on the list. Strong sophisticated hardware sales and price increases for records and tapes have been influential in this increase. The share of market (8.4%) is also up, despite the fact that the industry was hard hit by the recession of the early 1980s.

Video games, played both in the arcade and at home, have had a truly amazing impact on leisure spending. Since the mid-1970s, when video games were introduced, they have become a $6.1 billion per-annum business and command a 7.4% share of the leisure market. Experts feel that this new pastime has stunted the growth of the pop music and motion-picture industries, the two media hit hardest by the games' introduction. After slowed growth in 1982, new computer games using laser videodisc technology and Hollywood quality cartoons created a resurgence. The first cartoon game, *Dragon's Lair*, at $4000 per unit generated $30 million in sales before the first machine appeared in an arcade. The visuals were a great leap over the previous "dot and stick" games. *Dragon's Lair* produced by Don Bluth, was drawn by 50 artists who created the artistically beautiful but financially unsuccessful feature film *The Secret of N.I.M.H.* The new laser technology allows game discs to be interchangeable; as one game's popularity wanes, a new episode in that adventure or an entirely new game can be inserted. These games open a new avenue for TV and film artists. Motion pictures like *Tron* and *WarGames* reflected an attempt by filmmakers to lure audiences away from game arcades by using computer game themes. Now the thrust will be to create "movies" on laser discs to be played by audiences in the arcade or at home.

Radio has nearly tripled its dollar volume since 1970, but the $5.9 billion puts it in sixth place on the list. Radio is one of *four* media to show a decrease in share of the leisure dollar. The medium is now dominated by FM stations playing music formats, which appeal to very narrow target audiences. Music television (especially MTV) is a specter on radio's horizon; MTV has already replaced radio as the primary influence on record purchases.

Books remain in seventh place on the list with a 400% increase in dollar volume to $4.1 billion and a strong showing (5%) in terms of share of market. Book publishing has been hard hit by high interest rates (which have an impact on inventory and new ventures) and dramatic increases in manufacturing costs.

This scene from the movie *WarGames* (1983) reflects the nation's fascination with video games.

(Photo: New York Public Library at Lincoln Center, Courtesy United Artists, MGM/UA Entertainment Co.)

Motion pictures have lost significantly in share of market; the industry's share is down from 4.2% in 1970 to 3.7%, despite tripling its volume to $3 billion. The film business caters almost exclusively to the youth market, and that market is dwindling. Movie content will have to "age," and movie moguls will have to look for dramatic innovations once again. The industry's current health is based on increased ticket prices and a limited number of blockbusters that garner fabulous profits. Marketing costs have skyrocketed in the past ten years and now equal production costs.

Spectator sports have benefited from increases in population and media exposure and show strong growth potential. Battles between the National Collegiate Athletic Association (NCAA) and college football powers over ownership of TV rights to games are one indication of the economic value of sports on radio and television. Local station and cable rights for professional basketball and baseball may have to cover rapidly increasing costs, especially player salaries. The development and initial survival of the United States Football League (USFL) in no small measure reflects the financial support of ABC's and ESPN's royalty payments for TV rights.

Video recordings are another new entry on the leisure-activity list. Currently the industry depends on recent motion-picture releases for nearly all of its content. Sales and rentals amount to $1.4 billion and have become so important a source of ancillary income that many film unions have struck for profit participation in this area. Erotic content accounts for a sizable proportion of income. Playboy Enterprises is testing the waters with video versions of *Playboy* magazine on video cassettes as well as its cable channel.

Cultural events have lost nearly 40% of their share of the leisure market, and ticket prices have nearly tripled in the past 10 years for professional shows. Concerts and theater, opera, and dance performances, except for the "hot ticket" shows, are all suffering. Only rock concerts by "supergroups" continue to do well at the box office. Orchestras and opera and theatrical companies are looking to cable television for additional revenue, but thus far these arts ventures have not attracted large enough audiences to be profitable.

Four mass media showed decreases in share of leisure market: television, radio, motion pictures, and newspapers. Newspapers dropped 9.3 share points. With videotext and teletext video news services on the horizon, as well as 24-hour-a-day cable news now being available, newspapers must emphasize local information or their share will continue to decline. To shore up their industry, newspaper publishers are diversifying rapidly into other media.

LEADERSHIP IN MEDIA ECONOMICS   An examination of the major companies that produce media content is valuable because it illustrates the levels of involvement American corporations have in the economics of the media business. The following table displays the top 100 media companies in America. Several observations are worth making regarding the data in this table. The top 10 companies earn over $1 billion in media revenue annually; 80 corporations earn at least $100 million. The combined earning power of the top 100 companies is over $37 billion a year.

The Top 100 Media Companies

1982 Rank	1981 Rank	Company	1982 Revenues (in millions)			1981 Revenues (in millions)		
			Media	Total	% Media	Media	Total	% Media
1	1	American Broadcasting Cos.	2,530.0	2,660.0	95	2,300.0	2,440.0	94
2	2	CBS Inc.	2,450.0	4,120.0	59	2,180.0	3,960.0	55
3	4	Time Inc.	1,830.0	3,560.0	51	1,510.0	3,300.0	46
4	3	RCA Corp.	1,790.0	8,240.0	22	1,620.0	8,004.0	20
5	6	Gannett Co.	1,492.8	1,519.5	98	1,345.0	1,370.0	98
6	5	Times Mirror Co.	1,489.2	2,210.5	67	1,368.4	2,156.0	64
7	7	S. I. Newhouse & Sons	1,350.0	1,520.0	88	1,250.0	1,400.0	89
8	8	Knight-Ridder Newspapers	1,300.1	1,327.7	98	1,200.5	1,237.1	98
9	9	Hearst Corp.	1,300.0	N/A	N/A	1,200.0	N/A	N/A
10	10	Tribune Co.	1,240.0	1,430.0	87	1,170.0	1,410.0	83
11	11	New York Times Co.	890.6	933.7	95	796.6	841.7	95
12	13	McGraw-Hill	804.2	1,190.0	67	732.4	1,110.1	66

1982 Rank	1981 Rank	Company	1982 Revenues (in millions)			1981 Revenues (in millions)		
			Media	Total	% Media	Media	Total	% Media
13	12	Washington Post Co.	786.2	801.4	98	739.5[a]	753.4	98
14	14	Dow Jones & Co.	683.0	730.7	94	600.0	641.0	94
15	15	Capital Cities Communications	663.6	663.6	100	573.8	573.8	100
16	24	Westinghouse Electric Corp.	663.0	9,745.4	7	319.0	9,367.5	3
17	16	Dun & Bradstreet	584.1	1,500.0	39	553.4	1,330.0	42
18	18	E. W. Scripps Co.	575.0	631.9	91	500.0	550.0	91
19	17	Triangle Publications	549.4	549.4	100	502.2	502.2	100
20	21	Cox Communications	477.5	514.7	93	370.2	403.5	92
21	19	Cox Enterprises	425.0	425.0	100	419.5	419.5	100
22	29	Storer Communications	379.3	379.3	100	276.4	276.4	100
23	22	Field Enterprises	377.5	450.0	84	368.7	425.0	87
24	26	Harte-Hanks Communications	333.8	396.9	84	300.9	348.5	86
25	20	Metromedia Inc.	326.8	407.1	81	390.5	461.8	85
26	28	Ziff Corp.	320.2	N/A	N/A	300.0	N/A	N/A
27	25	Central Newspapers	315.0	315.0	100	304.5	304.5	100
28	30	Oklahoma Publishing Co.	302.9	302.9	100	266.8	266.8	100
29	35	Chronicle Publishing Co.	296.3	296.3	100	234.7[a]	234.7[a]	100
30	50	General Tire & Rubber Co.	288.2	2,470.0	12	160.9	2,180.0	7
31	36	News America Publishing	270.0	270.0	100	210.0	210.0	100
32	23	Meredith Corp.	266.0	449.1	59	236.7[a]	403.4[a]	59
33	48	Tele-Communications Inc.	265.6	282.6	94	167.7	181.4	92
34	33	Affiliated Publications	259.0	259.4	99	235.8[a]	236.1	99
35	31	Evening News Assn.	257.0	257.0	100	250.0	250.0	100
36	27	Reader's Digest Assn.	256.0	1,300.0	20	267.0[a]	1,200.0	22
37	34	Thomson Newspapers[b]	254.0	539.8	47	232.4	536.2	43
38	41	Media General	248.1	429.4	58	197.1	366.5	54
39	32	Cowles Media Co.	238.0	238.0	100	213.7	213.7	100
40	39	Landmark Communications	230.0	230.0	100	200.0	200.0	100
41	49	Viacom International	228.6	274.9	83	164.5	210.4	78
42	42	Multimedia Inc.	225.5	225.5	100	195.3	195.3	100
43	40	Pulitzer Publishing Co.	224.0	224.0	100	197.4	197.4	100
44	44	H & C Communications	210.8	210.8	100	188.3	188.3	100
45	37	Copley Newspapers	209.3	210.0	99	205.6	206.5	99
46	43	Freedom Newspapers	207.7	207.7	100	194.1	194.1	100
47	45	A. H. Belo Corp.	203.2	203.4	99	182.2	182.3	99
48	58	A. S. Abell Co.	185.0	185.0	100	133.0	133.0	100
49	52	McClatchy Newspapers	185.0	185.0	100	160.0	160.0	100
50	71	Warner Communications	183.8	3,980.0	5	110.5	3,240.0	3
51	47	National Geographic Society	181.1	280.4	65	170.7	272.7	62
52	70	American Express Co.	175.8	8,093.0	2	113.6	7,291.0	2
53	46	General Electric Co.	175.0	26,500.0	0.6	175.0	27,000.0	0.6
54	51	Houston Chronicle Publishing Co.	167.9	167.9	100	160.6	160.5	100
55	53	Playboy Enterprises	165.9	210.1	79	177.6[a]	221.5[a]	80
56	54	Journal Co.	165.8	290.0	57	162.4[a]	290.0	56
57	55	Penthouse International	165.0	175.0	94	150.0	160.0	94
58	56	Lee Enterprises	158.9	160.6	99	149.8	153.1	98
59	64	Wometco Enterprises	155.5	493.4	32	122.7	434.2	28
60	63	Donrey Media Group	147.4	147.4	100	125.0	125.0	100
61	82	Turner Broadcasting System	146.3	165.6	88	83.0	95.1	87
62	65	Blade Co.	141.4	141.4	100	122.6	122.6	100
63	57	National Enquirer	140.0	140.0	100	90.9	90.9	100

1982 Rank	1981 Rank	Company	1982 Revenues (in millions)			1981 Revenues (in millions)		
			Media	Total	% Media	Media	Total	% Media
64	74	Howard Publications	139.5	139.5	100	114.4	114.0	100
65	60	Oak Industries	139.0	545.7	25	130.0	507.1	26
66	66	Providence Journal Co.	132.0	312.0	42	121.0	262.0	46
67	59	Cahners Publishing Co.	130.0	160.0	81	100.0	150.0	67
68	—	Dispatch Printing Co.	127.2	127.2	100	110.4	110.4	100
69	62	Taft Broadcasting Co.	125.1	358.2	35	112.2	239.9	47
70	61	U.S. News & World Report	124.0	132.0	94	107.2	114.0	94
71	73	Harcourt Brace Jovanovich	122.4	573.3	21	107.0	539.3	20
72	72	Times Publishing Co.	119.5	119.5	100	110.0	110.0	100
73	69	Morris Communications Corp.	117.6	120.0	98	115.8	118.4	98
74	67	Petersen Publishing Co.	117.5	127.5	92	105.0[a]	113.0[a]	93
75	68	Seattle Times Co.	116.5	116.5	100	118.3	118.3	100
76	75	McCall Publishing Co.	110.0	110.0	100	97.2	97.2	100
77	89	Continental Cablevision	108.7	108.7	100	73.0	73.0	100
78	74	Rogers-UA Cablesystems	107.0	107.0	100	77.8	77.8	100
79	77	Jefferson-Pilot Corp.	101.1	1,020.0	10	91.4	978.7	9
80	83	Southern Progress Corp.	100.0	N/A	N/A	80.0	N/A	N/A
81	94	United Cable Television Corp.	99.8	99.8	100	62.8	62.8	100
82	76	Courier-Journal & Louisville Times Co.	98.0	160.0	61	93.1	153.2[a]	61
83	79	Scripps-Howard Broadcasting Co.	95.6	95.6	100	87.3	87.3	100
84	—	Ingersoll Newspapers Co.	95.0	95.0	100	87.5	87.5	100
85	—	Allbritton Cmmunications Co.	93.0	93.0	100	50.5	50.5	100
86	78	Des Moines Register and Tribune Co.	90.6	94.5	96	89.4	92.6[a]	97
87	90	Deseret Management Crp.	89.0	104.7	85	71.9	84.5	85
88	87	Outlet Co.	87.0	87.0	100	75.0	142.8	53
89	84	Bergen Evening Record Corp.	86.1	87.3	99	79.3	80.4	99
90	86	Park Broadcasting	85.0	91.0	93	75.0	80.0	94
91	80	Pittway Corp.	81.8	411.1	20	86.3	403.6	21
92	91	LIN Broadcasting Corp.	81.3	88.4	92	66.2	71.0	93
93	98	Sammons Communications	81.0	81.0	100	59.9	59.9	100
94	92	Knapp Communications	79.7	92.9	86	64.5	74.5	86
95	—	Maclean Hunter Communications[b]	75.0	427.1	18	60.2	341.2	18
96	93	Army Times Publishing Co.	73.7	104.2	70	63.3	94.4	67
97	95	Rollins Inc.	69.2	526.5	13	62.1	454.6	14
98	—	Cosmos Broadcasting Corp.	67.5	264.8	25	47.7	231.2	21
99	81	Worrell Newspapers	67.4	67.4	100	84.0	84.0	100
100	—	Rodale Press	67.0	96.0	70	55.0	85.0	65
		TOTAL	37,228.10					

[a] Restated figure.

[b] Media revenues represent U.S. holdings only. Total revenues are consolidated worldwide figures. Percentage figure consists of U.S. media percentage of total.

In the past 15 years big media companies have swallowed smaller media companies. Two events have occurred recently: (a) The biggest media companies have diversified into nonmedia areas; (b) even bigger nonmedia corporations have bought into media operations.

If we break down the top 100 companies in terms of investment as a percentage of total income, we find that several observations are important:

1. *Exclusively (100%) media.* These 35 companies do *not* have financial interests outside the media. Note that not one of the top 10 companies is in this group.
2. *Predominantly (91–99%) media.* These 21 companies earn nearly all their revenue from media enterprises. Thus, 56 of the top 100 companies are exclusively or predominantly involved in the mass communication industry.
3. *Substantially (51–90%) media.* There are 22 companies in this group. Thus, 78 of the top 100 companies earn at least 51% of their revenue from media enterprises.
4. *Moderately (11–50%) media.* There are 11 companies moderately involved in media. The number-four media company, RCA, leads this group, which includes other industrial giants, such as the General Tire & Rubber Company.
5. *Modestly (0–10%) media.* Eight corporations are involved modestly in media; Westinghouse, Warner Communications, American Express, and General Electric are the largest companies so involved.

If we analyze the same companies in terms of primary medium of revenue, another set of observations illuminates the economic clout of media lobbyists.

Dramatic advances from 1981 to 1982 were made by the following companies:

1. General Tire & Rubber grew from $160.9 million to $288.2 million, thus jumping from fiftieth to thirtieth place on the top 100 list.
2. Warner Communications moved up 21 rungs on the ladder. Expansions in the publishing and film industries placed it in fiftieth position.
3. American Express continues to invade media industries. It moved from seventieth to fifty-second place, yet only 2% of its revenue came from media.
4. Turner Broadcasting System, based on the strength of the first "SuperStation" (WTBS-TV) and two cable news services, doubled its revenue and moved from eighty-second to sixty-first place.
5. Dispatch Printing Company was the highest-placed entry of first-time corporations on the list; it was sixty-eighth. Five other companies also made first appearances on the list.

Rapid growth, diversification, and readjustment of economic position are part and parcel of the industries that provide news and entertainment for a nation that is becoming as information dependent as it is energy dependent. Media and media companies are among the most volatile in the economic marketplace. Media industries are growing economically and are becoming increasingly powerful politically.

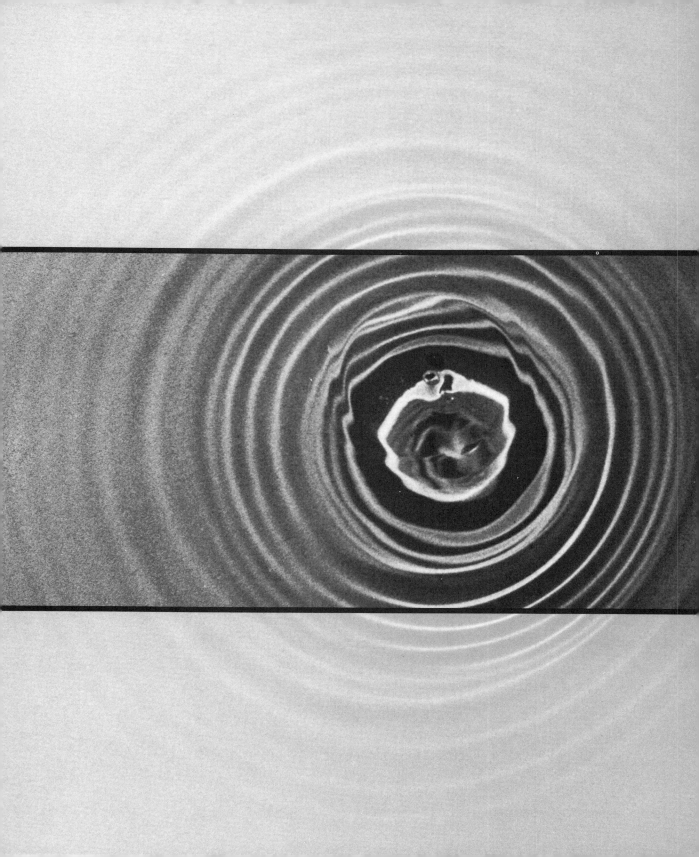

THE
ELEMENTS
OF
COMMUNICATION

PART **2**

Communicators  5

When Fred Hirsch graduated from Ithaca College 10 years ago with a degree in communication, he immediately set out for New York City to climb the network corporate ladder. Hirsch is still communicating to audiences in broadcasting, but far from being one of many radio news people at NBC, he is the chief reporter and announcer at radio station WDME in Dover–Foxcroft, Maine. As the *Wall Street Journal* reported his story, Hirsch is the station's business manager, advertising salesperson, and promoter. He also cleans the station's bathroom. Hirsch doesn't mind all these duties because he owns the station. Fred Hirsch is a communicator.

The process of communication starts with a communicator. The mass communicator, however, differs significantly from the individual communicator in interpersonal communication. When messages are exchanged on a person-to-person basis, the sender and the receiver are individual entities. In mass communication the receiver may be flesh and blood, but an individual sender is more myth than reality.

The communicator, or sender, in mass communication is rarely one individual. Even Fred Hirsch is only the visible portion of a vast and complex network of people. Many people, not simply those we actually see or hear, help shape the media message. A mass communicator is somewhat like the conductor of a symphony orchestra. One message comes

At home at radio WDME inside a converted railroad car in Dover-Foxcroft, Maine, station owner Fred Hirsch and wife Vickie represent occasional individual communicators who make up part of the conglomerate mass communicator.

(Photo courtesy Fred Hirsch.)

from many sources, and while the conductor may represent the orchestra, he or she is not the only communicator responsible for the message sent.

For example, when Mike Wallace appears as the correspondent on "60 Minutes," the audience may assume that Wallace is the person responsible for the story. Actually Wallace is chiefly a performer on a program written and edited by many others, including its executive producer, Don Hewitt. Indeed, the general rule in TV news is that the longer the broadcast, the smaller the role of the on-camera correspondent.

Hewitt in an article in *American Film*, acknowledges that the audience may misunderstand how the show's stories are put together. "I've felt for a long time that titles like 'producer' and 'executive producer' are misnomers," he says. "When TV news was just starting in 1948, they didn't know what to call us, so they borrowed from theater and movies. But I think it's caused great confusion and I think it's about time we eliminated those titles. I'm really more an executive editor than an executive producer. The man we call a producer is really a reporter."

In turn, the people who are called *correspondents*—Mike Wallace, Diane Sawyer, Morley Safer, Harry Reasoner, and Ed Bradley—often serve more as performers. They conduct the major on-camera interviews but do not participate in much of the research on their stories and frequently do not write their own scripts.

Given the system, it could scarcely be otherwise. An average story for "60 Minutes" takes a producer 6 to 8 weeks to complete, and each "60 Minutes" correspondent appears on three stories every 4 weeks.

"It's quite apparent that we can't do all, or even a lion's share of the reporting," says Wallace, who is generally credited with doing more of his own reporting than most. Wallace says that he serves an editor's role on his stories—reading material as it comes in, suggesting interviews, and talking with the producer about the direction of the story. "By the time you arrive at the filming stage, you're pretty well prepared," he adds.

Along with several colleagues, Wallace points out that television is a collaborative process by nature. "I love the process of working with a producer and a camera crew and an editor. That's what television always was, and always will be, and I think in general the system works well."

Therefore, even though Fred Hirsch and Mike Wallace are individual media communicators, the mass communicator in American media is usually a complex organization. Individuals at times seem to function as mass communicators. The animated films of Norman McLaren, for example, are essentially the work of a single individual. Because of McLaren's association with the Canadian Film Board, however, the characteristics of mass communicators, such as complexity, specialization, and a high degree of organization, are evident.

Performers or public personalities, then, are only one part of the conglomerate mass communicator. Too often, potential broadcasters, filmmakers, or newspaper reporters focus only on performance careers, not recognizing that mass communication is a *process* that goes beyond *performance*. Although performers are highly visible role models, they are often unrealistic or limited role models. Students of mass communication must recognize the vast network of media communicators that extends beyond performers.

CHARACTERISTICS OF THE MASS COMMUNICATOR

Competitiveness

Many features characterize the mass communicator in the United States, but one of the most significant is *competitiveness*. Mass communicators compete intensely for audiences and spend huge amounts of money to reach those audiences. The three major TV networks, for example, spend more than $3.5 billion annually on network programming. A half-hour pilot (a test program used to sell a series idea to a network or sponsor) costs anywhere from $250,000 to $500,000. The most tightly budgeted commercial motion-picture feature costs a minimum of $3 million including production, distribution, and promotion. Starting a small daily newspaper today would require at least $1 million, and a major metropolitan daily would take $10 to $15 million. Mass communicators spend these amounts of money sending messages because as complex organizations they compete to reach the largest or most significant audience.

Competition, then, in mass communication is a major force that has great impact on the communicator. In interpersonal communication individuals compete for the attention of another person. A busy signal on the telephone suggests communicator competition. Obviously this is minor compared to the intense competition in mass media. For example, newspapers compete with one another in terms of circulation figures; motion pictures compete for box-office income. Perhaps the most intense competition occurs in network television, where it is best symbolized by the emphasis on ratings. One rating point representing 1% of all American TV homes is worth millions of dollars to a network. Entire companies, such as A. C. Nielsen and the American Research Bureau, are devoted to research measuring the comparative standing of programs, magazines, advertisements, and networks.

Size and Complexity.   *Size and Complexity* are also important mass communicator characteristics. Successful mass communicators gain the opportunity to speak out; their weaker competitors lose that opportunity. The economic necessity to reach large audiences in order to survive normally requires a large organization. Size in this context requires some clarification, however. Certainly Fred Hirsch's station is not large. The average TV station in the United States employs only 60 full-time employees. Of the approximately 1800 book publishers in the United States, only 350 have more than 20 employees. Nevertheless, all media organizations, regardless of their internal size and structure, rely on networks of specialized people and organizations. Fred Hirsch's radio station, for example, relies on the vast resources and staff of the Associated Press news service. The smallest book publisher employs artists, copyeditors, and other editorial personnel on a freelance basis. Small newspapers use temporary reporters, called *stringers*, in the field. While not part of a paper's full-time staff, these people are a necessary part of the organization.

Complexity and size are closely related in mass media organizations. As size increases, complexity emerges. A large daily newspaper has many separate divisions, among them reporting, editorial, advertising, circulation, promotion, research, personnel, production, and management, to handle its work. CBS is known primarily as a TV network. But as the figure opposite indicates, the CBS Broadcast Group is only one of four separate divisions that include CBS Records, CBS Columbia, and CBS Publishing. The Broadcast Group itself has eight subdivisions.

Industrialization   Competitiveness, complexity, and size form the base from which several other common mass communicator features emerge. *Industrialization* is perhaps the most obvious feature. A glance at the stock-market section of a newspaper reveals the extent of industrialization in the mass media. Many mass communication organizations are part of large industrial conglomerates. The National Broadcasting Company (NBC) is a small part of

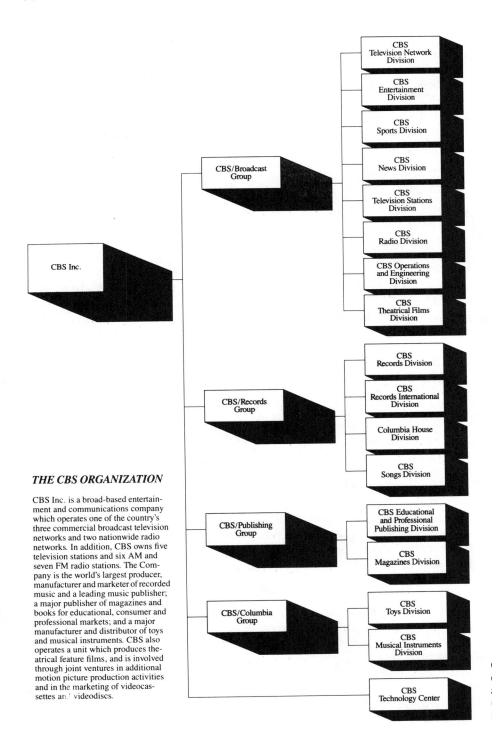

THE CBS ORGANIZATION

CBS Inc. is a broad-based entertainment and communications company which operates one of the country's three commercial broadcast television networks and two nationwide radio networks. In addition, CBS owns five television stations and six AM and seven FM radio stations. The Company is the world's largest producer, manufacturer and marketer of recorded music and a leading music publisher; a major publisher of magazines and books for educational, consumer and professional markets; and a major manufacturer and distributor of toys and musical instruments. CBS also operates a unit which produces theatrical feature films, and is involved through joint ventures in additional motion picture production activities and in the marketing of videocassettes and videodiscs.

CBS, Inc. has an organizational complexity appropriate to its size. (Copyright © 1984, CBS, Inc.)

a corporate giant, the Radio Corporation of America (RCA). Almost all major film studios are subsidiaries of larger corporations. Gulf & Western owns Paramount, Warner Brothers films are a product of Kinney Leisure Services, and Columbia Pictures is owned by Coca-Cola. Traditionally, motion-picture studios were identified with their production executives—Harry Cohn of Columbia, L. B. Mayer and Irving Thalberg of MGM, Darryl Zanuck of Fox, and Jack Warner of Warner Brothers—or with the major stars in their picture who were employees under long-term contract. Today, motion-picture stars not only move easily among major studios but often form their own companies, becoming conglomerate communicators in their own right. Studio production heads have been replaced by bankers, investment counselors, and corporate CEOs.

Book publishers are conglomerates with many different imprints: J. B. Lippincott is part of Harper & Row; Little, Brown is part of the Time Inc. media family. Most daily newspapers are part of large newspaper chains: Gannett, Newhouse, and Knight-Ridder are some examples. As with motion pictures, dominant personalities of print media, such as William Randolph Hearst, Henry Luce of Time Inc., Joseph Pulitzer, and William Allen White, have been replaced by the less well-known communicators associated with the major newspaper chains. To be sure, some editors, such as Ben Bradlee of the *Washington Post*, continue to function as public personalities, but the majority of newspaper editors today are less interested in their public image and more concerned about their managerial style and productivity.

Specialization

Specialization is a mass communicator characteristic that represents internal fragmentization. This fragmentization is perhaps nowhere more apparent than in the motion-picture industry. Feature films usually credit between 50 and 60 people with performing the jobs required to produce a motion picture. Many of these jobs are subdivided even further by trade unions. For example, under *painters* there may be a foreman, a color mixer, a sign writer, and a marbelizer. An organizational chart of a typical daily newspaper reveals about two dozen areas of specialization including three different subunits under *advertising*: display, national, and classified advertising. The photography department may have as many as 20 photographers, each one specializing in a different aspect of the job.

Representation

Still another mass communicator characteristic is *representation*. Representation is basically an external fragmentization of the mass communicator. Mass communicators have become so complex and must deal with so many different audiences that they often find it impossible to contact and make arrangements with all the individuals and organizations necessary to a smooth functioning of the organization. Mass communicator representatives include talent agents, managers, unions, program distributors, broadcast station representatives, and music licensing services.

In order to examine more fully the role of the mass communicator, let us look at some of the mass media in greater detail.

The radio and TV industries have three basic groups of communicators: networks, independent production companies, and local stations. Within each group are individual communicators who perform a wide variety of tasks.

BROADCASTING

Networks are organizations that provide TV programming and a limited supply of radio news and special-information services. On network television the idea for a program or a program series can, and often does, originate outside the network. By the time most programs or series are broadcast, however, they have come in contact with and have been influenced by many network people, all the way from stagehand to the chief executive of the network.

Networks

Today, the three major TV networks create few programs and concentrate on news, sports, and some documentaries. Of all TV network prime-time entertainment, 90% comes from program production or package agencies working in conjunction with network programmers. The function of the package agency is to develop a program or a program series. Package agencies employ writers, producers, actors, and technical personnel. This team of creators does everything short of braodcasting the program. Some production companies produce a pilot program independently and then attempt to sell a series to the network on the basis of the pilot. A more common practice is to produce a feature-film pilot with financial and creative support provided by the network on which the series is expected to appear. Showcases for this material have been developed by the networks, such as ABC's "Movie of the Week" and NBC's "World Premiere Movie." Package agencies also produce material directly for local TV station syndication. Series such as the game shows "Tic Tac Dough" and "Family Feud" are sold on a station-by-station basis rather than to the network.

Production Companies

As the telecommunication delivery system has expanded into cable, videodisc, video cassette, and satellite transmission, the number of video communicators has increased. Despite changes in the way content is delivered to audiences, however, the nature of the video communicator remains basically the same.

Although individual communicators vary from program to program, the process of production is similar. A writer creates the script, writing not only the performer's lines but also descriptions of what the viewer will see. A producer takes the script and assembles a creative staff to produce the show. A director coordinates the artistic efforts of the creative performers and technicians, including editors, camerapersons, sound-persons, set designers, and musicians. The performers add another dimension as they work with the total company.

Television program syndicators are also broadcast communicators. They are both passive and active senders. They are passive to the extent that they take off-network programs or feature motion pictures and sell them to individual stations in a package. They do not sell programs as such but merely the right to show the programs. They do not engage in program creation but simply distribute programs. Some producing and package agencies, such as Goodson-Todman, are actively engaged in distributing programs like "What's My Line?" for syndicated use by local stations. Some of the major program syndicators are the three networks and many of the major package agencies. Distribution is normally done by mail. In what is known in the industry as *bicycling*, each station, after airing a particular program, sends it to the next customer.

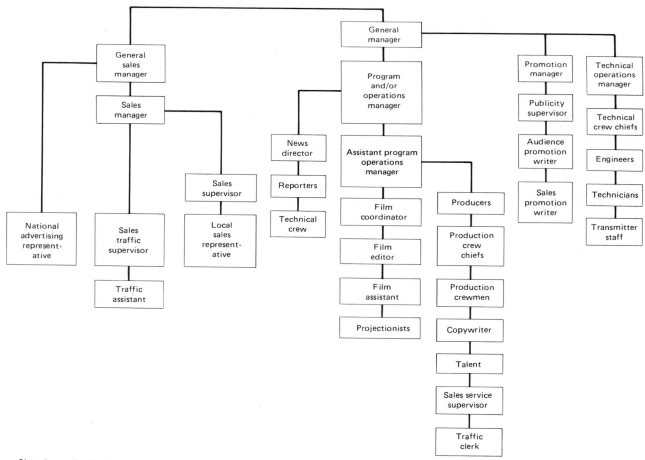

Structure of a Typical Large Television Station.

A local TV station generally employs its own staff to produce local programs. Local TV staff sizes range from over 100 at major-market stations to less than 20 at smaller organizations. The chart on the facing page illustrates the organizational structure of a typical large TV station. Even here, stations rely on outside senders such as the phonograph industry, jingle-package agencies, syndicators, and the networks for most of their program material. "Romper Room," for example, is a syndicated creative idea produced by local stations under guidelines established by the syndicator, who trains the local teachers who appear in the series.

Radio stations vary greatly in staff size. In New York, for example, WABC has over 50 employees, but more than half of all AM and FM stations employ fewer than 11 people full-time. The chart below shows the organizational structure of a typical radio station.

At the local level, radio stations depend on three outside creators for the bulk of their content: (a) the recording industry, which includes artists who write, arrange, and perform popular music and recording engineers who mix sound tracks to produce a master tape; (b) jingle-package companies, such as Music Makers of New York, which produce such items as station-break announcements, weather spots, and station identifications; and (c) format syndicators, which have emerged in recent years to become a dominant force in radio. The need to reach the right audience and obtain maximum numbers has led to extensive program-formula design in local radio. For a number of years, "top 40" was one of the few formats for local radio; today, over 50 major formats exist. These formats are often the product of format syndicators. Such companies as Drake-Chenault Enterprises not only provide the content but assist stations with promotion, publicity, and audience research. Such services add additional complexity and structure to the local station and further obscure the sense of an individual communicator.

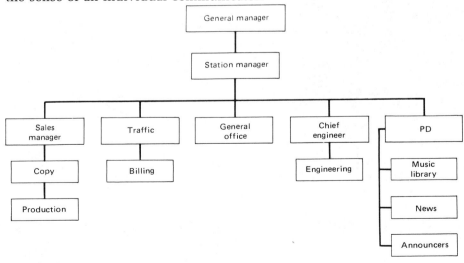

Organizational Chart for a Small-Market Radio Station. (Source: FCC)

Radio has taken on some attributes of a personal medium through the presence of the disc jockey, who is the bulwark of local radio programming. The disc jockey represents the individual thread that weaves together the material supplied by other creative teams. Often, his or her individuality is a major force in the station's popularity. Like the music, the role of the air personality is carefully designed. A good announcer sets the pace—he or she is the spirit of a radio station. The disc jockey provides the nonmusical muscle and showcases the product. For most radio stations, the DJ remains a key element in creating and executing the appropriate atmosphere for the desired audience. Today, with increased fragmentation and similar playlists on competing stations, the importance of personality is once again being stressed.

The announcer must develop a rapport with the audience. He or she must sound like a "real person," must speak the language of the listener. The day of the contrived, hype announcer has passed. Good jocks possess an understanding of their audiences and lifestyles. Their overriding message to the listener must be, "I'm one of you."

Undeniably, high-profile, identifiable personalities are an important element in cultivating station loyalty. In certain formats, such as album-

DJ Richard Neer lends his own personal style to radio WNEW-FM. (Courtesy WNEW-FM.)

oriented rock (AOR), however, the air personality must not eclipse the music, which is the absolute "star" of the radio station. The announcer must complement the music, not dominate it. Again, this is a function of a particular format.

Certain formats, notably talk shows, rely totally on the appeal of the personality. In most cases, morning radio also mandates a high-profile announcer.

MOTION PICTURES

The communicator in motion pictures assumes many of the characteristics and performs many of the functions of the broadcaster. In fact, the amount of TV production done by motion-picture studios adds to this similarity. Basically, the role of motion-picture communicators is not as complex as that of broadcast communicators because of the absence of such elements as networks and thousands of individual stations. Although theaters serve as the local exhibition outlet for film production, they are primarily passive outlets as contrasted with the more active involvement of stations in broadcast production.

Motion pictures have grown enormously in terms of production complexity. In the early twentieth century, production involved few people. Often one man—a Chaplin, a Sennett, or a Griffith—would conceive an idea, write the script, direct the film, and sometimes play the leading role.

In costume behind the cameras, Charlie Chaplin directs a scene from *The Gold Rush.*

(Photo: New York Public Library at Lincoln Center, Courtesy United Artists Corporation.)

Only a cameraman and a few extras were needed. The emergence of studios in the 1920s changed this. Huge organizations were built to produce an assembly-line product. Thousands of people became involved with the making of one motion picture.

The communicator role in motion pictures is perhaps the most specialized in all mass media. The figure below reveals some of the major and minor communicators involved in the production of a major motion

These credits for the feature film *2010* demonstrate the extent of specialization in the motion picture industry today. (Copyright © 1984 by MGM/UA Entertainment Co. All rights reserved.)

CAST

Heywood Floyd	Roy Scheider
Walter Curnow	John Lithgow
Tanya Kirbuk	Helen Mirren
R. Chandra	Bob Balaban
Dave Bowman	Keir Dullea
HAL 9000	Douglas Rain
Caroline Floyd	Madolyn Smith
Dimitri Moisevitch	Dana Elcar
Christopher Floyd	Taliesin Jaffe
Victor Milson	James McEachin
Betty Fernandez	Mary Jo Deschanel
Maxim Brailovsky	Elya Baskin
Vladimir Rudenko	Savely Kramarov
Vasali Orlov	Oleg Rudnik
Irina Yakunina	Natasha Shneider
Yuri Svetlanov	Vladimir Skomarovsky
Mikolai Ternovsky	Victor Steinbach
Alexander Kovalev	Jan Triska
Anchorman	Larry Carroll
Jessie Bowman	Herta Ware
Nurse	Cheryl Carter
Hospital Neurosurgeon	Ron Recasner
Dr. Hirsch	Robert Lesser
SAL 9000	Olga Mallsnerd
Commercial Announcers	Delana Michaels, Gene McGarr
Stunt Players	M. James Arnett, Jim Burk, Jim Halty, Robert Harman, Freddie Hice, John Meier, Gary Morgan, Mic Rodgers

CREDITS

Written for the Screen, Produced and Directed by	Peter Hyams
Based on the Novel by	Arthur C. Clarke
Director of Photography	Peter Hyams
Production Designer	Albert Brenner
Editor	James Mitchell
Visual Effects Supervisor	Richard Edlund
Music	David Shire
Casting by	Penny Perry
Costume Designer	Patricia Norris
Associate Producers	Jonathan A. Zimbert, Neil A. Machlis
Unit Production Manager	Neil A. Machlis
First Assistant Director	William S. Beasley
Second Assistant Director	Alan B. Curtiss
Set Decorator	Rick Simpson
Visual Futurist	Syd Mead
Film Editor	Mia Goldman
Assoc. Editors	Joanna Cappuccilli, Ross Albert
First Assistant Editor	Barbara Dunning
Second Assistant Editor	Greg Gerlich
Assistant Editors	Craig Herring, Ann Martin
Makeup Supervision	Michael Westmore
Script Supervisor	Marshall Schlom
Camera Operator	Ralph R. Gerling
Assistant Cameraman	Don E. Fauntleroy
Second Asst. Cameraman	Michael Wheeler
Chief Lighting Technician	John Baron
Key Grip	Tom May
Still Photographer	Bruce McBroom
Production Illustrator	Sherman Labby
Sound Design	Dale Strumpell
Production Sound Mixer	Gene Cantamessa
Boom Man	Raul Bruce
Rerecording Mixers	Michael J. Kohut, C.A.S., Aaron Rochin, C.A.S., Carlos deLarios, C.A.S., Ray O'Reilly, C.A.S.
Supervising Sound Editor	Richard L. Anderson
Sound Editors	Warren Hamilton, David Stone, Michael J. Benavente, Donald Flick, James Christopher
Apprentice Sound Editor	John Pospisil
ADR Editor	Vince Melanori
Music Editor	William J. Saracino
Technical Advisor	Dr. Richard Terrile
Special Effects Supervisor	Henry Millar
Special Effects Assts.	Dave Blitstein, Andy Evans
Flying Supervisor	Robert Harman
Hairstylist	Vivian McAteer
Propmaster	Martin Wunderlich
Men's Costume Supervisor	Bruce Walkup
Men's Costumer	Jim Kessler
Women's Costume Supervisor	Nancy McArdle
Transportation Coordinator	Randy Peters
Transportation Captain	Candace Wells
Stunt Coordinator	M. James Arnett
Production Coordinator	Katharine Ann Curtiss
Producer's Secretary	Barbara Allen
Production Controller	Steve Warner
Location Manager	Mario Iscovich
Unit Publicist	Don Levy
Effects Project Administrator	John James Jr.
Graphics	Arthur Gelb
Marketing Director	Elliot Fischoff

Visual Displays and Graphics by Video-Image

Video Effects Supervisor	Greg McMurry
Video Playback Coordinator	Rhonda Gunner
Video Computer Graphics	Richard E. Hollander
Computer Graphics Supervisor	John C. Wash
Video Technician	Pete Martinez

Production Associate	Steven Jongeward
Marine Technical Advisor	Dr. Jay Sweeney

Entertainment Effects Group, Los Angeles

Visual Effects Art Director	George Jenson
Director of Photography	Dave Stewart
Visual Effects Editor	Conrad Buff
Matte Department Supervisor	Neil Krepela
Mechanical Effects Supervisor	Thaine Morris
Special Projects	Gary Platek
Model Shop Supervisor	Mark Stetson
Optical Supervisor	Mark Vargo
Chief Engineer	Gene Whiteman
Animation Supervisors	Terry Windell, Garry Waller
Chief Matte Artist	Matthew Yuricich
Production Advisor	Jim Nelson
Business Manager	Laura Buff
Prod. Supervisors	Michael Kelly, Lynda Lemon
Camera Operators	John Fante, John Lambert, Mike Lawler, Bill Neil
Motion Control Technicians	David Hardberger, Mike Hoover, Jonathan Seay
Camera Assts.	Clint Palmer, Pete Romano, Jody Westheimer, Bess Wiley
Assistant Matte Cameraman	Alan Harding
Still Photographer	Virgil Mirano
Optical Printer Operators	Chuck Cowles, Bruno George
Optical Line Up	Phil Barberio, Ronald B. Moore, Mary E. Walter
Animators	Peggy Regan, Richard Coleman, Eusebio Torres
Technical Animators	Annick Therrien, Samuel Recinos, Rebecca Petrulli, Margaret Craig-Chang, Wendi Fischer, Juniko Moody
Stop Motion	Randall William Cook
Matte Artist	Michelle Moen
Key Effects Man	Bob Spurlock
Key Grips	Pat Van Auken, Ben Haller
Gaffer	Robert Eyslee
Effects Technicians	Bob Cole, Robin Kolb, Larz Anderson
Visual Effects Editor	Arthur Repola
Assistant Effects Editors	Jack Hinkle, Marty November, Dennis Michelson
Miniatures Crew	Jarek Alfer, David Beasley, Gary Bierend, Leslie Ekker, Kent Gebo, Bryson Gerard, Patrick McClung, Thomas Pahk, Robin Reilly, Milius Romyn, Christopher Ross, Dennis Schultz, Nicholas Seldon, Tom Silveroli, Paul Skylar, Ken Swenson
Miniature Mechanical Effects	Bob Johnston
Chief Moldmaker	David Shwartz
Chief Model Painter	Ron Gress
Starchild Personnel	Jon Alberti, Lance Anderson, Jon Berg, Tom Culnan, Gunnar Ferdinandsen, Mike Hosch, Stuart Ziff
Artistic Consultants	Brent Boates, Adolph Schaller
Video Systems	Clark Higgins
Design Engineers	Mark West, Mike Bolles, Rick Perkins
Electronics Engineers	Jerry Jeffress, Robin Leyden, Bob Wilcox
Software Programmer	Paul Van Kamp
Illustrator	Janet Kusnick
Cinetechnicians	George Polkinghorne, Mark Matthew, Ken Dudderar, Michael Nims, Joseph Ramos
Lab Technicians	Pat Repola, Brad Kuehn, Mike Lehman
Production Associates	Thomas Brown, Richard Johnson, Dan Kuhn, Sam Longoria, L. Mark Medernach, Laurel Walter
Production Accountant	Claire Wilson
Accountants	Kayte Westheimer, Leslie Falkinburg, Kim Ybiernas
Apprentice Matte Artist	Tanya Lowe
Addit. Miniatures Personnel	Adam Gelbart, George Pryor, Bob Wilson, Cynthia Czuchaj, Leslie Stetson
Prod. Administration	Jill Allen, Jamie Jardine, Mary Mason, Terry Platek
Digital Jupiter Simulation	Digital Productions
Addit. Display Material	Bo Gehring Associates
Prod. Assts.	Carl Brodene, Allen Cappuccilli, Dan Hutten, Brian Lee, Guy Marsden, Jon Schreiber, Harry Zimmerman
Projectionist	Don McLaren

Additional Optical Effects by Cinema Research
Filmed with a Louma Crane by Panavision, Inc.

The producers gratefully acknowledge the following for their assistance:

The Very Large Array Radio Telescope, an operating activity of the National Radio Astronomy Observatory, which is sponsored by the National Science Foundation
Marineland, Rancho Palos Verdes, California
Panasonic
Sheraton Hotels
Pan American Airlines
Ford Motor Company
Sanyo
3M Company
Adidas
Physio Control
Mag Instruments
Yamaha International
Lightning Sculpture by Bill Parker
Huffy
Carrera
Apple Computers, Inc.
Convergence Corporation
Calma G.C. Co.
Heartstart Incorp.
AT&T Systems
Aquarium World

Also Sprach Zarathustra!
by Richard Strauss
Lux Aeterna
by György Ligeti
Performed by
The North German Radio Chorus
Conducted by Helmut Franz
Courtesy of Deutsche Grammophon
a division of Polygram Classics
Electronic Music Produced by
Craig Huxley and David Shire
Synthesizer Programmed by Craig Huxley
Filmed in PANAVISION®
Titles and Opticals MGM
Prints in METROCOLOR®

Color Timer	Bob Kaiser

picture. Each person has a different task. The producer is an organizer, creating a structure in which other communicators can work effectively. The screenwriter produces a working film script. The film editor reviews the raw footage from the director and assembles the film into a meaningful form. The director has overall artistic control of the film's actual production.

Motion-picture credits are becoming more specialized than ever. *Star Trek II: The Wrath of Khan*, for example, credited Marc Okrand for Vulcan translation and Thaine Morris for pyrotechnics. *Dragonslayer* had its Latin adviser, its magic adviser, and several dragon movers. *Creepshow* listed the names of roach wranglers for its 25,000 cockroaches.

Some Hollywood movies today have technical credits six or eight times as large as their casts. Only 20 actors got their names on the screen for *Star Trek II*, but 127 behind-the-scenes men and women were credited. *Raiders of the Lost Ark* cited 232 technicians with such esoteric specialties as computer engineering and electronic-systems design; *Tron* matched its 44 actors and stuntmen with nearly 300 people whose faces did not appear on the screen.

The credit lists have lengthened largely because of the sophisticated special-effects movies that have poured out since *Star Wars*. No longer is it enough to have a gaffer (the head electrician), a best boy (the gaffer's right-hand man), and a number of grips (the equivalent of stagehands).

New categories such as synthevision technology, computer-image choreography, and object digitizing are all evidence of the computer-generated imagery that is increasingly a part of moviemaking.

In addition, communicator complexity has increased because most major movie studios have become parts of large industrial conglomerates. No longer is the motion-picture communicator a single studio with its hundreds of departments and divisions. Instead, the overlay of an industrial conglomerate has created new levels of corporate structure that must be considered. Gulf & Western is the corporate parent of Paramount Pictures. In addition to Paramount, Gulf & Western operates Famous Music, Inc., Desilu, Esquire, Inc., Simon and Schuster, Madison Square Garden Corporation and several other entertainment-based enterprises.

In the late 1960s, a relaxation of union rules governing the participation of various crafts in filmmaking permitted films to be made by fewer people. Such films as *Easy Rider* (1969) and *Billy Jack* (1971) were written, directed, and acted in by small groups of people and formed what many called a *new wave* in American film. For years we had the individualistic (auteur) films of foreign directors like Ingmar Bergman, François Truffaut, and Akira Kurosawa. In this country the experimental films of Andy Warhol, Jonas Mekas, and Kenneth Anger often involved little more than the creator and strips of film.

Nevertheless, major motion pictures like *Superman III* (1983), *Return of the Jedi* (1983), and *Poltergeist* (1982), with their huge casts, high costs, and complex organizations, illustrate that American films are still the product of many people working together. The real change in motion pictures has been a deemphasis on the studio and the elimination of many elements of general studio overhead that at times cluttered and overburdened a film with too many communicators. Lest one think that films are now being made on the "one person one film" principle, the slightly tongue-in-cheek Hollywood hierarchy should serve notice that motion pictures are still the products of complex corporate communicators.

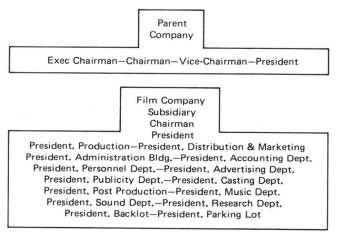

Ultimate Hollywood Executive Hierarchy. (Daily Variety Ltd. Reprinted by permission.)

PRINT MEDIA   For years the "byline myth" has dominated the concept of print media communicators. Many people have assumed that because one person's name precedes or follows a particular article or story, that person alone is responsible for the content. The stereotyped visions of individual entrepreneurial newspaper reporters created by such movies as *The Front Page* and *All the President's Men* have contributed greatly to this myth. In reality, the content of a newspaper or magazine or even a book is the result of the collaborative efforts of many individuals.

Print communicators work within large, organized, specialized, competitive, and highly expensive environments. Creative producers of print messages include researchers and reporters who find basic facts; writers who assemble material into effective messages; and editors who create ideas, manage their production, and evaluate the results.

In the jargon of the newspaper profession, legmen are researchers whose main task is to get the facts. They might station themselves at police headquarters and simply telephone leads into the home office. The reporter is both researcher and writer. In the magazine or book industry the researcher is often a fact checker who verifies the authenticity of the work of reporters and writers.

Writers play the key creative role in the production of print media messages. They often are the people with the original ideas, although some magazine and book writers are word technicians who take the ideas of others and dress them in effective language. The reporter is the key writer within the newspaper organization, the person who gathers the facts and composes the story. Indeed, the reporter is often the essential communicator in deciding whether any given event warrants mass communication.

The editor—whether copyeditor, assignment editor, or managing editor—is more an evaluator, or gatekeeper, of communication than its originator. But editors are part of the sending process to the extent that they supervise the entire package of communication through imaginative management and evaluation.

The masthead from *Time* indicates the many mass communicators who work on each issue. Like other mass media, the process of print mass communication involves hundreds of people.

RECORDING MEDIA

The recording media also demonstrate the basic mass communicator characteristics. A performer's name on a record simply indicates one of many communicators in the recording industry. For example, on the album "We Salute You" by the group AC/DC, in addition to the performers the following communicators are listed: producer, recording engineer, mixing engineer, three assistant engineers, and masterdisk engineer. Similar and more extensive credits grace most record album covers today. In addition, the conglomerate effect has been felt in the recording industry.

As a glimpse at the organizational chart shown on page 100 indicates, ABBA is not only the hugely popular Swedish pop group but also the source of a veritable corporate conglomerate. The chart, prepared by *Variety*, is based on a rough diagram sketched by Lars Dahlin, vice-president of Polar International AB, the holding company jointly owned by ABBA members and manager Stig Anderson. The chart doesn't necessarily reflect each and every one of the ABBA–Anderson holdings, but gives a representative sampling of the organization's scope.

THE INDIVIDUAL COMMUNICATOR

Given the enormous industrial complexity of today's mass media, the mass communicator has difficulty being an individualist. Nevertheless, complexity and size do not diminish the contributions of the many specialists who make up the conglomerate communicator. A corporate structure is not some sort of infernal machine that runs itself. It is run by individuals who are vital parts of the communication process at all levels.

TIME

Founders: BRITON HADDEN 1898-1929   HENRY R. LUCE 1898-1967

Editor-in-Chief: Henry Anatole Grunwald
President: J. Richard Munro
Chairman of the Board: Ralph P. Davidson
Corporate Editor: Jason McManus
Executive Vice President: Kelso F. Sutton
Senior Vice Presidents, Magazines: Philip G. Howlett, James O. Heyworth

MANAGING EDITOR: Ray Cave
EXECUTIVE EDITORS: Edward L. Jamieson, Ronald Kriss
ASSISTANT MANAGING EDITORS: Walter Bingham, Richard Duncan, John Elson
INTERNATIONAL EDITOR: Karsten Prager
SENIOR EDITORS: David Brand, Martha M. Duffy, William F. Ewald, José M. Ferrer III, Walter Isaacson, Stefan Kanfer, Donald Morrison, Henry Muller, Christopher Porterfield, Stephen Smith, George M. Taber
ART DIRECTOR: Rudolph Hoglund
CHIEF OF RESEARCH: Leah Shanks Gordon
OPERATIONS DIRECTOR: Gérard C. Lelièvre
PICTURE EDITOR: Arnold H. Drapkin
SENIOR WRITERS: George J. Church, Gerald Clarke, Otto Friedrich, Paul Gray, Robert Hughes, T.E. Kalem, Ed Magnuson, Lance Morrow, Frederick Painton, Roger Rosenblatt, R.Z. Sheppard, William E. Smith, Frank Trippett
ASSOCIATE EDITORS: Charles P. Alexander, Kurt Andersen, Patricia Blake, Tom Callahan, Richard Corliss, Spencer Davidson, John S. DeMott, William R. Doerner, John Greenwald, William A. Henry III, Russ Hoyle, Gregory Jaynes, Marguerite Johnson, James Kelly, John Kohan, John Leo, John Nielsen, Richard N. Ostling, Jay D. Palmer, Sue Raffety, J.D. Reed, George Russell, Alexander L. Taylor III, Evan Thomas, Anastasia Toufexis, Marylois Purdy Vega, Claudia Wallis, Michael Walsh
CONTRIBUTORS: Jay Cocks, Thomas Griffith, Charles Krauthammer, Melvin Maddocks, Jane O'Reilly, Kenneth M. Pierce, Richard Schickel, Mimi Sheraton, John Skow, Wolf Von Eckardt
REPORTER-RESEARCHERS: Rosemary Byrnes, Ursula Nadasdy de Gallo, Betty Satterwhite Sutter (Department Heads); Audrey Ball, Peggy T. Berman, Nancy McD. Chase, Oscar Chiang, Elaine Dutka, Georgia Harbison, Anne Hopkins, Nancy Newman, Jeanne-Marie North, Susan M. Reed, Victoria Sales, Zona Sparks, Susanne Washburn, Rosemarie Tauris Zadikov (Senior Staff); Peter Ainslie, Bernard Baumohl, Kathleen Brady, Richard Bruns, Robert I. Burger, Valence Castronovo, Helen Sen Doyle, Rosamond Draper, Kathryn Jackson Fallon, Cassie T. Furgurson, John Edward Gallagher, Cristina Garcia, Nelida Gonzalez-Alfonso, Robert L. Grieves, D. Blake Hallanan, Michael P. Harris, JoAnn Lum, Judith L. Marrs, Naushad S. Mehta, Katherine Mihok, Lawrence Mondi, Jamie Murphy, Adrianne Jucius Navon, Brigid O'Hara-Forster, Judith B. Prowda, Barry Rehfeld, Alfreda J. Robertson, Elizabeth Rudulph, Alain L. Sanders, Marion H. Sanders, David E. Thigpen, William Tynan, Sidney Urquhart, Jane Van Tassel, Linda Young
ADMINISTRATION: Martin I. Gardner, Charlotte J. Quiggle, Donald Sweet
CORRESPONDENTS: Richard Duncan (Chief); Dean Fischer, R. Edward Jackson, B. William Mader (Diplomatic); Washington Contributing Editor: Hugh Sidey Diplomatic Correspondent: Strobe Talbott
Senior Correspondents: Ruth Mehrtens Galvin, William Rademaekers, Sandy Smith, Peter Stoler, Frederick Ungeheuer
Washington: Robert Ajemian, Bruce W. Nelan, Sam Allis, Laurence I. Barrett, David Beckwith, Gisela Bolte, Jay Branegan, Douglas Brew, Anne Constable, Patricia Delaney, Hays Gorey, Jerry Hannifin, Carolyn Lesh, Neil MacNeil, Johanna McGeary, Ross H. Munro, Christopher Redman, Barrett Seaman, William Stewart, Bruce van Voorst, Gregory H. Wierzynski, John E. Yang New York: John F. Stacks, Dorothy Ferenbaugh, Marcia Gauger, Barry Kalb, Timothy Loughran, Thomas McCarroll, Elizabeth Taylor, Jack E. White, Adam Zagorin Boston: Richard Hornik, Joelle Attinger, James Bell Atlanta: Joseph N. Boyce, B. Russell Leavitt, B.J. Phillips Houston: David S. Jackson Chicago: Christopher Ogden, J. Madeleine Nash, Barbara B. Dolan, Lee Griggs, Don Winbush Detroit: Paul A. Witteman Denver: Robert C. Wurmstedt San Francisco: Michael Moritz, Dick Thompson Los Angeles: Benjamin W. Cate, Jonathan Beaty, William Blaylock, Steven Holmes, Joseph J. Kane, Melissa Ludtke, Richard Woodbury, Denise Worrell
Europe: Lawrence Malkin London: Bonnie Angelo, Mary Cronin, Arthur White Paris: Jordan Bonfante, Thomas A. Sancton Bonn: William McWhirter, Gary Lee Eastern Europe: John Moody Rome: Wilton Wynn, Roberto Suro Jerusalem: Harry Kelly, David Halevy Middle East: Roland Flamini Beirut: John Borrell Bahrain: Barry Hillenbrand Moscow: Erik Amfitheatrof Hong Kong: Sandra Burton, Bing W. Wong Bangkok: James Willwerth Peking: David Aikman Nairobi: James Wilde Johannesburg: March Clark New Delhi: Dean Brelis Tokyo: Edwin M. Reingold, S. Chang Melbourne: John Dunn Canada: John M. Scott, Ed Ogle Rio de Janeiro: Gavin Scott Mexico City: David DeVoss, Ricardo Chavira, Janice C. Simpson Caribbean: Bernard Diederich
News Desk: Suzanne Davis, Tam Martinides Gray, Susan Lynd, David Richardson, Jean R. White, Arturo Yáñez, Alison France, Blanche Holley, Jacalyn McConnell, Ann Drury Wellford
Administration: Emily Friedrich, Linda D. Vartoogian
ART: Nigel Holmes (Executive Director), Irene Ramp (Deputy Director); Arturo Cazeneuve, Renée Klein, Leonard S. Levine, Anthony J. Libardi, William Spencer (Assistant Directors); Lily Hou, Laurie Olefson, John White (Designers); Rosemary L. Frank, Dorothy D. Chapman (Copyers); Nickolas Kalamaras Layout: Burjor Nargolwala (Chief); John P. Dowd, John F. Geist (Deputies); Joseph Aslaender, Steve Conley, David Drapkin, Modris Ramans, Kenneth Smith (Deputies), Ralph Morse, Carl Mydans, Stephen Northup, Bill Pierce, David Rubinger, Ted Thai, Diana Walker, John Zimmerman
MAKEUP: Charles P. Jackson (Chief); Eugene F. Coyle (International); Leonard Schulman (Deputy); Peter J. McGullam
OPERATIONS: Susan Aitkin (Deputy Director); Susan L. Blair (Copy Chief); Stephen F. Demeter (Systems Manager); Lee R. Sparks (Production Chief); Eleanor Edgar, Judith Anne Paul, Joseph J. Scafidi, Shirley Zimmerman (Deputies); Trang Ba Chuong, Gary Deaton, Madeleine Butler, Bruce Christopher Carr, Joan Cleary, Barbara Collier, Kenneth Collura, Manuel Delgado, Sally George, Lucia Hamet, Evelyn Hannon, Garry Hearne, Judith Kaies, Theresa Kelliher, Claire Knopf, Agustin Lamboy, Jeannine Laverty, Marcia L. Love, Helen May, Emily Mitchell, Gail Music, Linda Parker, Maria A. Paul, Alma Routsong, Megan Rutherford, Marcia Schlafmitz, Craig Sturgis, Ricki Tarlow, Walter J. Tate, Jill Ward, Alan Washburn
LETTERS: Joan D. Walsh (Chief); Isabel F. Kouri (Deputy)
EDITORIAL SERVICES: Christiana Walford (Director); Peter J. Christopoulos, Benjamin Lightman, Alex Stack, Beth Bencini Zarcone

PUBLISHER: John A. Meyers
General Manager: Michael J. Klingensmith
Public Affairs Director: Robert D. Sweeney
Promotion Director: George P. Berger
Circulation Director: Robert D. McCoach
Business Manager: Allen M. Barr
ASSOCIATE PUBLISHER-ADVERTISING SALES DIRECTOR: Richard B. Thomas
U.S. Advertising Sales Director: John J. Crowley Jr.
Associate U.S. Adv. Sales Director: Charles D. Hogan

TIME, SEPTEMBER 17, 1984

Many individuals collaborate on the content of a single issue of *Time*. (Copyright © 1984 Time Inc. All rights reserved. Reprinted by permission from *Time*.)

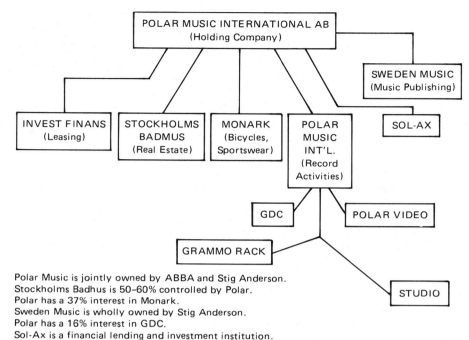

The conglomerate effect has been felt in the recording industry Polar International is jointly owned by ABBA members and the group's manager, Stig Anderson.

Polar Music is jointly owned by ABBA and Stig Anderson.
Stockholms Badhus is 50–60% controlled by Polar.
Polar has a 37% interest in Monark.
Sweden Music is wholly owned by Stig Anderson.
Polar has a 16% interest in GDC.
Sol-Ax is a financial lending and investment institution.

At times the human dimension of even something as vast and complex as network television rears its individualistic head, often in humorous ways. For example, in February 1979, during the showing of the NBC miniseries "Loose Change," a technician at the network inadvertently switched episodes, substituting Part 3 for Part 2. For 17 minutes, a national audience watched with puzzled expressions a drama that was out of synch with its internal reality.

Essential attributes of individual mass communicators are the ability to think, to see things accurately, to organize their thoughts quickly, and to express themselves articulately and effectively. Mass communicators have to be curious about the world, and about the people in it. Communicators are called on to make judgments, sometimes of vast importance, and they should be able to distinguish the significant from the insignificant, the true from the false. Mass communicators need to have a broad view of the world, but increasingly they must specialize in the communication field. Finally, they must know how to communicate. In mass communication this seemingly simple act becomes exceedingly complex, requiring many kinds of talents, abilities, and specialties. Above all, the sender must understand and respect the medium in which he or she works.

The training and education necessary to become a part of mass media institutions and the personal attributes of mass communicators are things

that are often misunderstood. Many potential mass communicators believe that technical training is the key to understanding the process of
mass communication. The technology of mass media often blinds students
to the fact that the *process* of mass communication involves more than
pushing a button or flipping a switch and that performers are but a small
part of the mass media communicator.

In his book *The Information Machines: Their Impact on Men and
Media*, Ben Bagdikian writes about "printed and broadcast news as a
corporate enterprise." He says that news is both an intellectual artifact
and the product of a bureaucracy. Distinguished journalism, he writes,
requires strong individual leadership; yet such journalism is often at odds
with the demands of corporate efficiency. Bagdikian predicts that daily
newspapers will find themselves increasingly in new corporate enterprises. As Edward Jay Epstein writes in his excellent study *News From
Nowhere: Television and the News*: "Before network news can be properly
analysed as a journalistic enterprise, it is necessary to understand the
business enterprise that it is an active part of, and the logic that proceeds
from it."

One must add, of course, that our complex, specialized, and industrialized corporate media enterprises have produced more information
and entertainment than any simplistic, individual, altruistic effort could
achieve. There is both good and bad in the system. But one cannot understand the mass communicator without seeing the individual as part
of a much larger organism.

6 Codes

Laurence Olivier talks soothingly to Dustin Hoffman, who is strapped in a chair, his head held in the grasp of a stranger. As Olivier's silken tones reach our ears, Hoffman's frantic eyes begin to dart about the screen. Olivier, as the villain, carefully prepares his instruments of torture, the tools of his profession.

The audience panics. They squirm in their seats. They grip the arms of their chairs or their dates. They may even look away as they giggle and groan. You see, they have placed themselves in Hoffman's shoes. The filmmakers have exploited the quintessential phobia of America's motion-picture audiences: going to the dentist.

We no longer fear for Hoffman's safety. We are calling up our own "remembrances of pains past." The most stupid question in the medical world rings in our ears: "Did that hurt?"

John Schlesinger, the film's director, is now the audience's dentist; William Goldman, the screenwriter, is the dental technician. They have their hands on the audience's throats as well as a drill in the mouth of the *Marathon Man*.

Our defenses are down. They have found a chink in our armor. Our "frames of references" have been breached. We understand this film at the gut communication level of pain. And the movie has just said, "Gotcha!"

(Photo: Museum of Modern Art/Film Stills Archive, Courtesy Paramount Pictures.)

As Sir Lawrence Olivier calmly drills into Dustin Hoffman's teeth, so director of *Marathon Man*, John Schlesinger, operates on the personal phobias of the audience.

Ideas are without existence until they find expression—and this expression is the art of the communicator. The *content* is *coded* using the syntax of the *medium*.

Three parts of the HUB Model form the *message unit* These three parts—the content, the code, and the medium—are stylistically inseparable. For example, the more knowledgeable a reporter is about an event (the *content*), the more fluent she is as a wordsmith (the *code*), and the more skillful she is in manipulating the news organization (the *medium*), the better the message presented.

News is news, right? Wrong! A radio bulletin, a newspaper story, or a report has media-code characteristics that shape the content. The length (time or space), the detail, the structure, the format, and the style of the news affect the message:

Radio news is radio news.

Television news is television news.

Newspaper news is newspaper news.

Unfortunately, news consumers do not always use a particular form of news as it was intended, or they become too dependent on readily available sources.

THE MESSAGE UNIT

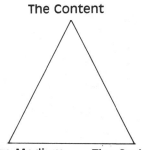

The Content

The Medium   The Code

The *message unit* takes the form of the equilateral triangle, the strongest geometric shape. The mass media *cannot* generate messages without the interaction of the content, the code, and the medium.

**THE MEDIA–CODE–
CONTENT
RELATIONSHIP**

A visual illustration of the impact of a medium and a code on content may be helpful: You are on your way home and you need to buy some vegetables. There are signs (a *medium*) on both sides of the road that read "fresh vegetables" (the *content*), and you know the prices of the two suppliers are identical. Two questions: Who has fresher vegetables? From whom will you buy?

Look at this figure. For a variety of reasons, most folks will choose to buy vegetables from the farmer on the left because the hurried nature of his code (the roughly lettered sign) implies that it was just lettered, which may mean fresher produce. The neatly lettered sign on the right is agribusiness and generally turns on fewer buyers.

Unimpressed?

Perhaps a second set of signs farther down the road will drive the concept home. Now look at this figure and decide where you want to try sky diving. OK? Those of you who picked the neat sign on the left will live long. Everybody else, start praying. Get the point? Would you even consider the outfit that put up that scrawled "sky-diving lessons"?

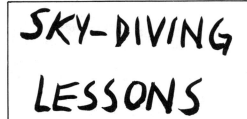

The *content*, then, must be wedded to the *code* of a specific *medium*. Exactly the same content ("fresh vegetables" or "sky-diving lessons") using the same medium (signs) can be radically altered by the code (the lettering). Every message unit is shaped by the interaction of the three elements involved.

1. *Content* is the data, the idea, the substance. It is the *communication*.
2. *Code* is the symbol system. And the symbols used have a significant impact on the content. It is communication *language*.
3. *Medium* is the organizational structure, the framework on which the ideas are woven. The technology, the tools, the practices, and so forth make each mass medium's expression of the same content different. It is the *organization*.

Each mass medium adds its unique contribution to traditional language structure. The syntax of each medium's symbol system also depends on an audience's past experiences with all other media as well as the one currently in use.

Mass media codes add a new set of symbols to traditional language structure. In other words, books, newspapers, magazines, radio, television, film, and recordings employ new languages. Each codifies reality differently; each makes its own statement in its own way. Edmund Carpenter has pointed out that, like theater, film is a visual–verbal medium presented before an audience. Like ballet, film relies heavily on movement and music. Like a novel, film usually presents a narrative depicting characters in a series of conflicts. Like painting and photography, film is two-dimensional, composed of light and shadow and sometimes color. But its ultimate definition lies in its unique qualities.

Each medium, then, has *unique* ways of coding content and structuring reality. The key questions are these: What do the media add to communication codes that are not found in interpersonal exchanges? Are there commonly shared symbols among media and groups of media? Are today's audiences trained to interpret these differences? Is one code–medium more effective than others with certain content?

To begin with, interpersonal communication uses all five senses:

We see messages (writing).
We hear messages (speech).
We touch messages (handshakes).
We taste messages (birthday cakes).
We smell messages (perfumes).

The mass media tend to depend largely on sight and sound. But the print media use different paper stocks—newsprint (cheap), magazines

MASS MEDIA SYMBOL SYSTEMS

(slick), books (permanent)—to tactile advantage. Print ads and children's books have "scratch and sniff" patches for olfactory smells and experiences. (In the 1950s "smellovision motion pictures" with scent jets under the seats failed.) Taste remains the least-experienced sense. The edible food advertisement may be around the next bend in the media road, however.

But, for practical purposes, the mass media depend on sight and sound. Only film and television can be seen as well as heard. The print media are deaf; the phonograph and radio are blind.

Despite sensory handicaps, motion pictures offer such visually and aurally powerful experiences that it seems we can taste, smell, and touch some movies. In *Tom Jones*, we get a "taste" of eighteenth-century England. It is a film that involves the eating and drinking of a parade of characters. The "eating" scene between Mrs. Waters and Tom Jones is a gourmand's delight. *Lawrence of Arabia* reeks of the animals, the heat, and the parched quality of the other images of this visually magnificent production. The fears and angers and hatreds that ultimately lead to a horrible climax help the audience "smell" this film when a character's "blood is up."

John Ford's westerns have a rough-hewn look that touches the audience's mind's eye. The coarseness of the sets and the costumes and natural

Making the most of a meal, Tom Jones and Mrs. Waters demonstrate the power of visual imagery to create the illusion of a multisensory experience.

(Photo: Museum of Modern Art/Film Stills Archive, Courtesy United Artists.)

Evocative imagery and realistic detail contribute to the intellectual and emotional impact of *Lawrence of Arabia*.

(Photo: Museum of Modern Art/Film Stills Archive, Courtesy Columbia Pictures.)

John Ford's *The Searchers* uses color, texture, and shapes to fullest advantage. Director Ford consistently frames John Wayne in doorways as the axis of his compositions so that the scene is dominated by Wayne's powerful presence.

(Photo: Museum of Modern Art/Film Stills Archive, Courtesy Warner Bros. Inc.)

vistas in these films cover the emotional softness of Ford's sentimentality for family as well as frontier. Audiences touch the rough adobe walls; the smooth, worn leather saddles; the weathered faces. And audiences are touched by the emotional quality of the great filmmaker's skill in coding universal messages of strength and vigor.

PRINT MEDIA CODES

The content of print is "hard copy." It exists in space, unlike electronic content, which exists in time. Essentially, the print media depend on printed words and still illustrations. The print communicator attempts to make the words flow and the visuals move through a design concept wedded to the ideas being presented.

Linear Progression

The print media depend on a linear progression.

1. The *book* is the most rigidly ordered of the print media. Content is paged in exact order to facilitate a detailed analysis of substantial dimension.
2. The *magazine* presents all or a major portion of a specific article or pictorial essay as a unit with completions scattered about later portions of the magazine to give the advertising exposure. Magazines are less ordered than books but more ordered than newspapers.
3. The *newspaper* is an information supermarket for news shoppers. Readers are attracted by major stories on the front page or the first page of major sections. Readers may or may not complete the stories on following pages.

Basic Style Considerations

The style of the printed page has been influenced tremendously by major art movements: cubism, futurism, surrealism, art deco, the Bauhaus movement, op-art, and the rest. Print designs have their roots as much in graphic design as information transfer. The overall language of a book, newspaper, or magazine (the *medium*) is to merge language (*code*) with the *content*.

The print media designer has to fill the surface with meaning and pleasure for the eye of the reader. Whether in books, magazines, or newspapers, the basic "canvas" in print communication is the paper page. This two-dimensional space (height and width) is usually higher than wider, seldom wider than high, and almost never square. In terms of page size the general progression seems to be (*a*) paperback book to (*b*) hardback book to (*c*) magazine to (*d*) tabloid newspaper to (*e*) blanket newspaper.

Some books rooted in visual design (art books) logically are paged larger than magazines, and some magazines go to extremes. *Reader's Digest, Jet,* and *TV Guide* are relatively smaller and *Rolling Stone* and *Billboard* relatively larger than other magazines.

Most page design in print is based on a grid principle. The layout for most word-based books is the simplest. Newspapers are the most predictable and magazines the most creative in their design practices. In terms of ideas, books and magazines are flowing space. **Page Design**

1. Not one page,

2. Not two facing pages,

3. But a flowing multipage section of the newspaper, article in a magazine, or chapter in a book.

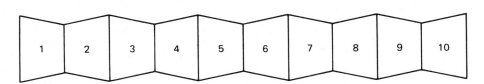

Pages need to be intellectually and visually joined in the minds of the audiences. There is space, then, not only within pages but among pages.

Gatefolds extend the images even more satisfyingly. The most famous example is the *Playboy* "playmate" foldout, which comfortably represents the human form in a three-page vertical or horizontal format.

Someone—perhaps the editor or designer but normally not the reporter or writer—organizes the spatial elements of the page to conform with the overriding intent of the message. The "designer" gives the page

1. *Symmetry*, whether symmetrical or asymmetrical
2. A sense of *proportion*
3. *Balance*, which gives a feeling of equilibrium
4. *Dimension*, or a sense of depth as well as height and width

5. *Contrast*, generated by sizes and shapes, lines and textures, values and colors, and signs and symbols that are recognizable to the reader

6. A sense of *movement* to give the eye *visual direction* through the page

All of this takes place within a basic design, called the *grid*, on the surface. This typographic grid is the systematic management of physical space. The surface (the page) is a constant within a given publication. But the arrangement of space is creatively variable within certain constraints: (*a*) type size; (*b*) number and width of columns; (*c*) numbers and sizes of visuals; (*d*) amount of text in individual units; (*e*) size of headlines; (*f*) lengths of captions; and (*g*) margins.

The Building Blocks of Print Communication

Successful communication occurs because of word choice, the logical organization of ideas, and the expression of those ideas with a compatible typeface and layout that contains the right pictures, illustrations, graphs, charts, and tables in position to give visual reinforcement to the total message.

Specifically, the building blocks of print communication are (*a*) copy set in columns; (*b*) headlines, headings, and titles; (*c*) photographs and illustrations; (*d*) charts, graphs, and tables; (*e*) captions; (*f*) margins and white space.

Copy. Print media organize copy in columns because columns make the page easier to read and give it visual rhythm. Columns also allow for horizontal as well as vertical ads. The copy is built out of letters into words into sentences into paragraphs into pages into articles in newspapers and chapters in magazines and books.

The *word* is a "learned" combination of letters, which when spelled correctly serve as a symbol for an idea or thing. The *line* is an optical arrangement of words with a spatial potential of less than to more than one sentence. The *sentence* is an action statement of words that normally includes a subject and verb. The *paragraph* is a complete idea, except in editorials and historical romances. The *column* is a series of ordered lines with width and height that are the essential copy blocks and the central style element of the printed page.

Headlines. Titles, headings, and headlines draw the eye's attention and the mind's involvement with the information unit. They are the "come-on" for the material they announce. Headlines summarize and analyze the content of the story. They set a mood or tone for the piece. They also index the page for the reader.

Photographs and Illustrations. The key elements of a visual are (*a*) size; (*b*) cropping; (*c*) position; (*d*) bordered or bled; (*e*) physical relationship to copy format; (*f*) intellectual and emotional relationship to the words; (*g*) physical relationship to other visuals on the page; and (*h*) the direction in which they force the eye.

In any printed story the purpose of the illustrations is to help carry the information load. The ideas presented by the visual must help the reader understand the content. The visual pleasure of a photograph must be a secondary consideration.

Charts, Graphs, and Tables. In a descending order of effectiveness, (*a*) the chart is best; (*b*) the graph is better; (*c*) the table is good. All three graphic displays must do the following:

1. Present the minimum data. If necessary, break the data down into multiple charts rather than one table (*simplicity*).
2. Force the eye to help the brain reach the conclusion (*effectiveness*).
3. Isolate the major points from the lesser points (*clarity*).

Captions. The caption must be more than a label. Somewhere (and the closer to the visual the better) the caption must explain or justify the visual if the visual is not self-justifying or self-explanatory. The problem with caption content is that it tends to be ignored by readers; points made in the caption often go unnoticed.

Margins and White Space. Blank areas serve to set off and highlight all the other elements. Margins and white space are critical in most print-media designs.

Print media use specific visual displays to aid the reader's content satisfaction. **Special Visual Displays**

1. The title, logo, and masthead identify the source. The slogan defines the focus.
2. The table of contents in books, magazines, and newspapers serves as a general guidepost. Index in books and periodical guides and newspaper reference systems provide detailed access.
3. The dateline adds a historical footnote.
4. The cover provides the basic statement of purpose; the identification mark (the logo); the visual trademark (because cover design is based on graphic decisions); and the headlines. The best covers are simple, but when complexity is needed, the cover format must make the ideas easy to handle. The cover must be a visual greeting.

Unquestionably, type is the single most important creative element in the design of print materials. The selection of type available is extremely large and getting larger. **Type**

Type is a tone of voice—the vocal quality of the silent eye. Headlines raise the voice, but shouting must be used sparingly or it will be heard rather than listened to. One of the main principles in selecting the type for *Mass Media IV* was readability. Will the pages be able to be read quickly and clearly? The typeface used to set *Mass Media IV* is Melior. It has a no-nonsense, up-front, scholarly voice.

Type can have a pictorial element. Used this way, it can be extremely effective in making the point. For example, take the three "power words" *fat*, *obese*, and *ugly*. Now see them as

These words have become "emotional" because of the design element.

Have you ever seen the word *1ne*? Do you understand what "1ne" means? Would it help to see that word in relation to similar ideas coded the same way? Look at the following list.

> 1ne
> 2wo
> 3hree
> 4our
> 5ive
> 6ix
> 7even
> 8ight
> 9ine
> 10n

Only in a series does this list have meaning. Alone, each line is meaningless, and so the type design has an "intellectual" as well as an "emotional" flavor.

Type elements include:

CAPITAL LETTERS
lowercase letters
1 2 3 4 5 6 (numbers)
P.u,n;c't:u?a(t"i"o-n) marks!
+ − ÷ × math signs
————————— lines

▓▓▓▓▓▓▓▓▓▓▓▓▓▓▓▓▓ ornamentation

Space   spaced   s p a c i n g

Dir
   e
   c
   t
    i
     o
      n

Individual pieces of type or letters have shape, SIZE, **Weight,** WIDTH, and *slope*.

1. Shape is the essential design of the face.
2. SIZE refers to measurement of height for most purposes from 6 points to 72 points. A point is about $\frac{1}{72}$ inch.
3. **Weight** is the thickness of the stroke.
4. WIDTH is the horizontal space the letter takes up.
5. *Slope* is the angle or lean of the letter in italic, bold italic, or oblique form.

All creative designs and decisions in print are for reader satisfaction— and perhaps writer, editor, publisher, and designer satisfaction as well. Legibility, instant communication, clarity, and simplicity lead to understanding and retention.

INDIVIDUAL PRINT MEDIA

Books

As Marshall McLuhan and others have pointed out, when writing was introduced, it did not simply record oral language; it was an entirely new language. It utilized an alphabet as its code. Nevertheless, bits and pieces of alphabets are meaningless in themselves. Only when these components are strung out in a line in a specified order can meaning be created.

The book is basically an extension of this alphabetized code with an even more uniform linear order. Using this linear order a book's code proceeds from subject to verb to object, from sentence to sentence, from paragraph to paragraph, from chapter to chapter. Events take place one after the other in books, rather than all at once as they often happen. A football play involves an explosion of simultaneous action that books cannot adequately describe. To do so, a book must restructure the reality in linear form. Books present an organized, logical, progression of words and pictures in a word-ordered world.

Because of its coded form, the book is an individual medium generally read silently and alone. A book is usually conceived of as a "serious" mass medium with a definite author or authority. The content is generally placed in some sequential order, either narrative, descriptive, or chronological. Thus a book tends to be read in a standard progression rather than selectively as are most magazines and newspapers. The code by which a book is structured also enables the audience to consume content at its own pace, even to reread portions of the content. A book therefore can deal with complex ideas and plots involving many issues or people; its language and code are best able of the print media to handle this complexity effectively.

Newspapers   Instead of a line-by-line development of the same idea, in newspapers there is an explosion of headlines and stories all juxtaposed and competing for attention. The front pages from the *New York Times* give some idea of this simultaneity of ideas. They also suggest that code systems are manipulated in different ways to reach different readers with different information. The *New York Daily News* is coded to attract a different reader from the *Times* reader and to accommodate the kinds of news it prints. *USA Today* has redesigned the newspaper to fit America's new information lifestyle that seems to survive on "headline news." The colorful design style uses extensive visuals as well as color photos and graphs and charts to illustrate the capsule news style. The overall newspaper code does not require sequential use but encourages selective reading by the audience. Through a balanced page makeup using multicolumn headlines with stories developed vertically beneath them, the newspaper gives the reader a choice.

Other noticeable coding characteristics are evident in the newspaper. The inverted-pyramid style of writing a story is one. With those coding style, the important information is given first. Less important items follow in an order of descending importance. The reader can stop anywhere and still have the essence of the story. The editor can cut the story easily at any point without destroying its meaning.

Short paragraphs and narrow columns are also characteristic of newspaper codes. The format of the newspaper and the audience dictate this. Newspaper columns are narrow because a short line is easier to read. Short paragraphs are easier to read than long ones and aid readers in assessing meaning. By breaking up a story, short paragraphs permit an audience to skim and read selectively.

Another newspaper code characteristic is the use of banners and headlines in different type sizes. Headlines in different sizes perform two func-

"All the News That's Fit to Print"

The New York Times

Late Edition

Weather: Mostly sunny and cool today, northwesterly winds; mostly clear tonight. Mostly sunny, mild tomorrow. Temperatures: today 50-53, tonight 33-37; yesterday 42-59. Details, page A24.

VOL.CXXXIV . . No. 46,221 Copyright © 1984 The New York Times NEW YORK, WEDNESDAY, NOVEMBER 7, 1984 80 cents beyond 75 miles from New York City, except on Long Island 30 CENTS

REAGAN WINS BY A LANDSLIDE, SWEEPING AT LEAST 48 STATES; G.O.P. GAINS STRENGTH IN HOUSE

Two Parties Still Split Control on Capitol Hill

House Power Battle

By STEVEN V. ROBERTS

Republicans cut into the Democratic majority in the House of Representatives last night, but their drive to shake the control of Democratic leaders seemed to fall short.

If last night's trends hold when the final votes are tallied, the House would continue to pose a major obstacle to President Reagan's legislative agenda, despite his overwhelming re-election victory.

Representative Thomas P. O'Neill Jr., the Speaker of the House, estimated that the Democrats would lose 10 to 12 seats from their majority of 99. In a television interview, he attributed the Democrats' strong showing to widespread desire in the country check Mr. Reagan's more conservative proposals.

G.O.P. Needed 25 Seats

"I believe they wanted the Democrats in there as a safety net," he said. Speaking of President Reagan, Mr. O'Neill said, "He really hasn't had coat tails."

The Republicans needed a gain of about 25 seats to give them a chance to form the sort of coalition with conservative Democrats that enacted many of Mr. Reagan's proposals during the first two years of his Presidency.

In many states, Democratic Representatives survived the Reagan landslide by distancing themselves from the national ticket and stressing their personal records of service to their constituents.

In North Carolina and Texas, the Republicans had a chance to make sweep-

Continued on Page A23, Column 1

Helms Senate Victor

By MARTIN TOLCHIN

Senate Republican candidates grasped President Reagan's coattails yesterday, but early returns indicated that they would be unable to solidify their control of the Senate.

Mr. Reagan, who spent the final week of his campaign appearing in behalf of Senate Republican candidates, seemed unable to translate his dramatic victory into significantly increasing the Republican margin in the Senate. But Democrats were similarly unable to make significant inroads into the Republican margin.

Should this pattern prevail, Mr. Reagan could expect to encounter the same resistance to some of his programs that he experienced in the last two years.

Helms Wins Bid

In the most acrimonious, expensive and closely watched Senate race, Senator Jesse Helms, Republican of North Carolina, leader of the New Right and a foe of abortion and supporter of organized school prayer, defeated Gov. James B. Hunt Jr., a moderate Democrat. The two had exchanged invectives right up to election day.

In Iowa, Senator Roger W. Jepsen, a Republican, was defeated by Representative Tom Harkin, a Democrat, in another campaign in which both candidates engaged in intensive negative campaigning.

Republicans appeared to have won an upset victory in Kentucky, where A. Mitchell McConnell, Jefferson County Judge, was narrowly leading Senator Walter D. Huddleston, a Democrat, although The Associated Press reported

Continued on Page A23, Column 3

The New York Times/Paul Hosefros

President and Mrs. Reagan claiming victory last night in Los Angeles.

MANDATE CLAIMED

Mondale Concedes Loss — Democrats Seek to Avert Realignment

By HOWELL RAINES

Ronald Wilson Reagan won a second term as President yesterday in an election that Republican leaders hailed as a sweeping personal triumph and a mandate for his policies.

Mr. Reagan secured clear landslide victories in both popular and electoral votes as he defeated Walter F. Mondale, the Democratic nominee, in at least 48 of the 50 states.

However, it remained unclear whether the powerful tide of support

Transcripts of speeches, page A21.

for Mr. Reagan ran deeply enough to carry enough Republican Congressional candidates into office to secure the "historic electoral realignment" that the President asked the voters to deliver.

With more than two-thirds of the popular vote counted, Mr. Reagan led Mr. Mondale by about 59 percent to 41 percent.

The President waited until after midnight, Eastern time, to claim the election that continued his tenure as the oldest man to occupy the White House.

Entering the ballroom of the Century Plaza Hotel in Los Angeles to the strains of "Hail to the Chief," Mr. Reagan received a tumultuous welcome from a crowd that chanted, "Four more years."

"I think that's just been arranged," said Mr. Reagan with a grin:

Policy Extension Planned

He said he would use his mandate to extend the economic and military policies of his first term. But, as if answering criticisms made by Mr. Mondale, he said he would also devote his second term to limiting nuclear weapons and to "lifting the weak and nurturing the less fortunate."

"You know, so many people act as if this election means the end of something," Mr. Reagan concluded in an indirect reference to the fact that this was the last election night of his career. "To each one of you I say, it's the beginning of everything," Mr. Reagan said. Then he stirred full-throated cheers by repeating an informal slogan of his campaign, "You ain't seen nothing yet."

Mondale Affirms Principles

Mr. Mondale, looking somber and drained, conceded shortly after 11:20 P.M., Eastern time. After complimenting the President on his victory, Mr. Mondale affirmed his commitment to the principles he had championed in a long, grinding campaign.

"Let us continue to seek an America that is just and fair," Mr. Mondale said. "Tonight especially I think of the

Continued on Page A20, Column 1

Economy the Key Issue

By HEDRICK SMITH

News Analysis

For all the careful orchestration of campaign rallies and political commercials, the televised debates, the partisan clashes over fine points of foreign and military policy, it was the economy that set the basic pattern for President Reagan's stunning re-election sweep yesterday and that fueled Republican gains in Congress.

In a very real sense the election returns followed the well-established script of the Reagan Presidency to make economic policy the central issue of American politics, according to a New York Times/CBS News Poll of 5,051 people as they left the voting booths. For Ronald Reagan vaulted into the White House in 1980 largely on the strength of his biting attacks on the economy under President Carter and his telling question, "Are you better off today than you were four years ago?"

In the midterm Congressional elections two years ago, he suffered a stinging setback with the recession that eroded Republican ranks in the House of Representatives. Now this year, interviews showed, the President won a resounding vote of confidence for his handling of the economy and used it to power a coast-to-coast landslide for a second term in the White House.

His strategists were quick to contend that he had won a mandate for future policies. But the Times/CBS News poll showed that it was the electorate's feelings about the economy more than Mr. Reagan's appeals to traditional values or any specific vision for the future of what he likes to call his "second American revolution" that moved solid majorities in every region of the country into the President's column.

Broad Coalition for Reagan

Indeed, Walter F. Mondale gained more support than Mr. Reagan on his vision of the future, according to the poll. By nearly 2 to 1, however, the voters rejected Mr. Mondale's argument that a tax increase was necessary to reduce the Federal deficit, and Mr. Reagan won a big margin among those who opposed raising taxes.

Most significantly, the Election Day survey found that almost three-fifths of the voters felt the economy was better off today than four years ago, and that

Continued on Page A20, Column 2

PRESIDENT SWEEPS THE TRISTATE AREA

Connecticut Landslide Gives G.O.P. the Legislature

By FRANK LYNN

President Reagan swept New York, New Jersey and Connecticut yesterday. But except for Connecticut, he generally failed to translate his landslide margin into Republican victories in the House of Representatives and local offices.

In Connecticut, the Reagan tide enabled Republicans to gain control of both houses of the General Assembly for the first time in a decade, and to win the post held by Representative William R. Ratchford, a Democrat who was seeking his fourth term.

The President's victory over Walter F. Mondale, his Democratic opponent, in both New Jersey and Connecticut was approaching record proportions of at least 300,000 and 600,000 votes respectively.

He won New York State by at least 500,000 votes, triple his 1980 plurality in the state. He lost traditionally Democratic New York City by 300,000 votes but almost made up the entire deficit on Long Island, with victories of more than 100,000 votes each in Nassau and Suffolk Counties. The President lost only one upstate county, Albany, also a traditional Democratic stronghold.

In a hotly contested House campaign that was the most expensive in the country, Andrew J. Stein, the Democratic Manhattan Borough President,

Continued on Page B4, Column 1

State of Siege Is Imposed in Chile

By LYDIA CHAVEZ
Special to The New York Times

SANTIAGO, Chile, Nov. 6 — President Augusto Pinochet imposed a state of siege in Chile today for the first time in six years.

He acted after months of political unrest and a day after his Cabinet resigned to give him a freer hand to deal with the situation.

"It is precisely to save democracy and liberty that now more than ever it is necessary to be inflexible with respect to the institutional order that rules us," the President said at a ceremony at which he announced a new Cabinet.

Greater Powers for President

Minutes after the ceremony, a nightly curfew from midnight to 5 A.M. was imposed.

The President already had considerable powers to combat terrorism under the previous state of emergency. The press could be censored and political leaders exiled.

The main difference seems to be that under the state of siege the Goverment can hold terrorist suspects without charges for an indefinite period and trials can be delayed indefinately.

The new Cabinet brought only two minor changes. General Pinochet reappointed Interior Minister Sergio Onofre Jarpa, the chief minister, whose decision to step down Monday was followed immediately by the resignation of 15 other ministers.

Mr. Jarpa's resignation had been thought to be in protest against the Government's hard line against the opposition. But his decision to remain in the Cabinet indicated that he agrees with the Government's position.

The Government has taken an in-

Continued on Page A12, Column 1

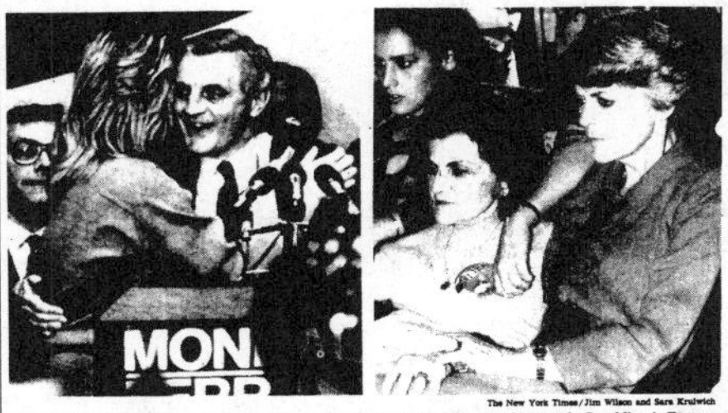

The New York Times/Jim Wilson and Sara Krulwich

Eleanor Mondale hugging her father as he appeared in St. Paul to make concession speech. Geraldine A. Ferraro was joined by her mother, Antonetta, and a daughter, Laura, in watching results at a Manhattan hotel.

Other News

Trade Talks With Russians

The United States and the Soviet Union plan talks in Moscow in January to explore ways to expand trade between the two nations. Page D1.

Catholics on Capitalism

A commission of conservative Roman Catholic business and professional leaders voiced strong support for American capitalism. Page A16.

About New York	B3	Living Section	C1-16
Around Nation	A14	Music	C20-21,C24-25
Books	C24	Obituaries	B8
Bridge	C18	Op-Ed	A27
Business Day	D1-27	Real Estate	B10
Chess	C19	Sports Pages	B12-16
Crossword	C24	Theaters	C21,C23
Dance	C24-25	TV/Radio	C25-27
Day By Day	B2	U.N. Events	A3
Editorials	A26	Washington Talk	B6
Going Out Guide	C11	Weather	A24

News Summary and Index, Page B1

Classified Ads	*B18-27*	*Auto Exchange*	*B16-18*

Nicaragua Said to Get Soviet Attack Copters

By PHILIP TAUBMAN
Special to The New York Times

WASHINGTON, Wednesday, Nov. 7 — Nicaragua has received a number of Soviet-built attack helicopters in recent days, a senior Administration official said Tuesday night. He said the White House viewed their delivery as a "very serious development."

In addition, Administration officials said they were concerned about a Soviet freighter apparently headed for Nicaragua that intelligence reports indicated was carrying crates that could contain MIG fighter aircraft.

A spokesman for the Nicaragua Embassy denied that helicopters had been delivered or that MIG's were on the way.

A senior Defense Department official said the Administration was considering a variety of responses to the delivery of the helicopters because they could have an important impact on the military balance in Central America.

Although they do not represent as serious an increase in Nicaraguan fire power as would the delivery of advanced fighter planes, he said, they presented a more serious "practical problem."

Specifically, he said, the helicopters, which Soviet forces have used extensively in Afghanistan to combat insur-

Continued on Page A12, Column 1

Bradley Wins Handily in Jersey Despite Strong Vote for Reagan

By JOSEPH F. SULLIVAN

Senator Bill Bradley, Democrat of New Jersey, easily won re-election to a second term yesterday.

With more than two-thirds of the votes counted, the 41-year-old Senator led Mary V. Mochary, a 42-year-old lawyer and former Mayor of Montclair, 63 to 37 percent.

Mr. Bradley gained his victory as hundreds of thousands of voters moved between the Democratic and Republican lines on the ballot to give President Reagan an overwhelming margin in the state as well.

Mr. Reagan held a a 64-to-36 percent lead over Walter F. Mondale with more than two-thirds of the votes counted. Mr. Reagan was leading in all 21 counties on his way to capturing the state's 16 electoral votes. The sweep would include Essex, Hudson and Mercer, three counties that he lost in 1980, when he won the state by 400,000 votes over President Jimmy Carter.

Mrs. Mochary telephoned Mr. Bradley at 8:45 P.M., 45 minutes after the polls closed, to congratulate him.

The Republican challenger was outspent by the incumbent, 3 to 1, and had to interrupt her campaign during the final three weeks to accompany her 44-year-old husband, Stephen, to the Stanford University Medical Center in California, where he is awaiting a heart transplant.

Mrs. Mochary said that she planned to leave for California this afternoon.

Mrs. Mochary, who talked to her supporters at the Somerset Hilton Hotel after telephoning Mr. Bradley, said she planned to run for office again, "and I'm not going to lower my sights."

Her comment prompted speculation she was thinking of running against New Jersey's other Democratic Sena-

Continued on Page B4, Column 5

The front page of *The New York Times* contains a variety of stories dominated by the major story. Banners and headlines draw the reader's attention into the stories in the blanket or standard-page-size newspaper. (Copyright © 1984 by the New York Times Company. Reprinted by permission.)

Election Final

DAILY ◉ NEWS

30¢ Wednesday, November 7, 1984   **NEW YORK'S PICTURE NEWSPAPER®**   Sunny. High 50. Details p. 29

RONAWAY!

FRITZ GETS BLITZED

Portraits by Harry Pincus

Bradley wins reelection in Jersey

Page 7

In contrast to *The New York Times*, the tabloid-page-size *New York Daily News* galvanizes the reader's attention and focuses it on the story of the moment. This stronger visual approach heralds a different news style on the pages to come. (Drawing by Harry Pincus. Copyright © 1984 by the New York News Inc. Reprinted by permission of the New York News Inc. and the artist.)

A third example of front page styles comes from *USA Today*, a national newspaper that resembles television's "headline news services". It does not provide in-depth coverage, but presents succinct reports of events in a visually arresting and colorful design. (Copyright © 1984 by the Gannett Publishing Company. Reprinted by permission.)

tions. They indicate the importance of the articles and give the reader a quick summary of the contents.

This coding process and its characteristics—inverted pyramid, story structure, narrow columns, short sentences and paragraphs, and headlines in different type sizes—extend naturally from the way people read newspapers. We do not generally sit down with a newspaper for hours; instead, we read selectively for short periods of time on the subway, in the office, or over breakfast. Few people read a newspaper from cover to cover. Some people read only one or two sections, such as sports or the comics, the front page, or the women's section. Newspaper codes are a natural outgrowth of the uses we make of the medium.

Magazines   Magazines follow several formats that are dissimilar to the newspaper. Instead of having many stories hit the reader simultaneously, magazine articles are published in a sequential plan according to the publication's philosophy. Most magazines print a table of contents that demonstrates their use of sequential organization. Within the page, however, magazines adopt a different style, demonstrating the creative use of juxtaposition, one story versus another, advertisements versus stories, photographs versus print, and color versus black and white.

Traditionally, the magazine reader makes five choices:

1. A reader who is familiar with the magazine will turn directly to *Time's* movie reviews or whatever else has priority in his or her use of that issue.
2. If the cover of *Newsweek* instigated the purchase, the reader will often go directly to the cover story.
3. The "professional" reader (researcher) will focus on the table of contents of *U.S. News and World Report*.
4. With a magazine structured around visuals, the reader will head straight for the centerfold in *Playboy*.
5. The reader who is "killing time" on an airplane or in an office or at the supermarket checkout line will riffle through *People Weekly* until something catches the eye and fills the time.

In magazines, single pages are usually vertical and the spread (two facing pages) is horizontal—but both should be laid out horizontally to get the best and most pleasing visual effect. In effect, layout breaks pages down into horizontal modules.

Because of the specialized nature of magazines, several design-code observations are important:

1. Although each issue's cover is unique, cover design is the visual signature of most periodicals.
2. Each issue has an overriding visual design, but special articles demand individual creative identity.

Newsweek

For God, Country—And Votes

Walter Mondale was on the attack last week, accusing Ronald Reagan of "moral McCarthyism" for his rhetoric in support of the religious right. The president responded by reiterating his commitment to the separation of church and state. Religion had become the surprise issue of Campaign '84—embodying the ideological schism between the candidates. NEWSWEEK explores the role of religion in U.S. politics and why church and state have always been hard to separate. *Page 24*

A World of Beauty Pageants

America's love affair with beauty contests is still going strong—and when Suzette Charles (above) turns over her crown to a new Miss America this week, a huge TV audience will be watching. Despite Vanessa Williams and attacks by feminists, beauty pageants draw millions of contestants and sustain a vast subculture of promoters, groomers and coaches.   *Page 56*

A Tory Landslide in Canada

A bilingual Conservative named Brian Mulroney swept to power in Canada, humiliating the Liberal Party, which has governed the country for 42 of the last 50 years. Mulroney's probusiness, pro-U.S. policies were good news for Washington. But he will have his hands full tackling Canada's ailing economy—and keeping the promises he made to win.   *Page 40*

Business Blasts Off

Space shuttle Discovery, which touched down last week, was a giant step for the commercialization of space. Dozens of firms are scrambling to establish outposts in private enterprise's newest frontier.   *Page 62*

More Gloss and Glitz

The new fall TV season features a parade of Tough Dolls and Soft Guys as network programmers present more of the same old sludge. Angela Lansbury stars in "Murder, She Wrote," the season's class act. *Page 74*

CONTENTS

News, as defined by this content page of *Newsweek,* has a broad base to which lifestyle and entertainment elements contribute significantly. The five major articles are identified as "top of the week" features, each with a summary and a small photo insert. The lower 40% of the page identifies general categories of news and the stories within each. (Copyright © 1984, by Newsweek, Inc. All Rights Reserved, Reprinted by permission.)

FROM BARBED WIRE TO A BEAM OF LIGHT.

Almost a century ago, Stromberg-Carlson began serving rural America with telecommunications systems—at first utilizing ordinary barbed wire fences as transmission lines. Through the years, we have steadily advanced our technologies and expanded our capabilities to become a widely acknowledged and trusted leader in the field.

Today, we continue in that long-standing tradition as the newest member of the Plessey Group of high technology companies. Plessey is a worldwide leader in the digital revolution that is merging computers, fibre optics and telecommunications to transmit and switch signals globally, from local exchanges to satellite earth stations.

A past rich with achievement. A wealth of opportunity for the future. Stromberg-Carlson now looks forward to serving our customers with a broader base of resources than ever before.

Stromberg-Carlson
Corporate Marketing Services (S-18)
400 Rinehart Road, Lake Mary, Florida 32746
(305) 849-3000
INFORMATION SERVICE BUREAU
Toll Free (800) 327-2217

Stromberg-Carlson
A PLESSEY TELECOMMUNICATIONS COMPANY

The two advertisements in this figure illustrate the dynamic use of print space for a company actively involved in the business of communication. The single-page ad utilizes vertical design principles, whereas the other ad changes the inherent shape of the magazine to a horizontal shape by using two adjoining pages. The single-page ad turns white space into black space, which draws the reader's eye into the visual of a man's face as a circuit board and humanizes technical advances. The copy emphasizes the importance that the company places on research. The ad introduces the parent company, Plessey Telecommunications, which, for some readers, will be less familiar than Stromberg-Carlson in the American market.

The two-page spread draws the eye into the barbed wire in the upper left-hand corner and then races it along the curved line into the optical fiber which explodes into the headline "From Barbed Wire to a Beam of Light." The copy in the white space capitalizes on the history and achievements of Stromberg-Carlson as the newest member of the international corporation, Plessey Telecommunications.

Both ads seek to import a positive image of a company in the midst of the hi-tech revolution and its own corporate change. (Reprinted by permission of Stromberg-Carlson.)

WE'RE COMMUNICATIONS.

As the newest member of the Plessey Telecommunications family, we've expanded our capabilities. In research and development, where we can draw on Plessey capabilities in materials, components and systems. In transmission where we offer the most advanced fiber optic technology and equipment. In service, where we now have technically staffed offices all over the world.

In every area of telecommunications we have greater resources to bring to the solution of your problems. But resources aren't the total solution.

Over the past century of service to telephone operating companies, we've learned that solutions come from dedication and concern. From knowledge of the customer's business. From day-to-day communications with customer managers and engineers.

Communications is our business. But more important, communications is our way of doing business.

Stromberg-Carlson
Marketing Services (S-18)
400 Rinehart Road
Lake Mary, Florida 32746
(305) 849-3000   (800) 327-2217

Stromberg-Carlson
A PLESSEY TELECOMMUNICATIONS COMPANY

WE'RE STROMBERG-CARLSON.
A PLESSEY TELECOMMUNICATIONS COMPANY.

3. Pictorial features offer limitless possibilities and are an art form in and of themselves.

4. The typeface becomes the fabric of the periodical and creates an overall gray scale, or visual tone.

5. Lines and decorative elements (borders, indentations, etc.) serve as fences to separate some ideas and glue to join others.

Again, much of the particular code system comes from the kind of readership and how the reader uses the magazine. For example, the page structure and layout of *Broadcasting* are much different from those of *People Weekly*. *Broadcasting* is a trade magazine read by media professionals interested in the content. The coding system of the magazine does not have to attract the reader as much as *People Weekly*'s system does. *People Weekly* makes extensive use of color, boxed inserts, and graphics

People Weekly is a broad based, entertainingly newsy approach to people in the news. The cover design spurs reader interest and spontaneous purchase. By way of contrast, *Broadcasting* is a trade journal whose cover's purpose is not to attract readership, although it has economic value as a place for an ad. (*People Weekly* cover copyright © 1984, Time Inc. All rights reserved *Broadcasting* cover copyright © 1984. Used by permission.)

to attract readers. The preceding page showed the two magazines' different coding styles, each designed according to the magazine's content and audience.

ELECTRONIC MEDIA CODES

The electronic media can be split into two combinations:

1. *Aural media.* Radio and sound recording are completely dependent on sound.
2. *Audiovisual media.* Motion pictures and television use all the sound techniques of aural media, all the design capabilities of print, and movement. Most important, film and television use the first three elements in combination with *sound.*

Sound

Essentially, sound can be categorized as (*a*) voice; (*b*) music; (*c*) sound effects; and (*d*) silence.

Voice. The voice can be that of singer (phonograph), announcer (radio), actor (film), or narrator–commentator (television). All four media, of course, use all four vocal entities.

Music. The music can be vocal or instrumental. The uses of music in mass media drama include

1. Main-title music over credits that prepare the audience for the film as an overture does in muscial theater
2. Music to identify characters, time period, and place
3. Music to support action
4. Music to establish mood
5. Music to state themes
6. Music to reinforce the visual style

Bernard Herrmann's score for *Psycho* does it all. It literally controls the emotions of the audience and makes them fear for their lives. It is the "music," not Norman Bates' "mother," that slashes at the audience. It meets and exceeds every criteria for a film score: It is the mood, the action, the theme and the characters. If you have the opportunity to view *Psycho* without sound, the point will driven home.

The kinds of music used for backgrounds in film and TV drama as varied as music itself. But film scores may well be the "classical music" of the twentieth century. Certainly electronic music and modern symphonic scores have found their intellectual haven in motion-picture art.

Sound Effects. *Star Wars* revolutionized sound even more than it did special visual effects. Sound effects can be (*a*) local, identified visually;

(Photo: Museum of Modern Art/Film Stills Archive, Courtesy Paramount Pictures.)

Music in film is an essential support for the other elements of filmmaking. As an emotional lubricant for the audience and a psychological force in the film, Bernard Herrmann's score for *Psycho* is a masterpiece.

(Photo: Museum of Modern Art/Film Stills Archive, Courtesy 20th Century-Fox.)

Star Wars revolutionized sound as well as visual effects. The voices of C3P0, Chewbacca, and R2D2, as well as that of arch-villain Darth Vader, spoke with new aural energy, while laser blasts, light swords, rocket sleds, and space ships blasted movie audiences with new sounds.

(b) background, accepted environmental source; (c) artificial, unique aural identity as in *Star Wars'* lasers, space ships, and so on.

Silence. The tension created by silence is often more effective than jarring sound. The film *2001: A Space Odyssey* is a textbook on the uses of silence.

Sound is paramount in aural media and in audiovisual media sound must be wedded to the visuals. Orson Welles's training in radio and theater brought an aural dimension to *Citizen Kane* that has reverberated in films over the past 40 years. Sound is at least as important as sight in creating illusions and realities in motion pictures.

Sight   All the visual techniques in television and film are built around *movement*, because both movies and television are *motion* pictures. The basic principles of still composition, balance, symmetry, line, value, shape, texture, color, dimension, contrast, and the rest are developed around the basic concepts of movement.

There are essentially two classifications, or elements, in telecommunication and film communication:

1. *Intrashot elements.* This is movement within the shot and includes movement of the camera; movement of actors, animals, and things; movement of the background.
2. *Intershot elements.* This is the movement created by editing shots together. Literally, a visual rhythm is created between shots.

Intrashot Elements. Composition is the overriding visual concern of every short, and each movement in a shot of camera, actor, or background requires a recomposition of that shot. Several basic elements have an impact on the composition.

Visual achievements tend to overshadow aural elements of Stanley Kubrick's *2001: A Space Odyssey*, nevertheless, this filmmaker's use of silence has a tremendous effect and accentuates the emotional tension of the film; it also points out that the vastness of space is silent, despite a science fiction film tradition that would belie this fact.

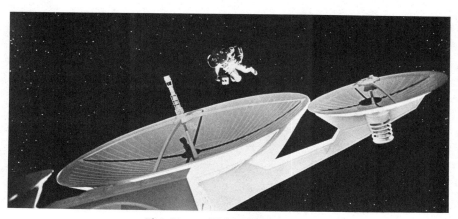

(Photo: Museum of Modern Art/Film Stills Archive, Courtesy Metro-Goldwyn-Mayer Inc.)

The *frame shape* has essentially three formats:

1. The regular film screen ratio, which is 1.33, to 1, or 1.33 units of width to each unit of height.
2. Wide-screen formats, which range from 1:65 to 2:55 to 1.
3. Television has the 1.33 to 1 ratio, but the rounded corners of the tube and the scanning system have an impact on the composition of theatrical releases shown on television.

Camera angles determine the viewpoint and area seen by the audience. Basically, *objective* camera angles are the least emotional views of an unseen observer; *subjective* camera angles offer a personal viewpoint and involve the audience emotionally; *point-of-view* camera angles offer a specific character's viewpoint (as though the camera is the actor's eyes).

Subject size depends on the distance from the camera and on the lens used. In descending order they are extreme long shot, long shot, medium shot, close-up, and extreme close-up.

The shots also involve more than one subject, and so there are two-shots (two characters), three-shots, and group shots. The shots also have foreground and background treatments.

The lens used also has an impact on size. Lenses fall into three general groupings: (*a*) Wide-angle lenses see more than the eye can; (*b*) telephoto lenses see less than the eye can and are used for close-ups at long distance (as a telescope does); (*c*) normal lenses approximate the eye. These three lenses have fixed focal lengths. The zoom lens has a variable focal length and approximates visually all three of the above lenses and incorporates them when zooming in or out.

The beautiful cinematography of *Barry Lyndon* duplicates the style of eighteenth century painting. Great care was taken to develop a lens that would allow "natural light" to illuminate the interior scenes. The candlelit scenes generate an emotional quality that is unique to the visual code potential of film in the hands of a director like Stanley Kubrick.

(Photo: Museum of Modern Art/Film Stills Archive, Courtesy Warner Bros., Inc.)

The depth of field (area in focus) also varies with each lens. It is greater with wide-angle (short) lenses than with telephoto (long) lenses.

Lighting is to film what paints are to canvas. The cinematographer paints with four basic lights: The *key light* is the primary light source (the sun or a lamp); the *fill light* softens the effects of the key light by eliminating harsh shadows; the *kicker*, or *backlight*, separates the actors from the background; the *background light* gives the composition depth.

Film stock is more than the difference between black and white and color. It has to do with contrasts (hardness—softness—hues) and the amount of light (speed) and filters and processing.

All these elements contribute to the overriding concern of the cinematographer: composition. The positioning of all the pictorial elements within the frame shape is the paramount consideration in filmmaking. Every shot must be a whole and contribute to the audiences's understanding and enjoyment of the film's themes, ideas, and story lines.

Intershot Elements. The second category of movement in film (and television) is the movement created by linking one image to the next. The movement between shots, or *intershot* movement, is an editorial function. And for many critics, editing is the heart and soul of audiovisual art. Cutting a film is the unique potential of the medium and may well be the most dynamic tool of the filmmaker's creative arsenal. The manipulation

The composition of a shot in a motion picture carries emotional values as well as information. By placing *Marathon Man*, Dustin Hoffman in the background and Laurence Olivier closer to the center, director John Schlesinger gives Olivier's character greater size (power) over Hoffman's character, despite the fact that Hoffman is pointing a gun.

(Photo: Museum of Modern Art/Film Stills Archive, Courtesy Paramount Pictures.)

In "The Odessa Steps Sequence" from *The Battleship Potemkin*, director Sergei Eisenstein uses dynamic editing to expand time, which enables him to explore the emotional content of rapidly occurring events. Yet, by cutting abruptly from image to image (general to specific, realistic to symbolic, long shot to close up), he manipulates the rhythm of the film so that the pacing seems to quicken, thereby accentuating the feeling of terror and panic implicit in the narrative. (Photos: Museum of Modern Art/Film Stills Archive.)

of a succession of visual and aural images generates both a kinetic and an intellectual energy, as well as moving forward the dramatic intent of the story line.

Editing manipulates both *real time* (the clock time the audience spends viewing) and dramatic time (the life length of the story and the characters that live the drama). Basically, editing moves the story line and facilitates action. *Continuity editing* is storytelling; it is slower, less frantic than *dynamic editing*, which is used in fast-paced action scenes. In both forms, editing controls time (speeding it up or slowing it down), establishes direction, controls pace and rhythm, generates spatial and emotional relationships of characters and locations, and reveals details of insights the audience needs to know.

The building blocks of the art of editing are these:

1. The *frame*, which is a single photographic image (sound films are shot and shown at 24 frames per second).
2. The *shot* is an individual moving image or length of film exposed from the time the camera begins running until it ends.
3. The *scene* is a dramatic unit in a single place at one time; it consists of one or more shots. If either time or place changes, a new scene begins.
4. The *sequence* is a major dramatic unit, made up of scenes, that completes exposition or character development or a theme or a dramatic action.

Films, then, are edited into shots, shots into scenes, scenes into sequences, and sequences into films.

Editing "builds" the film, and the editor's function is *the* critical element in restructuring electronic drama. The editing of a scene must be compelling and coherent because the audience must be both involved and able to understand the film. The editor performs a series of creative steps. First, he or she selects a specific shot from those available. Normally, only 10–20% of the available footage appears on the screen. Second, the selected shots are arranged so that the story line moves forward meaningfully. Third, each component shot is modified into a length that emphasizes the dramatic tone and action of the film.

The available footage is the raw material of the editor, who follows some general principles and some specific techniques to cut a film. For example, the techniques of editing include cuts (instantaneous changes from one shot to the next), dissolves (one shot gradually recedes as another gradually replaces it), wipes (a new shot shoves another off the screen vertically, horizontally, diagonally), and fades (goes to or comes from black). Traditionally, cuts are used between shots, dissolves between scenes, and fades between sequences. In principle, editing involves (a) *matching* images so that image size, positions, and direction match; (b) *cutting* on movement of an actor, object, or the camera; (c) *using reactions* as well as actions, depending on what is being done versus the impact of that action; (d) *parallel editing* that keeps the audience up to date on simultaneous actions occurring at different locations. Editing must, of course, always be done so that it keeps the attention of the audience engaged.

As the editor moves from raw footage to rough cut to fine cut, he or she must edit not only image to image and sound to sound but also image to sound. Synchronization of all this is the basic element here (and "sync" was the toughest problem to lick in the development of motion pictures).

Visually, the five elements of an art form—line, shape, value, texture, and color—dominate print. Film and television add a sixth element—*motion*. The illusion of movement in television and film occurs because the eye is unable to distinguish changes in the 525 electronic lines on the TV tube or the 24 still frames per second on the movie screen.

Aurally, the recording studio with "sweetening" techniques and 16, 24, 36, 48, and ad infinitum tracks mixed down can improve the live performance to an extent that the rock concert substitutes audience participation, "show biz" staging, and volume for the studio-mixed sound recording quality.

Although radio drama is in the doldrums, those of us old enough to remember will testify that in its heyday network radio generated pictures in our minds. The mass media "intensify" visual and aural experiences. Color photography is more intense than reality. The media codes generate a hyperreality that today is bigger and better and faster and more intense than ever before. We are willing to suspend belief for fantasies like *Return of the Jedi* or the re-created reality of docudramas like "Holocaust." Media codes transport us to new levels of experience. Certainly, a level of intense participation exists when the media environment and the content and the mass communicator's handling of codes take us up the stairway in *Vertigo* or transport us through the pages of Tolkien's *The Hobbit* or capsulize the week in *Sports Illustrated* or rock us to dreams with The Who's "Tommy."

Audiences have learned to "decode" new media languages and adjust to new dialects as they emerge. The naive movie audiences of the early 1900s have grown into a hardware-oriented generation of "film freaks" who want to know how the special effects work as well as experience the story line. Audiences have grown "more literate," which allows the film-maker to expand the lexicon of the medium. Audiences are not getting younger, they are getting better.

Both television and film attempt to fuse *form* and *content*. The form, or code, is neither identical to nor totally different from the content. The filmmaking process, like all other media, attempts to merge the medium, the code, and the content. This is what makes the creative process such a joy. The media are expanding human language.

Mass Media Gatekeepers

The words *Edited for Television* mean more than an occasional deleted word, sentence, or scene. They signal the presence of one of mass communication's most important and powerful elements: the gatekeeper.

When John Carpenter's graphically violent film *Halloween* was first shown on network television, it was heavily edited by NBC. As Robert Kapsis reported in an article in *American Film*: "Although the theatrical version contained only a few scenes of explicit violence, as the preliminary editing notes of NBC's Office of Broadcast Standards reveal, the network had a wide range of concerns in preparing the film for television." Consider, for example, this official list of recommended cuts pertaining to the first 30 minutes of *Halloween* (numbers refer to exact time the offensive material appeared):

> 2:00—Cut from shot at door to lights going off upstairs. Delete kids kissing on sofa.
>
> 5:00—Delete shot of nude girl at dressing table.
>
> 5:40—Delete shot of bloody breast. . . . Knife action must be tempered to one shot to establish action. No screams except for the one of Michael's name.
>
> 14:45—For God's sake.

  20:50—S – – –.
  21:00—Conversation among girls . . . delete reference to "Paul
    dragged me into the boys' locker room."
  22:25—Listen to Linda *screw* around.
  29:10—Two girls in the car . . . one girl gives the other one a
    joint.
  30:15—*Goddamn* kids.

The Office of Broadcast Standards at NBC was in fact a gatekeeper, deleting portions of the original message before it reached its TV audience.

Nearly everyone has played the communication game in which someone whispers a statement that is passed from person to person. By the time the message gets back to the originator, the content is often distorted and sometimes totally different from the original message. Each person in this communication chain has acted as a resistor or booster, emphasizing certain aspects of the message while deemphasizing others. In interpersonal communication each of us receives, makes judgments about, and modifies messages before we pass them along. Each of us acts as a checkpoint in the communication process—we refuse to transmit some messages, overemphasize others, and deemphasize still more. All of us, in effect, serve as gatekeepers, as checkpoints in the flow of communication. In mass communication these checkpoints are extremely important and have a critical effect on the content of news and entertainment.

THE CONCEPT OF THE GATEKEEPER

The word *gatekeeper* is essentially a sociological term used in mass communication research and may not even be recognized by many media professionals. The term was originally coined by Kurt Lewin in 1947 to describe the process by which a news item, traveling through channels, gains clearance at certain checkpoints along the way. Lewin called these checkpoints *gates*. The individuals or organizations who give clearance he labeled *gatekeepers*.

In the mass communication process gatekeepers take many forms. They are magazine publishers, newspaper editors, radio station managers, TV news directors, or movie producers. The gatekeeper's function is to evaluate media content in order to determine its relevance and value to audiences. Gatekeepers act as agents for both the communicator and the audience. As Alan Wurtzel, ABC's East Coast vice president for broadcast standards and practices, explained: "We have a contract with the audience. We tell them: "We're going to deal with some unusual scenes and in exchange we'll deal with them sensitively and carefully and you can trust us to do that." What is most important is that gatekeepers have the power to determine the nature and flow of certain kinds of information.

The model of mass communication developed by Bruce Westley and Malcolm MacLean graphically illustrates the concept of the gatekeeper in

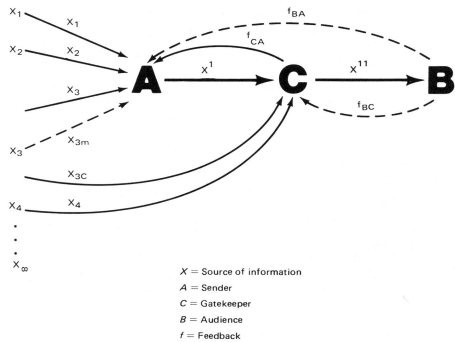

X = Source of information
A = Sender
C = Gatekeeper
B = Audience
f = Feedback

The Bruce Westley and Malcolm MacLean Model of Mass Communication. (From *Journalism Quarterly*, 34, Winter 1957.)

the mass communication process. The X's refer to events or sources of information (e.g., an accident or a speech delivered to a local audience). The mass communicator A in this example is a reporter who describes the accident or speech in the form of a news story. The gatekeeper C is the editor who deletes, deemphasizes, or adds to the reports of the accident or speech based on data that may or may not have been available to the reporter. The audience B then reads the news reports of the accident or speech in the newspaper. The reader may respond to either the editor fBC or reporter fBA regarding the accuracy or importance of the news story. The editor may also provide feedback to the reporter fCA. The news example can be extended to entertainment in the form of the previously noted NBC's Office of Broadcast Standards or the motion-picture industry's Classification and Ratings Administration (CARA), which assigns ratings to theatrical films.

Within this context it is important to distinguish clearly between gatekeepers and regulators. Both act to check, restrain, or clarify media content. Gatekeepers, however, are a part of the media institution and share its basic value system. Regulators exist outside the media and operate on different value systems. The U.S. Supreme Court may declare a certain film pornographic and halt its distribution; CARA may assign an X rating to a film and effectively restrict its audience to those age 17 or older. In the latter instance CARA is acting in behalf of the industry, for if the industry was not self-governing in terms of content and audience, it might find itself at the mercy of local, state, and federal regulations. The Supreme Court is operating on values different from those of CARA. The Supreme Court declares the film pornographic on the basis of an established value system; it rules that the film appeals to prurient interest and is wholly without socially redeeming value. The Court's decision has little to do with the box-office potential of the film or the value system of the industry.

It is important to understand that gatekeepers in mass communication are institutionalized within a system or organization. Often, as in the case of CARA, they are not personally visible. They are so vital to the proper functioning of the mass communication process, however, that they are institutionalized into formal roles and responsibilities.

Mass media systems do not simply *tolerate* gatekeepers, they create them. Historically, gatekeepers existed in the press in the singular form of owners—men like William Randolph Hearst, Joseph Pulitzer, and Henry Luce. Today's gatekeepers are not as socially visible, and rarely do they exist in the form of a single person. Gatekeeping in mass media today takes place primarily behind the scenes. Instead of individuals, there are departments (e.g., NBC's Office of Broadcast Standards) staffed by publicly faceless but enormously powerful people.

Gatekeeping has become such a necessary element in mass communication that it has often been formalized into codes of behavior. The now extinct NAB Radio and Television Code is perhaps the most prominent example of gatekeeping formalized into a code. Although less than half of all radio and TV stations subscribed to the code, and even though it is now officially dead, its "codes of conduct" involving such things as the advertising of hard liquor still carry great influence.

In addition to codes, media executives successfully manage their organizations by stressing the organization's values to their subordinates. The content of most newspapers or newscasts is not simply the result of the arbitrary choices of a few people; it results from a process. Richard Salant, while he was president of CBS News stated that "we do have a policy about live coverage of disorders and potential disorders." Clearly, Salant was functioning as a gatekeeper; equally important, he was indicating a value system that would be followed by reporters at CBS.

TYPES OF GATEKEEPERS

All mass media have a large number of gatekeepers. They perform a variety of functions and play several roles. They can delete a message or they can modify a message. They can stop a message by refusing to open a gate. The broadcast-standards department of a TV network can do this by simply refusing a proposed script. Local stations can also delete content or refuse to clear a network program, and in recent years the television networks have assisted the stations by feeding affiliates up to 20 hours a week of program material that might be controversial. Gatekeepers can alter a message by deleting limited portions of it. The following portions of a memo from the ABC network's department of broadcast standards provide a clear illustration of gatekeeping at work:

"Soap" represents a further innovation in the comedic/dramatic form presenting a larger-than-life frank treatment of a wide variety of controversial and adult themes such as: premarital sex, adultery, impotence, homosexuality, transvestitism, transsexualism, religion, politics, ethnic stereotyping (and other aspects of race relations), etc.

Accordingly, great caution will have to be exercised to carefully balance controversial issues; provide positive characterizations to balance ethnic stereotyping; delicate matters of taste will need to be handled with sensitivity and discretion; and the gratuitous, sensational or exploitative will need to be avoided.

"Soap" Part I

PAGE 5   Please delete ". . . the slut."
PAGE 6   Please delete "Some Polish slut."
PAGE 7   Avoid visual I.D. of *Penthouse* cover and photos.
PAGE 16   Please insure that Benson's self-effacing portrayal is always played tongue-in-cheek and that he continues to stay "one-up" vis-à-vis his antagonists.
PAGE 16   Please delete underlined—"*fruit* with acne."
PAGE 22   Please substitute for "Chocolate face."
PAGE 23   Delete "fruitcake."
PAGE 27   Here and elsewhere, Italian will require translation.
PAGE 28   In order to be able to treat the Mafia storyline here and throughout, it will be necessary to introduce a principal continuing character of Italian descent who is very positive and who will, through the dialogue and action, balance and counter any negative stereotypes.

All three networks have their own broadcast-standards departments. NBC employs 26 people, ABC's staff numbers 70 and CBS has 80 people on both coasts. They evaluate programs and commercials at several stages of development ranging from initial program ideas to specific words and scenes in scripts and productions. One of the pioneering writers treating strong social commentary, the late Rod Serling, continually ran afoul of broadcast standards and sponsors. "A Town Has Turned to Dust" on "Playhouse 90," for example, was based on the lynching of Emmett Till, a black youth, in Mississippi. Worried about reaction from the South and a possible boycott of sponsor U.S. Steel's products, the ad agency forced Serling to move the locale to New England and change the leading character from a black youth to a foreigner. The show's producer, the Theater Guild, backed the ad agency's demands.

Broadcast standards executives at all three networks agree that an increasing assortment of once-taboo topics, jokes, words, and sights now flows past their editing pencils without horrifying censors or audience.

The shift toward sensitive topics is evident. After ABC's treatments of nuclear war ("The Day After") and incest ("Something about Amelia"), censors say no taboo subjects are left.

"I don't think there's anything you can't present on television, given a balanced view and a degree of sensitivity," says Alice Henderson, vice president of program practices at CBS. Since the trailblazing "All in the Family," even sitcom plots can revolve around racism, drug abuse, and changing gender roles.

Yet in a "Buffalo Bill" abortion episode, a retort was doctored to eliminate even the initial "f" sound of an already bleeped epithet. "We're lagging behind society there," admits Ralph Daniels, NBC's vice president of broadcast standards. "The kinds of things said on T-shirts are not said on NBC in prime time."

Sponsors and their advertising messages are also subject to the gatekeeping process. NBC and ABC took a BIC disposable razor ad off the air because it did not meet their standards. Advertiser claims—in the BIC case comparisons of its razor to that of Gillette—cause the most problems for network standards.

Sometimes one medium serves a gatekeeping function that affects another medium. For example, several newspapers refuse to accept advertising of X-rated films. At the *Los Angeles Times,* a six-person committee decides whether a movie ad is acceptable; until 4 years ago, any ad that was in "good taste" was accepted. "But we had games played on us by some of the porn producers and distributors, recalls Gordon Phillips, the paper's director of promotion and public relations, in an article in *USA Today.* "They would put double meanings in their headlines, and they were using a few pictures we felt were not quite appropriate. So we banned X-rated films and all unrated pornographic films." Today, if ads for films rated G, PG, PG13, or R are not in "good taste," they are returned to the advertising agency or the exhibitor with suggestions on how to make the copy or the art acceptable.

Because they were considered objectionable by newspaper editors in several major cities, a series of *Doonesbury* comic strips depicting a journey through Ronald Reagan's brain were not run. A critic for a magazine may refuse to review a new book on the market. A radio station may refuse to play a recently released record because it deals with a controversial subject. Several radio stations, for example, routinely ban all records with drug-oriented lyrics.

Nonclearance of network TV programs by stations is a major gatekeeping function. Stations are responsible for all programming broadcast over their signal regardless of origination, and they refuse to clear network programs primarily for economic or objectionable-material reasons. (Low-rated network programs are not as profitable to the local station, especially if they can be replaced with low-cost syndicated or local programming that may have greater appeal to the station's audience.) The most extreme example of nonclearance for objectionable program material was the CBS production of the play *Sticks and Bones* in 1973. The play centered on a Vietnam veteran and was physically and psychologically violent. Its playing date coincided with the return to the United States of Vietnam prisoners of war, and the contrast between the play and the actual return was too harsh for many affiliates. Thus CBS postponed the program. It was eventually run by the network, but over half the affiliated stations refused to carry it.

All these gatekeeping decisions affect the ability of an audience to receive specific media experiences; therefore, deleting or stopping a message is a gatekeeper's most powerful role. But gatekeepers are not simply passive—negative forces opening or closing a gate on a message or a portion of it. They can also be a creative force.

A news editor can add to messages by combining information from other sources or by adding a story at the beginning of a newscast. A magazine-layout editor can increase the impact of a story by adding a significant number of pictures. An artist-and-repertoire person in a record company can send the master tape back for additional background music to improve the total sound. A movie producer can send a work print back to the editor or director to have scenes added. This process of adding to a message makes the role of a gatekeeper similar to that of a communicator, and indeed gatekeepers can be seen as part of the mass communicator concept in that they affect content. Nevertheless, gatekeepers function differently from communicators. The key distinction is that gatekeepers do not originate content; they alter it.

The following excerpt from *Esquire* magazine illustrates the gatekeeping process at work in magazine publishing:

> A good magazine is one that surprises its readers with a variety of imaginative and well-written stories. Putting together that mix is not easy and requires more people and more hours than most readers realize. What you are holding in your hands is the final step of a process we began many months ago.
>
> Ten weeks ago, for example, our political columnist, Richard Reeves, and our ethics columnist, Harry Stein, each mulled over several story ideas with our editors and finally decided that political campaigns and gossip were suitable subjects for April. About two weeks later they delivered their columns to the magazine, where it took another two weeks to edit, fact-check, and copy-edit them, as well as to come up with the accompanying illustrations.

Unless a major revision is required, the average column takes half a day to edit and two or three days to fact-check. Checking is a scrupulous process in which our researchers actually re-report the story, verifying every fact through printed sources or with experts on the subject. It's a tricky business because checking points can range from proper names to subtle implications. (One of our researchers, when faced with a deceptively innocent sentence referring to columns in Babylonian temples, found after an afternoon's digging that not all Babylonian temples had columns.) . . .

The editors of Esquire are an eclectic mix of writers, painters, philosophers, sports nuts, teachers, musicians, and political activists ranging in age from mid-twenties to mid-fifties. Put this group together and the resulting discussions are unpredictable, provocative, funny, and sometimes volatile. The only thing we all agree on is our commitment to quality journalism. . . .

All of our features go through the same editing, fact-checking, copy-editing, design, illustration, and production processes as our columns. As deadlines for closing approach, work hours stretch. Sometimes camaraderie runs high, while at other times mere civility is the best that people can manage.[1]

The gatekeeper also modifies the emphasis of the message. Murray Schumach notes this function in the film *Breakfast at Tiffany's*. The heroine, Holly Golightly, was an amusing girl with few moral inhibitions. Part of her humor was based on her indifference to promiscuity. But when Audrey Hepburn was cast in the role, it was considered improper to let the public see her depicted this way. As the film's director, Blake Edwards, said: "In the movie we don't exactly say what Holly's morals are. In a sense she can be considered an escort service for men. . . . Risque dialogue was deleted and she no longer discusses her affairs with men. Holly is now a patroness of the arts."[2] In newspapers, message emphasis is changed by headline size and story placement. Some radio station managers have "soul" programs for black listeners, but many such programs are slotted late at night when smaller audiences are available.

There is little question that gatekeeping represents enormous power and control. Nevertheless, gatekeepers retain their power only by exercising it within the shared value system of the media institution in which they work. A film editor who consistently cuts out a director's best scenes or an actor's most appealing camera angle will soon be out of a job.

The motion-picture industry's Ratings Board and its Appeals Board provide excellent examples of the shared value system at work. The movie *Poltergeist* (MGM/UA) has a very explicit body count of decaying corpses;

[1] Phillip Moffit, "The Editorial Process," *Esquire*, April 1980. Copyright © 1980 by Esquire Publishing, Inc.
[2] Murray Schumach, *The Face on the Cutting Room Floor* (New York: William Morrow, 1964), 142–143

Functioning as a gatekeeper, director of *Breakfast at Tiffany's* Blake Edwards chose to downplay character Holly Golightly's amoral attitude toward sex when Audry Hepburn was cast in the role. (Photo: Museum of Modern Art/Film Stills Archive, Courtesy Paramount Pictures.)

it was rated R by the film industry's Rating Board. With this rating, only those 17 years of age and older could see the film unaccompanied by an adult. Because *Poltergeist*, which concerns the ghostly possession of a tract house and its occupants, would obviously find its greatest audience among young teenagers, the studio appealed the decision. By a surprisingly lopsided vote, the Appeals Board, which consists of 24 members of organizations of movie producers and distributors and theater owners, overturned the R rating and granted *Poltergeist* a PG rating. The Appeals Board thus extended the *Poltergeist* message to younger audiences enhancing the film's economic potential.

The gatekeeping functions described in this chapter are usually accomplished through economic control, individual taste or bias, and ideology or value system. Economic control can exist in the form of broad policy, such as a corporation vice-president allowing no motion picture to cost more than a million dollars. Clearly, this places restraints on content and how it is presented. More often, economic control takes the form of simple space–time restrictions. A publisher may decide the news hole for today's paper will be 75 columns. The editor may have enough news to fill 125 columns, but to no avail. The producer of "The CBS Evening News" has approximately 20 minutes each evening to present the news of the day and must make hard decisions about which stories get on the air.

METHODS OF CONTROL

The control exercised by an individual personality has been and is the most common and most visible form of gatekeeping. Henry Luce determined much of what went into each issue of *Time*. Ben Bradlee made a critical decision by allowing stories by Woodward and Bernstein to appear in the *Washington Post* when there was great pressure to drop the reports. A similar decision by *Washington Post* editors to print a series by a reporter named Janet Cooke led to major embarrassment. After Cooke won a Pulitzer Prize for her series, it was discovered that she had fabricated much of the story. In this instance, the gatekeeping process dysfunctioned because the gatekeeper did not exercise the power to evaluate and alter the messages Cooke was sending. Rupert Murdoch clearly changed the style and content of *New York* magazine and the *New York Post*. There will always be key people in any media organization who will shape and influence media content. Bill Jackson, former editor of the *Sunday Courier Press* in Evansville, Indiana, stated that what got printed on the front page of his paper was what he decided was news.

The influence of ideology or value system is a little more difficult to recognize but is one of the most powerful gatekeeping methods. The conservative ideology of the *New Republic* clearly influences its content, as does the liberal philosophy of the *New York Times*. Les Brown comments in his book *Television: The Business Behind the Box*, "The ruling powers at the networks are decidedly Establishment in their politics and in general closer to the right of the political center than to the left." This would seem to affect the content broadcast by the networks.

Journalists—reporters, editors, publishers—have long subscribed to a code of ethics that defines and prescribes much of their work. The Radio Television News Directors Association, for example, has a Code of Broadcast News Ethics that emphasizes the basic premise that accuracy and comprehensiveness are criteria that take precedent over all other news motives.

A variety of people perform the gatekeeping function. Nevertheless, certain people or positions function more often and with greater influence as gatekeepers than others.

The major gatekeeper in the news media is the editor. In the face of today's tremendous news output, every news medium must be selective. Studies indicate that a typical large-city daily newspaper can carry as little as one-tenth of the news that comes into the newsroom on any given day. The same is true for news magazines because much more material is available to their editors than space limitations permit them to use. Editors determine which stories reach the public. They also decide what emphasis to give stories. Placement of a story on the front page of a newspaper as the cover article in a magazine or the lead story in a TV newscast can have significant influence on the number of persons who read or see it. The use of a larger headline in a newspaper can give a story more importance than it would otherwise have and thus attract more readers.

Although the editor is the most identifiable gatekeeper in a news operation, other persons assist in the gatekeeping function. To emphasize the complexity of this aspect of mass communication, let us examine the steps a story on President Reagan vetoing a congressional bill goes through before it appears in a local newspaper. The news source—in this case, President Reagan or his press secretary and certain congressmen—serve as the first gatekeepers. They are witnesses to and participants in the attempt to veto a piece of congressional legislation. They view the operation selectively, seeing some events and missing others, forgetting some events and misinterpreting others. Significantly, the fact that they are involved in the action affects their perception.

Reporters gathering information are the next people in the gatekeeping process. They may choose to believe President Reagan, who viewed the legislation as ill conceived, although Congress viewed the legislation as necessary. The reporters have to decide which facts to pass along, how to write or photograph them, and what perspectives to offer from their previous experiences in covering the federal government.

By the time the report gets to a wire service it has become part of a huge information flow. Wire-service editors must now decide what copy is worth passing along to regional and state bureaus, where a similar decision is made.

Finally, the story is pulled from the wire by a local newspaper's wire editor or a TV station's news director. Literally hundreds of stories are competing for space in the newspaper, and if President Reagan's action is seen as important, if there is space for it, and if no local news takes precedence, the story will be used.

Gatekeepers also operate in radio and TV news. Whereas newspapers have a space problem, broadcasters are limited by time. The editor of "NBC Nightly News" faces a selection and emphasis problem that is even more severe than that faced by the editor of the *New York Times*. Wire-service and staff reporters provide much more news than can possibly be used. Most TV network news programs are 30 minutes long, including commercials and credits. At most, only 10 to 15 stories can be covered

CBS "60 Minutes" executive producer Don Hewitt. (Courtesy Don Hewitt. Reproduced by permission of CBS News.)

in this time period. Thus, program length becomes a critical factor in news selection by broadcast gatekeepers.

Broadcast entertainment gatekeepers include writers, directors, producers, actors, editors, designers, musicians, and many other persons associated with a production. For example, "60 Minutes," has more than 60 people, including producers, researchers, film editors, and correspondents involved in the production of a single episode. Not all these people serve as gatekeepers, but most of them have the gatekeeping potential to evaluate and alter the flow of communication. Perhaps the key gatekeepers are the program producers. In "60 Minutes" these are Don Hewitt, the executive producer, and Philip Scheffler, the senior producer. Stephen Zito in his article "Inside 'Sixty Minutes'" notes Hewitt's function especially: "Hewitt makes up the show each week in much the same way a magazine editor assembles an individual issue of a magazine giving thought to length, tone, and contrast." Hewitt himself goes on to explain his gatekeeping role:

The Gatekeeper and Entertainment

It's all instinctive . . . I'm the least intellectual person I know. A lot of times I say to a producer, "I see it and I hear it but I don't feel it in the pit of my stomach." I don't make decisions intellectually, I make them viscerally. . . . When I get bored, I figure other people will get bored. I have the ability to put myself in the place of the viewer because I have the same short attention span he has. When an idea comes in, my first reaction is always, "Does anybody care? Is anyone gonna watch this?" It's not important in TV what you tell people; it's only important what they remember of what you told them.[3]

This attitude has led many people to criticize "60 Minutes" for what they feel is excessive bias and a limited point of view, especially concerning controversial issues.

Once a TV program is shot, the editor—a key gatekeeper—comes into play. This person can completely alter the message of the director. A fascinating glimpse of this process and its influence is found in the short film *Interpretations and Values*. The film shows how three editors cut a sequence from the TV series "Gunsmoke" and reveals how each editor saw the raw footage a little differently and stamped the film with his own interpretation.

Much the same gatekeeping process is involved in making a motion picture, although some differences occur because of the expanded scope and budget of a feature film. Whereas an episode of a TV series usually takes less than a week to shoot, a motion picture may involve months, even years, of work. A brief glimpse at one group of important gatekeepers in the motion-picture industry, editors, will help to illustrate this point.

Editors, like cinematographers, contribute greatly to the end result of a motion picture. Nevertheless, their contribution is, at its best, unobtrusive. Bad editing is obvious editing; but top film industry editors do have a style, and despite working closely with directors, they do exert an influence over the films they work on. Verna Fields is a well-known editor, having worked on such films as *What's Up, Doc?*, *Sugarland Express*, *American Graffiti*, and *Jaws*. Her work on *Jaws* was especially notable; she succeeded in creating much of the film's tension through editing, particularly in scenes involving the shark. Because it was obviously mechanical, the shark could not be left on the screen too long, or audiences would quickly perceive the illusion.

Dede Allen is another top editor; she has worked on such dissimilar films as Arthur Penn's *The Missouri Breaks*, Sidney Lumet's *Dog Day Afternoon* and *Serpico*, and George Roy Hill's *Slapshot*. Each of these films and directors has a distinct style, and Allen's contribution, although not as obvious as that of Fields in *Jaws*, is nevertheless important. Allen's value as an editor and gatekeeper lies in her ability to edit a film in a way that complements a particular director's style and intent.

[3] Stephen Zito, "Inside Sixty Minutes," *American Film* 2, no. 3 (December–January 1977): 31–36, 55–57.

From the previous discussion it becomes clear that the identity of the gatekeeper blurs with that of the communicator. When is the copyeditor or film editor a communicator rather than a gatekeeper? The distinction lies in *what* the person is doing. An individual who is creating is serving as a communicator. An individual who is evaluating another's creation is a gatekeeper. Obviously, the same individual may perform both functions at the same time: One person can evaluate a director's visual output and add a creative dimension to the film. A copyeditor's evaluation of a reporter's story also involves the creative editing of the total newspaper.

The regulator and gatekeeper roles are similar in one respect—both can stop messages from reaching audiences. As we noted previously the significant difference is that the *gatekeeper is part of the media institution,* but the *regulator is an external agent* of the public or government. Gatekeepers are further distinguished from regulators in that the gatekeeper, as noted, can add to as well as delete from mass communication messages.

The gatekeeper can have a potent effect on the mass communication process, especially if a society's media are controlled by an elite minority intent on restricting the public's rights to know. Former Vice-President Spiro Agnew brought this concern to the public spotlight in a Des Moines, Iowa, speech in 1969. Although he overstated the issue, he created controversy within the news media and focused attention on those individuals functioning as gatekeepers in TV network news. In a free society, however, where TV news is in competition with newspapers and magazines as well as other broadcast journalism, this potential misuse of the gatekeeping role is unlikely to occur. Obviously, the reactionary right and radical left sometimes feel that media gatekeepers in the United States devote too little time and space to these groups' views of what is news.

In practice, the gatekeeper's power is diffused because in mass communication the message is usually meant for such a large audience that one single cut from a script or a news story rarely produces a fundamental change in the nature of the communication event or in society itself. Nevertheless, live TV coverage of news events has demonstrated that gatekeepers can have a significant impact on mass communication. This fact was dramatically brought to light by TV coverage of the 1968 Democratic National Convention in Chicago. The interpretation and the subsequent impact of the convention were created in great measure by the selective coverage given the demonstrations outside the convention headquarters. Videotape editing demonstrated the impact gatekeepers can have when they present a selected view of events.

The concern expressed over the Chicago coverage has also been raised over television handling of riots in some large cities. Television cannot and does not simply "tell it like it is." It may record, but it does so under the influence of many communicators and gatekeepers who filter, amplify, or interfere with the message. The amplifying role used on television for news coverage has been severely criticized. Critics claim that by empha-

**THE IMPACT OF
THE GATEKEEPER**

sizing looting and destruction, TV gatekeepers may actually encourage observers to participate.

The same basic gatekeeping effects occur with an entertainment program, with the exception that the public usually does not feel the same concern over the deletion of a particular song or spoken vulgarity that it does when it suspects that what is being offered as news is untrue or that part of the truth is being withheld. For example, after an initial furor, gatekeeping issues involving "The Richard Pryor Show" were quickly forgotten. On the other hand, questions are still being raised about news coverage of events in Vietnam that happened years ago.

Thus, the basic effect of gatekeeping is that the message is altered in some way. Only when this alteration seriously distorts the public's view, however, does the gatekeeping function become unsatisfactory. The media can and do distort reality. This distortion generally occurs in one of two ways: systematic distortion or random distortion. Systematic distortion usually occurs through deliberate bias, whereas random distortion occurs primarily through carelessness or ignorance. A study of wire-news editors revealed a degree of systematic distortion at work when it was found that some editors, because of their particular bias and predisposition, would not carry certain stories. This can usually be corrected because it is highly visible to many people within and outside the particular mass media institution. Random distortion is often more dangerous and harmful. Here the role of the gatekeeper is not as easily discernible. Gatekeepers who operate by random distortion seldom have reasons for their decisions because their job may be so routine, so institutionalized, that they do not actually feel they are making decisions.

It is also clear that some gatekeepers are more important than others. Robert K. Merton has described several "influentials"—that is, certain individuals in any society who receive an unusually large number of messages. He further breaks down this category into "cosmopolitans" and "locals."[4] Cosmopolitans receive their information from outside the community, while locals function within the local society. These influentials exist as gatekeepers on a movie set, in a newspaper office, or at a TV studio. What is important about their presence in mass communication is that they are numerous, are fragmented into highly specialized positions, and may have an effect disproportional to their relative position and power.

In the final analysis, gatekeepers are a normal part of any communication process. Ordinarily, they create no great concern. With mass communication institutions organized the way they are, however, gatekeepers assume great importance because of their power to alter, delete, or stop media content altogether.

[4] Robert K. Merton, "Patterns of Influence: A Study of Interpersonal Influence and Communications Behavior in a Local Community," in Robert K. Merton, *Social Theory and Social Structure* (Glencoe, Ill.: Free Press, 1957), 387–420.

(Courtesy CBS News.)

CBS News Correspondent Ed Bradley covers activities on the floor of the Democratic National Convention in San Francisco in July 1984.

What is even more important is the fact that gatekeepers may be invisible to most people, and gatekeepers may be only barely aware that they are making decisions that affect the lives of millions of people. Gatekeepers have enormous power and control in the mass communication process. It is critical that we understand who they are and how they function.

8 The Media

The mass media, as institutions in American society, are composed of an intricate fabric of people, products, organizations, production units, service units, and associations. No doubt media institutions are among the most complex in our society; this makes their study intriguing, their operation demanding, their role vital, and their impact often difficult to determine.

An essential element of all communication is the medium that carries the message. When we communicate person to person, the medium consists of sound waves in the air, a letter delivered through the mail, or telephone wires and receivers. But in mass communication a vast, complex, and specialized technology characterizes the medium.

The figure below indicates in brief form the extent and complexity of mass communication in American society. Seven principal mass media institutions (newspapers, magazines, books, radio, television, motion pictures, and recordings) are broken down into basic media units—Time Inc., WGN-TV, Longman Inc., MGM, for example—that produce communication products such as publications, pictures, programs, and records. The basic media units themselves depend on a system of media service units that produce, distribute, exhibit, sell, manufacture, and represent corporations and individuals. These service units often represent clients from various media at the same time. The wire services, for example,

Media Institutions	Media Units	Media Products
Newspaper	New York Times Christian Science Monitor Oklahoma Eagle Ithaca Journal National Observer	Daily newspapers Weekly newspapers Sunday supplements
Magazine	Time Town and Country Playboy Ms. Journal of Communication	Weekly magazines Monthly magazines Quarterly magazines Comic books Journals
Book	Acropolis Books Longman Inc. Dodd, Mead, and Company University of Illinois Press Bantam Books	Hardcover books Paperback books

Motion picture	Universal Pictures
	Walt Disney Productions
	Metro-Golden-Mayer
	Avco-Embassy
		Feature-length motion
		  pictures
		Cartoons
		Documentaries
		Industrial films
		Television commercials
		  and programs

Radio	WBBM, Chicago KDKA, Pittsburgh WABC, New York WGBH, Boston WICB-FM, Ithaca	Radio programs and commercials
Television	KFMB-TV, San Diego WNYC-TV, New York KYW-TV, Philadelphia WXYZ-TV, Detroit WCCO-TV, Minneapolis	Television programs and commercials
Sound recording	Atlantic Records Columbia Record Company MCA Records RCA Records	Disk recordings Tape recordings Cassette recordings Cartridge recordings

Other	Kiplinger Washington
	  Letter
	Academic Media
	  Services, Inc.
		Personal, graphic,
		  audiovisual, mixed-
		  multi, and computer
		  media

The HUB Structural Chart of Mass Media.

Media Service Units	Media Associations

Production
Press associations
  API, UPI, Reuters, etc.
Syndicates
  King Features, United Features,
  etc.
Networks
  ABC, NBC, CBS, Mutual, etc.
Advertising agencies
  J. Walter Thompson, Leo Burnett,
  etc.
Public relations agencies
  Hill & Knowlton, Ruder & Finn, etc.
Independent production companies
  Associated Producers,
  Guggenheim Productions, Inc. etc.
	Media-Unit Owners
	American Newspaper Publishers
	  Association
	Magazine Publishers Association
	American Book Publishers Council
	National Association of Broadcasters
	Motion Picture Association of
	  America

Distribution and Exhibition
Motion-picture distributors
  Association Films, United World
  Films
Publication distributors
  American News Company, etc.
Motion-picture exhibitors
  Individual theaters and theater
  chains
Publication retailers
  Newsstands, department stores,
  etc.
Record distributors
	Media Professionals
	American Society of Newspaper
	  Editors
	National Conference of Editorial
	  Writers
	Society of Magazine Writers
	National Academy of Motion Picture
	  Arts & Sciences
	National Academy of Radio-
	  Television Arts & Sciences
	Radio Television News Directors
	  Association
	National Press Photographers
	  Association
	Sigma Delta Chi

Manufacturing
Printing-press, electronic, and
  photographic equipment
  manufacturers
Paper, ink, film, chemical, and
  record manufacturers
Printing, binding, film-processing,
  and record-pressing companies
Radio- and television-set
  manufacturers	

Representation
Talent agencies
  United Talent, Inc., Curtis-Brown,
  etc.
Artists' representatives
  American Society of Composers,
  Authors, and Publishers (ASCAP),
  Broadcast Music Inc. (BMI), etc.
Labor unions
  American Newspaper Guild,
  American Federation of Television
  and Radio Artists, American Guild
  of Variety Artists, etc.
Station and publication
  representatives
	**Service-Unit Owners and
	Professionals**
	Associated Press Managing Editors
	American Association of Advertising
	  Agencies
	Advertising Federation of America
	Public Relations Society of America
	American Institute of Graphic Arts
	Society of Independent Motion
	  Picture Producers
	Audit Bureau of Circulations

The HUB Structural Chart of Mass Media. (*continued*)

service newspapers, TV stations, and radio stations. In addition, a large network of management and professional associations represents the managers and communicators in their relations with one another and with other institutions in society.

Books come in a fairly standardized format, although there is variation in page size, binding, type of cover, and length. About 1700 publishing firms produce about 40,000 book titles in America each year. Of these firms, about 300 publishers, most of them located in New York City, produce the majority of books.

MEDIA INSTITUTIONS

The Book

Like books, newspapers are fairly standardized in format. They are printed on large sheets of paper, either blanket size (about 22 × 15 inches) or tabloid size (about 15 × 12 inches). About 1750 daily newspapers and 10,000 weekly newspapers are published in the United States, many of them as part of newspaper chains owned by large corporations. In this country only a small number of newspapers, such as the *Christian Science Monitor*, have national circulation. Most newspapers are edited for distinct metropolitan areas or communities.

The Newspaper

Magazines come in all sizes and shapes. Their pages are usually printed on heavier and higher-quality paper than newspapers and are stapled or glued between soft covers. About 10,000 different magazine publication units exist in the United States, many of them under chain ownership. Magazines have a broader range than newspapers, both in subject matter and in geographical distribution, but are designed to reach more specialized audiences.

The Magazine

Although the category of motion picture usually refers to feature-length dramatic films of from 90 to 180 minutes, there are many different kinds of motion pictures including documentaries, industrial films, commercial spots, and TV programs. Production has shifted away from large Hollywood-studio corporations to small, independent producers who use the old units (e.g., Warner Brothers and MGM) primarily for financing, promotion, and distribution services. Motion-picture studios are heavily involved in producing films for television. In addition, television uses motion-picture film for news and documentaries, series programs, and commercials, as well as for feature-length dramas.

The Motion Picture

Radio requires special equipment for transmission and reception. Transmission equipment is expensive and complex, but radio receivers using solid-state transistors are relatively inexpensive. Radio consists of two transmission systems, amplitude modulation (AM) and frequency modulation (FM). Radio is local rather than regional or national in ori-

Radio

entation, even though four national networks (ABC, CBS, MBS, and NBC) provide some national programming, primarily news. More than 98% of all homes in the United States have radio receivers; in the average listening area, most radios are capable of receiving at least six stations.

Television   The medium of television is also composed of two transmission systems: very high frequency (VHF, channels 2 to 13) and ultra-high frequency (UHF, Channels 14 to 83). The VHF stations normally reach more people because their signals cover a larger area using less power than UHF stations. This is reflected in the greater number of VHF stations compared to UHF stations. As with radio, TV stations are licensed by the federal government and regulated by the Federal Communications Commission (FCC). Three national TV networks (ABC, NBC, and CBS) dominate the medium, supplying 70–90 hours of programming per week to their affiliated stations' total program schedule of 100–110 hours.

Sound Recording   Like broadcast media, records and tapes require special production and playback equipment. Approximately 80% of all U.S. homes have phonographs or tape recorders, which use records and tapes produced by more than 1500 record companies. Four major and three emerging companies dominate record production in the United States. Record companies are also the largest suppliers of programming for radio.

(A detailed historical and structural analysis of the seven basic media institutions is contained in Part Three of this book.)

MEDIA UNITS   The mass communication industry resembles the operational organization of other corporate enterprises in the United States. Media products are produced, distributed, and exhibited through national corporations as well as local retailers. The basic media unit may be national or local, but whatever its primary function, the *basic media unit is that part of mass media held responsible for content*, even though the unit may not have produced or distributed the content. In fact, some basic media units actually create a relatively small portion of the content for which they are held accountable.

The local newspaper is held responsible for the news and entertainment it publishes, even though much of its content may come from outside sources such as syndicated feature or wire services. Most papers try to create a specific editorial policy on issues affecting their communities. They seek a distinct identity through layout, content, style, and coverage. The same is true of magazines. The responsible party is the particular staff that carries out the production of a publication that appears periodically under one title.

The book publisher—Longman, Harper & Row, Random House—is the basic media unit in the book industry. The publisher serves not only as producer and distributor but in a few metropolitan markets also operates retail bookstores.

The motion-picture's traditional pattern of having a studio serve as the basic media unit is changing as the movie industry moves through a transitional period. Small, independent producers are taking over a larger share of moviemaking. Because of the costs involved in production and the complex system of distribution, however, most feature films still rely on studio organizations—Paramount, 20th Century-Fox, MGM—as the basic media unit.

Radio and TV stations licensed by the FCC are directly responsible for all content broadcast, despite the fact that they create only a small part of it. For radio stations, the recording industry, wire services, network news operations, advertisers, and packaging agencies supply much of the content. Although the station organizes and supplements these services, it is still the responsible party and is required by law to serve "the public interest, convenience, and necessity" of the community. Networks, syndication companies, and advertisers dominate the content of television, but the station assumes responsibility for all programs telecast.

Sound-recording companies that produce records are the basic media units and the responsible parties in this medium.

MEDIA SERVICE UNITS

Media service units are extremely important to mass communication because so many of them service a variety of media units. Although these service units rarely are known to the general public—and touch the lives of consumers only indirectly—they often produce the bulk of mass communication, exercise control over its production, or provide necessary technical equipment and talent. These units can be categorized as production, distribution and exhibition, manufacturing, and representation.

PRODUCTION

Press Associations

Press associations are the primary news gatherers and processors for newspapers and broadcast stations. The largest American associations are the Associated Press (AP), a cooperative that sends teletype news and features to the more than 10,000 newspaper, magazine, TV, and radio media units that are members of the association; and United Press International (UPI), a private association that has more than 7000 media unit subscribers. These press associations, or wire services, as they are also called, produce material only for media units and not directly for the public. They have many offices and bureaus with experienced reporters, writers, and editors to process the news. The mass media are largely dependent upon them for national and international news and information and regional news features.

Syndicates

Syndicates provide feature and interpretative material, particularly for the print media. More than 200 syndicates exist that own the rights to the work of individual writers and commentators. These syndicates package, promote, and sell columns, analyses, comic-strip cartoons, and other features to individual newspapers, magazines, or other media units.

Networks

In radio and television, networks play a complicated and involved role. The most important networks in the United States are the American Broadcasting Company, the National Broadcasting Company, the Columbia Broadcasting System, and the Mutual Broadcasting System (radio only). They have become wealthy and powerful units of mass communication, buying and producing programs that they distribute to their affiliated radio and TV stations. The networks own stations of their own. These stations, known as "O & Os" (network owned and operated), serve as a critical element in the total corporation enterprise of ABC, CBS, and NBC.

Networks function by working out affiliation agreements with local stations willing to carry their programs. Fundamentally, the station gives a network the right to sell certain hours of the station's time at established rates to national advertisers. In return, the network agrees to provide programs and from 20% to 40% of the money normally charged by the local station when it sells the time itself. Network affiliation is dominant in television, unlike radio, in which a smaller percentage of stations are network affiliated. Most radio stations receive a free program service—primarily news—but little or no income from the networks.

In recent years, large numbers of regional and specialized networks have been organized to provide radio stations with content tailored to their specific formats. For example, ABC provides four separate network programming services: contemporary, entertainment, FM, and information. *Broadcasting Yearbook* lists almost 100 regional networks ranging from the Georgia Network to the Tobacco Radio Network, each providing unique content for their stations.

Advertising Agencies

Advertising agencies work for their clients' marketing operations. They produce advertisements and place them in the media. Leading agencies represent a variety of clients but normally do not represent competing products. For example, the Leo Burnett Company services accounts for nearly 40 corporations, including United Air Lines, Procter & Gamble, Maytag, Kellogg's, and Pillsbury, none of which competes with any other. Approximately 3400 advertising agencies operate in the United States, with a majority of the largest agencies that handle national accounts located in New York City.

Public Relations

Firms that specialize in handling public relations are also concentrated in New York City. But while ad agencies serve their clients' marketing needs by purchasing time or space in the mass media, public relations firms concern themselves with their clients' total communication problems. They counsel clients on the communication results of their actions, provide advice on a course of action needed to win public acceptance, and seek to publicize their clients to their publics (and publics to clients). While public relations firms may produce advertising, they engage primarily in publicity (free space and time in the mass media) and promotion (other communication efforts over a period of time) to persuade the public on their clients' behalf. Some attempts to determine the extent of public relations work have shown that a large percentage of mass media content originated with public relations firms.

Independent production companies perform a service for broadcast, film, and record media similar to that which syndicates perform for print media. Independent companies exist because of the great demand for a wide variety of programming in broadcasting. Although the idea for a program often originates with an individual, the programs are developed by program–package agencies. Today, except for network news, sports, and some documentaries, 90% of all TV network prime-time entertainment is produced by package agencies.

Independent Production Companies

The package agency develops the program and employs writers, producers, and actors—it does everything short of broadcasting the program. The packaging concept also extends to commercials for network and national spot advertising. Production companies generally subcontract all the production details to the ad agencies that create the specific advertisements. Program consultants, especially in radio, perform a significant function in selecting format and content for individual stations. In addition, some companies supply specific audio and video effects, including canned laughter, applause, and elaborate artwork (station ID slides, program credits) for TV programs.

Unlike radio and television, where the network serves as the distributor and the station as exhibitor, the other media, especially motion pictures, publications, and records, require complicated marketing, distributing, and exhibiting operations and facilities. Newspapers sometimes contract with a local dealer to distribute papers through a system of newsstands, delivery people, and the mail. Magazines make widest use of the mail system for distribution, but they often hire commercial firms to sell subscriptions. Book publishers in recent years have engaged in direct-mail selling and distributing, but they are still closely tied to bookstores, book dealers, and book clubs for distribution, often with complicated arrangements and large discounts. The "middleman distributor" has increasingly entered the book and magazine fields through jobbers that sell books to bookstores and distribution companies that sell books and magazines to newsstands, drugstores, supermarkets, and department stores. A similar apparatus exists for phonograph records and tapes.

DISTRIBUTION AND EXHIBITION

Distribution and exhibition are even more complicated in the motion-picture medium. Because of court rulings on antimonopoly procedures, no film company can engage in more than two of the following—production, distribution, and exhibition—unless it can demonstrate that the third activity will *not* restrain trade.

Today there are over 15,000 movie theaters in the United States. These theaters are primarily chain-owned by large exhibition companies, which in turn rent films from distribution companies, many of them affiliated with large production studios based in Hollywood. Currently more than 700 chains, each with 4 or more theaters, control better than 50% of all theaters in this country.

MANUFACTURING

The equipment and raw materials necessary for mass communication provide the basis for a large industry. One urban newspaper, the *Los Angeles Times*, has invested more than $65 million in printing press equipment alone. The *New York Times* uses more than 100 acres of trees to provide the pulp for one Sunday newspaper issue. Ink, chemicals, plastics, precision optical equipment, and complex electronic gear are all necessary for the operation of mass media.

Separate companies exist to provide printing and binding services for magazine and book publishers. Separate film-processing companies develop and print film for motion pictures and television, and separate record-pressing companies manufacture discs and tapes for the phonograph industry.

Finally, separate companies produce radio and TV sets for the individual home consumer. General Electric, RCA, Zenith, and others have become giant U.S. corporations. They earn more money by manufacturing radio and TV hardware than radio and TV stations and networks earn by broadcasting.

REPRESENTATION

Talent Agencies

Mass communicators are people with special talents, skills, and abilities. Increasingly they need special help in promoting their interests and protecting the value of their work. As a result, talent agencies have become an important part of mass media. Writers' agents help find publishers for authors' works, oversee the legal protection of their rights and properties in contracts, and help promote their fame. In return, these agents receive a share (usually 10%) of the author's profits. For actors and performers, particularly in the fields of radio, television, motion pictures, and phonograph recordings, talent agents play a crucial role. Often all dealings are made through the agent rather than with the performer, with the agent receiving 10–15% of a client's earnings.

Artists Representatives

Special note should be made of the work of representation in the field of music. Two giants—the American Society of Composers, Authors, and Publishers (ASCAP) and Broadcast Music Incorporated (BMI)—dominate the field. They exercise considerable control over published, recorded, and broadcast music, protecting the rights of artists and charging a fee to every media unit that uses their client's work through recordings or sheet music. This process is simplified by having the media unit pay a percentage of its income for the right to play the music licensed by ASCAP and BMI. For example, a small market, top-40 radio station may have to spend up to 5% of its gross time sales as payment for the music it plays on the air.

Unions have become an increasingly important part of mass media. **Labor Unions**
The American Newspaper Guild, founded in the 1930s, represents newspaper editorial personnel in salary negotiations and seeks to improve working conditions. Largely through its efforts, the salaries of reporters, photographers, copyeditors, and other professional staffers have risen to professional levels at many papers. The American Federation of Television and Radio Artists, the American Guild of Variety Artists, and the Screen Actors Guild, among others, perform similar services for mass communicators in the electronic media.

Professional and managerial associations represent a final aspect of **MEDIA**
mass media, and one of growing importance. Increased recognition of the **ASSOCIATIONS**
role of professional standards and responsibilities for mass communication in a free society has placed more emphasis on such associations. In those countries striving for a free and responsible press, especially in western and northern Europe, press associations or societies of journalists have been given considerable power to approve or license journalists, admitting only those who are properly trained or barring those who wilfully violate the standards of the profession. Such societies act for journalism in the same manner as the medical, legal, and accounting associations act for doctors, lawyers, and accountants.

In the United States these associations do not have, and perhaps never will have, as much power over individual journalists as they do in Europe, simply because the constitutional guarantee of freedom of speech and press would make any attempt to approve or reject journalists illegal. Nevertheless, many media associations have come into being, and these groups influence the communication profession and speak for their members in a variety of ways.

The owners of media units are well organized. Newspaper owners, magazine and book publishers, broadcasters, and film producers all have active associations that serve their needs, collect information, lobby for sympathetic laws, and promote their interests. In addition to national organizations such as the American Newspaper Publishers Association, media units often have state, country, or city groups, such as the Maryland–Delaware–D.C. Press Association or the Montgomery County (Maryland) Press Association.

In broadcasting, the National Association of Broadcasters (NAB) lobbies on behalf of broadcast stations with Congress. It also acts as a public relations firm for broadcasters.

In the film industry, the Motion Picture Producers Association handles a very important public relations effort, and its production-code division has created film ratings (G, PG, PG13, R, or X) for all films submitted by its members. The Recording Industry Association of America (RIAA) serves as a public relations arm and as an arbiter of production standards and controls for the sound-recording industry.

Media workers, too, have professional associations that promote their interests and advance their standards. The largest of these is Sigma Delta Chi, the National Society of Journalists, which has both campus chapters (at colleges where journalism and mass communication are taught) and professional chapters (for those working in the media). Other associations represent almost every communication professional, from editors and editorial writers to photographers, public relations people, advertisers, and cartoonists.

The Mass–Specialized Media Continuum

Although the mass media are characterized by complex organizations and operations, they do not all have an equally massive reach. The media can be charted on both a geographic continuum and an audience continuum. The geographic continuum shows that each medium has its own geographic boundaries.

National	Regional	Metropolitan	Local Neighborhood
Network television	Regional magazines	Daily newspapers	Weekly newspapers
National magazines		Local radio	
Books		Local television	
Films		City magazines	
National newspapers		Cable television	

A similar continuum can chart where the media fit with respect to the size of the audience or its heterogeneity. The medium that seeks the largest general national audience, of course, is network prime-time television; individualized data banks have the most personalized and exclusive audience.

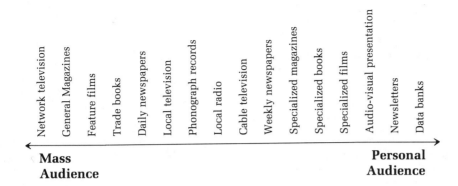

Network television
General Magazines
Feature films
Trade books
Daily newspapers
Local television
Phonograph records
Local radio
Cable television
Weekly newspapers
Specialized magazines
Specialized books
Specialized films
Audio-visual presentation
Newsletters
Data banks

Mass Audience   **Personal Audience**

OTHER MEDIA

Few other media are as completely institutionalized as the seven described thus far in this chapter. As new graphic and audiovisual media come into widespread use, they will become as institutionalized as the current mass media. Experiments with mixed-media and multimedia styles are producing new forms, usually combining still and motion pictures with recording and publications. Newest and most important are the computer-based media, which can publish, broadcast, store, retrieve, and manipulate communication in a variety of ways.

AUDIOVISUAL MATERIALS

Audiovisual materials have been so fully developed and widely used that we might consider them a new kind of communication medium. Most audiovisual equipment is built for small-group usage, but the equipment itself is standardized, and programs are being mass produced. Audiovisuals almost qualify as mass media, yet they retain their personal intimacy and allow for easy and inexpensive production of audiovisual presentations, even by amateurs.

Most audiovisual equipment falls into two categories: (a) filmed materials for visual presentation, which include still photographs (either for display or projection through opaque or overhead projectors), slides, and film strips (usually 35 mm) for projection; and (b) motion pictures for projection.

Audio materials for sound reproduction include disc recordings, audiotape recordings, and videotape recordings. Videotape, of course, includes sound and picture. Most sound reproduction is now synchronized with visual presentation, even with slides and film strips, and simple systems are available to program, synchronize, and mix sound and sight. The development of stereo tape and tape cassettes has enlarged the potential of the entire audiovisual field, providing compact and convenient packages of sound that rival the convenience of books for storage, retrieval, and easy access.

Closed-circuit broadcasting is another form of audiovisual presentation, one that is finding increased use in large-group meetings, conventions, internal organizational communication, and educational institutions to augment the communication process. Both closed-circuit radio and television are used in home and office, in shops and factories, and for personal communication.

Finally, audiovisual tools of all kinds are programmed and computerized to become teaching machines, capable of individualized communication and instruction. Large collections of instructional programs and programmed courses are available in slides, film strips, motion pictures, videotape, and tape cassettes.

MIXED-MEDIA PRESENTATIONS

Person-to-person communication which has long been the dominant form of communication in the classroom, church, synagogue, or town hall, is still the most effective way to send a message. Today, person-to-person meetings are widely used and fairly standardized in format to inform, persuade, educate, and even entertain us in business, the trades, professions, associations, and religious and social groups.

Meetings, seminars, conferences, and institutes have become such successful instruments of communication that they are regular affairs for most groups. These affairs may be held on an annual basis, semiannually, quarterly, monthly, or weekly—and not inconceivably, even daily. Most such meetings bring together people from diverse geographical locations; hotels have become common meeting grounds, and new hotels are being built with the latest audiovisual apparatus.

Sometimes the message, rather than the audience, is moved from place to place for different meetings. For example, the display and exhibit have become effective communication media. Here again, techniques of display and exhibit production have become formalized and standardized to the point where these new forms of communication might almost be considered mass media, although they provide for direct confrontation with their audience and lend a personal approach to the message.

The traveling display or exhibit has been used effectively for communicating across cultural barriers. The United States has used such shows in its overseas information programs. The Soviet Union has made effective use of this technique in a traveling exhibit of photographs, including hundreds of black-and-white and color pictures of life in Russia. This exhibit has been displayed in hotels in major cities around the United States and has received an enthusiastic American response.

In many of these person-to-person communication efforts, mixed-media presentations are used to enhance the communication's effectiveness. The grandest expression of a multimedia, mixed-media presentation is probably a world's fair; nations and cultures communicate with one another—through sight and sound and smell and touch—the way neighboring farm-

There are more than 68 special effects, screens that lower and rise on cue, real fog, real bubbles, and many panoramic scenes like this one in "The New York Experience". Presented hourly in the lower plaza of the McGraw-Hill Building in Rockefeller Center, this multi-media display tells the story of New York City, past and present. Even the seats swivel so that visitors can keep up with the action.

(Courtesy Trans-Lux Experience Corporation.)

ers might at a county fair. New forms of multimedia presentations, developed at world's fairs, have furthered the effective techniques of communication. Such presentations have ranged from posters and brochures to light-and-sound shows, from multimedia-screen projections to complicated, all-encompassing exhibits through which one might ride in a special car fitted with audiovisual–olfactory–sensory mechanisms that massage all the senses and provide for total communication.

The communication techniques developed for world's fairs have had wide application in other areas as well, including higher education and popular entertainment, from the multimedia center at the University of Texas to Disneyland in California to the Epcot Center at Disneyworld in Florida.

DATA BANKS AND INFORMATION CENTERS

Increasingly, American institutions—business, professional, or educational—are finding it necessary to provide for multimedia information centers, data banks, and libraries to ensure effective communication. These, too, are new media. A number of organizations now use a multimedia information center, complete with central projection core, control lectern, multiple rear and front projection screens, contoured chairs, and specially designed lighting and acoustics. The aim is to provide a total environment in which messages can be transferred with great effectiveness.

At the same time, our concept of information storage is changing. Libraries are no longer viewed only as places in which to shelve and store books and papers but also as information systems. When storage and retrieval of the library's contents are fully computerized, the library is really a data bank, and as such it is a new medium of communication.

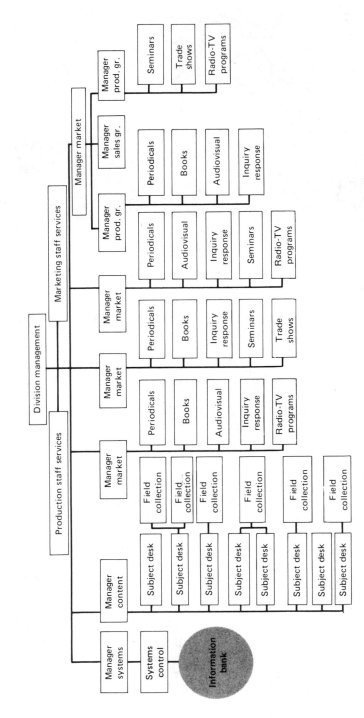

Organizational Chart for an Information Bank. (Source: Book Production Industry, February 1969.)

The advent of the home communications center, incorporating activities from shoppping and banking to education and actual employment, may ultimately drive people to seek entertainment outside the home. (Photo courtesy of AT&T Bell Laboratories.)

Such data banks are, in effect, publishers or broadcasters, not of mass communication, but of individualized reports and communiqués to fulfill the needs of the person who seeks specific data. These data banks are organized more like modern newspapers, magazines, and book publishers than like libraries. Like a modern newspaper's staff, data banks are engaged in data gathering. Such data banks may well become the newspapers, magazines, and book publishers of the future, producing materials on demand to fit individual needs.

The computer has become essential to mass communication. And the computer is rapidly becoming available to the mass market. The first computer, built in 1951, had about the same power as your pocket calculator, and it cost millions. Today's computers are far more powerful, much smaller and more compact, and cost pennies by comparison. Soon, computers may be used by audiences of mass media almost as much as by communicators. Indeed, computers will allow audiences to become part of the communication process, participating in the organization of mes-

THE ROLE OF THE COMPUTER

sages to fit their own needs. The combination of home computer, television, and telephone will turn households into communication centers. Many people will stay at home for work and education.

Alvin Toffler describes the future as the era of the "electronic cottage." And the electronic cottage of the late 1980s and 1990s will be quite different from the homes with TV sets in the past.

In the new electronic cottage we may turn to mass media not so much for entertainment as for information, education, and work. For rest and relaxation, we may well prefer to get away from video screens and computers. We may turn to real people and real participation for our entertainment. Toffler predicts that the now-booming home entertainment business of mass media may well go bust in the postindustrial age. "In fact," he says, "entertainment may turn out to be the least important aspect of the TV screen. People will be raging to get out of their houses."[1]

Social scientist John Naisbett calls this reaction the "high-tech, high-touch" syndrome. As we deal more and more with machines and technology on the job, he says, we want to turn more and more to the personal touch off the job. The rise of computers has been accompanied by a rise in human interaction groups; the rise of televised sports has been accompanied by great increases in jogging, tennis, racquetball, Little League, and hundreds of other rapidly growing popular participatory activities.[2]

The future of mass media may be considerably different from the present, and if so, these changes will certainly affect our way of life. The major use of mass media may shift to information and education. If that is the case, the importance of journalists will grow, for they will be called upon in ever-growing numbers to gather, process, and make judgments about the data that will be put into the storage banks for personal and specialized use.

The mass media of the future can offer far greater access to information than is available today. And if we have more information at our fingertips, we will be able to make more personal choices about the alternatives in our lives and about our lifestyles. The greater the array from which we can choose, the freer we will be as human beings.

Thus, if the mass media keep moving in the predicted directions, we can be optimistic about the future. Instead of turning us into mass robots manipulated by the big brothers of George Orwell's *1984*, the mass media can become the instruments that enable each individual human being to live a free, full, and rich personal life. That is the goal of a good society. But that future also depends upon the people who will shape the mass media of the future. The future depends upon those who are reading this book.

[1] Alvin Toffler, *The Third Wave* (New York: William Morrow and Co., 1980), 210.
[2] John Naisbitt, *Megatrends* (New York: Warner Books, 1982), 39.

Regulators 9

We live in an age of laws and regulations. Almost every element of our lives is governed by statutes and ordinances. The only exceptions, it seems, are those areas that our founding fathers felt were sacred to the democratic process—freedom of speech, freedom of worship, freedom to assemble, and freedom of the press. The framers of the U.S. Constitution wrote in the First Amendment:

> Congress shall make **no** law respecting an establishment of religion, or prohibiting the free exercise thereof; or abridging the freedom of speech, or of the press; or the right of the people peaceably to assemble, and to petition the government for a redress of grievances.

That guarantee has made mass media regulation in America different from media regulation in most other societies, for few countries have such a sweeping declaration of press and speech freedom as we. Nevertheless, it would be a mistake to think that the mass media in America are absolutely free of restraint or regulation. The First Amendment to the Constitution merely makes their regulation more complicated. Often, institutions other than government are involved in the regulation of mass communication.

When a word is "bleeped" off radio or television, do you know who is responsible for censoring it? When the publisher of *Hustler* magazine is tried in a Georgia courtroom for obscenity, do you know why? When you were in your early teens and tried to see a film rated R or X, do you know who kept you out of the theater?

In the first and third examples, the media were the censors; in the second example, a local jurisdiction had the authority to regulate the magazine's sale.

Many people assume that the federal government is responsible for these actions. In many national systems, the government *is* the chief censor and regulator of mass media, but in America the government is only one of many regulators. In fact, the U.S. government cannot censor the news media. Along with other institutions in our society, it can apply pressure only in some areas of mass communication to regulate and control quantity, quality, and direction.

We can identify five groups that, formally and informally, regulate the process of mass communication: government, source, advertiser, profession, and consumer.

THE GOVERNMENT AS REGULATOR

In American society, devoted to the twin freedoms of press and speech, government is the only agency capable of protecting those guarantees of freedom. Most American government regulations, but by no means all, are concerned with maintaining an environment of free communication and with protecting the individual's rights in the communication process.

Constitutional Guarantees

Freedom of the press was the result of a long struggle for individual rights and freedoms under Anglo-Saxon law. The way to press freedom was paved by documents such as the Magna Carta of 1215, the Petition of Rights in 1628, the English Bill of Rights in 1689, and the American Declaration of Independence in 1776. In the New World of the American colonies, where communication and independence were both important, freedom of speech and press became key elements in the sociopolitical fabric.

The First Amendment to the Constitution does not discuss limits of freedom. Court and legislative decisions have defined the meaning of the amendment, usually in the light of current trends and social conditions. The Constitution, as interpreted by the courts and lawmakers, controls the regulators and determines which of their actions are permissible under the American system.

Censorship

Censorship, meaning prior restraint or suppression of communication, has been held to be unconstitutional in all its many forms except one. Government agencies, both local and national, have from time to time attempted to censor communication, sometimes for the best motives. A

Minnesota legislature, for example, passed a "gag law" in the 1920s aimed
at restricting newspapers that were "public nuisances," specifically scandal sheets that made scurrilous attacks on the police and Jews. But in its
interpretation of the First Amendment, the U.S. Supreme Court found
this, as it has most other attempts at censorship, illegal. For example, in
1983, the Supreme Court struck down a Minnesota law that would impose
a tax only on newspapers and other publications. The justices said that
taxes imposed on other businesses also may be imposed on newspapers
and other publications. But taxes that single out the press can be a potential tool for censorship that abridges freedom of the press.

The famous "Pentagon Papers" incident in 1971 is another case in
point. A multivolumed Department of Defense study entitled *History of
U.S. Decision-Making Process on Viet Nam Policy*, was classified as top
secret but was leaked to the press. The *New York Times* and the *Washington Post* both decided to publish stories based on the material in the
47 volumes. The Justice Department obtained a temporary court injunc-
tion to prevent publication of the material. Because of its significance, the
case quickly went to the U.S. Supreme Court. In a 6–3 landmark decision,
the Court ruled in favor of the newspapers and freedom of the press.

Although the Court's decision clarified the First Amendment, it did
not really broaden the protection of freedom. The newspapers hoped that
the Court would rule that the First Amendment guaranteed an absolute
freedom. In the Pentagon Papers case, however, the Court held that the
government had not provided sufficient evidence justifying prior restraint
of the publications. This left the door open for courts in the future to
decide how much justification the government must provide in order to
censor a publication. But the six concurring opinions of the Supreme
Court justices all gave ample support to the general theory of freedom
from prior restraint by the government.

For years, motion pictures did not have this protection. In 1915 the
Supreme Court, in the case *Mutual Film Corporation* v. *Industrial Commission of Ohio*, upheld the right of individual states to censor motion
pictures on the grounds that they were "a business, pure and simple."
They were a "spectacle or show and not such vehicles of thought as to
bring them within the press of the country." In 1952, however, a Supreme
Court decision changed this somewhat and laid the groundwork for increasing freedom for motion pictures. In the case of *Burstyn* v. *Wilson*
involving the film *The Miracle*, the Supreme Court stated: "We conclude
that expression by means of motion pictures is included within the free
speech and free press guarantee of the First and Fourteenth Amendments.
To the extent that language in the opinion in the Ohio case is out of
harmony with the views here set forth, we no longer adhere to it."

Decisions since then have continually weakened efforts to censor movies. Not a single state now has a movie censorship board. Of the last four
states to have such a board, New York, Kansas, and Virginia phased theirs

Censorship of *The Miracle* (1952), a film which blended sex, religion, realism, and fantasy, resulted in a Supreme Court decision which sanctioned the application of the rights of free speech and free press to the motion picture medium.

(Photo: Movie Star News, Courtesy Warner Bros., Inc.)

out in the 1970s, and Maryland's was abolished in 1981. Only two cities—Chicago and Dallas—still require motion pictures to be submitted for examination prior to public showing.

It should be noted that when we speak of movie censorship, we are referring primarily to censorship of obscenity, and obscenity is not protected by the First Amendment. For example, Section 223 of the Federal Communications Act makes it illegal for anyone who uses the telephone to make comments or statements that are "obscene, lewd, lascivious, filthy, or indecent." Freedom of speech does not provide protection for such use of the telephone. The penalty for violation is a fine of up to $500 and imprisonment for up to 6 months. In 1983 the FCC used this statute to investigate the growing "Dial-a-Porn" business. Censorship of obscenity, however, does not give government the right to revoke licenses. In 1982 a small town in Utah passed a city ordinance prohibiting transmission of both pornographic and indecent material over cable television. A federal trial judge struck down the ordinance, calling it "overbroad" because it would have threatened revocation of the cable company's license for transmitting such films. In 1983 a Cincinnati cable firm was indicted for obscenity charges for broadcasting the Playboy channel programs, including the movies *Maraschino Cherry* and *The Opening of Misty Beethoven*. To some extent, the movie review boards have viewed themselves as consumer-protection agencies, not merely censors of obscenity. The Dallas Motion Picture Classification Board, for example, gives films a public rating to warn the moviegoer in advance; ratings are for explicit sex (S), excessive violence (V), drugs (D), rough language (L), nudity (N), and perversion (P).

Other forms of censorship, which exist in some countries and have been tried in the United States, have from time to time been declared unconstitutional. The print media, for example, are constitutionally protected from discriminatory or punitive taxes and from licensing that would amount to censorship.

It is legal to regulate some aspects of mass communication without causing prior restraint or suppression. The government has generally held that the morals of the community should be protected by restricting the importing or distribution or sale of certain kinds of communication that could be objectionable to the average person. These restrictions apply primarily to obscene publications, gambling and lottery information, and, in some cases, treasonous propaganda.

Restrictions on Importation, Distribution, and Sale

The Customs Bureau of the U.S. Treasury Department has the right to impound obscene material or gambling and lottery information. But a recent Supreme Court decision declared unconstitutional the role of Customs in restricting the importation of propaganda materials. In 1938, however, Congress passed the Foreign Agents Registration Act, which states that any person who represents a foreign government must register with the Justice Department and that any foreign publication that contains propaganda to influence the American public must be labeled propaganda. In 1983 the Justice Department attempted to restrict three Canadian films by forcing them to be preceded by a message stating that the films were political propaganda and expressed views not supported by the United States. The films were *If You Love This Planet*, an antinuclear film nominated for an Academy Award, and two films exposing the problems of acid rain, which was said to come from America: *Acid Rain: Requiem or Recovery* and *Acid from Heaven*.

The U.S. Postal Service exercises the right to restrict the distribution of obscene publications or lottery advertisements through the public mails. It can stop the mailing of such material and issue an order to refrain from further mailings. The Postal Service has greatly reduced its fulfillment of this responsibility in the past decade, however. It requires mailers of obscene materials merely to put a plain wrapper on the material with a label that the package contains obscenity. This supposedly protects those who do not want to be exposed to pornography. The Postal Service also requires mailers of pornography to remove from their mailing lists the names of all those who request such action.

The Supreme Court has upheld the right of local courts and legislatures to forbid the sale of obscene material. A person who violates a local ordinance against the sale of such material would be subject to arrest and punishment as called for in the ordinance. It was such a local jurisdiction that brought *Hustler* publisher Larry Flynt to court for distributing pornography.

It is important to note that in all cases of such restrictions by the Customs Bureau, the Postal Service, and local authorities, none has the right to censor or prevent publication. It should also be noted that social mores are changing rapidly, and certainly many forms of obscenity may not be considered as harmful today as in previous decades. The Customs Bureau is concerned primarily with confiscating pornography featuring children. Forms of obscenity that earlier might have been seized are now considered too benign to cause concern.

Criminal Libel

Government has assumed the right to protect society and the public from libel. Criminal libel is interpreted as a false and malicious attack on society that would cause a breach of the peace or disrupt by force the established public order. In this category of libel, sedition laws were enacted to regulate communication that might damage the state during wartime. Criminal libel might also apply to libelous statements made against groups or against dead persons who cannot defend themselves in a civil action; thus the state becomes the prosecutor and the libel a crime. Cases of criminal libel are extremely rare, however.

Libel of Government and Public Officials

Governments in totalitarian countries can suppress the critical press with criminal prosecution for seditious libel, but this is not possible in America. The trial of John Peter Zenger in New York in 1735 established the unqualified right of the press to criticize the government, even if the facts are false and the criticism malicious. Various attempts have been made by government to protect itself from such criticism, for example the Alien and Sedition Acts of 1798–1800. But the courts have steadily upheld the impunity of the press as goad and critic of government.

One of the most far-reaching U.S. Supreme Court decisions was *The New York Times Co.* v. *Sullivan* ruling in 1964. This ruling gave the press almost as much right to libel public officials as it has the right to criticize government. The case came about as the result of an advertisement appearing in the *Times* in 1960; the ad, it was claimed, libeled, among others, one L. B. Sullivan, commissioner of public affairs for Montgomery, Alabama. The Court allowed the publishing of defamatory falsehoods about public officials if the statements were made in good faith, if they concerned the official's public rather than his private life, and if they were not made in reckless disregard of the truth. In 1981, however, the U.S. Supreme Court refined and limited this ruling when it decided that government consultants were *not* considered "public figures" and thus, unlike individuals considered to be public figures, could bring suits for libel against the mass media. In this way, laws concerning libel and government regulation of mass communication are constantly being interpreted and clarified.

Contempt

Government also exercises the right to protect the administration of justice against the interference of mass media. If a journalist, for instance, in the course of professional work, disobeys a court order, disturbs a court-room, attempts to influence court decisions or participants, or (in some states) refuses to testify as to sources of news, that journalist can be cited for contempt of court. Court officials have used this power to subpoena reporters' notes, tapes, photographs, and film in an effort to use this ma-terial in court cases. However, 26 states have laws providing some pro-tection of the journalist's right not to reveal confidential sources of in-formation.

In a 5–4 decision in 1972, the Supreme Court ruled that journalists have no absolute privilege to protect their sources of information if they are subpoenaed to testify in court proceedings. Medical doctors do not have to reveal the nature of their relationships with their patients, nor lawyers with clients, nor ministers with parishioners, nor teachers with students, but the Court held that such a privilege does not apply to the relationship between a journalist and a news source. The ruling was made on the basis of three different cases. Paul Pappas of WTEV-TV (New Bed-ford, Massachusetts) had refused to tell a grand jury what he had seen in a Black Panthers headquarters. Earl Caldwell, a *New York Times* reporter, also had refused to testify about a Black Panther case. And Paul M. Branz-burg, a reporter for the *Louisville* (Kentucky) *Courier-Journal*, had refused to tell a state grand jury the names of individuals he had written about in a drug story.

Since that ruling, an increasing number of journalists have gone to jail for contempt of court after they failed to divulge information in court proceedings. For example, Peter Bridge, a former reporter for the *Newark* (New Jersey) *News*, was sentenced to an indefinite jail term for refusing to answer grand jury questions that went beyond his story about an alleged bribe attempt. He was ultimately released. In Fresno, California, four jour-nalists from the *Fresno Bee*—the managing editor, the newspaper's om-budsman, and two court reporters—went to jail in 1976 for an indefinite term for refusing to tell a judge the source of secret grand jury testimony used in a news story. They, too, ultimately were released. In 1981 the Supreme Court was still of the opinion that reporters should have no special protection from the courts. It let stand an order that a *Philadelphia Inquirer* reporter be jailed for refusing to answer questions about her source for a story about the Abscam undercover operation.

Congress also can cite journalists for contempt, as it did in the 1976 case of Daniel Schorr, the CBS reporter who refused to tell the House of Representatives how he obtained a copy of a congressional committee's report on intelligence activities. Congress ultimately decided not to pun-ish Schorr.

Restrictions on Court Coverage

The judicial branch of government can also restrict news media in their coverage of court news by closing the courtroom to reporters. For example, in 1975 a Nebraska judge ordered restrictions on news coverage in a mass-murder trial on the grounds that it was too sensational. But in 1976 the Supreme Court, in a unanimous decision, ruled that the Nebraska gag order, as it was called, was an unconstitutional restraint of freedom of the press. The Court did not rule out the possibility that such orders could be issued to protect the right of a defendant to a fair trial, but such orders should be issued only when there is a clear threat to the fairness of the trial.

In 1983 a U.S. district court judge issued gag orders barring CBS's "60 Minutes" from broadcasting a story about a New Orleans criminal case, saying it would prejudice the case. But a U.S. court of appeals in New Orleans postponed the trial so that effects of the publicity would not affect the jury, and the Supreme Court refused to change the ruling. Such battles between courts and the press will no doubt continue.

The problem of "free press versus a fair trial," the First Amendment versus the Sixth Amendment, has posed difficulties for both the news media and the courts. Journalists and lawyers have increasingly clashed over the issues of prejudicial publicity on the one hand versus censorship of the news on the other. Some restrictions have been eased, however. Long-standing rules forbidding cameras and broadcast equipment in the courtroom have been dropped in some states; cameras and microphones are now allowed on a limited and experimental basis. Some state bar and press associations have joined together to adopt guidelines for court coverage that would be acceptable to both sides, but national guidelines have thus far not been established.

In 1956 Colorado was the first state to relax its rules about cameras in the courtroom. By 1983, 40 states were in various stages of opening their courts to photographers, tape recorders, and video cameras. At present, 24 states have permanent laws opening their courts to cameras, 16 states have experimental programs. Congress has also changed its ban on TV coverage. The Senate is still off-limits to cameras, but a closed-circuit TV system has been installed in the House of Representatives. Cameras have been placed at various locations around the House, providing "gavel to gavel" coverage of floor proceedings. Live or taped broadcasts can be used by TV correspondents and networks. Some cable systems carry the floor proceedings in their entirety.

Protection of Property

The government also regulates communication by protecting right of communicators. The present copyright law was revised in 1976 for the first time since its original passage as a federal statute in 1909. The copyright law protects the property rights of authors, composers, artists, and photographers and establishes a system of penalties and a method of redress for violations of those rights. Among other restrictions, the 1976 revision also limits the amount of photocopying that can be done on copyrighted works and extends the life of a copyright. It is important to note that facts and ideas cannot be copyrighted, only the order and selection of words, phrases, clauses, sentences, and the arrangement of paragraphs.

The government has invoked "protection of property" as a means of restricting media access to a news event. In a few cases, the media have been cited for trespass in covering events such as fires. The news media contend that they should not have to obtain the permission of a property owner to enter the scene of a news event, but court rulings on such cases have not yet established clear precedents.

The government also protects property rights through the application of antitrust laws to the mass media. For example, newspaper mergers that eliminated actual or potential competition in a newspaper-market area were formerly considered a violation of the antitrust laws. But because so many newspapers have succumbed to financial pressures, antitrust law pertaining to newspaper mergers has been recast somewhat: a new "Failing Newspaper Act" gives newspapers special antitrust privileges.

Copyright laws were the center of attention in two major legal battles for the mass media in the early 1980s. The first was the debate over whether manufacturers of home video-recording equipment must pay copyright royalties to producers of TV programs because video-recorder owners tape movies and shows aired on television. Sony Corporation argued that owners of video recorders have a First Amendment right to copy publicly aired programming and replay the tapes as often as they like for their own, private use. Universal City Studios and Walt Disney Productions countered that there is no such right allowing wholesale, cost-free copy of copyrighted films. They said the practice illegally deprived them of fair compensation for use of their movies. If viewers could not record the programs, they would have to watch television, and the producers would receive royalties each time a program was aired. In 1984 the U.S. Supreme Court ruled that individuals do not violate copyright when they record video programs at home from their TV sets for their own individual use. But this case will continue to develop other legal ramifications.

The second battle was over who owns syndicated TV films. Rulings of the FCC have prohibited the three major national networks from directly owning most programming and syndication rights, since they are the prime distributors of the films. The networks sought the ownership rights, while the film and independent TV studios in Hollywood claimed that they should own the rights to TV films and syndicated programs.

Regulation of Broadcasting

Unlike other mass media, radio and TV stations are licensed by the government, but the government cannot censor or suppress any broadcast once the broadcaster has a license. The government began its regulation of broadcasting in the 1920s when major broadcasters requested its help to maintain order in the scramble for limited frequencies and channels.

Thus the notion developed that broadcasters use public property—the airwaves—and government has an obligation to administer property that is not private. In 1927 the Federal Radio Commission was established, and in 1934 it became the Federal Communications Commission (FCC), charged with regulating radio, telephone and telegraph, and later television. By the mid-1980s, however, reduction in the FCC's regulating powers was being pushed on a broad front.

Like the courts, the FCC interprets rather than makes the law. A broadcast station must be licensed by the FCC, and the license must be renewed. Formerly, a station was licensed for a period of 3 years. Now, radio stations are given a 7-year license and TV stations a 5-year license. At the time of renewal, the station and its programming were formerly reviewed, and if the commission ruled that the station had not acted in the public interest, the license could be rescinded. These reviews are now greatly reduced under deregulation. The FCC can still levy fines of up to $10,000 for specific violations of its rules and regulations. These regulatory powers do not give the FCC the right to censor.

Nonrenewals of licenses for single violations have been rare; it was the station's overall performance that was evaluated. Few licenses have been revoked, since the burden of proof fell upon the FCC, and the definition of "public interest" was vague. Nevertheless, the government does have more power to regulate a broadcaster than to regulate a publisher.

The FCC also has controlled the extent of broadcast ownership so that it could prevent monopolies. No one can own more than one AM, one FM, and one TV station in any one listening area. The FCC has also not given licenses to applicants who already owned a daily newspaper in the same market.

Prior to 1983, the FCC also regulated some broadcasting program content, especially in the areas of politics and public affairs. Section 315 of the FCC code required the broadcaster to furnish equal time and equal opportunity to all political candidates for a given office. Excepted were news programs, which were carefully qualified to allow debates between candidates of principal political parties when covered as a bona fide news event. In 1983 the FCC voted to abolish this requirement.

Another FCC regulation, the so-called Fairness Doctrine, charges broadcasters with the duty of seeking out and broadcasting contrasting viewpoints on controversial issues of public importance. The Fairness Doctrine is different from the equal-time provision of Section 315; the Fairness Doctrine requires broadcasters only to present contrasting views, not to give them equal time on the air. The constitutionality of the Fairness Doctrine was upheld by the Supreme Court in the famous *Red Lion Broadcasting Co. v. FCC* case of 1969. The Court ruled that the public's right to hear all points of view was more important than the broadcaster's right to express only one point of view.

The FCC set forth specific regulations, some of which it later modified, for cable television. Until the mid-1960s, the FCC paid little attention to cable television, regarding it as a passing phenomenon. But in 1972 the commission adopted a set of rules specifically for this expanding area of television. The rules established which broadcast stations the cable systems could transmit and which ones they could not; it required the systems to have a minimum 20-channel capacity; and it made provisions for an access channel. The commission also required, among other regulations, that cable systems build in the capacity for two-way circuitry, allowing for feedback from a subscriber to the system. But the FCC has relaxed many of these rules in an effort to allow cable systems to grow; for example, it has eased the rules on the stations that the system can carry and the rule on local origination and access.

In fact, most regulations on broadcasting were modified considerably in the early 1980s. Broadcasters spent years lobbying on Capitol Hill for deregulation of their industry, but the Reagan administration stimulated and speeded the process.

By the middle of the 1980s, radio was the most deregulated broadcasting medium. Stations were no longer obligated to devote a certain percentage of their programming to nonentertainment or public service programs. They were no longer required to ascertain the interests of their communities, maintain program logs, or produce a limited number of programs on issues relevant to their communities. Perhaps most important, stations were no longer required to limit commercials to 18 minutes per hour; they could run as many commercials as they wanted. Finally, the amount of paperwork required to apply for a license renewal was reduced drastically.

Deregulation of television has not come as swiftly, but by the mid-1980s, Congress and the FCC had agreed to eliminate the restrictions on TV stations and networks that had prevented them from owning cable systems. The FCC had voted to reduce requirements that TV stations broadcast a minimum amount of public affairs and news programming, and to ease the requirement that stations regularly assess community needs for guidance in programming. The commission had also recommended an end to the 16-minute limit on commercials during each hour of TV broadcasting. All FCC proposals must be approved by Congress before they become law.

Controversy over the Fairness Doctrine has continued. And much discussion has been held on making broadcast licensing periods indefinite. But licensing, some control of ownership, and some degree of regulation probably will always apply to the broadcast media in our society.

Regulation of Advertising

The Federal Trade Commission Act passed in 1941 was meant to regulate unfair competition in business, but checking dishonest advertising has become an important aspect of the commission's work. The FTC is also paying particular attention to advertising, especially TV commercials, aimed at children. Other government commissions have more specific tasks in the regulation of advertising. The Food and Drug Administration controls labeling and branding in the important area of food and drugs. The FCC does not regulate advertising on radio and television, but it does note whether a station is complying with the profession's own code (the National Association of Broadcasters' code), which seeks to limit advertising for hard liquor, for example, or overcommercialization). An act of Congress denied broadcasters the right to advertise cigarettes, although broadcasters can advertise pipe tobacco, cigars, and snuff. The Postal Service controls fraudulent advertising sent through the mails. And the Securities and Exchange Commission regulates advertising about stocks and bonds.

In all these cases, there is still no censorship or suppression on the part of the government. In can ask for voluntary compliance, and if the advertiser refuses, it can issue a cease-and-desist order. Violation of such an order can bring about a $5000 fine, 6 months in jail, or both. The FTC can also publicize deceitful advertising and thus warn the public.

In sum, the government can and does regulate and restrict mass media in certain areas, and in these areas the Supreme Court has determined that there is no conflict with the intent of the First Amendment of the Constitution. These regulations are aimed at protecting society from damage by mass media and protecting the rights of the media from damage by competing media, individuals, or the state.

THE CONTENT SOURCE AS REGULATOR

The content source is also a regulator, providing a form of regulation at the beginning of the communication process. As communication has grown massive and complicated, the forms of regulation used by the content source can be placed in fairly distinct categories.

Strategic Releasing

The content source regulates communication by strategically timing and packaging the message in a letter, a publication, or (if the content source has enough money) a radio, TV, or motion-picture production. The setting of the communication also gives the content source an opportunity to regulate the message, depending on whether the regulator chooses to release it to the media through a news release, a press conference, or an exclusive interview.

Strategic Withholding

The content source can also regulate the communication flow, blocking the media from getting a certain message or parts of a message. The government can do this by classifying documents or claiming executive privilege. The Freedom of Information Act of 1967 set forth the legal rationale for what can be withheld by the federal government and what cannot, and it established the judicial procedures to make the government prove in court why something should be withheld if challenged. Many states have statutes that set forth the categories of public records to which the media can and cannot have access.

For example, when President Reagan was shot in an assassination attempt in 1981, the White House press office withheld certain details of his injury soon after the shooting. The press office told journalists that the president was injured only slightly, that he was joking and laughing at the hospital, and that he would be back at work soon. Later, the officials said they had withheld information about the gravity of the president's wounds to avoid overreaction.

When U.S. troops landed on the tiny Caribbean island of Grenada in 1983, news about the invasion was withheld from the press for a number of hours. Even after the news was released, reporters were initially not allowed to go to Grenada for firsthand coverage. Later, a "pool" was established; only a few reporters were allowed to go to Grenada, on their return they shared their reports with a large number of grumbling and angry reporters waiting on a nearby island.

Another form of withholding has been to deny news media access to meetings. But in 1976 the "Government in Sunshine Act" was passed, requiring about 50 federal agencies, boards, and commissions with two or more directors to open their meetings and records to the public. There

(UPI/Bettman Archive)

A U.S. Navy warship cuts off a boat carrying newsmen trying to reach the island of Grenada (10/29/83) and orders them away from the "hostile zone". The boat chartered by ABC and CNN was forced to return to Union Island.

are 10 exceptions under which meetings may be closed, but in those cases, transcripts must be kept for scrutiny in case of legal action. Some states have passed sunshine laws to open meetings at state and local government levels as well.

The Reagan administration made strenuous efforts in the early and mid-1980s to reduce the effectiveness of the Freedom of Information Act and increase the penalties for government employees who leaked information to the press. The Intelligence Identities Protection Act of 1982 made it a crime to expose the identities of American intelligence agents. The Defense Department in 1982 also broadened its practice of giving employees lie-detector tests in an effort to prevent the leaking of information, and the Reagan administration urged Congress to pass a law making all government employees subject to lie-detector tests for the rest of their lives, to protect information. The Senate delayed voting on the issue.

Strategic Staging

The content source can also regulate the flow of communication by deliberately staging a situation or an event in such a way that a certain kind of message gets into the media. For example, a senator who wishes to express his point of view about a particular issue holds a hearing and calls a group of witnesses from whom he can elicit the kind of testimony that will get news headlines. The president, not wanting to see this point of view emphasized in the media, announces a trip to Europe to take place at the same time as the Senate hearing. The president takes many reporters with him, attracting daily coverage in the newspapers and newscasts, and overshadows the hearing called by the senator. Meanwhile, a citizens' group holds a rally on the steps of the Capitol to get media (and public) attention for its position on the problem. These concurrent events will affect what news and how much of it will be covered by the press.

The Iranians who took American diplomats and military personnel hostage in 1979 certainly used that staged event to capture the attention of the American people for 444 days. Indeed, many people believed the media was being held hostage by the situation. It was news that could not be ignored. Thus, the people who controlled the event also controlled the media.

THE ADVERTISER AS REGULATOR

Advertisers obviously play a role in the regulation of mass media, but theirs can be a subtle, unspecific control. David Potter, a historian who studied advertising as a force in molding the American character, wrote in his book *People of Plenty*:

> [I]n the mass media we have little evidence of censorship in the sense of deliberate, planned suppression imposed by moral edict (by advertisers) but much evidence of censorship in the sense of operative suppression of a great range of subjects. . . . The dynamics of the market . . . would seem to indicate

This photo taken on the first day of occupation of the U.S. Embassy in Teheran on 11/4/79 shows American hostages being paraded by their militant Iranian captors. The Iranians held the hostages and the attention of the media for 444 days.

(UPI/Bettman Archive)

that freedom of expression has less to fear from the control which large advertisers exercise than from the control which these advertisers permit the mass market to exercise.[1]

Individual instances can be cited in which advertisers have used their economic power to "regulate" the media. For example, advertisers in a Wisconsin town withdrew their advertising from the local newspaper to protest the use of its production shop to print an underground newspaper. Their action could have put the newspaper out of business, but the newspaper stood its ground and ultimately won the battle. The news offices of most mass media are separate from the advertising offices, and news officials rarely want to accept the dictates of advertising offices.

Theoretically, the more independent the medium can be from advertising, the less power of regulation the advertiser will have. Radio and television receive 100% of their revenues from advertising and run the risk of great pressure from sponsors. Newspapers and magazines, for the most part, receive one-third to one-half of their revenue directly from subscribers and have a less direct obligation to paid advertisers. Books,

[1] David M. Potter, *People of Plenty* (Chicago: University of Chicago Press, 1954), 184.

the record industry, and motion pictures, which receive 100% of their revenue directly from their audiences, can afford to ignore Madison Avenue.

THE PROFESSION AS REGULATOR

The gatekeeper, who as we have seen plays a key role in the flow of mass communication, voluntarily accepts codes of conduct that act as regulators of his or her actions. This is less important in the United States than in most other countries because the First Amendment prevents such codes from being absolutely binding on the communicator. In Sweden, for example, a journalist can be thrown out of the profession for violating a journalistic standard, but in the United States—since the Constitution guarantees anyone the right to practice journalism—such codes can be used only as voluntary guidelines.

Examples of important professional codes are "A Statement of Principles" of the American Society of Newspaper Editors and the "Code of Professional Standards" of the Public Relations Society of America.

Self-censorship has long been a important concept in the motion-picture and broadcast media. A motion-picture code was adopted by the industry in the 1920s in an effort to avert government censorship. The ratings of movies today by the industry is a form of voluntary self-censorship. The G (family), PG (parental guidance), PG13 (may be inappropriate for children under 13), R (no admission to those under age 17 without an accompanying adult), and X (no admission to all under age 17) ratings are not required by the government.

Self-regulation is also practiced in broadcasting. The major networks each have a "standards and practices" division that establishes standards and sees that they are followed. NBC's broadcast standards department numbers 26 people; ABC employs 70 people; and CBS has 80 people. Since television views itself as a family medium, it has usually adopted stricter standards than the movie industry, with the result that as television presents more movies, it has more work to do in censoring various aspects of these movies. In 1976, for example, when CBS showed the movie *Smile*, a satirical comedy about young women embroiled in a California beauty pageant, it had to remove certain scenes and words. A scene in which a plucked chicken got "smooched" by boisterous members of a fraternity at a fraternal initiation was cut by CBS. The words *sanitary napkin* were censored from a scene in which plumbers were complaining about discarded sanitary napkins clogging the pipes. This is self-censorship by media, not government censorship.

The so-called family viewing policy of the National Association of Broadcasters is an interesting example of government interference in professional codes. Family viewing stated that prime-time television should be restricted to programs that were appropriate for a general family audience, including children. Hollywood writers, actors, and program producers were in an uproar, complaining that family viewing restricted their freedom of expression; they claimed it was the FCC that inspired the policy, not the NAB, and brought a suit against the FCC. A district court in California agreed with the plaintiffs, ruling that family viewing violates the First Amendment and need not be enforced or followed by networks or stations.

THE CONSUMER AS REGULATOR

In a system of free mass communication, the consumer is perhaps the most important regulator of the media. In two areas—civil libel and right of privacy—consumers can resort to court procedures to help protect themselves from the media as well as help keep the media within acceptable boundaries.

Civil Libel

Libel is the false defamation of a person's character through printed or broadcast means. Slander is false defamation through spoken words. Defamation is communication that exposes a person to hatred, ridicule, or contempt; lowers him (or her) in the esteem of his fellows; causes him to be shunned; or injures him in his business or calling. The concept of defamation as a punishable act has a long history; the ancient Egyptians cut out the tongues of those found guilty of lying maliciously about their neighbors.

Those who feel that damage has been done them by communication can bring a civil suit against those responsible and seek payment for damages. The legal action is not much different from a lawsuit in which a person seeks to be paid for the actual damage to a car fender in an auto accident. In a libel suit, tradition holds that a person's reputation (unlike an auto fender) is a priceless commodity and that little just compensation can be paid for *actual* damages. Thus the plaintiff can ask for *punitive* damages, an amount of compensation so great that it will punish the libeler. Some punitive damages for libel have run into the millions of dollars, especially when the libel was shown to have been published with malicious intent.

The publisher or broadcaster of a defamatory statement can defend the publication or broadcast under certain conditions that might absolve the defamer completely or lessen the damages he or she may be ordered to pay. Truth is now accepted as an absolute defense for the publication of a defamation, and a defamer who can prove the truth of a statement can be absolved. Certain statements are privileged; that is, the publisher has a right to repeat them without fear of libel suits. Privileged statements are those recorded in legislative, judicial, and other official public proceedings. Also, statements made as a matter of fair comment or criticism about public matters are defensible even if defamatory.

Perhaps the most famous libel suit of the early 1980s was that brought by the singer and actress Carol Burnett against the *National Enquirer*. The

Enquirer had published a story indicating that Burnett had been drunk and disorderly in a Washington restaurant. She proved the description to be false and libelous, and a California court awarded her $1.6 million in damages, which was subsequently lowered to $750,000 by an appeals court.

The Right of Privacy

Individuals have the right to be private, even from mass media. Unlike libel, however, this right is a relatively new concept of communication regulation. Citizens have the right to recover damages from the media for intruding on their solitude, publishing private matters violating ordinary decencies, using their names publicly in a false manner, or using their names or likenesses for commercial purposes. Individuals can bring a civil action in court to seek compensation for damages done to them from such invasion of privacy.

There are instances when an individual may lose the right of privacy. For example, a person involved in a newsworthy act or a person who becomes newsworthy by virtue of public actions loses the right to privacy in those matters. Or someone who gives consent to an invasion of privacy—for example, by signing a waiver upon entering a studio to become a member of a TV audience—cannot recover any damages through loss of privacy.

Some states have passed laws that have added to the privacy of individuals but that may cause abuses. For example, Oregon passed a law in 1975 preventing police from disclosing the names and addresses of people arrested, detained, indicted, charged, sentenced, serving time, or released from prison in an effort to protect individuals who might have been falsely arrested or charged or sentenced. But the law in reality allows the police to carry out secret arrests, secret trials, or secret jailings in the name of protecting the few. Certainly no greater abuse could be perpetrated in a free and open society than police action without the scrutiny of the public through the watchdog eyes of the press. In such cases, it would seem, the right to know would be more important to a free society than the right to privacy.

Control through Consumption

No doubt the greatest amount of consumer regulation occurs in the marketplace. Publications that sell stay in business; those that cannot obtain or maintain an audience go bankrupt. Broadcast programs that do not attract large audiences go off the air. Because the media are in business to make a profit, they are usually sensitive to their customers and pay careful attention to the moods and habits of readers, listeners, and viewers. Of course, what the audience wants may not always be the best or most constructive content for the social good. Violence and sex seem to be more popular than news analysis and interpretation of public issues. Thus, control by the marketplace has to be balanced against other considerations to achieve social well-being.

Mass media are sensitive to individual responses, but as media grow the individual voice gets weaker. Increasingly, people have joined together in groups and associations to make their voices heard and their opinions felt. These groups have been able to pressure mass media, thus serving as regulators of mass communication. Nearly every religious, ethnic, occupational, and political group has an association that can speak for the members of the group, such as exerting pressure on television to stop portraying Italians as criminals, on newspapers to publish stories about gun laws, on radio to present antismoking commercials, on magazines to stop obscenity. One such pressure group, Action for Children's Television (ACT), petitioned the FCC for a rule barring advertisements on children's shows. The efforts were a major force behind all three networks' appointments of executives to supervise children's programming. Such pressure is also often applied to the media through government regulatory agencies. For example, enforcement of the FCC's Fairness Doctrine is most often triggered by complaints from individual groups with opinions different from those broadcast.

One segment of the population that is increasingly applying pressure on all media is women. Women's groups have lobbied in various forums for more balanced coverage and an end to employment discrimination by the mass media. For example, a number of women complained about the first edition of this textbook, saying that it contained too many sexist references, such as the constant use of the word *newsman*. As a result, the authors were encouraged (not forced) by their editor to change or modify such references in the second edition. We were happy to comply with the request, for the earlier edition did reflect outdated usage, and more important, the changes improved the book.

In 1976 the National Commission on the Observance of International Women's Year produced a set of guidelines for mass media coverage of, and employment of, women. No doubt, these guidelines are studied seriously by mass media communicators and gatekeepers, for the mass media certainly will not continue to be mass if they offend so large a segment of their audience.

10 Filters

The child's adage "sticks and stones will break my bones, but *names* will never hurt me" is a defense mechanism. It is a way to *filter out* the epithets. When a word attacks your sensibilities, what do you do? How do you respond? Do you hide the hurt and react rationally, or do you allow the wound to show and respond with an expletive?

The power of words, signs, symbols, codes, and actions lies with the receiver more than the sender. We can filter out the emotional content of power words, or we can allow them to anger, frighten, annoy, or manipulate us.

You meet a dapper older fellow and say, "Haven't you lost some weight?" Why, you just made his day! Or, how about meeting a female friend and saying, "Hey, aren't you putting on some pounds?" Why is there so much power in the concept of being told you are overweight? The mass media have played a major role in the "thinning of America."

Mass communication has power only if the audience's filters allow it to be powerful. The listener–viewer–reader's response is based on a willingness to respond. Audiences are difficult to manipulate; their filters are the protective, interpretive devices that create problems for mass communicators.

THE FILTRATION CONCEPT

In spite of mass communication on all sides today, we speak increasingly of a communication gap. The rich do not seem to communicate with the poor. Whites and blacks seem unable to overcome communication barriers. Protestants, Catholics, and Jews still seem to have difficulty finding many common areas for discourse. Even within families, gaps develop as fathers and mothers fail to speak the language of their children.

Filtration is the process of removing impurities, of separating particles from liquids or air, or eliminating certain light and sound wavelengths. When the filtering is over, one is left with less, yet one hopes it is more.

In mass communication, messages must struggle one against the other because there are so many of them. The average American is involved in thousands of communication exchanges a day. Communication overload is a reality, and our filters help us eliminate the useless, the annoying, and the unwanted. To some extent, filtration is our communication life vest.

The filtering process depends on internal "frames of reference" within each individual member of the audience. Filters are the complex mechanisms we use to "decode" messages. Your filters are a part of you; they are learned, and they can be relearned. They can be improved, and their improvement will make you a better audience member. Filters are, in effect, frames of reference.

OUR SENSES AS FILTERS

No two people see the world exactly alike. Our perception depends upon the way we have conditioned our eyes, ears, fingers, mouth, and nose. Our responses to the world are dependent on (a) the fidelity of our seeing, hearing, touching, tasting, and smelling; (b) the training of these senses.

ONE MAN CROSSES SIXTH AVENUE WHILE ANOTHER CROSSES THE AVENUE OF THE AMERICAS

(Drawing by Ziegler, Copyright © 1984 The New Yorker Magazine, Inc.)

Why does one person take better photographs than another? She has *learned* to see better compositions.

Why does a blind person hear things a sighted person cannot? He has *trained* himself, consciously and unconsciously, to listen more carefully.

Why does a weaver choose the fibers she does? Her sense of touch is *developed* through practice of her craft.

Why can one person enjoy cooked cabbage or raw oysters or retsina wine or steak tartare or—believe it or not—even chicken, while another gags at the mention of them. The one who enjoys has *cultivated* a taste for these delights.

Why can't a smoker understand that her home, her car, her clothes, her hair, and her breath reek of cigarette smoke? She has *reoriented* her olfactory mechanism to disregard or enjoy these smells. The nonsmoker has not.

Our physical sensors are the receivers we use to gather in the communication around us. They are our communication response mechanism.

CONDITIONS OF FILTRATION

Four basic sets of conditions have an impact on our ability to filter messages: (*a*) informational or lingual filters or conditions; (*b*) physical filters or conditions; (*c*) psychological filters or conditions; and (*d*) cultural filters or conditions. These *filters* or *conditions* are the ways in which we learn or are trained to receive or ignore messages in our daily communication activities.

Informational or Lingual Filters

Each of us has learned a variety of languages and the responses to those codes. When you do not know the signs and symbols, you are at a serious disadvantage. Egyptian hieroglyphs slept for centuries until the work of Jean François Champollion unlocked the secret of the Rosetta stone. Champollion discovered that the Egyptian symbols were syllabic and alphabetic rather than pictographs. The mysteries and the glories of ancient Egypt became readable once the message was filterable.

During World War II a major victory took place when code books and decoding mechanisms were found aboard a German submarine. From that time onward, the messages of the German High Command were understandable when intercepted.

Scientists working to contact other intelligent life forms believe mathematical and scientific *constants* may be the only language we would have in common. Perhaps the series of radio pulses (one pause, one–two pause, one–two–three pause, and so one, using only pure numbers) would be the best start because that truth is scientifically constant in the universe. The message is being coded to be filtered.

Without accurate informational filters, *no positive communication can occur.* If you cannot decode the message, you cannot communicate. Specialized codes of science and technology baffle us not because we lack

VARIETY

PRICE
$**1**50

NEWSPAPER
Second Class P.O. Entry

Published Weekly at 154 West 46th Street, New York, N.Y. 10036, by Variety, Inc. Annual subscription, $75. Single copies $1.50.
Second Class Postage Paid at New York, N.Y. and at Additional Mailing Offices
©COPYRIGHT, 1984, BY VARIETY, INC., ALL RIGHTS RESERVED

Vol. 316 No. 5   USPS 656-960   **New York, Wednesday, August 29, 1984**   02371   **112 PAGES**

DISK BIZ BASKING IN SALES GLOW

RETAILERS REPORT GAINS OF 15-20%, UNITS UP TOO

By KEN TERRY

The disk biz is booming again, with many U.S. retailers reporting year-to-year gains of 15-20% through August. Since average record prices haven't risen in the past year, it's clear that these increases in dollar volume are being matched by proportional advances in unit sales.

If demand for prerecorded music holds up through Christmas — and most dealers think it will — the industry could see a 15% boost in the annual dollar value of shipments. That would drive volume up to $4.387-billion from $3.815-billion for 1983 (including both retail and direct marketing sales). But,

while this figure would exceed the $4.131-billion highwater mark reached in 1978, the year of "Saturday Night Fever" and "Grease," the corresponding unit figure of 665,000,000 would still fall far short of the 726,200,000 units shipped in 1978.

These statistical quandaries, however, are of no concern to the nation's record retailers, who are enjoying their best year since the decade began. Assuming that the artistic product remains good and that record labels don't raise prices across the board, the dealers believe their prosperity will continue well

into next year.

The current boom in LP, cassette and compact disk sales is only partly attributed to the general economic recovery. Equally important, say retailers, are the mass appeal of new releases, the lessening of competition from videogames, the growth of the market for portable cassette players and the increased exposure of artists on MTV and other television outlets.

Nevertheless, the optimism engendered by economic growth has certainly had a marked impact on the disk biz. "People buy more rec-
(Continued on page 92)

Homevid-Film Battle Raging Anew In Gaul

By JACK MONET

Paris, Aug. 28.

The French homevid-film industry war flared anew this week as Thorn EMI topper Jacques Chazeau assailed cinema professionals, "closely linked with the government," who he alleged were smothering the development of h.v. commerce and unfairly favoring the pay-tv service Canal Plus, which starts Nov. 4.

Chazeau disclosed Monday (27) that he also quit the French professional association of homevid distribs, the SNEV, two months ago. He cited lack of support from the SNEV on issues arising from court-ordered seizures of multimedia-multinational Thorn EMI's vidcassette title "Tchao Pantin" (*Variety*, Aug. 15).

Chazeau named no names, but did reserve his most bitter remarks
(Continued on page 26)

Jacksons May Not Sell Out In Philly, Poor Distribution

By HARRY HARRIS

Philadelphia, Aug. 28.

The Jacksons' Victory Tour, nearing its biggest venue yet via a Labor Day weekend gig at John F. Kennedy Memorial Stadium Saturday (1) through Monday, may find a considerable number of the 63,-547 available seats unoccupied.

Ticket sales were still sluggish Monday (27), with several factors cited. Among them were too-short notice before rescheduling from Oct. 5-7; poor ticket distribution,
(Continued on page 29)

Ohio Fair Sets Record; State Asks More Use Of Exposition Grounds

Columbus, Ohio, Aug. 28.

For the fourth straight year, the Ohio State Fair, which closed at midnight Aug. 19, racked up a record attendance mark of 3,671,302 persons, 5.4% higher than the 1983 mark of 3,481,640. Three strong weekend entertainers helped push
(Continued on page 108)

Black Group Is Set To Picket N.Y. Production

By ANDREW KIRTZMAN

Seeking to head off a threatened series of pickets and demonstrations at shooting locations throughout the city, two major union leaders and a City Hall labor negotiator met Thursday (23) with black leaders intent upon integrating New York's production industry.

After a long and often heated meeting, members of The Motion Picture Project, an organization recently formed by the Black Muslims and Fightback, a black activist group, said the pickets would commence as scheduled.

"We feel that if City Hall plays a major role, then we can foresee some type of change," said Mustafa Majeed, codirector of the Project. "But as far as things go now, there's been no change and there's going to be demonstrations. We're going to picket every motion picture on the streets."

Majeed was not specific about the planned pickets, other than to
(Continued on page 108)

Abe Lastfogel, 86, Wm. Morris Giant, Succumbs In L.A.

Hollywood, Aug. 28.

Abe Lastfogel, 86, guiding force at the William Morris Agency for more than 60 years, died Saturday (25) night of a heart attack at Cedars-Sinai Medical Center in Los Angeles.

Lastfogel entered the hospital Aug. 10 to have his gall bladder removed. He suffered side effects from the surgery, however, and one mild heart attack before being fatal-
(Continued on page 96)

Samuel Goldwyn

GOLDWYN GOLD

21 MOTION PICTURE CLASSICS
SAMUEL GOLDWYN TELEVISION SYNDICATION

NEW YORK · 200 WEST 57TH STREET · SUITE 706 · NEW YORK, N.Y. 10019 · (212) 315-1010
LOS ANGELES · 10203 SANTA MONICA BLVD. · SUITE 500 · LOS ANGELES, CA 90067 · (213) 552-2255

ALL NEW:

GLOBAL TV PRICE CHART

(See page 76)

intelligence but because we do not possess the necessary lingual skill. That is why in mass communication the primary directive of the conglomerate communicator is to code the content *not* in his or her language but in a symbolic form the audience can filter accurately and easily.

As the world grows more complex, the problems of cross-occupational communication, in one sense at least, grow greater rather than smaller. As people become more specialized in the functions they perform, their filters become more specialized. They acquire a specialized vocabulary and language for their tasks. Engineers do not speak the language of doctors. The people who live in a neighborhood may have less in common with one another than they have with professional colleagues whom they meet only occasionally. We have to make new maps of the world informationally.

Specialized media have developed to accommodate the growing specialization of people. Almost every day, a new publication is born in America to serve a distinct audience, whether it is a group of prosthetics specialists or an association of terrazzo and mosaic experts. These new media vehicles for new audiences develop new languages, which require specialized informational filters.

The front page of *Variety* may drive the point home. The "show biz" jargon is made up of nontraditional symbols. But as one reads along and becomes familiar with the style, one's informational filters "clock-on." The theatrical nature of the words becomes not only comprehensible but more meaningful than standard English. You don't even need a Rosetta stone. That's show biz!

The better information we have, the better we see, hear, touch, taste, and smell communication. The informational or lingual filter is *the* essential filter in the receiving and decoding of messages.

Physical Filters   Our sensory perception is heightened, diminished, accepted, or rejected by two sets of physical characteristics: internal physical conditions and external physical conditions.

Internal physical conditions refer to the well-being or health of the individual audience member. A person who is physically ill filters messages differently from the way he or she does in good health. A migraine headache, a bleeding ulcer, or an abscessed tooth can radically alter message filtering. The pain of a smashed thumb affects the sense of touch so intensely that sight and sound are impaired. In some cases, physical discomfort may heighten the communication experience. For example, Pepto-Bismol commercials are filtered differently when we have upset stomachs from the way they are when we are feeling well. In the extreme, the absence or impairment of one sense significantly heightens the effectiveness of another. Blind individuals tend to develop acute hearing—blindness filters motion-picture messages negatively but may increase positively the filtering of phonograph music.

External physical conditions refer to the environment or surroundings in which we receive messages. If the room in which you are reading this book is too hot, too cold, too dark, or too noisy, the environment will affect your senses and the way you filter the content of this page. The purpose behind the construction of most motion-picture theaters is the development of the most satisfactory environment possible for viewing films. Every sense is catered to in order to improve the way movies are filtered. Compare this situation to the way you watch a movie on television. The room is lighted. People wander in and out. The phone rings. Commercials interrupt. Your senses are bombarded by a competing array of stimuli. No wonder seeing a movie in a theater is a better experience than seeing the same movie at home. We filter these two experiences in entirely different physical environments. Every medium is affected in significantly different ways by the way people feel and the physical surroundings in which they use the medium.

These two physical conditions also relate to two major problems mass media communicators must face: information overload and clutter.

Information overload is a fact of life. There is just too much communication in our lives. The amount of mass communication would overwhelm us if we let it, and so audience members at times just shut the mass media off with switches on the hardware and filters in their heads. Because there is so much to digest in print, we are a society of speed readers. We physically filter all but the necessary words.

Look at the three triangles in this figure. There is an error in each triangle. Find the error.

If you have not found the error, look again. Each triangle repeats a word (Snake in *the the* grass. Busy as a *a* beaver. Paris in the *the* spring). Because the phrase was familiar, and because we all speed-read, we misread. There is too much to read; we cope by deleting what we think is unnecessary. Information overload leads to filtering out some of the wheat with the chaff.

Unfortunately, time has not expanded to meet the demands of increased mass communication, and so we physically react with more intense philtering. *Philtering?* you mean *filtering.* No, "philtering" stops the reader a microsecond and makes that person concentrate. The communicator is trying to combat your filters with philters.

Clutter is a broadcasting term that refers to too many bits and pieces of information in a time slot. For example, in the average 2-minute commercial break, we see four 30-second ads. Because of clutter, advertisers must ensure that their spots stand out amid the clutter.

Often, the adult viewer "shuts down" during the commercial breaks or gets something to drink or talks to other viewers or goes to the bathroom. It is the opposite with many toddlers. They play during the show and run in to watch the commercials. Why? Television ads are intense visual experiences.

Information overload leads us to filter the messages printed in these word triangles.

Psychological Filters

Each of us has a personality based on individual experiences. That personality has a variety of formats. We are more than one-dimensional; we are multifaceted. Our personal receptivity to a specific communication is based on psychological sets. These psychological sets are complex, and under various conditions psychological filters can reflect a variety of responses to the same content.

Our psychological sets, in effect, are what make us intellectually and emotionally selective regarding the communication process. These psychological sets define other people, situations, and events. As receivers of messages, we know that certain situations, individuals, interactions, symbols, words, etc., have more impact than others.

We structure our perception of the world in terms that are meaningful to us, according to our frames of reference, our filters. This process has been described as selective exposure, selective perception, and selective retention. Wilbur Schramm defines three problems that communicators must expect as they try to communicate meaning. First, receivers will interpret the message in terms of their own experiences and the ways they have learned to respond to them. For example, a jungle tribesman who has never seen an airplane will tend to interpret the first airplane he sees as a bird. Second, receivers will interpret messages in such a way as to resist any change in strong personality structures. For instance, a person strongly committed to the Democratic party will tend to ignore the campaign information of the Republicans. Third, receivers will tend to group characteristics from their experiences so as to make whole patterns. To illustrate, notice how we need just a few strokes of a cartoonist's brush, creating a steel helmet, to enable us to summon up an image of a conservative hardhat.

Rape is a powerful word psychologically because it connotes one person brutalizing another. Ask a group of men if they have been raped. There

Zoran Jovanović

(Copyright © 1983 by the New York Times Company. Reprinted by permission.)

are sometimes responses such as "not lately," which often gets a big laugh. Then ask those same men if they have seen *Deliverance*, a film in which a man is raped by another man. Now the situation changes and the laughter is absent. Most men understand the terror of the concept, and the psychological impact is sobering. The filter changed with the situation rather than the symbol or source.

So, the litany of power words depends on the source and the situation as well as the symbol, because our psychological filters are discerning.

The filters—our senses—are colored, distorted, and polarized by our culture. Edward T. Hall, a cultural anthropologist, has written effectively about the role of culture in human communication efforts, especially in his book *The Silent Language*, in which he shows how culture affects the way a person sends and receives messages. We are fully aware, he says, of "the broad extent to which culture controls our lives. Culture is not an exotic notion studied by a select group of anthropologists in the South Seas. It is a mold in which we are all cast, and it controls our daily lives in many unsuspected ways."

Cultural Filters

One can identify 10 separate kinds of human activity that are "primary message systems." These are interaction, association, subsistence, bisexuality, territoriality, temporality, learning, play, defense, and exploitation (or use of materials). These systems vary from individual to individual and from culture to culture. They constitute a vocabulary and a language of their own, a silent language of which most of us are not aware.

Consider *temporality*, for example. To the average American of European origin, time exists as a continuum; there is a past, a present, and a future. Such a person is able to compartmentalize time, to see distinctions in time, to do one thing at a time. The American–European culture is basically linear, and that is perhaps one cultural reason for this perceptual phenomenon. But to the Navajo Indian, time has no limits. The American Indian culture, without written language, is not linear. For the Navajo, time has no beginning, middle, or end. Time starts when the Navajo is ready, not at a given point. The future has little reality because it does not exist in the Navajo's time; nor does the past.

Territoriality is also a cultural message system. The average American of European origin has a strong sense of space and knows where things belong and to whom they belong. Individuals with this cultural background establish their rights to territory. For example, students take certain seats in a classroom; they become *their* seats, and the students might well return to the same seats throughout a semester, as if they had established rights to them. But to typical Hopi Indians, space does not belong to anyone; they are apt to settle down wherever it suits them, regardless of whose territory they are invading.

Obviously the Hopi and the Navajo have different message systems regarding time and space from those exhibited by Americans of European origin. This cannot help but affect their message intake and output on any subject where temporality and territoriality are involved. We can make an almost endless list of cultural traits and subcultural habits of mind that influence our patterns of communication and our ability to make the act of communication a mutual sharing of a common understanding.

Cultures are social systems that share common attitudes, mores, beliefs, and opinions. In a pluralistic society such as ours, the subgroups to which we belong are often stronger in molding our cultural communication filters than is the parent society. The enduring subcultural attitudes, beliefs, and opinions, however, are undergoing homogenization carried out by the mass media.

In terms of youth movements, the disco contest in *Saturday Night Fever* has been replaced by *Urban Cowboy's* mechanical bull which in turn has been replaced by the break dancers of *Beat Street*. The political and cultural minorities using the mass media have modified America's responses to blacks, Chicanos, women, and gays to an extent one would not have predicted 30 years ago. But because there is so much to react to so quickly, we continue to fall back on cultural stereotypes.

Stereotyping was discussed at length by Walter Lippmann in a pioneering work, *Public Opinion*, published in 1922. He borrowed the term "stereotyping" from the printing industry. It refers to the plates, molded from type, used to reproduce printed copies, each one exactly the same as the original. Lippmann used the term to characterize the human tendency to reduce perceptions to convenient categories, cataloging people, ideas, and actions according to our frames of reference for the purpose of easy recognition.

"The pictures inside people's heads," Lippmann wrote, "do not automatically correspond with the world outside." Yet the pictures in our heads are our public opinions, and when those pictures "are acted upon by groups of people, or by individuals acting in the name of groups, they are Public Opinion with capital letters." The Public Opinion is the "national will" that is supposed to govern democratic societies; and mass media are supposed to inform the public about the truth of the world outside. But communicators themselves cannot keep from shaping the news in terms of the pictures in *their* heads and the stereotypes of their audiences.

We can see one example of stereotyping in our attitudes toward people of other nations. Two social psychologists, William Buchanan and Hadley Cantril, studied the images that one national group had of another and found a definite tendency to ascribe certain characteristics to certain people. For example, Americans think of Russians as cruel, hard-working, domineering, backward, conceited, and brave. Americans think of themselves as peaceloving, generous, intelligent, progressive, hard-working, and brave. The British think of Americans as intelligent, hard-working, brave, peace-loving, conceited, and self-controlled. Buchanan and Cantril

Groups subject to stereotyping, like these gay and lesbian activists, sometimes use public demonstrations to protest prejudice, employing mass media to publicize their views.

(Photo by Mark Glickman.)

found that people in countries that were on friendly terms tended to use less derogatory adjectives in describing one another's characteristics and that people invariably described their own nation in flattering terms.

THE INTERACTION OF FILTERS

The four filtering conditions—informational–lingual, physical, psychological, and cultural—are constantly working together with varying individual impact on our communication sensors—our sight, sound, touch, taste, and smell. At times, one filter can short out the others:

1. We cannot read Italian, and the letter we receive is in Italian (*information–lingual*).
2. We are in severe pain, and so it doesn't matter who scored in the game on the tube (*physical*).
3. The movie is about Vietnam; someone in my family died in that war, and so I will not go to see it (*psychological*).
4. Your parents object to rock 'n' roll so much that it doesn't matter how loud you turn it up. They still can't hear what you hear (*cultural*).

In each case, one condition is so strong that it overrides all others; but in most receptions, situation filters interact with unequal influence depending on the message.

In the figure below the visual tries to emphasize that filtering is imperfect and no one best pattern exists. Remember, *filtering* messages is *reaction* and usually requires immediate and imperfect responses in an environment choked with communication. Filtering the mass communication process is the audience's survival mechanism.

FORMULA AND STYLE IN MASS COMMUNICATION

For a variety of reasons, the mass media actually reinforce certain views of the world. First, the media have to simplify reality. Because of the limits of time and space, the mass communicator must reduce most messages to their simplest elements. There is never enough time on the air or enough space on the page to tell everything in detail. Audiences themselves usually do not have enough time or energy to digest great detail.

Second, the message must be framed in terms that are understandable and acceptable to the audience. In general the media give favorable pre-

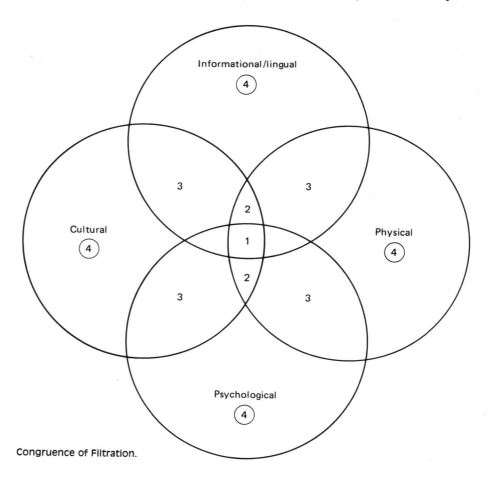

Congruence of Filtration.

sentation to ideas that their audiences approve and unfavorable presentation to ideas that are not approved. For example, during the 1930s and 1940s, the American media never pictured President Franklin D. Roosevelt on crutches, in a wheelchair, or in any other posture that would have emphasized his disability. In the 1970s the media seemed bent on full coverage of every slip and fall made by Presidents Johnson, Nixon, Ford, and Carter. The American people had undoubtedly changed their notion about their president and wanted to see him as an ordinary human being.

Third, mass media achieve simplification and audience identification be resorting to easily structured molds and readily recognizable formulas, themes, and attitudes. The news story is a highly structured message with a lead and a body usually composed in an inverted-pyramid style, almost always containing the answers to certain questions such as who, when, where, why, what, and how. This enables the reporter, editor, copyreader, and even printer to deal with the material quickly and easily, filtering from the news story that part of the message that is meaningful to them. The same is true of the editorial, the feature story, the column, and other parts of the printed newspaper or magazine.

Fourth, formulas and themes vary with the times and cultural patterns. But they reinforce the culture and enhance the stereotype view through our filters. We might say that the mass media, because of limitations of time, space, and audience, deal largely in caricature rather than in portraiture, deliberately selecting features for quick recognition and easy identification in a few strokes, instead of presenting a full picture, rich in detail and complexity, which might be closer to reality.

MEDIA ACCULTURATION

The mass media also seek to make positive changes in our social system, and indirectly, in the audience's filtration system. Even if it is stereotyped, oversimplified, and structured, mass communication can make possible the consensus and understanding among individual components of society, bringing people together on some common ground. The mass media are important to the process of acculturation, where one culture modifies another.

An excellent example is the eight-part TV show "Roots," adapted from the novel by Alex Haley, about the search of a black man for his ancestors in Africa and in American slavery. The show was one of the most widely viewed and popular TV presentations in the history of television, gaining a larger audience than the TV showings of *Gone With the Wind* or the Super Bowls. "Roots" probably could not have attracted such a large audience in the 1940s or 1950s. The mood in America about racism and blacks changed and in the late 1970s this change made it possible not only to elect a president (who scorned racism) from the Deep South but also to produce a popular program about the evils of slavery.

Yet the dramatic marvel of "Roots" was that it told the story of the evils of slavery and racial discrimination in a way that millions of whites could identify with and say, "That's my story, too." Thus, while white attitudes toward blacks and black history will no doubt be modified by "Roots," in the same way blacks will see themselves in different terms as a result of molding the story in terms demanded by mass media. In such ways, mass media quicken the historical process of acculturation; the mutual interpenetration of minds and cultures goes forward at a rapid pace.

Perhaps in no society known to humankind has the process of acculturation gone forward so quickly as in America. Here, the great melting pot has taken people with different filters from diverse backgrounds and environments of Europe, Africa, and Asia and has made of them one new culture where the vast majority, regardless of what their grandparents did or where they came from, now speak the same language, live in the same kind of split-level house or high-rise apartment, study in the same kind of school, drive the same kind of car, and eat the same kind of hamburgers and apple pie at the same kind of drive-in restaurant.

For this, mass media are largely responsible. They have increasingly modified our filters, changed our frame of reference, and given us a way of looking at and perceiving the world around us.

Audiences  11

Books, newspapers, magazines, radio and TV programs, motion pictures, and sound recordings are produced solely to be consumed by audiences. Communicators, gatekeepers, and regulators work for audiences. The entire news and entertainment industries exist only because there are audiences. Unquestionably, audiences are the crux of the mass communication process. Audience members are the most studied, most catered to, and most economically important element in the study of the mass media. They are the media's *raison d'être*.

Distinctions need to be drawn between the terms *public* and *audience* and the conditions that differentiate mass communication *audiences* from interpersonal communication *receivers*.

The *public* refers to a total pool of available people, whereas *audience* refers to the individuals who actually use the content produced by a basic media unit. For the mass communicator, the public is an abstraction; the audience is a reality because audience members actually consume what the media produce. An individual has only to exist to be a part of the public, but a person must take action to become a part of an audience. The individual must read or listen or watch. The members of the audience are *active participants* in mass communication. They select, buy, con-

THE CONCEPT OF THE AUDIENCE

sume, are affected by, and act on mass media content. Human beings are not vegetables in the media cooker. Audiences interact with the media, and the results are complex and powerful.

We have already seen (in Chapter 5) how the sender becomes a conglomerate communicator when the mass media become involved in the communication process. The destination also changes from one person, who remains a discrete, discernible, recognizable, individual receiver in close physical or emotional (or both) contact with the sender in interpersonal communication, to part of the total *audience* in mass communication. Individuals are examined as parts of larger aggregates called *readership, listenership,* or *viewership.* Readers, listeners, and viewers make up mass communication audiences. Note the use of the plural here. It is not a singular audience because there are many audiences, over time, for any given unit of media content. Mass communication audiences exhibit five basic characteristics:

1. The audience tends to be composed of *individuals* who are apt to have commonly shared experiences and are affected by similar interpersonal social relationships. These individuals choose the media products they use by conscious selection or habitual choice. Some people react to audiences as unthinking masses, following the line of thought developed by Gustave LeBon in *The Crowd,* where the masses (*the* mass audience) follow a leader (a TV program or magazine) in zombielike obedience. The "crowd mentality" and "mass audience" are not well-thought-out concepts. The audience member remains an individual throughout the mass communication process.

2. The audience tends to be *large.* Charles Wright says: "We consider as 'large' any audience exposed during a short period of time and of such a size that the communicator could not interact with its members on a face-to-face basis."[1] There is no numerical cutoff point intended in the definition of *large.* Audience size is relative. A "large" audience for a hardback textbook might be a "small" audience for a prime-time network TV special.

3. The audience tends to be *heterogeneous* rather than homogeneous. Individuals within a given audience represent a wide variety of social categories. Some basic media units increasingly seek specialized audiences, but even these groups tend to be more heterogeneous than homogeneous. In actuality, audiences for some basic media units are relatively narrow in scope. For example, the target audience for "Soul Train" is young black Americans in predominantly urban markets. *Ms.* magazine has a relatively limited audience based on sex, age, and sociopolitical views. The younger, college-educated female is more likely to

[1] Charles Wright, *Mass Communication: A Sociological Perspective,* 2d ed. (New York: Random House, 1975), 6.

read *Ms.* than is her older, grade-school-educated grandmother. The audience for *Mass Media IV* is very specialized, but its readers are still part of a mass communication audience. To coin a phrase, audiences exhibit a "selective heterogeneity." Certainly most mass media are available to a heterogeneous public if not actually used by a heterogeneous audience.

4. The audience tends to be relatively *anonymous.* Communicators normally do not know the specific individuals with whom they are communicating, although they may be aware of general audience characteristics. For example, Linda Ronstadt does not personally know the individuals who are listening to her latest record.

5. The audience tends to be *physically separated* from the communicator. Thus, the final episode of "M*A*S*H*" came into the audience members' environment weeks after the episode was shot and miles from the studio where it was produced. Audiences are separated from the conglomerate communicator in both time and space.

Audiences are also identified with a variety of subclassifications. We talk about *available audiences* in television (those who have their sets on) versus the *actual audience* (those who are tuned to a specific show). Print-readership studies focus on *primary readers* (those who buy the publications) versus *pass-along readers* (those who use the magazine or whatever secondhand). Advertisers are interested in *target audiences*, those individuals who match prospective buyer characteristics or are "heavy users" of a specific brand or product class.

Audience research is good business. It helps the communicator put together content he or she thinks audiences want to use.

No mass medium through its basic media units serves all parts of the public. In fact, most basic media units serve only a fraction of the American populace. Even radio and TV stations that use the public's airwaves, which theoretically belong to all Americans, serve only those people who listen to or view their programs. Although stations are licensed to serve the *public* interest, convenience, and necessity, in reality they serve *audience* interests, conveniences, and necessities. No medium reaches all the people, but the total media system attempts to accomplish the feat of reaching most of the people, most of the time—profitably.

In *Theories of Mass Communication,* Melvin DeFleur and Sandra Ball-Rokeach analyze three perspectives of how audiences interact with the mass media and the messages the media carry.[2] In effect, these two so-

THEORIES OF MASS COMMUNICATION AUDIENCES

[2] Melvin DeFleur and Sandra Ball-Rokeach, *Theories of Mass Communication,* 3d ed. (New York: Longman, 1975), 202–225.

ciologists are looking at the effects of mass media—audience interaction, or how the audience acts on the content of the media.

The *Individual-Differences Perspective* describes audiences in terms of behaviorism, where learning takes place on a stimulus-response basis. Here there is no uniform mass audience—the mass media affect each individual audience member differently in terms of that individual's personal psychological makeup derived from past experiences.

Using the Individual-Differences Perspective in the figure below the individual audience members in (A_1, A_2, A_3) act on the media content by selectively attending and perceiving the same messages using different, individual filters. Therefore, each individual responds differently (A_1 produces R_1; A_2 reacts as R_2; and A_3 responds as R_3). This perspective suggests that each of us responds independently to the same message.

The *Social-Categories Perspective* takes the position that there are social aggregates in American society based on the common characteristics of sex, age, education, income, occupation, and so forth. Since these social aggregates have had commonly shared experiences, audience members have similar social norms, values, and attitudes. Here there are broad audience groups (e.g., working mothers, males aged 18–49, southern white females with two children) who will react similarly to specific message inputs.

Using the Social-Categories Perspective in the chart opposite the members of the audience (A_1, A_2, A_3) are culturally linked and share a common frame of reference; therefore their responses to the same message are similar given that other conditions remain the same.

The Individual-Differences and Social-Categories perspectives, in combination, produce the "who says what to whom with what effect" approach to mass communication. DeFleur and Ball-Rokeach evaluate this approach in the following manner:

A visualization of the individual-differences perspective illustrates the behavioral nature of this concept. When an audience member is exposed to a media experience the individual responds differently from others based on his or her unique personal makeup.

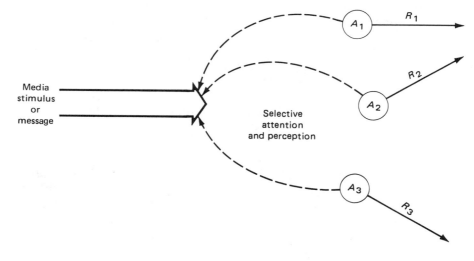

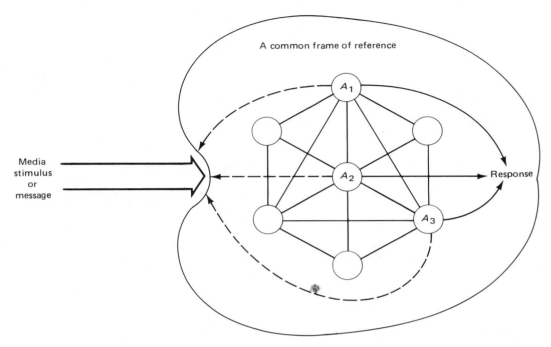

A visualization of the social-categories perspective, which recognizes that audience members are individuals, but adds that individuals belong to social aggregates and as such may respond in ways similar to other members of their group.

While these two perspectives on mass communication remain useful and contemporary, there have been further additions to the set of variables intervening between media stimuli and audience response. One additional elaboration of the S-R formula represents a somewhat belated recognition of the importance of patterns of interaction *between* audience members.[3]

The *Social-Relationships Perspective*, based on the research of Paul Lazarsfeld, Bernard Berelson, Elihu Katz, and others, suggests that informal relationships significantly affect audiences. The impact of a given mass communication is altered tremendously by persons who have strong social relationships with the audience member. As a result, the individual is affected as much by other audience members' attitudes as by the mass communication itself.

Using the Social-Relationships Perspective in the following figure, the audience members (A_1, A_2, A_3, and an opinion leader [OL]) receive a message. Here, however, it is not the media stimulus that has the significant impact; the informal interaction with others and a significant other (opinion leader) creates a common response. Audience member A_3 has

[3] Ibid., 206.

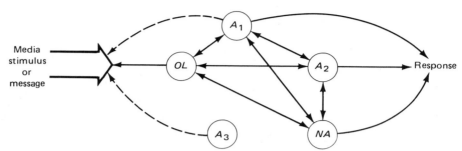

A visualization of the social-relationships perspective suggests that interpersonal interaction occurs before, during, and after the mass communication event and that these interactions are significant in terms of individual reactions to media content. The model also suggests that there are *opinion leaders* (OL), influential individuals who may be relatively important in our thinking as we make up our minds on a given issue.

no observable reaction, but an individual (NA) who did not receive the media message but did interact with audience members now reacts as they do. The interaction, rather than the message in isolation, has the significant impact.

Audiences and Perspectives

If we combine aspects of all three perspectives, we come up with the following description of a possible audience "theory": No one mass audience of our media system exists; rather, a variety of audiences exists for each media event. All of us are members of a large number of audiences, but each audience member reacts individually. This individual reaction may be similar, however, to that of other audience members who

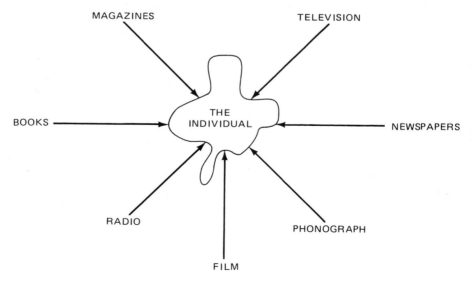

This implosion model of mass communication visualizes two concepts: the audience is central to the business of mass communication; and our media opinions are shaped under a constant bombardment from all sides.

have shared common experiences. Our interaction with other audience members, nonmembers, and opinion leaders also has an impact on how we respond and may lead to a common reaction. As a result of being a member of an audience, an individual is changed by the total media experience, not just the content of that experience.

Marshall McLuhan describes the audience situation in terms of the concept *implosion*. In this description the audience is central to mass communication and is under constant bombardment from the media. Instead of talking about an information explosion, we may need to refer to an information *implosion*..

IMPLOSION AND THE AUDIENCE

McLuhan argued that it is the medium itself, not the content of that medium, that "massages" the audience.

> Societies have always been shaped more by the nature of the media by which men communicate than by the content of the communication. The alphabet, for instance, is a technology that is absorbed by the very young child in a completely unconscious manner, by osmosis so to speak. Words and the meaning of words predispose the child to think and act automatically in certain ways. The alphabet and print technology fostered and encouraged a fragmenting process, a process of specialism and of detachment. Electric technology fosters and encourages unification and involvement. It is impossible to understand social and cultural changes without a knowledge of the workings of media.[4]

The individual American resides in an information vortex and is pummeled on all sides by the mass media. There is some justification for an inverted HUB Model of Mass Communication. Actually, it is the medium, the content, how it is presented, how it is received, and a multitude of other factors that affect individuals in the audience; but the media are *imploding* on all of us, all the time.

The media distribution of information implodes inwardly on the individual. The media are so pervasive, they are almost impossible for audiences to escape. In addition, each individual is a member of a great number of audiences and receives thousands of mass messages daily. We have developed barriers that resist most mass communication and filter in those messages that might be helpful for a particular need.

There are informational, physical, psychological, and cultural limits to our ability to perceive and understand. As the mass media provide more and more information, and entertainment and implosion increase, an audience's filtering systems become more complex and more difficult to penetrate.

---

[4] Marshall McLuhan, *The Medium Is the Message* (New York: Bantam Books, 1967).

The inverted HUB model of mass communication reverses the flow of the process. It forces the audience inside where it is caught in the environment of a mediated society protected to some extent by audience filters. The *effects* of the process are implied by the shape "the audience" which has been bombarded by the mass media. Feedback also takes on a much weaker visual dimension because some viewers, listeners, and readers feel powerless to resist manipulation.

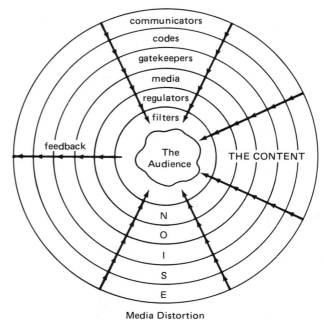

Media Distortion

AUDIENCES OF MEDIA

Print Media

Every time we commit ourselves to newspapers, books, and magazines, we become part of the audience of that specific book or given issue of a magazine or newspaper. When business people talk about print readership, they normally refer to circulation (i.e., those who buy the product). Media people, in point of fact, do not know exactly *what* is read or *who* reads it. So when we talk about readership, we are referring to those people *who do not necessarily buy but whom we hope read* the media product in question. Financial commitment generally precedes actual consumption, however, and so we can assume that the buyers have a high probability of becoming readers. The buyer and his immediate family are *primary readership*. If someone outside the buyer household uses the issue in question, we call him or her *pass-along readership*. Pass-along readership is an important aspect of the magazine audience because every reader is a potential reactor to the messages and a potential customer for the products advertised.

The readers of books, newspapers, and magazines meet the audience criteria established earlier:

1. Each basic media unit has a variety of audiences, not just one audience.

2. The audiences for books, newspapers, and magazines are very large. Many of these items sell millions of copies, even though they specialize in a select body of content.

WHAT SORT OF MAN READS PLAYBOY?

His taste is respected among wine buyers and cellars, but that doesn't mean he lives in a cave. PLAYBOY readers buy a quarter of the wine sold in the U.S., but they know there are surprises that the most full-bodied Burgundy can't offer. So our man can let the rest of the testers educate their palates while he relaxes with a more passionate discovery. If he is the talk of the tasting—well, everybody heard it through the grapevine.

Playboy solicits readership among individuals who may wish to identify with this idealized reader prototype. (Reproduced by Special Permission of *Playboy*. Copyright © 1982 by *Playboy*.)

3. Although specialized books and magazines seek specific audiences, they are available and used by a wide variety of individuals. Newspaper audiences are heterogeneous even for a selective newspaper like the *Los Angeles Free Press*, which is an example of what has been called the alternative press. The *Los Angeles Free Press* is different from the *Los Angeles Times* and has a more selective clientele.

4. Print media audiences are relatively anonymous. Publishers try to identify the characteristics of prospective audiences but seldom personally know the users.

5. The reader is physically removed from the writer. The audiences read after something is written (time). The audiences do not read over the author's shoulder (space).

Reading is individual, private, and personal. Words are written to be read by one person at a time. Reading is the act of one person, which makes print audiences a collection of individuals.

Recorded and Broadcast Media

Broadcast and record audiences are collections of groups of individuals. These electronic audiences may listen as individuals (as is usually the case in radio and record listenership), in small family group (as is usually the case with television), and in small-to-large nonfamily gatherings (party or discothèque use of the phonograph or jukebox).

Record listenership is assessed by record sales. Radio and television audiences are determined by audience-rating services, which attempt to determine not only the size but also the characteristics of the individuals using these media. Unlike what happens with print media, audiences occasionally use radio, television, and recordings as a group, although individual members maintain their personal identity.

The Motion-Picture Medium

Movies are seldom viewed by a solitary individual and almost always by group audiences, although drive-in movies provide something akin to a solitary experience. Even though an individual may become deeply involved in a given film, he or she remains an individual. There is a variety of movie audiences that are massive, heterogeneous, relatively anonymous, and physically removed from the communicator.

The movie audience and the content of films seem to be in an ever-narrowing spiral that is becoming younger and more elitist in an industry where $18 million average feature-film costs have driven up the cost of a movie tickets. Perhaps in no industry is the audience so closely tied to the individual young pocketbook as in film. The film audience is not only young but urban and economically viable.

AUDIENCES IN MEDIA ENVIRONMENTS

Each medium creates or modifies the environment in which it is used. In like manner, the physical conditions in which media are used affect the audience response.

Reading Environments

Print media are highly mobile; they can be used almost anywhere if the user is literate and there is light to read by. Interestingly, some print-use environments establish physical constraints on the user. The library, presumably a place where intense concentration is required, usually de-

Newspaper reading is a multi-environment activity often involving mobile situations.

(Photo by Brendan Beirne.)

mands quiet. Reading a textbook or studying for a test may require low-level sound. Freedom of movement is not restricted, however. It is amazing how irritating noise can be in a library but how unobtrusive it becomes on the subway ride to work. The rider–reader conditions himself or herself to the use of magazines, newspapers, and books in this noisy environment.

All of us learn to use media in a variety of environments. When these environmental conditions are altered, the audience member may become upset. Today's older generation learned to study quietly, and parents cannot fathom their children's use of rock music for background purposes while doing homework. The amount of retention required affects the reading situation. Reading for pleasure and reading for school are different acts and require different levels of concentration because each requires us to acquire different amounts and kinds of information.

The reading of a magazine, newspaper, or book can take place in many environments. Studying, however, tends to require environments that have little distraction. Nevertheless, the tremendous mobility of most printed matter allows readers to function anywhere they can establish satisfactory physical and psychological environments.

Radio has great mobility if the audience member owns a portable radio or has a car radio. In addition to having the physical device, the radio user must also have an electrical source, be it dry-cell batteries, the car battery, or the standard alternating current. The automobile environment requires primary concentration on driving. For this reason, one hopes that the radio get less attention than the road. Despite this, the audience mem-

Listening and Viewing Environments

ber is captive unless the driver turns the radio off or leaves the car. The portable radio has no single physical setting for its use; portable use is inhibited where radio volume would disturb others, but the development of the Sony Walkman has solved this problem.

The TV set tends to be located in a specific place, often modified for that experience, generally in the living room or family room. If a household has two or more sets, the extra sets generally go into bedrooms. There are portable TV sets, but the TV receiver tends to be less portable than radio or print. The TV room is often the focus of family activity, and normal distractions and interruptions are accepted as part of viewing. Americans use television as a social activity; interaction during viewing is not only permissible but encouraged.

The record environment depends greatly on whether the phonograph or tape deck in use is the portable that belongs to the youngsters or the family stereo. The portable usually gets around more, and because it has little sound quality, needs to be played louder. The stereo is often housed in a visible area—immovable and supreme. The portable and the 45-rpm record can be adapted to new environments by means of an increased volume. The album and the stereo modify the environment in which they are kept. Perhaps the best phonograph environment is provided by headsets, which eliminate other aural stimuli.

The motion-picture environment is the least portable and most institutionalized of all media. Watching a movie at home, on television, or in the classroom is completely unlike the experience we have in the movie theater. The movie house is created to increase the involvement of the audience with the film experience. The screen is huge, the place is dark, the seats are designed for comfort, interruptions are minimal, and the sound is usually good. Without question, motion pictures operate in the best of all possible controlled media environments.

The "Walkman" radio set has greatly expanded the listening environment of the audience. (Photo by Brendan Beirne.)

THE ECONOMIC VALUE OF AUDIENCES

In commercial mass media operations, *the audience is a by-product* of the content a specific media vehicle produces. *People Weekly* magazine sells copies of its issues to consumers, who, in turn, are sold to advertisers as *circulation* or *total readership,* which includes *pass-along readership.* those individuals who read someone else's copy of the magazine. The estimated audience (based on ratings) of NBC's "Hill Street Blues" or a local radio station's daypart are sold the same way. All advertising media seek out and serve audiences that have economic value to particular advertisers of specific goods and services.

Advertising Efficiency

Advertisers seek to reach the largest number of consumers at the lowest possible price. Advertisers tend to use media vehicles that provide the best cost efficiency. This cost efficiency, or cost per thousand (CPM) readers or viewers, is a means of assigning relative value to media audiences.

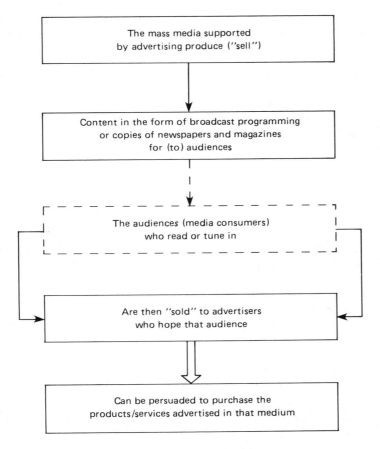

The mass media supported
by advertising produce ("sell")

Content in the form of broadcast programming
or copies of newspapers and magazines
for (to) audiences

The audience*s* (media consumers)
who read or tune in

Are then "sold" to advertisers
who hope that audience

Can be persuaded to purchase the
products/services advertised in that medium

The Dual Consumer Model

$$CPM = \frac{\text{Advertising cost}}{\text{Audience size (in units of 1000)}}$$

Under normal conditions, newspapers with large circulations have higher advertising rates than papers with fewer readers; when a newspaper's audience increases, its rates go up. For example, a large daily newspaper charges a one-time advertiser about \$15,000 to use a full-page ad to reach its approximately 800,000 daily readers. On Sunday the paper charges \$18,750 for the same-size ad because Sunday circulation exceeds 1 million. When the cost efficiency of the two editions of the paper is compared, the CPM circulation is the same because the higher cost is offset by the increase in circulation of the Sunday edition.

Cost Efficiency

Daily	Sunday
$\dfrac{\$15,000 \text{ cost of ad}}{800,000 \text{ circulation}} = \$18.75 \text{ CPM}$	$\dfrac{\$18,750 \text{ cost of ad}}{1,000,000 \text{ circulation}} = \$18.75 \text{ CPM}$

In terms of advertiser cost, both editions have the same efficiency ($18.75), based on paid circulation estimates made by the Audit Bureau of Circulation.

The Effect of Audience Characteristics on Advertising Costs

Advertisers must know more about audiences than *how many* people use a particular media product; they need to know *what kinds* of people use a given newspaper, magazine, radio, or TV station. In television, for example, total audience size is usually less important than the characteristics or composition of a program's audience. If we compare two network programs, this point may become clearer. For example, an advertiser for a diet beer, if such a product exists, has to choose between buying one 30-second spot during a situation comedy for $100,000 or another during a football game for $150,000. The sitcom reaches 15 million viewers, while the football game reaches only 10 million viewers.

CPM Total Audience

Situation comedy	Football game
$\dfrac{\$100,000 \text{ cost of spot ad}}{15,000,000 \text{ total audience}} = \$6.67 \text{ CPM}$	$\dfrac{\$150,000 \text{ cost of spot ad}}{10,000,000 \text{ total audience}} = \$15 \text{ CPM}$

Comparing CPMs, the sitcom ($6.67) seems to be a better buy than the football game ($15) because it has a larger total audience. But the advertiser's target audience is men age 18–49, and so the situation changes markedly. The sitcom has only 5 million male viwers (18–49), while the football game has 8 million male viewers (18–49).

CPM Men (18–49)

Situation comedy	Football game
$\dfrac{\$100,000}{5,000,000 \text{ men } (18\text{–}49)} = \$20 \text{ CPM}$	$\dfrac{\$150,000}{8,000,000 \text{ men } (18\text{–}49)} = \$18.75 \text{ CPM}$

At this point the football game ($18.75 CPM men 18–49) becomes a more efficient buy than the sitcom ($20 CPM men 18–49). Football, then, is a better buy for this advertiser because it reaches more of the target audience at a lower unit cost.

The diet beer's best audience would be in terms of "heavy user" data that disregard traditional demographic variables and rely totally on product consumption. The situation comedy has only 1.5 million people in this new target audience, while the football game has 5 million heavy users.

CPM Heavy Users

Situation comedy	Football game
$$\frac{\$100,000}{1,500,000 \text{ heavy users}} = \textbf{\$66.67 CPM}$$	$$\frac{\$150,000}{5,000,000 \text{ heavy users}} = \textbf{\$30 CPM}$$

At this point the football game ($30 CPM) becomes more than twice as efficient as the situation comedy ($66.67 CPM). This is true in spite of the fact that (a) the situation comedy spot cost $50,000 less than the football spot; (b) the situation comedy had a substantially larger (5 million) number of total viewers.

Current Advertising Efficiencies

Obviously, cost-per-thousand audience data vary between media and between competitors within a medium, but some benchmarks are available. Television CPMs run from $2 for "daytime" to $8 in prime time. Radio CPMs vary by market, but $2–6 are benchmark costs. Cable household CPMs are harder to predict because of less consistent audience research data; a $5–10 range probably covers the major services. The cable services CNN, MTV, ESPN and USA are close, but there commercial lengths (up to 2 minutes) are therefore very attractive for advertisers who can use a longer format to "tell their story" to the viewer/consumer. There is evidence that the demographics of cable audiences are good in terms of providing "upscale" audiences.

Print CPMs for newspapers run about $10 for a *full page* ad in the major markets. Interestingly, smaller newspapers are less efficient; and CPMs go up as markets decrease in size. Sunday-paper cost efficiencies traditionally are about 10% lower than the same paper's weekday editions. Magazine CPMs are higher than those of newspapers, but that is because magazines tend to reach very specialized target audiences.

EFFECTS OF AUDIENCES ON MEDIA CONTENT

The reality of the media marketplace is that audiences affect media content more than the content affects them. In a capitalistic mass media system a "post facto" system of cultural democracy emerges, where audience expenditures of time and money serve as the votes that determine the next wave of content. The seemingly never-ending series of historical romances with implicit sex and the strings of horror novels that serve up explicit violence exist because of audience demand. "New wave" rock 'n' roll gathered momentum slowly until MTV video clips generated an audience demand that radio stations could no longer ignore. *Star Wars* begat *The Empire Strikes Back, Return of the Jedi,* and lord knows how many imitators. *Jaws* spawned *Jaws II* and *Jaws 3-D.* The same situation prevails in television: "Dallas" led to "Falcon Crest," "Dynasty," and "Knots Landing." Movies are imitated as TV series. The film *Alice Doesn't Live Here Any More* became "Alice" on CBS and then a spinoff, "Flo," was developed. The TV series "Star Trek" became *Star Trek: The Motion Picture; Star Trek II: The Wrath of Khan;* and later *Star Trek III: The Search for Spock* continued a favorite story of "trekkies" begun 20 years earlier in one TV episode.

The audience–consumer influences the content of media in a variety of ways. The audience–consumer can change the content by personally communicating with the people who produce it. The buyer of a southern newspaper can write a letter to ask the editor to get the hockey scores printed in that paper. The consumer can telephone the local TV station to complain about the inaccuracy of the weather reports. The audience member can go to see the general manager of the local radio station to ask that the station cease to play certain records. Obviously, the basic media unit can reject these requests outright. But when the communicator feels that the complainer may speak for a sizable portion of the audience, changes may be made.

The audience–consumer can join with others to form pressure groups that, as a body, attempt to change the media content, as did the Legion of Decency (a Roman Catholic organization that rated the moral tone of motion pictures and had a powerful influence on the decision-making process of the Motion Picture Code Office and Hollywood filmmakers) in the 1930s, 1940s, and 1950s. The audience–consumer can refuse to spend time or money on the basic media unit. The buyer can refuse to subscribe to the local newspaper. The consumer can refuse to watch a TV series. The audience member can refuse to listen to the local radio station. If audience size decreases appreciably, the media content will change.

This method is the most effective because it is the hardest on the media economically. The newspaper, magazine, TV station, and radio depend on audiences to attract advertisers. The size of a basic media unit's audience affects its revenue, and this may be the most accurate index of the value our society places on that particular newspaper or station. When a movie becomes a smash hit, similar films are made until the public fails to support them financially. Thousands of records are produced annually, and the public selects those that it finds valuable from the ones "plugged" on their favorite radio stations.

Theoretically, at least, the media have a responsibility to meet the needs of American audiences. When a basic media unit succeeds in satisfying the wants of one or more audiences, it will be rewarded financially. The audience affects the content of books, films, TV programs, and records by financially rewarding or punishing the people who produce them. The

The success of the movie *The Big Chill* (1983) means that its creators and artists will continue to work in the high risk motion picture environment.

(Photo: Museum of Modern Art/Film Stills Archive, Courtesy Columbia Pictures.)

Rolling Stones are a cultural success because the consumers deem it so. Stephen King is an economic success because audiences buy his books. Lawrence Kasdan will direct additional films because *Body Heat* and *The Big Chill* were successful; audiences came to see them.

EDUCATION OF THE CONSUMER– AUDIENCE–PATRON

Artists have always needed patrons to produce art. Our time is no different from previous ages except that the "common person"—the audience—has become the major source of patronage. Today, audiences support the work of popular artists, and mass media display their works. Consumers support what they *like*, what their culture has taught them is worthwhile. Audiences pay for movie tickets, videotapes, phonograph albums, and books. Audiences pay for newspapers and magazines through subscriptions and single-copy sales, as well as by buying the products and services advertised. The content on radio and TV stations, and on cable and satellite services, also must be supported financially. It is a valueless exercise to bemoan the lack of quality in media content for two reasons. First, there is excellent content available if the media consumer shops the content wisely and takes advantage of the quality material. Second, the mass media will produce "better" print and electronic programming when there is an audience that will spend time and money on it.

There must be a growing concern to educate "critical consumers" who can make conscious decisions, knowledgeable choices about why and how they use the media. It is not a matter of "improving the media" because media are changing in many ways for the better. Certainly audiences are becoming more sophisticated. The concern must be in "improving the audience" so that it can handle the content and put it to the desired use. A media-educated audience is also better prepared to eliminate negative media effects.

Feedback 12

One evening Dan Rather accepted a telephone call early in the second broadcast (feed) of the "CBS Evening News," which is not the sort of thing an anchor usually does while a broadcast is in progress. This call, however, came from the president of the United States, Ronald Reagan, who wanted to take issue with the way the "CBS Evening News," in its first "feed" had characterized the administration's announcement of an intention to limit arms sales to Taiwan. After the second "feed" repeated the Taiwan coverage, Rather interposed a report of the president's telephoned remarks. This occurrence of immediate, direct, and personal feedback on television was dramatic, but in mass communication it is the rare exception rather than the rule.

Communication, by its definition, is a two-way process, a cooperative and collaborative venture. It is a joint effort, a mutual experience, an exchange between two parties—a sender and a receiver. The communication experience is not complete until an audience is able to respond to the message of the communicator. That response is called feedback. In mass communication, however, feedback assumes different characteristics.

Interpersonal feedback
enhances and enlivens
this communication
experience.

(Photo by Brendan Beirne.)

CHARACTERISTICS   In interpersonal communication the receiver usually responds natu-
OF FEEDBACK   rally, directly, and immediately to the message and sender. We may flutter
our eyelids or raise an eyebrow, ask for explanation or repetition, or even
argue a point. In this way a message is shaped and reshaped by the participants until the meaning becomes clear. The sender and receiver interact and constantly exchange roles.

Many responses to mass communication resemble those in interpersonal communication. An audience member may respond by frowning,
yawning, coughing, swearing, throwing down a magazine, kicking a TV
set, or talking back. None of these responses is observable to the mass
communicator, however, and they are all ineffective responses unless they
lead to further action—writing a letter, making a phone call, canceling a
subscription, or turning off the TV set.

Because of the distance in time and space between communicator and
audience in the mass communication process, feedback in mass communication assumes different characteristics from interpersonal feedback.
Instead of being individual, direct, immediate, one-time, and personal,
mass communication feedback is representative, indirect, delayed, cumulative, quantitative, institutionalized and costly.

Despite what seem to be complicating obstacles—obstacles not worth
the effort in overcoming—feedback for mass communicators is extremely
important. All of us want our communication to be efficient; that is, we
want to achieve the goals of our communication with as little effort as

An unusual example of "talking back to the TV set" occurs as a young woman prepares to throw a brick at the screen when Howard Cosell appeared on "Monday Night Football."

(AP/World Wide Photo)

possible. Mass communicators are similarly concerned. Communicating by mass media involves enormous expense that has to be justified to executives and stockholders. The communicator must bring a return on the investment, must demonstrate that his or her communication is efficient; and feedback is necessary to provide the proof.

For example, A. C. Nielsen Company's 1984 estimate of U.S. television households was 83.8 million, up 0.6% from 1983 and the smallest year-to-year increase in recent memory. Nielsen's persons-per-household estimates have also gone up from 2.62 to 2.63 per home. Both of these measurements sound minuscule and insignificant but the important age demographics of 18–49 and 25–54 will be up about 2%, and it is this type of exactness that media communicators need. Each national rating point in 1984 was worth 838,000 homes, 5000 more than before.

Therefore, feedback in mass communication is not simply desirable, it is required. Because it is required, the mass media have gone to elaborate lengths to ensure that it is received on a regular basis. Let us look in more detail at the characteristics of mass communication feedback.

Representative Feedback

The audiences of mass media are so large that it is impossible to measure feedback from each member. Instead, a representative sample of the audience is selected for measurement, and the response of this sample is projected scientifically to the whole. A letter to the editor or a change of channels may be noted by the mass communicator, but these responses have little significance unless they can be shown to be statistically representative of the feelings and actions of a large portion of that medium's total audience. In measuring the feedback of mass media audiences, the specific responses of every individual are replaced by a representative sampling of the total population.

Sampling is perhaps the least understood and most controversial aspect of mass communication survey research. Sampling is a statistically valid technique in which a portion of the population is used in order to arrive at answers about the entire population. In determining the size of the sample, the idea is to use as few units as possible and still maintain reasonable accuracy. What makes for "reasonable accuracy" varies, but the standard rule of thumb in media audience research is that samples of less than 100 are often unreliable and samples of more than 1000 are seldom needed. A. C. Nielsen, for example, uses a national sample of about 1700 households to determine national TV ratings. It may be difficult to accept that 1700 homes can represent all the TV homes in the United States, but sampling technique is a proven method that has stood the test of time.

A. C. Nielsen, like most research companies, takes great care to create a national sample that is representative of the whole population. They use a sample drawn from U.S. census maps by a method known as *multistage area probability sampling*. Basically, the method guarantees that the number of sample members from each geographic area is proportionate to the total population of the area. For its individual-market ratings, Nielsen uses special, current telephone directories.

As developments in media technology expand, however, especially in television, questions are being raised about traditional sampling methods. Special attention has been focused on the A. C. Nielsen national TV ratings because of their effect on the TV industry. The Nielsen sampling process involves a small, randomly dispersed sample with no weighting made to correct for sample imbalances. The process works when the viewer has the option of choosing among 5 or so programs, but it is overly taxed when the viewer has the option of viewing any of 30, 40, or even 100 channel opportunities. With the advancement of cable and satellite technology, which promises to bring 100 channels and more into the cable-TV household, a much closer look must be given to the sampling process that affects Nielsen's audience measurements.

In the past, when TV viewing was confined to broadcast, most of it network, a distortion in Nielsen's sample was not critical, for all viewing was restricted to the same programming regardless of household characteristics. Today's TV usage can include either network or nonnetwork broadcasting, cable, or a new electronic mode like video cassette or videodisc playback, TV game display, or two-way communication functions. The need to discern accurately from among these opportunities grows in importance as costs continue to escalate. Any inconsistencies in the composition of the Nielsen sample may well distort audience selection and levels. Sensitive to such criticism, Nielsen uses diaries to supply demographic information. For example, the Nielsen figures include tune-in estimates for each network television program by 17 different age and sex categories. Cable viewership is now measured in its national sample for areas in which the cable network is available in 15% of all TV homes.

Indirect Feedback

Rarely does a performer on television or a reporter for a newspaper receive any direct response from audience members. Rather, the feedback comes through a third party: a rating organization or a polling company. Even when a performer or reporter receives a telephone call from a listener or a letter from a reader, the response seldom offers much opportunity

34 PROGRAM AUDIENCE ESTIMATES (Alphabetic)   2ND JAN. 1984 REPORT

AUDIENCE COMPOSITION — VIEWERS PER 1000 VIEWING HOUSEHOLDS BY SPECIFIED CATEGORIES

PROGRAM NAME (WK#/DAY/START/DUR/NET/TYPE)	T/C SEASON / PROG POS	STATIONS WK1 WK2	KEY	AVG AUD %	AVG SHARE %	AVG AUD (0,000)	TOTAL PERSONS (2+)	LADY OF HOUSE	WORK ING WOM	WOMEN TOTAL	18-34	18-49	25-54	35-64	55+	MEN TOTAL	18-34	18-49	25-54	35-64	55+	TEENS TOTAL	TEENS FEM	CHILD TOTAL	CHILD 6-11
WEEKDAY DAYTIME CONT'D																									
NEWSBREAK-3.57 M-F 3.57P 2 CBS N	75	188 187 / 94 94	A	7.3	19	612	1297 798 148			869	208	390	345	369	448	210	59^	93	77^	83^	111	119	102	99	62^
			B	6.5	19	545	1329 825 154			921	251	439	384	404	436	187	61	86	61	78	94	135	92	86	43
ONE LIFE TO LIVE M-F 2.00P 60 ABC DD	79	202 203 / 99 99	A	9.2	28	771	1227 759 232			854	429	582	456	322	214	244	109	168	120	106	55^	63^	57^	66^	13v
			B	8.3	27	696	1314 793 243			908	458	653	511	344	203	228	117	163	112	80	54	104	75	74	23
2.00 - 2.30			A	9.1	28	763	1227 756 237			852	432	586	462	325	204	256	116	178	136	114	53^	61^	56^	58^	8v
2.30 - 3.00			A	9.3	29	779	1211 758 225			853	427	578	451	318	218	225	99	155	103	96	52^	63^	55^	70^	14v
PEOPLE TO PEOPLE-M-F(S) 1 M-F 11.00A 30 ABC U		184 / 88	A	2.8	11	235	1383 804 123^			902	430^	574	433^	408^	213^	361^	72v	107v	60v	90v	254v	51v	21v	69v	47v
PRESS YOUR LUCK M-F 10.30A 30 CBS QP	80	161 161 / 83 83	A	6.0	23	503	1223 562 125			696	205	316	249	254	356	333	111^	178	152	129	143	43^	32^	151	66^
			B	4.6	20	385	1260 660 142			750	202	336	300	309	379	315	110	173	138	107	136	59	35	136	51
PRICE IS RIGHT 1 M-F 11.00A 30 CBS AP	77	204 202 / 99 99	A	8.8	32	737	1288 610 137			716	217	331	265	270	368	365	110	168	148	124	174	44^	26^	163	42^
			B	7.2	30	603	1306 668 116			756	224	351	306	288	373	366	113	170	142	125	179	54	32	130	44
PRICE IS RIGHT 2 M-F 11.30A 30 CBS AP	77	204 202 / 99 99	A	11.6	41	972	1254 640 138			740	213	335	281	293	380	337	95	153	136	130	165	37^	22^	140	35^
			B	9.5	38	796	1314 679 117			764	228	353	309	297	375	369	113	172	138	132	181	55	31	126	42
RYAN'S HOPE M-F 12.30P 30 ABC DD	80	177 177 / 94 94	A	5.7	18	478	1207 647 226			754	374	488	391	260	194	276	94^	185	163	142	70^	52^	38^	125	27v
			B	5.0	18	419	1269 743 220			846	436	596	461	288	198	229	100	153	112	86	68	85	58	109	24
SALE OF THE CENTURY M-F 10.30A 30 NBC QG	74	159 157 / 88 88	A	5.1	19	427	1527 774 100^			801	198	412	365	354	375	431	131^	194	201	150	222	70^	33^	225	65^
			B	4.6	19	385	1437 737 113			804	225	395	327	331	375	367	110	177	155	145	171	90	57	176	64

This sample page from the National Nielsen Television Report illustrates the complex quality and quantity of institutionalized feedback. (Courtesy the A.C. Nielsen Company.)

for direct interaction or substantially changes specific media content unless that response is felt to be representative of a large part of the audience. Because mass communication feedback is filtered through a third party, such as a rating organization, there is less variety in form and type of feedback. As we discuss later, one form—quantitative feedback—dominates. In effect, a rating organization such as Arbitron or Simmons acts as a gatekeeper in reverse, altering, modifying, or even preventing feedback from reaching the communicator.

Delayed Feedback　　　Mass media feedback is also delayed in time from the moment of original transmission. There are overnight TV ratings, but most network ratings are published weekly. Local-TV reports are published three to eight times a year, depending on the size of the market. Letters to the editor must go through the mail and face even further delay because of periodical publishing deadlines. The following letter to the editor, which contains feedback that significantly alters the original communication, appeared in *Business Week* 6 weeks after the original article.

> The statement in "Magic Chef's new recipe calls for upscale appliances" (Product Development, June 20) that Magic Chef replaced "heavy, expensive, die-cast aluminum doors with plastic doors" on its microwave oven line to cut more than 20 lb. from the weight and pare the price tag by at least $200 is both untrue and unfair.
>
> The large weight savings looks questionable, but the cost saving is unbelievably high.
>
> LARRY BUCHTMANN
Sunnymead, Calif.

The article should have stated that changes in design and production in addition to the door contributed to the weight saving and that the price reduction stemmed in part from a more competitive pricing strategy by Magic Chef.

Surveys and polls take time to conduct and study. The reaction of the communicator to feedback from the audience is also delayed by the particular technological and industrial characteristics of a medium. For example, once a motion picture is "in the can" it can be modified in only minor ways after audience reaction to preview screenings.

Michael Cimino's film *Heaven's Gate,* for example, was scheduled to be released late in 1980. Preview screenings resulted in such universally negative feedback that the $33 million film was not released. Here was the ultimate consequence of delayed mass communication feedback: the potential loss of a huge amount of money because the content was completed, at great cost, before significant audience reaction was received. In other instances, feedback from preview audiences can be used to modify content in positive ways. James Bridges used a preview of his film *Mike's Murder* which he describes as "disastrous" to make major changes. The preview forced Bridges to think twice about a particular sequence in which the title character is killed. According to an article in the *New York Times*, Bridges stated: "We had knives and a cut throat and blood spurting onto the wall." He decided to eliminate the sequence altogether and simply suggest the murder. While toning down the volume Bridges also decided to alter the film's musical score to include more dramatic and traditional music by John Barry.

Even in the daily newspaper, immediate modifications and corrections are played down and put on the back pages because they are not timely and newsworthy. Before the first episode of a new network TV series appears in the fall, 13 episodes of that series have usually been completed. Thus, because of the financial investment and contractual commitments involved, poor ratings (negative feedback) almost never spell the immediate termination of a new TV program; this occurs at the end of the first or fall quarter (the 13-week period from September to December).

Feedback to this book occurs primarily through published reviews and letters to the authors. Because the authors and publisher felt more feedback was required, however, you will find a form at the back of the book to fill out and return. Response to even this improved feedback is delayed until the next edition is published. The effect of delay, for this book or for other forms of mass communication, is the necessity of continuing inefficient communication beyond a natural stopping point. So, despite the mass communicator's great concern over efficiency, by the very nature of the feedback process, a great deal of inefficiency is built into the original message.

Cumulative Feedback

In mass communication, the immediate and individual response is infrequent and therefore not too important; emphasis is placed on the collective or cumulative responses over a substantial period of time. Since the response is delayed, there is seldom any change for immediate reaction, and so the communicator accumulates data over time from a variety of sources. The communicator stores the data, and this information influences future decisions, especially concerning what the public wants in the way of media content. The spinoff concept in TV programming is evidence of this. "The Mary Tyler Moore Show," for example, was very successful for several years. Its cumulative feedback and success was attributed to the various characters in the series including Mary's two female friends, Rhoda and Phyllis, and her boss, Lou Grant. Consequently, series were created around all these characters. The cumulative success of "Rich Man, Poor Man" stimulated the use of the anthology drama on prime-time television. Motion pictures such as *Indiana Jones and the Temple of Doom* (1984), *Star Trek III: The Search for Spock* (1984) and *Oh God You Devil* (1984) are the result of cumulative feedback on the original

Cumulative feedback on an original television series has resulted in an entire series of movies. Pictured here, Lieutenant Uhura (Nichele Nichols) wields a phaser in *Star Trek III*.

(Photo: Movie Star News, Courtesy Paramount Pictures.)

motion picture. The enormous success of *People Weekly* magazine spawned a large number of similar efforts (*Us, We, Self*). These print spinoffs were the result of favorable cumulative feedback received by *People Weekly* in the form of subscriptions and newsstand sales.

hour (the standard time unit of measurement) is so small, research organizations such as Arbitron compile cumulative audience figures known as *cumes*. For a radio station, cumes can represent many different listeners over different quarter hours or the same quarter hour over a number of weeks. Cume persons are identified as the estimated number of different persons who listened at home and away to a station for a minimum of 5 minutes within a given daypart. The table on the facing page illustrates how this feedback is broken down.

Quantitative Feedback

For the most part, mass communication feedback is sought and measured in quantitative terms. Examples include box-office figures for motion pictures, ratings for TV programs, sales figures for records and books, and circulation figures for newspapers and magazines. So critical are accurate

Average Quarter-Hour and Cume Listening Estimates

	Adults 25–49						Adults 25–54					
	Total Area		Metro survey area				Total Area		Metro survey area			
Station call letters	Avg. pers (00)	Cume pers (00)	Avg. pers (00)	Cume pers (00)	Avg. pers rtg.	Ave pers shr.	Avg. pers (00)	Cume pers (00)	Avg. pers (00)	Cume pers (00)	Avg. pers rtg.	Ave pers shr.
WABC	543	12608	476	10780	.9	4.7	595	14031	524	11975	.6	4.5
WADO	322	2467	322	2467	.6	3.2	398	2872	398	2872	.5	3.4
*WALK	1	64	1	64			3	140	3	140		
WALK FM	32	555	32	555	.1	.3	37	805	37	781	.1	.3
TOTAL	33	590	33	590	.1	.3	40	840	40	516	.1	.3
WBAB	39	480	39	480	.1	.4	39	480	39	480	.1	.3
WBLI	152	1775	151	1713	.3	1.5	157	1613	156	1751	.2	1.3
WBLS	648	7561	639	7448	1.2	6.4	672	7862	663	7749	1.0	5.7
WCBS	403	9270	342	7777	.6	3.4	517	11754	438	9891	.7	3.7
WCBS FM	668	10012	644	9535	1.2	6.4	685	10452	660	9927	1.0	5.6
WCTC	26	439	26	439		.3	33	597	33	597	.1	.3
WCTO	49	660	49	660	.1	.5	55	785	55	785	.1	.5
WEVD	36	583	36	583	.1	.4	40	899	40	599	.1	.3
*WHLI	52	614	52	614	.1	.5	78	1077	78	1077	.1	.7
WHM	353	6436	322	5885	.6	3.2	474	7593	439	6878	.7	3.7
WHUD	99	1118	53	634	.1	.5	143	1577	71	784	.1	.6
WINS	371	9342	368	9271	.7	3.7	472	11637	469	11566	.7	4.0
WJIT	242	2111	242	2111	.4	2.4	300	2263	300	2283	.5	2.6
WKHK	317	3852	286	3540	.5	2.8	346	4309	315	3955	.5	2.7
WKTU	779	9422	778	9360	1.4	7.7	786	9702	785	9540	1.2	6.7
*WLIB	79	1005	79	1005	.1	.8	87	1122	87	1122	.1	.7
WLIR	58	942	58	928	.1	.5	58	968	58	954	.1	.5
WMCA	161	2497	156	2384	.3	1.6	255	3533	250	3420	.4	2.1

reliable numbers that since 1914, the print media have used the services of the Audit Bureau of Circulation, which impartially audits and reports on the paid circulation of newspapers and magazines. Mass media critics provide qualitative judgments via book, photograph, movie, and TV reviews. But the mass communicator is more interested in knowing how many people responded rather than how one person (e.g., a critic) responded, unless the critic's view can affect or represent a number of people. The review of a book, record, or movie, particularly the review by a well-known critic in a big city who writes for a large circulation newspaper or magazine, can seriously affect purchases or attendance; but in television the review of a particular program has little impact because it usually takes place after the telecast. Little or no consistent critical evaluation of newspapers, magazines, or radio is available to audiences. Numbers are what count in mass communication. As the A. C. Nielsen Company states in one of its promotional brochures, "[t]hese are quantitative measurements. The word rating is a misnomer because it implies a measurement of program quality—and this we never do. Never!"

This fact creates some problems. When you consistently measure the success or efficiency of your message in terms of *how many* responses rather than *what kind* of response, you are severely limiting your ability to judge the quality of your message. A TV program may have a large audience at 9:00 P.M. on Tuesdays, not because it is a good program, but because the competition is weak. Placed in another time slot or on another day, the same program may fail. In network television, for example, Saturday night is known as "the graveyard" because fewer people watch television this night than on any other night.

Communication research firms today are sensitive to this criticism and are increasingly analyzing the why and who as well as the what of media audiences. A. C. Nielsen supplements its audimeter figures with diary responses; and more and more communicators are utilizing interviews and detailed questions to go beyond a simple quantitative measure of response. The Arbitron Ratings Company specializes in radio ratings using the diary method. By such means, a radio station manager can determine where the audience lives, how long they listen, when they listen, their age and sex, where they listen, and when they switch stations.

The quality of quantitative feedback varies with the questions being asked. In terms of *how many people are exposed*, media research data are excellent within the limits of statistical error. As to *who the audience is*, the feedback is also superior within these statistical limits. In terms of *how messages are perceived*, and *the effects of this perception*, reliable feedback is extremely limited, however.

Institutional Feedback

Mass communication feedback is institutionalized. That is, large and complex organizations are required to accomplish meaningful feedback to mass communication. Research organizations such as the A. C. Nielsen Company, the American Research Bureau (ARB), and Pulse, Inc. provide quantitative feedback data for broadcasting in the form of ratings. Companies such as Simmons and Politz survey print media audiences. Standard Rate and Data Service provides information on newspaper costs and circulation. Market research and public opinion survey groups, such as Gallup, Harris, and Roper, go directly to the public to find out what messages have come through and what changes have resulted in levels of information, attitudes, and actions.

Most media institutions not only purchase the raw data but also seek an analysis of the information by the research institution. In fact, little feedback is developed or interpreted directly by the majority of mass communicators.

This "third party" function regarding the indirect nature of mass communication feedback further complicates the issue. Because an organization is collecting responses and then communicating them to the sender, a gatekeeping function sets in with all its potential concerns and problems. The broadcast industry recognized the potential problems and established the Broadcast Ratings Council. The council functions as an accrediting agency and checks on such areas as sample design, fieldwork, and type of reporting. In essence, mass communication feedback is mass communication in reverse, with many of the characteristics of conglomerate communicators, gatekeepers, regulators, and so forth.

Finally, mass communication feedback is expensive. The expense is the result of most of the other characteristics. Measuring a national audience for a long time and with precise sampling methods is costly. The institutions and organizations that provide this service are in business to make money, and as a result, feedback in mass communication is expensive. Arbitron, for example, prices its service according to a broadcast station's commercial rates; these fees range from $2633 a year for small stations to $85,000 a year for large stations with the average for all stations approximately $17,000. Because of the costs involved, elaborate or qualitative feedback is not common in mass media. Sales figures, TV sets in use, average listeners per quarter hour, and circulation statistics are relatively gross measures of feedback. Rarely do media communicators know audience attitudes or ideas, even though this information may be important. Cost is a mass communication feedback characteristic that, in the final analysis, limits feedback and prevents the media communicator from knowing as much as he or she wants and needs to be efficient and effective.

Costly Feedback

It should be obvious by now that feedback is essential for communicators using mass media. Whether the originator of the message is an advertiser, a public relations official, a politician, or an entertainer, all need to ask questions concerning responses to their message. Examples of the information required by mass communicators include radio–TV set counts, audience size, audience characteristics or demographics, buying habits, product use, station image, and public opinion.

TECHNIQUES OF OBTAINING FEEDBACK

The answers to these questions are obtained through research, using scientific methods developed by sociologists, psychologists, and survey researchers. As noted, correct sampling procedures are a critical aspect of such research. Although there are many ways to conduct mass communication research, four techniques are common to most research organizations:

1. The *personal interview* is used in media research because it can provide lengthy, detailed responses that involve personal interaction of the respondent and interviewer. It offers the greatest flexibility in questioning methods. The drawbacks of this method are that it is time-consuming, relatively expensive, and often depends on recall rather than the immediate responses of audience members. As a result of these and other drawbacks personal door-to-door surveys have declined in recent years.

Pulse, Inc. uses in-person interviews for local radio broadcast ratings reports.

2. The *telephone coincidental* is a method that provides immediate feedback as to what an individual is doing at the time of the phone call. It is fast, simple, and relatively inexpensive. Extremely lengthy and detailed answers are difficult to obtain, however, and because of the prevalent use of the telephone as a sales tool, many people called in such surveys are suspicious and refuse to cooperate. Therefore, coincidental telephone surveys normally require large samples. This method also automatically limits the sample to people with phones, to those who have not moved recently, and to those at home, or not using the phone when called. Despite these drawbacks, however, the telephone coincidental method provides the most accurate information on TV-audience size.

Telephone recall is another method of collecting audience data, primarily TV sets in use or program viewing. It is less reliable than the telephone coincidental because it relies on respondent memory, although advances in polling techniques in recent years have improved the results.

3. The *diary* method, whereby respondents keep a log of their own or their family use of media, has the advantage of providing a continuous record over a substantial period of time (usually a week). Detailed information regarding viewer habits and consumer behavior also can be obtained. Major disadvantages are failure to maintain the diary, thus depending on recall to fill in data, and forgetting to return the diary. Arbitron, the major rating service that uses diaries, reported that in 1980 only slightly over 40% of the sample homes returned usable diaries. In 1981 and 1982, however, only 13.2% of the radio diaries and 13.4% of the TV diaries were unusable. The diary method is also more expensive than the telephone technique although not as expensive as the personal interview. In addition, the diary has room for only 22 different channels, not enough to accommodate viewers in heavily cabled cities. Diary keepers are supposed to keep a quarter-hour record of what programs all family members and visitors have watched for 5 minutes or more during a week. The diaries also have a space to record the names, ages, and sex of family members. The incentive for cooperating is normally 50¢ but can run to $2 for hard-to-reach categories. Arbitron uses its diaries for local market ratings only.

4. The *mechanical device*, such as the audimeter used by the A. C. Nielsen Company, records the minute-by-minute use of the TV set. But the audimeter only supplies information as to whether the set is on and the station to which it is tuned. No data are provided as to who the viewers are or even how many viewers are watching. Also, because of the expense of setting up a sample home with a meter, the sample, especially in the A. C. Nielsen surveys, is relatively permanent. Each meter remains in place for 5 years. Arbitron is also beginning to develop a metered rating

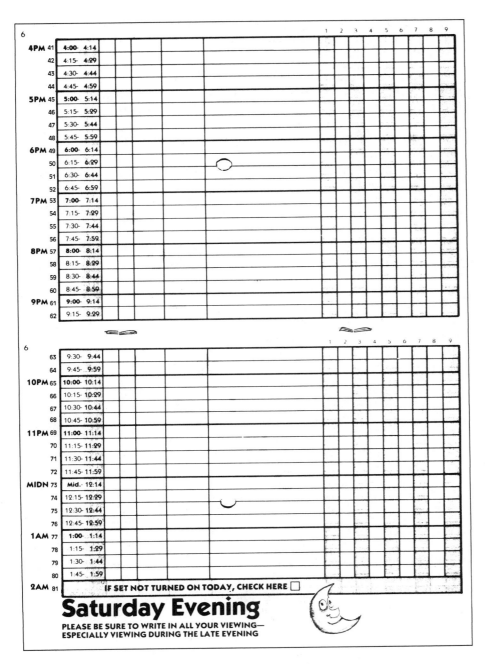

When completed, this page from an Arbitron diary can provide detailed feedback on TV viewer habits, however, the low response rate of participating viewers results in very small samples. (Courtesy the Arbitron Company.)

system in major cities. People who allow Arbitron to install the meters are given free TV repairs, reimbursement for the electricity used, and a $10 thank-you check.

Another technique used by a number of mass communication organizations is the so-called preview theater. Here a random sample of people are shown various TV programs, advertisements, or both in a theater and respond to the messages by pushing buttons or turning dials signaling like–dislike feelings. The American Research Institute of Los Angeles uses this technique. It is gaining in popularity because it provides data that show how people react at different stages of the message, not simply at the end. Of course, the motion-picture "sneak preview" has existed for almost 50 years. Today, however, it is used in increasingly sophisticated ways that involve detailed audience questionnaires and follow-up interviews with selected viewers.

The ways in which these research methods have been used tend to fall into general patterns. The diary and the mechanical device are used almost exclusively in providing feedback for the broadcast media. The personal interview and telephone coincidental serve as essential methods in public opinion surveys. The telephone coincidental survey is also used as a fast method of obtaining broadcast-audience information, and the personal interview is used almost exclusively for print feedback.

INDIVIDUAL MEDIA FEEDBACK

The Motion-Picture and Sound-Recording Media

For both commercial films and records, record sales and box-office receipts are key determinants in the kinds of feature-length movies and singles or albums that will be produced in the future. For both films and records, critics have some impact, but the communicator usually focuses on ticket and record sales rather than reviews. The following figures are from *Variety* and *Billboard* magazine. These figures represent a major form of feedback for movie and record producers in that they reveal the number of people buying a particular product during a limited time.

In addition to gross ticket sales the charts reflect movement up and down the list, indicating a picture's or record's relative popularity from week to week and its performance against competition.

Although this feedback cannot alter the content of a completed film or recording, it can affect the booking and distribution of a film or record and can greatly influence the future production of films and records with similar themes. One has only to look at the top grossing films of the late 1970s and early 1980s to see the pattern of spinoff, reproduction, duplication, and sequel at work.

As the cost of producing and marketing a feature-length motion picture soars, few individuals or corporations are willing or able to risk huge sums of money on untried or unproven themes. As a result, sequels to successful movies like *Jaws*, *Star Wars*, and *Superman* are commonplace. The reissue

Wednesday, August 29, 1984   *VARIETY*   **PICTURE GROSSES**   9

50 Top-Grossing Films

(WEEK ENDING AUGUST 22)

Compiled by Standard Data Corp., N.Y.

TITLE	DISTR	THIS WEEK $	RANK	LAST WEEK $	RANK	CITIES	FIRST RUN	SHOW CASE	SCREENS	AVG. PER SCREEN	WEEKS ON CHART	TOTAL TO DATE $
TIGHTROPE	WB	3,398,900	1			16	4	249	253	13,434	1	3,398,900
PURPLE RAIN	WB	2,068,218	2	2,925,197	1	20	5	190	195	10,606	4	13,220,948
GHOSTBUSTERS	COL	2,061,218	3	2,423,812	3	20	7	245	252	8,179	11	52,030,113
RED DAWN	UA	1,955,304	4	2,429,000	2	20	5	251	256	7,637	2	4,493,171
THE WOMAN IN RED	ORI	1,431,700	5			16	4	191	195	7,342	1	1,431,700
REVENGE OF THE NERDS	FOX	1,398,607	6	1,595,263	4	18	12	150	162	8,633	5	5,483,078
THE KARATE KID	COL	1,103,064	7	1,253,281	7	20	9	148	157	7,025	9	17,024,881
DREAMSCAPE	FOX	1,003,100	8			16	4	122	126	7,961	1	1,003,100
SHEENA	COL	964,300	9			16	6	238	244	3,952	1	964,300
GREMLINS	WB	841,778	10	1,340,073	5	19	9	125	134	6,281	11	39,837,019
CLOAK AND DAGGER	U	698,376	11	1,271,100	6	19	6	171	177	3,945	2	1,938,250
INDIANA JONES-TEMPLE OF DOOM	PAR	641,769	12	835,042	8	19	5	90	95	6,755	13	49,106,622
THE PHILADELPHIA EXPERIMENT	NW	479,532	13	400,001	15	7	1	97	98	4,893	3	1,387,833
MEATBALLS PART II	TST	260,000	14	52,542	28	1		73	73	3,561	4	908,876
THE MUPPETS TAKE MANHATTAN	TST	255,807	15	579,994	11	12	5	95	100	2,558	6	7,136,247
BACHELOR PARTY	FOX	228,852	16	562,697	12	7	2	47	49	4,670	8	9,987,093
JUNGLE BOOK	BV	212,030	17	673,675	9	14	12	46	58	3,655	16	8,130,102
ADVENTURE OF BUCKAROO BANZAI	FOX	174,884	18	169,000	19	5	3	26	29	6,030	2	342,944
THE NEVERENDING STORY	WB	153,636	19	629,978	10	15	10	28	38	4,043	5	5,268,231
ANOTHER COUNTRY	ORC	114,318	20	96,500	24	8	7	2	9	12,702	10	730,228
UNDER THE VOLCANO	U	105,151	21	135,300	21	9	8	6	14	7,510	10	1,059,858
THE BOSTONIANS	ALM	105,000	22	79,000	26	2	1	2	3	35,000	3	298,129
GRANDVIEW USA	WB	91,223	23	541,415	13	7	2	21	23	3,966	3	1,548,997
BEST DEFENSE	PAR	90,566	24	220,650	18	4	2	38	40	2,264	5	5,898,757
THE LAST STARFIGHTER	U	81,041	25	330,058	16	9	4	17	21	3,859	6	5,747,742
REPO MAN	U	72,136	26	41,697	33	4	4		4	18,034	10	497,669
SAMS SON	IVS	71,100	27			4	1	18	19	3,742	1	71,100
METROPOLIS	CIM	68,600	28	45,000		4	4		4	17,150	1	112,142
LES COMPERES	EUR	58,971	29	61,283	27	8	8		8	7,371	21	1,137,933
JOY OF SEX	PAR	58,281	30	274,133	17	4	1	15	16	3,642	3	763,283
CAREFUL HE MIGHT HEAR YOU	FOX	53,500	31	84,500	25	5	4	2	6	8,916	10	555,693
THE 4TH MAN	SPF	50,122	32	45,183	30	5	4	2	6	8,353	8	443,226
TOP SECRET	PAR	48,000	33	530,000	14	1		10	10	4,800	9	5,453,709
THE GODS MUST BE CRAZY	TLC	43,120	34	25,553	37	2	2		2	21,560	6	201,768
ONE DEADLY SUMMER	UCL	36,455	35	25,500	39	3	3		3	12,151	4	191,352
ROMANCING THE STONE	FOX	33,997	36	138,000	20	4	3	8	11	3,090	21	19,068,813
PHAR LAP	FOX	33,000	37	46,445	29	2	2		2	16,500	6	350,378
FIRST NAME-CARMEN	SPF	32,600	38	37,000	35	1	1		1	32,600	3	110,416
GABRIELA	UAC	23,713	39	31,769	36	4	3	2	5	4,742	15	497,677
THE NATURAL	TST	20,150	40	125,700	22	4	3	3	6	3,358	15	13,956,276
THE ROPE	UCL	19,500	41	5,700		2	2		2	9,750	14	517,249
STAR TREK 3/SEARCH FOR SPOCK	PAR	17,820	42	111,521	23	3	2	2	4	4,455	12	20,104,489
BALLAD OF NARAYAMA	KNO	17,200	43	4,200		2	2		2	8,600	5	99,304
ERENDIRA	MMX	16,836	44	25,503	38	3	3		3	5,612	17	576,149
AFTER THE REHEARSAL	TPH	14,587	45	13,400	45	2	2		2	7,293	9	229,907
A QUESTION OF SILENCE	QRT	13,585	46	17,838	42	1	1		1	13,585	2	68,006
ANOTHER TIME ANOTHER PLACE	GWN	13,000	47	9,400	49	2	2		2	6,500	6	81,444
ENTRE NOUS	UAC	12,700	48	14,800	43	1	1		1	12,700	30	1,821,365
BEYOND REASONABLE DOUBT	SAT	12,000	49	8,500		1		2	2	6,000	1	70,627
SUGAR CANE ALLEY	ORC	11,800	50	18,428	41	2	2		2	5,900	19	581,303
ALL OTHERS		160,418		276,709			39		39	4,113		8,848,167,654
GRAND TOTAL		$20,931,565		$20,561,340		232		2732	2964	7,061		9,154,108,051

SURVEY FOR WEEK ENDING SEPTEMBER 8, 1984

Billboard HOT 100

SEPTEMBER 15, 1984, **BILLBOARD**

THIS WEEK	LAST WEEK	WKS. ON CHART	TITLE—Artist (Producer) Writer, Label & Number (Distributing Label)
1	1	18	WHAT'S LOVE GOT TO DO WITH IT—Tina Turner ● (Terry Britten) T. Britten, G. Lyle; Capitol 5354 — WEEKS AT #1: 3
2	2	13	MISSING YOU—John Waite (John Waite, David Thoener, Gary Geresh), J. Waite, C. Sanford, M. Leonard; EMI-America 8212
3	3	9	SHE BOP—Cyndi Lauper (Rich Chertoff), C. Lauper, S. Lunt, G. Corbett, R. Chertoff; Portrait 37-04516(Epic)
4	6	7	LET'S GO CRAZY—Prince And The Revolution (Prince and the Revolution), Prince and the Revolution; Warner Bros. 7-29216
5	5	13	STUCK ON YOU—Lionel Richie (Lionel Richie, James Anthony Carmichael), L. Richie; Motown 1746
6	7	9	IF THIS IS IT—Huey Lewis And The News (Huey Lewis And The News), J. Colla, H. Lewis; Chrysalis 4-42803
7	10	7	DRIVE—The Cars (Robert John "Mutt" Lange, Cars), R. Ocasek; Elektra 7-69706
8	8	12	THE WARRIOR—Scandal Featuring Patty Smyth (Mike Chapman), H. Knight, N. Gilder; Columbia 38-04424
9	4	14	GHOSTBUSTERS—Ray Parker, Jr. ● (Ray Parker, Jr.), R. Parker, Jr.; Arista 1-9212
10	13	14	THE GLAMOROUS LIFE—Sheila E. (Sheila E., Starr Company), Sheila E.; Warner Bros. 7-29285
11	9	17	SUNGLASSES AT NIGHT—Corey Hart (Jon Astley, Phil Chapman), C. Hart; EMI-America 8203
12	12	10	LIGHTS OUT—Peter Wolf (Michael Jonzun, Peter Wolf), P. Wolf, D. Covay; EMI-America 8208
13	18	9	CRUEL SUMMER—Bananarama (Tony Swain, Steve Jolley), T. Swain, S. Jolley, Bananarama; London 810127-7(PolyGram)
14	17	6	COVER ME—Bruce Springsteen (Bruce Springsteen, Jon Landau, Chuck Plotkin, Steve Van Zandt), B. Springsteen; Columbia 38-04561
15	20	9	DYNAMITE—Jermaine Jackson (Jermaine Jackson), A. Goldmark, B. Roberts; Arista 1-9190
16	15	11	ROCK ME TONITE—Billy Squier (Billy Squier, Jim Steinman), B. Squier; Capitol 5370
17	11	16	WHEN DOVES CRY—Prince ▲ (Prince), Prince; Warner Bros. 7-29286
18	26	5	I JUST CALLED TO SAY I LOVE YOU—Stevie Wonder (Stevie Wonder) S. Wonder; Motown 1745
19	21	10	WHEN YOU CLOSE YOUR EYES—Night Ranger (Pat Glasser), J. Blades, A. Fitzgerald, B. Gillis; Camel/MCA 52420
20	24	7	HARD HABIT TO BREAK—Chicago (David Foster), S. Kipner, J. Parker; Full Moon/Warner Bros. 7-29214
21	14	19	IF EVER YOU'RE IN MY ARMS AGAIN—Peabo Bryson (Michael Masser), M. Masser, T. Snow, C. Weil; Elektra 7-69728
22	25	5	TORTURE—Jacksons (Jackie Jackson) J. Jackson, K. Wakefield; Epic 34-04575
23	23	8	WE'RE NOT GONNA TAKE IT—Twisted Sister (Tom Werman, Julia's), D. Snider; Atlantic 7-89641
24	27	4	LUCKY STAR—Madonna (Reggie Lucas), Madonna; Sire 7-29177(Warner Bros.)
25	19	11	ALL OF YOU—Julio Iglesias & Diana Ross (Richard Perry, Ramon Arcusa), Tony Renis, Cynthia Weil, J. Iglesias; Columbia 38-04507
26	16	14	ROUND AND ROUND—Ratt (Beau Hill), DeMartini, Pearcy, Crosby; Atlantic 7-89693
27	22	20	I CAN DREAM ABOUT YOU—Dan Hartman (Jimmy Iovine, Dan Hartman), D. Hartman; MCA 52378
28	36	6	CARIBBEAN QUEEN (NO MORE LOVE ON THE RUN)—Billy Ocean (Keith Diamond), K. Diamond, B. Ocean; Jive/Arista 1-9199
29	31	7	THE LUCKY ONE—Laura Branigan (Jack White, Robbie Buchanan), B. Roberts; Atlantic 7-89636
30	33	6	THERE GOES MY BABY—Donna Summer (Michael Omartian), B. Nelson, L. Patterson, G. Treadwell; Geffen 7-29291(Warner Bros.)
31	34	8	GO INSANE—Lindsey Buckingham (Buckingham, Fordyce), L. Buckingham; Elektra 7-69714
32	39	5	ARE WE OURSELVES?—The Fixx (Rupert Hine) Curnin, West Oram, Woods, Greenall, Brown; MCA52444
33	37	7	I'M SO EXCITED—Pointer Sisters (Richard Perry), A. Pointer, J. Pointer, R. Pointer, T. Lawrence; Planet 13857(RCA)
34	38	8	ONLY WHEN YOU LEAVE—Spandau Ballet (Tony Swain, Steve Jolley, Spandau Ballet), G. Kemp; Chrysalis 4-42792
35	40	5	BOP 'TIL YOU DROP—Rick Springfield (Rick Springfield, Bill Drescher) R. Springfield; RCA 13861
36	41	4	SOME GUYS HAVE ALL THE LUCK—Rod Stewart (Michael Omartian), J. Fortgang; Warner Bros. 7-29215
37	43	5	ON THE DARK SIDE—John Cafferty and the Beaver Brown Band (Kenny Vance) J. Cafferty; Scotti Bros. 4-04594(Epic)
38	28	11	LEAVE A TENDER MOMENT ALONE—Billy Joel (Phil Ramone), B. Joel; Columbia 38-04514
39	44	4	FLESH FOR FANTASY—Billy Idol (Keith Forsey), Idol, Stevens; Chrysalis 4-42809
40	54	2	WHO WEARS THESE SHOES?—Elton John (Chris Thomas), E. John, B. Taupin; Geffen 7-29189
41	48	3	SWEPT AWAY—Diana Ross (Daryl Hall, Arthur Baker), D. Hall, S. Allen; RCA 13864
42	32	15	SAD SONGS (SAY SO MUCH)—Elton John (Chris Thomas), E. John, B. Taupin; Geffen 7-29292(Warner Bros.)
43	46	6	(WHAT) IN THE NAME OF LOVE—Naked Eyes (Arthur Baker), R. Fisher, P. Byrne; EMI-America 8219
44	29	9	RIGHT BY YOUR SIDE—Eurythmics (David A. Stewart), Lennox, Stewart; RCA 13695
45	49	4	STRUT—Sheena Easton (Greg Mathieson), C. Dore, J. Littman; EMI-America 8227
46	51	3	SHINE SHINE—Barry Gibb (Barry Gibb, Karl Richardson), B. Gibb, M. Gibb, G. Bitzer; MCA 52443
47	50	4	YOU TAKE ME UP—Thompson Twins (Alex Sadkin, Tom Bailey), T. Bailey, A. Currie, J. Leeway; Arista 1-9244
48	52	5	THE LAST TIME I MADE LOVE—Joyce Kennedy & Jeffrey Osborne (Jeffrey Osborne) B. Mann, C. Weil, J. Barry; A&M 2656
49	61	2	DESERT MOON—Dennis DeYoung (Dennis DeYoung), D. DeYoung; A&M 2666
50	42	17	DANCING IN THE DARK—Bruce Springsteen (Bruce Springsteen, Jon Landau, Chuck Plotkin, Steve Van Zandt), B. Springsteen; Columbia 38-04463
51	30	12	STATE OF SHOCK—Jacksons ● (Michael Jackson), M. Jackson, R. Hansen, M. Jagger; Epic 34-04503
52	35	12	SEXY GIRL—Glenn Frey (Barry Beckett, Glenn Frey, Allan Blazek), J. Tempchin, G. Frey; MCA 52413
53	45	7	WHAT THE BIG GIRLS DO—Van Stephenson (Richard Landis), V. Stephenson, J. Buckingham, S. Buckingham; MCA 52437
54	NEW ENTRY		BLUE JEAN—David Bowie (David Bowie, Derek Bramble, Hugh Padgham), D. Bowie; EMI-America 8231
55	47	10	17—Rick James (Rick James), R. James; Gordy 1730(Motown)
56	56	6	THE MORE YOU LIVE, THE MORE YOU LOVE—A Flock Of Seagulls (Steve Lovell), M. Score, A. Score, S. Maudsley, P. Reynolds; Jive/Arista 1-9220
57	67	3	A GIRL IN TROUBLE (IS A TEMPORARY THING)—Romeo Void (David Kahne), D. Iyall, P. Woods, P. Zincavage, D. Kahne; Columbia/415 38-04534
58	73	2	I FEEL FOR YOU—Chaka Khan (Arif Mardin), Prince; Warner Bros. 7-29195
59	80	2	WAKE ME UP BEFORE YOU GO-GO—Wham (George Michael), G. Michael; Columbia 38-04552
60	NEW ENTRY		WHAT ABOUT ME?—Kenny Rogers With Kim Carnes And James Ingram (Kenny Rogers, David Foster), K. Rogers, D. Foster, R. Marx; RCA 13899
61	63	6	STRANGER—Stephen Stills (Ron Albert, Howard Albert), S. Stills, C. Stills; Atlantic 7-89633
62	57	12	HIGH ON EMOTION—Chris DeBurgh (Rupert Hine), C. DeBurgh; A&M 2643
63	NEW ENTRY		BETTER BE GOOD TO ME—Tina Turner (Rupert Hine), Knight, Chinn, Chapman; Capitol 5387
64	65	6	JUST THE WAY YOU LIKE IT—The S.O.S. Band (J. Jam, T. Lewis), T. Lewis, J. Harris, III; Tabu 4-04523(Epic)
65	55	10	TWO SIDES OF LOVE—Sammy Hagar (Ted Templeman), S. Hagar; Geffen 7-29246(Warner Bros.)
66	66	8	STRAIGHT FROM THE HEART (INTO YOUR LIFE)—Coyote Sisters (David J. Holman, Roger Paglia), L. Kunkel, T. Berg; Morocco 1742(Motown)
67	74	3	ON THE WINGS OF A NIGHTINGALE—The Everly Brothers (Dave Edmunds), P. McCartney; Mercury 880213-7(PolyGram)
68	79	2	STRUNG OUT—Steve Perry (Steve Perry), S. Perry, C. Krampf, B. Steele; Columbia 38-04598
69	53	13	PANAMA—Van Halen (Ted Templeman), E. Van Halen, A. Van Halen, M. Anthony, D.L. Roth; Warner Bros. 7-29250
70	62	5	TURN AROUND—Neil Diamond (Denny Diante) N. Diamond, B. Bacharach, C. B. Sager; Columbia 38-04541
71	59	16	BREAKIN'...THERE'S NO STOPPING US—Ollie And Jerry (Ollie E. Brown), O.E. Brown, J. Knight; Polydor 821 708-7(PolyGram)
72	60	17	ALIBIS—Sergio Mendes (Sergio Mendes, Robbie Buchanan), T. Snow, T. Macauley; A&M 2639
73	77	3	IN THE NAME OF LOVE—Ralph MacDonald With Bill Withers (R. MacDonald, W. Eaton), R. MacDonald, W. Salter, B. Withers; Polydor 881221-7(PolyGram)
74	82	2	LAYIN' IT ON THE LINE—Jefferson Starship (Ron Nevison), C. Chaquico, M. Thomas; Grunt 13872(RCA)
75	58	17	INFATUATION—Rod Stewart (Michael Omartian), R. Stewart, D. Hitchings, R. Robinson; Warner Bros. 7-29256
76	68	12	SHE'S MINE—Steve Perry (Steve Perry, Bruce Botnick), S. Perry, R. Goodrum; Columbia 38-04496
77	64	5	SATISFY ME—Billy Satellite (Don Gehman) Chauncey, Byrom, Walker; Capitol 5356
78	75	21	JUMP (FOR MY LOVE)—Pointer Sisters (Richard Perry), M. Sharron-S. Mitchell, G. Skardina; Planet 13780(RCA)
79	78	15	HOLD ME—Teddy Pendergrass And Whitney Houston (Michael Masser), M. Masser, L. Creed; Asylum 7-69720(Elektra)
80	85	2	NEW GIRL NOW—Honeymoon Suite (Tom Treumuth), D. Grehan; Warner Bros. 7-29208
81	89	2	BODY ROCK—Maria Vidal (Phil Galdston, Sylvester Levay), S. Levay, J. Bettis; EMI-America 8233
82	NEW ENTRY		SUGAR DON'T BITE—Sam Harris (Steve Barri, Tony Peluso), B. Roberts, D. Weiss; Motown 1743
83	87	2	PRETTY MESS—Vanity (Bill Wolfer, Vanity), Vanity, B. Wolfer; Motown 1752
84	76	23	SELF CONTROL—Laura Branigan (Jack White, Robbie Buchanan), G. Bigazzi, R. Riefoli, S. Piccolo; Atlantic 7-89676
85	NEW ENTRY		I CAN'T HOLD BACK—Survivor (Ron Nevison), F. Sullivan, J. Peterik; Scotti Bros. 4-04603(Epic)
86	86	4	ANYWHERE WITH YOU—Rubber Rodeo (Hugh Jones), B. Holmes, P. Milliken; Mercury 880175-7(PolyGram)
87	72	18	LEGS—Z Z Top (Bill Ham), Gibbons, Hill, Beard; Warner Bros. 7-29272
88	70	11	MAMA, WEER ALL CRAZEE NOW—Quiet Riot (Spencer Proffer), N. Holder, J. Lea; Pasha 4-04505(Epic)
89	NEW ENTRY		YOU, ME AND HE—Mtume (J. Mtume), J. Mtume; Epic 34-04504
90	NEW ENTRY		BULLISH—Herb Alpert Tijuana Brass (Herb Alpert, John Barnes), J. Cameron; A&M 2655
91	88	28	BORDERLINE—Madonna (Reggie Lucas, John "Jellybean" Benitez), R. Lucas; Sire 7-29354(Warner Bros.)
92	81	20	EYES WITHOUT A FACE—Billy Idol (Keith Forsey), Idol, Stevens; Chrysalis 4-42786
93	69	11	MY, OH MY—Slade (John Punter), N. Holder, J. Lea; CBS Associated 4-04528(Epic)
94	NEW ENTRY		MIDNITE MANIAC—Krokus (Bruce Fairbairn), M. Storace, F. Von Arb; Arista 1-9248
95	83	19	ALMOST PARADISE...LOVE THEME FROM FOOTLOOSE—Mike Reno And Ann Wilson (Keith Olsen), E. Carmen, D. Pitchford; Columbia 38-04418
96	71	8	THE ONLY FLAME IN TOWN—Elvis Costello & The Attractions (Clive Langer, Alan Winstanley), E. Costello; Columbia 38-04502
97	90	14	TURN TO YOU—Go-Go's (Martin Rushent), Caffey, Wiedlin; I.R.S. 9928(A&M)
98	84	6	CAN'T WAIT ALL NIGHT—Juice Newton (Richard Landis), B. Adams, J. Vallance; RCA 13863
99	91	22	DANCE HALL DAYS—Wang Chung (Chris Hughes, Ross Cullum), Hues; Geffen 7-29310(Warner Bros.)
100	96	14	I'M FREE (HEAVEN HELPS THE MAN)—Kenny Loggins (David Foster, Kenny Loggins), K. Loggins, D. Pitchford; Columbia 38-04452

◯ Bullets are awarded to those products demonstrating the greatest airplay and sales gains this week (Prime Movers). ● Recording Industry Assn. of America seal for sales of 1,000,000 units (seal indicated by dot). ▲ Recording Industry Assn. of America seal for sales of 2,000,000 units (seal indicated by triangle).

Sheet music suppliers are confined to piano/vocal sheet music copies and do not purport to represent mixed publications distribution. ABP — April Blackwood Pub.; ALM — Almo Publications; B-M — Belwin Miss; B-3 — Big Three Pub.; BP — Bradley Pub.; CHA — Chappell Music; CLM — Cherry Lane Music Co.; CPI — Cimino Pub.; CPP — Columbia Pictures Pub.; CRIT/JG — Criteron/Joe Goldfeder; HAN — Hansen Pub.; HL — Hal Leonard; IMM — Ivan Mogull Music; MCA — MCA Music; PSP — Peer Southern Pub.; PLY — Plymouth Music; WBM — Warner Bros. Music.

HOT 100 A-Z

Record Sales Figures (for week ending September 8, 1984) from *Billboard*. (Copyright © 1984, Billboard Publications, Inc. Compiled by the Billboard Research Department and reprinted with permission.)

of successful films has also become a prominent feature of the past several years. Such movies as *Jaws, Blazing Saddles,* and *Close Encounters of the Third Kind,* among others, often bring as much revenue in reissue as in the original run.

Economic feedback is also critical to the careers of the talent employed in the film and recording media. Unless the efforts of a singer or director sell, that individual cannot remain in the business, no matter how accomplished he or she may be.

One other form of feedback important to both media is professional recognition of excellence symbolized by the giving of awards. The Oscars and Grammys are important forms of feedback to film and recording artists. These awards can and often do serve as recognition of a specific film or recording, or they can be used as rewards for exceptional careers. The most important effect of this feedback, however, is monetary. An award brings increased sales for a film or record and gives the performers additional leverage with future employers.

As Mike Melvoin of the National Academy of Recording Arts and Sciences says, "There's a measurable sales impact to a Grammy and even a nomination." In 1983 the group Toto collected several Grammys and as a result its album *Toto IV* returned to the top 10 list and stayed there for another 12 weeks. The 1984 sweep for Michael Jackson and *Thriller* boosted sales from 25 million to over 30 million. In motion pictures an already established hit benefits less from an Oscar win since the audience has already turned out for it. *Terms of Endearment,* 1984's big Oscar winner, attracted the infrequent moviegoer and a repeat audience but did not increase its total box office gross dramatically. On the other hand, *Annie Hall* earned an extra $10 million after it won the best picture award in 1977 and *Gandhi*'s best picture Oscar added over $16 million to the $38 million it had already taken in at U.S. box offices.

Broadcasting

For both radio and television, critics' feedback has little impact, and awards in the form of Emmys are often used by actors and other talent to criticize TV business decisions. As Richard Low, vice president of Young and Rubicam advertising agency says, ". . . we are buying because a program delivers an audience. The prestige of an Emmy may be a factor in deciding to buy time . . . but only slightly."

Feedback in the form of volume of radio or TV set sales as well as subscriptions to community-antenna television systems also has little direct effect on programming practices of stations or networks because it provides no information about specific content; it merely implies that the medium is popular.

In radio and television four forms of feedback are dominant. These are homes using television (HUT), rating, share, and cumulative audience (cume). HUTs are television-only feedback; cumes, as described earlier, are radio feedback.

Radio feedback has become increasingly sophisticated in recent years. Age and sex represent only a small portion of the information available to agencies and advertisers. Information based on income, marital status, family size, presence of children, occupation, employment status, home ownership, education, race, and geo-demography is available. Research companies such as Simmons define specific demographic groups and then repackage the information into "clusters"—socioeconomic profiles of prospective product users. As Ray Nordstrand, president of WFMT–FM in Chicago says: "After all, in most cases you're not interested in just the lowest cost-per-thousand bodies, you want prospects, people who are qualified to buy your product."

As the figure indicates, HUT measures the number of homes that are using television at a given time.

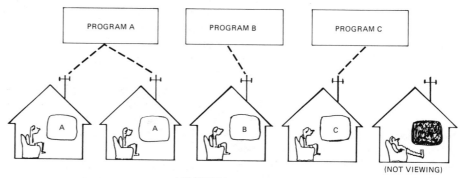

Homes Using TV (HUT). The percentage of homes using TV at a given time.

4 OF 5 HOMES USING TV = 80%

Ratings are a further refinement of broadcast feedback and are expressed as the percentage of individuals or homes exposed to a particular program.

The ratings most of us are familiar with are the national ratings compiled by the A. C. Nielsen Company. Actually, Nielsen compiles four different ratings, the most important being those involving network TV programs. The national TV ratings obtained by Nielsen are a percentage of the estimated number of U.S. households watching certain TV programs at a particular time. A program rating of 20 means that 20% of all U.S. homes equipped with TV sets are watching that program. In the mid-1980s there were about 83 million TV homes. Thus a rating of 20 meant that over 16 million homes were tuned to that program.

To calculate a rating you need two numbers: (a) the total population of homes with television; and (b) the number of TV homes watching a certain program. To obtain the rating for a particular program you divide the number of homes watching a certain program by the total number of homes with television.

Homes with television $= 80,000,000$

Homes tuned to Program A $= 30,000,000$

Rating for Program A $= \dfrac{30,000,000}{80,000,000} = 37.5\%$

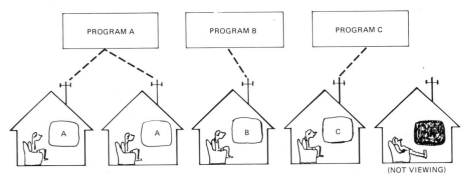

PROGRAM A RATING = 2 OF 5 HOMES = 40 RATING
PROGRAM B RATING = 1 OF 5 HOMES = 20 RATING
PROGRAM C RATING = 1 OF 5 HOMES = 20 RATING

Rating. The percentage of individuals exposed to a particular program.

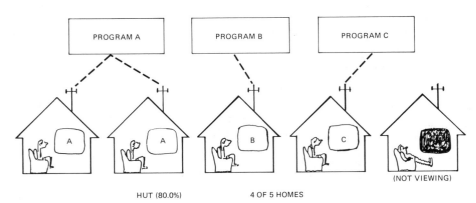

HUT (80.0%)   4 OF 5 HOMES

PROGRAM A - SHARE . . . . 2 OF 4 HOMES = 50
PROGRAM B - SHARE . . . . 1 OF 4 HOMES = 25   100%
PROGRAM C - SHARE . . . . 1 OF 4 HOMES = 25

Share. The percentage of HUT tuned to a particular program.

It should be reemphasized that these ratings usually represent households, not individuals, and that they are based only on homes with TV sets.

A share is an equally important measurement of the broadcast audience. A share is a measure of homes watching a TV program based on homes *watching* television at that time, whereas a rating measures homes watching a program based on all homes *with* television. The percentage of the TV audience accounted for by a share provides a more accurate measure of how a particular program did in competition with other programs broadcast at the same time.

$$\text{Homes using television} = 50,000,000$$
$$\text{Homes tuned to Program A} = 30,000,000$$
$$\text{Share for Program A} = \frac{30,000,000}{50,000,000} = 60\%$$

The Nielsen Television Index Reports also carry ratings for various audience groups based on age, sex, family size, location, income, and so forth. For example, if we consider women aged 18–49 (a primary target audience of a large number of advertisers), a rating is a percentage of that universe: women aged 18–49 who reside in a TV household. The table below provides feedback in the form of ratings—percentages for the syndicated program "To Tell the Truth" according to a specific kind of audience. The program was viewed, for example, in Providence by 32% of all TV households in the station's market area. The 43% share figure indicates the percentage of households watching television at that time who were tuned to "To Tell the Truth." The information is further broken down by estimating figures (in thousands) for people aged 18–49 and 18–34, and for two groups of housewives. This kind of information is obtained

Selected Market Ratings Analysis of "To Tell the Truth"

Market		Station	Rating	Share	Rating	Share	Homes	Total	18–49	18–34	Housewives Total	Under 50
			ADI		METRO							
Providence	(WED)	WJAR	32	43	38	51	215	218	61	34	183	51
Chattanooga	(THURS)	WDEF	25	36	29	48	60	51		11	47	20
Spokane	(MON)	KXLY	24	39			64	52	20	14	46	17
Memphis (6:30 CST)	(WED)	WREC	29	41	29	42	159	161	68	37	137	55
Albany	(FRI)	WTEN	23	36	27	42	97	93	43	25	79	37
Columbus, O.	(FRI)	WTVN			20	39	98	87	39		77	
Phoenix (6:30 CST)	(MON)	KOOL	23	43	24	45	93	85	24		80	
Indianapolis	(WED)	WISH	22	33	25	38	162	155			138	
St. Louis (6:30 CST)	(THURS)	KTVI	20	33	18	31	184	163	58		145	49
Fresno	(THURS)	KMJ	22	37	25	42	54	50	24		46	21
Roanoke	(MON)	WSLS	28	39	35	49	91	90	44	21	77	36

SOURCE: Arbitron Television Syndicate Program Analysis.

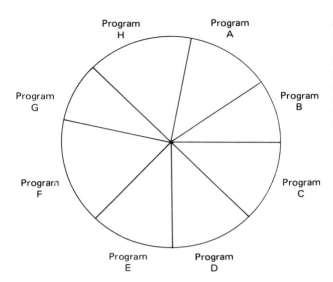

Program H   Program A

Program G

Program B

Program F

Program C

Program E   Program D

An "audience pie." A *share* is the number of homes that watch a program during a given time expressed as a percentage of all persons who watched television during that period.

by using diaries, because it deals with *viewers* rather than *sets*. In using this feedback, mass communicators place as much importance on the share as on the rating because a share indicates how many households watching TV tuned into a program, thus providing a more significant measure of head-to-head popularity.

The most specialized ratings are based on product usage, a practice initiated in the mid-1960s by the Brand Rating Index (BRI). Here, viewers are reported as percentages (ratings) of users of a product class. For example, a BRI rating of 20 indicates that 20% of the viewers are heavy users of a product class (e.g., gasoline, prepared cereal, beer). The rationale for this system is that the advertiser on TV is more interested in feedback that indicates results in terms of product use than in terms of audience characteristics and demographics. This feedback is obtained through personal interviews to get product information and diaries to get viewer information.

Ratings to obtain radio and TV feedback for local markets are also prepared by Statistical Research, Inc., Pulse, Inc., Trendex, and the American Research Bureau (ARB). Each organization uses a different method of obtaining feedback. Statistical Research, Inc. uses the telephone coincidental method for network radio research. Pulse, Inc. uses the personal interview aided recall method for local radio ratings. Trendex uses the telephone coincidental method for local TV and radio ratings. ARB uses the diary method for local radio and is also the major competitor of Nielsen in providing local TV feedback.

Local TV ratings for more than 200 markets are reported nationally from one to seven times a year depending on market size and demand; the most common time frame is four times a year. In addition, Arbitron and Nielsen provide continuous daily and weekly reports in four (ARB) and six (Nielsen) major cities. Arbitron also provides ratings to over 250 radio markets, usually twice a year.

Ultimately, HUTs, ratings, shares, and cumes lead to the most critical form of feedback for media: cost per thousand (CPM). This is the most widely used comparative tool for evaluating the efficiency of a particular medium. A CPM represents the advertiser's cost in reaching 1000 of its target population using a specific medium or combination of media. A CPM is calculated as follows:

$$\frac{\text{cost}}{\text{audience}/1000} = \text{CPM}$$

A CPM, then, is used to evaluate alternatives.

The main criticism leveled at ratings is the emphasis placed on them by networks, stations, and advertisers. Low ratings bump programs off the air because a program with a rating of 10 costs its sponsor twice as much for each home reached as does a program with a 20 rating. A television program stays on the air or is canceled almost exclusively according to how much it costs the sponsor of the program to reach 1000 people.

As long as we have a commercial system of broadcasting in the United States, ratings will play an important role in the medium. Broadcasters and advertisers must know what they are getting for their money in television and radio as in any other advertising medium.

Print Media   Feedback for books, newspapers, and magazines comes from critics, award committees, and sales. All three provide a good indication of a book's success. For newspapers and magazines, the most important feedback comes from subscription and sales figures on a regular basis. Most

We Use CPM to Evaluate Alternatives

	Cost: 30	Delivery (000)		CPM	
		Homes	Women	Homes	Women
Program A	$30,000	8,000	5,000	$3.75	$6.00
Program B	$40,000	12,000	10,000	$3.33	$4.00

	Cost Page 4-Color	Delivery (000)		CPM	
		Total Women	Women 25–54	Total Women	Women 25–54
Women's Day	$57,270	19,706	11,919	$2.91	$4.80
Good Housekeeping	$45,235	17,498	9,865	$2.59	$4.59

newspapers and magazines subscribe to the Audit Bureau of Circulation, which verifies their circulation figures. This information indicates *only* the newspaper's and magazine's paid circulation. Additional feedback on both media is provided by readership studies conducted by companies such as Politz and Simmons, but these studies are not made with the regularity of broadcast ratings. In terms of advertisers, considerably more feedback on a repetitive basis would be helpful.

The effect of telephone calls and letters from readers has in the past not had significant impact on the print media. This form of feedback has often been considered "crank mail," unless the print media are barraged by a huge quantity of mail over a period of time. Nevertheless, there is a growing sensitivity to reader opinion as reflected in letters to the editor. The media are so complex that the audience often feels powerless to change them. In spite of the competition in the media marketplace, subscription cancellation and even advertiser boycott of print media are often relatively ineffective forms of feedback.

Recording Media

Sales of records and tapes are primary forms of recording feedback. And because recorded music is so much the content of radio, play lists that indicate how often a record is played on a particular station also are important forms of feedback.

Most music-oriented radio stations have long participated in obtaining some recording feedback by monitoring best-selling albums and singles at local record stores. With prices up and sales down, however, stations can no longer rely on record sales to indicate music popularity. Also, statistics on record sales do not always pinpoint favorite songs or match listening patterns. Recently, more sophisticated research programs have been introduced, designed to profile and provide insight into the characteristics of the average listener. The new wave of research is concerned with the "passive" listener, the person who does not call the radio station's request line or buy many records but who listens to radio on a regular basis.

A new form of research known as *call-out* plays short musical excerpts over the phone and is virtually limitless in potential. Although many stations have adopted call-out strictly for tracking the appeal of individual songs and artists, other programmers have used it to explore their listeners' lifestyles—to find out where they eat, what they eat, how much they earn, how many concerts they attend, what kinds of cars they drive, what they think of a particular announcer, when they want news, etc.

Other forms of research include *auditorium testing*, in which a large group is asked to rate music or other program-related elements. Personal interviews are also frequently employed wherever possible, for example at shopping malls.

THE IMPACT OF   Given the reliance on institutionalized and largely quantitative feed-
FEEDBACK   back, it is no wonder the average viewer feels helpless in terms of having
an impact on specific programs or programming practices. Still, individual or group feedback can have an effect if it is directed at the right target.
Often this takes the form of going beyond the local communicator to other
agencies or groups, which in turn can exert pressure on the particular
medium.

Many dissatisfied audience members of radio and TV stations write to
the Federal Communications Commission rather than the specific station.
The FCC—under public pressure—then will provide the station with indirect feedback that might be more effective than that of the local audience. For example, WLBT-TV in Jackson, Mississippi, lost its license in
1969 because of indirect feedback on that station's policy in regard to
racial issues. Action by the FCC can also serve as feedback for other stations, indicating that certain actions are frowned upon. Television is not
the only medium where this kind of feedback is effective. The action by
the Motion Picture Producers Association in establishing a production
code and self-regulating agency was a result in part of public feedback to
Congress, which was then transmitted to the film industry. In addition,
public reaction to increased violence and nudity in film has been communicated to other media, the local newspapers, and national magazines,
which in turn transmit it to the film industry. In the early 1980s religious
groups used economic threat and boycott to pressure advertisers to drop
their sponsorship of programs containing what they thought was too much
violence and sex.

Public feedback over references to drugs in rock music lyrics led the
FCC to send a notice in 1971 to radio stations, reminding them that they
were responsible for putting this material on the air. The stations, in turn,
pressured the recording industry for changes in the music or printed lyrics
of all new releases so that they could be evaluated in the light of the FCC
policy statement.

There is some indication that the public feels its direct, negative feedback goes unheeded when sent directly to the media. Letters alone usually
cannot keep a TV series on the air or change the content of movies or the
lyrics of rock music. This is, in part, correct—a few letters are ineffective.
Nevertheless, a massive barrage of letters, telephone calls, or a boycott by
regular users of a medium can have some effect. Reform feedback in mass
communication must consist of extensive long-term pressure on the appropriate source in order to be successful in accomplishing major change.

Equally important to the consistent long-term frame of reference is the
organized group responding to a specific issue. In the past this has been
one of the more effective means of supplying a media communicator with
important feedback. In the early 1970s the TV series "Maude" was the
subject of organized group feedback as several church organizations opposed the showing of a two-episode program dealing with abortion. The

groups were concerned that the programs did not condemn abortion, and as a result of their pressure, over 30 network (CBS) affiliates refused to clear the episode. Similar actions by the National Rifle Association in 1975 resulted in a CBS documentary "The Guns of Autumn" being shown with only minimal sponsor support as advertisers refused to run spots in fear of the powerful NRA's threat of boycott of their products. Another example is the Reverend Jerry Falwell's threatnened boycott of sponsors of ABC's controversial drama "The Day After."

NOISE

All along the route of a message from communicator to audience and back, there are many possibilities for distraction, and this element of the communication process should not be minimized. This breakdown in mass communication is called interference, static, or noise. In person-to-person communication, these distractions occur in various ways: One person may look away, or another person may interrupt the flow of conversation. In mass communication the possibilities of interference are greatly multiplied. Noise or static can result from weak signals, clutter, competing messages, distractions in the environment, and audiences burdened by information overload.

Weak Signals

Weak signals, such as poor sound levels in radio, distorted pictures on television, or poor quality of paper and printing in newspapers, magazines, and books, can result in a message reaching an audience in distorted form or not at all. This type of technical noise is the most easily controlled since the sender has direct influence on the source of the noise.

Clutter

Clutter, such as the variety of sounds and images in broadcasting, the jumble of stories splashed on the newspaper page, or the profusion of books and magazines lined up on the newsstand rack, can cause so much competition for the mind of an audience that it turns off and receives no messages or receives so many different and conflicting messages that none make any impression. This is especially prevalent in commercial radio where a 5-minute segment can contain as many as seven or eight message units.

An example of clutter in books may be found in the copy of this text that you are now reading. If you bought a used copy at your college bookstore, you probably discovered that it was not a "clean" copy. One or more readers before you underlined, wrote in the margins, and in general created visual and cognitive noise for you as a reader. The following example illustrates how this clutter can create visual and cognitive confusion by creating emphasis and distraction instead of allowing the reader the opportunity to read the material "cleanly."

IMPORTANT FOR TEST [handwritten]

Feedback 201

sequently, series were created around all these characters. The enormous success of "Rich Man, Poor Man" stimulated the use of the anthology drama on prime-time television. Motion pictures such as *Jaws II* (1978), *The Empire Strikes Back* (1980) and *Superman II* (1981) are the result of cumulative feedback on the original motion picture. The enormous success of *People* magazine spawned a large number of similar efforts (*Us, We, Self*). These print spinoffs were the result of favorable cumulative feedback received by *People* in the form of subscriptions and newsstand sales.

ALSO note movie into TV spinoffs [handwritten]

Quantitative Feedback For the most part, mass communication feedback is sought and measured in quantitative terms. Examples include box-office figures for motion pictures, ratings for television programs, sales figures for records and books, and circulation figures for newspapers and magazines. So critical are accurate reliable numbers that since 1914, the print media have used the services of the Audit Bureau of Circulation, which impartially audits and reports on the paid circulation of newspapers and magazines. Mass media critics provide qualitative judgments via book, photograph, movie, and television reviews. But the mass communicator is more interested in knowing how many people responded rather than how one person (e.g., a critic) responded, unless the critic's view can affect a number of people. The review of a book, record, or movie, particularly the review by a well-known critic in a big city who writes for a large circulation newspaper or magazine, can seriously affect purchases or attendance; but in television the review of a particular program has little impact because it usually takes place after the telecast. Little or no consistent critical evaluation of newspapers, magazines, or radio is available to audiences. Numbers are what count in mass communication. As the A. C. Nielsen Company states in one of its promotional brochures, ". . . these are quantitative measurements. The word rating is a misnomer because it implies a measurement of program quality—and this we never do. Never!"

This fact creates some problems. When you consistently measure the success or efficiency of your message in terms of *how many* responses rather than *what kind* of response, you are severely limiting your ability to judge the quality of your message. A television program may have a large audience at 9:00 p.m. on Tuesdays, not because it is a good program, but because the competition is weak. Placed in another time slot or on another day, the same program may fail.

Communication research firms today are sensitive to this criticism and are increasingly analyzing the why and who as well as the what of media audiences. A. C. Nielsen, for example, supplements its audimeter figures with diary responses; and more and more communicators are utilizing interviews and detailed questions to go beyond a simple quantitative measure of response. The Arbitron Company specializes in radio ratings using the diary method. By such means, a radio station manager

[handwritten marginalia: JAWS 3-D and III / WAR GAMES / *movie* / print / New York Times review / Vincent Canby / PAULINE KAEL / how about Siskel and Ebert? / teacher used old example of Ben Casey don't know?]

Information Overload

Information overload also can interfere with the message. The audiences of mass media receive so much continuous information that the barrage often distracts from the meaning of the message. The difference between clutter and information overload is that information overload results primarily from the continuous barrage of messages. We are surrounded by mass media messages, and given the number of exposures bombarding the audience, it is remarkable that any messages come through.

It is important to distinguish between interference, or noise, and filters. Both elements have the ability to distort the sender's message. The key difference is the ability of senders to control noise, at least partially, and their inability to control filters. In other words, a sender can work to eliminate noise by reducing static, increasing power, or reducing the number of messages. Nevertheless, distortion can still occur because of audience filters. The sender has little or no control over filters.

AMPLIFICATION

Those messages that actually get through the maze of mass communication do so because they are amplified. Somewhere along the line a message gets amplified so that it stands out from the other facts and ideas clamoring for our attention. Amplification might be the result of front-page headlines, frequent reproduction of the same message in many media over a period of time, or the approval of a third party. The very fact that one message gets into the media, while others do not, serves to emphasize that message and deemphasize others. Gatekeepers play a critical role in this process, as the analysis in Chapter 7 demonstrated.

Strong signals can amplify the message. Bold, black type in a front-page headline can make one item stand out more loudly than another. Powerful radio transmission, color television, technicolor and stereophonic wide-screen movies, slick paper, and artful typography can add to the effectiveness of a message.

Repetition of the message over a period of time can also amplify it. A person whose name is mentioned in the headlines day after day becomes a household word, acquires status and prestige; people listen to that person more carefully than they would if they had never heard the name. Products, ideas, and events, too, can be amplified if they are repeated in the mass media.

Endorsement may be one of the most important elements in achieving amplification of a message. An attractive woman is often used to endorse an idea. A baseball hero, movie star, or popular politician can also amplify a message by veryifying it for the sender, or approving it. John Houseman is paid very well for his effectiveness in selling a financial service, as is Karl Malden for selling traveler's checks.

SUMMARY

Feedback is critical not only to the success of communication but ultimately defines the process of communication. Feedback in interpersonal communication is simple, direct and immediate. In mass communication feedback assumes different characteristics. As John Gehron, general manager of WLS-AM and FM in Chicago, so aptly characterized mass communication feedback: "Radio research used to be easy. I used to be able

"The quality of Smirnoff is classical.

Its value merits a standing ovation."

PINCHAS ZUKERMAN, world-renowned violinist.

"When I play, I strive for the highest quality in my performance.

"I look for the same standards in my vodka. I know that Smirnoff® vodka is distilled from the finest grain, and then checked 47 times for quality and smoothness. In short, it offers a virtuoso performance. You may pay a little more, but you'll find Smirnoff is worth more.

"When it comes to vodka, Smirnoff plays second fiddle to none."

Smirnoff
LEAVES YOU BREATHLESS®

There's vodka, and then there's Smirnoff.

Pinchas Zuckerman's personal endorsement of Smirnoff vodka combined with some clever copy serves to make this ad stand out thereby amplifying its message. (Copyright © 1983 by Ste. Pierre Smirnoff Fils. Reprinted by permission.)

to stand on a street corner with a traffic light on a hot summer day and, as the cars stopped with their windows rolled down, I could quickly tell what people were listening to on their radio. And then technology changed things. Air conditioning came along, windows rolled up and it was a quiet street corner." The efforts to roll down the windows of mass communication are a major and necessary part of the process of communication.

The Effects of Mass
Communication

13

As each mass medium emerged in the twentieth century, eu-
phoric proclamations announced that the new communication
tool would create a "brave new world." When the prediction did not
become reality, rumblings were heard that the same mass medium was a
menace to the public health and safety of the next generation. It is important to remember that the mass media are neither saviors nor the devil's
handmaidens. Yet the issues remain: How do the mass media influence
us? What are the effects of mass communication on individuals, groups,
and society?

In the 1930s we began to look for answers to these questions by using
empiricism. Empirical research into the impact of mass communication
uses techniques borrowed from the social sciences. If we compare communication research strategies with those used in the physical sciences,
it becomes obvious that inquiry into the attitudinal and behavioral impact
of the mass media is not now what we hope it will become. Remember,
systematic analysis in the field is barely 50 years old, and so our tools
are primitive. And communication has been dabbled in by researchers
trained in a variety of disciplines, generating conflicting results. These
results, in turn, have been misinterpreted and popularized by public interest groups for their own purposes. It often seems that much of our
research is continually trying to invent the wheel.

THE STATE OF THE ART Given the problems in studying the effects of mass communication, why do we persist? Why continue the discussion? Why look for the answers to questions that we have not fully framed?

Because it is important! Because we need to know!

Admittedly, media science is in its infancy. But we are beginning to gather the wherewithal to emerge as an independent social science. We are beginning to produce scholars who understand the mass media as well as research techniques.

What we think we know about the effects of mass communication has come from numerous field studies and laboratory experiments. Three basic methodologies have contributed to the current body of knowledge:

1. *Historical research* investigates past and current media events in order to make comparisons; recently, content analysis has broadened that endeavor.

2. *Survey research,* using representative, random, or stratified samples of audiences, has assessed media effectiveness in the diffused environment of the "real world" to determine who watches, listens, and reads what the media produce.

3. *Experimental research,* done in the controlled environment of the laboratory, has contributed much toward determining specific short-term changes in behavior and attitudes as they relate to mass media content.

As should be expected, differences in design, methodology, and manipulation of the data have produced some disagreement among researchers and practioners. We are not positive of the meaning of some of the results we have as to the effectiveness of mass communication in our society. Also, we are more confident in some research areas than in others.

Mass communication research is currently facing up to a serious deficiency: Most of what we have done is short term rather than longer term. This is the case because longitudinal studies are (*a*) *costly*, and funding is inconsistent; (*b*) *topical*, and data have been collected to prove a point; (*c*) *time-consuming*, and researchers in the academic setting are pressed to produce results that can be published quickly; (*d*) *difficult to sustain* when human subjects are required for a study of sensitive issues such as violence or erotica; (*e*) subject to *methodologies that change*, and some collected data cannot be compared with information gathered at an earlier date; (*f*) *evaluated by very powerful pressure groups* that dispute answers that conflict with their position on the issue, affect their economic base, or both.

Mass communication inquiry uses a battery of mathematical and statistical models, techniques, and tests to collect, evaluate, and validate data. We use partial and multiple correlations, parametric and nonparametric statistics, analysis of variance, and high-speed computers. In the laboratory we manipulate the *independent* variable as the *dependent* variable is held constant and *extraneous* variables are controlled. A variety of *treatments* are tested on *experimental groups* large enough to determine if the *probability level* is *significant* when we compare results with a *control group*.

Some of you are confused by this litany, but it illustrates why the remaining discussion of research findings does not include these details. From this point onward, we attempt to distill what is known in ways that the beginner can comprehend.[1]

TRADITIONAL CONCERNS OF MASS COMMUNICATION RESEARCH

It is a fact that the mass media affect the course of human development. It is a fact that a causal relationship exists between exposure to the mass media and human behavior, even if it is not always possible to establish absolute cause-and-effect relationships for every individual in every situation. There are many variables in complex combinations in all media experiences. In 1948 Bernard Berelson framed his famous and cogent reply to questions about the effects of communication: "Some kinds of *communication* of some kinds of *issues*, brought to the attention of some kinds of *people* under some kinds of *conditions*, have some kinds of *effects*."[2] This statement remains valid today. As to delineating these effects, Berelson, in conjunction with Morris Janowitz, commented:

> The effects of communication are many and diverse. They may be short-range or long-run. They may be manifest or latent. They may be strong or weak. They may derive from any number of aspects of the communication content. They may be considered as psychological or political or economic or sociological. They may operate upon opinions, values, information levels, skills, taste, or overt behavior.[3]

This quotation, too, remains an accurate summary of the overall state of our knowledge. But we are learning more details about the "some kinds" of communication.

---

[1] In doing so, a huge amount of information is condensed and interpreted, which always generates honest disagreement. But, at this time, for the anticipated readership of this book, we feel we have chosen the best course of action. Some research is neglected, some may seem to be misinterpreted, but we are attempting to clarify complex issues in a very short space. We apologize if we have not given sufficient attention to concepts, results, and studies that you feel are essential and welcome feedback regarding how to make this important body of information more accurate and understandable for the beginners it is designed to inform.

[2] Bernard Berelson, "Communications and Public Opinion," in *Mass Communication*, ed. Wilbur Schramm (Urbana: University of Illinois Press, 1949), 500.

[3] Bernard Berelson and Morris Janowitz, eds., *Reader in Public Opinion and Communication*, 2d. ed. (New York: Free Press, 1966), 379.

The effects of exposure to content in the mass media are seldom, if ever, simple, direct, or totally dependent on a specific experience. But media exposure is one of the important variables.

Research has focused primarily on the following:

1. Three general areas[4]
   a. The effects of mass communication on *cognition and comprehension*
   b. The effects of mass communication on *attitude and value change*
   c. The effects of mass communication on *behavioral change*, including both antisocial behavior (negative change) and prosocial behavior (positive change)
2. Three specific topics
   a. The effects of *violence* in the mass media on American society
   b. The effects of *erotica* in the mass media on American society
   c. The effects of the mass media on *children*

The issues of comprehension, attitude, and behavior change are summarized first. The specific topics of erotica, violence, and children are then examined in relation to historical and current research.

COGNITION AND COMPREHENSION

The communication process begins with gaining an audience's attention, then proceeds to generating awareness (cognition), and finally—optimally—results in comprehension. In mass communication, cognition is affected by the fact that the individual does not read all pages of the newspaper or listen to every minute of a newscast with equal attention. Audience members selectively expose themselves to media content; but by constant, repetitive exposure, the media can become highly effective on a wide variety of issues. Retention of information over a long time span is least probable when the individual has no personal interest in the information.

Comprehension (as with all media effects) is in large measure the result of the interaction of media content with the direct, personal experiences of audience members. A person's ability to recall a media event also depends on repeated exposure to the stimulus and some reinforcement via interpersonal relationships. For example, if an individual has a brother in a trouble spot in the Middle East, the very mention of that area will increase awareness on the individual's part because he *needs* that information and is gratified by it (needs and gratifications).

[4] Walter Weiss, "The Effects of the Mass Media of Communication," in *Handbook of Social Psychology*, 2d ed., ed. Gardner Lindzey and Eliot Aronson (Reading, Mass.: Addison-Wesley, 1968), 2:77–195. This section is a modification of Weiss's comparison of research in Chapter 38 of the *Handbook*. Weiss's summary is one of the best available to date and is a must for students interested in media effects. The *Handbook* remains an excellent source of historical data as well.

Although Americans have one of the best overall information systems in the world, considerable misunderstanding occurs because people misinterpret, fail to hear, or refuse to accept the facts. Evidence also suggests that audience members' predispositions on a given issue create subtle, unconscious misconceptions in spite of repeated exposure to messages that contradict these notions. In other words, comprehension on a given issue can be distorted by personal beliefs.

Wilbur Schramm points out that "the mass media can widen horizons. . . . They can let a man see and hear where he has never been and know people he has never met."[5] Obviously this is an important effect of mass media in developing societies in terms of *the diffusion of innovations,* but it is also relevant in any society caught up in rapid growth and change.

Mass media audiences may suffer from an information overload to the point where they are actually narcotized by communication. They react with apathy rather than action. So many voices are heard, so much static and interference are on the line, that audiences tend to block out everything; no message comes through loud enough and clear enough for them to participate and be involved in the action. When there is information overload, the media can turn off audiences as well as turn them on. At times, there is simply too much communication to handle.

In media research on attitudes, there is general agreement that the mass media have an effect on the values of a society and the attitudes of individuals. The extent, speed, and longevity of the effects remains in question.

ATTITUDE AND VALUE CHANGES

Most research evidence supports the hypothesis that mass media can create new opinions more easily than they can change existing ones but that reinforcement of existing beliefs is the main effect of most mass communication experiences. One reason for this reinforcement is the self-protective human process of selective exposure, selective perception, and selective retention. We tend to expose ourselves only to messages that agree with our existing opinions; we tend to avoid communication that is unsympathetic to our predispositions.

Psychologists have shown that when exposed to messages with which we disagree, we tend to perceive only those elements that fit our preconceptions. Finally, we tend to retain facts and ideas that agree with our existing opinions. Leon Festinger has studied this phenomenon and named it *cognitive dissonance.*[6] Basically, "dissonance" replaces the word *inconsistency* and "consonance" replaces *consistency.* Festinger's main hypothesis is that the psychologically uncomfortable existence of

[5] Wilbur Schramm, *Mass Media and National Development* (Stanford, Calif.: Stanford University Press, 1964), 127.

[6] Leon Festinger, *A Theory of Cognitive Dissonance* (Evanston, Ill.: Row, Peterson, 1957).

dissonance motivates a person to try to reduce it and achieve consonance. In addition to trying to reduce dissonance, the person actively avoids situations and information that would increase it. For example, a man who continues to smoke knowing that smoking is harmful tries to reduce the dissonance. He rationalizes that he enjoys smoking so much that it is worth the chances of ill health, or he rationalizes that if he stopped smoking he would put on weight, which could be equally bad for his health.

Not only do the mass media reinforce what we already believe, they also "enforce the normal attitudes and behavior patterns of society." Two sociologists, Paul F. Lazarsfeld and Robert K. Merton, have pointed out the effects of mass communication on organized societal values. "Publicity closes the gap between 'private attitudes' and public morality,'" they write.[7] The mass media expose deviations to public view, and this exposure usually forces some degree of public action against what had been privately tolerated.

Considerable research has also verified the "bandwagon effect"; people adopt opinions because they are, or seem to be, the opinions of a large number of other people. This social conformity is most commonly demonstrated in advertising, which frequently uses such phrases as "nine out of ten," "more people use," or "millions recommend." Studies also show that small, cohesive minority groups have an unusual amount of resistance to the bandwagon effect but that most people, lacking the support of a strong, active reference group, simply go along with the majority.

> The mass media bestow prestige and enhance the authority of individuals and groups by legitimizing their status. Recognition by the press or radio or magazines or newsreels testifies that one has arrived, that one is important enough to have been singled out from the large anonymous masses, that one's behavior and opinions are significant enough to require public notice.[8]

This prestige enhancement is known as *status conferral*, and the news media not only confer it on persons in the news but on those who report the news. News "stars" are considered to be very powerful in terms of generating attitudes about events as well as providing information about them. News may also be *dysfunctional* and cause an effect that was unintended.

According to some sociologists and psychologists, news, which is invariably about deviations and abnormalities in society, may actually create anxieties among readers, listeners, and viewers. This anxiety could result in *privatization*, where individuals feel overwhelmed by the news

---

[7] Paul F. Lazarsfeld and Robert K. Merton, "Mass Communication, Popular Taste and Organized Action," in *Mass Communication*, ed. Wilbur Schramm (Urbana, Ill.: University of Illinois Press, 1960), 499.

[8] Ibid., 498.

and react by turning inward to a private life over which they have more control. There is considerable support for the idea that heavy users of mass media develop negative attitudes about the world.

Many media users, in fact, turn to the mass media to be *turned off*. The escapist function is an important use of mass media and has many socially valuable results. We turn to soap operas and musicals in "living color" not just to get away from our problems but also to find emotional release, vicarious interaction, a common ground for social intercourse, and stimulation of our imagination, and mental and physical relaxation. All these, in turn, affect our attitudes and values in ways we do not yet completely understand.

BEHAVIORAL CHANGE

Research has investigated both antisocial (negative) and prosocial (positive) changes in individual behavior to determine what the media's influences are on specific kinds of behavior. Among the behaviors studied are voting, play patterns, and aggression.

As we allocate our discretionary or leisure time, the time allotted to the mass media is significant. Mass media dominate leisure-time activity in our society. New media usually generate high public interest if participation in them requires no skills (e.g., TV viewing, radio listening, and moviegoing). In effect, what happens is that mass communication experiences are so attractive and rewarding that the individual consciously gives up or modifies other activities in order to partake of them.

The mass media are often employed to stimulate interest in specific activities such as homemaking, sewing, or cooking. Most studies indicate that special-interest programs develop passive rather than active behavior on the part of the viewer. For example, audiences watch Julia Child; they enjoy her performance. But apparently few audience members ever try a specific recipe. They may go out and buy a cookbook, however, which they then use on occasion.

In regard to *family life patterns*, studies have investigated various aspects of home behavior. In general, the media studies—specifically of television—indicate that television has not had a marked effect on family lifestyles. At a superficial level, members of a family spend slightly more time together viewing television as a group until a second TV set is purchased.

In terms of *passivity*, the media do not make a person more passive unless the individual has a very strong predisposition to be so anyway. The specific fear that TV viewing negatively affects school work seems to be unfounded. In fact, TV viewing may actually contribute to a faster start for some children. The bedtime of children also has not been changed markedly by television.

Julia Child's entertaining and often humorous lessons in the art of French cooking, like other special interest programing, tend to develop passive rather than active behaviorial response on the part of her viewers.

("The French Chef," Copyright © WGBH Educational Foundation.)

Considerable research has been devoted to the effects of mass communication on *voting behavior*. The mass media seem to be relatively ineffective in converting a voter from one party affiliation to another. Few voters seem to be influenced by specific political commercials for a candidate they dislike. The critical role of the media apparently is to reinforce existing political attitudes and maintain party-member support.

As for adopting a *specific behavior*, it takes considerable time for this to occur and depends on several factors. Included in these factors are the

(Courtesy CBS Records)

Tie-dyed clothes and shoulder-length hair, once a symbol of radical politics and nonconformity, ultimately became popular fashion in the late 1960's. Here, contemporary punk rock group The Clash displays its sense of style.

number of people involved in the decision; the economic and social risk necessary; the future ramifications of the action; the extent of departure from current practices; and the compatibility of the new behavior with the personality, values, and motives of the individual. The same factors influence change in purchasing behavior, wearing clothes, using "miracle cleaning agents," joining protest marches, participating in common-law marriages, adopting children of minority percentage, and other behavioral modifications. The interaction of media exposure and other personal experiences becomes the critical force in behavioral change.

Since the 1930s, numerous studies have been reported, but unfortunately not enough of them have been replicated. In addition, articles have appeared in the popular press that misrepresent or misinterpret study results and stress sensational or unsubstantiated findings.[9] Over the past

HISTORICAL PERSPECTIVES

[9] A number of articles and books have gained wide public acceptance without acceptable evidence or corroboration. This is the case with *subliminal persuasion*, which suggests that messages below the threshold of awareness can persuade audiences to make consumer purchases. This is not based on fact, and there is no evidence to support this notion. Another fixation to muddy the water of mass media effects is the discovery of sex and death symbols in a limited number of print advertisements. These symbols can be discovered only after the closest scrutiny. "Pop scholarship" immediately assumed the existence of a plot that was somehow poisoning our minds. This premise was accepted in some quarters without the slightest shred of evidence. Such "scholarship" must stop. We have enough real problems in the area of mass communication research without creating straw men.

50 years a number of major works have appeared; several of them require a brief review.[10]

1. *The Payne Fund studies* from 1929 to 1932 evaluated the influence of motion pictures on children. These 13 studies, published in 10 volumes, focused on audience composition and content analyses of themes. Results suggested that movies can affect information acquisition, modify cultural attitudes, stimulate emotions, and disturb sleep. Results even suggested that some films can produce negative "morals" and behaviors in some children. This report reinforced existing public concern and led to an industry self-censorship system that lasted until the 1960s.

2. *The "Invasion from Mars" study* was hastily done after the Orson Welles radio broadcast "War of the Worlds," which occurred on 30 October 1938 and panicked an estimated 1 million listeners, who believed the drama to be real. The major findings were these: (a) The excellent quality of the production, designed around fictional news reports, contributed to the panic; (b) people who tuned in too late to hear disclaimers and who could not verify the broadcast's authenticity from another source were most likely to panic; (c) individuals with "weak" personalities, lower education levels, and strong religious beliefs were most susceptible to panic; (d) once frightened, people stopped listening altogether or would not believe that all was well despite other stations being on the air; and (e) political tension in Europe and a depressed economy at home created cultural conditions that contributed to the overall panic. In the aftermath of the broadcast, standards were mandated to prevent similar broadcasts. The power of radio was real.

3. *The "People's Choice" study* analyzed voting predispositions in the 1940 presidential elections. For the first time, the tools of the social scientist were used in a large-scale field study of communication. The study found that political propaganda activated voters to remain loyal to their political beliefs rather than change parties. Variables such as religion, socioeconomic status, age, occupation, and urban versus rural residence were identified as important. The study also suggested that media content moves through a "two-step flow" in which opinion leaders influence less active information seekers, and these interpersonal social contacts are more important than exposure to the media.

[10] Shearon Lowery and Melvin L. DeFleur, *Milestones in Mass Communication Research: Media Effects* (New York: Longman, 1983). The authors provide individual reviews of 11 major studies undertaken from the 1930s to the 1970s. This work is highly recommended as a comprehensive overview, even though it does not suggest that it is a complete study of many of the major works or that it selectively eliminates others.

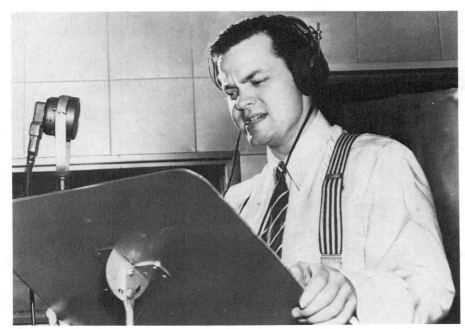

Orson Welles' top convincing radio performance in *The War of the Worlds* (1938) exposed the tremendous power of the medium by generating widespread panic.

(AP/Wide World Photos)

4. *The "Why We Fight" studies* brought filmmakers and social scientists together at the beginning of the Second World War to create, produce, and test informational and motivational training films. Results showed the effects to be a product of a variety of factors in addition to the films. Yet the films proved (*a*) to be effective in imparting information, although the information was clearly forgotten over time; (*b*) to have had *little* effect on opinions regarding the war; and (*c*) to have had *no* effect on recruits' motivation to serve their country. Results also demonstrated the value of one-sided presentations on less-well-educated soldiers and two-sided arguments on better-educated inductees.

5. *Project Revere* (1951–1953) studied military propaganda but also was interested in airborne leaflet distribution to contact soldiers and noncombatants behind enemy lines. Results demonstrated that messages were *leveled* (shortened to fewer words), *sharpened* (emphasized select ideas), and *assimilated* (expanded) as they were passed along through interpersonal channels after the initial contact with the leaflets (medium).

6. *Interpersonal Communication Research* by Carl Hovland and Elihu Katz working with Paul Lazarsfeld had an impact on our understanding of mass communication effects in the 1940 and 1950s. The authors examined information and opinion exchange

within social groups and shed light on the influence of source credibility, fear appeals, order of presentation, and explicit and implicit message variables. They also presented a more thorough analysis of the "two-step flow" theory. These studies found that there were many different opinion leaders depending on the content area. Most important, people interact over media content, and *the interaction influences the effect* perhaps more than the content.

7. *The Wertham "Comic-Book" studies,* published in 1954, analyzed *the effects of selected sexually oriented or violent comic books on emotionally disturbed children.*[11] Wertham's findings were based on his clinical work; he observed and solicited reports that such content contributed to the negative behavior of children with problems. The sensationalism of the media's coverage of Wertham's studies led to severe economic problems for comic-book publishers and the imposition of an industry "seal of approval" self-censorship. Interestingly, the hardest survivors among comic books today are the types that Wertham condemned.

The studies discussed thus far found a variety of effects and led to public consternation and strict self-regulation of motion pictures, radio, and comic books. This body of work strongly suggests that the media can have an impact on comprehension, attitudes, and behaviors and that individuals react *differently* under the same situation. This conclusion negates the "magic bullet theory" and the belief that interpersonal interaction before, during, and after a media event is a (if not *the*) major determinant of the effect of that particular mass communication experience.

EARLY STUDIES OF TELEVISION

Since the early 1950s, most research on the effects of mass communication has focused on television, especially the effect of television on children. A review of some of the significant work of the 1950s and 1960s reveals a variety of important information.

1. *Television and the Child* by Hilde Himmelwaite, A. N. Oppenheim, and Pamela Vance[12] was suggested by the British Broadcasting Corporation (BBC) and funded by the Nuffield Foundation to assess the impact of television on children in England. Begun

---

[11] Frederic Wertham, *Seduction of the Innocent* (New York: Rinehart, 1954). Wertham's work is *not* documented by subject description and is difficult to apply beyond the two qualifications noted in the text: (1) *violent and sexually oriented content;* and (2) *emotionally disturbed children.* Yet press reports and personal appearances and writings by Wertham attempt to expand his work to include *all* comics and *all* children. His studies from 1948 to 1954 do not seem to justify this expansion.

[12] Hilde Himmelweit, A. N. Oppenheim, and Pamela Vance, *Television and the Child* (London: Oxford University Press, 1958). This book was the first major longitudinal study of TV's effects and makes a significant contribution to our understanding of the emergence of a new medium in a modern industrial society (Great Britain).

in 1954 and reported in 1958, this field study matched pairs of children aged 10 and 11 and 13 and 14 in four cities in England. The study utilized questionnaires, observational techniques, mother's diaries and viewing, interviews, personality measures, teacher's opinion studies, and school performance to gather information. It even compared children prior to television's coming to town and after its arrival. The 11 studies found the following: (a) Age, sex, emotional maturity, and personal need reflect taste and lead to program selection; (b) the more active, more intelligent, and more socially interested child needs television less; (c) parental example is significant as to what and how much is viewed on television; (d) TV viewing influences children's ideas about jobs, success, and social surroundings; (e) TV dramas can frighten children, especially if it is realistic violence and is viewed alone and in the dark; (f) parental viewing with children reduces fright, but most children enjoy the excitement; (g) knives are more fearful than guns, fisticuffs have little impact, and verbal aggression is often more frightening than physical acts of violence; (h) TV viewing takes time away from other leisure activities but does not seem to have an impact on learning or school performance; (i) viewing violence on television has little impact on the normal, active child but does seem to affect the emotionally disturbed, heavy viewer; (j) television affects children but not to the degree that they are fundamentally changed; and (k) supervision of viewing and interaction with children by adults is the critical intervening variable in short-term and long-term effects of television on children.

2. *Television in the Lives of Our Children* by Wilbur Schramm, Jack Lyle, and Edwin Parker included 11 studies funded by the National Television and Radio Center that were conducted from 1958 to 1960. They focused on the uses of gratifications, or *functions*, that television served. The researchers found the following: (a) There are no harmful physical effects (eyestrain, loss of sleep, etc.) from watching television; (b) television helps children acquire information and stimulates interest in subjects not otherwise available; (c) children who are passive, under stress, possess inferior social skills, or are less intelligent make greater use of television; (d) as brighter, socially active children age, they use television less; (e) children use television for thrills and play and seem to like being mildly frightened; (f) adults and children alike seek out and use TV content to gratify certain needs. The major conclusion of the studies was this:

> For some children, under some conditions, some television is harmful. For other children, under the same conditions, or for the same children under other conditions, it may be beneficial. For most chil-

dren, under most conditions, most television is probably neither harmful nor particularly beneficial.[13]

3. *The Effects of Mass Communication* by the late Joseph Klapper has been neglected of late because of his association with the TV industry (employment by CBS) and his role as defender–apologist for industry positions on the effects of violence. Klapper's work is a summary of previous research and advocates the "phenomenistic" approach to television effects. His position was that television and other mass media must be viewed as only one of many factors rather than *the* factor in any consideration of the effects of the mass communication process on human behavior. Klapper suggested several generalized principles: (*a*) Children's reactions vary based on uses, gratification, and group associations; (*b*) the content is *not* as powerful as we would like to believe and mass communication normally is *not* an ordinary and sufficient cause, but a part of other "mediating factors and influences"; (*c*) regardless of other conditions, the mass media tend to reinforce rather than change; (*d*) when mass media do have an impact, it often is a result of other variables being inoperative or because the individual is actually desirous of change; (*e*) media have measurable psychophysical impacts, but these are probably of short duration; and (*f*) media impact is influenced by the situation, the social climate, and the person's condition, as well as by the content.[14]

4. *The People Look at Television*, funded by CBS and published in 1963, is a study of public *attitudes* toward the effects of television rather than a study of the effects themselves. It emphasizes that parents and other adult viewers felt that television had relatively little effect on them, but that they were concerned about the effects on children and about the amount of suggestive material on television.

5. *Experimental and field studies* done in the 1950s and 1960s demonstrated that violent TV content, regardless of the existence of other variables, led to aggressive behavior in children. The *"Bobo Doll"* experiments of Albert Bandura with others tested his social learning theory and suggested that *children learn personalities.* These experiments were concerned with modeling, or imitative behavior, stimulated by TV violence, whether that violence was rewarded or punished. Bandura argued that TV violence has both a learning and a motivating effect. Bandura's much publicized article in *Look* magazine (1963) went beyond what his data dem-

---

[13] Wilbur Schramm, Jack Lyle, and Edwin Parker, *Television in the Lives of Our Children* (Palo Alto, Calif.: Stanford University Press, 1961), 13. This was the first of many studies about the influence of television on children, and it remains a major contributor to our understanding of this process.

[14] Joseph T. Klapper, *The Effects of Mass Communication* (Glencoe, Ill.: Free Press, 1960), 8–9.

onstrated; many felt it strayed back to the "magic bullet" approach. Nevertheless, the research did demonstrate a relationship between TV violence and aggression in children in the laboratory setting.

The *aggression-machine experiments* of L. Berkowitz used a button-pushing situation where helping or hurting could be simulated after viewing violent content. Both college students and children exhibited more aggression as measured by the length of shocks after exposure to TV violence. An instigation theory was suggested that media violence somehow instigates aggressive behavior, especially when the violence appears to be justified. Violence presumably triggers aggression.

The *catharsis experiments* of S. Feshbach (1955) posited the opposite result from that of Berkowitz, that TV violence reduced aggression by defusing the need and predisposition to act aggressively. When these experiments were replicated by pro-aggression researchers, they found nothing to corroborate cathartic effects. In the 1960s Feshbach continued work in support of his theory and found TV violence to *decrease* aggression in aggressive boys but *increase* it in nonaggressive boys. This finding was again challenged by other researchers.

Comparing the major field studies and experiments presents a confusing if not conflicting picture of the effects of television. The experimenters demonstrate that TV violence does make a difference in aggression, regardless of the other variables. The Himmelwaite *et al.*, Schramm *et al.*, and Klapper works argue that TV violence is one of many factors in the environmental mix and that other factors may be more powerful than the content of television when it comes to negative attitudes or antisocial behavior.

GOVERNMENTAL INVOLVEMENT

Throughout the 1950s and 1960s politicians were uneasy about the impact and power of mass media, especially television, and about that medium's effects on children. Senators Estes Kefauver (1954), Christopher Dodd (1961), and John Pastore (1968) held hearings on subjects related to the mass media and social ills. When cities exploded in violent expressions of civil disobedience in the 1960s, the violence and pornography that were widely available in mass media were suspect as a contributing cause. Three massive governmental investigations sought answers to, and possibly scapegoats for, America's ills.

In June 1968 President Lyndon Baines Johnson created the National Commission on the Causes and Prevention of Violence in America to evaluate conditions that led to the domestic turmoil: assassinations, antiwar protests, inner-city riots, etc. A portion of the report submitted by the Media Task Force in December 1969 was a massive volume titled *Violence and the Media*. Among other findings, it included essays that linked violent media content to violent social behavior. The report suggested that TV portrayals of violence dominated the schedule (80% of programs) and refuted the networks' claim that violence had been reduced. The report implied that violent TV content was a contributor to turmoil in the streets. George Gerbner's violence scale was the measurement used. It was and remains a controversial instrument because of its all-inclusive definition of violence; it includes comic action and does not adequately adjust for the explicitness or degree of the violent act and its outcome. The report implied that television was culpable, and because television was and is a very visible target, lingering doubts remain.

Further political discussion and public disturbances led to *Television and Social Behavior: The Surgeon General's Report,* which was completed by the Surgeon General's Scientific Advisory Committee on Television and Social Behavior. The Surgeon General was directed by Congress, at the urging of Senator Pastore, to study TV violence as a public health hazard. The committee's selection, research decisions, and summary report (*Television and Growing Up: The Impact of Televised Violence*), were all controversial. The political debacle that followed the report involved the blackballing of social scientists by the TV industry; questionable funding practices; and a much-criticized, politically compromised summary volume that many of the researchers felt misrepresented the findings of their 23 reports. In the studies, Gerbner continued to find high levels of violence in his content analyses; other researchers found that television could teach aggressive behavior; still other researchers decided that TV viewing decreases with age and developed a sociocultural description of heavy users of violence; and content analyses described how the media portrayed an America with few blacks and Hispanics and depicted traditional stereotypes of women. In effect, the report seemed to repeat previous work and appeared to be an unwise expenditure of funds. It was widely quoted and roundly criticized. Senator Pastore was so unhappy with the hedging and qualifications of the summation that he instituted another round of hearings to get to the bottom line—that television had a provable causal relationship with negative human behavior and needed to be changed.

In 1967 Congress established through Public Law 90-100 the Commission on Obscenity and Pornography, which, on 30 September 1970, submitted its report contradicting many strongly held beliefs of politicians and citizens alike. The commission's majority report has gone the way of many other scientific–bureaucratic undertakings. The findings of the commission have been attacked, and the report's proposed legislation has been ignored.

The Commission on Obscenity and Pornography was unable to reach unanimous agreement on the effects of obscene material. The findings of the majority are these:

1. In the nonlegislative area, the major media involved in providing pornographic materials are paperback books, magazines, and films; however, with the advent of the new cassette videotape units, pornographic materials might become available more readily for use in the home.

2. In the legislative area, all local and state laws as well as federal statutes (Statutes 18 U.S.C. Sec. 1461, 1462, and 1465; 19 U.S.C. Sec. 1305; and 39 U.S.C. Sec. 3006) prohibiting the sale of pornographic materials to consenting adults should be repealed, because

  a. There is no empirical evidence that obscene materials cause antisocial attitudes or deviant behavior, although the material is sexually arousing.

  b. Increasingly, large numbers of persons (most frequently middle-aged, middle-income, college-educated males) use pornography for entertainment and information, and these materials even appear to serve a positive function in healthy sexual relationships.

  c. Public opinion studies indicate that the majority of Americans do not support legal restriction of adult uses of pornography and legal attempts to control the distribution of obscene material have failed.

  d. Obscenity laws are an infringement on Americans' constitutionally guaranteed right to freedom of speech.[15]

The commission also stated:

Although the empirical evidence suggests that pornography is in no way harmful to children, the commission, on ethical grounds, felt that obscene material should not be made available without direct parental consent to persons under eighteen. The commission also argued that unsolicited mailings and public displays should be prohibited.

In other words, the majority of commissioners believed that there is *no empirical evidence* that pornography is harmful and that government at all levels should repeal obscenity laws for consenting adults. Three members of the commission objected to the findings on moral grounds (as did the Nixon administration) and questioned both the scientific studies and legal interpretations of the majority report of the Commission on Obscenity and Pornography.

Erotica in the mass media is sexually oriented content that has as its purpose the physical and emotional arousal of the consumer. Books, magazines, and films are the traditional mass media for erotica, but sound recordings, cable television, and video cassettes are active in the distribution process. Erotica is a cultural term, whereas pornography has a legal, albeit a vague and arbitrary, definition at times.

Pornography is any obscene material. Obscenity is based on these legal criteria: (a) The dominant theme, taken as a whole, must appeal to a prurient (morbid and unhealthy) interest in sex; (b) the material must be

---

[15] *The Report of the Commission on Obscenity and Pornography* (New York: Bantam Books, 1970), 53–72.

patently offensive and affront comtemporary community standards; and (c) the material must be without redeeming social value. If a book or movie is shown to possess all three characteristics, it is legally obscene; in some communities, the distributor, exhibitor, and seller are liable for prosecution for making such material available to the public. A major change in dealing with pornography was the redefinition by the U.S. Supreme Court in 1973 that "community standards" were *local, not national*. This means that something can be erotica in San Francisco but pornography in a small town in the Midwest.

Pornographic content falls within the definition of erotica, but not all erotica is obscene.

The intensity of erotic stimuli vary from mild "cheesecake" photos to explicit "stag films." Research in the field is in its infancy because of social pressures and other difficulties in conducting it, and because of problems in obtaining financial support. In general, mild erotica seems to generate a pleasurable emotional state in subjects, but there appears to be a linkage between erotica and aggressive behavior. There may also be a systematic sexual excitation transfer to negative kinds of behavior if other release is not possible. Arousal from erotica seems to have two major response patterns: If the material is perceived as entertaining, the subjects usually enjoy it; but if they are bored, their response borders on disgust. Interestingly, the higher the arousal level, the more likely it is that the material will be judged pornographic. Studies also indicate that satiation occurs with repeated exposure, and the user loses interest. Recent studies also seem to indicate that male and female responses are growing more alike and that exposure to erotica and the resultant arousal levels affect how subjects perceive attractiveness in others and the receptiveness of others to their own sexuality.

Limited research has been done relating erotica to anxiety, guilt, socially threatening situations, liberalism–conservatism, and intellectual versus anti-intellectual variables. Without question, additional research is necessary before any final conclusions can be reached, but new findings suggest that arousal from sexual material may instigate more aggressive behavior than arousal from violent content. Relatively little experimental research takes place on this topic because of the difficulties in finding financial support and research subjects. Masters and Johnson, among others, continue medical research on human sexuality that is tangentially related to this topic. One hopes that it may provide the necessary insights into this area of mass media content.

The three government studies reported earlier cost a great deal of money and generated a lot of political heat. In the long run the major contribution of these studies may well be that they prepared a new generation of researchers and provided the impetus and funding for a decade of active research in the field of mass media effects.

Prior to 1971, there were approximately 300 research titles relating to **CURRENT**
media effects. Over the next 10 years, another 2500 works appeared. Thus, **RESEARCH**
about 90% of the research on media effects is recent.[16]

Most of that research revolves around three key words:

1. Television (medium)
2. Violence (content)
3. Children (audience)

Thus, what is really the subject of the research is the effect of television
violence on children.

Television is studied because it is the most pervasive medium we have
ever had. Children are studied because they are perceived as the most
vulnerable audience segment and because they spend a significant amount
of time watching television.[17] Violence is focused on because it is a central
dramatic action in most TV programs and because there are very real
concerns about its impact on youngsters.

Two other areas of interest to researchers are the effects of TV advertising on children and the effectiveness of television in imparting prosocial attitudes and behaviors to children.

Television is one of the most active participants in the socialization of **EFFECTS OF**
the young. Television consumes more time in our children's preschool **TELEVISION**
lives than any other waking activity. It is second only to school and, later, **VIOLENCE ON**
work as they grow up. There is evidence that heavy TV viewing by chil- **CHILDREN**
dren can lead to unimaginative play and cause them to develop a negative
view of the world. Children are relatively passive viewers of audiovisual
thrills, and viewing is habituating.

Children's emotional responses tend to fall across a continuum from
joy to excitement to surprise to fright to distress to fear. Youngsters seem
to enjoy mild fright, and they seek out TV programs that produce this
emotion.

There can no longer be any question that TV violence is arousing and
that arousal can lead to aggressive behavior in normal children. The re-

---

[16] Robert Liebert, Joyce N. Sprafkin, and Emily S. Davidson, *The Early Window: Effects of
Television on Children and Youth*, 2nd ed. (New York: Pergamon Press, 1982). This work
provides a comprehensive review of the research literature and expresses the major social
concerns of political action groups and social scientists. It is highly recommended for
anyone interested in a secondary source on this topic. It is a major resource as to prosocial
behavior.

[17] U.S. Department of Health and Human Services, *Television and Human Behavior: Ten
Years of Scientific Progress and Implications for the Future* (Washington, D.C.: Government Printing Office, 1982). This project was funded by the National Institute of Mental
Health and is a truly superior literature review and summary. The research volume contains a number of studies not otherwise available. It is *highly* recommended and serves
as the major source for the section on TV violence and children.

search overwhelmingly substantiates these premises. Under very special circumstances, aggression can become antisocial behavior. Audience research gives us a relatively clear picture of the child who is an inordinately heavy user of television, one who is *habituated*.

Among children, there is also a correlation between heavy TV viewing and lower socioeconomic background, and children from disadvantaged homes rate violent behavior as more acceptable and more enjoyable to view on television than do youngsters from more economically advantaged backgrounds. In addition, children whose parents are heavy TV viewers invariably imitate that behavior.

We also know that children who are heavy users of television seek out violent programming and that as they grow older, they differ from light uses of television in the following ways. Heavy TV viewers (a) believe there is more violence in the world they live in; (b) are more accepting of violence in their society; and (c) are more distrustful of others.

Socially deviant children who are prone to violent behavior enjoy violent TV content, and their exposure to TV violence stimulates antisocial behavior in the real world. Unquestionably, the viewing of TV violence by emotionally disturbed youngsters must be viewed as a *catalyst* for, if not a cause of, aggressive, antisocial actions. The correlation is stronger in boys than in girls.

The Intervention of Adults

The research literature indicates that the single most important intervening variable in mitigating negative effects of television is the parent (or older sister or brother or other adult), who acts as an opinion leader. Adults can take positive action regarding children's TV viewing (a) by setting an example and avoiding habitual viewing patterns; (b) by controlling the amount of time spent viewing; (c) by supervising the kinds of programs viewed; and (d) by viewing television with children and interacting with them before, during, and after the exposure.

A child does not have an inalienable right to view as much television as he or she wants. When attractive alternative activities are made available, children can break habitual viewing patterns. Parents who do not participate in the viewing decisions of children, especially "problem" children, are creating a potentially serious societal problem.

Research unfortunately indicates that parents in most American families do not restrict either how much television their children watch or what TV shows their children view. And seldom, if ever, do parents discuss TV programs with their children. One reason why most parents do not worry about their children's TV viewing may be that parents do not know how much television their children watch. Yet, even as parents fail to supervise their children, more than half the adults in America express the opinion that excessive TV viewing is responsible for the poor state of education in America.

Adults must be made aware of the TV-viewing problem and must be encouraged to exercise their responsibilities. The alternative is to impose censorship on TV content, and that solution may be even more dangerous to the health of future generations.[18]

Political action groups have had limited success in changing TV advertising directed at children. Action for Children's Television (ACT) prodded the National Science Foundation into sponsoring a review of research as to the effects of advertising on youngsters. The findings, which appeared in 1977, reported the following:

EFFECTS OF TELEVISION ADVERTISING ON CHILDREN

1. Children do *not* understand that the primary intent of advertising is *to sell*.
2. Children do *not* understand disclaimers.
3. Commercials on television are effective in developing active consumerism in children.
4. As a result of seeing TV commercials, children attempt to persuade parents to make certain purchases, which on occasion leads to conflict between parent and child.
5. Very strong evidence exists that TV advertising generates product awareness but that children become less accepting and finally skeptical of advertising claims by the time they reach their teens.
6. Very young children have difficulty perceiving the difference between advertising and program content.[19]

This report and other actions by ACT contributed to the following changes in TV advertising directed at children:

1. The discontinuance of children's vitamin ads
2. Characters in shows no longer selling products
3. Advertising time being limited on weekends
4. Premiums being discontinued in association with breakfast cereals.

[18] National Science Foundation, *Research on the Effects of Television Advertising on Children: A Review of the Literature and Recommendations for Future Research* (Washington, D.C.: Government Printing Office, 1977).

[19] Expertly crafted films like *Kramer vs. Kramer* and *Ordinary People* are emotionally arousing for adults. Can you imagine their effect on unsupervised youngsters? They deal with young people's deepest fears: verbal aggression and intimidation, being unlovable and rejected, and divorce. They may have more of an impact on the young than the stylized violence of *Raiders of the Lost Ark* or the silly sex of *Porky's*. Parental reassurance is important after a problem film. If viewed with the family, complex films have significantly less impact, especially, if they are then discussed with the family. Motion-picture sex and violence are significantly more graphic and gratuitous today then in the past, and such films are rapidly filling the hours of programming needed by pay cable services as well as TV networks. Some children may not benefit from these film experiences. Parental supervision and participation in media experiences is highly recommended.

EFFECTS OF TELEVISION ON PROSOCIAL LEARNING

If TV content can lead to antisocial behavior, it has the potential to be used to educate and socialize children in positive ways. Studies show that TV programs help children's cognitive process at the three levels from *perceiving* to *comprehending* to *remembering*. We have found that the process improves with age but that the very young do not understand much of what they view and tend to forget the little that they do understand. Specialized program content can lead to imaginative play and positive behaviors such as altruism, friendliness, and self-control. And studies have shown that special "diets" of controlled TV programs can result in prosocial behaviors among behaviorally disturbed children.

The development of prosocial learning content is suspect because it is associated with cultural "mind control." Some people believe that the imposition of selected socially acceptable, middle-class values may actually be a handicap to the disadvantaged children they are designed to help.

A number of TV series have attempted prosocial learning; among them are "Sesame Street," "The Electric Company," and "Mister Rogers' Neighborhood." All appeared on public television. The three commercial networks, especially CBS, have actively developed Saturday morning programs—including "Fat Albert and the Cosby Kids," "The Harlem Globetrotters Popcorn Machine," "U. S. of Archie," "Shazam," and "Isis"—to impart positive social values. The CBS network also has conducted extensive research to find out about the effectiveness of these shows. "Afterschool Specials" and learning units at ABC use commercial techniques and rock music. The NBC network has generated fewer prosocial programs and less research.

The most researched TV series is the Children's Television Workshop's "Sesame Street." Some impressive results of the research indicate that children do learn as a result of watching the show. Nevertheless, children from disadvantaged families—the target audience of the series—are less likely to watch it than other children.

UNDERSTANDING THE EFFECTS OF MASS COMMUNICATION

The study of mass communication continues to be the study of variables. We are studying leaves (variables) to describe a tree (the problem). Even if we study a thousand leaves, we may not be able to describe the tree. We have not learned enough about media effects to reach many conclusions, but the research is beginning to suggest hypotheses. The research is also becoming more systematic, organized, and consistent. Nevertheless, many variables and combinations of variables remain.

There are five primary sets of variables: environment variables, content variables, media variables, audience variables, and interaction variables.

1. *Environmental variables* include the political, economic, and social conditions that exist at the time of exposure. The radio broadcast "War of the Worlds" created panic in part because of the

troubled economic situation and the dangerous international conditions in the 1930s. The viewing environment itself also contributes to a show's impact. The motion-picture theater with its comfortable seats, large screen, and controlled environment is relatively free of interruptions. But a dark house on a stormy night can be fearful for a child (or an adult) with or without TV violence.

2. *Content variables* are manipulated by media artists. Most of the frightening films or TV programs we view use the following variables to arouse feelings of fear: (a) explicit violence; (b) a combination of erotic elements with violence; (c) realism in the violent acts and settings; (d) weapons of violence (knives are more threatening than guns or fistfights); (e) verbal aggression and threatening action, which have a strong impact on children; (f) sympathetic villains, who are more difficult to understand than the "good guys and bad guys"; (g) character–audience identification that makes violence directed at the character more real; Violence directed at youngsters and animals is the most fear-inducing for children; (h) vulnerable characters; (i) familiarity with continuing characters; and (j) a relative powerlessness on the part of characters to control the situation.

3. *Media variables* refer to the style of the stimulus material using the inherent codes of a given medium. Loud music and flashy visual techniques such as camera angles, deep shadow lighting, erratic camera movement, and rapid editing contribute to arousal regardless of content.

4. *Audience variables* are very significant because they involve the personality characteristics of individual audience members. Individuals who have had previous experiences with certain stimulus material will react differently from those who are unfamiliar with it. Normal people will respond differently from disturbed individuals. You will respond differently based on your physical health or the degree of tension or anxiety or stress you are under. Are you tired or alert?

5. *Interaction variables* are dependent on the presence of others in the audience with whom we communicate before, during, and after the experience. Most of us have been "set up" by our friends to be frightened before a film begins. We have held each other's hands or tried to defuse tension by yelling or laughing. We have talked afterward to release our tension or have hidden around the corner and jumped out to startle others or have been startled by them. We know that children are less affected by violence when their parents also view the show and interact with them.

The Model of Media Effectiveness attempts to visualize the interaction of these five sets of variables that contribute to the impact of a specific media experience in terms of both short-term and long-term impact. The modification of individual variables in any of the sets does indeed have an impact on the effectiveness of a given TV program or motion picture or other media experience. Short-term effects of TV violence and erotica in media are arousing; the degree of aggression that viewing such content leads to depends upon the production values, the viewing situation, and the individuals involved. Positive interaction with adults significantly reduces or eliminates negative behavior on the part of children. Repeated exposure to specific kinds of media content is hypothesized to have an effect on long-term comprehension, attitudes, and behaviors in both pro-social and antisocial ways.

All these factors are at work, yet in the popular literature it is the *content stimulus* that is most often singled out for censure. Why should this be so?

Scenes of violence and sexual activity have been a part of art throughout history, but the explicitness (realism) and sense of participation is intensified by television and movies. In addition, the pervasiveness of these media has opened them to wider audiences, including children. Parental control becomes more difficult because of the ready availability and the general permissiveness of society as a whole.

Despite the fact that many intervening variables generate specific cause-and-effect relationships, scientific research strongly suggests that the mass communication experience plays a role in human behavior.

THE COMPLETED PROCESS   Finally, let us put all the elements of mass communication together again in the HUB model, and picture once again how the process works. In this figure, three different kinds of messages are pictured.

Message A might be the transmission of a story about the Super Bowl. As it goes from the original source to the communicator, who encodes it into the proper language, the message becomes amplified. It has no trouble passing through the gatekeepers, and the medium too amplifies the message. There is some interference with the message at the filter stage, however, since the story is about an event that does not quite fit everyone's cultural concepts. Nevertheless, it reaches most of its intended audience, and there is some feedback to the communicator commenting in both negative and positive terms.

Message B might be the transmission of news about a violent campus protest. The message has no trouble passing through the elements of the mass communication process and is enlarged upon, amplified, and repeated all along the way. The message is coming through loud and clear. The feedback, too, is strong. Action is taken as a result of the message in almost direct proportion to the strength of the message.

Message C might be the release of a press statement by a political candidate. The message was amplified by a communicator, but somehow it was not put into the proper code or did not have sufficient news or communication value, and so it did not pass the barrier of the gatekeeper and get into the mass media. Nevertheless, there was some feedback; the communicator of the message at least got the message that the message was not perceived as important by the gatekeepers.

Using such a model, we could draw a diagram of every communication act. This, of course, is only a rudimentary picture of the process, and we should not be fooled into thinking that such a complex process as mass communication is as simple as we have tried to show it. However, the HUB model is designed to identify the elements in the process and to illustrate graphically that mass communication is a process, not simply a performance. The key to understanding mass communication is to think of it as a continuous two-way process with several elements, all of which have key characteristics. It has been the purpose of Part Two to describe and analyze these elements and their characteristics in order to prepare you to better understand the media that symbolize the process, which is the subject of Part Three.

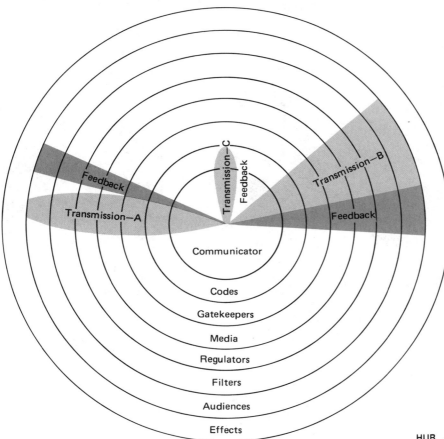

HUB Model of Mass Communication.

MEDIA OF MASS COMMUNICATION

PART 3

Books 14

At the University of Maryland, as well as at many other educational institutions in America, the campus is dominated by a citadel to one of the mass media—the book. As you approach the library, you see engraved in stone various quotations extolling the power and the virtue of books. One of the stone quotations, by Thomas Carlyle, reads: *In books lies the soul of the whole past time.*

(Courtesy of the University of Maryland)

The library of the University of Maryland occupies the center of its sprawling campus.

In such worshipful tones we have revered the book as a medium and an institution. Books have played a dominant role in education since the development of movable type. A large part of that education has been of the self-help, or self-instruction, variety, for which the book has been indispensable. Books have also provided entertainment. And books are becoming a journalistic medium by providing timely and in-depth information.

Books are not just dusty tomes of obscure and specialized information in libraries and institutions of learning. In spite of the advent of the popular press and the electronic media, books play a greater role in our society than ever before. Book production is increasing, and so is book reading.

The reason, perhaps, is that the book is still the most convenient and most permanent way to package information for efficient storage, rapid retrieval, and individual consumption. When we compare the book with the newer media, we can recognize the special qualities of the book as a valuable communication tool.

HISTORICAL PERSPECTIVES

Books have had a long history. As far back as 2400 B.C., clay tablets about the size of shredded-wheat biscuits were used as we use books today. In Babylonia these clay tablets were inscribed with cuneiform characters recording legal decisions or financial accounts. In 700 B.C., an entire library of literary works written on such tablets existed in Nineveh in Asia Minor.

In this artist's visualization, a Babylonian scribe reads cuneiform characters pressed into tablets of wet clay. (Courtesy National Geographic Magazine)

The development of paper was the first great technical advance in book production. The earliest form of paper was papyrus, believed to have been used as a writing material in Egypt as early as 4000 B.C. In the second century B.C., finding papyrus difficult to procure because of conflict with the Egyptians, the king of Pergamon sought improvements in the preparation of animal skins for writing purposes, leading to the development of parchment. Parchment became the chief medium for writing until the tenth century A.D., which saw the introduction of a new writing material made from linen pulp.

Developments in bookbinding were also important. The earliest form of paper books, called *volumen*, consisted of rolls of papyrus or parchment, wound around a stick. Such scrolls were difficult to handle and impossible to index or shelve for ready reference. In the fourth century A.D., the Romans developed a new form of binding, called *codex*, in which scrolls of paper were cut into sheets tied together on the left side between boards, forming the kind of book we still use today. Codex binding opened a new world for books: The reader could leaf through the book and find the passage he wanted; he could begin to compare passages of books; he could set up a table of contents and an index and put material into some order.

Technical Advances

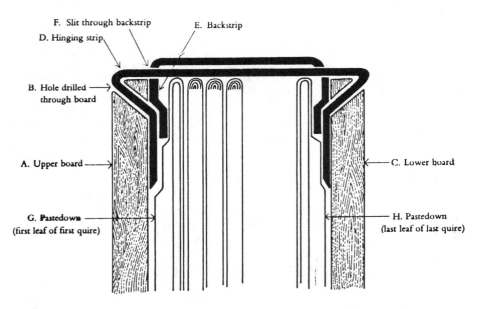

This diagram of codex binding, in cross-section viewed from above, reveals the structure of a fifth century Egyptian illuminated manuscript of the *Acts of the Apostles* written in Coptic. (From *Twelve Centuries of Bookbinding, 400–1600* by Paul Needhan, The Pierpont Morgan Library, New York, 1979. Reprinted permission of the Pierpont Morgan Library.)

The Development of Printing

The most important single innovation for book publishing was the invention of the printing press and movable type. The Chinese were the first to develop printing, sometime during the ninth century, and the oldest known printed book is *The Diamond Sutra*, printed in China in A.D. 868 and made up of seven sheets pasted together to form a 16-foot scroll. But the Chinese did not carry their invention much further. In Europe, books were hand-copied until the fifteenth century, when Johannes Gutenberg, in Mainz, Germany, put together a wine press and movable type to make a usable printing system.

The craft of printing spread rapidly in Europe; more than 30,000 different books were produced during printing's first 50 years. Most of these books were religious or Latin classics and were printed in Latin or Greek. As more people came into contact with books and learned to read, printers slowly began to produce crude versions of these classics in native languages, and they began to publish more popular subjects, such as works on history, astronomy, and supernatural phenomena.

The first printed books looked much like the hand-copied volumes of the Middle Ages. The style of type was Old English, which resembled the handwriting of the monks who had copied manuscripts in florid letters. Because the type style was not easy to read, the book was not too useful for information. The spread of the printed word caused new type styles to be designed, and families of type styles began to grow. As more people began to read books, type style itself began to be vulgarized or simplified. Gothic type, made up of black, bold, square letters, was easier to read than ornate text type. This new type expressed a feeling of simplicity and directness. Roman type was a combination of Old English and Gothic, with some ornateness and some simplicity in the design of the letters, much like the type styles in use today.

Each development in the production of books—whether in paper, binding, printing, typography, or broader distribution through popular translations—brought the book closer to the common person, and each de-

ABCDEFGHIJ KLMNOPQRSTU VWXYZ abcdefghijklmnopq rstuvwxyz 1234567890

ABCDEFGHIJ KLMNOPQRSTU VWXYZ abcdefghijklmnopq rstuvwxyz 1234567890

ABCDEFGHIJ KLMNOPQRSTU VWXYZ abcdefghijklmnopq rstuvwxyz 1234567890

As printed material proliferated, Roman type (right), combining features of Old English (left) and Gothic type (center), became favored for its balance of legibility and design.

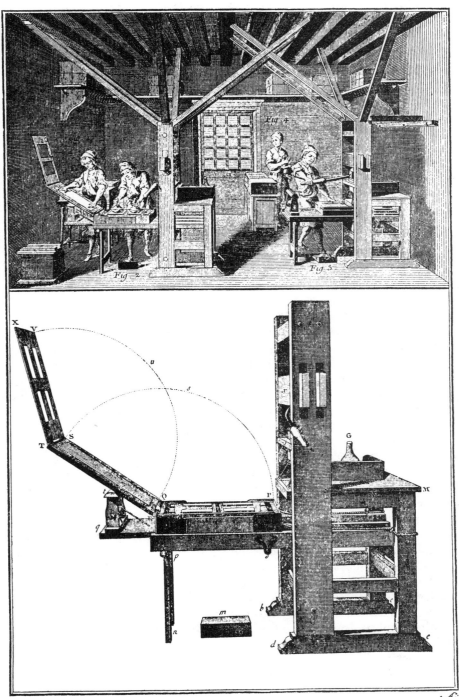

This diagram shows printers at work on an eighteenth century press.

273

velopment further paved the way for the ultimate mass production and dissemination of the book as a mass medium.

Books in Early America

Books were, of course, important to the development of America. They allowed explorers to pass along their discoveries, and accelerated accumulation and distribution of this knowledge.

Nineteen years after the Pilgrims first set foot at Plymouth Rock, Stephen Daye became the first printer in North America, establishing himself at Cambridge; and a year later, 1640, he published his first book, *The Whole Book of Psalms*. The first American Bible was published in 1663; it was soon translated into the language of the Massachusetts Indians for missionary work.

More popular works gradually made their appearance. Most famous of these was *Poor Richard's Almanac*, published by Benjamin Franklin every year from 1733 to 1758. Franklin wrote the almanac under a pseudonym, Richard Saunders, and, between meteorological reports, filled the books with wise and witty sayings. In 1731 Franklin had started the first subscription library in America, the Library Company of Philadelphia. One of the first American inventors, a scientist as well as an eminent statesman, Franklin was also one of America's pioneer mass communicators, making important innovations not only in book publishing but in magazine and newspaper publishing as well.

Until the nineteenth century, however, books were relatively scarce, and the elite and affluent were most likely to possess or read books. A man's library was often a mark of his place in society. The aristocrats of Virginia, for example, prided themselves on their leather-bound volumes of classics. One of the best collections belonged to one of the greatest statesman among them, Thomas Jefferson; his personal library was purchased by Congress in 1815 to start the Library of Congress.

Development into a Mass Medium

For the first 350 years of printing, the production of books changed very little. The type was set by hand, the paper was handmade, and the wooden press was hand operated. At the beginning of the nineteenth century, such slow production did not matter, since only about 10% of the population was able to read. But by the end of the nineteenth century, 90% of America's population had become literate. As literacy increased, the demand for books soon exceeded the supply, and during the nineteenth century mass production techniques came to the book business.

The first technological innovation was the invention of a machine in France in 1798 that could make paper in a continuous roll rather than in single sheets. Press innovations were made about the same time with the development in England of an iron press (to replace wood) and the Germans' addition of steam power (to replace hand production) and a cylinder that could make impressions (replacing the flat-bed press). It was not until 1846 that an American invented a rotary press where the type also was put on a cylinder. And in 1865 another American put paper rolls together with a rotary press for the first high-speed printing. Type continued to be hand set until 1884 when Ottmar Mergenthaler of Baltimore invented the linotype to set type by machine.

These developments in technology were accompanied by rapid change in the editorial side of book publishing. To fill the rising demand for books that could be produced more quickly and cheaply, book publishing be-

The nineteenth century invention of the linotype machine did much to accelerate book production. (New York Public Library Picture Collection)

came a more organized business. A few major publishers emerged, and they sought writers to produce books quickly for the new market.

The nineteenth century saw the emergence of the popular book, a cheaply produced and often sensational treatment of some popular theme, either fictional or nonfictional. The development of fast printing methods and cheap paper in the 1840s opened the way for the dime novel. Thus the world of books, which had formerly been devoted primarily to works of philosophy, religion, literature, and science, also became inhabited, during the latter half of the nineteenth century, by popular heroes of adventure, romance, the wild West, and Horatio Alger success stories. Books came to be judged by the book industry not so much on their intrinsic merit as their popularity: How many copies were sold? How much money did they make? This best-seller concept would become basic to all mass media.

Current Developments in Book Publishing

Until the end of World War II, book publishing in America remained essentially the same industry it was in the late nineteenth century. Most firms were still relatively small, family-owned publishing houses, usually specializing in one kind of book, such as adult trade books, specialized professional books (e.g., books for medicine, law, or science) or textbooks for elementary or secondary schools or colleges.

In the half dozen years immediately after World War II, changes began to take place that resulted in massive improvement and a sustained growing period for book sales. From 1952 to 1970, the book industry increased at a rate of more than 10% each year. In the 1970s, the industry grew 16.5% a year. By 1983, the gross sales of books exceeded $8.5 billion a year, with textbooks accounting for the lion's share of that market.

The growth in book publishing over the past 25 years can be attributed to four specific developments within the book industry and American society: (a) the development of book clubs; (b) the emergence of paperback books; (c) changes in the organization of publishing firms; and (d) the boom in American education.

Unlike magazines and newspapers, books cannot depend upon subscription sales, which guarantee that the consumer will purchase and receive continuing installments of the publication over a regular period. The purchase of a book is usually a one-time action to fill a specific need. The book club was a new distribution technique that revitalized book publishing. Book clubs began to develop in the 1920s, providing a kind of automatic subscription for books and regular ordering each month through the mail, in a habit-forming pattern. By the mid-1980s, more than $650 million was grossed annually by the industry through book-club sales.

A second element in the growth of book publishing was the emergence of the paperback book. Europeans were the first to publish cheaply bound

Book Publishing Industry Sales, 1972–1983 (Millions of Dollars)

	1972 ($)	1977 ($)	1977 Pct chg from '72	1982 ($)	1982 Pct chg from '77	1982 Pct chg from '72	1983 ($)	1983 Pct chg from '82	1983 Pct chg from '72
Trade (Total)	444.8	887.2	99.5	1355.5	52.8	204.7	1595.2	17.7	258.6
Adult Hardbound	251.5	501.3	99.3	671.6	34.0	167.0	807.6	20.3	221.1
Adult Paperbound*	82.4	223.7	171.5	452.0	102.1	448.6	531.6	17.6	545.1
Children's Hardbound	106.5	136.1	27.8	180.3	32.5	69.3	190.3	5.5	78.7
Children's Paperbound	4.4	26.1	493.2	51.5	97.3	1071.3	65.7	27.6	1393.2
Religious (Total)	117.5	250.6	113.3	390.0	55.6	231.9	454.9	16.6	287.1
Bibles, Testaments, Hymnals & Prayerbooks	61.6	116.3	88.8	163.7	40.8	165.8	182.0	11.2	295.5
Other Religious	55.9	134.3	140.2	226.2	68.4	304.7	272.9	20.6	388.2
Professional (Total)	381.0	698.2	83.2	1230.5	76.2	223.0	1373.0	11.6	260.4
Technical & Scientific	131.8	249.3	89.2	431.4	73.0	227.3	491.0	13.8	272.5
Business & other Professional	192.2	286.3	49.0	530.6	85.3	176.1	561.2	5.8	192.0
Medical	57.0	162.6	185.3	268.5	65.1	371.0	320.8	19.5	462.8
Book Clubs	240.5	406.7	69.1	590.0	45.1	145.3	654.4	10.9	172.1
Mail Order Publications	198.9	396.4	99.3	604.6	52.5	204.0	554.5	−8.3	178.8
Mass Market Paperbacks Racksize	250.0	487.7	95.1	665.5†	36.5	166.2	706.1	6.1	182.4
University Presses	41.4	56.1	35.5	122.9†	119.1	196.9	129.9	5.7	213.8
Elementary & Secondary Text	497.6	755.9	51.9	1051.5	39.1	111.3	1149.7	9.3	131.0
College Text**	375.3	649.7	73.1	1142.4	75.8	204.4	1228.6	7.5	227.4
Standardized Tests	26.5	44.6	68.3	69.7	56.3	163.2	79.7	14.3	200.8
Subscription Reference	278.9	294.4	5.6	396.6	34.7	42.2	443.0	11.7	58.8
AV & other Media (Total)	116.2	151.3	30.2	148.0	−2.2	27.4	143.0	−3.4	23.1
Elhi	101.2	131.4	29.8	130.1	−1.0	28.6	124.3	−4.5	22.8
College	9.2	11.6	26.1	7.9	−31.9	−14.1	7.6	−3.8	−17.4
Other	5.8	8.3	43.1	10.0	20.5	72.2	11.1	11.1	91.4
Other Sales	49.2	63.4	28.9	77.1	21.6	56.8	80.0	3.8	62.6
Total	**3017.8**	**5142.2**	**70.4**	**7844.3**	**52.5**	**159.9**	**8592.0**	**9.5**	**184.7**

* Includes Non-rack size sales by Mass Market Publishers of $113.5 million in 1982 and $139.9 million in 1983.
** The Statistical Service Center conducts an independent survey for the Higher Education Division. In 1982, this survey of 43 college publishers, which represent the majority of known college publishing, reported sales of $863.9 million. The 1983 survey is not yet complete and will be reported in the final Table S-1. The AAP statistical agent and the U.S. Department of Commerce have been unable to reconcile their figures with the special college survey.
† Previously reported 1982 figures revised to conform to information available at a later date.
SOURCE: *Publishers Weekly*, June 22, 1984, p. 34.

books on a large scale, giving readers access to a much broader range of books than they could otherwise afford. The growth of paperback publishing spurted during World War II, when millions of servicemen needed inexpensive reading material that could easily be carried in their pockets. Today, paperback books are a staple item at almost every newsstand, drug-

The demand for low cost reading material has resulted in the high marketability of paperback books.

(Photo by Brendan Beirne)

store, corner grocery, supermarket, bus depot, train station, and airport. Paperbacks are no longer limited to the 75-cent variety; the average mass market paperback costs $3.13.

A new dimension was added to book publishing in the mid-1970s: the development of the managed book. Publishers began to put books together in the same way that movie producers and magazine executives assemble their products. A managed book begins in editorial boardrooms, not in an author's imagination. Editors and publishers look at demographic charts and opinion polls and decide what kind of book is needed and what will sell. They then hire out various pieces of the job in order to get it done rapidly. Good examples of this kind of publishing are the books produced by Time-Life and American Heritage.

The growth of the industry has been marked by important changes in the organization of publishing firms. Many are now large public corporations with wide distribution and public listing on the stock market. Often these corporations have diversified their publishing activities into broad ranges of books, including trade, juvenile, elementary, secondary,

Average Price of U.S. Hardcover Books, per Volume, 1977–1983*

Dewey classifications	1977	1980	1981	1982	1983 Total volumes	1983 Total prices	1983 Average prices
Agriculture (630–639; 712–719)				$29.08	369	$10,242.31	$27.76
Art (700–711; 720–779)				26.88	1,121	30,014.41	26.77
Biography				19.68	1,556	30,761.05	19.77
Business (650–659)				23.48	1,133	27,219.22	24.02
Education (370–379)				20.41	615	13,111.96	21.32
Fiction				13.57	2,070	29,274.00	14.14
General Works (000–099)	$22.45	$23.34	$25.15	26.93	1,507	39,363.99	26.12
History (900–909; 930–999)				23.70	1,591	37,844.54	23.85
Home Economics (640–649)				15.80	710	10,316.88	14.53
Juveniles				8.74	2,520	23,049.96	9.15
Languages (400–499)	$14.55	$20.14	$20.65	22.09	374	8,448.23	25.26
Law (340–349)				29.30	1,126	34,057.60	30.25
Literature (800–810; 813–820; 823–899)				20.39	1,249	26,612.82	21.31
Medicine (610–619)				33.01	3,007	99,279.95	33.02
Music (780–789)				25.28	266	6,401.12	24.06
Philosophy, Psychology (100–199)	$14.17	$20.18	$21.61	22.75	1,019	25,557.44	25.08
Poetry, Drama (811; 812; 821; 822)				18.12	659	12,775.36	19.39
Religion (200–299)	11.98	15.55	16.58	16.61	1,252	19,943.85	15.93
Science (500–599)	23.78	32.67	33.97	35.20	2,589	94,466.67	36.49
Sociology, Economics (300–339; 350–369; 380–399)				23.81	5,564	138,166.99	24.83
Sports, Recreation (790–799)				18.61	685	13,065.55	10.07
Technology, (600–609; 620–629; 660–699)				31.27	1,884	64,358.63	34.16
Travel (910–999)				19.29	281	5,158.81	18.36
Total	**$17.32**	**$22.48**	**$24.33**	**$23.26**	**33,106**	**$799,541.44**	**$24.15**

* Volumes priced at $81 or over eliminated.
SOURCE: *Publishers Weekly*, September 7, 1984, p. 47.

college textbook, scientific, and technical-book publication. In addition, these corporations have been steadily merging into giant conglomerates, which often include other media as well.

The most important development in the growth of book publishing has been the boom in American education. Textbooks now account for more than one-third of the total gross sales of books; in 1945 they accounted for only one-fifth. If we added together all books falling generally within the educational category, including encyclopedias and professional books, they would account for more than half the book industry's sales. Among the mass media, the book has a particular usefulness for conveying

Average Prices of U.S. Mass Market
Paperback Books, per Volume, 1981–1983

	1981 volumes Average prices	1982 volumes Average prices	1983 volumes		
			Total volumes	Total prices	Average prices
Agriculture	$2.54	$3.61	7	$ 35.65	$5.09
Art	5.49	8.45	6	27.80	4.63
Biography	3.82	4.29	49	227.05	4.63
Business	4.63	3.89	8	40.15	5.02
Education	3.96	4.25	6	33.25	5.54
Fiction	2.47	2.72	2,838	8,135.40	2.88
General Works	3.62	3.90	48	255.40	5.32
History	3.53	4.25	25	110.45	4.42
Home Economics	4.34	4.68	77	360.95	4.69
Juveniles	1.79	2.04	223	500.30	2.24
Language	3.41	3.61	20	68.45	3.42
Law	3.08	3.50	2	5.90	2.95
Literature	3.41	3.65	32	127.05	3.98
Medicine	3.66	5.08	31	160.50	5.18
Music	—	5.67	2	10.90	5.45
Philosophy, Psychology	2.83	3.57	90	390.55	4.33
Poetry, Drama	3.21	3.41	18	88.30	4.90
Religion	2.70	3.55	22	84.95	3.86
Science	4.45	4.70	17	72.35	4.26
Sociology, Economics	3.43	4.05	43	182.70	4.24
Sports, Recreation	3.04	2.90	171	592.50	3.47
Technology	4.20	4.33	47	188.80	4.02
Travel	3.22	7.55	18	178.65	9.92
Total	**$2.65**	**$2.93**	**3,790**	**$11,878.00**	**$3.13**

SOURCE: *Publishers Weekly*, September 7, 1984, p. 46.

information as well as providing entertainment. As a tool of education, it is still far superior to other media, and this fact has been an essential element in the growth of publishing in the United States.

BOOKS AND THE MASS MARKET   Aside from textbooks and educational books, which students are obligated to buy, what kind of book achieves mass circulation in America? An analysis of best-selling books is useful in understanding the publishing industry; it is also revealing of American society and culture. The list of best-selling books throughout our history does not include many books by Nobel Prize winners or literary critics' choices. Most best-selling books are self-help books. The top three best-selling hardcover books from 1895 to 1975 were cookbooks, and the best-selling paperback of all time is a book on baby and child care. Not far behind the cookbooks and child-

Subjects of Paperbound Trade Books
Published in the United States, 1981–1983

	1981	1982	1983
Agriculture	5	4	7
Art	8	9	6
Biography	74	65	50
Business	9	13	8
Education	14	11	6
Fiction	3,097	2,971	2,859
General works	86	60	49
History	43	38	25
Home Economics	109	80	78
Juveniles	240	222	230
Language	20	7	20
Law	4	1	2
Literature	44	38	34
Medicine	35	28	31
Music	1		2
Philosophy, Psychology	80		90
Poetry, Drama	16		18
Religion	26	22	22
Science	17	14	17
Sociology, Economics	52	49	43
Sports, Recreation	178	209	172
Technology	11	17	48
Travel	4	23	18
Total	**4,175**	**3,985**	**3,835**

SOURCE: *Publishers Weekly*, September 7, 1984, p. 45.

care books are the sex manuals. *The Sensuous Woman, The Happy Hooker,* and *Everything You Always Wanted to Know About Sex but Were Afraid to Ask* have all sold more copies in paperback than any hardcover book other than the *Better Homes and Gardens Cook Book*.

One publishing phenomenon that should be noticed is the work of Dr. Seuss. Five of his children's books are among the top 10 best-selling hardcover books. Their titles ring with familiarity for all of us who used to be children: *Green Eggs and Ham; One Fish, Two Fish, Red Fish, Blue Fish; Hop on Pop; Dr. Seuss's ABC; and The Cat in the Hat.*

The latest mass market book genre is the lush, sexy paperback romance, called the "bodice-ripper" in the industry. In 1971 Avon Books tested the historical romance market with the publication of *The Flame and the Flower*. It sold 3 million copies, and soon every paperback publisher was in the "bodice-ripper" business. These romances became the second-largest mass market paperback sellers (after general fiction) in the mid-1970s.

Book Rankings
Best-Sellers

TOP TEN BEST-SELLING FICTION BOOKS, 1983

1. *Poland* by James A. Michener (Random House).
2. *The Little Drummer Girl* by John le Carre (Knopf).
3. *Pet Sematary* by Stephen King (Doubleday).
4. *Return of the Jedi* adapted by Joan D. Vinge (Random House).
5. *The Name of the Rose* by Umberto Eco (Helen and Kurt Wolff/Harcourt Brace Jovanovich).
6. *Christine* by Stephen King (Viking).
7. *White Gold Wielder* by Stephen R. Donaldson (Ballantine/Del Rey).
8. *Space* by James A. Michener (Random House).
9. *Changes* by Danielle Steel (Delacorte).
10. *Hollywood Wives* by Jackie Collins (Simon & Schuster).

TOP TEN BEST-SELLING HARDCOVER BOOKS, 1983

1. *In Search of Excellence* by Thomas J. Peters and Robert H. Waterman Jr. (Harper & Row).
2. *Megatrends* by John Naisbitt (Warner).
3. *Motherhood: The Second Oldest Profession* by Erma Bombeck (McGraw-Hill).
4. *The One Minute Manager* by Kenneth Blanchard and Spencer Johnson (Morrow).
5. *Jane Fonda's Workout Book* by Jane Fonda (Simon & Schuster).
6. *The Best of James Herriot* by James Herriot (St. Martin's Press).
7. *Blue Highways* by William Least Heat Moon (Atlantic/Little Brown).
8. *Creating Wealth* by Robert G. Allen (Simon & Schuster).
9. *On Wings of Eagles* by Ken Follett (Morrow).
10. *Growing Up* by Russell Baker (Congdon & Weed).

TOP TEN BEST-SELLING TRADE PAPERBACKS, 1983

1. *Color Me Beautiful* by Carole Jackson (Ballantine).
2. *Living, Loving & Learning* by Leo F. Buscaglia (Fawcett).
3. *The Color Purple* by Alice Walker (Pocket/Washington Square Press).
4. *Thurston House* by Danielle Steel (Dell).
5. *Garfield Eats His Heart Out* by Jim Davis (Ballantine).
6. *Items From Our Catalog* by Alfred Gingold (Avon).
7. *The One Minute Manager* by Kenneth Blanchard and Spencer Johnson (Warner).
8. *Life Extension* by Durk Pearson and Sandy Shaw (Warner).
9. *Garfield Sits Around the House* by Jim Davis (Ballantine).
10. *Thin Thighs in 30 Days* by Wendy Stehling (Bantam).

TOP TEN BEST-SELLING MASS MARKET PAPERBACKS, 1983

1. *Truly Tasteless Jokes* by Blanche Knott (Ballantine).
2. *Master of the Game* by Sidney Sheldon (Warner).
3. *The Parsifal Mosaic* by Robert Ludlum (Bantam).
4. *The Valley of Horses* by Jean M. Auel (Bantam).
5. *The Man From St. Petersburg* by Ken Follett (NAL/Signet).
6. *Different Seasons* by Stephen King (NAL/Signet).
7. *When Bad Things Happen to Good People* by Harold S. Kushner (Avon).
8. *Christine* by Stephen King (NAL/Signet).
9. *Return of the Jedi* by James Kahn (Ballantine/Del Rey).
10. *Truly Tasteless Jokes Two* by Blanche Knott (Ballantine).

SOURCE: *New York Times*, February 3, 1984.

The Book Publishing Industry Compared to Newspapers and Periodicals, 1972–1981, (Millions of Dollars)

Item	Newspapers			Periodicals			Books		
	1972	1977	1981	1972	1977	1981	1972	1977	1981
Establishments, number	8,116	8,867	(NA)	2,535	2,994	(NA)	1,205	1,745	(NA)
With 20 or more employees	2,120	2,147	(NA)	453	525	(NA)	307	346	(NA)
Employees* (1,000)	350	349	419	67	70	80	57	60	64
Payroll	3,168	4,306	6,289	709	1,020	1,564	558	830	1,123
Value of receipts	8,263	13,056	20,050	3,511	6,057	9,843	2,857	4,794	6,760
Cost of materials	2,044	3,539	5,793	1,404	2,289	3,790	960	1,544	2,166
Value added by manufacture**	6,220	9,519	14,258	2,110	3,763	6,075	1,936	3,262	4,623
New capital expenditures	360	554	1,023	57	86	171	48	78	153
Fixed assets, gross value	3,639	5,026	8,037	588	725	1,135	512	680	958
Inventories, yearend	153	382	682	198	350	586	629	992	1,325

* Represents the average number of production workers plus the number of other employees in mid-March.
** Derived by subtracting the cost of materials, supplies, containers, fuel, purchased electricity, and contract work from the value of shipments. This result is then adjusted by the addition of value added by merchandising operations, plus the net change in finished goods and work-in-process inventories between the beginning and end of the year.
SOURCE: U.S. Bureau of the Census, *Census of Manufactures, 1977*, Industry Reports, series MC 77-I-27A and *Annual Survey of Manufactures*, M81 (AS)-1.

By the mid-1980s major paperback publishers were estimating that romance books constituted a large share of their total sales.

THE SCOPE OF BOOK PUBLISHING

Book publishing is smaller than the newspaper and magazine industries, but it is growing. From 1970 to 1980, book publishing grew at a slightly greater rate than did newspapers—165% growth for books compared with 153% for newspapers. American publishers currently produce about 55,000 titles yearly.

There are about 1,700 book publishers in the United States, but the industry is dominated by a few large publishing houses. The larger publishers are conglomerates with many different imprints. Many old-line companies have merged with conglomerates: J. B. Lippincott is now part of Harper & Row; Little, Brown is now part of Time Inc.; Dial Press is now part of Doubleday; and so on.

The book publishing industry has traditionally been headquartered in New York City, which still is the home of one out of three of the large publishers. The number of publishers in New York is declining slightly, however, and substantial growth is taking place in the West, particularly California, and in the South. New York publishers account for about 45% of the industry's total receipts.

Subjects of Books Published in the United States, 1981–1983, Based on the Dewey Classification System

Categories with Dewey decimal numbers	1981 Titles				1982 Titles				1983 Titles			
	Hardbound and trade paperbound only			All hard- and paper- bound	Hardbound and trade paperbound only			All hard- and paper- bound	Hardbound and trade paperbound only			All hard- and paper- bound
	New books	New editions	Totals		New books	New editions	Totals		New books	New editions	Totals	
Agriculture (630–639; 712–719)	393	76	469	474	338	97	435	439	451	114	565	572
Art (700–711; 720–779)	1,450	235	1,685	1,693	1,453	260	1,713	1,722	1,650	240	1,890	1,896
Biography (920; 929; B)	1,407	379	1,786	1,860	1,447	240	1,687	1,752	1,818	267	2,085	2,135
Business (650–659)	1,031	302	1,233	1,342	979	335	1,314	1,327	1,289	339	1,628	1,636
Education (370–379)	1,006	152	1,158	1,172	887	148	1,035	1,046	925	128	1,053	1,059
Fiction	1,906	653	2,558	5,655	2,042	406	2,448	5,419	2,258	353	2,611	5,470
General Works (000–099)	1,428	229	1,657	1,743	2,055	283	2,338	2,398	2,410	308	2,718	2,767
History (900–909; 930–999)	1,813	465	2,278	2,321	1,696	443	2,139	2,177	1,776	495	2,271	2,296
Home Economics (640–649)	848	151	999	1,108	886	133	1,019	1,099	1,109	138	1,247	1,325
Juveniles	2,761	201	2,962	3,102	2,677	150	2,827	3,049	2,838	129	2,967	3,197
Language (400–499)	629	112	741	761	447	122	569	576	522	127	649	669
Law (340–349)	1,128	316	1,444	1,448	1,065	385	1,450	1,451	1,356	398	1,754	1,756
Literature (800–810; 813–820; 823–899)	1,477	256	1,733	1,777	1,454	250	1,704	1,742	1,675	248	1,928	1,957
Medicine (610–619)	3,128	625	3,753	3,788	2,691	510	3,201	3,229	3,308	663	3,971	4,002
Music (780–789)	298	101	397	398	265	77	342	346	335	80	415	417
Philosophy, Psychology (100–199)	1,141	244	1,385	1,465	1,151	242	1,393	1,465	1,227	261	1,488	1,578
Poetry, Drama (811; 812; 821; 822)	1,047	120	1,167	1,183	925	96	1,021	1,049	1,111	105	1,216	1,234
Religion (200–299)	1,905	347	2,252	2,278	1,762	291	2,053	2,075	2,108	303	2,411	2,433
Science (500–599)	2,781	577	3,358	3,375	2,604	506	3,110	3,124	3,079	524	3,603	3,620
Sociology, Economics (300–339; 350–369; 380–399)	6,627	1,122	7,749	7,807	6,319	1,081	7,400	7,449	7,142	1,285	8,427	8,470
Sports, Recreation (790–799)	921	165	1,086	1,264	832	150	982	1,191	1,005	158	1,163	1,335
Technology (600–609; 620–629; 660–699)	1,866	436	2,302	2,313	1,911	400	2,311	2,328	2,396	530	2,926	2,974
Travel (910–919)	372	96	468	472	352	107	459	482	448	116	564	582
Total	**37,259**	**7,359**	**44,618**	**48,793**	**36,238**	**6,712**	**42,950**	**46,935**	**42,236**	**7,309**	**49,545**	**53,380**

SOURCE: *Publishers Weekly*, September 7, 1984, p. 44.

Top Ten U.S. Book Publishing Companies in 1982, by Total Revenues

Rank	Company	1982 Revenues (millions)
1	Time Inc.	$485.0
2	McGraw-Hill	389.3
3	H.B.J.	327.5
4	Times Mirror	302.0
5	SFN	252.1
6	Mattel (Western Pub.)	246.0
7	Torstar	237.6
8	Scott & Fetzer	235.6
9	Prentice-Hall	220.9
10	Houghton Mifflin	189.7
	Total	$4059.2

SOURCE: *Publishers Weekly*, Feb. 3, 1984, p. 292.

U.S. Book Audience Preferences in Fiction, Based on Total Fiction Books Purchased, First Half of 1984

Type of Fiction	Percentage
Mystery/Spy/Suspense	19
Romance	18
Popular fiction	12
Historical	11
Action/Adventure	11
Science Fiction	10
Western	4
Humor	3
Occult/Supernatural	3
War/Military	1
Other	6
Don't know	2
Total	**100**

SOURCE: The Gallup Survey, from *Publishers Weekly*, September 7, 1984, p. 32.

U.S. Book Audience Preferences in Nonfiction, Based on Total Nonfiction Books Purchased, First Half of 1984

Type of Nonfiction	Percentage
Reference/Instruction	16
Historical	16
Biography	15
Religious	9
Health/Diet/Exercise	7
Home & Garden/How-to Books	6
Leisure	6
Cook books	5
Investment/Economics/Income Tax	3
Other	12
Don't know	5
Total	**100**

SOURCE: The Gallup Survey, from *Publishers Weekly*, September 7, 1984, p. 32.

The Book Audience

The average American does not spend as much time reading books for pleasure as the average European does. A survey completed in 1978, however, indicates that more than half of all Americans read some books (55%); of those, 25% had read 10 or more books in the past 6 months and were considered moderate to heavy book readers. Six percent of Americans read no books.

Generally, women read more books than men; 60% of American women are book readers, whereas only 49% of the men are. Young people read more books than old people. In fact, book reading declines steadily with age, whereas newspaper and magazine reading seems to increase with age. Textbook reading in school undoubtedly plays a major role in those statistics. Reader education also plays a role: The more education a person has, the more he or she is apt to be a book reader.

THE STRUCTURE AND ORGANIZATION OF BOOK PUBLISHING

The book publisher is essentially a middleman between author and reader. In most small firms the publisher contracts for all the services necessary for the production and distribution of his publications—including the work of artists, designers, copyeditors, paper dealers, printers, binders, salesmen, and distributors. Even some of the largest book publishers use outside services for some production aspects, and only a handful of major publishers have their own printing facilities.

Demographic Data on American Adults Who Have Purchased a Book in the Past Seven Days

	1983 (%)	1984 (%)		1983 (%)	1984 (%)
All Adults	21	20	**Annual Household Income**		
Sex			$30,000 and over	29	29
Male	20	18	$20,000–$29,999	26	21
Female	22	21	$10,000–$19,999	17	17
			Under $10,000	14	11
Age			**Women's Employment**		
18–24	26	23	**Status**		
25–34	26	22	Employed full-time	29	26
35–49	26	23	Employed part-time	25	24
50 and older	13	14	Not employed	15	16
Education			**Region**		
College	33	30	East	22	21
High School graduate	18	16	Midwest	18	18
Less than high school			South	19	17
graduate	8	7	West	26	25

SOURCE: The Gallup survey, from *Publishers Weekly*, September 7, 1984, p. 32.

The publisher operates at the center of a large number of services and specialists between the author and the reader. Within the publisher's offices, generally speaking, says book publisher Henry Z. Walck, "No more than forty to forty-five percent of the publisher's staff work is in the editorial, manufacturing, advertising, and selling departments. The shipping clerks, invoice clerks, accountants, yes, the top executive officer, frequently find their particular operations not much different from those in a plumbing business or that of selling cornflakes."[1]

The larger the firm, the more specialized each individual's function must become. Editors themselves have increasingly specialized tasks. Managerial editors are responsible for planning and managing publishing programs. These editors are decision makers, deciding what books to publish, what authors should write the books, and how the product should be packaged and promoted. Production editors are technicians rather than planners, performing the technical steps necessary to convert a manuscript into a finished book. This includes such tasks as supervision of copyediting, rewriting if needed, registering copyright, proofreading, and indexing.

[1] Daniel Melcher, *So You Want to Get into Book Publishing* (New York: R. R. Bowker, 1967), 10.

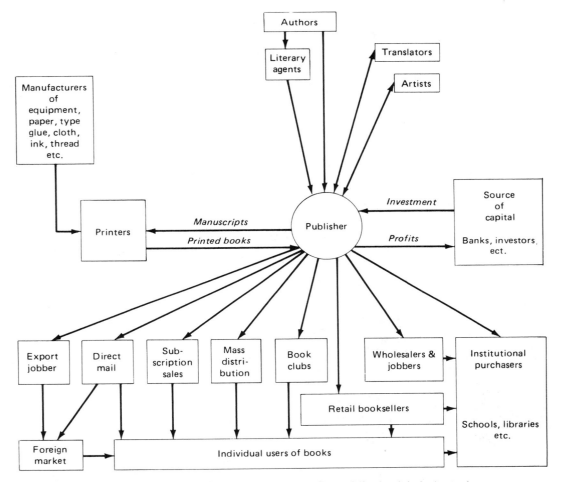

The Book Publishing Industry. This diagram depicts the structure of the book industry and visualizes the interaction of a variety of institutions with publishers. (Reprinted from *A Guide to Book Publishing*, with permission of the R. R. Bowker Company. Copyright © 1966 by Xerox Corporation.)

The other jobs in book publishing—whether in selling, promoting, distributing, or producing—are also specialized. Artists, designers, advertising copywriters, and promotion specialists are of increasing importance and concern. There are many different and challenging jobs in book publishing, and as one publisher says: "The qualifications necessary for many of these positions are not unique to publishing; they are the same as required by most other business enterprises for similar jobs. Book publishing is a business, and as such it offers opportunity to almost anyone who has a business skill or professional talent."

KINDS OF BOOK PUBLISHING

Today we speak of book publishing in terms of three broad areas: general, professional, and educational.

General Books

These books are also often called *trade books* because most of them are sold to the public by the trade, meaning bookstores. General trade books include reference works, children's books, "how-to-do-it" books, fiction, poetry, humor, biography, and religion. Children's books, or "juveniles" or "junior books," represent a rapidly growing segment of the trade field. Often ideas for trade books, and even complete manuscripts, come from freelance writers, except in the reference-book field. The typical large publisher may receive annually up to 25,000 unsolicited manuscripts or book outlines and ideas, only a fraction of which will be published. Trade books are generally sold through bookstores and to libraries for general public consumption. Reference works and encyclopedias are more often sold by subscription, through the mail, or by house-to-house salesmen.

The rapid development of high technology and its resultant social change have created an increasingly important role for professional books. (Photo by Brendan Beirne)

Books written for professional people have become increasingly important because of our constantly changing and rapidly developing society. The professional person, no matter what the occupation, must keep up with the changes in his or her field or run the risk of obsolescence. Hundreds of books are published each year for lawyers, doctors, engineers, scientists, businessmen, teachers, and executives. Professional books are most often written by specialists in the various professions and are often produced at the suggestion of a book editor familiar with the occupation. Such books are usually sold through direct mail or in special technical or campus bookstores, and almost always at prices higher than those of trade books.

The largest area of publishing is that of educational books. There are more than 50 million students in primary and secondary schools; about 11 million people are studying in colleges, universities, and technical institutes; and more than 25 million adults are enrolled in evening courses, on-the-job training, or home-study programs. This represents a giant audience for educational textbooks, workbooks, supplementary reading, reference works, and laboratory materials.

Most of these books are written by teachers, college professors, or specialists. As with professional books, they are often written at the suggestion of an editor or publisher who sees the need for a particular text, but ideas for educational books often come from educators who have developed new materials or new ways of looking at old subjects. The essential element of distribution for educational books is the *adoption*. Textbooks are not selected by the individual student but usually are adopted by the teacher for an entire class. In some cases, a book can be adopted for an entire school, an entire school system, or even a statewide school system.

Professional Books

Educational Books

The book is becoming an important medium of journalism and is being rediscovered by journalists. Because of improvements in the speed of production, books are increasingly being used for timely news and interpretation, especially when a subject needs more in-depth development.

This has stimulated the relationship between literary writing and journalism. Novelist Truman Capote, for example, used the techniques of the journalist to produce *In Cold Blood*, a factual work of literary merit that was the forerunner of many similar books. And journalists have increasingly used literary techniques to bring color and action to their books, for example, Theodore H. White's *The Making of the President*, a series of books about recent presidential elections. Using the book as their medium, journalists can add dialogue, description, and dramatic pacing that bring factual events to life.

Bob Woodward and Carl Bernstein, the *Washington Post* reporters who broke the Watergate story, turned to books to tell the full story of the events

THE BOOK AS A JOURNALISTIC MEDIUM

leading to the downfall of the Nixon administration. *All the President's Men* and *The Final Days* are journalistic books that read like fiction. The authors have been criticized for overdramatization, for imagining scenes, for lack of sufficient attribution, and for failure to document their sources fully. These are all journalistic sins; but by using these novelists' techniques, in book form, the writers were probably able to show the whole Watergate episode better than other media could.

The work of such writers as Robin Moore represents another dimension in the new role of books in journalism. Moore is the author of *The French Connection*, *The Green Berets*, and *The Washington Connection*. He em-

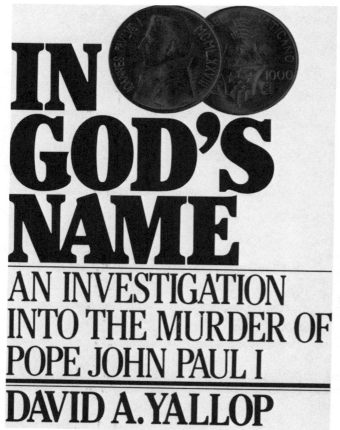

The investigative techniques of the journalist are enlivened by the literary style of the mystery writer in David Yallop's *In God's Name*. (Copyright © 1984 by Poetic Products Ltd. Reprinted courtesy Bantam Books, Inc.)

This biography of Prince appeared in bookstores only weeks after the movie *Purple Rain* had made him a superstar. (Photo by Paul Natkin/Star File Photos. Courtesy Perigee Books, The Putnam Publishing Group.)

ploys a team of investigative reporters to research all the facts about a current public problem or situation—in the books mentioned, drug addiction, combat elites, prostitution, political scandal. He then puts all the facts together in the form of a novel. Moore calls his form of journalism *faction*.

Books can now be produced almost as rapidly as newspapers and magazines, which enables the book to be a news medium. Within a week after the return of the 52 hostages from Iran, for example, a publisher had a major book out on the newstands called *444 Days*. Paperback publishers were able to bring out copies of the *Pentagon Papers* in book form within hours after the Supreme Court had ruled that the government could not stop their publication.

THE FUTURE OF BOOKS

The book has always been a very personal medium, but new technologies will make books even more personalized in the future. In the past, the high costs of older print processes and of mass advertising needed to reach an intended audience meant that publishers could only produce books that would have relatively high sales. New technologies allow the publisher to use market research to find a specific or specialized audience, computers to organize and arrange that audience so that it will be easily reachable, and less expensive printing processes to produce highly specialized books for a small number of readers at affordable prices.

Publishers can also use new word processing equipment to further reduce costs and make more books available. Authors can become their own typesetters by doing their writing on a video display terminal, and the disk or tape that is produced can generate the computer composition for camera-ready copy needed to make the plates for printing. In addition, readers can now publish their own books. Information stored on microfilm or microfiche can be retrieved by computer and assembled into a customized book.

CHARACTERISTICS AND ROLES OF BOOKS

Books are marked by several distinguishing characteristics. They are, first, the only medium to which we attach some permanence. We throw away magazines and newspapers. The sounds of radio and visual images of television pass immediately, although this is changing somewhat with the increased use of home video recorders. Phonograph records are a bit more permanent, but they wear out, break, become dated, and are hard to store. Movie film is also difficult for the private individual to store. But any person can put together bookshelves and keep books for a lifetime. The permanent storage of books has been institutionalized through libraries. All this gives books a reuse rate far higher than that of other media. The book can be retrieved, referred to, and reused better than other forms of communication.

More than most media, the book is personal. One can sit alone with a book, at leisure, whenever the mood strikes. One can read a book at one's own pace—can stop and start at will—and can leaf through the book and find a special passage. There is no need for speed; time is of little concern. Because this is so, the author of a book can develop a subject much more completely than can the originator of any other mass communication medium.

The book carries with it an aura of more dignity and respect than most other media, perhaps because it has been so closely identified with education, intellectual activity, and the recorded wisdom of humankind. People who would not think twice about wrapping their garbage with the "Week in Review" section of the *New York Times* might keep on their bookshelves a superficial romance bound in book form. We tend to have a reverence for the book that transcends our reverence for all other media.

Newspapers | 15

Newspapers are as indispensable to democracy as books are to learning. Indeed, newspapers and modern democracies grew up together, and it is doubtful that a democracy could exist without newspapers that are free from government regulation and restraint. Each day more than 100 million people in America rely on newspapers to provide accurate, timely, and useful information to help them plan their daily lives. Newspapers provide the facts and analysis that allow informed citizens to make effective and responsible decisions, not only in coping with the complexities of modern living, but also in protecting the rights and liberties of a free society.

From the earliest days of newspapers, monarchical and authoritarian governments were challenged by newspapers spreading information to the people. Information has always been powerful, and as people acquired more information, they acquired more power over their own destinies, and their ruler's power over their lives was lessened. So newspapers have often been suppressed by authorities.

The founding fathers of America, hoping to establish a free and democratic society, knew that a free flow of information was essential to citizens seeking their rights and freedoms. They knew that newspapers were the key to the free flow of information, and so they insisted on the freedom of newspapers to pursue the truth and publish it, whether the government agreed with the truth or not. Thomas Jefferson summed up this political philosphy when he said:

> The basis of our government being the opinion of the people, the first object should be to keep that right; and were it left to me to decide whether we should have a government without newspapers, or newspapers without a government, I should not hesitate a moment to prefer the latter. But I should mean that every man should receive those papers and be capable of reading them.

HISTORICAL PERSPECTIVES

The regular publication of news goes back more than 2000 years to at least 59 B.C., when the Romans posted public news sheets called *Acta Diurna*. The word *diurna*, meaning "daily," has been an important part of news ever since. The words *journal* and *journalism* have their roots in the same word, "day," and the daily, current, or timely aspect of news has always been an essential factor in newspapers.

But for much of the past 2000 years, the communication of news has been carefully guarded. Through most of the days of the Roman Empire and the Dark Ages, the distribution of news came under the strict control of both secular and ecclesiastical authorities. Even after the development of the printing press in the mid-fifteenth century, it was another 150 years before the political climate changed sufficiently to allow the beginnings of the modern newspaper.

Early Development of the Newspaper

During that 150 years (and long thereafter), printers had to fight monarchs for the right to publish. William Caxton, the first English printer, set up his press in 1476 and worked in relative freedom for 50 years, largely because he did not print any news. When Henry VIII came to the throne of England, he feared the power of the press, and by 1534 he had set up strong measures to control printing. For more than a hundred years after that, the British maintained repressive restrictions on printers; some were hanged and many were imprisoned for defying the authority of the Crown.

As Edwin Emery points out in his history of journalism, *The Press and America*: "It is significant that the newspaper first flourished in areas where authority was weak, as in Germany, at that time divided into a patchwork of small principalities." The first prototype newspaper, a rudimentary version, to be sure, was published about 1609, probably in Bremen, Germany. In that same year a primitive newspaper appeared in Strasbourg, and another in Cologne in 1610. By 1620, primitive newspapers were being printed in Frankfurt, Berlin, Hamburg, Vienna, Amsterdam, and Antwerp.

The first English prototype newspaper was printed in London in 1621. From that year to 1665, various *corantos* and *diurnals* ("current" and "daily" forms of publication) made their appearance. These often took the forms of tracts and broadsides, rather than newspapers. Their production accompanied a growing freedom from governmental control, climaxed by the ringing declarations of the poet John Milton. In 1664, in his essay *Areopagitica*, he expressed the basic rationale of a free press in the democratic society:

> [T]hough all the winds of doctrine were let loose to play upon the earth, so truth be in the field, we do injuriously by licensing and prohibiting to misdoubt her strength. Let her [truth] and falsehood grapple; who ever knew truth put to the worse, in a free and open encounter?

In 1665 the first true English-language newspaper, in form and style, was published in Oxford, then the seat of the English government. It was called the *Oxford Gazette*. When the government moved to London some months later, the newspaper moved too, and became the *London Gazette*. Thirty-seven years later, in 1702, the first daily newspaper, the *Daily Courant*, was published in London. In those 37 years, English printers of newspapers had won many rights, including the freedom to publish without a license.

In the British colonies, where people did not have full British citizenship, printers did not yet enjoy the same rights and freedoms. Thus, the first newspaper in the American colonies, *Publik Occurances, Both Forreign and Domestick*, published on 10 September 1690, was banned after its only issue because its printer, Benjamin Harris, did not have an appropriate license from the Crown.

Newspapers in Early America

Fourteen years later, the *Boston News-Letter* was started, published under the authority of the Massachusetts governor. Nevertheless, in its lifetime from 1704 to 1776—when it ceased publication because of the American Revolution—it was rebuked by the government on occasion, and publication was suspended several times.

Most early colonial newspapers, like their European counterparts, existed primarily for the purpose of spreading information about business and commerce. Produced by printers, not journalists, they contained some local gossip and stories, but many of them were concerned chiefly with advertising and often had the word "advertiser" in their title. They told about ship comings and goings, market information, import and export news, and trade tips. But the colonial printers who published these newspapers could not help but inject stories about political conditions that affected their businesses, and they expressed their opinions on such political matters. As they smarted under their second-class British citizenship, they began to express in their editorials their bitterness over the policies of the Crown.

In 1721 James Franklin, a colonial printer, began publication of the *New England Courant*. When he published a sarcastic comment about the British governor, he was thrown into jail; his 13-year-old brother, Benjamin, took over the paper. This started Ben Franklin on a lifetime of writing, printing, and publishing. Later Franklin went to Philadelphia to start his own print shop and newspaper, and before he was 40 he had become the first "press lord" in America, having founded a chain of print shops and newspapers in which he held partial ownership.

Another colonial printer who ran afoul of the Crown was John Peter Zenger, printer of the *New York Weekly Journal*. In 1734 Zenger was thrown into jail for libeling the governor. But a jury of colonists ultimately freed Zenger when a shrewd Philadelphia lawyer, Andrew Hamilton, made a convincing argument of the point that Zenger's facts had been true and that men should be free to print the truth, even if it is damaging.

The case eventually led to the legal interpretation that newspapers could print anything, even attacks on follies and abuses of government, if they could prove their criticism was based on facts. This gave journalists an unprecedented power in the modern world.

The Zenger case emboldened the colonial newspapers to take up the attack against the colonists' status as second-class citizens. Increasingly, political activists among them used the pages of colonial newspapers to arouse public opinion against the abuses of British authority, leading finally to the Declaration of Independence and the Revolutionary War.

The historian Arthur M. Schlesinger, Jr., in his book *Prelude to Independence: The Newspaper War on Britain 1764–1776*, demonstrates

Andrew Hamilton addresses the court in this artist's conception of the John Peter Zenger trial. The verdict left government and public figures open to attacks from the newspapers *provided* they could prove their criticism to be based on fact. (Courtesy State Library of New York.)

clearly that colonial newspapers were powerful weapons in the battle for freedom from the Crown. Some of the founding fathers were newspaper writers and press agents who fought for independence through the pages of the colonial press. Among them were Samuel Adams, Thomas Paine, Thomas Jefferson, John Adams, John Dickinson, Benjamin Franklin, and Richard Henry Lee.

After the revolution, colonial newspapers again served to encourage social action, helping to persuade the liberated citizens to ratify the Constitution and adopt a democratic form of government. Another historian, Allan Nevins, in a booklet titled *The Constitution Makers and the Public, 1785–1790*, describes how James Madison, Alexander Hamilton, and John Jay sent essays to colonial newspapers urging support for the new constitution. Today we know those "press handouts" as *The Federalist Papers*. It was, says Nevins, "the greatest work ever done in America in the field of public relations." Little wonder, then, that newspapers were so important to the new nation of America.

Although the first American "daily" newspaper, the *Pennsylvania Evening Post and Daily Advertiser*, was started in 1783, it was not until half a century later that newspapers began to reach a truly mass audience. Until the 1830s, newspapers were fairly high priced and aimed at a relatively elite audience of political influentials. They were politically biased, often functioning as organs for a particular party or political viewpoint.

Technical advances in printing early in the nineteenth century made communication for the masses more feasible. Most important was the development of the cylinder press, which speeded the printing process enough to allow for mass production. One New York printer, Benjamin Day, used the new, fast press to start a trend in journalism. In 1833 he began the *New York Sun* and sold it for a penny rather than the usual 6 cents. By hiring newsboys to hawk the newspapers on the streets, he succeeded in making up in volume what he lost in individual sales. The *New York Sun* became the publishing success of journalism and started the era of the "penny press," the first mass circulation medium.

In order to sell penny papers on a mass basis, the newspapers had to contain material of interest to many people. This economic factor led to the development of the profession of news gathering. The man most responsible was James Gordon Bennett, a printer like Day, who started the *New York Herald* in 1835, two years after Day had started the *Sun*. Day and Bennett both realized that to sell papers on the streets of New York, they had to have good stories and interesting headlines.

Bennett started the practice of hiring writers to go out and find the stories, and the modern news reporter was born. He sent men to the police stations to get stories about crime, to city hall for stories about politics. He sent reporters into New York harbor in boats to meet ships coming in

The Penny Press— The First Mass Medium

James Gordon Bennet (shown here), along with Benjamin Day, were the "fathers" of the mass circulation newspaper. (Photo: New York Public Library Picture Collection.)

from Europe so that his paper could be the first with foreign news. And when the telegraph came into use in the 1840s, he was the first to station a correspondent in the nation's capital to wire stories about Congress and government back to New York City.

The penny press proved to be a great business success. Only 15 months after Bennett's *Herald* was born, it had a circulation of more than 40,000, and the number of readers grew steadily. Other newspapers were started, such as Horace Greeley's *New York Tribune* and Henry Raymond's *New York Times*. With circulation ultimately reaching the hundreds of thousands, these papers and their editors became powerful forces in mid-nineteenth century society, playing an influential role in the Civil War, the industrial revolution, westward expansion, and American urbanization. Similar newspapers soon were started in cities across the country.

Yellow Journalism and Muckrakers   Mass circulation newspapers became big business by the end of the nineteenth century. The papers were highly competitive, for the most part independent, and were no longer tied to any one political party or group. Circulation was built largely through sensational news coverage or spicy features, with bold headlines and extra editions carrying the latest news.

"Newspaper barons"—men who had built newspaper empires through aggressive promotion—emerged toward the end of the nineteenth century. Joseph Pulitzer developed a strong *St. Louis Post-Dispatch* and then bought the *New York World* in 1883. The *World* had a circulation of 20,000 when Pulitzer took it over; less than a decade later, by 1892, he had raised its readership to 374,000. Pulitzer stressed sound news coverage combined with crusades and stunts to win his readers; in 1889 he sent a young reporter with the pseudonym of Nellie Bly around the world to beat the record of the fictitious Phileas Fogg, hero of Jules Verne's *Around the World in Eighty Days*. Nellie completed the trip in 72 days, and circulation of the *World* soared as readers kept up daily with her reports of her trip.

Another press lord, William Randolph Hearst, entered journalism as the student business manager of the *Harvard Lampoon* and then received the *San Francisco Examiner* as a gift from his wealthy father. In 1895 he purchased the *New York Journal* and copied many of Pulitzer's techniques to compete with the *New York World*. Knowing that headlines would sell papers, Hearst did not stop at reporting the news—he sometimes created news to get banner stories. Some historians have accused Hearst and the *Journal* of fomenting the Spanish-American War in 1898 to get more exciting stories and thus more subscribers.

In 1889, the same year as Nellie Bly's globe-circling trip, Pulitzer's *World* produced the first regular comic section, soon to be printed in color, in a Sunday paper. The most popular cartoon was a strip called *The Yellow Kid*, a feature that gave the name of "yellow journalism" to the whole era of sensational newspaper practices.

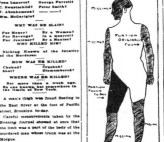

In addition to its frequent use of lurid headlines to attract attention, the yellow press encouraged reporters to investigate corruption. (Courtesy Bell & Howell Company)

According to the newspaper historian Frank Luther Mott, yellow journalism was based on sensationalized coverage of crime news, scandal and gossip, divorces and sex, disasters, and sports. Its distinguishing features were scare headlines, sensational pictures and photographs, stunts and faked stories, comic strips, Sunday-supplement features, and crusades for the downtrodden and the lower classes. Similar elements often have been part of other new mass media.

The crusading element was most important. The yellow press, with hundreds of thousands of regular readers, exercised great influence on public opinion. By exposing graft and corruption in society, newspapers found they could not only sell more papers but could also perform a service to society. A new breed of reporter began to develop, one who was interested in investigating the sins of society and the hidden perversions of power. These men, to use Teddy Roosevelt's expression, "raked the muck of society."

The so-called muckrakers did much social good. For example, Lincoln Steffens exposed graft and corruption in city governments and helped bring about municipal reform. Ida Tarbell's exposé of the Standard Oil Company helped to strengthen antimonopoly laws. Samuel Hopkins Adams's investigation of the patent-medicine business led to federal food and drug regulations. These writers worked in the magazine and book fields as well as newspapers, but they typified a new breed of newspaper journalist.

By the beginning of the twentieth century, the daily newspaper had become a power for good and evil in society. It was the first and most influential mass medium.

The Modern Newspaper

In the twentieth century the American newspaper grew into more maturity and responsibility. During the first 30 years of the new century, some of the old newspaper giants of the nineteenth century declined and fell, including the *World* and *Sun*. In *The Compact History of the American Newspaper*, John Tebbel says this marked "the transition from propaganda and personal journalism to the conservative newspapermaking of a new generation of businessmen soon to rise." In the twentieth century corporate caution replaced the old individual newspaper flamboyance.

One of the reasons for the change was economic. James Gordon Bennett had started the *New York Herald* in 1835 with an investment of $500. By 1900, it would have taken $1 million to start a New York newspaper, and by mid-century, at least $6 million. The amount of investment required for a large metropolitan newspaper plant today is usually $10–15 million. The *Los Angeles Times*, for example, estimates that it has more than $65 million invested in printing equipment alone. Enterprises with that sort of money at stake cannot afford to be reckless.

One consequence of rising costs and big-business operations has been the death of many newspapers and the merger of many others. In New

York City, most of the giants of the nineteenth century merged, becoming the *New York World, Telegram,* and *Sun;* the *New York Herald Tribune;* and the *New York Journal-American.* And all of these ultimately merged in the 1960s into the *New York World-Journal Tribune,* and then died.

The front page of *The New York Daily News* is frequently dominated by eyecatching photographs and sensational headlines. (Reproduced with permission of *The New York Daily News.*)

The same happened, though perhaps less dramatically, in other American cities.

Sensational journalism did not die completely in the twentieth century. An important manifestation of it was the so-called jazz journalism of the 1920s, marked by the rise of tabloid newspapers, smaller in size than regular "blanket" newspapers. These papers usually made extensive use of photographs and were dominated by one or two major headline stories. Such a paper is the *New York Daily News*; started in 1919, it grew swiftly in the 1920s, with sex and sensation as its stock in trade. Its circulation was the largest in the country until the mid-1980s, when it was eclipsed by the *Wall Street Journal*.

In the twentieth century, daily newspapers have had to withstand rising competition from many sides. The new mass media—radio, television, and movies—have grown to challenge the premier position of the newspaper as mass communicator. The automobile revolution, the suburban exodus, the death of the inner city, and growing leisure time for sports, recreation, and entertainment, have also changed the place of the newspaper in the daily life of the twentieth-century individual.

Twenty Largest U.S. Newspaper Companies, Ranked by Daily Circulation

	Daily circulation*	Number of dailies	Sunday circulation*	Number of Sunday editions
Gannett Co. Inc.†	4,483,483	85	3,472,915	56
Knight-Ridder Newspapers Inc.	3,651,369	29	4,347,439	22
Newhouse Newspapers	3,202,759	27	3,551,315	21
Tribune Co.	2,756,062	8	3,702,702	7
Dow Jones & Company Inc.	2,558,341	21	388,884	10
Times Mirror Co.	2,340,844	7	2,934,891	7
News America Publishing Inc.	2,087,681	5	1,120,243	3
Scripps-Howard Newspapers	1,459,880	16	1,576,782	7
The New York Times Co.	1,367,338	21	1,911,659	10
Thomson Newspapers Inc. (U.S.)	1,294,711	84	804,802	38
Cox Enterprises Inc.	1,196,448	18	1,363,987	13
Hearst Newspapers	969,193	14	1,927,760	8
Capital Cities Communications Inc.	965,063	9	824,015	5
Freedom Newspapers Inc.	849,413	29	802,983	19
Central Newspapers Inc.	804,641	7	842,223	4
The Washington Post Co.	774,167	2	1,052,185	2
Cowles Newspapers	713,398	6	1,081,659	6
The Copley Press Inc.	708,071	11	641,976	6
Evening News Association	690,289	5	788,203	1
Donrey Media Group	617,690	49	588,257	42

* Average for 6 months ended 30 September 1983.
† Includes estimated average of 1,041,667 for *USA Today*.
SOURCE: Morton Research, Lynch, Jones & Ryan, from *Facts About Newspapers*. Reston, VA.: American Newspapers Publishers' Association, 1984, p. 16.

Chain ownership of newspapers is a twentieth-century phenomenon that developed to offset rising costs and growing competition. In chain ownership different newspapers, owned by a single corporation, gain the advantage of management efficiency. Among the larger and more important newspaper chains in the United States are those of Hearst, Scripps-Howard, Copley, Gannett, Newhouse, Thomson, Knight-Ridder, Dow Jones, Harte-Hanks, and Tribune Company newspapers.

Today a number of great American newspapers are economically sound, politically independent, and socially responsible, despite competition and high costs. For nearly a century, the *New York Times* has maintained its reputation as the newspaper of record. (It is kept in libraries as the official record of the day's events.) Two other great newspapers claiming a national audience are the *Wall Street Journal* and the *Christian Science Monitor*, both of which have won wide respect for their coverage of important news and their penetrating analysis of events. The *Washington Post* rose rapidly during the 1950s and 1960s to challenge the *New York Times*, as did the *Los Angeles Times*, under the dynamic leadership of Otis Chandler. Other great newspapers of the twentieth century are the *Baltimore Sun, Kansas City Star, Louisville Courier-Journal, Milwaukee Journal, Minneapolis Star-Tribune,* and *St. Louis Post-Dispatch*, to name a few.

The "alternative" press has become a medium of communication that has a direct and personal appeal to select subcultures within our society. The newspapers are not "underground," as they are sometimes called, **THE "ALTERNATIVE" PRESS**

Twenty-Five Largest U.S. Daily Newspapers

Rank		Total daily circulation	Rank		Total daily circulation
1	Wall Street Journal	2,081,995	13	Philadelphia Inquirer	536,065
2	N.Y. Daily News	1,374,858	14	Long Island Newsday	533,384
3	USA Today	1,332,974	15	Boston Globe	510,261
4	L.A. Times	1,057,536	16	Cleveland Plain Dealer	492,002
5	N.Y. Times	970,051	17	Miami Herald	451,206
6	N.Y. Post	963,069	18	Newark Star Ledger	432,238
7	Washington Post	768,288	19	Houston Chronicle	427,560
8	Chicago Tribune	762,882	20	Dallas Morning News	340,502
9	Detroit News	657,015	21	Boston Herald	325,086
10	Detroit Free Press	631,087	22	Buffalo Evening News	320,028
11	Chicago Sun Times	628,285	23	Rocky Mountain News	319,177
12	San Francisco Chronicle	539,450	24	Arizona Republic	314,460
			25	Milwaukee Journal	306,055

SOURCE: Circulation figures from ABC FAS-FAX for the period ended March 31, 1984.

The Guardian

Viewpoint:
Another look
at Flight 007
Page 18

INDEPENDENT RADICAL NEWSWEEKLY   SEPTEMBER 12, 1984   90¢

Cuba travel fight brews

By DENNIS SCHAAL

The right to travel from the U.S. to Cuba, already sharply restricted by the Reagan administration, came under further attack last month when the Treasury Department demanded to see the records of the only U.S. travel agent arranging passage to Cuba.

In one subpoena, served Aug. 14, the Treasury Department directed New York City-based Marazul Tours to turn over all documents concerning travel it had arranged to Cuba since 1982. Two days later a second subpoena demanded that Marazul turn over its records of advertising a Cuban National Commission of Jurists' conference in Cuba scheduled for later this month, for which the travel agency had sent an advertising brochure to some 2000 U.S. attorneys. Among other things, the subpoena covers the mailing list used by Marazul to distribute the brochure.

With the support of the American Civil Liberties Union (ACLU) and the Center for Constitutional Rights (CCR), Marazul is resisting complying with the subpoena in full. In particular, it has refused to supply the government with names of some 2000 North Americans that it has already sent to Cuba. Marazul also denies having a copy of the list of lawyers who received the brochure about the conference.

SUBPOENA DELAYED

On Aug. 31 representatives of the ACLU and the National Lawyers Guild met with Treasury Department officials to request that the subpoenas, which had a Sept. 5 deadline, be modified or withdrawn. But a day before the compliance deadline, it was learned that the Treasury Department had delayed the initial subpoena until Sept. 11 for modification. The National Lawyers Guild had been preparing to go to court to block the subpoenas on First Amendment grounds and at Guardian presstime, the subpoena concerning the lawyers conference was withdrawn.

Although the subpoenas have not yet been
(Continued on page 6)

Struggle scorches South Africa

By SUE DORFMAN

As South Africa's new apartheid parliament opened last week, the atmosphere was explosive. In a manner violently reminiscent of the 1960 Sharpeville rebellions and the 1976 and 1977 Soweto uprisings, state security forces and black South African township residents were once again in battle.

On Sept. 3, rebellions and police attacks in five black townships around Johannesburg left over 29 known dead and over 200 wounded. Police used tear gas, rubber bullets and birdshot against protesters armed with stones

and petrol bombs. On the same day, a bomb tore through the Department of Internal Affairs offices in central Johannesburg, injuring four people.

The uprising has been mainly attributed in the U.S. press to recent rent increases and school boycotts, but the protests over rent hikes and student demands have been building for many months. Anger and protest over the "new deal parliament" that excludes the participation of 23 million black South Africans has also been a key feature of South African political life for nearly a year. And Pretoria's refusal to settle conflicts with anything but violence reflects longstanding policy.

What is new is the escalation of activity from all sectors of the society. Those opposing the regime have significantly expanded their use of boycotts, strikes, petition drives and armed struggle. Those collaborating with the state by clinging to their positions in the new parliament and town councils have meanwhile resorted to sharply increased harassment, intimidation, arrests, pass raids, forced removals and armed attacks.

Since Aug. 30, 29 people have been listed officially as dead in the wake of rebellions in African townships. Affected areas include Tembisa, northeast of Johannesburg, and the townships of Sharpeville, Sebakeng, Boiostatong and Evanton.

Sharpeville, where the most violent unrest was said to have occured, has long been a symbol of black resistance to racist rule. Sixty-nine people were killed there during the 1960 uprisings. The total number of those killed, injured or arrested was not known at presstime.

(Continued on page 14)

Apartheid pits blacks against 'coloreds;' few colored or Indian-origin South Africans fell for 'separate elections' scheme last month, which leaves blacks on the outside.

An example of a successful "alternative" newspaper, *The Guardian* retains a traditional format, yet makes no attempt to hide a strong editorial slant in its selection and treatment of feature stories. (Courtesy *The Guardian*/115J.)

but are publicly available. They came into vogue during the 1960s, and by the end of that decade several hundred were in existence.

Today there is considerable flux in the fortunes of the alternative press. Many of the papers that were started during the rebellious years of the 1960s by flower children, hippies, war protestors, social and sexual reformers, and university activists have died. Others, such as *Rolling Stone* and the *Village Voice*, have become so successful that they can hardly be considered alternatives anymore; they are now part of the establishment press.

These papers are printed by inexpensive offset methods; are often sold on the streets rather than by subscription; and usually deal with sensational materials, either sexual, social, or political.

In order to divorce themselves from the traditional press, the young people who ran the alternative press often deliberately cast off accepted newspaper forms. The papers were sometimes garish, obnoxious, gaudy, biased, amateurish, vulgar, crude, slanted, and obscene. These tabloids specifically sought to combine unorthodox style with their content of dissent. The rejection of newspaper conventions, said the editors, like the rejection of American society, is vital—style and content are inseparable and must reject present societal and press conventions.

The alternative press appears to satisfy a need not fulfilled by the usual news media. Their editors argue that traditional "objective" reporting is impossible and, indeed, that subjective reporting should be the norm. Although some of the content is designed simply to shock, much of the "news" in these papers simply cannot be found in regular newspapers. The success of some of these papers cannot be discounted. Alternative papers have been found on some military bases, college campuses, and in high schools.

THE SUBURBAN AND THE SPECIALIZED PRESS

The development of photo-offset printing and cold-type composition, plus the automation and computerization of typesetting, enabled reporters to set their copy in type as they composed it and made small newspapers for a specialized audience economically feasible in the 1970s. The result has been the growth of small weekly newspapers to serve the local community and specialized weekly newspapers to serve distinct ethnic or cultural groups. In fact, the suburban press was the fastest growing form of journalism in the 1970s.

As people moved out of the central city and into the suburbs they continued to rely on their metropolitan daily for news until cheaper forms of printing made local newspapers possible. In the typical suburban communities of Washington, D.C., for example, dozens of new weeklies emerged in the 1960s and 1970s. One company, the Journal Publishing Company, by using a central plant with automated equipment, was able

Edstan Drive Traffic Discussed

Having considered a number of alternative ways for slowing down traffic and making Edstan Drive safer for pedestrians — especially schoolchildren — the borough may have to fall back on its periodic police radar checks to accomplish its objectives.

As residents of this designated-by-ordinance through street know too well, it is a convenient bypass for those traveling to and from work when the daily jam-ups occur on Moonachie Road and at the intersection of Redneck and Moonachie Avenues. In recognition of numerous complaints about this situation, the Mayor & Council recently surveyed all 78 homeowners as to their desires to have sidewalks installed along the length of that street, but only 14 of the survey forms had been returned as of Tuesday.

Some 20 residents attended a special open session of the governing body prior to last Thursday's work meeting and their comments ranged from asking for enforcement of the "no thru traffic" signs (which, they were told, are unenforceable but are intended to serve as a deterrent), to making part of the street one-way at various hours (also of questionable legality), to installation of traffic signals at one or more intersecting streets (state DOT approval not likely). A mayoral proposal to install stop signs at Jefferson (southbound) and Truman (northbound) also seemed unlikely to be approved.

(Continued on page 8)

INDEPENDENT photo

Radar in operation Tuesday morning at Edstan and Truman.

Serving Wood-Ridge & Moonachie

WOOD-RIDGE INDEPENDENT

VOL. L, No. 26   **15c Per Copy**   **Thursday, June 28, 1984**

JOINS RANKS — Ptl. Joseph Abitante (right), Vice President of Wood-Ridge PBA Local 313 presiding at the June 20th meeting, administers the oath of office to newly-appointed Ptl. Thomas Faivre. The 28-year old officer, who resides in Englewood, became the 16th member of the recently-formed organisation. He had been a member of the Bergen County Sheriff's Department in the capacity of Corrections Officer at the County Jail for the past 3½ years before coming on the Wood-Ridge P.D. on January 1st of this year. Ptl. Faivre was unanimously accepted by the membership.

60 Plus Club

by Peggy Anthony

Social Meeting of the Sixty Plus Club was held on June 21st; attendance was 101.

EMD Reorganizes

A re-organization meeting of the Evening Membership Department of the Woman's Club of Wood-Ridge was held recently at the home of Virginia Smirle, newly-installed Chairman of the Wood-Ridge E.M.D.

The following are the new Committee Chairmen: American Home, Ruth Stumm; Music and Drama, Doris Genton; Social Services, Elsie Mae Scherba; Hospitality, Ruth Cashnelli; Membership, Christine Bagdzinski; Program, Janet Nieradka and Trudy Wells; Public Relations, Beatrice White; Ways and Means, Florence Kotter, Jean Rodemeyer, Evelyn Shedd; Cheerio, Dolores Dill; Education, Lillian Habermann; Breakfast With Santa, Ruth Stumm; and Parliamentarian, Evelyn Shedd.

Children's Films

The film, Noah's Animals, will be shown in the Children's Room of the Wood-Ridge Memorial Library on Wednesday, July 11th at 1:30 p.m.

Crossing Guards Sought in W-R

The Wood-Ridge Police Department is now accepting applications for the positions of both full-time and relief school crossing guards for the 1984-85 school year. Interested persons are asked to come to headquarters (85 Humboldt St.) or to call 939-0476.

We had a guest speaker, Mr. Shannon from Short Line Tours. He showed a movie on a trip to Atlantic Canada. It was most interesting and made you feel you wanted to get up and go there now.

On Thursday, June 14th, we had a nice trip to The Old Mill Inn at Spring Lake, where we had a lovely luncheon, and then went on to the boardwalk at Asbury Park.

Our best to Edna Owens, who suffered a fractured elbow in a nasty fall; to Fanny Conti, who is recuperating from an operation; and to all others who have been ill. A speedy recovery to all.

Next outing is to Granite, where we always have a real good time.

Bus Ridership To Be Promoted By Meadowlands Chamber

In a continuing effort to "get more people out of their cars and onto buses," the Meadowlands Chamber of Commerce has embarked on a marketing plan designed to increase the use of NJ Transit services, according to Richard Fritzky, the chamber's executive director.

"As the Meadowlands District has grown," Fritzky said, "more and more people are driving to work alone and clogging the highways. We plan to contact most of the 85,000 people who work in the Meadowlands District with the message, 'take the bus.'"

NJ Transit has given the Chamber a $5,000 grant for a four-month program. In addition, the transit corporation is printing 70,000 copies of a ride guide for the Meadowlands District, and 2,000 posters urging people to make more use of the bus transportation available.

"We feel if people are more aware of the convenience of bus service and how economical it is compared to car travel, more area workers will use the bus," Fritzky said.

The Chamber will initially contact its more than 600 members asking for cooperation in getting the message to their employees and then reach out to all firms with offices and plants in the Meadowlands District.

The ride guide, entitled Meadowlands Connections, "will be very valuable. We intend to list every bus route, the stops and the timetables so that people have a quick and convenient single source of information on public transportation.

EARLY DEADLINE FOR NEXT WEEK'S ISSUE

With Independence Day being next Wednesday, the deadline for submitting all copy, pictures and advertising for the Thursday, July 5th issue of the Independent will be 12 NOON on Monday, July 2nd. Thank you in advance for your cooperation.

Holiday Closings

All banks as well as the Post Office will be closed on Independence Day, Wednesday, July 4th. The office of the Independent will also be closed(see notice of early deadline above).

This Week In...

WOOD-RIDGE

Mon., July 2nd — 8 p.m., Shade Tree Commission, Boro Hall (subject to postponement; check with Boro Office on Monday before 4 p.m.)

Thurs., July 5th — 7:30 p.m., Board of Health, and Municipal Court (at Boro Hall).

• • • • •

MOONACHIE

Tues., July 3rd — 7:30 p.m., Board of Education caucus, Craig School.

WRHS Students Excel In Youth & Government Program

Members of the Wood-Ridge High School Tri-Hi-Y and Hi-Y Service Club recently attended the 46th YMCA Youth and Government Program at the convocation in Trenton.

Joseph Solda's bill to provide Advanced Emergency Life Support Systems was one of the first bills to be passed. Tina McKeever, Vincent Minervini and Sandra Ruppert helped to draw up this bill.

A bill to provide Tuition Incentives for Prospective Teachers, sponsored by Vincent Minervini, also passed. Theresa Ciardi assisted with this bill.

Christopher Trause was appointed to the Governor's Cabinet as Attorney General.

Sandra Ruppert was awarded a certificate of honor for her election to the 1984 Youth Conference on National Affairs. Christopher Trause and Theresa Ciardi will also participate in this conference.

Other students participating in the program were: Annmarie Haley, Terence McKeever, Mary-Ann Morreale, Elisa Quinzer and John Reitz.

Principal Paul J. Moran, attended the conference as an advisor and resource person. Vincent Morreale, an alumnus of WRHS and Fordham University, served as Senate Advisor. Elizabeth Marcellaro was bill expeditor.

Superintendent of Schools Mr. Thomas Gallagher visited the sessions in Trenton to observe the program first-hand and to lend his support.

In an incident involving a young man who collapsed upon exiting the pool at the hotel, Joseph Solda applied emergency paramedic assistance.

The Youth and Government Program is coordinated and directed by Elizabeth Marcellaro and Gretta Ostrovsky.

Morreale Heads W-R Dem Men

Former Councilman Peter J. Morreale was elected President of the Wood-Ridge Men's Democratic Club for the year 1984.

Morreale, who served as Borough Council president in 1973 and has once before served as Men's Democratic Club President, is presently serving as Chairman of the Wood-Ridge Zoning Board of Adjustment. He was elected unanimously, as were George Hohn, Vice President; Harry Lynch, Treasurer; and Henry Zajac, Secretary.

President Morreale called upon Democratic Council candidates John Molinelli and James Silvestri to tell the membership about their campaign plans. Candidate Molinelli announced that he and Silvestri had selected Mayor Herb Gorab and Councilman Harvey Young to act as their co-campaign managers. Silvestri and Molinelli pledged a positive, issue-oriented campaign.

Councilmen Ed Roes and Gary Cosgrove were also asked to speak to the membership.

In closing, President Morreale commented that the turnout for the meeting was one of the largest in recent months. He also commented on the fact that several long-time Democrats were in attendance and he viewed that as a positive sign of increased party unity. He urged members to bring Democratic friends to the next meeting and advised that he was appointing Vice President Hohn as Membership Chairman to initiate a Club membership drive.

Lower production costs resulting from technologically advanced printing methods, have stimulated the proliferation of small suburban newspapers devoted to reporting local news. (Courtesy the Wood-Ridge Independent.)

within a short time to start five new suburban weeklies in the Washington area—the *Montgomery Journal, Prince Georges Journal, Alexandria Journal, Arlington Journal,* and *Fairfax Journal*—each serving a specific Washington suburb with news about the local community that could not be provided by the *Washington Post.* With the closing of the *Washington Star,* the suburban *Journal* papers decided to publish 5 days a week to provide better community and suburban coverage for the Washington, D.C., area. Other cities appear to be moving in this direction as well.

Other specific groups in our society have been able to develop their own newspapers. Foreign-language papers—Spanish, German, even Korean—are flourishing. Newspapers serving specific ethnic groups are also thriving.

Even within a community, the lowering of publication costs has made a proliferation of specialized publications possible. This is true within a corporation, an association, a university, and other institutions. At the University of Maryland, for example, until the mid-1960s, the campus was served by only one newspaper, the *Diamondback,* a student daily. Since then, cheaper printing has brought into existence dozens of campus newspapers, each serving a specialized audience. The faculty and administration have their weekly newsletters; the black students have a weekly newspaper; the fraternities and sororities, the commuter students, some of the dormitories, and some schools and departments regularly produce a publication for their members.

Special-interest groups are also producing newspapers for mass circulation, carrying the news from their perspective rather than a general, objective point of view. For example, in the 1980s a daily newspaper called the *Washington Times* was started in Washington, D.C. It was published by a group with backing from Sun Myung Moon, the Korean religious leader who has stimulated a growing religious movement. The *Washington Times* was a professional-looking newspaper with news stories, color photographs, editorials, features, and some advertising; but its general slant was toward Moon's philosophy.

THE BLACK PRESS

An exception to the huge growth of a specialized press has been the black press, which has been declining in circulation. Nevertheless, in the 1980s it is still a potent voice. The black press was started in America more than 150 years ago when John B. Russwurm and the Reverend Samuel E. Cornish published the first issue of *Freedom's Journal* in 1827.

Prior to the Civil War, more than 40 newspapers were published for blacks. Many of them were short-lived; all suffered extreme pressures. The most prominent was the *North Star,* founded and edited by Frederick Douglass to "attack slavery in all its forms." By 1890 there were 575 black newspapers in America. Many of them became great voices of the black

Serving the Italian-American community, *Il Progresso* is one example of the many foreign language newspapers currently thriving in the United States. (Courtesy *Il Progresso*.)

community, especially newspapers such as the *Chicago Defender*, the *New York Amsterdam News*, the *Baltimore* and *Washington Afro-American*, the *Milwaukee Courier*, the *San Francisco Sun*, the *Columbus Times*, and the *Los Angeles Sentinel*.

Since *Freedom's Journal*, more than 3000 black newspapers have been founded in the United States. Only 220 are still being published, but they are stronger than ever, with a total circulation of about 4 million. Ad-

New York Amsterdam News

VOL. 75, NO. 36, SATURDAY, SEPTEMBER 8, 1984   **The new Black view**

50¢ · Outside NYC · 60¢
© 1984 The New York Amsterdam News

Black officers threaten to sue city over exam

Editorial:

The Amsterdam News endorses:

In this political year, it is perhaps more important than ever before for Blacks and Hispanics to go out in record numbers to vote, in order to assure the beginning of political empowerment for the 53 percent of the citizens of this city — Blacks, Hispanics and Asians — who are not represented at all on the most important body in this city — the Board of Estimate.

The fight for political representation on the Board of Estimate — Mayor, Comptroller, President of the City Council and the five borough Presidencies — does not occur until 1985. But we must begin now to vote for and elect those of consequence and competence to retain or take seats in the Congress, the State Senate, and Assembly, as well as the District Leaderships and a lone seat in the City Council now filled by appointment. Only in this way might a cadre of professionals be on board when we move to form a truly representative government in this city for all of its citizens.

Jesse Jackson has in so many ways been a lynchpin, focusing on the major issues that immediately affect our lives and creating, in that focus, the necessity for coalition, as well as intense voter registration. He has fostered the idea of a rainbow embracing those who have been locked out of the political process — primarily the poor, who come in all colors; but most particularly the Black, Hispanic and Asian poor, who, due to America's peculiarity, when one speaks of difference, find themselves locked out, not only due to poverty, but to skin color, nose angle and racial inheritance. The fact of the matter is, one can be a "rich" Black, Hispanic or Asian, yet find oneself locked out equally by a process of electoral politics that seeks to divide people along racist lines, while at the same time pitting minority against minority in order to assure the continuation of morally bankrupt and sometimes politically corrupt machines.

We can no longer allow ourselves to fall victim to the schemes of some of the existing county leaderships that have purposely run Blacks and Hispanics against each other, as well as Blacks against Blacks, and Hispanics against other Hispanics, thereby maintaining an incumbent who does not represent either group. There are heavily populated minority communities served by an incumbent not particularly sympathetic to their dreams, needs or aspirations. To be sure, there are some incumbent candidates who are notable excep-
(Continued on page 12)

IT'S . . . O.K. like us, we were baffled, but as this masquerader told us "anything goes on Labor Day." (See page 8 for more carnival pictures)

Jesse: Let us boot out Ron

By SIMON ANEKWE
Amsterdam News Staff

"I choose to support Mondale/Ferraro and fight the Reagan/Bush regime," the Rev. Jesse Jackson thundered through the microphone to some 900,000 participants at Monday's West Indian-American Labor Day Carnival and Parade along Brooklyn's Eastern Parkway.

"Let's elect Mondale together. Let's retire Reagan together. It's time for a change," said the former Democratic Presidential candidate, as he fulfilled his last week's promise to "hit the ground running on Labor Day," on behalf of the Democratic ticket.

But vote not just for Walter Mondale and Geraldine Ferraro his running mate, Jackson stated. Blacks should vote for the 435 Democratic candidates for Congress at the November election. "There's Simeon Golar in Queens," he added about the Black challenger in the 6th C.D. race.

And the road to the election of the Democratic candidates he supported would

be voter registration, Jackson stated; with the largest such effort in the nation set to start in the next few days. "Your votes do count," he told his listeners.

He talked about the narrow margins of victory in the 1960, 1976 presidential races and in Reagan's victory over Jimmy Carter in 1980. "We (Continued on page 20)

Result is biased, they say

By J. ZAMGBA BROWNE
Amsterdam News Staff

A group of Black police officers say they will go to court to challenge the results of a controversial sergeants examination in which Blacks scored very poorly.

The Guardians Association claims the test was discriminatory because only 1.6 percent of the Black candidates and 4.4 percent of the Hispanic candidates earned passing grades compared to 10.6 percent for whites.

Marvin Blue, president of the Guardians said his group's challenge is based on a New York State guideline which stipulates that if the results of a police exam for a group of candidates fall sharply below a certain percentage point, that test should immediately be de-
(Continued on page 20)

AT CARIB CARNIVAL — The Rev. Jesse Jackson spoke to nearly a million revelers out on Eastern Parkway, Monday, at the West Indian-American Labor Day Carnival. Percy Sutton who introduced Jackson and Jewell Jackson McCabe are closest to his right; with Simeon Golar and Albert Vann to his left. (Lem Peterkin Photo)

The *New York Amsterdam News* is the largest paid-circulation black newspaper in America today. (Courtesy the *New York Amsterdam News*.)

vertising linage is growing; although it is still a minor fraction of establishment newspaper advertising, it has doubled in the past 25 years.

The New York *Amsterdam News*, founded in 1909, is the largest paid-circulation black newspaper, with about 100,000 readers. Seven of the black newspapers in history have been dailies; five, including the *Am-*

sterdam News, are still in existence. The oldest are the *Atlanta Daily World*, launched in 1932, and the *Chicago Daily Defender*, started in 1956. The *Columbus Times* and the *New York Challenge* were started in the 1970s.

The black press established its own organization in 1940: the National Newspaper Publishers Association. But the black press declined in the decades after the war, as blacks became increasingly assimilated into white culture. James D. Williams, director of communications for the National Urban League, in a booklet titled *The Black Press and the First Amendment*, wrote that

> there were other factors that also began to operate against the black press; the general decline in newspaper readership as more and more people turned to television; the dispersal of black persons outside the central city where the black papers were available; the continued indifference of major advertisers to black media . . . and a decline, in some instances, of the quality and quantity of the reporting.

THE SCOPE OF NEWSPAPERS Newspapers maintained a strong and healthy economic posture throughout the 1970s and that seems to be continuing into the 1980s. The number of daily newspapers in the United States in the mid-1980s is about 1700. The peak number was reached just before World War I in 1914 when 2250 individual dailies were published. In 1973 newspaper circulation

Number of U.S. Daily Newspapers, 1946–1983

Year	Morning	Evening	Total M&E*	Sunday
1946	334	1,429	1,763	497
1950	322	1,450	1,772	549
1955	316	1,454	1,760	541
1960	312	1,459	1,763	563
1965	320	1,444	1,751	562
1970	334	1,429	1,748	586
1975	339	1,436	1,756	639
1980	387	1,388	1,745	735
1981	408	1,352	1,730	755
1982	434	1,310	1,711	768
1983	441	1,288	1,699	770

* There were 30 "all-day" newspapers in 1983. They are listed in both morning and evening columns but only once in the total.
SOURCE: *Editor & Publisher*, from *Facts About Newspapers*. Reston, VA.: American Newspaper Publishers Association, 1984, p. 2.

Circulation of U.S. Daily Newspapers, 1946–1983

Year	Morning	Evening	Total M&E	Sunday
1946	20,545,908	30,381,597	50,927,505	43,665,364
1950	21,266,126	32,562,946	53,829,072	46,582,348
1955	22,183,408	33,963,951	56,147,359	46,447,658
1960	24,028,788	34,852,958	58,881,746	47,698,651
1965	24,106,776	36,250,787	60,357,563	48,600,090
1970	25,933,783	36,173,744	62,107,527	49,216,602
1975	25,490,186	36,165,245	60,655,431	51,096,393
1980	29,414,036	32,787,804	62,201,840	54,671,755
1981	30,552,316	30,878,429	61,430,745	55,180,004
1982	33,174,087	29,313,090	62,487,177	56,260,764
1983	33,570,242	29,041,494	62,611,741	56,714,895

SOURCE: *Editor & Publisher*, From *Facts About Newspapers*. Reston, VA.: American Newspaper Publishers Association, 1984, p. 3.

in America hit a peak, with more than 63 million copies printed each day. Since then, daily circulation has hovered around the 62 million mark. By the mid-1980s, four newspapers sold more than a million copies each day: the *Wall Street Journal*, the *New York Daily News*, the *Los Angeles Times*, and *USA Today*.

After a period of decline, the number of weekly newspapers is beginning to rise again. In 1960 there were 8138 weeklies in America, but that number had dropped to 7466 by 1977. By the mid-1980s, there were about 7600 weeklies in operation. Weekly newspaper circulation has shown steady growth over the last 20 years, from 21 million in 1960 to more than 44 million in the mid-1980s. Average circulation also rose to its highest level.

Although the number of newspapers and their circulation have been relatively stable, newspaper advertising, both national and local, has grown enormously. In the mid-1980s, ad revenue reached an all-time high of more than $18 billion, more than triple the revenue from advertising in 1970. Newspapers also received a larger share (27.2%) of the advertising dollar than the other media but that share was down a few percentage points from the 1970s.

Group ownership of newspapers has continued to grow. In 1910 there were only 13 newspaper groups; in 1980 there were 163. Nearly 1100 dailies are published by groups, or about 62% of all American newspapers. One of the fastest-growing is Gannett, which by the mid-1980s published 85 dailies and 34 nondailies, with a combined circulation of nearly 5 million.

Weekly U.S. Newspapers and Circulation, 1960–1984

Year	Total weekly newspapers	Average circulation	Total weekly circulation
1960	8,174	2,566	20,974,338
1965	8,061	3,106	25,036,031
1970	7,612	3,660	27,857,332
1975	7,612	4,715	35,892,409
1980	7,954	5,324	42,347,512
1981	7,602	5,389	40,970,890
1982	7,666	5,875	45,035,092
1983	7,626	5,808	44,295,042
1984	7,547	5,710	43,092,465

SOURCE: National Newspaper Association and American Newspaper Representatives, Inc. From *Facts About Newspapers*. Reston, VA.: American Newspaper Association, 1984, p. 14.

Newspaper Share of Advertising Revenue Sales and Percentages, 1982–1983

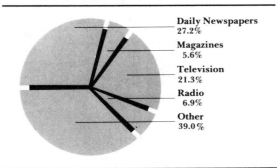

Daily Newspapers
27.2%

Magazines
5.6%

Television
21.3%

Radio
6.9%

Other
39.0%

SOURCE: McCann-Erickson Inc. From *Facts About Newspapers*. Reston, VA.: American Newspaper Publishers Association, 1984, p. 8.

Newspaper Workforce:
Distribution of Employees at a Typical
U.S. Metropolitan Daily Newspaper

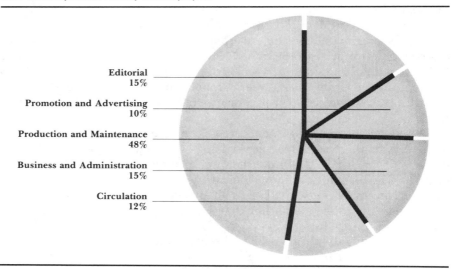

Editorial
15%

Promotion and Advertising
10%

Production and Maintenance
48%

Business and Administration
15%

Circulation
12%

SOURCE: Jon G. Udell, *Economics of the American Newspaper*, 1978, From *Facts About Newspapers*. Reston, VA.: American Newspaper Publishers Association, 1984, p. 13.

Gannett, in fact, is the publisher of *USA Today*, a national newspaper launched in 1982 that has already become a publishing success. The newspaper is edited in the Washington, D.C., area, but is printed by Gannett printing plants around the country. The content is transmitted to the printing plants by satellite, with regional issues containing some regional content. After little more than a year of operation, *USA Today*'s total circulation was more than a million a day, making it the third largest-circulation newspaper in the country. By the mid-1980s, Gannett's executives were exploring the possibilities of European and Pacific editions, to make *USA Today* an international paper.

Newspapers are also profitable businesses on the whole. *Fortune* magazine's analysis of the top 500 manufacturing industries in 1979 showed that newspapers, broadcasting, and motion-picture production and distribution companies had an average profit of 9.6%, which is higher than that of many industries. Of newspaper expenses, 37% went to employees. Another large share of costs, 28%, went to buy paper, a cost that has been rising sharply in the last decade.

Although newspapers face increased competition from other media, especially local radio and television, the number of newspapers that compete with one another is declining.

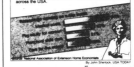

Its content transmitted to local printers by satellite, *USA Today* is a highly successful national newspaper. (Reprinted with permission of *USA Today*.)

Newspapers are one of America's largest manufacturing employers (behind only the steel, auto manufacturing, and auto parts manufacturing industries). Newspapers employ about 425,000 people. Most newspaper employees, 48%, work in production and maintenance, including printing. Editorial personnel make up only 15% of the newspaper's total work force. The number of women working in the business has increased by more than 45,000 since 1975. In 1983 there were 165,300 women working for newspapers, or almost 39% of the total work force.

Newspaper salaries have grown, too. In 1984 the minimum salary for a *New York Times* reporter who had served his or her apprenticeship was

Personal Characteristics of American Newspaper Readers and Nonreaders

Characteristic	Readers	Nonreaders
Sex		
Male	45.7	45.3
Female	54.3	54.7
	N = 5869	N = 285
Age		
Under 30	25.7	26.6
30–59	52.4	40.4
60 and older	21.9	33.0
	N = 5848	N = 282
Race		
White	87.6	75.8
Nonwhite	12.4	24.2
	N = 5869	N = 285
Education		
Less than high school	33.8	68.7
High school	50.6	28.9
Junior college	2.1	.4
Bachelor's	9.4	1.4
Graduate school	4.0	.7
	N = 5839	N = 284
Marital status		
Married	67.2	51.9
Widowed	9.4	18.2
Divorced or separated	9.2	16.5
Never married	14.3	13.3
	N = 5868	N = 285
Number of children		
None	25.6	22.1
One or two	38.6	37.8
Three through five	29.7	25.6
Six or more	6.0	14.6
	N = 5843	N = 281

SOURCE: *Journalism Quarterly*, Spring 1981, p. 11.

$843 a week, or about $44,000 a year. That same reporter would have made $164 a week in 1960.

Newspapers reach 108 million Americans every day, or 7 out of 10 adults. Every week 9 out of 10 adults read at least one newspaper. An average of 2.17 people read each newspaper delivered to a household. The average newspaper reader is more likely to be "mature" rather than either young or old, to be a college graduate rather than a high school dropout, to have a higher income rather than a lower one, to be white rather than nonwhite, and to be stable rather than mobile.

Newspaper reading habits usually develop in early adolescence and continue to grow until the retirement years. The average reader picks up a newspaper 1.9 times and reads 1.2 different papers. Almost everybody

The Newspaper Audience

Percentage of Frequent Readers of Newspaper Content, by Type of Reader

News category	Type I (N = 62) young optimists	Type II (N = 107) traditional conservatives	Type III (N = 128) progressive conservatives	Type IV (N = 52) grim independents
Weather	46.7%	50.4%	50.0%	59.6%
Housing aids	24.2	9.3	12.5	11.6
Astrology	29.0	27.1	18.8	11.5
Art and music	9.7	9.3	12.5	1.9
Travel	8.1	11.2	10.1	9.6
Gardening	8.1	20.6	14.8	15.4
Book reviews	4.8	6.6	8.6	0.0
Food	20.9	31.8	20.3	7.6
Society news	14.5	28.0	10.2	1.9
Letters to the editor	50.0	62.6	62.5	44.2
Puzzles and games	17.7	14.0	9.4	5.7
Advice columns	43.6	62.6	39.1	25.0
Classified ads	29.0	28.1	26.6	27.0
Local sports	29.1	21.5	39.1	51.9
National sports	32.3	31.8	43.7	51.9
Local news	72.5	79.4	81.3	73.1
National news	62.9	76.6	76.6	71.1
World news	51.6	69.1	68.0	61.5
Local deaths	35.4	63.6	41.4	23.0
Church news	11.3	23.4	13.2	11.5
Comics	35.4	29.9	37.5	25.0
News about people	35.5	38.3	30.5	13.5
Business	43.6	39.3	53.9	50.0
Editorials	40.4	57.0	62.5	42.3
TV and movie reviews	22.5	24.3	21.1	28.8

SOURCE: *Newspaper Research Journal*, November 1979, p. 13.

reads a newspaper sooner or later. Only 9% of Americans have not seen a weekday paper in the past week nor a Sunday paper in the past month. In the five weekdays, 52% read a paper every day and 84% read a paper on at least one weekday. More newspaper reading occurs in the afternoon than in the morning, but newspaper reading falls off dramatically after dinner, perhaps because people are turning instead to television.

Children's reading of newspapers grows with age. The 9 minutes of newspaper reading per day by 6- to 8-year-olds stretches to 19 minutes a day for 15- to 17-year-olds. But 19 minutes is only a small fraction of the time children spend watching television each day. Nevertheless, as children's newspaper reading increases, their TV watching decreases.

THE STRUCTURE AND ORGANIZATION OF NEWSPAPERS

Like all mass media, the newspaper is a highly structured, carefully organized, and exceedingly complex mechanism. Literally millions of words come into the large metropolitan daily each day, from many sources. These words must be sorted, selected, checked, evaluated, edited, rewritten, set in type, laid out, made up into pages, printed, and distributed to readers, all in less than 24 hours. In order to accomplish this task with a maximum of reader interest and a minimum of error, the newspaper mechanism must work like a well-oiled machine, with each part running in its place and operating in smooth relationship to the next.

The operation of a newspaper is usually divided into three parts: editorial, business, and production. Although the most important of these,

Newsprint Use by the World's Leading Newsprint Consumers, 1982*

Nation	Metric tons	Percent of total
United States	10,115	40.6
Japan	2,620	10.5
Britain	1,283	5.2
West Germany	1,084	4.4
U.S.S.R.	1,068	4.3
Canada	934	3.8
France	581	2.3
Australia	546	2.2
Netherlands	366	1.5
Sweden	308	1.2
Italy	300	1.2

* Total World Demand (1982 Est.)—24,913,000 metric tons (Total includes Peoples' Republic of China.)
SOURCE: *Newspaper and Newsprint Facts at a Glance, 1982–83.* New York: Newsprint Information Committee, 1983, p. 8.

for our purposes, is the editorial side, the newspaper could not function without the other two. The business manager is in charge of both classified and display advertising. Without these, the newspaper as we know it could not exist. The business manager is also in charge of selling or promoting the newspaper and is responsible for getting it properly distributed, through a circulation department, which is usually made up of independent distributors and a network of newspaper carriers. The business manager is in charge of the bookkeeping and accounting for the entire organization.

The production manager, also essential to the operation, is in charge of the printing plant, which usually includes composition or typesetting; engraving or photographic platemaking; stereotyping or casting of the type

Most Frequently Covered Stories and the Amount of Space Devoted in a Typical Midwestern Daily Newspaper during 1981

Event	Number of stories on topic during 1981 (Pages 1 and 3)	Percent of stories ¼ page or more
1. The economy (Reagonomics, high interest rates, recession)	216	12
2. The Middle East conflict (Israel and Arab countries)	139	9
3. Poland crisis	111	7
4. The return of the hostages	64	39
5. Murders in Atlanta	59	7
6. Coal talks—United Mine Workers	57	0
7. Space shuttle	52	29
8. U.S. defense policies	52	6
9. Air traffic controllers	46	9
10. PCBs	42	5
11. Attempt on Reagan's life	38	32
12. Local school funding	37	0
13. Problems in Northern Ireland	36	17
14. Chill in U.S.-Soviet relations	34	9
15. AWACs sale	31	13
16. Problems with auto industry	28	11
17. School redistricting	27	11
18. El Salvador	26	15
19. Social Security	24	12
20. Cuts in federal social programs	23	9
21. Sandra Day O'Connor	22	14
22. Pope shot	20	10
23. Steven Judy execution	19	16
24. Sadat assassination	15	53
25. Reagan and the new administration	14	7

SOURCE: *Newspaper Research Journal*, Fall 1983, p. 72.

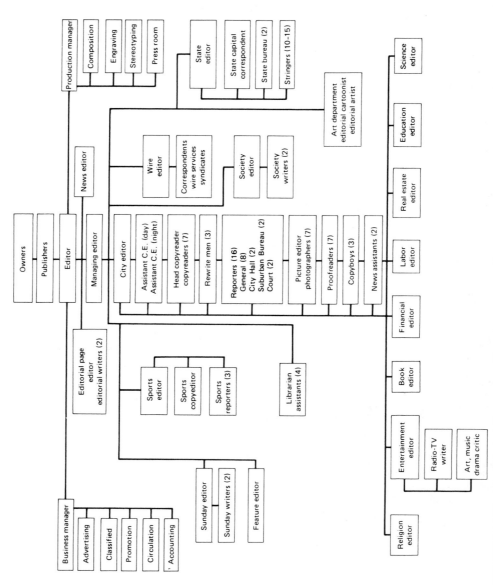

Organizational Chart for a Typical Newspaper with a Circulation of 100,000. (Based on *The Structure and Layout of Editorial News Departments*, ANPA Research Institute Bulletin 1008, January 26, 1970.)

Single Copy Sales Price of U.S. Daily and Sunday Newspapers, 1965–1983

Daily

Year	5¢	10¢	15¢	20¢	25¢	30¢	35¢	40¢
1965	456	892	3	2	—	—	—	—
1970	46	1,507	139	5	1	—	—	—
1975	4	428	1,153	137	10	1	—	—
1980	—	41	497	644	555	9	7	1
1981	—	30	290	437	960	17	15	1
1982	—	14	143	272	1,227	29	16	3
1983	—	10	91	183	1,306	80	24	3

Sunday

Year	5¢	10¢	15¢	20¢	25¢	30¢	35¢	40¢	45¢	50¢	55¢	60¢	65¢	70¢	75¢	80¢	85¢	90¢	95¢	$1.00
1965	21	128	190	143	45	5	—	—	—	—	—	—	—	—	—	—	—	—	—	—
1970	2	89	115	140	161	30	35	3	—	4	—	—	—	—	—	—	—	—	—	—
1975	—	37	61	49	170	58	157	37	3	51	1	4	—	—	1	—	1	—	—	1
1980	—	5	50	25	84	29	121	30	6	291	—	23	5	1	46	—	1	2	—	5
1981	—	—	33	16	77	24	88	21	3	313	4	22	2	—	117	—	3	—	—	—
1982	—	—	21	17	77	14	61	17	1	326	1	23	6	1	160	1	5	2	1	15
1983	—	—	5	12	88	8	44	15	3	309	1	26	5	1	170	1	6	3	—	60

SOURCE: *Facts About Newspapers.* Washington, D.C., American Newspaper Publishers Association, 1984, p. 5.

into curved plates to fit on the cylinders of the press; and finally the press itself, usually a gigantic machine with more than a million moving parts.

Many mass communicators also work on the editorial side of the newspaper. The typical daily newspaper with a circulation of 100,000 has about 75 full-time editorial staff members. The main function of the editorial department is to gather information, judge its importance, evaluate its meaning, write and display it in ways that will attract and hold the attention of readers, and put it through the cycle of production until it reaches the printed page.

The process requires a complex organization for the typical newspaper. The important decisions are often made in committee. The editors meet at the start of each news day to draw up a list of assignments from their knowledge of events that have taken place or will soon occur. As the reporters complete their assignments, they and the editors together in further conferences during the day develop the way in which the news and opinions will be played in the newspaper. This kind of constant team effort is an essential aspect of newspaper work.

THE TECHNOLOGICAL REVOLUTION

A series of technical and electronic developments in the past few decades has brought about a revolution in the editing and production of the newspaper. They are:

1. The perfection of photo-offset lithography, a technique of printing from photo-sensitive plates rather than with raised letters. By the mid-1980s, more than 1400 daily newspapers were being printed by the offset method.
2. The perfection of photo composition to set type by photographing letters rather than cast type with hot metal on a linotype machine.
3. The perfection of an optical character reader (OCR) that can scan letters on a page or videoscreen and automatically set the material in type.
4. The introduction of the computer to automate many of the functions of composition and printing and to store and retrieve material.
5. The development of video display terminals (VDT) for direct transmission of copy into an automated system.

The use of VDT promises to be a significant change. Most major newspapers have already revolutionized their newsrooms with the new equipment. Many other papers use VDT systems for circulation, accounting, and advertising and will convert them to editorial uses.

In a VDT system, the reporter types the story on a typewriterlike keyboard, but the words appear on a videoscreen in front of the reporter rather than on a sheet of paper. Editing copy on the screen can be done much

(AP/Wide World Photos.)

Video display terminals (VDTs) such as these at the New York City headquarters of Associated Press have already revolutionized the newsrooms of most major newspapers.

faster than editing on paper because a reporter can add or delete words, sentences, or paragraphs with a single push of a key. The reporter transmits the story to the memory bank of the computer, where it can later be retrieved by the copyeditor for further editing. The story then goes to the automatic typesetter, which can produce camera-ready copy, in the prescribed typeface and size, with a headline, to be pasted up for a negative from which the final plates are made for printing. Systems are already being used to automate page layout and pagination as well.

Newspapers will soon turn to computers and electronics to deliver the paper as well as process the news and publish it. Several systems are already perfected and should be in wide use within a decade.

Teletext is a system already in use in Britain; the British Broadcasting Corporation operates the world's first and most extensive newspaper delivered by television. Called CEEFAX, it is available 16 hours a day. It uses a TV set and a decoder. By pressing a button on a recall pad, you can bring an index page to the screen. By keying in a three-digit number, you can get a headline page, the weather, highway conditions, or the latest sports scores. Whenever you want to read it, you can get whatever news of the day is stored in the system. By pressing another button, you can return to your TV show. And you can instruct your set that you want your show to be interrupted by news bulletins flashing on the screen whenever they are sent along the system.

Teletext is the transmission of information buried inside a TV signal that can put the written word on any properly equipped TV screen at the demand of the viewer and at almost the moment of its creation. The key phrase is "at the demand of the viewer." It is not the rolling news bulletins common on CATV channels. You can read what you want when you want it. The CEEFAX viewer can create his or her own special-interest newspaper from among the more than 100 pages that are constantly available on each BBC channel.

What makes Teletext different from television is the *written* word. Television deals with the *spoken* word, which is fleeting and gone after it has been uttered. But the written word allows the reader to set the pace, to go back and reread at will. The message remains available until it is changed by the editor at his video display terminal.

The news or the message of the content of the communication gets into the Teletext system in the same way that it does in modern newspapers. Reporters write their stories at a video display terminal. Editors edit the stories on their VDTs and then they are put into the system, for the viewer to call up at his or her leisure.

Viewdata is another system now being tested that may soon be in wide use. It is an interactive system, a two-way system where question-and-answer dialogue is possible. The store of data in this system is limited only by the size of the data base at the other end of the telephone line, not by the amount of information that can be serially transmitted in a given period of time.

In the Viewdata system, the TV set is modified and connected to the telephone. The user dials a local newspaper or an information source, and the selected pages appear on the screen. The first experimental use of Viewdata was in Coral Gables, Florida, where 200 homes were hooked into the system. People in these homes could browse through thousands of frames of information, from horoscopes to headlines, from baseball scores to the L.L. Bean catalogue.

As time passes, the alternatives for newspaper communication will grow. And as home computers become a widespread reality, these systems will become home terminals, and persons in the home will be able to tap information from gigantic data bases. The important element here is that the readers will be able to create their own newspaper. They will be able to tailor their TV screen to their own choosing, sifting out the material they want and eliminating everything else.

Of course, this means that there will be a greater need than ever for a larger data base. We will need more reporters to gather information and more editors to select and prepare the information for the data base.

Also, these new systems of delivering the day's news to the home via the TV screen will not do away with the printed version of the newspaper. People will continue to demand the printed word. The newspaper is highly portable. We can read it wherever we choose, be it at the breakfast table, on the train, or at our desks. And it is separable: Father can read the financial pages while mother is reading the editorials and the kids are reading the comics. That luxury will continue to be demanded by many people.

Videotext displays allow the TV home viewer to retrieve specific, up to date, written news stories from a central system at the touch of a button.

With the development of new media in the twentieth century, the role of the newspaper in society has changed. The newspaper is no longer the fastest medium, and its responsibility for carrying bulletins and headlines of the day has been taken over by radio and television. The "extra" edition that typified newspaper publishing through World War II for any major news break has all but vanished. Radio and television can do a better job of skimming the surface of events around the world and providing hourly "extra" editions of the news.

But the newspaper has the advantage of being a better display case, or bulletin board, of news. At a glance, readers can survey the layout of the newspaper and quickly know what is happening. They have better control over elements of the news on which they want to spend their time. Readers can be more selective, choosing items that are important to them and pursuing them as far as time will allow. Thus the newspaper can offer a greater variety of information, and it can go into greater depth with the information.

Daily and weekly newspapers play an essential role in the community, therefore, providing the small details of day-to-day and week-to-week information that sew together the fabric of society. They announce births, marriages, and deaths; tell what is for sale; explain laws and customs; help citizens form opinions about issues close to home; and lighten the day with feature stories about local personalities and events.

Newspapers are turning more and more to investigative and interpretive reporting, forms of journalism that are not as adaptable to radio and television. Newspaper stories are getting longer and are going into greater depth; increasingly, newspapers let radio and television serve the function of providing spot news and headlines.

For the newspaper of the future, the key role will increasingly be local community reporting, specialized and in-depth coverage, and information and advertising display.

CHARACTERISTICS AND ROLES OF NEWSPAPERS

16 Magazines

Midway between the book and the newspaper stands the magazine, a mass medium that enjoys some of the advantages and disadvantages of both. Like books, magazines have the space and time to develop a subject fully. Like newspapers, magazines are published periodically at regular intervals and can maintain the currency of their subject matter. And more than either of these other print media, magazines can be produced in a wide variety of styles, formats, sizes, typography, color, and paper. Many people in the mass media will argue that magazines are the ideal print medium.

Magazines have had their ups and downs and have changed considerably in their nearly 300 years of history. The most important change for American magazines in the past 30 years has been the decline of the general-interest magazine and the rapid growth of specialized magazines. The rise of television was certainly a factor in this change, but so was the increased need for highly specialized current information in our highly developed technological age.

The word *magazine* means a general "storehouse"; it comes from the French word *magasin*, meaning "store" or "shop." Indeed, the earliest magazines, appearing in France, were really catalogues of booksellers' storehouses. These were issued periodically; after a while, essays, reviews, and articles were added. The names of early magazines, often called *museums* and *repositories*, reflected their nature as collections of varied items of general interest.

From the beginning, magazines have often been started by young persons with new ideas and little money. The first English publication of a magazine was really a cross between a newspaper and a magazine; called the *Review*, it was published in London starting in 1704. It had four small pages in each issue and was printed as often as three times a week for 9 years. Daniel Defoe, a nonconformist and dissenter who went on to become one of the great men of British letters, was the author, editor, and publisher. Defoe wrote and published news; articles on domestic affairs and national policy; and essays on literature, manners, and morals.

In the fifth year of the *Review*'s publication, 1709, an imitator was started, testimony to the fact that Defoe's idea had been a good one. The *Tatler* was produced by Richard Steele, who was later joined by Joseph Addison; together they also published the *Spectator*. They printed political, international, and theatrical news, coffeehouse gossip, and moralistic essays. They also carried extensive advertising, a feature that was to become a necessary aspect of almost all magazine publishing. The *Tatler* and the *Spectator* provided some of the first magazine contributions to English literature in the guise of informal essay and short story.

In 1731 the first publication was started that carried the name *magazine*; this was the *Gentlemen's Magazine*, founded by Edward Cave. He produced varied reading fare, but perhaps his most important contribution was his publication of reports of debates in Parliament. Eventually Cave hired the famous Dr. Samuel Johnson to write these reports, and Johnson ultimately used this experience to found his own magazine, the *Rambler* (1750–1752). By 1750, the *Gentlemen's Magazine* had the amazing circulation of 15,000 copies, and a number of imitators were being published in London. Half a century after the first magazine appeared, more than 150 periodicals were being printed in England.

HISTORICAL PERSPECTIVES

About 35 years after the first English magazine was published, the new medium appeared in the American colonies, and Benjamin Franklin was again one of the pioneers. In 1740 he announced his plans to publish the *General Magazine and Historical Chronicle, for All the British Plantations in America*. A competitive printer in Philadelphia, Andrew Bradford, seizing upon Franklin's idea, rushed his own magazine into print and beat Franklin by 3 days. Thus American magazine journalism was born in a state of competitiveness that has marked it ever since.

Bradford's *American Magazine, or a Monthly View of the Political State of the British Colonies* lasted for only three issues, and Franklin's only six, but they inspired more than a dozen other magazine efforts in colonial

Magazines in Early America

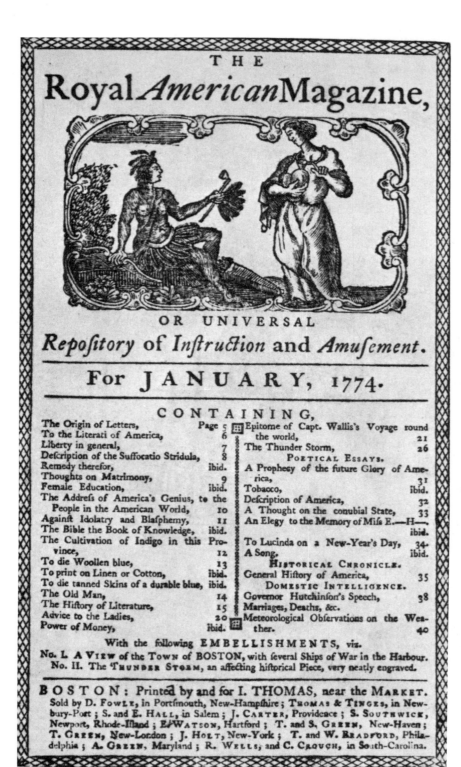

THE
Royal *American* Magazine,

OR UNIVERSAL
Repository of *Instruction* and *Amusement*.

For JANUARY, 1774.

CONTAINING,

With the following EMBELLISHMENTS, viz.

No. I. A VIEW of the TOWN of BOSTON, with several Ships of War in the Harbour.
No. II. The THUNDER STORM, an affecting historical Piece, very neatly engraved.

BOSTON: Printed by and for I. THOMAS, near the MARKET.
Sold by D. FOWLE, in Portsmouth, New-Hampshire; THOMAS & TINGES, in New-bury-Port; S. and E. HALL, in Salem; J. CARTER, Providence; S. SOUTHWICK, Newport, Rhode-Island; E. WATSON, Hartford; T. and S. GREEN, New-Haven; T. GREEN, New-London; J. HOLT, New-York; T. and W. BRADFORD, Philadelphia; A. GREEN, Maryland; R. WELLS; and C. CROUCH, in South-Carolina.

The *Royal American Magazine* published essays, poems, and engravings and reported local current events. (New York Public Library Picture Collection.)

America. No American magazine before 1800 lasted more than 14 months, and advertising support was scarce. The average circulation was about 500 copies, although each issue passed into many hands. Magazines covered a wide range of general topics, including religion, philosophy, natural science, political affairs, and literature. These magazines were a unifying force in the new nation, and they numbered among their authors and editors many of the great names of early America, including Franklin, Noah Webster, Philip Freneau, and Thomas Paine as editors; and George Washington, Alexander Hamilton, John Jay, Benjamin Rush, John Hancock, and Richard Henry Lee as authors. Paul Revere was the foremost magazine illustrator of the day.

After the turn of the nineteenth century, magazines blossomed into a national force, and some were started that would last a century and a half. They influenced education, spreading the new nation's ideas and culture, building literacy, and shaping public opinion. In the 1820s, 1830s, and 1840s, magazines played the same role that radio would later play in the 1920s, 1930s, and 1940s. "This is the age of magazines," wrote a poet in the *Cincinnati Literary Gazette* in 1824. Edgar Allan Poe, magazine editor and writer, wrote in the 1830s: "The whole tendency of the age is Magazineward. The magazine in the end will be the most influential of all departments of letters."

Most famous among these magazines was the *Saturday Evening Post*, started in 1821 (although it claimed lineage back to 1728 and Ben Franklin's *Pennsylvania Gazette*). It lasted until the late 1960s, when it became a victim of high production and mailing costs and competition from specialized magazines. Another was the *North American Review*, founded in 1815. It lasted until 1938, numbering among its contributors the literary figures of the nation.

As literacy spread in the nineteenth century, magazines became a literary force, building a national literature of American fiction, poetry, and essays. *Harper's Monthly* and the *Atlantic Monthly*, both founded in the 1850s, were among several dozen widely influential literary magazines. These publications provided the launching pad for most American literary giants of the nineteenth century, including Henry Wadsworth Longfellow, Washington Irving, Ralph Waldo Emerson, Henry David Thoreau, Mark Twain, Henry James, Nathaniel Hawthorne, John Greenleaf Whittier, and Oliver Wendell Holmes.

The Magazine as a National Medium

With the coming of the Civil War, magazines played an increasingly journalistic role, informing the nation and influencing public opinion. Magazines were widely used by antislavery groups to spread information about slavery and antislavery activities and to mold public opinion on the issue. Most famous among them was William Garrison's *Liberator*, started in 1831 and ceasing publication in 1865, when its goal of liberation had been attained.

With its firsthand coverage of the Civil War, *Harper's Weekly* advanced the development of magazine journalism. (Courtesy *Harper's Magazine*.)

Magazines became reporters and interpreters of the social and political scene, increasingly dealing with public affairs. *Harper's Weekly*, founded in 1857 (sister publication to *Harper's Monthly*), got its great chance to further magazine journalism during the Civil War. It sent a staff of writers and artists to the battlefields for firsthand coverage of the war. Among them was photographer Matthew Brady, whose Civil War pictures are still regarded as among the best in photojournalism. During Reconstruction, magazines were in the forefront of the fight against political corruption, led by such publications as the *Nation*, whose militant editor, E. L. Godkin, shaped his magazine into a leading commentator on current affairs and a fighter for democratic principles.

After the Civil War, magazines began to reach a national audience, particularly for special-interest groups. Farming magazines had already emerged as a separate publishing field. Among them was the *Tribune and Farmer*, published by Cyrus H. K. Curtis, who would go on to establish one of the largest magazine empires in history. Magazines for women also came into their own, particularly with the founding of the *Ladies' Home Journal*, published by Curtis and edited by Edward Bok, one of the great innovative editors of magazine history. Other women's magazines that grew to nationwide circulation by the end of the century were *Good Housekeeping*, *Woman's Home Companion*, *McCall's*, *Harper's Bazaar*, *Vogue*, and *Vanity Fair*.

By the end of the nineteenth century, magazines were a mass medium. Improvements in printing, especially the automatic typesetting machine of Ottmar Mergenthaler, perfected in 1884, dramatically increased production speed. Prices were lowered, and the "dime magazine" became a counterpart to the penny press. The number of magazines increased by nearly 500 percent in a 20-year period, going from 700 in 1865 to 3300 in 1885. By 1900 there were at least 50 well-known national magazines, many of them with circulations of more than 100,000. One, Curtis's *Ladies' Home Journal*, had a circulation of over a million. By 1908, another Curtis publication, the *Saturday Evening Post*—which Curtis had taken over when it was failing—had also reached a circulation of a million copies per issue.

With a nationwide audience, magazines became a vital political and social force. Nowhere can this be seen better than in the socially conscious magazine writing of the muckrakers. Magazines actually were ahead of newspapers in using their pages to expose crime and corruption, fraud and manipulation. Chief among such publications was *McClure's Magazine*, founded by S. S. McClure in 1894. He used his pages to expose oil monopolies, railroad injustices, political shenanigans, and life-insurance trickery (among others). He was so successful, both in winning audiences and in reforming society, that other magazines followed McClure's muckraking, including *Cosmopolitan*, *Munsey's Magazine*, *Collier's*, and *Frank Leslie's Popular Monthly*, which became the *American Magazine*.

THE SATURDAY EVE

August 23, '30

5c. THE COPY

Sir Arthur Conan Doyle—William Hazlett Upson—George Wharton Pepper
Mary Pickford—Barrett Willoughby—Benito Mussolini—Robert Winsmore

Started in 1821, the *Saturday Evening Post* became closely associated in this century with illustrator Norman Rockwell who designed many of its covers. (Reprinted from the *Saturday Evening Post*, Copyright © 1930 The Curtis Publishing Company.)

Between 1894 and 1904, the American magazine came of age as a mass medium and proved itself to be a powerful institution in society.

The Magazine in the Twentieth Century

Magazines have continued to change and enlarge their scope in the twentieth century. Innovation in the magazine field seems to have come particularly from individual genius, often the vision of the young with new ideas and fresh talent.

The digest has become a major publishing phenomenon of the twentieth century, sharing with all mass media one basic purpose: saving people time by giving them the cream off the top, making it appetizing, palatable, and easily digestible. None has achieved this better than the *Reader's Digest*, which before the middle of the twentieth century had the largest circulation of any magazine; but by the mid-1980s, its position had been challenged by another media digest, *TV Guide*. The *Reader's Digest* was the product of a young man, DeWitt Wallace, and his wife, Lila, both children of poor Presbyterian ministers. In 1922, while still in their 20s, the Wallaces borrowed the necessary funds to give their idea a try. In the 1980s their magazine was being sent each month to nearly 18 million subscribers in the United States alone, and other editions were sent to millions more all over the world.

More important even than the digest phenomenon has been the emergence of the news magazine as a national force. Another far-from-wealthy son of a Presbyterian missionary, Henry Luce, founder of *Time*, *Life*, *Fortune*, and *Sports Illustrated*, must be given much of the credit for building the weekly news magazine into a viable journalistic medium. Luce was a young man just out of Yale in 1923 when he and Britton Hadden founded *Time*. Like the *Reader's Digest*, it has not changed much since its early editions. And its imitators, including *Newsweek* and *U.S. News & World Report*, follow its format.

Luce was also a pioneer in modern photojournalism, founding *Life* magazine to report news through pictures. *Life* was not the first picture magazine, but it was the first to use photography as a regular journalistic tool to inform, entertain, persuade, and sell. *Life* had imitators, too, including magazines such as *Look*. Although *Life* is again in print, in December 1972 *Look* became a casualty of the rising costs in the magazine business.

The city magazine, once the only form of magazine, has come back into its own in the twentieth century. The most successful and most influential of these magazines has been the *New Yorker*, founded in 1925 by former newspaperman Harold Ross. He built it into a magazine that has lived up to his original prospectus, which described it as a sophisticated "reflection in word and picture of metropolitan life. It will be human," Ross wrote at the beginning. "Its general tenor will be one of gaiety, wit, and satire. . . . The *New Yorker* will be the magazine which is not edited for the little old lady in Dubuque. . . ." It has not reached the circulation heights of some magazines that are edited for more average tastes, but it has influenced scores of other metropolitan magazines. By the early 1980s, the city magazine was enjoying unusual growth. By the mid-1980s, every major city and many states and regions had their own magazines—some had more than one. For example, in the Washington, D.C., area alone, a half dozen city magazines were flourishing.

The twentieth century has seen the rise of magazines devoted to higher culture, too. Some of these magazines, in their articles on art, science, history, philosophy, and current affairs, are similar to some of the earliest

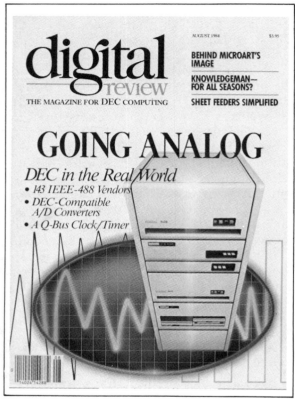

The twentieth century renaissance of the city magazine, started in 1925 by the *New Yorker*, has blossomed with hundreds of contemporary metropolitan and regional publications. Pictured here is just one of San Francisco's city magazines. (Courtesy San Francisco Magazine, Inc.)

Magazines dealing with computer technology constitute a fast growing trend in contemporary magazine journalism. (Copyright © Richard Krieglar, Courtesy American Artists Rep. Inc.)

magazines. Chief among these have been *National Geographic* and *Smithsonian*. Often produced without advertising, in a book binding with hard covers, and with lengthy articles and lavish illustrations, these magazines are aimed at educated, affluent readers. The *Smithsonian*, in fact, has been a major magazine success story of the 1970s and 1980s, growing in a few years to one of the largest circulations in the industry.

Other trends in the twentieth century should not be overlooked. True-confession and movie-fan magazines reach an enormous audience, as do specialized publications, from *Farm Journal* and *Presbyterian Life* to *Hairdo & Beauty*. The "little magazine" of poetry and criticism is another twentieth-century phenomenon, as are esoteric or scientific journals such as *Biotechnology & Bioengineering* or *Journal of Applied Polymer Science*. The association magazine, the trade journal, and the house organ are all growing types of twentieth-century magazine journalism.

The success of *Ebony* illustrates the growth of the specialized magazine aimed at a single target audience. (Courtesy of *Ebony*.)

Perhaps the most remarkable development has been the increasing growth and success of specialized magazines aimed at a single target audience. Ethnic groups are increasingly being served by their own magazines, such as *Ebony* and *Sepia* for blacks. New magazines have been started for Italian-Americans, German-Americans, and other ethnic groups. Specialized groups of many kinds have turned to magazines as a means of providing communication among those with similar interests, including such magazines as *Advocate*, the largest and most influential news magazine for the gay community, and *High Times*, a slick magazine for members of the American counterculture.

One of the most successful magazine types begun since World War II has been the sexually explicit men's magazine. *Playboy*, the prototype, was started by Hugh Hefner when he was only a few years out of the University of Illinois, with some experience at *Esquire*. *Playboy* has ushered in a new era of hedonism in American popular culture, with stress on sophisticated food, drink, and frank sexual pleasure. Begun in 1953, *Playboy* reached a circulation of nearly 6 million before it began to decline in the early 1980s. *Playboy* has had a profound influence on other men's magazines, many of which left hunting, fishing, and sports cars behind to imitate *Playboy*'s content.

In the 1970s a new kind of woman's magazine emerged, edited for the "independent woman." Unlike earlier magazines for women, such as *Good Housekeeping* and *Ladies' Home Journal*, these new periodicals did not carry articles on cooking, homemaking, sewing, housecleaning, and child rearing. They published articles on politics, career development, and sex. Some, like *Playgirl*, an imitation of *Playboy*, published centerfold pictures of nude men. Others, such as *Ms.*, spread the news of the women's movement. Among these new magazines for women are *Working Woman*, *New Woman*, *Self*, *Savvy*, and *Woman's World*.

Special Problems   In the 1950s and 1960s television threatened to capture advertising dollars from the general magazine, causing some to predict that the mass circulation magazine would be killed. Magazines fought back by playing what they called "the numbers game," building circulation figures to compete with television for national advertising. Some magazines turned from their traditional newsstand sales to concentrate on subscription selling. They hired high-powered subscription sales organizations to attract subscribers at any cost. These organizations often used young people for door-to-door, high-pressure selling campaigns, offering long-term bargain prices or package deals with many publications for the price of one. The sales organization owned the subscription, collected the money from the subscriber, and sold the subscription to the magazine publisher.

In effect, such magazines were buying subscribers in order to produce large numbers of readers to attract advertisers. They earned no money from the subscriber; indeed, they had to pay to get the subscriber. And they had to lower their price far below value to keep the subscriber. In 1968 the average magazine cost the buyer 54 cents, but it cost the publisher perhaps four or five times that amount to produce. The publisher hoped to make up the difference through revenue from large advertising sales.

Such economics ultimately put some of the large mass-consumer magazines out of business. *Colliers*, the *Woman's Home Companion*, and the *Saturday Evening Post* failed in the 1950s and 1960s. They did not go under for lack of readers, however. When the *Saturday Evening Post* died, it had more than 4 million regular subscribers. But the magazine did not have the right audience (young, with discretionary income) to attract advertisers, who were not interested in reaching its older, more conservative audience.

In spite of these failures, the magazine field is not by any means dying. In the 10-year period from 1962 to 1971, 160 magazines went out of business. But in the same period, 753 magazines were born. By the mid-1980s, magazine circulation and advertising revenue were at an all-time high. Magazine publishers were also no longer selling their product cheaply to attract masses of subscribers in order to get advertising.

Advertising revenue for magazines has increased, too. One reason for this was that advertisers acknowledged what the publishers called *media imperatives*. The publishers divided the adult population into four segments: (*a*) the heavy magazine reader and the light TV viewer (the *magazine imperative*); (*b*) the light reader and the heavy viewer (the *television imperative*); (*c*) the heavy reader and heavy viewer; and (*d*) the light reader and light viewer. Through audience research, publishers demonstrated that the "magazine imperative" group was better educated, more affluent, and more apt to buy the products advertised than was the "television imperative" group. Obviously, then, it was in the advertisers' interest do do more of their advertising in magazines.

Publishers also encouraged single-copy sales, which have a larger margin of profit than subscriptions. A single copy of *Newsweek*, for example, costs $1.75 at the newsstand, with 52 issues a year; this is twice as much as the annual subscription rate of $46. More people will buy magazines on a single-copy basis when they are available, not just at corner newsstands, but in drugstores and supermarkets as well. Supermarket sales have turned out to be remarkably profitable, so much so that magazine distributors have developed "family reading centers" in stores. Other magazines are sold only as single copies. *Family Circle* and *Woman's Day*, for example, both in the top 10 largest circulation magazines in the country, are sold only in grocery stores and supermarkets; there are no mail subscriptions. Other magazines are moving in this direction.

Another reason for encouraging single sales has been the rising cost of postage. The U.S. Postal Service started a phased increase for second-class mailing in 1970; by the mid-1980s, publishers were paying three to four times more for mailing than they did in 1970. Naturally publishers must look to other means of selling and distributing products.

Increasingly, magazines are using computers and new demographic data to make their advertising and editorial content more selective. For example, a magazine's production and circulation can be coordinated so that circulation can be broken out into 25 megamarkets, 50 megastates, and a group of top-spot zip-coders. Advertising can even be placed by selected geographical regions to reach any number of predetermined markets. For less money, the advertiser is able to reach a more appropriate market for the product, either on a regional or reader-interest basis.

Time magazine, for example, now has the technology available to customize its editorial content to the extent of giving the reader at least one article per issue that meets one of his or her preselected interests. Thus, the same issue of *Time* might bring to a sports fan an issue with an article on pro football; her next-door neighbor, a science buff, will get an article on electronic engineering. Such magazines can have mass and selectivity, both, with wide appeal to advertisers as well as consumers.

The ability to target one's audience also has made possible the controlled-circulation magazine. The magazine is sent only to certain people, sometimes on application by the reader, sometimes on identification by the publisher. For example, two magazines in Washington, D.C., *Regardie's* and *Washington Dossier*, are sent free to households and businesses targeted by market research and demographic studies as "active" and economically successful. These are the spenders that advertisers are eager to reach—and the magazines are full of ads—even though the addressee has never indicated an interest in the publication.

One of the best examples of this new kind of magazine publishing is *Nutshell*, with which many college students are familiar. By the mid-1980s, millions of copies of *Nutshell* were being distributed free at hundreds of colleges and universities across the country. The magazine carried ads wrapped around more than a dozen student-oriented features about campus fashion, college football, film schools, and draft registration.

Nutshell is only one of 10 such magazines published by the 13–30 Corporation of Knoxville, Tennessee. It is another success story of young people in the magazine field. The corporation was started by two men who met as undergraduates at the University of Tennessee in 1967, Philip Moffitt and Christopher Whittle. The numbers "13–30" represent the age limits within which the corporation seeks its audience for its advertisers.

THE SCOPE OF MAGAZINES

More than 10,800 magazines were published in the continental United States in 1984. This total included only those magazines that were publicly available and did not count private, institutional, or in-house publications. The 10,800 figure represented a significant growth from 1979, when 9700 magazines were published. Most magazines were published on a monthly basis. Magazines were published in every state of the union in 1984, but nearly a third of them were published in New York.

Magazine ownership is broadly spread, and the largest U.S. publishers do not produce many different magazines. Time Inc. publishes six magazines; Reader's Digest Association publishes only one; Triangle Publications, publishes two, including *TV Guide* and the Washington Post Company publishes a single magazine, *Newsweek*.

Reader's Digest has a monthly circulation of more than 17.9 million in the United States (and another 12 million foreign) making it the biggest seller overall; most of its circulation (better than 90%) comes from subscription sales. *TV Guide*, with more than 17 million copies sold weekly, has the second-highest circulation of any magazine in America, most of it (over 60%) from single-copy sales. *National Geographic* has a circulation of more than 10.6 million, all of it by subscription; the magazine

Total Number of U.S. Magazines (Not Including Nonregular and Institutional Publications)

Year	U.S. Periodicals
1974	9,755
1979	9,719
1984	10,809

SOURCE: Ayer Director of Publications. Philadelphia: Ayer Press, 1984.

Number and Circulation of Consumer Magazines or Magazine Groups, 1953–1983.

Year	No. of magazines or groups	Per-issue circulation
1953	258	163,034,506
1956	282	185,730,889
1959	274	185,589,166
1962	278	200,657,742
1965	275	215,486,748
1968	287	237,101,335
1971	293	242,453,893
1974	316 ·	248,822,947
1977	373	263,948,552
1980	407	286,447,087
1983	457	305,240,173

SOURCE: Audit Bureau of Circulation Reports on General and Farm Magazines. From *Magazine Newsletter of Research.* New York: Magazine Publishers Association, August 1984, p. 3.

Twenty Five Leading A.B.C. Magazines Average Paid Combined Circulation per Issue, Second Six Months of 1983*

Rank		Circulation	Percentage change versus 1982
1	Reader's Digest, The	17,937,045	+ .2
2	TV Guide	17,066,126	+ .4
3	National Geographic	10,626,224	+ .1
4	Modern Maturity	9,296,187	+ 11.6
5	AARP News Bulletin	8,760,153	+ 13.4
6	Better Homes & Gardens	8,041,951	− .6
7	Family Circle	7,193,079	− 2.8
8	Woman's Day	7,025,290	+ 1.3
9	McCall's	6,358,293	+ 1.4
10	Good Housekeeping	5,393,087	− 1.8
11	Ladies Home Journal	5,252,444	+ 2.3
12	National Enquirer	4,706,165	− 8.1
13	Time	4,615,594	+ 3.4
14	Playboy	4,209,324	− 6.5
15	Redbook	4,019,611	+ 4.0
16	The Star	3,689,337	− 8.0
17	Penthouse	3,500,275	− 7.3
18	Newsweek	3,038,832	+ .5
19	Cosmopolitan	3,038,400	+ 3.8
20	People	2,781,542	+ 4.1
21	Prevention	2,769,560	+ 8.4
22	American Legion	2,507,338	− 1.0
23	Sports Illustrated	2,448,486	+ 3.7
24	Glamour	2,275,743	+ 7.4
25	Southern Living	2,213,878	+ 3.4

is not sold on the newsstands. More than 50 magazines have circulations of a million or more; they represent only 13% of the total consumer magazines but account for more than 66% of the sales.

Since World War II, magazines have been growing faster than newspapers. From 1950 to 1980, magazines grew by 81% while newspapers grew only 16%. By 1983, the 457 consumer magazines audited by the Audit Bureau of Circulation (ABC) had a per issue circulation of more than 266 million copies. On the average, those magazines sold 34% of their issues on the newsstand and 66% through regular subscriptions.

Magazine advertising revenue has continued to increase; in 1983 it reached a record high of almost $4.2 billion. On the expense side, the biggest item for magazine publishers is personnel. Unlike newspapers, most magazines do not own expensive printing equipment but contract out that part of the process. A large share of magazine costs goes to sales promotion and magazine distribution, including 13 cents on every dollar for postage. Magazine industry salaries are about the same as salaries in the newspaper business for comparable work. A general editor at *Newsweek* makes a slightly lower minimum salary ($747 a week, as of June 1984) than a *New York Times* reporter makes as a minimum after an apprenticeship ($843 a week).

The Magazine Audience

A single magazine issue is read longer and by more people than a single newspaper issue; a book is read longer and by more people than either a magazine or a newspaper. The average magazine copy is read by 4.26 adults, and each adult reads the magazine over a period of several days.

Average Magazine Cover Price and One-Year Subscription Price

	1983 price
Single Copy	$ 1.97
One-Year Subscription	21.53

SOURCE: *Magazine Newsletter of Research*. New York: Magazine Publishers Association, August 1984, p. 17.

Production Costs for the Average U.S. Magazine

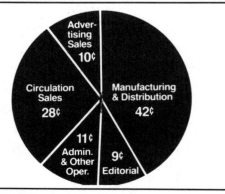

SOURCE: Price Waterhouse Study for Magazine Publishers Association, 1983. From *Magazine Newsletter of Research*. New York: MPA, August 1984, p. 18.

Total Adult Reading of the Average Magazine Copy, per Copy

Number of adult readers	4.26
Reading days per reader	3.2
Total adult reading days (4.26 readers × 3.2 reading days)	13.63
Reading time per reader	62 minutes
Total adult reading time (4.26 readers × 62 minutes)	264 minutes (4.4 hours)
Copy kept accessible	28.8 weeks (median)
Percent exposed to average ad page	85%
Per-reader exposures to average page (MPX)	1.7x
Total adult exposures per page (4.26 readers × 1.7x)	7.2

SOURCE: *Magazine Newsletter of Research*. New York: Magazine Publishers Association, August 1984, p. 5.

Magazine Audience Demographics

	Average month	
Adults	Read 1+ magazines	Average No. of issues
18–44 Years	95.8%	10.9
Attended/Graduated college	97.3	11.5
$25,000 and over household income	95.8	10.6
Professional/managerial	97.2	11.4

SOURCE: *Magazine Newsletter of Research*. New York: Magazine Publishers Association, August 1984, p. 5.

Magazine reading varies with the seasons; less reading is done in the summer than in the colder months. Most magazines are read in the home, and most reading takes place after dinner. Women read slightly more magazines than men, and magazine readership rises with income and education. Children are reading more magazines these days, and an increasing number of them have their own subscriptions.

Surveys of magazine reader actions suggest that readers tend to take more action as a result of their reading than is usual as a result of other media activities. A relatively large percentage of magazine readers discuss what they read with others and seek information about advertised products.

Audience Exposure to Magazines,
Compared to Other Media, by Demographics

	Index of media exposure			
Demography	Magazines	TV	Newspapers	Radio
Age				
18–24	118	94	90	121
25–34	110	89	90	107
35–44	112	89	106	104
45–54	96	94	110	99
55–64	92	115	113	86
65+	61	127	97	74
Education				
Attended/graduated college	131	85	119	97
Graduated high school	100	100	100	106
Did not graduate high school	63	118	74	94
Household Income				
$40,000+	133	81	129	103
$30,000–39,999	120	84	113	102
$25,000–29,999	102	88	110	99
$20,000–24,999	96	97	103	106
$15,000–19,999	96	101	94	99
$10,000–14,999	86	111	87	101
Under $10,000	69	127	71	92

SOURCE: *Magazine Newsletter of Research.* New York: Magazine Publishers Association, August 1984, p. 6.

THE STRUCTURE AND ORGANIZATION OF MAGAZINES

Because magazines come in different sizes and shapes and are aimed at different kinds of readers, no one organizational or operational pattern could fit them all. Each magazine develops its own way of organizing and operating to get its special job done. Some magazines—those that deal heavily in news and timely subjects—are organized in much the same manner as newspapers. Others that deal in less time-bound material are set up much like book publishing firms.

Because they do not have to worry about daily printing schedules, magazines do not need an expensive investment in printing equipment but can accomplish the same purpose by contracting with established printers. Some magazines, even famous ones such as the *Atlantic Monthly*, operate out of a few small offices, with a few editorial hands, a couple of typewriters, some furniture, and a supply of typing paper. Everything else, including production and distribution, can be handled by outside help.

The editorial staff of a magazine usually includes as chief executive an editor who has overall responsibility for establishing policies and making final decisions. A managing editor or executive editor has the responsi-

Editorial Content of Selected ABC-Audited Consumer Magazines in 1983

Type of editorial	1983 editorial pages distributed		1983 editorial pages per U.S. household
	(000)	(%)	
National affairs	12,058,196	6.7	143
Foreign affairs	9,580,511	5.3	113
Amusements	7,460,913	4.1	87
Beauty and grooming	6,649,838	3.7	79
Building	5,277,120	2.9	62
Business and industry	6,852,685	3.8	81
Children	3,594,198	2.0	43
Gardening and farming	3,506,651	1.9	40
Food and nutrition	17,750,996	9.8	209
Health/medical science	10,677,107	5.9	125
Home furnishing/management	13,254,461	7.3	155
Sports	12,522,452	6.9	147
Travel and transportation	7,254,010	4.0	85
Wearing apparel/accessories	8,564,554	4.7	100
Culture/humanities	28,009,391	15.5	330
General interest	15,878,670	8.8	187
Miscellaneous	7,416,209	4.1	87
Fiction and stories	4,721,662	2.6	55
Total Editorial	181,029,624	100.0	2,128

SOURCE: R. Russell Hall Co., Audit Bureau of Circulation, and Sales Management Survey of Buying Power, 1983. From *Magazine Newsletter of Research*. New York: Magazine Publishers Association, August 1984, p. 10.

bility for carrying out the editor's policies and for running the day-to-day operation. Staff editors head various departments within the magazine or handle various functions, such as picture editing, copyediting, or layout and production. Often staff writers on magazines are called editors.

Many magazines have contributing editors, who work either full time or part time in the office or out in the field; they often are specialists in certain categories and help the magazine discover material, find appropriate writers, approve the authenticity of the writer's copy, or do some writing themselves.

Another distinguishing feature of many magazines is the editorial board, a fixture not used by newspaper or book publishers to the same extent. The editorial board is often composed of leaders in the field to which the magazine is directed. They serve to give the magazine direction and authority.

In the past, magazines have depended largely on freelance contributions for their editorial content. The editor could sit back and wait for the mailman and then publish the best of what contributors sent in. There are literally hundreds of thousands of people who would like to be freelance writers for magazines, and many of them try. *Harper's*, for example, receives more than 20,000 unsolicited manuscripts each year, even though the magazine does not publish unsolicited material. While many free-lancers can supplement their incomes from part-time magazine writing, only a handful of professionals make a substantial salary from full-time free-lance writing.

Increasingly, magazines are using staff-developed and staff-written material. Schedules are too demanding and story development too complicated to allow the editors to wait and see what comes in the mail. Editor and staff determine the audience they are reaching, the type of material the audience needs and wants, and the subjects available for development into appropriate magazine articles and stories. Then they produce the material to make sure it fits their needs and their time schedules.

Even the *Reader's Digest*, ostensibly a selection of the most interesting articles from other magazines, in reality cannot depend upon other magazines to produce all the material it needs to fulfill the demands of its readers. The *Digest* editors often produce their material themselves, sometimes placing it in other magazines and then "borrowing" it for the *Reader's Digest*, or sometimes writing an article for a famous person and then "buying" it from that person for *Digest* publication.

KINDS OF MAGAZINES Generally, magazines are divided into consumer (or general interest) and specialized (including children's, professional, and trade publication) magazines.

Consumer magazines are generally broken down further into various categories, including women's (e.g., *Redbook*), men's (*Playboy*), sophisticated (*New Yorker*), quality (*Atlantic Monthly*), romance (*Modern Screen*), news (*U.S. News & World Report*), sports (*Sports Illustrated*), travel (*Travel and Leisure*), exploration (*National Geographic*), humor (*Mad*), shelter (*Better Homes & Gardens*), class (*Smithsonian*), and city (*Washingtonian*).

Specialized magazines can also be broken down into different kinds of publications as follows: juvenile (e.g., *Boy's Life*), comic (*Superman*), little literary (*Prairie Schooner*), literary (*Paris Review*), scholarly (*Journalism Quarterly*), educational (*College & University Journal*), business (*Nation's Business*), religious (*Christianity Today*), industrial or company (*Western Electric World*), farm (*Farm Journal*), transportation (*Railway Age*), science (*Scientific American*), and discussion (*New Republic*).

The specialized magazines, aiming their editorial fare at specialized reading audiences, have been growing at a rapid rate. A recently completed 20-year survey of this group showed that entertainment guides grew 256%, sports publications grew 247%, and business magazines expanded by 76%. According to *Advertising Age*, "publishers themselves believe that the future of specialized magazines is the rosiest of any industry group."

The business-publication field is one of the fastest-growing specialties in magazine journalism. Some magazine publishing houses have developed large groups of such magazines, serving varied trade and business groups, from automobile dealers to zookeepers. Many such magazines are distributed to a prime list of readers, some free of charge. The publisher makes his profit by selling advertising to merchants who want to reach these specific groups.

THE COMICS

One popular form of mass communication that deserves special consideration is the comic, which is either a cartoon, comic strip, or comic book. Although the comic strip and cartoon often appear in newspapers, we treat this form of communication as part of the magazine medium. The comic as a form has most of the characteristics of the magazine even in its form as a supplement to newspapers.

To qualify as a comic the item must meet certain specific criteria. A comic must develop a narrative within the panel, strip of panels, or pages. A comic must use continuing characters from one panel strip or page to the next panel strip or page. A comic must include dialogue or descriptions as part of the panel, rather than serve as a pictorial adjunct of another feature in the newspaper, magazine, or book. Most comics are printed by high-speed, low-definition presses on newsprint, which affects the degree of subtle detail possible.

Five classes of comics serve mass communication functions:

1. The single-picture (panel) newspaper features such as *Grin and Bear It*, *The Family Circus*, or the cartoons in the *New Yorker*, *Playboy*, and other magazines.
2. The black-and-white multipanel, daily newspaper comic strip, such as *Dick Tracy*, *B.C.*, or *Mary Worth*.
3. The multicolor, weekly, Sunday supplement, which is a collection of strips either continuing the daily newspaper feature's story line or a separate story. Nearly all strips are both daily and Sunday features, but many papers will carry more comic strips on Sunday than during the week.
4. Multipage color narratives in magazine form, which are issued monthly, bimonthly, or quarterly, and are called comic books (*Action Comics*).
5. Antiestablishment, social–political–economic commentary comics, or underground comic books, which are usually published irregularly in black and white (*Zap*, *Despair*, and the like).

Historical Background

From 1890 to 1914, three American artists—Richard Felton Outcault, James Swinnerton, and Frederick Opper—and two newspaper press lords—Joseph Pulitzer and William Randolph Hearst—battled to create

Richard Felton Outcault's "The Yellow Kid," the first newspaper comic, became, in 1899, the first published comic book, Vol. 1, No. 1 pictured above.

(New York Public Library Picture Collection.)

newspaper comics. Outcault's *Down Hogan's Alley* appeared in Pulitzer's *New York World* in the early 1890s and featured a nightshirted ragamuffin involved in unsavory lower-class goings-on. In 1896 the newspaper experimented with the use of yellow ink on the ragamuffin's nightshirt. The color test became a regular feature—*Down Hogan's Alley* became *The Yellow Kid*. Hearst hired Outcault away from Pulitzer, and both Pulitzer's *World* and Hearst's *Journal* ran *Yellow Kid* comics. Hearst printed the first comics section in 1896. The daily strip format emerged in the first decade of 1900 as the comics became a strong circulation builder.

From 1914 to 1929, syndicates such as King Features emerged, supplying publications with a large selection of syndicated strips by a stable of creators. Nearly every newspaper in the country carried a comics section, and "funny papers" were a major part of the industry. During this period most of the strips emphasized a humorous view of family life and its problems. By 1925 the *New Yorker* had begun its now famous one-line panel of cartoons. Today such cartoons appear in many general-reader magazines.

In the 1930s three major creators began careers: Milton Caniff's *Terry and the Pirates* and later *Steve Canyon* participated in and sometimes predicted political and military events; Al Capp's *Li'l Abner* became a sharp satirical comment on American society—nothing was sacred—and his attacks were savage; and the Walt Disney organization contributed two great characters to American pop culture—*Mickey Mouse*, the gentle, helpful, playful, and somewhat inept caricature of Americans, and *Donald*

Duck, a satirical picture of the rascally, distempered, and ornery man, constantly attacking his fate.

The comic book emerged during the economic depression of the 1930s. First came strip reprints in a format called *Funnies on Parade. Detective Comics* (1937) was the first to structure its content upon one theme. Then in 1938 the most popular superhero of all time, *Superman,* appeared in *Action Comics.* By 1940 there were more than 40 comic-book titles; in 1941, 168 titles. At U.S. Army posts during World War II, comic books outsold all other magazines ten to one.

Like many other Americans, comic characters went to war, thus contributing mightily to the propaganda effort. Some of the strips' heroes even entered the war before the United States did, joining the RAF or the Flying Tigers. In this way the comics may have helped psychologically to prepare the American public to support the war effort and glorify the American fighting man. Special "war" strips appeared, including *Male Call, G.I. Joe, The Sad Sack,* and *Johnny Hazard.* Possibly the most important comic characters of the war years were Bill Mauldin's dogfaces, Willie and Joe. These single-panel cartoons depicted the seriocomic life of the average GI. In 1945 Mauldin won the Pulitzer Prize for his work.

From 1946 to the present, several major events have characterized the development of the comics, including an anticomics campaign that attempted to link comics to the rise in juvenile delinquency. The attacks led to the development of the Association of Comic Magazine Publishers (ACMP) in 1947. A code was drafted to safeguard children from comic books that presented nudity, torture, sadism, and frightening monsters. The code also banned racial, ethnic, and religious slurs; negative marital story lines; ridicule of law officers; profanity; and detailed descriptions of criminal acts. The ACMP later became the Comics Magazine Association of America (CMAA) and developed a 41-point code. By the mid-1980s, 90% of the industry was submitting materials for code approval, allowing them to display the code seal on their products.

Another characteristic evident in the postwar era was the emergence of the gentle comic strips of anxiety, which contain strong comment. *Pogo* (1949), by Walt Kelly, revolutionized both the style and political scope of the strips, becoming so important as to incur the wrath of Senator Joseph McCarthy. *Miss Peach* (1957), *B.C.* (1958), and *The Wizard of Id* (1964) provided gentle fantasies.

The most spectacular comic of all times is *Peanuts* (1950) by Charles Schulz. Schulz's creations seem to speak to the anxieties of our times through the eternal loser, Charlie Brown. He and his friends may be the best literary explanation of American lifestyles in the 1960s. *Peanuts* also is the all-time success story in the comics business; it is a $150 million-a-year empire. The cartoon appears in more than 1400 papers around the world. It has generated hundreds of books in a dozen languages; a Broadway play; a line of greeting cards; seasonal TV specials; and an entire products industry that includes sweatshirts, baseball caps, dolls, bed-sheets, tie clips, stuffed animals, and calendars.

Perhaps the most important change on the comics page in newspapers is the trend away from ongoing, serialized stories to strips in which each day's story or joke or message stands alone. The continuity in these comics is not supplied by a story line but by recurring themes and a regular cast of characters.

Another change is the trend away from action–adventure strips. The nature of humor has also shifted away from broad slapstick to a more sophisticated and literate humor.

Until recently, most women in the comics were in subservient or domestic roles. *Wonder Woman* and *Brenda Starr* were two exceptions. New women have equal billing in several strips, and modern women like *Cathy* and *Sally Forth* have their own strips. *Cathy* began as small drawings that a 26-year-old advertising executive, Cathy Guisewife, sent to her mother to describe an unhappy love affair. It was the first comic strip about a liberated, independent woman. In its first 4 months, *Cathy* was bought by 89 newspapers.

Blacks were also relegated to subordinate roles or ignored altogether in the comics of the past. *Mandrake the Magician* had an African sidekick, and Daddy Warbucks had an East Indian giant named Punjab who visited occasionally, but they were exceptions; these characters were stereotyped and inconsequential. Now, blacks appear frequently in several popular comics; and they are the major characters in *Luther*, *Friday Foster*, and *Kudzu*. Blacks figure prominently in the wholly integrated strip *Wee Pals*, which often pokes fun at sensitive racial issues. In one *Wee Pals* strip, for example, a small black boy says he does not want to go to an integrated school because "I don't like going to school with girls." In another, a white playmate asks a black friend for a piece of candy. When he refuses, the playmate says, "Don't be so niggardly." In the last panel the white boy is seen writing himself a note: "Next time, use the word 'miserly.'"

Civil rights and feminism have not been the only agents for social change on the comic page. *Doonesbury*, by Garry Trudeau, is the classic example of this socialization process—a comic strip that deals, often in harsh terms, with these and other major issues of the time. *Doonesbury*'s potshots at politicians and social classes creates so much controversy that it further complicates what one editor calls "the most disorderly process in the newspaper business—the entire comics apparatus: which ones to buy, where to run them, how much to pay for them, and when to drop them." Newspaper wars were fought over *Doonesbury*.

The Scope of Comics

About 300 syndicated comics are regularly available in newspapers today. The artists who draw them split the fees 50–50 with the syndicates that sell them, and the most successful can earn six-figure yearly incomes. Overall, the sale and production of comics and related merchandising generates annual revenue in the hundreds of millions of dollars.

One of the most-read parts of the daily newspaper is the comics section; 6 of every 10 readers read the comics every day. More than 100 million persons read the Sunday comics section. A major strip may appear in more than 1000 papers across the world. Nearly every paper has a comics section supplied by the syndicates. The business is dominated by 25 syndicates led by King Features, which handles about 65 of the available 300 strips. *Puck*, a Sunday comics section, has a multinewspaper circulation of 14.5 million.

More than 100 comic-book publishing companies (dominated by the 25 largest) publish 300 titles and sell in excess of 250 million copies annually. Pass-along readership of these comics is estimated to be three readers to every buyer. Normally a company prints about 200,000 copies of an issue, but *Classics Illustrated*, which are skeletal versions of important literary works, remain on the stand indefinitely, and most titles have sold a million copies or more. The heavy users of comic books are children aged 7–14, and they tend to be good readers rather than poor ones.

The comic form is used for religious, educational, and political messages as well as campaigns against smoking, drinking, and narcotics abuse.

Despite continuing complaints about them, the comics are a dynamic part of pop culture. They are easy to read, socially relevant, entertaining, and provide wish fulfillment and escape for the reader. The comics have influenced broadcast programming, films, plays, art forms, and advertising.

NEWSLETTERS

The rise of the newsletter is a twentieth-century journalistic phenomenon, even though the newsletter is one of the oldest forms of journalistic communication. Letters were used for news and general communication in ancient Greek and Roman civilizations and throughout the Middle Ages. The Fugger newsletters, produced in several German city-states in the fifteenth and sixteenth centuries by the Fugger banking house, were among the forerunners of the modern newspaper. Written in letter form, they contained financial and economic information that helped spread the mercantile revolution among the merchants and businessmen who read them. The modern newsletter is often used for a similar purpose.

The father of the modern newsletter was probably Willard M. Kiplinger, who started the *Kiplinger Washington Letters* in 1923. A Washington reporter for the Associated Press, Kiplinger was hired by a New York bank to produce reports on government information vital to banking and business interests. Kiplinger put this information in a letter that he regularly sent to the bank. He reasoned that he might sell the information in his letter to other banks and to businessmen as well.

He typed the four-page letter on his own typewriter, had it mimeographed and later printed by offset, without any fancy makeup or advertising. Underscoring and capitalization were used to provide some graphic effects, but Kiplinger was primarily interested in distilling information to

More than 4000 commer-
cial newsletters like this
one are being published
today.

SOCIAL SCIENCE MONITOR
FOR PUBLIC RELATIONS AND ADVERTISING EXECUTIVES

Volume VI, Number 1   January 1984

MEDIA AND POLITICS IN 1984

The dominant event in 1984, many predict, will be the national
elections. The primaries, the party conventions, and the November
elections may color much of the news and influence many national and
international developments, from the stock market to diplomacy and war.
Communication, not issues, will probably be the dominant factor in
candidate selection, campaign strategy, and election victory.

Researchers and analysts have been working overtime to discover
what lessons could be learned about communication from the 1980
elections. And what they have learned has many implications for the
communicator, whether in politics or not. Here is a summary of two
important new books on the subject:

TELEVISED POLITICAL REALITY HAS BECOME "REAL POLITICAL REALITY"

Austin Ranney, former president of the American Political Science
Association and resident scholar at the American Enterprise Institute,
says in his new book, Channels of Power, that TV will be the dominant
factor in 1984 politics. And whether TV's version of reality is accurate
or not, it has become the reality.

Prior to television, he says, political influence came through
political socialization (parents, schools, churches, party affiliation)
and the two-step flow of communication, from influence leaders to the
people. But TV has overridden the "two-step flow" and bypassed the
"opinion leaders." Most of the talk that most Americans hear about
politics comes to them as they sit in front of their television sets
after the local news and weather forecasts have been aired and before
their favorite "sit-com" or cop show comes on, he says.

Ranney's study of television and politics has led him to the
following conclusions:

● ### NETWORK NEWS IS BIASED AGAINST THE POLITICAL ESTABLISHMENT

Ranney finds that network news does not suffer so much from political
bias as it does from journalistic bias. The bias is more apt to be caused
by economic constraints, time limitations, and legal ramifications than by
ideologies.

Network newspeople, he says, take the anti-establishment stance in
part because they feel it is their professional obligation and in part

(Copyright © Communication Research Associates, Inc.)

its essence. Each typewritten line carried a complete thought. He wrote
so that each line would be easy to read and readily remembered. He did
not feel constrained to follow normal journalistic restrictions of objectivity
and attribution to sources. Kiplinger made analyses and predictions for
his readers, taking them into his confidence.

In reality, Kiplinger was writing a personal letter to each of his subscribers, giving them his interpetation of the facts. He opened his letter with "Dear Reader" and closed it with his own signature, printed in blue ink. This feature alone cost him thousands of dollars in postage because he had to send his letter by first-class mail, rather than by the second-class rate available to news publications. But the extra cost was worth it to Kiplinger because he wanted to have a form of communication that was warm, personal, and intimate. The *Kiplinger Letters* have been widely imitated. Others preceded them and others followed them, but none has been as successful or as widely copied.

By the mid-1980s more than 4000 commercial newsletters were being published. A commercial newsletter, as defined by the Gale Research Company, publisher of the newsletter directory, is a publication that is usually reproduced as a typewritten page, without elaborate makeup or printing. It does not carry advertising, since its essential feature is the personal relationship it attempts to develop between author and reader, without any middleman to sponsor or subsidize the communication. Thus the commercial newsletter must charge a subscription, and sometimes the rate can be very high. Some newsletters cost as much as $1000 a year, if there are few subscribers and the information is of vital importance. The *Kiplinger Letters* cost about $36 a year, about average for the field.

Not counted in the 4000 commercial newsletters are the many thousands of subsidized newsletters used to promote or persuade, or as internal organs of communication within an organization or a group. Nearly every congressman today uses some form of newsletter to communicate personally with constituents. Newsletters are used by professional associations, church groups, factory workers, fraternal organizations, university administrations, alumni associations, labor unions, and most other organized units in our society.

Newsletters have become so well established that there is now a *Newsletter on Newsletters* and a Newsletter Clearinghouse. In 1977 a new group was founded in Washington, D.C., the Newsletter Association of America, to serve the special interests and needs of those who write, edit, and publish in this special medium.

A typical newsletter publishing company is Phillips Publishing Inc. of Washington, D.C. Started by Thomas Phillips in 1974, only 6 years after he graduated from journalism school, the company now publishes more than 20 newsletters. Phillips started with consumer newsletters offered at a relatively low subscription rate and aimed at a large general audience. He soon discovered that there was another and perhaps better market in the professional newsletter, with a relatively high subscription rate, aimed at a small, specialized market. He decided to enter both markets. Thus, some of his newsletters are aimed at the general consumer in finance, travel, and government affairs. They range in price from $27 to $39 per year. The others are aimed at professionals in the telecommunication industry and are priced at $127 to $247 per year.

The newsletter is quick, inexpensive, simple to produce, and useful. Just about anybody with a typewriter, a copying machine, and a mailing list can get into the newsletter business. Succeeding at the business is not so simple, however. Many newsletters have short lifetimes and make only a fleeting impression.

CHARACTERISTICS AND ROLES OF MAGAZINES

Of all the media, magazines have the largest number of individual and diverse production units. They require the least investment of organized business and the smallest budget to operate. "Find me a list of names and I'll create a magazine for it," said one bold magazine entrepreneur. He was not far off base. Magazines have been published for almost every group in our society.

In addition to this sort of selectivity, magazines have greater flexibility than all media other than books. The magazine publisher can create a package in almost any size, shape, or dimension and can achieve change and variation with ease.

The magazine has the advantage of a greater intensification than newspapers, radio, or television can usually manage. With a longer lead time and less-pressing deadlines, magazine editors can afford to take a longer look at issues, to penetrate problems more deeply in order to do a better job of interpretation and analysis.

Magazines have an advantage over books in that they are usually timely enough to deal with the flow of events. And they have the power to sustain a topic over a period of time in a series of issues, achieving a cumulative impact, whereas books must settle for a single impression.

One of the primary roles of magazines as mass media is their role of custom-tailoring mass communications. Magazines, unlike other media, are ideally suited to small groups, whether they are organized by culture, race, religion, geography, or subject. Even the mass general-consumer magazines, as we have seen, are finding ways to specialize in tailoring their product for a specific region or interest group.

Magazines do not have the permanence of books, but they are not as temporary as newspapers and not nearly as fleeting as broadcast messages. While the newspaper's lifetime is usually a single day, weekly magazines often last 2 or 3 weeks and monthlies for several months. Quarterlies are often bound and kept permanently.

Motion Pictures 17

It is very difficult to characterize motion pictures in today's society. Traditionally movies have been identified with eras or styles, such as films of the 1930s, film noir, musicals, Westerns, or science fiction. But contemporary films refuse to be typecast.

Part of the problem is the simple lack of historical distance. Compounding it is the speed by which much of the change took place. Instant trends have been the norm over the last 20 years of motion-picture making. With the exception of James Bond and an assortment of sharks, flying men in red suits, and Jedi warriors, very few film cycles of any length were established. In 1964–1965, with the huge success of *My Fair Lady*, *Mary Poppins*, and *The Sound of Music*, musicals were in. Two years later, with such disasters as *Star* and *Dr. Dolittle*, musicals were out. Following *The Graudate* (1967), *Easy Rider* (1969), and *Alice's Restaurant* (1969), youth films were booming. Two years later, with Elliot Gould and others leading the way in such films as *Getting Straight* (1970), *The Magic Garden of Stanley Sweetheart* (1970), and *The Landlord* (1970), the youth-film boom was busted. Old-fashioned love was flowering once again in 1970 with *Love Story*, but less than 2 years later *The Godfather* exhibited a different form of affection. *The Exorcist* (1973) started a brief occult cycle, but *Jaws* (1974) replaced it with a monster of a different kind. *Halloween* (1978) continued the horror cycle, but the industry soon jumped on an outer-space bandwagon generated by the phenomenal success of *Star Wars* (1977). This has proved to be the most enduring cycle, as *Return of the Jedi* (1983) and *Superman III* (1983) box-office receipts have documented. All of this serves to illustrate the number of directions in which recent American films have been traveling. Hollywood's search for a lost audience, for a successful formula, and for a return to past glories has continued unabated throughout the 1960s, 1970s, and into the 1980s.

Changes in the industry, content, and overall pattern and structure of American motion pictures began in the late 1940s and early 1950s. The large production studios, for years symbols of power and prestige, have been reduced to a financing and distributing role and only occasionally produce a film. Production companies are set up for individual films, and while the independent film is here to stay, it bears little resemblance to the low-budget shoestring films of a decade ago. *Indiana Jones and the Temple of Doom* and *Star Trek III: The Search for Spock* were both independent productions; but in form, style, and content they are little different from the blockbusters churned out by the studio system for decades. Motion pictures today in some sense resemble what they were at their beginning—products of individual taste and concern reflecting both what the audience wants and what individual communicators want to say. This, of course, was not always so and brings us to the beginning of our discussion—a brief historical overview of the medium.

HISTORICAL PERSPECTIVES

The motion picture is the child of science. Many traces of antiquity, such as cave drawings and shadow plays, are evidence of the universal quest to re-create motion. Very early, this quest was taken up by the scientist as well as the artist.

The Prehistory of the Motion Picture

A number of discoveries, inventions, and theories occurred with some regularity throughout history and demonstrated our continued fascination with reproducing motion. A variety of camera-projection devices were developed, including Alberti's *camera lucida*, della Porta's use of da Vinci's *camera obscura*, and, most important, Kircher's magic lantern. Nevertheless, none of these devices went beyond the ability to project drawn pictures of still life. There was no photography and no motion.

Before motion pictures could exist, therefore, several major discoveries had to take place. The following discoveries, all occurring in the nineteenth century, formed the scientific base of cinematography: (*a*) discovery of the persistence of vision; (*b*) development of photography; (*c*) development of a motion-picture camera; (*d*) development of motion-picture projection techniques; (*e*) integration of motion, projection, and photographic concepts into cinematography.

This final evolutionary process began with Peter Mark Roget presenting his theory of the persistence of vision in 1824. Roget demonstrated that through a peculiarity of the eye, a visual image is retained on the retina for a fraction of a second after it actually appears. Motion pictures are simply a series of motionless images (still frames) presented before the eye in rapid succession. Persistence of vision allows these still images to blend, creating the illusion of motion.

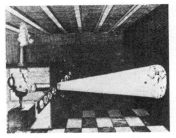

Kircher's magic lantern, shown in this seventeenth-century illustration, provided a crude form of projection.

Soon after Roget published the results of his findings, a variety of motion devices incorporating his discovery were invented. Although they carried such imposing names as the stroboscope and the phenakistiscope, they were basically parlor toys in which drawn figures were animated.

The next required component was a system of projection. Projection in a crude form had existed for some time in the form of Kircher's magic lantern (1646), but it was not until 1853 that Baron Franz von Uchatius projected moving images visible to large numbers of persons. This was accomplished by a series of individual projectors each containing a phase drawing. It was not until the 1890s that the motion-picture projector as we know it today developed out of experiments by Thomas Edison and Thomas Armat in the United States and the Lumière brothers in France.

Despite these advances in projection, the pictures used to simulate motion were still being drawn. The next step in the development of cinematography actually involved two separate steps: the invention of photography, and, from this, the development of motion-picture photography. Still photography resulted from the efforts of Nicephore Niepce and Louis J. M. Daguerre, who presented copperplate photography to the public for the first time in 1839. Subsequently, photographs were used instead of drawings in the available projection devices. In the most elaborate demonstration of projection, Henry Heyl, in 1870, projected photographs onto a screen in front of 1600 people in Philadelphia.

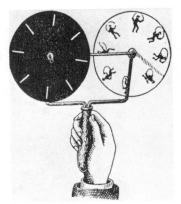

The phenakistiscope, a nineteenth century parlor toy, gave the illusion of figures in motion.

In order for these developments in motion, projection, and photography to be integrated, however, special cameras, film, and projectors were needed. A camera that would take pictures faster than the still camera was essential. A number of attempts were made to solve this problem, including Eadweard Muybridge's famous demonstration of the gait of a galloping horse in 1877. A more successful step came in 1882 when Dr. E. J. Marey developed what he called a "photographic gun," which could take a series of pictures in rapid succession. But his camera still used individual plates. Flexible-roll film was necessary for the complete development of a motion-picture camera.

An American preacher, Hannibal Goodwin, invented roll film, but George Eastman became its greatest promoter with the development in 1888 of his Kodak camera. He was not concerned with cinematography, however, and did nothing to develop motion-picture film.

It remained for William Dickson, an assistant of Thomas Edison, to perfect the first motion-picture camera using roll film. There is some con-

E. J. Marey's chronophotographic gun could take still pictures in rapid succession.

Eadweard Muybridge, in order to win a bet, set out to prove that all four feet of a galloping horse are sometimes in air at the same time. By constructing a row of cameras operated by trip wires, he was able to take a series of individual still pictures which documented the position of the horse at various stages of its run. (Photo: Museum of Modern Art/Film Stills Archive.)

fusion as to exact dates, but it appears that by 1889 Dickson and Edison were taking moving pictures. In 1891 Edison applied for patents on the Kinetograph as a photographing camera and the kinetoscope as a viewing apparatus and soon afterward began producing short film strips.

Edison's kinetoscope was a "peep show" device allowing viewing by only one person at a time. Edison was, in fact, slow to realize the importance of projection. At least a dozen other men began working on projection, including brothers August and Louis Lumière in France. In 1895 they demonstrated their projection device, the cinematographe, and shortly after began producing films. Edison soon realized his shortsight-

(Photo: The Bettman Archive, Inc.)

A Kinetoscope Arcade in
San Francisco, circa 1899.

edness, and taking advantage of the efforts of the Lumières and American
inventor Thomas Armat, developed the Vitascope projector. On 23 April
1896, in Koster and Bial's Music Hall in New York, Edison's Vitascope
projector was used for the first public showing of motion pictures in the
United States.

The first subject matter of the newly developed art of motion pictures
was simple pictorial realism. The motion-picture medium began as a recording device. Such films as *Arrival of the Paris Express*, *Venice Showing
Gondolas*, *Kaiser Wilhelm Reviewing His Troops*, and *Feeding the Ducks
at Tampa Bay* emphasized the ability of the camera to record reality. Few
of these films ran more than a minute, and they were often run backward
to pad the presentation and amaze the audience.

The Beginnings

Despite the initial excitement, people soon tired of various versions of
Niagara Falls, fire engines racing down a street, and babies smearing their
faces with porridge. Motion pictures soon began to develop themes involving a story and sustained narrative. An important factor in this rapid
development was that film, unlike some of the more traditional art forms,
had the solid traditions and skills of photography and the theater behind
it. In addition, when a new technique was discovered, it was quickly
imitated by other filmmakers.

Generally of short dura-
tion, early reality films
recorded natural phenom-
ena or public events such
as the Jeffries-Sharkey
fight of 1899.

(Photo: The American Mutoscope
and Biograph Co., Reproduction
from the collections of the Library of Congress.)

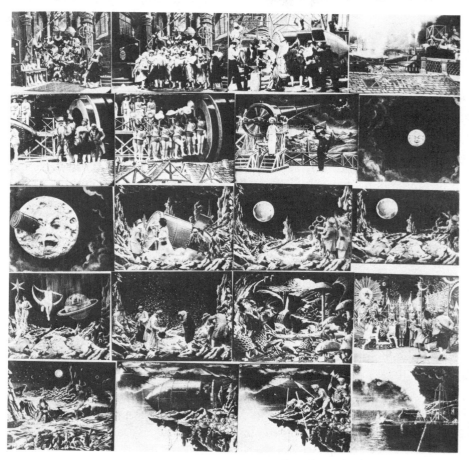

George Meliès was the
first to incorporate dra-
matic narrative into filmmaking as illustrated in *A
Trip to the Moon* (1902).

(Photo: Museum of Modern Art/Film Stills Archive.)

As early as 1896 the French filmmaker George Meliès began to create motion pictures with a story line. Meliès discovered new ways of seeing, interpreting, and even distorting reality. He contributed much to the development of the motion picture, including the invention or development of many standard optical devices such as the dissolve, split screen, jump cut, and superimposition. Meliès' most important contribution, however, was his approach to film as a means of telling a story, not simply recording reality. Unfortunately, he was unable to move beyond his theatrical and magical background. His films were always a series of artificially arranged scenes shot from the fixed view of a spectator in a theater.

Developments in England and America soon propelled the motion picture into its unique means of expression. In America it was Edwin S. Porter who is credited with the initial development of narrative film. In two films, *The Life of an American Fireman* (1902) and more importantly *The Great Train Robbery* (1903), he demonstrated the power of editing as a means of film construction. The significance of *The Great Train Robbery* lay not only in its technique of building up an effective continuity of action through editing but also in the timeliness of its arrival. Despite the camera trickery of Meliès, audiences had begun to tire of films that simply moved. *The Great Train Robbery* presented a fresh approach and offered the public new excitement.

Edwin S. Porter explored the techniques of film editing to provide continuity of action in *The Great Train Robbery* (1903).

(Photo: Museum of Modern Art/Film Stills Archive.)

Narrative Development

The years between 1906 and 1916 were the most important period of artistic development in motion-picture history. It was the time of the feature film, the first film star, the first distinguished director, the first picture palaces, a place called Hollywood, and above all, the development of film as a unique and individual means of expression.

Some historians have aptly labeled this time "the age of Griffith." It was David Wark Griffith who took the raw material of film and created a language, a syntax, and an art. His contributions were many, but more than anything else Griffith made film a dynamic medium. Beginning with *The Adventures of Dolly* (1908) and culminating with *The Birth of a Nation* (1915) and *Intolerance* (1916), Griffith freed the motion picture from strictly theatrical bounds. He pioneered a more natural acting style, better story organization, and most important, a true filmic style. Rather than simply use film as a moving photograph or portable theater, he developed a language that emphasized the unique characteristics of the film medium, such as editing, camera movement, and camera angle.

To say that these years were the age of Griffith is not to deny the emergence of other notable film styles and important artists. Mack Sennett and his Keystone company developed their unique brand of slapstick comedy. Charlie Chaplin moved beyond Sennett's slapstick humor with a deeper, more philosophical edge. William S. Hart made realistic Westerns, and Mary Pickford was the screen's most popular personality.

D. W. Griffith (seated at right) pioneered most modern filmmaking techniques.

(Photo: Museum of Modern Art/Film Stills Archive.)

The nickelodeon appeared in 1905 as the first permanent motion picture theater. (Photo: Museum of Modern Art/Film Stills Archive.)

The businessman also played an important role in this period. Since most inventors of cinematic devices did little to exploit their devices commercially, it remained for individual entrepreneurs like B. F. Keith, Major Woodville Latham, and Thomas Talley, among others, to bring showmanship to the motion picture. The early commercial development of motion pictures began with vaudeville houses. Films started out as "headliners" but ended up as "chasers" moving patrons out of the theater between shows. Motion pictures then moved to slightly more permanent homes as projectors were installed in empty stores and music halls. There were also a number of traveling film shows, "electric theaters" as they were called. In 1905 the nickelodeon appeared as the first permanent motion picture theater—so named because a nickel was the price for admission. By 1907 there were more than 3000 of these small theaters, and by 1910 over 10,000 nickelodeons were scattered over the eastern half of the country.

Making motion pictures became a prosperous and thriving enterprise. Between 1905 and 1910 narrative films grew longer and more costly, as well as more popular and profitable. Porter's *Dream of a Rarebit Fiend* (1906), for example, cost $350 to make and grossed more than $350,000. The Vitagraph Company, which started in 1896 with capital of $936, showed profits of over $900,000 by 1912. The trappings of an industrial empire were not yet apparent, however. There was no star system, no million-dollar salaries, no Hollywood. These would all come about as a reaction against a monopoly called the Motion Picture Patents Company (MPPC). Formed in 1909 through the pooling of 16 patents, it controlled virtually every aspect of motion-picture production, distribution, and exhibition in the United States for more than 3 years.

The final stage of early economic development included a savage war between the MPPC and independent and foreign producers. It was a battle with one of these producers, Adolph Zukor, that precipitated the final developmental stage. Zukor acquired the rights to the French film *Queen Elizabeth* (1912), starring Sarah Bernhardt. In order to exhibit it, he had to apply to the MPPC for permission. It refused, and so he went to an independent exhibitor. The picture was a success, and the experience led Zukor to form his own company, Famous Players in Famous Plays, the forerunner of Paramount Pictures. Heartened by Zukor's stand, other independent producers began showing films without permission of the MPPC. Pressure was applied by the trust, and as a result many individuals moved west to escape its control. The move to California came gradually, but by 1914 it had attracted such men as Cecil B. DeMille, Jesse Lasky, Zukor, and others. Some prospered and many failed. Nevertheless, most of Hollywood's major studios trace their origins back to the independents who between 1910 and 1914 fought the MPPC.

The epic scale of Griffith's *The Birth of a Nation* (1915) and other feature-length films made nickelodeons obsolete and initiated the age of the movie palace.

(Photo: Movie Star News.)

One important effect of this conflict was the establishment of Hollywood as the center of motion-picture production. Other important results were the introduction of feature-length films, the rise of the star system, and the construction of elaborate motion-picture theaters. For obvious financial reasons, the trust had limited all films to one reel and blocked actor identification. For the independents, longer films and stars became an effective way of attracting customers. To accommodate the influx of star-studded, feature-length films, new theaters were constructed. With such films as *The Birth of a Nation*, motion pictures moved out of the nickelodeons and into their own grand palaces.

By 1917 the MPPC had been dissolved by the courts. Even though brief, the MPPC fight produced lasting results including the founding of an industrial empire, the birth of many production companies, feature-length films, the star system, Hollywood, and above all, a new respectability for film.

By World War I motion pictures were firmly established as an artistic and economic reality. The war further strengthened America's position in the international film market because virtually all the major film industries of Europe were either shut down or had their production severely curtailed. By 1919, 80% of the world's motion pictures were made in Southern California. By 1920 average weekly movie attendance in the United States was 40 million and growing rapidly.

International Awakenings

Following World War I, there was a great deal of international development in film. The war-ravaged film industries of Germany, France, and Russia were quickly reconstructed and began producing films. Movements in these three countries were especially important because of the contributions they made to film theory and aesthetics. In Germany, for example, two types of film emerged: the expressionistic film, a part of the art movement of the same name; and the realistic "street films," so named because city streets played an important part in them. The street films had a distinct impact in bringing to film a new sense of naturalism and realism. The camera was also used with a new sense of personal perspective and movement. Important films of these two movements included *The Cabinet of Dr. Caligari* (1919) and *The Joyless Street* (1925).

The Russians, most notably Lev Kuleshov, Sergei Eisenstein, and V. L. Pudovkin, contributed greatly to the theory of film editing. The Russian concept of montage—the creation of meaning through shot juxtaposition—had a significant impact upon Russian film and was used by Eisenstein and Pudovkin, especially, to produce films of stunning force and deep meaning. Key films here were Eisenstein's *Potemkin* (1925) and Pudovkin's *Mother* (1927).

In France, motion pictures displayed an abstract and surrealistic form through the work of interested intellectuals and creative filmmakers such as René Clair, Jacques Feyder, and Luis Buñuel. In such films as *Entracte*

The Cabinet of Dr. Caligari (1919) is notable for its expressionistic stage design.

(Photo: Museum of Modern Art/Film Stills Archive.)

The unforgettable images in *Potemkin* (1925) achieve most of their impact through Eisenstein's use of montage.

(Photo: Museum of Modern Art/Film Stills Archive.)

(1925) and *Un Chien Andalou* (1929), these men extended the boundaries of film beyond narrative into the world of deep symbolism and pure form.

All this international energy had a distinct yet diffused impact on the American film industry. Few of the actual film forms and theories were incorporated by Hollywood; however, the talent that produced them was absorbed. Not long after they achieved international reputations, such directors and film stars as Emil Jannings, F. W. Murnau, Greta Garbo, and Marlene Dietrich came to the United States to make films. The result was the gradual weakening and ultimate destruction of most of the national foreign movements.

Meanwhile, Hollywood was busy providing films that were essentially a reflection of the roaring twenties. Companies became studios, which grew in size and power. Salaries rose, huge stages were constructed, and many backlots contained entire towns. By the mid-1920s, 40% of a film's budget went to pay for studio overhead.

Hollywood in the 1920s

Three kinds of films dominated the final decade of silent film: the feature-length comedy, the Western, and the comedy of manners. In this era, many critics believe, film comedy reached its zenith. The comedic style of the time moved away from the broad, farcical slapstick of Mack Sennett toward a more subtle, sophisticated format, characterized so brilliantly by, among others, Charlie Chaplin, Harold Lloyd, and Buster Kea-

Buster Keaton's in a scene from his most famous film, *The General* (1926).

(Photo: Museum of Modern Art/Film Stills Archive.)

ton. In such films as Chaplin's *The Gold Rush* (1925) Keaton's *The General* (1926) and Lloyd's *The Freshman* (1925) silent comedy achieved the pinnacle of artistic film achievement.

The Western matured with the development of the "big" feature best represented by John Ford's *Covered Wagon* (1923), James Cruze's *Iron Horse* (1924), and William S. Hart's *Tumbleweeds* (1925). The "B" Western, especially the romantic melodramas of Tom Mix, also became prominent, providing contrast not only to the spectacular Westerns of Ford and Cruze but to the stark realism used so effectively by Hart.

The third film form was a direct result of the social conditions of the time. The mores of the country were freer and more open than at any time in its history. The comedy-of-manners film was a reflection of this increased sophistication as it concentrated on high society, glittering wealth, and personal freedom. Such films as Cecil B. DeMille's *Male and Female* (1919) and *Why Change Your Wife* (1920) appealed directly to this new sense of freedom.

The Arrival of Sound

Despite the fact that the 1920s were years of increased prosperity for the motion-picture industry, the end of the era found Hollywood experiencing a profound uneasiness. As a result of a series of major scandals in the early 1920s, a motion-picture-code office was formed to police both the content of films and the behavior of the people who made them. This, coupled with the increasing popularity of radio and the automobile, created an attendance problem. In order to save the industry and win back the lost audience, something new was needed.

Warner Brothers was a small studio on the verge of bankruptcy in 1926. Having little to lose, it invested its remaining capital in a new sound system called Vitaphone. On 26 October 1927 it presented the first talking feature, *The Jazz Singer*, starring Al Jolson. The motion-picture industry, reluctant at first to abandon silent film completely, soon recognized the public's acceptance as permanent and moved to total sound production.

The effect of sound on motion pictures was profound and lasting. Sound's impact upon content was evident from the start with a rush toward the musical. The more a film talked, sang, or shouted, the better it was. Swept aside in the rush were many unique forms, most notably silent-comedy.

Individual stars were also greatly affected. Buster Keaton, Charlie Chaplin, Harold Lloyd, and other silent comics, whose basic style was visual, were hampered. In addition, many stars found that their voices were displeasing to audiences. The careers of such major silent-film stars as Charles Farrell and Norma Talmadge were greatly limited because of unsatisfactory vocal quality.

The impact upon audiences was most important. In 1927 an average of 60 million people attended motion pictures every week. By 1929 this

The era of the silent film
came to an end in 1927
when Al Jolson starred in
The Jazz Singer, Holly-
wood's first talking fea-
ture film.

(Photo: Movie Star News, Courtesy Warner Bros., Inc.)

figure was over 110 million. This success gave the industry a tremendous
financial boost and helped it over the worst years of the depression.

The expense of making sound films also brought a new financial domination in the form of such companies as Western Electric, RCA, and their
respective financial backers, Kuhn-Loeb and the First National Bank of
New York. When RCA, which made sound equipment, bought a film company and theater corporation, it set up a powerful new studio, RKO. The
eastern banking interests gained a significant hold on the entertainment
industry and its products. Despite Hollywood's domestic success, its dominance of the world market diminished because, although silent films had
a universal language, sound films required expensive dubbing of foreign
languages for overseas distribution.

Like other elements of the time, film reflected the tensions, crises, and
deepening social awareness in the United States. One reaction to the time
was the documentary film, beginning with Robert Flaherty's work in the
early 1920s and continuing under John Grierson's influence in England.
The United States initially failed to exploit the documentary's potential,
but in 1936 Pare Lorentz produced *The Plow That Broke the Plains*. Lorentz was soon made head of the U.S. Film Service, and along with other
directors, such as Willard Van Dyke, he created several powerful films,

**Hollywood in the
1930s**

Although thin on plot, *Flying Down to Rio* (1934) first introduced the dance team of Ginger Rogers and Fred Astaire.

(Photo: Museum of Modern Art/Film Stills Archive, Courtesy RKO Studios.)

including *The River* (1937), *Ecce Homo* (1939), and *The Power and the Land* (1940). For a variety of political reasons, however, the service was legislated out of existence in 1940, and it took the catastrophe of World War II to revitalize the documentary form.

Another response to the needs of the time was the social-consciousness film. Such films as *The Public Enemy* (1931) and *I Was a Fugitive from a Chain Gang* (1933) asked their audiences to view men and their actions as a part or the result of the social conditions of the time. A third response was escapism. As the economic depression deepened, the studios turned toward more musical and comedic themes in an attempt to provide their audiences with another reality. Hollywood produced a wave of Busby Berkeley and Fred Astaire–Ginger Rogers singing and dancing spectacles, such as *Footlight Parade* (1933), *Gold Diggers of 1935* (1935), and *Flying*

Down to Rio (1936). These were soon accompanied by "screwball" comedies, such as *It Happened One Night* (1934), directed by Frank Capra, and "The Thin Man" series starring William Powell and Myrna Loy.

The 1930s were also the golden age of the studio system. Production was almost completely centered in seven dominant companies: MGM, Paramount, Warner Brothers, RKO, Universal, Columbia, and 20th Century-Fox. Each studio had its own stars and unique style.

Toward the end of the 1930s, with war imminent in Europe, American studios began to produce strongly patriotic films, and some cautious steps were taken in portraying future allies and enemies in such films as *Foreign Correspondent* (1940) and *The Ramparts We Watch* (1939). Until Pearl Harbor, however, the United States was technically a neutral nation, and most film companies were wary of economic reprisals by Axis governments.

World War II

After Pearl Harbor, Hollywood began to produce patriotic war films with Japanese and Germans immediately becoming stock, stereotyped villains. The image of the American fighting man was equally stereotyped. American audiences did not want realistic war dramas detailing the horrors they read about in newspapers or heard on radio. As the war continued to wear on, the studios turned to more and more escapist fare. More than half of the 1300 films produced from 1942 to 1944 had themes unrelated to the war. As a result of a war-weary civilian population seeking escape, the studios enjoyed enormous success and profits reached new heights.

The story of postwar film is essentially a chronicle of decline and frustration for Hollywood and the major studios but rebirth and growth for foreign and independent films. After the war, American studios resumed standard operating procedures, producing a steady supply of films designed for the mass public's tastes and habits. Before the 1940s were spent, however, four events occurred that forced major changes in the traditional Hollywood structure: (a) the rise of television; (b) the House Un-American Activities Committee hearings; (c) the Supreme Court divorcement ruling; and (d) the emergence of a vigorous international film movement.

The Postwar Era

The advent of network television in 1948 diverted much of the audience from its traditional twice-a-week motion-picture habit. Between 1950 and 1960 the number of TV sets in the United States increased by 400%, while motion-picture attendance fell by 50%.

The fear of communism in the United States, labeled the "red scare," had a number of effects. The most devastating was the blacklist in which many talented craftsmen and artists were labeled as communists because of alleged left-wing activities and were banned from the industry. Experimentation and initiative in content were discouraged, and producers either fell back on old patterns or grasped at experimental technological straws.

The third blow was the 1950 *Paramount* decision of the U.S. Supreme Court, which forced the Hollywood studios to end vertical integration by which one corporation produced, distributed, and exhibited films. Film companies were forced to divest themselves of one of the three operations. Most major companies sold off their theater chains and stayed in production and distribution. This, in effect, caused the collapse of the basic industry monopoly and ended the absolute control the major Hollywood studios had held on the American film market for 30 years.

Coincidental to these domestic happenings, and to a certain extent because of them, a strong international film movement emerged. Beginning with neorealism in Italy, vital national cinemas developed in the late 1940s and early 1950s. Japan walked off with the Venice Film Festival award with Akira Kurosawa's *Rashomon* in 1951, and suddenly American audiences became aware of other sources of motion pictures. Foreign films were available not only from Japan but from England, France, Italy, Sweden, and India. With this availability yet another aspect of studio monopoly was undermined.

Motion pictures in the United States were no longer *the* mass medium, and at the time their future as *a* mass medium looked shaky. Attendance figures dropped off sharply. The industry frantically responded with such technological innovations as stereophonic sound, wide screens, and 3-D viewing—anything television could not duplicate. These attractions were built on passing fancies, however, and the basic fact of a changing audience was ignored. Attempts to inject new vigor or new themes were fought consistently. This is clearly illustrated by Otto Preminger's unsuccessful fight to obtain the industry's seal of approval for two films, *The Moon Is Blue* (1953), an innocuous comedy about adultery, and *The Man with the Golden Arm* (1956), a film dealing with drug addition.

In 1953, the motion picture industry introduced 3-D glasses in an attempt to win back audiences who had defected to television.

(Photo: New York Public Library at Lincoln Center, Courtesy 20th Century-Fox.)

Unlike *The Sound of Music* (1965), one of the biggest money makers in the history of film, most of the high-budget spectaculars of the late 1960s and early 1970s were financial disasters.

Hollywood tried to win back its lost audience and regain some of its former prestige by emphasizing size. The spectacle had been a part of Hollywood ever since *Birth of a Nation* (1915), and in the 1960s this film form was looked upon as the savior of the Hollywood system. *Cleopatra* (1963) should have been a warning signal; it was the most expensive and most publicized film made to this time, and it was a monumental box-office failure. But 2 years later *The Sound of Music* (1965) became one of the biggest box-office successes in history, earning more than $80 million in rentals. The major studios, with their confidence bolstered by *The Sound of Music*, set into motion a series of spectacles, among them *Dr. Dolittle* (1968), *Star* (1969), *Goodbye Mr. Chips* (1970), and *Tora! Tora! Tora!* (1971). All were failures that plunged many of the studios to the point of bankruptcy and led to their eventual takeover by non-Hollywood business interests.

Some cracks began to appear in Hollywood's facade. One change was the reorganization of United Artists in 1951. Originally organized in 1919 as an independent outlet for the films of D. W. Griffith, Charlie Chaplin,

The success of the low budget film *Marty* (1955), encouraged recently reorganized United Artists to continue to provide distribution for independently produced films.

(Photo: New York Public Library at Lincoln Center, Courtesy United Artists Corporation.)

Douglas Fairbanks, and Mary Pickford, United Artists was revamped in 1951 to carry out precisely the same function—providing distribution for independently produced films. With such films as *The African Queen* (1951) and *Marty* (1955), United Artists began to provide new hope for the independent filmmaker. From this beginning, the roots of the "new American cinema" emerged.

The Film Revolution   In the 1960s Hollywood and its traditional picture values declined even further. A new cinema emerged to take its place; a cinema difficult to characterize except perhaps in what it rejected. The films of the 1960s and early 1970s were the products of a changing society, a society in which relevance, awareness, and freedom of expression became watchwords. Motion pictures no longer existed exclusively as a product to be passively consumed by a mass audience. New filmmakers were searching for new audiences, who in turn were seeking a new kind of involvement in the film experience.

Hollywood did not die in the 1960s, but it did experience radical change. Most of the major studios were used as financing and distributing agents for independently produced features, but the traditional system of motion-picture production, distribution, and exhibition did not undergo transformation easily.

Perhaps the most important force at work was the so-called New American Cinema, which was essentially the surfacing of what used to be called underground films. There have always been films that were shot away from normal production sources. They have been called art, avant-garde, experimental, "new wave," or even pornographic. Perhaps the major film trend of the 1960s was that such films acquired a legitimacy that saw them exhibited virtually without restriction. Essentially, what happened was a juncture of the art–experimental film with the underground film through the normal channels of production, distribution, and exhibition.

One of the first underground features to surface and receive wide public distribution was Shirley Clarke's *The Connection* (1961). This was soon followed by Jonas Mekas's *The Brig* (1964) and Kenneth Anger's *Scorpio Rising* (1966). By the late 1960s, this movement, coupled with the troubles of the major studios, had catapulted the independent filmmaker into a position of prominence. Dennis Hopper's *Easy Rider* (1969) was the watershed of this trend, for it finally convinced the major studios that a low-budget ($370,000) independently produced film could be a blockbuster (over $50 million in rentals).

The significance of *Easy Rider* was not in its artistic merits, although it certainly possessed them, but in the fact that talents outside the Hollywood mainstream (Dennis Hopper, Peter Fonda, Jack Nicholson, Karen Black) could produce and star in a film with massive audience appeal on a small budget. It showed a new way to mine gold in the American audience.

Dennis Hopper and Peter Fonda on the road in *Easy Rider* (1969), a watershed film in the development of the "New American Cinema." (Photo: Museum of Modern Art/Film Stills Archive, Courtesy Columbia Pictures Industries, Inc.)

There was a great deal of talk in the late 1960s and early 1970s of a new film generation, of an audience that was more sophisticated and would demand more from film than entertainment. An indication of this growing awareness was the expanding film curriculum in high schools, colleges, and universities. The American Film Institute's guide to college film courses listed more than 4000 courses being offered at more than 1000 schools. Film majors numbered in excess of 8000. This new awareness, coupled with formal instruction in film production and consumption, produced an audience that was more perceptive and more knowledgeable about film than ever before. As Robert Evans, former head of production at Paramount, said in 1971: "The main change has been in the audience. Today people go to see *a* movie, they no longer go to *the* movies. We can't depend upon habit anymore."

New audiences are basic to a new cinema. They were and are the driving force behind it. Motion pictures were no longer appealing to an audience composed of a cross section of the American population. It was estimated that some 75% of the film audience of the 1970s was between the ages of 16 and 30. This was obviously a young and flexible audience. Their effect on motion pictures was dramatic. On the one hand, many of them demanded that film do more than simply provide escape; it should, in their view, make statements, take sides, and promote cause. On the other hand, they were using film as escape, as pure entertainment.

They Shoot Horses Don't They? (1969), for example, revealed a sordid side to the often fondly remembered dance marathons of the 1930s. The outstanding success of such films as *Tell Them Willie Boy Is Here* (1969), *Five Easy Pieces* (1970), *Z* (1969), *Joe* (1970), *M*A*S*H* (1969), *Little Big Man* (1970), *Dirty Harry* (1971), *The Last Picture Show* (1971), *A Clockwork Orange* (1972), and *Cabaret* (1972), among others, pointed to an increased awareness of film as a medium for social comment.

Nevertheless, what was thought to be a permanent trend turned out to be simply another cycle. The social-consciousness film movement that had begun with *Easy Rider* quickly faded. By 1973–1974 a new cycle of films had appeared: the disaster film. Headed by *The Poseidon Adventure* (1973), this cycle dominated film production for two years with such films as *Airport 1975, Earthquake,* and *The Towering Inferno.* This trend was short-lived, however, as audiences grew tired of being guinea pigs for ambitious special-effects artists who filled vapid plots and surrounded dull acting with all sorts of magical tricks. Aside from this minicycle, 1974 was a year of great diversity with such films as Francis Coppola's intense character study, *The Conversation,* Sidney Lumet's witty *Murder on the Orient Express,* Roman Polanski's searing picture of the 1930s' Los Angeles underworld in *Chinatown,* Art Carney's wistful portrayal of the problems and beauty of old age in *Harry and Tonto,* and John Cassavetes's continued exploration of the human condition in *A Woman Under the Influence.*

(Photo: The Bettman Archive, Inc.)

Princess Leia (Carrie Fisher) places a message for help in Artoo-Detoo. The record breaking profits of *Star Wars* (1977) fed the film studios' "blockbuster psychology."

With *Jaws* in 1975 the era of the mega-rental film began in earnest, and in 1977 *Star Wars* exploded previous box-office records into outer space.

Star Wars was *the* film of 1977 and of film box-office history. The success of this film immediately revived the long dormant science-fiction genre, and a new cycle began. The new cycle was less one of content or style and more one of formula and financial success characterized by the obsessive use of sequels and reissues. The blockbuster psychology of the studios made it almost impossible to be offbeat and personal. The 1980s continued with more of the same, resulting in fewer films and bigger budgets, especially for advertising and publicity, as hype too often substituted for quality.

In addition to *Star Wars*, 1977 saw the birth of two other "sequel series:" Sylvester Stallone in *Rocky* and Burt Reynolds in *Smokey and the Bandit*. As the second and third most popular rental films of the year they inspired (some would say "conspired to") a succession of baby Rockys and Smokeys that are still going strong. *Grease* was the big film of 1978, followed in turn by *Close Encounters of the Third Kind* (actually released in late 1977) and *Animal House*. *Jaws II* and a reissue of *Star Wars* made the top 10 box-office list as well. *Superman* led the way in 1979 and was quickly followed by the Spielberg–Lucas dynasty beginning in the 1980s. *The Empire Strikes Back* more than doubled the box-office rentals of the number-two film, *Kramer vs. Kramer*, in 1980; *Raiders of the Lost Ark* and *Superman II* held forth in 1981. The year 1982 starred *E.T.*, as well as

(Photo: Movie Star News, Courtesy Universal Studios.)

Rocky III, Star Trek II, a reissue of *Raiders of the Lost Ark*, and Spielberg's
third film in the top 20, *Poltergeist*.

Although relatively few in number the feature film follow-ups have
exerted an extremely potent box office appeal. In 1981 and 1982 sequels
and follow-ups to major films (nine and eleven titles respectively) accounted for 12% of all domestic rentals for each of those years. This is a
startling performance given over 500 new and reissued pictures in the
marketplace each year.

Key films for each year were; 1981: *Superman II, For Your Eyes Only,
The Great Muppet Caper, Halloween II, The Final Conflict, Friday the
13th Part 2* and *Shock Treatment*; 1982: *Rocky III, Star Trek II: The Wrath
of Khan, Friday the 13th Part 3, Airplane II: The Sequel, Halloween III,
Grease 2* and *Trail of the Pink Panther.*

The sequel syndrome of the 1980s may be a continuing phenomenon;
*Return of the Jedi, Superman III, Octopussy, Jaws 3-D, Porky's II, Smokey
and the Bandit Part 3* and *Psycho II* dominated 1983 box-office statistics.
However, there are signs that some cracks are beginning to appear because
both *Jedi* and *Superman III* generated less return revenue (people seeing
a film twice and even three and four times) and met with decidedly less
than universal critical acclaim. In 1984 series and sequel films continued

to do well with the issue of *Indiana Jones and the Temple of Doom, Star Trek III: The Search for Spock, Cannonball II, The Muppets Take Manhattan, Oh God You Devil* and *Friday the 13th Part 4*.

Despite these minitrends, the real profile of the American feature film in the late 1970s and early 1980s was one of isolated success. As several contemporary critics noted, among the Hollywood studios and independent production companies, strategy in production replaced style, and the emphasis in commercial filmmaking was focused almost totally on the mega-box-office success. In 4 of the last 5 years of the 1970s, one huge box-office success spawned a host of attempts at duplicating that success (*Jaws* in 1975, *Star Wars* in 1977, *Grease* in 1978, and *Superman* in 1979).

When one looks at films today, the only word that comes to mind is conformity; it is conformity not so much in style as in the attempt to duplicate what has proven commercially successful. One of the significant effects of this trend has been the decline of the foreign film. The 1960s saw a tremendous surge in foreign films, but by 1972 Ingmar Bergman's *Cries and Whispers* could not find an American distributor. Today, the foreign film that successfully cracks the U.S. theatrical market is a rare commodity. Most illustrative of this trend is the history in recent years of films made in France and Italy, traditionally two leading suppliers of import films to America. None of the locally popular films starring French superstars Alain Delono and Jean-Paul Belmondo have shown up on American marquees as have few, if any, of the many comedy hits coming from Italy. The current practice of major U.S. distributors is to set up a separate "classics" division to handle what they term mainly "arty" imports. Independent distributors concentrate primarily on importing European art films or fantasy and sex films, letting the middle range of popular hits remain at home.

The key to understanding the conformity and noticeable lack of individuality in American films of the early 1980s is simple economics. As the average cost of producing a feature film has risen from $1 million in 1972 to over $11 million in the mid-1980s, the small film—financed, made, and distributed outside the major studios—has become all but obsolete. As the studios themselves have become small parts of large conglomerates, films have become the means to an end (profits) rather than the end itself.

Filmmaking today is controlled by a few major studios that are in turn controlled by conglomerate owners. The individuals who run these and other film conglomerates, such as MCA and Transamerica, have decided to devote their money to large "blockbuster" films and to eliminate small films. If one looks at the top 10 box-office films of 1982, this pattern becomes obvious. The big film of the year, *E.T.*, was essentially a *Star Wars* clone. *Rocky III* speaks for itself. *Star Trek II* continued the science-fiction theme, and *Poltergeist* gave Steven Spielberg a sweep of the big-money stakes of 1982. *Annie* and *The Best Little Whorehouse in Texas*

Top 10 Box-Office Films, 1982

1. *E.T.*
2. *Rocky III*
3. *On Golden Pond*
4. *Porky's*
5. *An Officer and a Gentleman*
6. *The Best Little Whorehouse in Texas*
7. *Star Trek II: The Wrath of Khan*
8. *Poltergeist*
9. *Annie*
10. *Chariots of Fire*

Feature-Film Production Costs, 1983

Type of film	Budget range	Average cost
Hard-core pornography	$80,000–150,000	$120,000
16-mm independents, student features	$20,000–500,000	$120,000
Independent-distributed programmers (horror, action, comedy)	$200,000–2,000,000	$1,000,000
Foreign TV features	$400,000–1,000,000	$750,000
Foreign theatrical features	$500,000–7,000,000	$2,000,000
Made-for-TV films		
Pay cable	$1,000,000–4,000,000	$3,500,000
Network	$1,800,000–3,000,000	$2,100,000
Independent production for major distributor pickup	$2,000,000–10,000,000	$5,800,000
Major distributor in-house films	$5,000,000–40,000,000	$11,500,000
Network TV miniseries (6–18 hours)	$12,000,000–40,000,000	$2,000,000 (per hour)

Horror Film Production

Year	U.S.	Foreign	Total
1978	35	23	58
1979	38	33	71
1980	66	55	121
1981	70	45	115
1982	34	35	69
1983 (est.)	35	25	60

were Broadway success stories hoping for a repeat, and *On Golden Pond* had not one but three surefire, run-to-the-bank stars (Henry Fonda, Katharine Hepburn, Jane Fonda). Only *Chariots of Fire* represented any degree of individuality.

As the cost of making films has risen, the stylistic and thematic freedoms of the early 1970s have given way to the action-dominated and star-populated conformity of the 1980s. While small, personal films like *The Elephant Man* (1980), *Diner* (1982), and *Local Hero* (1983) are still made, they represent a dying breed. The current trend is toward content–theme cycles of increasingly shorter duration; we almost have "seasons" as on television. The key is to start a new trend or get on the bandwagon quickly, before the audience gets bored.

A perfect illustration of the bandwagon effect is the horror film cycle of the late 1970s and early 1980s. After steady and in some years spectacular increases in box office rentals, horror films in 1983 suffered badly as domestic rentals for the genre fell by 50%. Only 19 horror films in 1983 earned $1 million in domestic rentals, compared to 31 in 1982, 22 in 1981, and 26 in 1980. The following chart illlustrating the decline in horror film production since 1980 indicates the general public's disenchantment with the game, an inevitable result of the relentless imitation in the exploitation film market.

There is no guarantee of success any longer. Previous "guarantees" included studios such as MGM; stars such as Gable, Cooper, Tracy, Newman, McQueen, and Hoffman; directors such as Ford, Bogdanovich, Peckinpah, Altman, and Kubrick; and audience habits such as going to the movies regularly.

The feature film of the 1980s bears little resemblance to its counterpart of the late 1960s. Part of the reason for this is the motion-picture industry's code, which no longer censors films but simply suggests suitable age levels for particular films. These ratings (begun in 1968) include G for general audiences, PG for parental guidance suggested, PG-13 for special guidance for children under 13, R for restricted to individuals at least 17 years old or those accompanied by a parent or guardian, and X for no one under the age of 17 admitted.

Freedom from industry censorship has led to a dramatic increase in the sexual and violent content in motion pictures. Sex and violence have been a part of motion pictures from the beginning; but industry codes, state and local laws, or both always checked "excesses." The rating code and changes in society have led to new standards in treating sex and violence in film. For examples, in earlier days, actual sexual activity was suggested, not shown. In 1972 a movie entitled *Deep Throat* changed all this, and "hard core" sex films appeared. By the end of 1972 an estimated 700 theaters were showing "porn" films exclusively. This, too, was a cycle that quickly faded. The lasting results are not to be found in the occasional hard-core film that makes the national circuits but in the more open and free treatment of sex as a theme and activity in most contemporary films.

Much the same could be said regarding violence. Although violence has had a long history in films, formerly there were rules that governed its use. These rules were graphically broken in the late 1960s by such films as *Bonnie and Clyde, Bullitt, The Wild Bunch,* and *The French Connection.* Violence became explicit; audiences saw bullet holes, blood, and torn flesh. The horror films of the late 1970s and early 1980s, which began with *Halloween* (1978), saw most of the rules of the game broken. No taboos were too sacred. Heads were severed, eyes were gouged out, stomachs were split open; in general, the human body was subjected to every imaginable form of mutilation until the effect became almost comic.

Whether audiences would "buy it" was, and is, the real issue. As long as the public is willing to accept violence, filmmakers are going to produce it. Some, like Samuel Z. Arkoff, former board chairman of American International Pictures, may demonstrate a social conscience and set "a limit on the number of blood bags used," but the attitude of most seems best summed up by producer Joe Hyman, "The effect on society? I don't give it a thought. Psychiatrists don't have the answers, why should I?"

Film and Television

In the mid-1970s the patterns begun in the 1950s intensified and solidified. Motion-picture attendance decreased steadily as the number of TV sets increased. What started out as competition moved to cooperation and, ultimately, coexistence. What appeared to be a destroyer at one time has turned out to be a savior. Without television, Hollywood would not have survived, even in its diminished existence. Of the 20,000 odd jobs in Hollywood today, 50% are in television. Ninety percent of all prime-time television (8:00 P.M. to 11:00 P.M.), is on film. More important, motion pictures make up a significant part of this prime-time programming. As former motion picture producer William Fadiman noted in *Hollywood Now*: "More people than ever before are seeing Hollywood films, but most of them are not paying Hollywood for the privilege." Motion pictures account for more than half of all network prime-time programming and up to 80% of the air time on nonaffiliated independent stations. Universal Studios turned out 80 feature films in 1972, breaking an industry record set back in 1927. Fewer than 25 of these films, however, were for theatrical release.

Television has become the new "B" movie and provides the same function for the industry that "B" movies have always provided—a substantial, reliable, steady income. New markets in cable and pay television hold great potential, and it is clear that television and motion pictures are firmly and permanently linked together. This linkage is causing concern in the boardrooms of major studios, however. It's a simple case of numbers. Five years ago, 80% of a film's revenues came from its box-office performance. But by 1990 domestic theater attendance could drop more than 50% to about 500 million, according to Jay M. Gould, president of Economic Information Systems. The loss of that audience could force moviemakers to rely on sales to television and other nontheater markets for as much as 50% of their revenue.

For the film companies, that is bad news. They split the box-office gross with theater owners almost 50–50 but take a smaller percentage of sales in other markets. In pay television, the studios generally keep only about 20% of the revenue. For example, HBO virtually dictates how much it will pay for a film.

A clear shift has occurred in motion-picture revenue. Studios can no longer depend on a steady income from theatrical distribution rights because the distribution of content has undergone a radical change in the past few years.

It is difficult to say where motion pictures stand at the present; they are ultimately in the hands of the people who make them and the people who view them. This constant interaction reflects change and growth, and if anything is a constant for this medium, it is change.

The motion picture continues to be one of the primary recreational outlets for the American people, although it is nowhere near as significant as it was 35 years ago. The industry peaked in 1946 with estimated box office receipts of $1.7 billion from 4.1 billion admissions. Since then the decline in admissions was precipitous until 1962, when it leveled off. Admissions have been relatively stable for more than 20 years.

Despite declining admissions, box office receipts have risen dramatically in the past four years due to ticket price increases. In 1983 the motion picture industry had its most successful year ever. Total theater receipts for the first 7 months of the year were over 10 percent above those for 1982. Viewers paid a record $2.6 billion to see a series of hit pictures, which included *Risky Business*, *National Lampoon's Vacation*, *Return of the Jedi*, *Trading Places*, and *Staying Alive*. Although receipts (including both box office and concession revenues) were generally less dramatic

THE SCOPE OF MOTION PICTURES

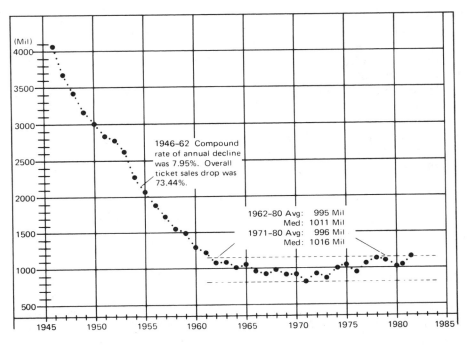

1946–62 Compound rate of annual decline was 7.95%. Overall ticket sales drop was 73.44%.

1962–80 Avg: 995 Mil
         Med: 1011 Mil
1971–80 Avg: 996 Mil
         Med: 1016 Mil

United States Theatrical Film Admissions (1946 to 1983). An unbroken annual decline in ticket sales occurred from 1946–1962. Perhaps not by coincidence, 1962 was the year that television had reached 90 percent penetration of U.S. homes, culminating its period of explosive growth. Since 1962, admissions have stabilized in the range of 1 billion per year. The low point was in 1971, at 820 million tickets. Annual Ticket Sales Data: MPAA, *Variety*. Chart © 1984 A. D. Murphy.

From 1973 to 1983, box office receipts rose from
$1.6 billion to $3.7 billion,
an increase of over 230%.

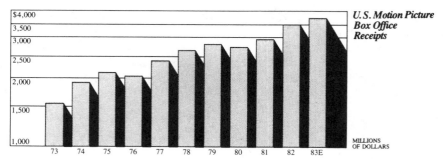

(Source: Motion Picture Association of America.)

during the rest of 1983, they reached an estimated total of $3.7 billion, 9 percent above the prior year.

Theater admissions totaled 1.176 billion in 1982, the highest attendance since the 1.225 billion recorded in 1960. The 1982 admissions figure represented an increase of 109 million, or over 10 percent above the prior year. Total attendance in 1983 reached approximately 1.196 billion, almost 2 percent above 1982.

Increases in ticket prices continued unabated in 1982. The average composite ticket price in 1982 was $2.94, almost 10 percent above the prior year. The consumer price index (CPI) figure for admission prices, which includes not only admission prices to motion picture theaters but also opera houses, concerts, and other legitimate entertainment, rose 6.2 percent. During the first 7 months of 1983 the composite ticket price increased by 7.4 percent bringing the cost of the average ticket over $3.00.

Seasonal swings in the domestic theatrical film box office have long been a fact of industry life, despite a lot of wishful thinking to the contrary. But an analysis of week-to-week fluctuations within the year, created by industry analyst A. D. Murphy and published in *Variety*, shows a remarkably steady and recurring annual profile of film attendance within the United States.

The opposite graph depicts the weekly box office (b.o.) gyrations. Weekly data over a 15-year period were utilized, and ticket-price inflation has been removed in order to eliminate distortion. A "normal" 52-week year has been used for standardized comparisons.

The overall analysis shows that business tends to slide in January approximately 40 percent, and then tends to stabilize until the Washington's Birthday holiday weekend upturn in February.

Next comes the slack period in late winter until the spring school vacation/Easter season when business perks up again to a slightly higher level than at Washington's Birthday.

The post-Easter weeks represent another, and deeper, b.o. sag. Memorial Day weekend business soars, but b.o. then rapidly (though briefly) declines until the waves of summer vacation school closings and business vacation periods propel business to another relative high for the year around July 4.

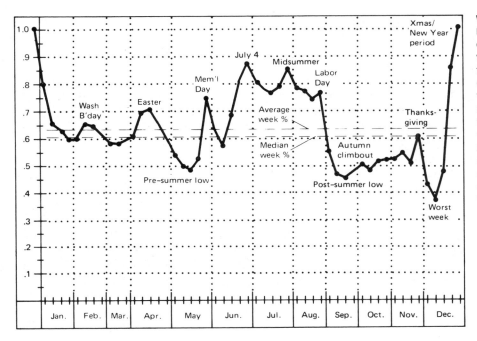

Weekly Fluctuations in U.S. Film Attendance. The chart shows the ratio of weekly film theater attendance to a base reference—the *final* week in a year, given arbitrary value of 1.0. Dashed lines show the *average* and *median* week ratios. The time base used is 1969–1983. Evidently, the idea of an "average" week is specious, given the wide fluctuations in a year. Data: MPAA, *Variety*. Chart © 1984 A. D. Murphy.

After July 4, summer business experiences a slight midsummer decline before rising again in late July/early August, followed by another mild sag until the Labor Day weekend climax of that season.

The sharp September slump bottoms out late in that month, followed by a stable, slightly rising trend through October and November. But just before Thanksgiving week, there's a tapering off before the holiday upturn.

Next come the worst weeks of the year—early December, when business has fallen to its lowest relative point. This situation changes quite markedly as Christmas approaches, with b.o. levels tripling between the second week of the month of New Year's Day week.

According to *Variety*, major Hollywood producers and independents produced 184 feature motion pictures in 1982, 10 percent below a year earlier. The total of 184 was the lowest since 1976, when 174 pictures were produced. Domestic movie-making dropped 37 percent, from 126 pictures in 1981 to only 79 pictures, while overseas production by U.S. producers increased by 33 percent, from 79 in 1981 to 105 in 1982. Pressed to reduce budgets, producers and production companies found a solution overseas in both lower labor costs and more favorable rates of exchange.

Feature film production by the major studios declined from 101 in 1981 to 85 in 1982, and the mix of filming changed sharply. Domestic production dropped from 81 pictures in 1981 to only 50 in 1982, while foreign starts increased from 20 in 1981 to 35 in 1982.

Films by independent producers followed a similar pattern—a total of 99 in 1982, down from 104 in 1981. Of the 1982 total, 29 were filmed in the United States and 70 were produced overseas.

Feature film production through August 1983 was running ahead of 1982. During this 8-month period the major producers started 77 pictures, compared to 58 in the same period of 1982. Of the 77, 45 were filmed in the United States and 32 overseas. Independent productions were also running ahead of the previous year, with 68 pictures having been started through August 1983, compared to 57 a year earlier. Of the 68, 35 were domestic while 33 were made outside the country. About 40 films, each with a production cost of $15 million or more, were released domestically in 1984.

According to industry estimates, the average feature production cost of the major U.S. companies has increased many times since the beginning of World War II. In 1941, average cost per feature was $400,000. In 1949, this had risen to more than $1 million. The average negative cost of theatrical film in 1972 was $1.89 million. In 1982 it reached $11.3 million and in 1983 $11.8 million. The average production budget is divided as follows:

Story Costs	5%
Production and direction costs	5
Sets and other physical properties	35
Stars and cast	20
Studio overhead	20
Income taxes	5
Contingency fund	10

There were an estimated 18,772 theater screens in the United States as of June 1983: 15,837 of them indoors and 2935 drive-ins. This was an increase of 3 percent in the total number of screens over 1982, with indoor screens increasing by 4.7 percent and drive-ins decreasing by 7.3 percent.

California, still the world's capital of motion picture production, notwithstanding the proliferating level of runaway filming, also is the world's champion in moviegoing, with the number of screens-per-state as the measurement. It is far out front with 2014. Texas is second with 1339, and New York next with 1071. Florida trails with 942, Ohio with 803 and Pennsylvania with 751.

The average number of full- and part-time employees in the industry in 1982 was 214,000, down from the 222,000 registered in 1979, 1980 and 1981 and up only slightly from 192,000 in 1960. In fact, unemployment in the motion picture industry is at an all time high.

The nature of the motion picture audience has changed considerably over the past 20 years. What was primarily an adult audience has now become a youth audience. Almost 75 percent of the motion picture audience is under 30 years of age.

Some 60 percent of U.S. moviegoers go to a neighborhood theater; 65 percent prefer single features to double bills; 80 percent consider the subject matter of a film important in deciding what to see; 30 percent consider the stars important in deciding what to see; 70 percent prefer American films to foreign films; 83 percent prefer color to black-and-white films; 39 percent of moviegoers are influenced by movie critics; 47 percent of drive-in admissions are from the suburban market; 87.5 percent of moviegoers are aware of the MPAA ratings; 74 percent of the movie audience is under 30 years of age; and only 7 percent is 50 and over.

THE STRUCTURE AND ORGANIZATION OF THE MOTION-PICTURE INDUSTRY

The film industry is divided into three major parts: (a) production—the creation of films; (b) distribution—the supplying of films to markets; (c) exhibition—the displaying of films to the public. In the past all three functions were performed by one company. But, as noted earlier, in the late 1940s the Supreme Court ruled that the practice of vertical integration (control of production, distribution, and exhibition by one company) restrained free trade. Today most companies only produce and distribute films with exhibition controlled by individual theaters or chains.

Production

The making of films is a complex operation involving the talents of many people, including directors, cinematographers, producers, editors, lighting and sound crews, designers, musicians, costumers, makeup crews, choreographers, and actors. The size of a film crew is one of the key reasons that production budgets are high.

In recent years the industry's unions, long one of the prime contributors to exorbitant production costs, have relaxed many of their requirements to allow skeletal crews and lower minimum wages for low-budget films. This shift in policy was forced upon the unions by economic conditions. If Hollywood was to survive, labor costs had to be reduced. Still, personnel costs account for well over 50% of an average feature film's production budget.

Because of rising personnel costs, filmmakers have been forced to cut back their nonproduction expenses. In the 1940s almost 40% of a film's budget went to cover studio overhead, which involved upkeep of the backlots and equipment and an extensive bureaucracy of production and nonproduction personnel. Today a typical independent production company's permanent staff consists of a small secretarial pool, a good accountant, and the producer. Studio overhead currently accounts for barely 20% of production costs.

The heart of the motion-picture business in the 1980s lies beyond the studio gates. More and more films are being shot on location in the United States and Europe rather than on Hollywood backlots. In fact, only one such backlot exists, that being the part-working lot, part-tourist attraction at Universal Studios. With the advent of portable equipment, location shooting is much easier and less expensive than in the past. For most films the sound stage has become unnecessary, especially since the development of the Cinemobile Mark IV in the 1960s. This studio—bus contains dressing rooms, bathrooms, space for a large crew, and a full complement of lightweight equipment.

The key word today in film production is *conglomerate*. Currently, six major film studios account for over 75% of all American films. On the surface this does not seem to be any different from the patterns of the 1930s and 1940s, but there is a basic change in the production structure of the major studios. Today these studios are primarily financing and distributing agencies; the actual production is done by hundreds of individual corporations put together or packaged specifically for one film.

Much of this change took place in the late 1960s when such nonestablishment filmmakers as John Cassavetes, Andy Warhol, Dennis Hopper, Peter Bogdanovich, and Francis Ford Coppola proved to Hollywood that magical names on the marquee were not necessary for success. With 75% of box-office revenue coming from an audience under the age of 30, it was the independent talent, often young itself, that was succeeding. As these filmmakers succeeded, they began to achieve financial independence. Directors such as Francis Ford Coppola, Robert Altman, Martin Scorsese, Steven Spielberg, and George Lucas formed their own production companies, and the studios became the bank and the distribution system. Because of individual successes, such as Cimino's *The Deer Hunter* (1979), many directors persuaded the studios to allow them almost total artistic and budgetary control. With Cimino's $30 million disaster *Heaven's Gate*, however, accountability once again became a key word. Ultimately, filmmakers who don't make money don't make films, as Peter Bogdanovich so successfully demonstrated. The studios with their moguls have been replaced by corporate presidents and boards of directors.

This trend has given rise to new financial arrangements in which stars and directors take a percentage of a film's potential profit rather than a high salary, making them partners in a collaborative enterprise. Of course, only major stars can command such a contract.

Today the package rules American filmmaking. The package rather than the idea is the key to getting a film made. The idea is a starting point, but preferably it should be presold to the widest possible audience. The idea should have a director, screen writer, and star who have solid track records; and if a successful marketing plan can be developed for the idea, the film may receive the necessary financial backing. *Grease* (1978) is a perfect example of the packaged product: It was presold through a record-breaking Broadway run, starred hot box-office stars Olivia Newton-John and John Travolta, appealed to a broad audience, and was marketed through a nationwide media advertising campaign that cost over $5 million.

As indicated, the primary distributors of motion pictures are the major **Distribution** studios that traditionally produced films. Most independent producers release their films through one of these established studios in two major markets, foreign and domestic.

The foreign market is extremely important because it can account for over 50% of the total annual revenue for most American films. In a great many nations of the world, U.S. Films dominate both the exhibition schedule and box-office receipts. The popularity of the American film product is so great that most European nations limit the number of weeks U.S. films may be shown in local theaters. Rights to American films shown abroad are normally retained by the parent company. This contrasts with the practice of foreign film producers, who sell American distribution rights to their films.

Domestic distribution of films involves the normal channels used to move any product from producer to consumer. Six major studios dominate film distribution in the United States: Columbia, MGM/United Artists, Warner Brothers, 20th Century-Fox, Paramount, and Universal. A group of minor studios are also important, especially in the distribution of low-budget independent films. These include Avco-Embassy, American-International, Cinerama, Allied Artists, and National General. The majors and minors account for 80–90% of annual film revenue in the United States.

Film-distribution operations involve the booking of films into theaters. Licenses between the distributor and exhibitor include both price and nonprice agreements. The process of block booking—requiring theaters to buy groups of films rather than individual films—has been outlawed, and so every film is leased separately.

Local theater owners bid competitively for films. This usually involves a specific guaranteed minimum against a percentage of the gross receipts. For example, the theater owner pays an amount ($1000 per week) or a percentage of the gross receipts (60% of one week's ticket sales), whichever is higher. This procedure saves the exhibitor from losing too badly if the film is a flop and helps the distributor if the film is a major success.

In the motion-picture business in the 1980s the distributor is still the major risk-taker. This is the case because distributors are the prime borrower of funds to produce films. They finance or provide the collateral for 9 of every 10 films. If the cost of the movie exceeds production estimates, it is the distributor who provides the necessary capital to complete it. Because of this, the distributor receives his return before the producer does. One-third of the distribution gross (total receipts minus the exhibitors' share) is retained to cover distribution costs; the remainder is sent to the bank to retire the standard 2 year loan. Before the producer earns any sizable sum, the film must earn roughly 2.5 times its production costs. Thus, a film like Cimino's *Heaven's Gate* with a cost of approximately $30 million would have to earn over $75 million before the producer could realize any profit. In effect, interest and distribution costs of a film run about 150% of the production costs. Marketing costs in film are among the highest—if not *the* highest—for any major consumer product. The risk in film is increased by the fact that the economic life of a film is extremely short; in most cases about 25 weeks account for two-thirds of its total gross. Maximum gross in the shortest time is a critical aspect of film distribution.

Exhibition The local theaters and drive-ins are the final link in the structure of the motion-picture industry. Here, also, concentration of ownership is dominant. More than half the theaters in the United States are owned by 700 theater chains. Some 70% of an average film's gross comes from 1000 key theaters. These bookings in major population areas mean the difference between financial success or failure for a film. The larger theaters (over 400 seats) account for 80% of the total dollar volume of most features. Nine of every 10 large houses are owned by the theater chains with the largest, ABC-Paramount, owning over 500 theaters, most of them in metropolitan areas.

Films are exhibited in either roadshow, popular-release, or four-walling patterns. Roadshow is used only for blockbuster films, such as *E.T.*, *The Empire Strikes Back*, and *Return of the Jedi*. It requires a large marketing investment and must have a good long-run potential. Tickets are usually sold at only one theater per market. If the film does not do well in this hard-ticket exhibition, it is immediately changed to popular release, where the film is booked in as many theaters as possible. The trend today is away from roadshow exclusive releases and toward limited popular release and, in most instances, saturation booking. *Flash Gordon* (1980), for example, was saturation booked into all the medium and large markets. This was done primarily to recoup the investment as quickly as possible and to lessen the effect of poor reviews and word-of-mouth reaction.

A more recent trend in exhibition patterns is four-walling, whereby the film's producer bypasses normal distribution channels and contracts directly with the local theater owner. For low-budget, limited-audience-appeal films, this is a popular method because the costs normally given to the distributor are put into local advertising.

Sunn International has made a science out of marketing a film just the way toothpaste or dog food is marketed. Using sophisticated marketing techniques, Sunn identifies key target audiences and the types of films that are not currently being developed and then creates films that will appeal to those audiences. The success of such films as *The Life and Times of Grizzly Adams* (1975) and *In Search of Noah's Ark* (1977) demonstrates the viability of this approach. The exhibition pattern of Sunn films is designed to reach the right audience and take advantage of each film's particular entertainment value.

Success in film exhibition depends on a number of factors including trade advertising, word of mouth, critical reviews, the weather, local publicity, previous box-office results, the season of the year, the number and quality of competing films in the area, the content of the film, and the film's rating by the code of authority. Thus the predictability of a film's success is difficult to assess until the film is released for public appraisal. Here, the exhibitor often assumes great risk. As Marvin Goldman, president of K-B Theatres in Washington, D.C., explained in *Variety*, "the business has gone from a buyer's market in the '40s and '50s to a seller's market today. Then, on the biggest film, the exhibitor, or movie theater owner, paid the distribution company 50 percent of the gross over a certain time period, and the average moive called for 30 to 35 percent." Today, with approximately 100 movies being made each year—compared with 500 during the 1940s and 1950s—the companies can be choosy. And they command a large chunk of the money from a theater owner to show their films.

In the mid-1970s, the distribution companies instituted the "90–10" clause in most contracts involving the exhibitors' leasing of films. Under that clause, if a theater realized gross revenue of $10,000 during the first week a movie was shown, an agreed-upon deduction of $4000 was retained by the theater to cover house expenses. Of the remaining $6000, the movie company got 90%, or $5400, and the theater received only $600.

The industry later instituted a "70–floor" clause that guaranteed them at least 70% of the house's weekly gross. The film company had a choice of that arrangement or the 90–10, whichever offered more money. Using the same $10,000 example, the distributor would choose 70% or $7000 of the $10,000 gross. "Ninety-five percent of the movies we buy today— and that applies to every studio—have one or the other clauses in effect," says Goldman.

When it comes to bidding for a new picture, the distribution companies also have the upper hand. Only 23 states do not permit the practice of blind bidding. As the term implies under that system a theater owner must bid, and subsequently lease, a film without first seeing it. In the 1960s, fewer than 10% of the films offered were the result of blind bidding. In the late 1970s, that percentage rose to 85 percent.

The role and function of motion pictures has changed greatly in the past 30 years. Once a major source of recreation, motion pictures today serve as a primary source of content for another medium, television. Before the advent of videotape recording in the mid-1950s, TV reruns were possible only when films were used or when filmed kinescopes were made of a live performance. In the early 1970s most regular evening network dramas were filmed. Feature films made up an important block of network

CHARACTERISTICS AND ROLES OF THE MOTION PICTURE

Multitheaters are often located on the periphery of suburban shopping malls, thus avoiding shortages of parking space and other problems of the inner city. (Photo by Brendan Beirne.)

schedules with all three networks running multiple "nights at the movies" and "movies of the week." Motion pictures today are made with one eye clearly focused on television as a source of income; in fact, many films are presold to the networks before production starts.

Newer theaters in the United States reflect the changes taking place in our society. They are often twin or multicinemas with 200 to 500 seats per theater and are located in peripheral shopping centers or malls; the theaters are leased rather than owned. A new theater often seeks identification with the shopping area, has few parking problems, gains maximum traffic and exposure, and does not face inner-city problems. The multitheater operates with one lobby, one concession stand, and one projection booth to cut costs. Important features can be run in both theaters, or the theaters can cater to two audiences with different films. A key trend in contemporary exhibition patterns is that concessions account for over half the revenue in most theaters. Thus theaters can still make money charging $1.50 for "twilight" screenings as long as they charge $2.50 for the popcorn.

Audiences go to a *movie* rather than to *the movies*. Nevertheless, despite increased competition from television, motion pictures hold a unique position in American leisure patterns. Many singular elements make the motion picture attractive. For one, the film experience is of a high technical quality that stimulates strong involvement. The picture is a large, high-definition, colored, visual image. The sound is also of high quality. The theater is designed to encapsulate the viewer. It is dark, the chairs are comfortable, there are relatively few interruptions, food is available. Every aspect of filmgoing is designed to heighten the impact of film experiences and create viewer involvement. Film is the most realistic of all media, and it is primarily this attribute that contributes to the great persuasive power inherent in film.

The motion picture is perhaps the most international of the media. Its primarily visual symbol system and easily dubbed sound make the entire world a film marketplace. It has become a selective medium catering to the tastes of an audience that is younger, less discriminating, and weaned on television. The industry is youth oriented, and current film themes reflect this audience's ambitions and tastes.

In summary, motion pictures have changed greatly over their relatively short history. But they still function as they always have, providing entertainment to a large number of people in a unique and involving way.

Radio ⌐18

The Green Hornet, Johnny Dollar, Ma Perkins, Helen Trent, Fred Allen, Joe Penner, Rudy Vallee, and Al Jolson. Unfamiliar names to most of us, but for almost 30 years, they and others made up what is affectionately known as radio's "golden age." Today we identify radio with such codes as AOR, C/W, beautiful music, MOR, and soul. These cryptic code words and symbols represent the various kinds of recorded music that make up the sound of a radio station.

In the 1950s and 1960s, the radio industry in the United States changed radically in order to survive the competition of television. Many in the industry thought radio was dead. Radio not only survived television; it developed new forms that have made it one of the most dynamic and successful mass media.

There are now more radio stations than ever. Frequency-modulation (FM) radio has grown from an experimental toy into the dominant programming vehicle in contemporary radio. Radios are in 99% of American homes and 95% of American cars. Radio is a flexible, adaptable, individual, personal medium. Although it functions primarily as a medium for playing recorded music, it is as alive, dynamic, and popular as it was 30 years ago. Radio experienced one golden age, but unlike most mass media, grew and changed to experience another. How it got to that point is the subject of history, and it is here we begin.

HISTORICAL PERSPECTIVES

The brief history of radio is broken into time periods of irregular but logical length corresponding to the medium's major developments. Oddly enough, for a medium less than 80 years old, we start early in the nineteenth century.

1840–1919

Radio developed out of scientific advances made in the fields of electricity and magnetism. The first transmission of an electromagnetic message over wire was made in 1844 by Samuel F. B. Morse. A country expanding rapidly westward needed the enormous potential of the telegraph, and by 1861 a transcontinental, high-speed, electric communication system was signaling coded messages across the United States. The first transatlantic cable was laid in 1858, and by 1870 a web of underseas cables linked the Western world and its economic outposts. The replacement of Morse code with voice transmission occurred in 1876 when Alexander Graham Bell used undulations in electric current to produce vocal communication by wire. The telephone's ability to code, transport, and decode voice transmissions personalized electric communication in a way that was impossible with the telegraph.

During the same period that the telegraph and telephone were demonstrating and perfecting long-distance communication by wire, James Maxwell predicted (1864) and Heinrich Hertz demonstrated (1887) that variations in electric current produced waves that could be transmitted through space *without* wires at the speed of light. These theories stimulated much experimentation, the most successful being Guglielmo Marconi's work in the late 1890s. Marconi received a patent for his wireless

Guglielmo Marconi as a young inventor with his first transmitting device.

(Photograph 1895, The Bettman Archive, Inc.)

telegraph in 1897 and by 1901 was transmitting wireless dot-dash transmissions across the Atlantic. Through the work of such men as Reginald Fessenden and Lee De Forest, high-quality wireless *voice* communication carried by electromagnetic waves became possible, thus setting the stage for radio broadcasting.

Radio broadcasting required more than technology, however. People had to change their thinking about wireless communication. Two individuals talking back and forth is not broadcasting. The intellectual retooling needed to transform radio *telephoning* into radio *broadcasting* had to wait until people thought in terms of one person talking to a mass audience. Public and industrial appetites had to be whetted to create a demand for radio broadcasting.

From 1910 to the outbreak of World War I, radio amateurs brought new noise to the night as they chattered to each other from their basements, attics, or pantries. It was a time of neighborhood experimenters who pieced together radio sender–receivers in order to carry on conversations with others of the same inclination.

During this period, the U.S. government passed two major laws concerning the use of radio. The first was the U.S. Wireless Ship Act of 1910, which required all passenger ships to carry radio-transmission equipment. The second was the 1912 Radio Act, requiring all radio operators to be licensed by the Secretary of Commerce. The 1912 act was the first comprehensive attempt to regulate all phases of radio communication. When the United States entered World War I in 1917, the federal government took over all radio operations, and the medium marked time until the end of the war.

Nevertheless, the stage was being set for the development of broadcasting. One of the visionaries of the medium was a young man named David Sarnoff. In 1916 he wrote a memo to his boss at American Marconi proposing a new use for radio.

> I have in mind a plan of development which would make radio a "household utility" in the same sense as the piano or phonograph. The idea is to bring music into the house by wireless. . . . The receiver can be designed in the form of a simple "Radio Music Box" and arranged for several different wave lengths. . . . The main revenue to be derived will be from the sale of the "Radio Music Boxes" which if manufactured in lots of one hundred thousand or so could yield a handsome profit.

Sarnoff's idea erred only in the major source of revenue.

After the war ended, an organized attempt was made to develop radio broadcasting as opposed to point-to-point communication. With fewer than 1000 radio sets in the entire nation, regular radio programming began with the broadcast of the Harding–Cox election returns over KDKA in   **1920–1928**

Coverage of the Harding-Cox election returns (November 2, 1920) on KDKA Radio, Pittsburgh, gave birth to modern broadcasting, opening a new era in communications.

(Photo courtesy of Westinghouse Broadcasting and Cable, Inc.)

An early broadcasting studio of one of almost 600 radio stations licensed in 1922.

(Photo: The Bettman Archive, Inc.)

Pittsburgh on 2 November 1920. Almost overnight, hundreds of stations were started and began to broadcast music, politics, sports, drama, and vaudeville. By the end of 1922, close to 600 stations had been licensed by the Secretary of Commerce. By 1923, over a million people a year were listening to programs broadcast from concert halls, theaters, and athletic fields.

As programming expanded, the public bought more radio sets. Additional hours of programming became available, and audiences grew more discriminating. Listener tastes soon forced broadcasters to provide a greater variety of entertainment.

As the broadcast industry developed, the revenue from the sale of radio sets proved insufficient to support radio's mass entertainment and information services. A new method had to be found to pay the bill for the public's insatiable appetite for radio programming. To solve this problem two developments occurred: Radio stations were linked into networks so that the increased cost of expanded programming could be shared; and merchants were asked to support the system by advertising their goods and services on the stations. The American Telephone and Telegraph Company (AT&T) and set manufacturers formed a network in 1923 to provide expanded program-distribution service. After a lengthy, fratricidal war over the use of Bell transmission facilities, AT&T withdrew from the program-distribution business in 1926. This left the door open, and a new corporate giant, The Radio Corporation of America (RCA), took over from AT&T. Formed in 1919 as a sales outlet for radio manufacturers, RCA soon became the dominant force in broadcasting. RCA immediately consolidated its position and formed the National Broadcasting Company (NBC). In 1927 the Columbia Broadcasting System (CBS) was formed and with its 16 affiliates set out to do battle with NBC's 48 affiliates and 2 networks, the Blue and the Red.

Now that radio was becoming big business, something had to be done about the chaotic state of signal transmission so that broadcasting could more efficiently serve the public and economic interests. In 1926 a series of court cases ruled that Secretary of Commerce Herbert Hoover did not have legal jurisdiction under the Radio Act of 1912 to regulate broadcasting. As more and more stations went on the air, they began to interfere with one another. Chaos reigned; it was obvious that immediate legislative action was needed if broadcasting was to survive.

The broadcast media, unlike other media, are physically limited by the number of channels or spaces available in the radio spectrum. The Berlin Conference (1903) and the Havana Treaty (1925) established international rules for using radio frequencies, but internal domestic use of the allocated channels was left to individual governments. A growing awareness that the airwaves were a natural resource that belonged to the public also began to affect the legal decision-making process.

Congress passed the Radio Act of 1927, which created a temporary Federal Radio Commission to straighten out the radio mess. The FRC was made permanent in 1929. Congress created the Federal Communications Act in 1934; the act expanded and clarified the 1927 act and established the Federal Communications Commission to regulate telephone, telegraph, as well as radio communication systems, in the public's interest, convenience, and necessity. This act remains in effect today, modified, of course, by prevailing political, social, and economic conditions.

1929–1945   With its technical problems solved, radio was free to grow almost unrestricted. By the late 1920s the medium had achieved a high degree of program sophistication and was on the verge of entering a new stage of development. One of the major areas of growth was in broadcasting advertising. The broadcast historian John Spaulding has suggested that the 1928–1929 program year marks the point at which radio became a mass advertising medium. That year, radio reached a level of financial stability and program sophistication that made advertising on a wide scale feasible. In turn, the economic stability provided by advertising set the stage for the advent of the golden age of network radio.

During the first half of the 1930s, a number of new radio program types evolved. Network programs drew increasingly large audiences as living rooms became the entertainment centers of a nation locked in the squeeze of a depression. Advertising revenues increased during this period of economic crisis, however, rising from over $25 million in 1930 to more than $70 million in 1940.

In fact, the network economic picture was so good in 1934 that a fourth radio network, the Mutual Broadcasting System (MBS), was formed to challenge NBC–Red, NBC–Blue, and CBS. By 1935 MBS had 60 affiliates competing with the 80 to 120 affiliates of the established networks. As network competition intensified and program costs increased, broadcasters needed to know more about the size of their audience. By 1935 a number of research organizations were providing data on the size and composition of radio audiences. With more than 22 million American radio homes, programming successes became advertising bonanzas.

The second half of the 1930s was a time of refining and polishing established formats rather than a period of extensive program innovation. The networks continued to dominate, especially in advertising revenue and program production. More than 50% of all radio advertising dollars went to the four national networks. In 1941 alone, that sum was $75 million.

Two major legal actions also occurred at that time. In 1935 the American Bar Association in Canon 35 ruled that at the discretion of the presiding judge, broadcast journalists could be prohibited from using radio equipment in the courtroom to cover trials. In 1941 the FCC's "Mayflower decision" forbade broadcasters to editorialize. These two actions reflected to some extent the media bias of society, which identified print as information media and radio (and later, television) as entertainment media. The Mayflower ruling was overturned later in the decade, and broadcasters may now editorialize. There is also increased but by no means universal radio and TV coverage in courtrooms.

Of the 850 stations on the air in 1941, 700 were affiliated with one of the four networks that dominated radio broadcasting. Only three corporations made up the radio oligopoly at that time, however, since NBC had both a Red and a Blue network. The Federal Communications Commission, recognizing the long-range consequences of the situation, forced NBC to divest itself of one network. The Supreme Court upheld this decision, and NBC sold its Blue network operation to a group of businessmen who formed the American Broadcasting Company (ABC) in 1943.

World War II brought domestic production of radio equipment to a standstill. Despite the fact that the number of radio receivers decreased during the war years, advertising revenue continued to climb. The public's demand for war information doubled the number of news programs in the first half of the war, but as war weariness set in during the last 18 months of the conflict, entertainment programs began to squeeze the news out of time slots as Americans sought escape from reality.

Significant among the many program types of this period was radio drama. Produced live (the networks banned recordings until the late

The cast of "Gang Busters" gathers around the microphone. Two sound effects men fire safety pistols for the live broadcast.

(Photo: The Bettman Archive, Inc.)

1940s), the form flourished with such series as "The Mercury Theater of the Air" and "Columbia Workshop" and produced several memorable programs including Orson Welles's famous 1938 Halloween presentation of "The War of the Worlds." In addition, playwrights such as Norman Corwin and Arch Obler wrote material directly for radio.

1946–1959   When the war ended, radio broadcasting quickly resumed its prewar pace. During this time, however, television began its phenomenal rise to preeminence as America's major leisure-time activity. By 1948 television was here to stay, and the handwriting was on the economic wall. Radio was saved, however, temporarily, by the FCC's 4-year freeze on TV-station allocations.

Other changes also were taking place that would affect radio in the future. The first change made FM frequencies available for commercial use, and by 1948 over 600 FM stations had been licensed. With the growth of television, however, FM was put on hold until 1958 when FM stations again began to expand. The second change adjusted the distance required between AM stations to allow for multiple use of channels previously used by clear-channel stations. As a result, when the restrictions on TV's growth were removed by the FCC in 1952, radio's economic situation was further strained by the fact that 3000 stations were now competing for audiences and revenue. The networks' domination of radio programming ended because their programming lost its economic base as reduced audience size brought in fewer advertising dollars. Also, the networks were busy establishing themselves in TV programming, and radio was quickly shuttled to the back of the bus. The once all-powerful radio networks were suddenly relegated to minor programming roles. By 1960 the last of the networks' major programming forms, the daytime soap opera, went off the air.

The networks no longer provided revenue to affiliates, only a national news and specialty service, and they accounted for only 5% of total radio advertising revenue in 1960. The only major network programming innovation of the period was NBC's "Monitor" weekend service, which was basically a modification of the disc-jockey format for a national audience.

Local stations quickly moved into this vacuum, mostly out of necessity. Nevertheless, once the reality of having to provide local programming and still make money sank home, local-station programming rapidly developed, primarily around the omnipresent disc jockey, a stack of records, a skeletal news and sports operation, and anything else that provided for and attracted audiences at a low cost. Total advertising revenue stumbled along from 1953 to 1956 as local salesmen attempted to make up the slack created by the continued slide of network revenue, which hit an all-time low of $35 million in 1960. Despite the network crash, additional AM stations plunged into the business so that by 1960, 3500 AM stations were competing for the radio audience. More than 1000 of these stations reportedly lost money from 1956 to 1960. The number of FM stations grew to 700, but they were used chiefly as an auxiliary service that simulcast the programming service of AM stations.

The 1960s were a period of great economic growth for radio. More than 150 million radios were sold at a retail value of $6 billion. Advertising revenue totaled more than $8 billion during the 10 years from 1960 to 1969. Network radio stabilized, and revenues increased slowly.

1960 to the Present

In the 1960s and 1970s FM radio grew at a phenomenal rate. There are many reasons for this growth. In 1961 the Federal Communications Commission permitted FM stereo broadcasting, and by the mid-1960s more than 50% of all FM stations were stereo operations. In 1965 the FCC ruled that AM–FM combinations in cities of over 100,000 population could no longer duplicate more than 50% of either station's programming. This "50–50 ruling," as it was called, affected approximately 330 stations and greatly opened up the FM market. A wide variety of station operations and formats appeared in the late 1960s because FM could now exist on extremely low-cost programming appealing to very specialized audiences. There were and are stations that broadcast nothing but classified ads, stations with programming for the blind, stations that play only "golden oldies," all-talk stations, and all-news stations. As the number of FM stations, receivers, and listeners increased, FM's financial status improved enormously. Today there are five times as many FM stations as in 1961, and the advertising money for FM has surpassed that of AM.

In this period AM radio grew too, but it grew more slowly, partially due to a freeze on new AM license awards from 1962 to 1964 and again from 1968 to 1973. The problem of limiting AM growth because of lack of spectrum space was a severe one; finally, in 1973 the FCC issued stringent rules for new AM applications.

As a result, the differences in AM and FM listenership have steadily diminished and in the top 10 markets the FM share of the radio audience has tripled, from 20% to almost 60%. The battle between AM and FM is more like a rout, with FM the winner. Following is the breakdown of listening preference according to age group. On average, FM stations sell for far more than AM stations, and the only factor holding down the percentage of FM's advertising income is the lack of FM car receivers.

Age	FM	AM
12-24	84%	16%
25-34	73%	27%
35-49	59%	41%
50 +	44%	56%

Today industry observers offhandedly discuss the likelihood of AM's "survival." However, technology is creating new opportunities for AM radio. More than 200 AM stations are now broadcasting in stereo. In addition, digital systems will offer both AM and FM radio even clearer signals. The system works by encoding sound in computer language. Digital players read music from a coded disc with a laser beam, eliminating the static common to traditional vinyl records.

Network radio made a slow but steady climb out of the abyss of the late 1950s. A major innovation occurred in 1968 when ABC Radio developed four separate radio services for affiliates. Recognizing that the audience for radio had become increasingly segmented by age group and lifestyle, ABC offered radio stations news and public affairs features fine-tuned to particular audiences.

Currently five major networks—ABC, NBC, CBS, Mutual, and RKO—dominate the field. Leading the pack is ABC with over 1800 affiliates. Each network offers multiple programming services, in effect creating internal multiple networks. In addition, hundreds of smaller networks have come into existence, such as Satellite Music Network, CNN Radio, and Transtar. As Walter Sabo, vice-president of ABC Radio Networks, said, in an interview with this author, "The key to success for any network is to provide stations with services they can't do themselves." Network radio will continue to exist as long as it lives by this idea. Rather than broadcast, networks now narrowcast, linking specific audiences with programs that speak their "language."

Few people would have predicted even moderate success for radio in the mid-1950s. But, 25 years later, radio has emerged from the ashes of its golden age to assume a new identity as a tough hybrid capable of not only competing with television but in many cases surpassing it.

(Drawing by Ziegler. Copyright © 1984 The New Yorker Magazine, Inc.)

A statistical profile of radio in the mid-1980s reveals a strong, vigorous, dynamic medium meeting a wide variety of listener needs and interests. There are more stations on the air, more sets in use, and more listeners than ever before.

The following tables and charts provide vivid evidence of radio's size and structure. These statistics, however, reveal more than simply a profile of contemporary strength. They also provide a picture of a remarkable transition over the past 30 years, from a national network-dominated prime-time medium of comedy, drama, and variety programs to a local, selective, highly personal medium serving a variety of listener needs.

Perhaps nowhere else is radio's growth and change more evident than in the size and composition of the basic media units or stations. The table below reveals that the number of radio stations has almost doubled in the last 20 years. Contributing most significantly to this unprecedented

THE SCOPE OF RADIO

Date	AM		FM	
	Authorized	On Air	Authorized	On Air
Jan. 1, 1954	2636	2521	580	560
Jan. 1, 1955	2774	2669	559	552
Jan. 1, 1956	2935	2824	557	540
Jan. 1, 1957	3125	3008	554	530
Jan. 1, 1958	3295	3196	590	537
Jan. 1, 1959	3440	3326	695	578
Jan. 1, 1960	3527	3398	838	688
Jan. 1, 1961	3667	3539	1018	815
Jan. 1, 1962	3911	3693	1128	960
Jan. 1, 1963	3924	3810	1128	1081
Jan. 1, 1964	4039	3937	1249	1146
Jan. 1, 1965	4077	4009	1468	1270
Jan. 1, 1966	4129	4049	1657	1446
Jan. 1, 1967	4190	4121	1865	1643
Jan. 1, 1968	4249	4156	2004	1753
Jan. 1, 1969	4300	4237	2114	1938
Jan. 1, 1970	4344	4269	2651	2476
Jan. 1, 1971	4383	4323	2795	2636
Jan. 1, 1972	4411	4355	2971	2783
Jan. 1, 1973	4431	4382	3162	2965
Jan. 1, 1974	4448	4395	3360	3135
Jan. 1, 1975	4477	4432	3617	3353
Jan. 1, 1976	4513	4463	3752	3571
Jan. 1, 1977	4536	4497	3969	3743
Jan. 1, 1978	4569	4513	4130	3972
Jan. 1, 1979	4599	4549	4310	4089
Jan. 1, 1980	4651	4558	4463	4190
Jan. 1, 1981	4700	4589	4588	4374
Jan. 1, 1982	4763	4634	4736	4467
Jan. 1, 1983	4828	4685	4970	4505
Jan. 1, 1984	4897	4733	5240	4649

growth is the remarkable rise of FM stations. In 1960 there were less than 700 FM stations on the air while in 1984 there are 4649, over a 400% increase. The impact of FM station growth on total station growth has been significant. AM stations have increased by less than 800 in the last 20 years. However, FCC rulings regarding so-called "clear channel" stations have provided room in the AM portion of the electromagnetic spectrum for even more growth in future years.

Radio networking exploded in the early 1980s, but has now leveled off to some degree. Since 1982, ABC has launched three new radio networks—ABC Direction Network, ABC Rock Radio Network, and ABC Talkradio—and has introduced several new programming services within each. And ABC is not alone in expanding. Along with the introduction of 24-hour satellite networks there has been a proliferation of syndicated bartered networks. What happened is that there have been so many new entries into the business that there has been some fractionalization of total inventory. The influx of new competition was the reason that network radio didn't see price increases.

The following table profiles the major radio networks along with the name of the satellite and transponder they use as well as an affiliate count.

Network	Satellite	Affiliates
ABC Radio Network* Talkradio	Satcom I-R, 23	1725 (combined)
Associated Press Network	Westar III, 1	1125
CNN Radio Network†	Satcom III-R, 14	157
CBS Radio Network RadioRadio	Satcom I-R, 19	850 (combined)
Music Country Network‡	Westar III, 1	122
Mutual Broadcasting	Westar IV, 2	850
NBC Radio Network The Source Talknet	Satcom I-R, 19	664 (combined)
National Public Radio	Westar IV, 2	288
RKO Radio Networks (I and II)	Satcom I-R, 19	575
Satellite Music Network	Satcom III-R, 3	363
Sheridan Broadcasting§	Satcom IV, 7	115
Transtar Radio Networks¶	Telestar 301, 5 Westar III, 2;	160
UPI Radio Network	Westar III, 1	750
Wall Street Journal Report	Westar III, 1	80

* Contemporary, Direction, Entertainment, FM, Information and Rock networks.

† Affiliate count includes separate affiliate lists for two weekly programs: *Top 30 USA* and *Top 40 Satellite Survey*. Basic affiliates total 550 for both networks.

‡ Co-venture of AP Network and *WSM* Inc. Nashville.

§ 100 of 115 affiliates are receiving programming via satellite.

¶ Adult contemporary format is on Westar system, country and 'light' contemporary (Format 41) are on Telestar.

As the National Association of Broadcasters annual financial survey of radio stations in 1982 confirms, the financial outlook for the radio industry is on the rise. The profit margin for "the typical radio station" rose from 3.5% in 1981 to 9.4% in 1982. The survey also showed that 67% of the 1618 radio stations participating in the survey reported profits, while only 58% of the 1704 stations participating in the 1981 survey reported profits.

According to the survey, advertising revenues rose 21% in 1982 and national and regional spot sales climbed 37%. Local sales increased 19% over the 1981 results. Total operating expenses also rose 11.2% in 1982. Sales and promotion costs, the survey said, climbed 32% over 1981, and payroll costs also grew 14%.

FM station revenues continued to increase more rapidly than those for AM stations because FM stations are now reaching an audience comparable in size to the AM audience and their revenues are growing from a smaller base. Total FM revenue data are not available because approximately half of the FM stations report their revenues jointly with their associated AM stations.

Revenues, Profits, and Expenses of a Typical Radio Station, 1981–1982

	1982	1981	Percent change
Total Time Sales	**$562,500**	**$465,000**	+ 21.0
Network compensation	0	0	0.0
National radio spot	79,200	57,700	+ 37.3
Local advertising sales	483,300	407,300	+ 18.7
Total Broadcast Revenues	**542,300**	**457,600**	+ 18.5
Nonbroadcast revenue	1,100	1,000	+ 10.0
Trade-outs and barter	22,200	15,500	+ 43.2
Total Operating Expenses	**491,200**	**441,800**	+ 11.2
Engineering	29,700	28,300	+ 4.9
Program (news and production)	138,000	122,400	+ 12.7
Sales (advertising and promotion)	133,200	101,100	+ 31.8
General and administrative	190,300	190,000	+ 0.2
Selected Expense Items			
Total salaries	250,300	219,700	+ 13.9
Depreciation and amortization	32,600	24,200	+ 34.7
Cost of outside news service	7,300	7,100	+ 2.8
Music license fees	13,600	10,800	+ 25.9
Pretax profit	51,100	15,800	+223.4
Pretax profit margin	9.42%	3.46%	5.96*
Full-time employment	14	14	0

* Percentage point difference.

Year	Radio homes (millions)
1949	40.8
1950	42.1
1951	43.6
1952	44.8
1953	45.0
1954	45.4
1955	46.2
1956	47.2
1957	48.2
1958	48.9
1959	49.5
1960	49.5
1961	49.5
1962	51.1
1963	52.3
1964	54.9
1965	55.2
1966	57.0
1967	57.5
1968	58.5
1969	60.6
1970	62.0
1971	62.6
1972	64.1
1973	67.4
1974	68.9
1975	70.4
1976	71.4
1977	72.9
1978	74.6
1979	76.5
1980	78.6
1981	80.5
1982	84.3
1983	84.3

The number of radio homes leveled off in 1983 at 84.3 million, which represents 98% of all U.S. homes. This figure is more than double the 1949 figure when network radio was at its zenith. There are an estimated 470 million radio sets in the U.S., 347 million (74%) in homes and 123 million (26%) out of homes. The average household has 5.7 sets. Forty-one percent of the radio audience have six or more sets, and 60% of all homes are equipped with clock radios. The chart below shows where home radios are located.

Almost 1/2 Of All Rooms Have Radios. Radios Are Heard In:

67.0%	Living Rooms
58.4%	Bedrooms
49.8%	Kitchens
21.9%	Dens/Family Rooms
9.3%	Dining Rooms
7.2%	Bathrooms
38.4%	Other Rooms
41.0%	All Rooms (Avg.)

Locations of Home Radio Sets. (*Source: Radio Facts*, 1984. Courtesy Radio Advertising Bureau.)

The variety of sounds, formats, and styles which make up contemporary radio programming is displayed in the accompanying table, where historically we can see the tremendous variety and fluctuation of radio formats. The eight major formats in themselves are somewhat misleading in that they represent a much wider variety of individual sounds and styles. Middle of the Road (MOR), for example, can mean a number of sounds ranging from 1940s big band music to the lush sounds of Ray Conniff, to the stylized vocal renditions of Frank Sinatra or Barbra Streisand. As a result of this format's ambiguity and broad general appeal, it declined from a high of over 17% of the top 25 markets to just over 4% in 1980. This table compared to a 1983 update reveals that radio formats are fluid and reflect current trends in music with almost volatile frequency. Note the fluctuation in the popularity of Country/Western music, especially. It should be noted that the 1983 table, represents over 8000 radio stations, whereas the preceding only covered the top 25 markets. This clearly accounts for the large number of country stations.

In summary, a statistical profile of radio reveals a massive medium with a highly fragmented audience. Radio is a local rather than a national

Trends in Radio Formats, 1976–1980 (Listeners 12 Years and over, Monday to Sunday, 6 a.m. to Midnight)

	1976	1977	1978	1979	1980	Percent Change from 1979
Adult Contemporary			12.0	19.3	20.4	+6
Top 40	19.5	19.9	14.1	7.9	9.2	+17
Disco		1.5	2.6	3.4	1.1	+35
Urban Contemporary					3.5	
Mellow/Soft		1.4	1.4	1.5	1.4	−7
AOR		6.1	8.2	9.9	12.5	+26
Progressive	7.7	4.2	1.4	.5	.1	−80
MOR	17.4	13.9	9.7	7.1	4.5	−28
Big Band/Music of Your Life					.6	
Good Music	15.5	14.9	13.6	14.5	14.8	+2
Country	6.7	7.3	7.6	7.7	8.7	+13
News	5.2	5.2	5.8	6.5	6.4	−3
Black	5.0	4.4	4.5	5.3	2.7	−49
Talk	3.3	2.9	3.0	2.5	4.0	+60
Classical	1.4	1.3	1.3	1.3	1.7	+31
Oldies	1.2	.4	.2	.7	1.3	+86
Spanish		1.6	1.6	1.7	2.0	+17
Jazz				.7	.7	+17
Others	17.1	15.0	13.0	9.6	4.4	−54

Source: McGavren Guild Format Study.
Note: Figures are for share of audience in the top 25 markets among AM and FM stations combined.

Stations Programming a Full-Time Format as of July 1983

Format	Number of Stations	Percent of Total
Country	2233	27.7
Adult contemporary	1933	23.9
Top 40	809	10.0
Nostalgia/MOR	687	8.5
Beautiful music	524	6.5
Religious	510	6.3
AOR	294	3.7
Black R&B	207	2.6
Oldies	173	2.1
Diversified	155	1.9
News/talk	135	1.7
Spanish	126	1.6
Soft rock	83	1.0
Classical	58	0.7
All news	48	0.6
Ethnic	43	0.5
Urban contemporary	37	0.4
Jazz	19	0.3
Total	8,071	100.0

medium in terms of stations, content, audience, and source of income. Radio listening habits are personal and stations program selectively to satisfy individual needs within a relatively homogeneous group. Above all, the data clearly demonstrate the health and strength of radio today as it has adjusted with remarkable speed and accuracy to meet the needs of a new audience at new times with new programming.

THE STRUCTURE AND ORGANIZATION OF RADIO

A variety of factors affect radio's structure and organization. The local radio station is the basic media unit responsible for almost all content, but several media service units are deeply involved in radio programming. The phonograph or music industry provides the bulk of most stations' programming at little or no cost for the records, although stations are charged an annual fee for music rights by Broadcast Music Inc. (BMI) and the American Society of Composes, Authors, and Publishers (ASCAP). Networks provide primarily a service of national news and features. The wire services (Associated Press and United Press International) are the backbone of most radio news departments.

Station organization varies greatly, depending on the size of station, type of programming, size of market, and amount of competition. At very large stations, specialized tasks and departments exist in the news, sales, and programming areas. At medium-sized stations, announcers double as newspeople, salespeople, or engineers, as well as entertainers. At small stations, the program manager may also be the sales manager; there is often no news staff, and, normally, all announcers are licensed engineers.

Computers have had a revolutionary effect on radio as in every other form of contemporary life. The most dramatic impact is in programming; computers literally carry out many programming, production, traffic, and engineering functions. Keyboard operators, using microcomputers, perform many of the duties traditionally handled by several groups of station personnel.

Radio stations are highly competitive, especially in the big markets, and pay scales reflect this competitiveness and the size of the station's market. High salaries and specialized roles exist only in very large stations, however. The vast majority of people working in radio stations earn what at best could be termed modest salaries.

Kinds of Radio Stations

Technologically, there are two basic kinds of radio stations: amplitude-modulation (AM) stations and frequency-modulation (FM) stations. The standard bank of frequencies (535 to 1605 kilocycles) is used for AM broadcasting. The FCC has assigned FM broadcasting to frequencies between 88 and 108 megacycles (1000 kilocycles equals 1 megacycle).

Because over 4600 AM stations are licensed for broadcast on 107 channels, an intricate system of accommodation has been established with three major variables: power, signal direction, and hours of operation. AM stations are divided into four classes within three channels:

1. Clear-channel stations operate clear channels, usually with 50,000 watts of power. These stations are designed to serve remote rural areas as well as large urban populations. There are 45 authorized clear channels with one 50,000 watt (Class I) and two to several dozen medium- and low-power stations (Class II) on each channel.

2. Regional channels that accommodate 30 to 50 stations (Class III) each with power ranging from 1000 to 5000 watts.

3. Local channels on which small stations operate with a maximum power of 1000 watts during the day and 250 at night. There are six local frequencies, each used by 100 or more stations (Class IV).

To further lessen interference problems, most AM stations are required to directionalize their signal and to operate within assigned hours.

Three classes of FM stations are in operation today; they are defined primarily by power and antenna elevation. The maximum power–height combination is 100,000 watts and 2000 feet. Class A stations have an effective coverage area of 15 miles; Class B stations cover 30 miles; and Class C stations, 60 miles. The reason for the exceptionally high antennas and power is that FM signals are direct signals that reach only to the horizon, unlike AM signals, which encompass both ground and sky waves.

Part of the reason FM listening has increased so dramatically in recent years is the quality of its signal. Because of its location in the VHF band, the FM signal is almost totally free of static. The FM signal can also reproduce sounds with greater cycle range than AM and has a larger dynamic range than the AM signal. Because the FM signal is 20 times the width of an AM channel, stereophonic sound is possible through multiplexing.

Radio stations in the United States are identified by call letters using letters beginning with *K* or *W*. Except for a few early stations, such as KDKA in Pittsburgh, stations east of the Mississippi River have call letters beginning with *W*, while *K* is assigned to stations west of the Mississippi. Most early broadcast call signs used three letters, but these were quickly exhausted; today, most stations have four-letter call signs.

One additional classification for radio stations is their categorization as commercial and noncommercial or educational. Of the more than 1100 educational radio stations today, only 24 are AM, these dating from the early years of radio. In 1945 the FCC reserved 20 FM channels between 88 and 92 MHz for noncommercial educational stations. Since then, the number of noncommercial stations has grown slowly but steadily to slightly over 1000.

There are five dominant commercial national radio networks: CBS, NBC, Mutual, ABC, and RKO. These networks provide a national news service to their affiliates and a few sports programs, features, and commentaries. The financial conditions of network radio operation dictate that only a limited number of stations in the lineup receive payments from the national service, and those that do receive only a nominal sum. At ABC, for example, the majority of affiliates pay the network for the service.

Kinds of Radio Networks

In 1970 National Public Radio began the development of a network radio service designed to provide programming for noncommercial educational stations. Funded through the Corporation for Public Broadcasting, NPR has expanded rapidly in the past 10 years to almost 250 affiliates. At one time educational radio was little more than a classical jukebox or huge lecture platform, but today it provides a unique alternative to commercial radio. The NPR affiliates face an uncertain future, however, as President Reagan's economic plan calls for a 50% cutback in federal funding by the mid-1980s. This coupled with management problems has created a diminished role for NPR. With the exception of two premiere news programs, "All Things Considered" and "Morning Edition," NPR network programming is virtually nonexistent. Many of the program innovations of the 1970s have been eliminated or severely reduced because of financial problems.

In addition to the major national networks, hundreds of smaller regional or specialized program, networks either interconnect stations for a specific program (e.g., a football game) or provide various special programming (e.g., black news or religious information).

Station Programming

Most radio programming today is based on format broadcasting in which a station selects a segment of the audience (those aged 18–24, for example) and attempts to reach only that segment throughout its entire schedule.

A big term in broadcast circles these days is *audience fragmentation*. Throughout the country, so-called mass-appeal radio stations are being outperformed by stations serving individual segments of the population. Much in the same manner as magazines, radio is now a medium of specialization. Programmers, taking into account factors ranging from age to income to geographical location, are targeting their product at specific audience "cells."

Targeted broadcasting is further linked to the "lifestyle" concept. Knowledge regarding a listener's lifestyle—interests, tastes, attitudes, habits, and values—can be attributed to radio's ability to profile the psyche of a listener with startling accuracy and reliability. The result of this kind of research is an uncovering of irritants and frequently a restructuring of a station's program mix to appeal directly to a specific lifestyle group.

RADIO FORMATS

A direct by-product of targeted radio has been the advent of formats. *Broadcasting* magazine lists over 60 program formats or sounds, but most stations fall into the following major categories: (a) adult contemporary; (b) top 40–contemporary; (c) album-oriented rock (AOR); (d) country; (e) beautiful music; (f) soft rock; (g) urban contemporary; (h) big band–music of your life; (i) all news; (j) news–talk.

These 10 formats are somewhat misleading in that they represent a much wider variety of individual sounds and styles. For example, AOR can mean a number of sounds ranging from hard rock, classic rock, and new wave. As a result of this format's volatile nature it is constantly undergoing change. Radio formats are fluid and reflect current trends in music. Country–western music, for example, has fluctuated widely in popularity, and there has been a tremendous growth in recent years of progressive or urban contemporary music.

Adult contemporary

The most-listened-to radio format in America. Its popularity may be due in part to confusion as to what constitutes "adult contemporary." At some stations, the format is merely a convoluted top-40 presentation; other stations have developed a full-service product featuring everything from meteorologists to financial experts. Personality is usually an important element.

Typical artists: *Barbra Streisand, Neil Diamond, Beach Boys, Spinners, Beatles.*

Audience target: *Adults 25–49 age group.*

**Top 40–
contemporary**

The mass-appeal format of the 1960s and 1970s is eroding. The teen base that was the mainstay of many AM radio giants has fractionalized and scattered. The influx of FM radio and a drop in younger demographics has forced the repositioning of many top-40 stations to a more subdued and adult approach (adult contemporary). Top 40 does, however, live and continue to score well in a variety of forms on the FM band. It is a prime example of a format that has been greatly altered in this newly competitive environment.

Typical artists: *Hall & Oates, Commodores, Billy Joel, Olivia Newton-John.*

Audience target: *12–24 age group.*

**Album-oriented rock
(AOR)**

Considered by many the most volatile of all formats, AOR features a steady diet of rock 'n' roll. Successful stations with the format carefully research music and are aggressive promoters. In many markets, AORs are considered the new teen stations, thus there is a heightened concern about "image." A variety of theories prevail regarding program attitude and music selection. One includes a pure hard-rock stance, frequently referred to as "chain saw." Another theory has programmers concentrating on classic rock. Most programmers agree that we are in the midst of a "musical lull." Listeners to AOR are among the heaviest of radio users.

Typical artists: *Rolling Stones, The Who, Bob Seger, Genesis.*

Audience target: *adults 25–49 age group.*

Country

Country may be the AM format of the 1980s. Programmers throughout the nation are opting for country formats. Some offer a "cityfied" music selection stretching the criteria to include artists ranging from Dan Fogelberg to Linda Ronstadt. Others offer a mainstream blend concentrating on "pure" artists like Willie Nelson and Conway Twitty. Stations frequently offer a mix of news and other information sercices.

Typical artists: *Barbara Mandrell, Kenny Rogers, Tammy Wynette, Anne Murray.*

Audience target: *25–50 age group.*

Beautiful music   Call it dentist-office music, if you will, but beautiful music remains one of the biggest formats in America. Utilizing instrumentals and light vocals assembled in blocks of about 15 minutes, these stations usually feature minimal talk. Many are computer operated, thus eliminating the need for live announcers and other operational costs.

Typical artists: *Ray Conniff, Hollywood Strings, Frank Sinatra, Sergio Mendes.*

Audience target: *25–54 age group.*

Soft rock   Soft rock is a spinoff of album-oriented rock concentrating on "mellow" music acts from the mid- to late 1970s and early 1980s. Trademark is generally a low-key announcing style with minimal personality.

Typical artists: *Dan Fogelberg, Joni Mitchell, Beatles, Fleetwood Mac.*

Audience target: *Females 18–34 age group.*

Urban contemporary   Disco radio that has grown up. This is the logical extension of contemporary hit radio with accessible "dance" music. Urban contemporary has proved viable only in highly ethnic communities and generally features a "wide" up-tempo playlist. Key personalities are usually integral in success formula.

Typical artists: *Kool & The Gang, Earth, Wind & Fire, Commodores, George Benson, Foreigner.*

Audience target: *12–34 age group.*

Big band   There has been a recent resurgence of big-band music on radio. Stations using the format are highly music oriented. The minimal personality involvement will most likely change as the format, in its latest incarnation, matures.

Typical artists: *Tommy Dorsey, Tony Bennett, Glenn Miller, Frank Sinatra.*

Audience target: *Adults 50 and over.*

All news   Easily the most expensive to run of all radio formats, and so usually confined to major markets. Stations are highly structured with frequent time checks, weather forecasts, and story repetition. Many have successfully integrated short features. Some employ two-voice announcer concept. All-news stations are highly reliant on morning listening.

Audience target: *25–54 age group.*

Hybrid of all-news radio. Most stations feature extensive news commitment supplemented with high-profile talk personalities utilizing
guests and telephones. Hailed as the most important AM format of the
decade, it has proven enormously successful in some major markets.

Audience target: *25–50 age group.*

The significant increase in specialized music formats has prompted the
appearance of syndication companies that provide tapes of selected music
cuts programmed up to 24 hours in length. These syndication companies
offer stations tapes of music that change hourly and provide different
moods, rhythms, and styles. Seasonal changes are also incorporated into
the tapes. Bill Drake of Drake-Chenault Enterprises is the largest and most
influential program syndicator–formatter. Formats are basically an economic issue. Stations want the best-quality programming for the least
money; syndicated formats allow this economic principle to exist.

Most radio programming is based on a limited number of standard and
inexpensive components:

1. Recorded music is provided at little or no cost by most record
   companies as a means of exposing the public to their new releases.
   The kind of music played has come to serve as a label for stations
   and to indicate the kind of audience who listens to them.
2. News is the second most important part of radio. National news
   and features are provided by the networks. Some stations have
   extensive local news operations, but most depend on wire services for nearly all the news they broadcast.
3. Disc-jockey talk binds the music, news, sports, weather, and advertising into a cohesive unit. But announcer creativity is limited
   by the style of the station. Many "rock jocks" seem to have been
   made on an assembly line, and any member of a station's stable
   of announcers sounds similar to all the others.
4. Local sports, especially high school and college sports, are major
   features on many stations.
5. Finally, advertising pays the station's bills. In radio, the most
   lucrative times of the day are the two "drive time" periods when
   people are going to, or coming from, school or work.

At present radio is a mass medium with a highly fragmented audience   **CHARACTERISTICS**
and revenue base. Radio is a local rather than a national medium both in   **AND ROLES OF**
terms of its sources of audience and income. Radio listening habits are   **RADIO**
personal, and stations program selectively to satisfy individual needs
within a relatively homogeneous group. Radio, adapting to the nature of

our society, has used technological advances to become mobile. Listeners use radio as a secondary activity to accompany the work or play of the moment, and advertisers use radio to supplement the primary medium in their advertising mix.

Local   Radio has become a local as opposed to a national medium in terms of its sources of audience, income, and programming. Until the 1950s radio was the prestige mass medium, controlled by national advertisers and networks. Network affiliation assured affiliated stations of extensive programming, audience, and revenue.

In the 1980s, local stations attract the audiences, earn the revenue, and provide much of the programming. Nevertheless, syndicated and network program services have assumed much of the local stations' programming role. Local disc jockeys, newspeople, and other personalities operate within a local frame of reference; but program sources in radio are increasingly national in character.

Fragmented–   In the mid-1950s, radio broadcasters were in the position of needing
Selective   more programs but having less money to pay for them. Since both talk and music were relatively cheap, radio rebuilt its programming around music, news, and sports. What evolved has come to be called formula, or format, radio.

Very quickly, AM and FM broadcasters realized that general radio was dead. The more variety a specific station offered, the more its audience dwindled. Television had assumed the role of general entertainer. Stations began to develop variations of the music, news, and sports formula, based on types of recorded music. Audience research indicated that certain formats attracted select segments of the available audience. Top-40 stations held a virtual monopoly on the teen and subteen groups, while country–western stations had strong appeal not only in the South and the Southwest but also for vast numbers in the large northern metropolitan areas. Middle-of-the-road (MOR) stations attracted another segment.

Broadcasters began to program selectively to serve one portion of the population. The FCC granted licenses for racially and ethnically oriented stations, which specifically set out to establish themselves as radio services for minority groups within the community. Stations today seek to create a distinct personality on a program formula. Radio stations program selectively in order to corner a special segment of the listener–consumer market. Then, if any advertiser wants to reach the black market, the teen-age market, or the young housewife market in a given area, that advertiser must deal with the station that programs selectively for the audience in question. The following table, from the Washington, D.C., market, graphically illustrates this diversity with over 30 different formats.

AM–FM Radio, Washington, D.C.

AM radio stations			FM radio stations		
Dial	Format	Call letters	Dial	Format	Call letters
570	Classical Music	WGMS	88.1	Progressive Music	WMUC
630	Pop Music/Talk (ABC Information)	WMAL	88.5	Arts/Information (NPR)	WAMU
730	Continuous Country Music	WRMR	89.3	Jazz Community Radio (Pacifica)	WPFW
780	Religious/Sacred Music	WABS	90.1	Jazz/Information	WDCU
900	Adult Contemporary	WLMD	90.9	Arts/Information (NPR)	WETA
950	Christian Music	WCTN	91.9	Educational/Cultural	WGTS
980	News/Talk (NBC)	WRC	93.9	Urban Contemporary	WKYS
1050	Beautiful Music	WGAY	94.7	Adult Contemporary	WLTT
1120	Gospel: Talk/Music	WUST	95.5	Adult Contemporary Music	WPGC
1150	24-Hour Comedy	WJOK	96.3	Progressive Black Music	WHUR
1220	Inspirational/Devotional	WFAX	97.1	Up-Tempo Familiar Music	WASH
1260	Personality/MOR (RKO)	WWDC	98.7	Country	WMZQ
1290	Popular Music	WAGE	99.5	Beautiful Music	WGAY
1310	All News	WEEL	100.3	Album Soul	WOOK
1340	Inspiration/Information	WYCB	101.1	Album Rock	WWDC
1390	Big Band/Swing	WEAM	102.3	Progressive Music	WHFS
1440	Country	WVBK	103.5	Classical Music	WGMS
1450	Adult Contemporary (SBN)	WOL	104.1	Hit Oldies	WXTR
1460	Contemporary	WPRW	105.1	Album Rock	WAVA
1500	All News (CBS)	WTOP	105.9	Continuous Country Music	WPKX
1530	Country, Gospel	WPWC	106.7	Adult Contemporary	WEZR
1540	Contemporary Latin Music/News	WMDO	107.3	Contemporary Music (ABC-FM)	WRQX
1560	Hit Oldies	WXTR			
1580	Adult Contemporary Music	WPGC			
1600	Oldies (Mutual)	WINX			

Personal

Closely allied to radio stations' selective programming is the fact that listening to radio has become a personal activity. No longer does the family unit gather around the console radio to be entertained in a group situation. People tend to listen to the radio as individuals, and radio station announcers attempt to develop "personal" listening relationships with radio audiences. How many times have you heard a disc jockey single out specific individuals for attention? "I'm sending this song out to Tom and Donna, and Don and Karen." The radio talk show builds a loyal audience of individuals who call to express their personal views or argue with those individuals with whom they disagree. Entire formats are now built around the talk-show concept.

You might see a couple of teenagers stroll down the streets as they listen as individuals to the same station on two personal radios. This personal orientation is possible because there are 1.3 radios for every individual in the United States. In kitchens, radio is listened to for weather reports in order to send children off to school properly dressed. Upstairs, teenagers tune in on the latest number-one hit in the country. On the way to work, people listen to traffic reports on the automobile radio. The individual listens in relative isolation, seeking to gratify a personal entertainment or information need of the moment.

Mobile   The United States has been called a "society on wheels," and radio has the ability to get out and go with its American audiences. This ability to participate in the individual's daily routine has been made possible by the new mobility of radio.

The phenomenal increases in radio sales in recent years result in great measure from the production of three specific kinds of radio receivers: the car radio, the portable radio, and the clock radio. Home radios, usually small AM-FM sets, constitute little more than 15% of all radio sales.

The trend toward increased mobility began immediately following World War II, although production of car radios had been an important part of total radio production as early as 1930. By 1951 auto-set production exceeded that of the home-receiver class for the first time and has continued to be the leading type of set manufactured for the past 15 years. Today, 95 of every 100 new cars are radio equipped.

During the 1950s and 1960s, portable production also topped home-receiver production, excluding clock radios. The tremendous surge in portability was made possible by the transistor, which reduced set size and cost. The sale of transistor radios exceeds $30 million a year, which is 200% above the 1952 level, and Americans spend more than $100 million a year just to keep transistor radios going in a mobile society.

Secondary and   The final characteristics of radio are its use as a secondary activity by
Supplementary   listeners and a supplementary medium by advertisers. Radio is to drive a car by, study by, or relax at the beach by. No longer does an audience eagerly cling to the radio for every sound. Radio is no longer the primary entertainment activity in our society, and with the added mobility of the radio, it goes along as a companion for the activity of the moment. An automobile radio is secondary to the prime function of the car itself—to go somewhere. We need traffic reports to get there, and radio provides them. The most recent development that enhances radio's usefulness as a secondary item is the clock radio. It does not jolt you awake; it sings or talks you out of the bed and into the day. Its primary function is not to entertain or provide information; it is basically an alarm clock.

National and local advertisers with sizable budgets use radio to supplement the major medium of an advertising campaign. Most local advertisers use newspapers primarily but keep the campaign supported with radio ads. Major national advertisers usually spend only a small portion of their total budget on radio. Nevertheless, Radio Advertising Bureau studies have shown that radio can effectively and efficiently reach con-

(Photo by Brendan Beirne.)

The development of the transistor made possible greater radio portability.

sumer prospects that television misses. Most of the nation's top advertising agencies spend less than 10% of their national clients' budgets on radio. The major exceptions to the rule are the automobile and related industries, which extensively use "drive time" to hit the available audience going to or coming from work.

In summary, radio has clearly survived the competition from television and has evolved into a new and remarkably solid medium. Radio is now a companion medium, fine-tuned to meet almost any need. This unique ability will continue to provide it with an audience and revenue capable of sustaining future expansion.

19 Television

As you begin to read this chapter, reflect back for a moment on the 18,000 hours in your life that you have spent watching television. For most of you, TV viewing has been, in terms of raw time, the dominant activity of your waking life. You have spent more time watching assorted heroes, villains, and fools on the tube than you have spent in school, in church, or at any other organized activity. Many of you can date your lives by moments on television: You were born around the time television brought the horror and sorrow of Robert Kennedy's and Martin Luther King's assassinations to a stunned nation; at the same time your brother or sister enjoyed a new program called "Sesame Street"; President Nixon resigned in an emotional television farewell to a Watergate-weary population as you started school; your junior high school social studies teacher assigned "Roots" as a discussion topic in class; you went through high school with images of "J.R." being shot, American hostages being freed, and another American president falling wounded before an assassin's gunfire.

You are not the first TV generation, but you have been witness to one of the most intense and active periods in the history of television. For most Americans, television is *the* source of entertainment, *the* most reliable source of news, *the* most dynamic form of advertising, and an integral part of their total lifestyle. This is even more impressive when you consider that television as we know it today is not yet 40 years old. If there are such things as historical periods, one title for the second half of the twentieth century must surely be the Age of Television.

The history of television in the United States breaks down into several fairly well-defined units. The first is the prehistory of television encompassing the early theoretical research leading up to the first video experiments in the mid-1920s.

HISTORICAL PERSPECTIVES

Like radio, television grew out of the intense experimentation in electricity in the late nineteenth century. Basic research in electromagnetic theory by James Clerk Maxwell and Heinrich Hertz led to more practical experimentation culminating in the work of Guglielmo Marconi. Coincidental with this research in wireless communication in the 1880s was the work of Paul Nipkow, who experimented with mechanical scanning-disc methods of sending pictures by wire. Most of the early experiments in television employed the mechanical method, including work in the 1920s of Charles Jenkins in the United States and John Baird in Britain. Research in television slowed down with the tremendous surge of radio in the early twentieth century. Nevertheless, work on an electronic TV system was begun in the United States by Philo T. Farnsworth and Vladimir Zworykin. Both men contributed basic inventions, including most significantly Zworykin's camera tube, the iconoscope, which he patented in 1928.

Prehistory: 1884–1925

Barely 3 years after radio broadcasting became a reality, a crude, all-electronic TV system was available, although much of its early use was not successful. The first real transmission of television occurred in 1925 with Jenkins's mechanical method. Zworykin's method of electronic scanning was simpler, however, and eventually produced a better picture. Experiments with electronic television were conducted throughout the world in the 1920s, including the work of Alexanderson and Farnsworth in this country and Baird in England. The Federal Radio Commission (later the Federal Communications Commission) granted the first experimental license for visual broadcasting to RCA's W2XBS in April 1928. That same year, the General Electric Company broadcast the first TV drama over W6X in Schenectady, New York.

Early Development: 1925–1947

Experimentation continued throughout the 1930s, chiefly by Zworykin and his team of engineers working at RCA, and by 1937, 17 stations were operating under noncommercial experimental license. The first major public demonstration of television occurred at the 1939 World's Fair in New York City with President Franklin D. Roosevelt's appearance on television the hit of the fair.

Dr. Vladimir K. Zworykin demonstrates the cathode ray television system developed at Westinghouse in 1929.

(Photo: The Bettman Archive.)

Commercial TV operations were scheduled to begin 1 September 1940, but the FCC rescinded its original authorization in March 1940. The delay was ordered by the commission because it felt that RCA had indulged in an unwise promotional campaign to sell its transmission and receiving equipment that would retard further TV research and experimentation.

In January 1941 the National Television System Committee (NTSC) suggested TV standards to which the FCC reacted favorably, and the start of commercial telecasting was rescheduled for 1 July 1941. On that date both the DuMont and CBS stations aired programming. But it was RCA's WNBT that ran the first spot commercial (Bulova Watch Company) and sponsored programs, Lowell Thomas's news program (Sunoco), "Uncle Jim's Question Bee" (Lever Brothers), and "Truth or Consequences" (Procter & Gamble). By the end of 1941, some 10 commercial stations were serving 10,000 to 20,000 television homes, half in New York and the rest in Chicago, Philadelphia, and Los Angeles.

World War II interrupted TV's growth and delayed its national appearance. Commercial telecasting ended early in 1942, although experimental telecasts on six stations continued on an irregular basis. Advertisers were encouraged to use the facilities free of charge. Although the war was detrimental to the immediate development of television, it had positive effects as well. Chief among them was the development of better electronic techniques and equipment, the most important of which was the image-orthicon tube.

The single most important event affecting TV's future during World War II was the 1943 duopoly ruling that forced NBC to divest itself of one of its two radio networks. This decision created another economically strong national radio operation (ABC) that enabled the ABC-TV network to evolve and survive during its early years.

Following World War II, the rapid development of television was further retarded by problems involving the placement of television in the electromagnetic spectrum and the $1 million price tag attached to building and equipping a TV station. In 1945 there were 6 commercial stations on the air, and by 1947 only 11 more had been added. At this time many broadcasters thought that FM radio would be the next important medium.

By March 1947, however, the FCC had set aside Channels 2 to 13 in the VHF (very high frequency) band, and more and more receivers were appearing on the market. By this time, too, AT&T had begun to install intercity coaxial cable, making possible network interconnection. The rush for TV facilities was on, and CBS, because of misplaced TV priorities during World War II, belatedly joined in. There was a definite need for more stations because people were buying the high-priced sets as fast as they were being produced. Over a million sets were sold in 1948 at an average price of $400. By early 1948, 19 stations were on the air, 81 had FCC authorization, and 116 applications were before the FCC. At this time it became obvious that the commission would have to reevaluate TV broadcasting to prevent station interference, since only 12 VHF channels were available to serve the total system.

During this period, three major factors significantly affected the future of video broadcasting: (a) the Federal Communications Commission's "freeze" on TV station allocations; (b) the development of TV networks; and (c) the evolution of video programming formats.

The Formation of the American Television System: 1948–1952

The Freeze. By the fall of 1948 there were 36 TV stations on the air in 19 markets and another 73 licensed in 43 more cities. In order to solve technical-interference problems, provide for the increased demand for licenses, and study color TV systems, the Federal Communications Commission froze new-station allocations from 30 September 1948 to 1 July 1952. During these years the RCA compatible-color system was adopted, UHF Channels 14 to 83 were added to VHF Channels 2 to 13, and 242 station allocations were reserved for educational television. This third class of stations—public, noncommercial, and educational—was established through the efforts of Commissioner Frieda B. Hennock, despite the lack of support from most educators and universities.

While the freeze was on, 108 of the 109 commercially licensed stations went on the air, and TV homes jumped from 1.5 million to 15 million. Between 1948 and 1952 one of every three American families bought a TV set at an average cost of $300. Although no new licenses were being granted, growth was possible during this period because almost every major population area was being served by at least one TV station.

The Networks. The generally accepted date for the arrival of national television networking is the 1948–1949 TV season (September to August). In January 1949 the Midwest and the East Coast were linked by coaxial cable. The West Coast linkup occurred in September 1951. Since not every station was able to carry live feeds, however, many new stations had to depend on kinescopes (films of electronically produced pictures) for network programming.

The birth and survival of the television networks depended on these factors: (a) a financially sound parent company that could survive the lean years of television development; (b) ownership of key stations in the largest population centers to provide local revenue and guarantee that the network's series would be aired in those markets; (c) expertise in national radio operations that provided both financial support and a ready-made lineup of affiliates to carry programs; (d) a backlog or quick development of talent and programs that would attract large audiences for national advertisers.

The American Broadcasting Company, the Columbia Broadcasting System, and the National Broadcasting Company were able to meet these criteria and survived. The key, of course, was financial strength. NBC lost over $18 million in its first 4 years of network TV operation. The Mutual Broadcasting System, which did not own any radio stations, was the weakest national radio operation and was never able to develop the resources necessary to enter television. The DuMont Television Network, owned by Allen B. DuMont Laboratories, an early pioneer in TV operations, did not have a radio network, financial strength, station ownership, or programming experience; despite early promise and some limited performance, it collapsed completely in 1955.

Programming. In these early years of network and station development most of the content of television came from radio-programming formats. The quiz shows, suspense programs, Westerns, variety shows, soap operas, and comedies were direct descendants of developments in radio. In fact, most of TV's early hits were exact copies of radio series transposed intact to television, such as "Suspense," "The Life of Riley," "The Aldrich Family," "The Lone Ranger," "Break the Bank," and "Studio One." Television's first stars were radio personalities, including Red Skelton,

Burns and Allen, Arthur Godfrey, Jack Benny, and Edgar Bergen. The networks also adopted other traditional radio programming, such as news, sporting events, and live coverage of special events like the 1948 and 1952 political conventions and election returns.

Local stations attempted to provide programming in those early years to fill the gaps left in the network schedules. Much of it was of poor quality, however, and as a result the syndicator emerged early as an important source of TV content. In 1950 the first package of theatrical films found its way into the local marketplace.

The financial base of television was clear from the start. The public was acclimated to radio commercials and accepted them as the means of paying for their programs. Also, the networks had contractual agreements with sponsors. Structurally, TV economics was simply an extension of radio economics, and because of this, television developed much faster than expected.

Despite its affinities to radio, television was still a new medium. Its own particular pattern of adoption in society coupled with its unique properties were prime factors in the rapidly changing pattern of programming. Television, like newspapers and radio before it, was initially not a household medium. As newspapers were first read in coffeehouses, television was first viewed by many in local bars and taverns. This factor plus the inherent visualness of television were strong reasons for sports programming making up as much as 30% of all sponsored network evening time in 1949. As the TV set became more of a household item, the programming changed to reflect this. Children's and women's programming became more important, as did family entertainment such as variety shows.

The end of TV's birth and its rush into childhood came in 1952 when the FCC issued its Sixth Order and Report. The report did more than end the freeze. It was essentially a master plan for TV development in the United States. Television was on the brink of fulfilling its destiny as the dominant leisure-time activity for most Americans.

This slice of television history contained the most fantastic growth spurt ever experienced by a mass medium. As one would expect, there was a great rush to obtain station licenses immediately following the end of the freeze. By 1955 there were 439 stations on the air. Set sales mushroomed as more stations began broadcast operations. The 15 million TV homes in 1952 expanded to 26 million in 1954, 42.5 million in 1958, and reached 45 million homes by 1960. In this period the percentage of TV-equipped homes in the United States grew from 33% to 90%. Station and network profits kept pace with this growth as gross industry revenues increased from $300 million in 1952 to $1.3 billion in 1960.

The Golden Age of Television: 1952—1960

The dominant networks of this period were CBS and NBC, primarily because of their network radio experience, available capital assets, top-quality talent, and large number of affiliated stations. The ABC network had many problems, primarily the lack of affiliates. The death of the DuMont network in 1955 eased ABC's need for more affiliates to a limited degree. This factor, plus the merger with United-Paramount Theaters, helped increase ABC's competitiveness, but throughout the 1950s it ran a poor third to CBS and NBC.

The FCC's Sixth Order and Report was designed to ease problems that faced the industry, but the implementation of these changes took considerable time. Seventy new channels were opened in the UHF band, but since most TV sets were built to receive only VHF signals, special adapters and antennas had to be purchased in order to receive UHF stations. Although 120 UHF stations were operating in 1954, they were in an extremely poor competitive position, and as a result their numbers fell to only 75 in 1960. This situation continued until 1962 when Congress passed legislation that required that all TV sets produced after 1 January 1964 be capable of receiving both UHF and VHF signals.

Color television in the form of RCA's electronic system began to emerge slowly following FCC approval in 1953. The first color sets were manufactured in 1954 and sold for about $1000. The high cost of both receivers and broadcast equipment dictated a slow growth, however. The season of 1954–1955 was the first color season, with NBC programming 12 to 15 hours a week.

Several factors were responsible for the public's slow response to color television: (a) Set costs were extremely high; (b) ABC and CBS refused to move into color programming because it would have given NBC the competitive edge, since most compatible-color patents were held by NBC's parent company, RCA; (c) the electronics industry already had a thriving business in black-and-white sets, and they too would have to do business with RCA. Many manufacturers chose to experiment with, rather than produce, color sets, and as a result, as late as 1960 there were no color series on ABC or CBS.

By 1966 all three networks were running a complete all-color, prime-time schedule. This growth in available color programming led to a boom in sales of color sets, and by 1972 50% of U.S. homes with television had color receivers. Today, over 80% of American TV homes have a color-TV set. What is equally important, color-equipped homes use their sets approximately 20% more than black-and-white homes.

Another important technical development that occurred in the 1950s was the move toward film and videotape programming. With the development of videotape in 1956, live telecasting, with the exception of sports, specials, and some daytime drama, soon became a thing of the past. By 1960 virtually all network prime-time programming was on film or videotape. Two reasons for the rise of recorded programming were: (a) Errors could be corrected before they were broadcast, thus improving the artistic quality of the program; (b) the program could be rerun, cutting the skyrocketing costs of program production.

Programming in the 1950s continued the trends of the early years with a mixture of sports, family situation comedies, and variety–vaudeville shows. The variety–vaudeville show format was led by the self-proclaimed "Mr. Television" Milton Berle. Beginning in 1948, Berle captured the screens of American households on Tuesday night as host and star of "Texaco Star Theater." Ed Sullivan, with the "Toast of the Town" (later "The Ed Sullivan Show"), represented a saner and more broadly entertaining show that lasted for over 20 years. One of the most creative comedy–variety shows of the time and a classic of television's golden age was "Your Show of Shows," starring Sid Caesar and Imogene Coca. Family situation comedy was a format taken directly from radio with such series as "The Goldbergs," "The Life of Riley," and "Our Miss Brooks." However, it was "I Love Lucy," first arriving in 1951, which set the standard for this type of comedy. Children's programs were very popular led by "Howdy Doody" with Buffalo Bob Smith and a host of puppets and Burr Tillstrom's more adult "Kukla, Fran, & Ollie," starring Fran Allison. Two important program additions were the adult Western, starting with "Gun-

(Photo: Movie Star News.)

The zany comedy of Milton Berle's TV variety show in the 1950s earned him the title "Mr. Television."

None of the early TV sitcoms attracted so great a following as "I Love Lucy."

(Photo: Movie Star News.)

In 1955, "Gunsmoke" pioneered the TV adult Western.

(Photo: Movie Star News.)

smoke" in 1955, and the big-prize game shows, beginning with "The $64,000 Question" in 1956. Westerns reached their peak in 1959–1960 with 32 Westerns in prime time, but gradually declined until, by the mid-1970s, none were on network schedules. The quiz scandals in 1959 revealed that some participants had received answers prior to their appearance on the shows or had been coached in their responses to heighten tension. This notoriety killed off the prime-time big-money quiz shows, although game shows continue to be a staple of daytime programming.

"Live" drama reached its zenith in the mid-1950s with such programs as "Studio One," "Playhouse 90," and "The Armstrong Circle Theater." But television's voracious appetite for new material soon made it impossible to sustain high artistic standards. The form began to blend with other dramatic types and gradually faded from the scene. Today, with the exception of "The Hallmark Hall of Fame," British Broadcasting Corporation (BBC) imports on public television, and limited network specials, quality drama on television is rare.

Program experimentation began to dwindle as network competition set in. In the late 1950s, Westerns, situation comedies, and crime-detective dramas accounted for over 50% of all prime-time programming. Everyone

Jack Barry reads a question for contestant Charles Van Doren in the booth behind him. The quiz show "Twenty-One" succumbed to public scandal when Van Doren confessed that he had been given the answers.

(Photo: New York Public Library Picture Collection, Courtesy NBC Television.)

"Robert Montgomery Pre-
sents" was one of the live
television dramatic series
which flourished in the
mid 1950s.

(Photo: The Bettman Archive, Inc.)

seemed to be jumping on various bandwagons, duplicating whatever was popular at the moment.

The TV quiz scandals in 1959 seemed to herald an end to the age of euphoria. According to the *Tenth Annual Videotown Report* published in 1957 by Cunningham & Walsh, television had become accepted as a routine part of life and had lost much of its former novelty and excitement. A public opinion poll taken by Sindlinger in 1959 revealed a sharp drop in the public's estimation of television following the quiz scandals. Congress began a series of investigations focusing particular attention upon the relationship among advertisers, agencies, and broadcasters. Much of this concern was strikingly capsulated by FCC Chairman Newton Minow in 1961 when he criticized television, calling it "a vast wasteland."

The 1950s were a time of experimentation and change for television. A whole new generation of programs, stars, and techniques came into being. By 1960 the trial period was over. Television was ready to both settle down and grow up. The tensions created by these two trends would highlight TV's maturing years.

The two words *progress* and *criticism* sum up much of the public's attitude toward television in the period since 1960. Criticism of television became popular as politicians, educators, social scientists, minority groups, and parents all took turns attacking the medium. Of particular public concern was television's role in the violence that seemed so much a part of America in the 1960s and 1970s. Countless studies focused on TV's effects, especially on children. The results have generally concluded that everyone knows television has an effect, but few are sure exactly what this effect is and how it works. The medium's advertising effectiveness is clearly evident, however, by the $2 billion investment made annually by advertisers.

Television's impact on the political process became apparent in the 1960s, beginning with the Nixon–Kennedy debates in 1960, continuing in 1968 with TV's coverage of the Democratic convention in Chicago, and highlighted further by the Carter–Ford debates in 1976, the Reagan–Carter debates of 1980, and the Reagan–Mondale debates of 1984. The role of television in the political campaign process grew tremendously and created concern over packaged candidates and election by commercial slogan.

Networks continued their domination of programming. By 1969 they provided almost 64% (77.5 hours per week) of their affiliates' program-

Progress and Criticism: 1961 to the Present

Jimmy Carter and Ronald Reagan are seen squaring off before a national audience during the 1980 presidential television debates in this photo from an NBC monitor.

(Photo: AP/Wide World Photos.)

ming. As revenue and profits increased, criticism seemed to keep pace. The FCC proposed a plan whereby 50% of all prime-time programming would have to be non-network originated, but this proposal was never implemented. In the 1971–72 season, however, the FCC did institute a ruling cutting network prime-time programming from 3.5 hours to 3.0 hours per evening in the 7:30 to 11:00 P.M. (EST) time block.

As TV homes exceeded the 90% saturation mark and viewing levels reached 6 hours per day in the average TV household, a great deal of concern was generated over programming. Pressure groups succeeded in altering some of this programming. Violence on television was somewhat curtailed because of pressure brought to bear following the assassinations of President John F. Kennedy, Martin Luther King, and Robert Kennedy. An overhaul of Saturday morning cartoon shows occurred in the 1970–1971 season to appease critics. Perhaps the most dramatic and effective attack came against the cigarette industry by the Surgeon General's Office with its claims that cigarette smoking was dangerous to a person's health. Pressure by the Surgeon General resulted in all cigarette advertising being taken off the air on 2 January 1971. A short-lived "family hour" was implemented in 1975–1976 with less than successful results. The idea was to limit the first hour of prime-time programming to material suitable for the entire family, but the result was a mishmash of weak comedies and variety programs that proved to be poor lead-ins for later programs. The concept was phased out in 1976.

All cigarette advertising, such as this Old Gold live TV commercial, was taken off the air in 1971.

(Photo: New York Public Library Picture Collection.)

Television enabled millions of viewers to share in Astronaut Ed Aldrin Jr.'s moonwalk while it was actually happening—the Apollo 11 Moon Landing, 1969.

(Photo: The Bettman Archive, Inc.)

Any historical overview of television in the 1960s finds itself overwhelmed by the sheer number of events, people, and issues in the TV spotlight. In this decade three events stand out: the Vietnam war, the assassination and funeral of President Kennedy, and the *Apollo 11* moon landing. All three events are competitors for the label of TV's finest hour. Instead of simply hearing or reading about the war, the president's funeral, or the moonwalk *after* they happened, the American public was able—through television—to witness and participate in the events *as* they were happening. At times this witnessing was inspiring, as when television went to the moon. At times it was frightening, as when suspected presidential assassin Lee Harvey Oswald was murdered by Jack Ruby in full view of the nation, or when a captured Vietcong soldier was shot in the head as cameras recorded the scene. At times it was illuminating, as when dogs and water hoses were turned on civil rights demonstrators and police fought with protestors in Chicago during the 1968 Democratic convention. (Many remember the chant "The whole world is watching" as police pummeled protestors.) The 1960s were anything but peaceful, and television was on hand providing dramatic witness, perhaps even dramatic stimulation, to the turmoil. Much of the world *was* watching and was being changed in the process.

In the area of program content, motion pictures became a major part of the network's prime-time fare. The ABC network broke new ground by showing *The Bridge on the River Kwai* in 1966, and by the 1970s the networks were engaged in a furious bidding war for recent and successful motion pictures. In addition, programs such as "That Was the Week That Was," "The Smothers Brothers Comedy Hour," and "Laugh-In" began to challenge a number of taboos, and television in general got in step with a more permissive society. Perhaps the single most important commercial programming development was the appearance of the adult situation comedy. It started in 1971 with "All in the Family" and proliferated throughout the first half of the decade until it made up over 25% of the nation's prime-time schedule in 1976–1977. Such programs as "Maude," "Soap," "Sanford and Son," "Alice," "Mary Hartman, Mary Hartman," and "Three's Company" regularly used abortion, premarital sex, narcotics, and religious evangelism as comic material. The entertainment industry responded to the civil rights movement by integrating programs and commercials; blacks such as Bill Cosby, Diahann Carroll, Redd Foxx, and Flip Wilson became successful series stars. Professional football became the national TV sport, and NBC made it possible for the fledgling American Football League to survive economically by exposing the junior league to national audiences and paying large sums for TV rights to the games. ABC did much the same for the United States Football League in 1983. Late-night talk shows became part of the three-network competition but were quickly reduced to one as no one could compete against the long-established "The Tonight Show." "Sesame Street" emerged as public broadcasting's first "star" and helped focus attention on the almost anonymous fourth network. The late 1970s and early 1980s gave rise to the miniseries. With the appearance of "Rich Man, Poor Man," "Roots," "Holocaust," "Winds of War," and "The Thorn Birds," among others, the miniseries became a strong programming factor that threatened to alter television's long-standing seasonal structure built on 13- and 26-week series.

Soap operas became major media events in the 1970s and 1980s. Soap operas were, of course, a staple of daytime radio with series such as "The Romance of Helen Trent" and "Ma Perkins" lasting over 20 years. They made the transition to television in the early 1950s but were considered only incidental to network strategy until the middle 1970s when, led by the long-running "The Guiding Light," several of the more popular programs went to an hour format. The form achieved major programming status in the late 1970s as it began to treat increasingly realistic and adult themes. Such series as "General Hospital" and "Ryan's Hope" took on cult status as the audience for soap operas extended beyond the housewife to incorporate college students and adult males.

Hollywood&Vinyl/The Miniseries

TEXT: PAUL RUDNICK
ART: BILL McKEARN

In which two aspiring network assistants sneak a peek at a rough cut and plot to remake history

A GEORGE WASHINGTON MINI-SERIES?! NOBODY'S GONNA WATCH THIS, AND IT'S SWEEPS WEEK. WHAT'LL WE TELL THE CHIEF?

I KNOW, LET'S RECONCEPTUALIZE IT AS "ROOTS," BUT FOR WASPs! TAKE A D.A.R. GIRL, TRACE HER BACK TO THE FIRST CABIN ON THE MAYFLOWER — CALL IT "STREAKS"!

WHAT IF WE MADE IT MORE NUTTY? WE COULD SHOW GEORGE WASHING-TON FORGETTING TO PUT HIS TEETH IN, OR BETSY ROSS SEWING ON 14 STARS, YOU KNOW— "COLONIAL BLOOPERS"!

OR TRY THIS. WE HAVE A SLAVE FAMILY MOVE INTO MONTICELLO AND DO CRAZY ZANY THINGS THAT TEACH US SOMETHING — CALL IT "THE JEFFERSONS"!

WELL, WE'VE ALREADY GOT PATTY DUKE AS THE WIFE, BUT MAYBE SHE COULD BE WACKY, ALWAYS GETTING INTO SCRAPES WITH HER BEST FRIEND, DOLLY MADISON. SORT OF "I MARRIED MARTHA."

A LIBERTY BELLE WHO'S REALLY CRACKED.

BUT GEORGE REALLY LOVED HIS BEST FRIEND'S WIFE, AND WE'VE GOT JACLYN SMITH. LET'S MAKE HIM A REAL PERVERT— "SOMETHING ABOUT GEORGE"!

WELL, WHY NOT JUST GO SOFT-CORE THEN, AND TOSS IT ON CABLE? "HOUSE OF PAINE."

"AN ACT OF CONGRESS."
"MOTION FROM THE FLOOR."
"MIDNIGHT RIDE."
"BREECHES OF PROMISE."

OKAY, NOW PUT IT ALL TOGETHER: SEX, COMEDY, GUEST STARS. WE GET JACLYN OUT ON THE RARITAN, GAVIN MACLEOD AS GEORGE, ERIN MORAN AS MOLLY PITCHER WITH THE HOTS FOR BEN FRANKLIN. WE'LL TELL THE CHIEF TO SELL IT AS—"CROSSING THE DELAWARE — A SPECIAL 8-HOUR LOVE BOAT."

(Courtesy Esquire Magazine.)

Attractive soap stars such as Emma Samms and Tristen Rogers have helped to broaden the appeal of "General Hospital." (Photo: American Broadcasting Companies, Inc.)

Network and local news also took on an enlarged and more important role. Network news on television began in 1948 with a 15-minute program on CBS, "Douglas Edwards with the News." This program length remained the standard until 1963 when all three networks expanded to a half-hour newscast. Along with the increase in time, news grew in prestige and as a source of revenue. Soon a star system developed in network news, led by the anchors for the network news evening program. Walter Cronkite of CBS became the dominant broadcast journalist of the 1970s and along with David Brinkley, John Chancellor, Dan Rather, and a host of others, became a network star.

On the local level the commercial success of news programs led to a show-business style aptly dubbed "happy talk." News became choreographed and packaged much like any other entertainment programs, much to the chagrin of critics and journalists.

Television today is faced with coming to grips with its past and confronting new technologies that threaten the basic structure of the industry. James Rosenfield of CBS made this position very clear when he stated that television was facing its fourth major trial, the "trial of technology." Indicating that television had survived three previous trials—acceptance as a medium, cultural integration, and maturity—he expressed deep concern over what he called "unregulated competitors" for the TV audience.

The major changes in television in the 1980s have not been in programming but in the manner in which programming is distributed to and

CBS News Correspondent Dan Rather (right) with Walter Cronkite (left), now a Special Correspondent for CBS News, converse at the Democratic National Convention in San Francisco in 1984.

(Courtesy CBS News.)

received by the American public. The technological developments of the 1960s and 1970s have spawned a new era in program delivery systems involving satellites, cable television, and video cassette and videodisc players.

SATELLITES

When the Communications Satellite Act was passed in 1962, the United States officially got into international television. The act provided for the vate corporation that came into existence on 1 February 1963. COMSAT actually operates an international satellite system in behalf of a consortium of countries called International Telecommunications Satellite Organization (INTELSAT). The first satellites, *Telstar* and *Relay*, went up in 1963 and provided intercontinental coverage of the funerals of Pope John XXIII and President Kennedy among other events. In 1965 the first commercial satellite, *Early Bird*, was launched by COMSAT. By 1969 satellite usage had increased, much of it for Vietnam war coverage via *Lanai Bird*, the Pacific counterpart of *Early Bird*. By 1971 a full-scale international communication system existed, with three synchronous satellites in fixed positions over the Atlantic, Pacific, and Indian oceans as well as a large network of earth stations.

Recent developments have focused on domestic satellites. The United States entered the field in 1973 with RCA leasing transmission time on Canada's *ANIK II* to relay signals between the two coasts. In 1974 ABC Radio began transmitting service to its four radio networks via satellite.

As network distribution costs via AT&T long lines increased steadily in the 1970s, the use of domestic satellites increased as well. In 1976 KPLR-TV in St. Louis was granted an FCC license for a satellite earth receiver, and other stations soon followed suit. In 1977 the Public Broadcasting System began construction of a satellite interconnect system that eventually would provide direct satellite-to-earth-station distribution for all PBS television and NPR radio stations. By the early 1980s satellite distribution of programming was being used by a wide variety of networks, production companies, and even local stations. Ted Turner's station WTBS-TV in Atlanta, Georgia, began to distribute its local programming to cable systems by satellite in 1979. By the early 1980s, Turner had developed CNN (Cable News Network), a news service sent to cable systems across the country, opening the way for a wide variety of special networks that fed programs to cable systems.

The key to satellite distribution of programming is not simply the satellite itself but two other elements, a transmission station on the ground known as an "uplink" and a receiving dish or "downlink." The uplink sends a signal up to the satellite which amplifies and retransmits the signal to the downlink, which in turn feeds a cable system, a local station or in the case of DBS, direct satellite to home. As earth stations become tech-

The satellite earth station at Raisting, Upper Bavaria, is the largest in the world. Pictured here is one of its five antenna systems. (Photo courtesy Siemens AG Communications.)

nically, economically, and legally easier to construct, the possibilities of direct satellite to home distribution become more obvious allowing DBS to bypass the station or cable delivery system.

These developments are causing concern, however. Satellites compete directly with AT&T's ground networks and, in the case of direct transmission to individual receivers, with local stations The economic consequences of direct satellite-to-home transmission (DBS), especially, are great. Nevertheless, the potential for expanded program service at a reduced cost makes the risk worthwhile. Early in 1981 COMSAT filed for permission with the FCC to provide a DBS (direct broadcast satellite) program service. Other corporations soon followed suit, and the potential of DBS service is fast becoming reality.

CABLE TELEVISION

Cable television, CATV (Community Antenna Television), has made even more dramatic strides. In 1960 there were only 640 operating systems in the United States with a total of 650,000 subscribers. By 1970 cable had grown to almost 2500 systems and 1.3 million subscribers. In 1983 over 5700 systems were serving over 33 million TV households with predictions of 50 million homes by 1992.

What began in the late 1940s as simply a master receiving antenna for isolated communities has grown to the point where it clearly poses an economic threat to local broadcasters. Cable television is a major programming force in today's TV environment. It no longer exists simply to serve rural areas or even to bring a local–regional station's signal into individual homes. Cable has developed a programming life of its own by augmenting its local station service with distant signal importation, such as Atlanta's WTBS-TV, local origination programs, and special services such as Home Box Office (HBO). With FCC deregulation of cable in the early 1980s, cable is now free to compete in the open marketplace for audiences and advertising dollars. Growth in cable penetration and programming is occurring at a phenomenal rate.

Major cities, among them Dallas, New Orleans, Cincinnati, Pittsburgh, and Boston, are being wired and added to the cable universe. This expansion is adding subscribers to the industry roll at a rate of 250,000 subscribers per month.

Cable operators are building supersystems in the new markets. Many will offer 50 channels, and some more than 100, although about 30 channels seems to be the maximum at present. And nearly all the big urban systems are being built with interactive capability, permitting the subscriber to send signals back to the cable headend. This capability opens up a host of new service and revenue possibilities.

The cable operators are also upgrading existing cable systems, expanding channel capacity to 20 or more channels to increase services and revenues and make the systems less vulnerable to competition.

The widespread introduction of satellite-delivered pay television revolutionized the industry in the latter half of the 1970s, providing an enormous leap in revenues without significant additional capital investments. Multipay, the selling of two or more pay services to the same home, has proved viable and is counted on to fuel the construction and operation of the high-capacity urban systems. Pay-per-view pay television (PPV) and advertising are seen as the most immediate sources of additional revenues.

Tulsa Cable

Channel	Programming services
1	Not available
2	KJRH: Tulsa NBC affiliate
3	KTVT: Ft. Worth independent/WFAA: Dallas ABC (after midnight)
4	KSHB: Kansas City independent
5	Movie Five (cable operator's own movie channel—not pay)
6	KOTV: Tulsa CBS affiliate
7	KXTX: Dallas/WOR New York (after midnight)
8	KTUL: Tulsa ABC affiliate
9	USA Cable Network
	Tulsa Cable Sports: live, local events
10	SPN: Satellite program network
11	PBS: Public broadcasting service
12	The weather channel
13	Program guide (listing)
14[a]	HBO: Home Box Office
15[a]	Cinemax
16[a]	Escapade/The Playboy Channel
17	WTBS: Atlanta independent
18	CNN: Cable News Network
19	CNN2: News updates every half-hour
20	Nickelodeon (children) and ARTS (cultural)
21	WGN: Chicago independent
22	Religious channel
23	KOKI: Tulsa independent
24	Education channel: college credit and noncredit courses
25	ESPN: Entertainment Sports Programming Network
26	MTV: Music Television
27	Education channel: public schools
28	Education channel: public schools
29	Sports information
30	CBS Cable: cultural
31	Classified advertising
32	KGCT: Tulsa independent
33	MSN: Modern Satellite Network
34	Stock quotes
35	Not programmed yet
36	Not programmed yet

[a] Premium pay channels.

And the so-called two-way services—videotext, security, teleshopping, telebanking—promise new revenues for the latter half of the decade.

Cable has become the medium of choice. Operators (and, ultimately, subscribers) have a panoply of programming to choose from, all delivered conveniently to their backyards by satellites. A survey by *Broadcasting* magazine in 1982 found no fewer than 47 program services—35 basic and 12 pay—with 15 others in the wings. The table from the Tulsa market, provides graphic evidence of this diversity.

Many factors cloud the future of cable, however, the most important being financial. While cable's rapid expansion into a $5 billion industry has secured a foothold in TV's future, the growth has strained resources on every level. Advertising revenue is coming in more slowly than expected as advertising agencies are experimenting with cable instead of investing in it. Production costs of original cable programming have risen, and local cable operators are squeezed between programmers demanding higher prices for their product and subscribers demanding more service for the same fee. Most of the problems have originated with cable's high hopes for itself. To support the promise of something for everybody many companies promoted market projections to unrealistic levels. They estimated and developed revenue levels on the basis of 60–70% penetration when 45% was more realistic.

It seems clear that cable will succeed only to the extent that it provides a strong alternative to existing programming. If cable chooses to utilize its potential for minority-interest programming, two-way transmission, multi-channel programming, and "custom tailored" programming, it will not only survive but prosper. If it chooses merely to relay existing signals, performing the role of conduit, it will most likely fail. The "shakeout" period is now cable's reality. As one industry spokesperson said: "Tough climbs like this are a healthy sign. They remind us we are a growing industry."

PAY TV   With the tremendous growth in cable television, the potential for pay TV–cable increased greatly. Pay TV has been around since the early 1950s, but most systems lost money and quickly folded. The FCC finally instituted rules in 1970 permitting pay TV over the air or by cable.

In 1975 RCA's *SATCOM I* satellite was sent into space, enabling HBO and, later, two smaller rivals, Showtime and the Movie Channel, to transmit movies to local cable systems. Since then, the living room has rapidly been supplementing the theater as an arena for watching motion pictures, and the amount of money collected from home viewers has soared. The fees paid by subscribers for a monthly diet of movies increased tenfold in the last 5 years, to an expected take in 1983 of almost $2.4 billion, versus $3.5 billion at the conventional theater box office.

The rental of these films to HBO and other pay-cable services brings in more than $500 million a year to the film companies, and this source of income has been growing recently at a rate more than 20 times faster than box-office ticket sales. Some movie executives believe that, in less than 3 years, pay-TV revenues for them will be larger than the $1.3 billion or so they took in in 1983 for renting films to theaters.

Programming on pay cable typically includes first-run motion pictures and sporting events. A greater variety is emerging, however, including X- and R-rated films on "adult cable" and cultural programming provided primarily by the BBC over cable rather than its traditional U.S. outlet, the PBS stations. Prices for pay TV vary according to the system, but most subscribers pay $10–15 a month for Home Box Office programming or similar services.

Over-the-air pay TV, or subscription television (STV), has also grown in the last 5 years, although at a much slower rate than pay cable. As a result of FCC deregulation in 1977, STV finally got off the ground with two stations in Los Angeles and New York. By the early 1980s more than 25 stations were operating, all of them in large urban areas. Programming on STV is similar to cable, but because it can offer only one channel to a subscriber (versus the tiered service possibilities of cable), many feel its future is limited to noncable areas. Indeed, by mid-1983 STV subscribership had slipped from a high of 1.4 million to 1.1 million. The Entertainment Channel, a pay-TV network created by RCA folded in 1983 after only 9 months of operation with over $80 million in losses. The problems of STV merely underscore the challenges facing other pay-TV delivery systems such as multipoint distribution services (MDS) and direct satellite to home reception (DBS). The formula for success in pay television is no longer simply offering people the latest *Star Wars* or *Indiana Jones* blockbuster. Instead "made for pay" series and sporting events are being bought on an exclusive basis by the pay networks. Further development of pay television includes pay-per-view television. A few programs have been marketed with mixed to negative results. However, as more cable systems develop the ability to turn individual channels on and off the pay-per-view audience may grow into a legitimate profit center.

LOW-POWER TELEVISION

Low-power TV is a new kind of television station, licensed to broadcast over a geographic area between 10 and 15 miles in radius. A full-power station covers about 80 miles. Low-power stations are inserted on the VHF and UHF spectra, but emit signals so weak that they do not interfere with full-power stations on the same channels in nearby cities. Before low power, for instance, Stillwater, Minnesota, couldn't use Channel 5, which is allocated to St. Paul. Now a broadcaster in Stillwater can send out a low-power signal over Channel 5 without impinging on the larger station's signal.

Low-power stations are modeled on the "translator" or repeater stations used for some time in rural areas to pick up and rebroadcast remote signals. Translator operators were forbidden to originate their own material until 1981, when the FCC lifted the restriction.

The nation's first LPTV station was Channel 26 in Bemidji, Minnesota and despite some early promise growth has been slow. The primary problem is financial. To survive in the localized form for which it was intended, LPTV stations have to carry a high volume of ads. Advertisers, even, in small communities, want the most and best audience for their dollar and so the pressure is on most LPTV stations to supply popular off-network and/or syndicated programming. This ultimately defeats the intent of LPTV and the future of the medium may ultimately be with large corporations, such as Park communications, which have applied for large numbers of LPTV licenses, who have the financial resources to acquire programming and stay in the market over the long haul.

TELETEXT AND VIDEOTEXT

Teletext and videotext are the two newest stars on the horizon. By linking the power of the computer to the television set they have the ability to transform an entertainment medium into an information age appliance.

Videotext uses a telephone line, or two-way cable, to connect the TV set to a central computer, and thus is interactive. A popular and simplified version of on-line computer time-sharing, videotext allows thousands of individuals to communicate with a single computer in order to retrieve information or conduct transactions. For a monthly subscription fee plus telephone charges, the videotext subscriber uses a small keyboard to bank, shop, play games, do research, and conduct a variety of other transactions.

Teletext is a one-way technology that delivers textual and graphic information to TV sets as part of the standard broadcast signal. Digital data are "inserted" into a few lines of the TV picture called the "vertical blanking interval."

The information is presented on "pages," which the viewer can call up on his screen by punching a number on a decoder. Most teletext "magazines" contain about 100 pages of information, typically including news headlines, weather reports, sports scores, videogames, and stock prices. Teletext is generally supported by advertising and is free to anyone who buys a decoder. Thus teletext promises to be more widely available than videotext, even though it can't do as much.

By the end of 1983 both NBC and CBS as well as Time Inc. had developed videotext services. However, technical standards in the form of competing system incompatability remain a problem and for the near future growth will be slow and carefully measured.

The late 1970s witnessed a tremendous surge in new forms of video technology, including home video cassette or videodisc record systems, video games, and the possibility of new uses of the TV screen with home computers and multiband cable systems.

The 1980s have carried this surge to the point of a new media revolution, a revolution of technology centered on delivery and distribution. While cable television and satellites have been steadily encroaching on the traditional network long-line distribution structure, their progress has been measured and in many instances encouraged by the networks. The revolution involving video cassettes, videodiscs, and home computers promises to be neither measured nor encouraged by the networks.

Home video recording dates back to the 1960s, but it was not until 1972 that Sony produced the first video cassette machine for business and education. In 1975 Sony brought out the Betamax for home use; the market expanded in 1977 with the introduction of a different and technically incompatible VHS system. Today, VHS sales are double Beta sales. VCR unit sales increased 250% to 2 million in 1982, and sales in both 1983 and 84 exceeded 4 million units, bringing VCR penetration to at least 12 million or 12% of American homes.

The VCR boom is being fed by lower prices and added features that increase the versatility of the basic machines. Many models now feature two week advance programming, remote control and "scanning" which gives the viewer the ability to "fast forward" the picture to avoid commercials. New developments permit "zapping," the elimination of the commercial altogether. Also fueling this expansion is the growth of the "software" or programming. Surveys indicate that over 80% of VCR owners buy or rent prerecorded programs, mostly movies. An estimated 10 million prerecorded video cassettes were sold in 1984 and for every sale there are approximately 10 rentals bringing the total to 100 million.

The Sony Betamax, introduced in 1975, was the first video cassette recorder available for home use. (Courtesy Sony Corporation of America.)

The videodisc, once thought of as the shining star of the video revolution, has been essentially the story of great promise unfulfilled. After four years of "hard sell" RCA pulled out of the field in 1984 leaving the laser system developed by Pioneer and North American Philips with the market to itself. The laser system has primarily seen industrial use and the home potential of the video disc remains unfulfilled.

The videodisc may, however, ultimately play the lead role in the video revolution, after all. Essentially the disc can turn a TV set into an interactive instrument with multiple uses. The key to the videodisc's role in shaping the future of television lies not so much in simply providing an alternative means of distributing a series such as "Dallas" or the movie *Superman III* but in the videodisc's power and potential as an information-processing and storage medium. When linked with a home computer, the videodisc can perform myriad functions ranging from interactive teaching lessons to providing vicarious travel in which an individual can travel in a foreign country through programmed response patterns.

The immediate future of videodiscs rests with the concept of "video publishing" in which videodisc programs are marketed much like books or records. Corporations like RCA with its SelectaVision disc system are releasing catalogues of movies and selected TV series for home consumption. The networks themselves are also bidding to program this market.

All of these new technologies have ultimately had their impact on the home receiver. Now being described as a "home video terminal" the set of tomorrow here today has incorporated special input and output jacks for video devices, higher resolution tubes and circuitry to accommodate computers and teletext and built-in tuners that substitute for the cable-TV converter box. In addition such features as stereo amplifiers and speakers, remote control and giant screen size have spurred record sales of color television receivers—over 14 million in 1984.

The last 20 years have been witness to the most intense and dynamic media–society relationship in history. Television was said to have created a "new" politics, a "new" generation, and a "new" society. In turn, events of the time forced television to mature, to expand its role beyond that of entertainer and become a positive force in society. Some say television has not matured enough. That is probably true. But television is young as a national medium. The 1950s saw its childhood, the 1960s its stormy adolescence, and the 1970s its slow maturity. In the 1980s the medium seems headed toward adulthood, but with that status comes the possibility of radical changes in TV structure and content.

PUBLIC BROADCASTING SERVICE (PBS)

After languishing for over a decade, educational television (ETV) began to flex its muscles in the 1960s with the passage of federal funding legislation in 1962. The pivotal event in ETV's growth was the Public Broadcasting Act of 1967, which ranks with the 1952 Sixth Order and Report as one of the most important events in educational television. In effect, the 1967 act provided for the first interconnected network of ETV stations. Most important, it provided educational television with the long-needed financial support necessary for it to become a creative force in American life. Without the 1967 act, many ETV stations would never have been built or modernized.

The act established the Corporation for Public Broadcasting, which in turn established the Public Broadcasting Service (PBS) in 1970. After a lengthy and damaging struggle between CPB and PBS for control of the systems, PBS emerged in 1973 as the voice of the system with CPB continuing its role as program funder. PBS manages TV programming, production, distribution, and station interconnection, which is primarily by satellite. The most important single programming development during the early years of the PBS system was the creation of the Children's Television Workshop (CTV), producers of "Sesame Street" and "Electric Company," among other programs. An independent nonprofit corporation, CTV's only ties to public broadcasting are partial funding by CPB. Another important programming source is the British Broadcasting Corporation, which has supplied such series as "Civilisation," "The Forsythe Saga," and "Upstairs, Downstairs." In 1980, however, the BBC entered into a 10-year agreement to sell its programming in the United States to a cable network, threatening one of PBS's best courses of prestige programming.

Financing is at the heart of public broadcasting's present role and future potential. Throughout the Nixon administration, there was controversy resulting primarily from CPB's increasing development of public affairs programming, including several controversial programs and series. New legislation under President Ford provided for a federal matching plan and 5-year financing. This $634 million bill became law in 1976 and assured public broadcasting of a relatively stable financial base for the first time

Where PBS Funding Comes From

Programming budget for 1982: $135.9 million

Source of revenue
  Business: $38.6 million (28.5%)
  Public television stations: $33.6 million (25%)
  Corporation for Public Broadcasting: $20 million (14.5%)
  Other federal agencies (National Endowment for the Arts, National Endowment for the Humanities, National Science Foundation, Office of Education): $16.8 million (12%)
  Independent producers and independent production companies: $15.1 million (11%)
  Educational institutions, associations, state and local governments, individuals: $6.5 million (5%)
  Foundations: $5.3 million (4%)

SOURCE: Public Broadcasting Service.

in its history. However, the Reagan administration's proposed cuts have clouded the future of public television, and PBS is seeking new sources of revenue.

Funding, of course, is at the heart of the survival of the system. As the preceding table indicates, a funding shift has occurred in recent years with private business rather than the federal government the major source of funds. Second on the list are the local stations, which raise money through program underwriting, membership drives, auctions, and other promotions. Many stations are pushing membership drives and local fund-raising efforts to the saturation point and as a result are beginning to explore other means of obtaining operating revenue including limited sale of time and programs.

THE SCOPE OF TELEVISION

Despite the continuing avalanche of criticism about television, TV viewing, TV households, and prime-time TV network audiences reached new record levels in 1983.

Television viewing in August 1983 averaged 6 hours 55 minutes per TV home per day, an increase of 7 minutes over 1982 and a jump of 85 minutes over the 1965–1966 average. This represents the highest use ever. The graph below shows this growth in television use and breaks the total use figure into February and July totals (traditionally the highest and lowest viewing months, respectively). Both months had significant increases in TV usage.

As the next graph indicates, prime-time on Sunday nights attracts the

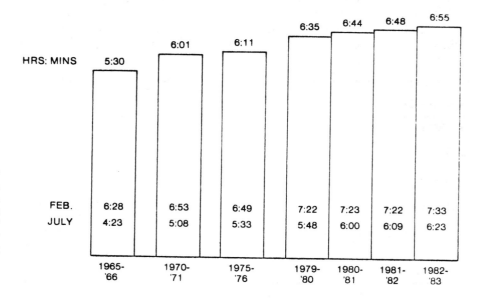

Average Hours of Household TV Usage per Day, 1965–1966 to 1982–1983. From Nielson estimates based on total U.S. TV households, September through August; 48-week average excluding unusual days.

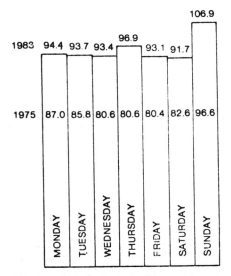

1983 94.4 93.7 93.4 96.9 93.1 91.7 106.9

1975 87.0 85.8 80.6 80.6 80.4 82.6 96.6

MONDAY · TUESDAY · WEDNESDAY · THURSDAY · FRIDAY · SATURDAY · SUNDAY

Television Viewing by Night of the Week. (November. Total persons aged two and over.) Based on 8 p.m. to 11 p.m. eastern time, except 7 p.m. to 11 p.m. Sunday.

BY HALF HOUR
% SHARE-NOVEMBER 1983

	WOMEN			MEN			TEENS 12-17	CHILDREN		TOTAL PERSONS 2+ (MILLIONS)
	18-34	35-54	55+	18-34	35-54	55+		2-5	6-11	
8-8:30 PM	14	12	16	13	11	11	9	9	5	101.8
8:30-9 PM	14	12	16	13	11	11	9	9	5	104.8
9-9:30 PM	15	14	16	14	12	11	9	6	3	101.1
9:30-10 PM	16	15	16	15	12	11	8	5	3	98.7
10-10:30 PM	16	16	16	15	13	11	7	3	2	87.7
10:30-11 PM	17	16	17	16	13	11	7	3	1	80.8

Persons Viewing Prime Time Television by Half Hour. (Percentage share for November 1983.)

largest audience. Thursday night has moved into second place displacing Monday night, and Saturday night continues to receive the least attention.

Television viewing increases through the day, hitting a peak between 8 and 10 p.m. The 8:30 to 9:00 p.m. half hour is the most viewed time, and women account for the greatest share of viewing during prime time.

In terms of total viewing, women 55 years and older do the most TV viewing—41 hours and 13 minutes a week in November. That's 10 hours, 34 minutes more than average. Female teens watch the least—24 hours, 16 minutes a week. Children 6 to 11 were next to last, an average 24 hours, 50 minutes a week. TV households viewed an average of 52½ hours of television per week during November 1983. As the chart below indicates, however, household characteristics affected that average with the highest use in households of three or more people. Also, pay cable households view significantly more television, as do houses with children. Viewing by income level was basically similar in pattern, with lower-income households generally viewing more television.

The number of TV households is also increasing every year. The accompanying chart shows that in January of 1984, there were 83.8 million homes with at least one set. This represents 98% of all U.S. homes. Of these, 90% had color sets and 55% had two or more sets.

These households exist in virtually every area of the country, but it is the top five markets which are considered most important as they con-

---

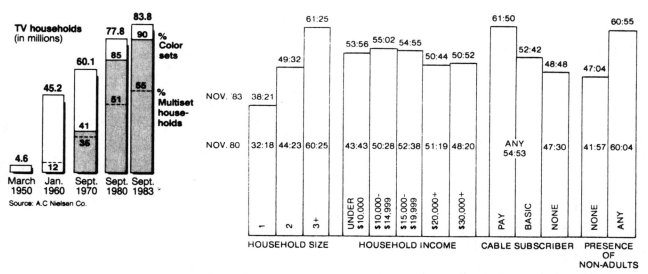

Hours of TV Usage per Week by Household Characteristics. Based on 24-hour viewing days, Monday through Sunday.) (Source: Nielson estimates: National Audience Demographics Report.)

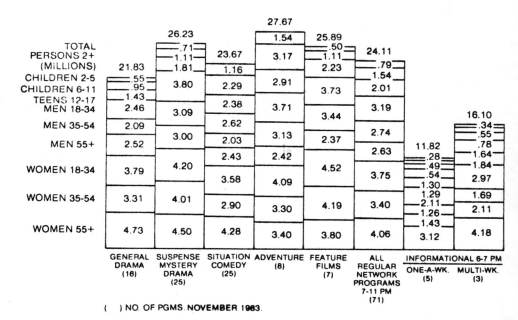

Audience Composition by Selected Program Type. Regularly scheduled programs, 6 p.m. to 11 p.m. Average minute audiences.

Top ADI Markets, 1984–1985

Market (ADI)	Percentage of U.S. TV households
1. New York	7.72
2. Los Angeles	5.13
3. Chicago	3.55
4. Philadelphia	2.97
5. San Francisco	2.42
6. Boston	2.28
7. Detroit	1.94
8. Dallas-Forth Worth	1.77
9. Washington, D.C.	1.75
10. Houston	1.69
11. Cleveland	1.64
12. Pittsburgh	1.44
13. Minneapolis-St. Paul	1.36
14. Miami	1.36
15. Atlanta	1.34

Source: Arbitron Ratings Co.

stitute almost 22% of all TV households. The table below breaks down the top 15 markets.

Adventure programming, which was last in 1982, attracted the largest prime-time network audience in November 1983. Feature films, first in 1982, slipped to third, while suspense/mystery drama remained in second. The following table breaks down the major program types by total persons and various audience categories.

The number of TV stations, although limited by spectrum space and frequency allocation continues to grow. Both VHF and UHF stations increased dramatically in 1984, primarily due to LPTV (low power television) regulations.

Television continues to prosper financially. As reported by the National Association of Broadcasters and illustrated in the table below, the typical U.S. TV station had a pretax profit of $1,253,100 in 1982, up 24.7% from $1,004,900 in 1981. That derived from total 1982 net revenues of $5,377,800 (up 6.1%) and total expenses of $4,124,700. Total time sales for the typical TV stations were $6,299,300, composed of $497,600 in network compensation, $2,965,900 in national and regional advertising, and $2,835,800 in local advertising. The 1982 pretax profit was the best since 1978, largely because the expense increase was held to 3% over 1981 ($4 million).

The 1982 expense figure included $1,573,900 as the payroll at a median station with 78 full-time employees and 7 part-time workers. The salary dollar was apportioned as follows: news, 25.8 cents; sales, 21.0 cents;

TV Stations on the Air

	VHF	UHF
1973	510	187
1974	513	184
1975	514	192
1976	511	190
1977	515	196
1978	515	201
1979	515	209
1980	516	218
1981	519	237
1982	517	260
1983	519	294
1984	539	357

Source: Television & Cable Factbook 1982–1983 Edition, Television Digest, 1983, Washington, D.C.

Typical 1982 TV Station Revenues and Expenses, All Stations

Revenue and Expense Items	Typical Dollar Figures ($)	Typical Percent Figures (%)	Revenue and Expense Items	Typical Dollar Figures ($)	Typical Percent Figures (%)
Total Time Sales	**6,299,300**	**100.0**	SALARIES;		
			Engineering	271,200	17.2
Network compensation	497,600	7.9	Program and production	309,000	19.6
National and regional advertisers	2,965,900	47.1	News	406,300	25.8
Local advertisers	2,835,800	45.0	Sales	330,800	21.0
			Advertising and promotion	47,900	3.0
			General and administrative	208,700	13.3
Total Net Revenues	**5,377,800**		Total Salaries	1,573,900	100.0
Political advertising revenue	158,300				
Revenues other than time sales	107,000		Total cost of broadcast rights	336,700	
Trade-outs and barter	121,500		Music license fees	83,500	
			Rating services	71,200	
			Travel and entertainment	66,000	
EXPENSES			Depreciation & amortization	434,400	
Engineering	461,900	11.2	Interest	4,000	
Program and production	1,051,300	25.5	Utility costs	96,100	
News	543,200	13.2	Bad debt expense	34,700	
Sales	515,400	12.5	Legal & auditing fees	22,400	
Advertising and promotion	182,600	4.4	Corporate allocation charges	71,200	
General and administrative	1,370,100	33.2	Employee fringe benefit costs	188,400	
			Station insurance costs	32,800	
Total Expenses	**4,124,500**	**100.0**			
			Pretax Profit	1,253,100	
			Profit Margin		23.30%

programming and production, 19.6 cents; general and administrative, 13.3 cents, and advertising and promotion, 3.0 cents.

Cable television continues to grow at a rapid pace. As of 1983, there were 5800 operating cable systems in the United States, serving some 15,665 communities. Another 1939 franchises are approved but have not been built. Pennsylvania has the most systems (351) and California the most subscribers (2.6 million). Operating systems currently reach about 34.1 million subscribers, perhaps over 95 million people—44% of the nation's TV households. The largest (Cox Cable in San Diego) has about 225,000 subscribers. Tele-Communications, Inc. is the largest multiple system operator (MSO), with more than 2.2 million subscribers. Industry revenues in 1982 totaled approximately $2.8 billion. The average monthly fee (basic service) is $7.94. An estimated 3250 systems originate programming in their own studios, the average for 23 hours weekly. Over 700 systems (14% of all systems) accept advertising on their local origination channels (excluding automated channels), with rates from $2 to $400 per

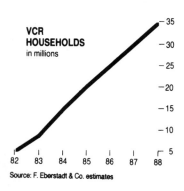

VCR
HOUSEHOLDS
in millions

Source: F. Eberstadt & Co. estimates

Service	Systems	Subscribers (Dec. 1983)	Subscribers (May 1982)	Per cent change
HBO	5,200	13,500,000	8,500,000	59%
Showtime	2,900	4,750,000	3,000,000	58%
Cinemax	2,000	2,700,000	1,500,000	87%
Movie Channel	2,700	2,600,000	2,200,000	19%
Playboy	320	577,000		—
Disney	1,136	531,000		—
HTN Plus	400	250,000	155,000	61%
Bravo	101	155,000		—
Galavision/SIN	160	120,000	100,000	20%
Spotlight	237	750,000	300,000	117%

30-second spot. Most cable systems derive less than 5% of their gross revenues from advertising.

Pay cable is on approximately 4800 systems and reaches 15 million subscribers in 50 states. Most pay cable operators are reporting close to 44% penetration of their subscriber count. As the table below shows, HBO is by far the largest pay network, with over 13 million subscribers at the end of 1983.

A final statistical note on the scope of television which will clearly impact on the medium's future is revealed in the accompanying graph. Video revolutions are proclaimed so often that the figures in the graph may seem like another false alarm. However, more than 10 million U.S. homes have at least one VCR and that figure is rising fast.

As the previous data show, television from other leisure time activities continues to grow and prosper, despite criticism and competition. However, the pattern of growth is changing as new technology continues to have an impact.

THE STRUCTURE AND ORGANIZATION OF TELEVISION

Television's basic function is programming, and the ways in which programs are produced, distributed, and exhibited are the basis for the organization of the TV industry.

Program production is the responsibility of networks, stations, and program production companies. Distribution is the critical function of the networks using the ground facilities of the American Telephone and Telegraph Company (AT&T) and satellite transmission. The exhibition of programs is the primary role of local stations. The structure of television in the United States can be analyzed best by discussing the two critical participants in programming: the networks and local stations.

The Networks

At the present time the primary forces in commercial television programming are three national networks: the American Broadcasting Company (ABC), the Columbia Broadcasting System (CBS), and the National Broadcasting Company (NBC). These three commercial networks generate over 40% of commercial TV's total income.

The networks are organized much like stations into four main areas: programming, sales, engineering, and administration. Within each of these major divisions are many units, such as news and sports, each with a separate administrative structure. At CBS, for example, the CBS/Broadcast Group has six major divisions: CBS Radio, CBS Television Stations, CBS News, CBS Television Network, CBS Entertainment, and CBS Sports. Under the CBS Radio Division there are 15 discrete units, among them Engineering, Program Practices, Research, and Network Sales.

Networks exist only to the extent that they provide a service to stations through an affiliation contract. This contract sets the terms by which the network pays the station for the right to use the station's time to program its offerings. Stations, in effect, *clear* time from their own schedules and sell it to the networks for a price based on the individual station's local rate for an hour of its time. Rates range from $10,000 an hour at the network-owned stations in New York City to under $100 at stations in small markets.

The key function of the TV networks is to provide their affiliated stations with programming that will be viewed by a large aggregate audience. The network makes its money by selling this aggregate audience (measured by ratings) to advertisers. Without successful programs the networks would not survive. Like local stations, the networks get most of their programming from outside production organizations. Approximately 90% of the networks' prime-time schedule is produced cooperatively with these program production agencies. For an annual program season, more than 30 separate production companies prepare programs for the networks, which spend in excess of a billion dollars a year for the right to broadcast the programs.

The networks currently provide about 65% of all programming hours broadcast by their affiliates during the four blocks of time that make up the TV week. The rest is filled by the local stations with local or syndicated programs.

The most important time period in television is called *prime time* (8:00–11:00 P.M. EST) and is dominated by the three networks. By FCC regulation the networks may provide up to 3 hours of programming per night. During these hours the most expensive and elaborate programs are aired and the TV audience is the largest.

The dominant forms of prime-time network programming today are action–adventure series, situation comedies, and movies. Specials and miniseries are also prominent as the networks continue to experiment with program stunting and other strategies to win the audience rating race. The only "live" programming—transmitted at the time of the event—are various sports events such as ABC's "NFL Monday Night Football" and certain news programs. All other programs are either filmed or video-taped. The one innovation in the last 10 years has been to tape programs before a live audience to try and achieve a certain degree of spontaneity. Programs such as "Cheers" and "Three's a Crowd" utilize this process. All programs are telecast in color.

The second most important time for television networks is *weekday daytime* (7:00 A.M.–5:00 P.M.). This time is taken up with quiz and game shows, news shows like NBC's "Today" or ABC's "Good Morning America," reruns of networks series, and soap operas. Programming philosophy assumes that audiences are composed primarily of women and children. At one time treated lightly by the networks, daytime programming has become increasingly important to network success because of the relatively low production costs of the shows and the rather constant audience.

Weekend daytime (7:00 A.M.–5:00 P.M. Saturday and Sunday) has also taken on greater importance for the networks in recent years as the audience for children's programming and sports has increased in size and purchasing power. Even Sunday morning, the traditional "dead zone" of broadcasting, is now programmed heavily with network news and public affairs as well as syndicated religious programming.

Fringe time (5:00–8:00 P.M. and 11:00 P.M.—1:00 A.M.) is the fourth time period for TV programming and consists primarily of network and local news, syndicated programs, talk shows, and movies. As the demand for TV time by advertisers has increased, fringe time has become more important to the networks. ABC began programming nightly news updates during the Iranian hostage crisis in 1980 and subsequently developed its popular late-night network news program "Nightline." The contract negotiations and manipulations involving Johnny Carson and his late-night talk show also demonstrated the value of the late-evening audience.

Besides exercising production control, the networks also assume economic responsibility for distributing programs, using the coaxial cable and microwave facilities of AT&T, and the satellites. This cost alone amounts to over $75 million a year.

Each network owns VHF (very high frequency) stations in major metropolitan areas. These network-owned-and-operated stations (O&Os), along with the other 700 affiliates, provide for the exhibition of network TV programs. The dominance of the networks in programming is further strengthened by the fact that successful network series often turn up in syndication programming carried by the local stations.

In addition to the national networks, numerous regional and special-program networks such as CNN and ESPN offer programs for local broadcast and on cable systems. These networks service national, regional, and local advertisers and are becoming increasingly important in sports, religious programming, and news.

Stations

The local station is the key element in the total structure of broadcasting. The actual broadcasting or airing of programs is done by stations in each market. Although all stations are local, most are affiliated with one of the three networks. Stations enter into an affiliation contract with a network in which they agree to carry the network's programs in exchange for payment. No network payments are made for most sports, news, and late-night programs. In addition, a specific number of advertising slots in these programs, usually at station breaks, are left open for local sales.

The local network-affiliated station's schedule generally consists of 65% network shows, 25–30% syndicated programs, and 5–10% locally produced programs. The syndicated programs are dominated by feature-movie packages, old network series, game shows, and talk shows. Locally produced programming consists primarily of the six o'clock and eleven o'clock news, noontime and morning talk shows, plus a local children's series such as "Romper Room."

The local stations's role, then, is primarily as an exhibitor of programs created by someone else. Administrative personnel of a station seldom preview the episodes of a series before they are aired, and, in effect, stations have little control over much of the programming they telecast. Despite this fact, the station assumes responsibility for the content of all programs it broadcasts and is held legally accountable for all content broadcast.

No two TV stations are exactly alike, but certain basic functions are common to most commercial stations. In a typical TV station there are four primary activities: programming, sales, engineering, and management. The organization of a noncommercial station is the same except for the absence of a sales operation. A general manager performs the overall supervisory function for a station, but no one category is most important. Programming incorporates the greatest diversity of any of the units because it includes on-air personalities, writers, producers, directors, and editors, among others. The sales function in a large station is handled by a sales or advertising department with a sales manager and a number of

TV: Average Number of Employees

Full-time	Part-time	ARB marketsize ranking
90	8	1–10
103	7	11–25
88	6	26–50
70	3	51–75
55	5	76–100
42	5	101–125
37	6	126–150
30	4	150+
(60)	(5)	(Nationwide average)

SOURCE: *Broadcast Management*, 2d ed. (New York: Hastings House, 1976).

salespeople. In a small station one person may constitute a whole area or may handle programming in addition to sales. Engineering involves all personnel used in running cameras, slides, and film projectors, as well as those used to maintain technical engineering standards. The following table provides some data on local station employment.

Unlike radio, all TV stations are classified as local outlets. As local outlets, they can be typed according to several classifications: technical, market size, or network affiliation.

Technically, TV stations are grouped according to where their signal falls in the electromagnetic spectrum. The two bands into which all TV signals are placed are very high frequency (VHF) and ultra high frequency (UHF). Channels 2 to 13 are VHF. Channels 14 to 83 are UHF. This technical classification is very important because stations located in the VHF band reach a greater geographical area with less power and a clearer signal than stations in the UHF band. Thus, almost without exception, VHF stations are more powerful, better established, and more profitable than their UHF counterparts.

Another important classification of TV systems is market size, or the number of households a TV station reaches. In order to be consistent, advertisers use the Arbitron Area of Dominant Influence (ADI) to define market size. The ADI concept divides the country into 209 markets, each made up of the counties that cluster around the signal of a particular TV station. Generally there are three basic market-size groups: (a) major, the 100 largest ADIs in the country, (b) secondary, ADIs with populations ranging from 50,000 to 125,000; (c) small, ADIs with less than 50,000 population. Market size is vital in TV broadcasting. National advertisers buy time on stations according to market size; stations in major markets get most of the national advertising dollar, while the small-market station must depend heavily on local advertising.

The third important basis for TV station classification is whether the station is independent or network affiliated. Most TV stations want network affiliation because networks are capable of providing the more popular types of programs and therefore attracting a larger audience. About 85% of all U.S. commercial TV stations are network affiliated. A station is seldom independent unless it is in a market with four or more outlets and all three networks already have affiliates.

CHARACTERISTICS AND ROLES OF TELEVISION

Television today is huge, complex, costly, continuous, and competitive. It is a mass entertainer, mass informer, mass persuader, and mass educator.

Television is universal; more than 98% of America's homes have TV sets, and viewing television is the dominant leisure-time activity in our society, occupying 6.5 hours per day in the average household.

TV viewing is an in-home activity, and although multiset homes are increasing, TV usage is still a family or small-group activity rather than an individual or large-group experience. The content of the medium is dominated by national organizations that seek to provide general programming for massive, heterogeneous audiences, although special content for limited, homogeneous minorities is rapidly increasing.

The medium is the costliest of the electronic media because of the demand placed on it by the 18-hour daily schedule of most stations. Only television among the advertising media has sight, sound, motion, and color. This makes it the most dynamic sales tool available. This accounts for the fact that today it costs advertisers an average of $100,000 for 30 seconds to advertise on network prime-time television.

As we have pointed out, the primary role of the magazine is the custom tailoring of mass communication. Television's primary role is just the opposite. Television specializes in the mass distribution of mass communication. It is the channel through which stream mass-produced messages for the widest possible dissemination. With virtually the entire population having access to television 18 hours a day, 365 days a year, it is the mass medium for reaching most of the people most of the time. Because of this, television is perhaps the least flexible of the mass media. While it can and does provide instant coverage of many important national and international events, the majority of TV time is taken up with programs and schedules that have been put together a year or two in advance.

In a more critical sense, television has a number of primary social roles, two of which stand out: reflecting society and evaluating society. Aubrey Singer, a leading executive of the British Broadcasting Corporation, has stated that television's most common role as practiced today is that of "one of the many windows through which we observe, transmit, and reflect our valuation of society to each other. It has little to do with the initial creation of a spiritual trade wind. It is only a sort of air conditioner that processes and gets this wind into homes more quickly." Television has been criticized strongly for assuming this primarily passive role in society. Too often, TV critics say, television is simply a passive conduit, neutral to a fault and rarely engaging and challenging its audiences.

Television has another role, however, and on occasion plays it. Despite television's essentially passive nature, there are times when it does act in its own right; when, according once again to Singer, it uses its power of communication not merely to convey other people's images but to "create out of its own genuine statement." Many people feel that the TV coverage of the assassination and funeral of President Kennedy plus the coverage of the *Apollo 11* moon landing were times when television did create genuine statements, perhaps not so much out of its particular design or structure, but merely by being there to record the event as it was happening.

The future of television seems to rest in the ability of audiences to control and use it for their own purposes. The technological revolution will have a major impact on traditional broadcasting. *Broadcasting* as we have traditionally defined it may soon be replaced with narrowcasting in which producers will send out messages to small clusters of demographically linked groups, who in turn will manipulate and "massage" the content for their own purposes. The new technologies offer many opportunities for producers and consumers alike. Many industry people, however, fear that greed and failure to take risks will waste the expanded opportunities. Bob Klein, a communication consultant, said:

> If the new media offer merely more of the same we will pander rather than elucidate . . . we will downgrade rather than lift. We can be a promised land where the new technologies grow and offer a legacy . . . or we can, through greed, fail to grasp this incredible opportunity . . . leaving behind nothing."

The decision on how to program these new channels of communication should not be the choice of *Gilligan's Island*, *The Dukes of Hazzard* and 50% annual profit. It must be the choice of intellectual growth, quality, diversity and reasonable profit.

20 Sound Recording

"**H**ave you heard from rock 'n' roll lately? How's it doin'?'', she asked.

"Great! But you've got to *see* it to believe *in* it!" he said.

"But I can't find it on the radio," she said.

"Yeah, radio has died and gone to, Lennon forbid, AOR heaven," he crooned.

"Who'd have thought that old eight-track would spin out of chartland?'' she bluesed.

"Ain't it a shame? Elvis, where are you when I need you? I never thought rock would get old!" he bluesed.

"Hey, man, it's still happenin', *beatin'* it up down under, on the Continent, in reggaeland, and at the music clubs," she souled.

"New music can't get no satisfaction without a *radiomigration* card!" he wailed.

"Where you been, baby? The sound has moved. It's livin' with some new wave, preppie vee-jays over in cable TV," she rocked.

"IWANTMYMTV!"

"What was that?"

What was what?"

"IWANTMYMTV!"

"That!"

"Oh, that's just Saint Mick, England's oldest teen!"

"What's he want?"

"I WANT MY MTV!"

"Don't we all!" they videoed.

No mass medium has meant more to the youth revolution in America and around the world than the record business. No purchase has been more important, more time-consuming, and more costly than the ultimate in sound systems—except for a car. And that vehicle had better have a stereo cassette deck!

In 1977 the phonograph celebrated its centennial. In 1978 record and tape sales jumped 18% to a new high of $4.1 billion and in 1979 the bottom fell out.

HISTORICAL PERSPECTIVES

To say the least, the future of the music business is unsettled. Sales are still dropping. Radio has gotten extremely conservative. Home taping and pirating are estimated to cut total sales by 50%. Attendance at concerts is off, except for supergroups, such as the 1984 tour of The Jacksons. The music consumer has become a fickle, aging beast. The video game business is siphoning off teen consumers' spending power. Overhead and production costs are out of hand. The music goes round and round, but the lament of the industry is that business goes down and down. So, what's new! The sound recording industry has always been the most volatile and least predictable of the mass media.

The use of the term *recording* is generic and refers to a variety of sound-reproduction systems including cylinders, discs, records, reel-to-reel tapes, cartridges, cassettes, video music productions on Beta and VHS formats, as well as laser audiodiscs and videodiscs.[1] Like other electronic media, the phonograph requires machines to record and play back the content; unlike the others, consumers of sound recording have direct control over what they use. Individuals buy records and play them when and where they want. Recordings stop time in the sense that the event can be repeated because it is stored on records and tapes.

Definition of Terms

There are major periods in the history of the recording business:

Major Historical Periods

1. **1877–1923**, the period of discovery, experimentation, and exploitation

---

[1] Music productions on 1/2-inch videotape formats and videodisc are hybrids, combinations of video (single-camera "film" techniques) displays of essentially record-business content. It is sound recording with pictures. But the *sound* is key. At present, video music is a sales promotion element of the record business, but as all else in this business, things are changing.

2. **1924–1945**, the period of technical improvement, financial disaster, and consumer ambivalence

3. **1946–1963**, the period of technical rebirth, the death of network radio, and the birth of rock and roll and its audiences

4. **1964–1978**, the period of the rise and dominance of FM radio, big business's financial excesses, and cultural–musical involvement in sociopolitical action

5. **1979 to the present**, a period of space-age computer technology, the emergence of music video, and economic and cultural recession of America as the innovative force in rock music

1877–1923   The use of music in mass communication extends farther back in history than its adoption by the recording medium. Music was *published* long before it was *recorded*. Beginning with musical "broadsides" in the eighteenth century, which combined editorial comment with musical satire, published music soon developed a separate identity in the form of sheet music. During the Revolutionary War, continuing in the War of 1812, and reaching a peak during the Civil War, sheet music provided inspiration and the lifting of military morale for millions of mothers, wives, and soldiers. Sheet music is still published today, but the phonograph has replaced it as the dominant medium of communicating music, not only to young people, but to audiences of all ages

Two men working on different continents contributed to the birth of the phonograph. In April 1877 Charles Cros filed a paper with the French Academy of Science that described a system of sound reproduction, but the French physicist never produced a working model. In the United States, Thomas Edison and his machinist, John Kruesi, actually built a functional sound record-playback device in December 1877. This phonograph used a hand-cranked metal cylinder wrapped in tinfoil for recording purposes, but Edison applied for patents on a disk system as well as the cylinder. Having invented what he considered to be a dictating machine. Edison did little to exploit his invention. For the next decade, his phonograph was little more than a traveling sideshow, exhibiting the marvels of a "talking machine."

Chinchester Bell and Charles Sumner Tainter in 1881 began work on an improved version of Edison's phonograph using wax cylinders. They applied for a patent in 1885 for a gramophone that utilized wax-coated cardboard cylinders instead of tinfoil. By 1886, however, Edison had returned to work on a reusable solid-wax cylinder called the phonogram. Jesse H. Lippencott's purchase of the business rights to both the Edison and Bell-Tainter devices in 1888 brought an end to what was becoming a serious patent dispute. The dream of Lippencott was that the phonograph would become the major means of business communication by using reusable cylinders that lasted from 2 to 4 minutes at a time. In 1889

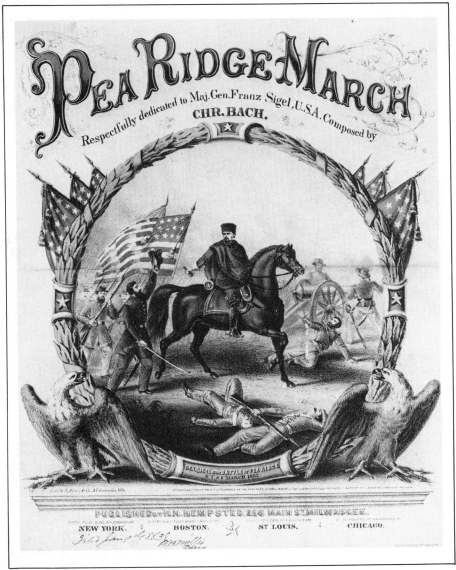

(Photo: The Bettman Archive, Inc.)

Music was published long before it was recorded. From the Revolutionary War on, reaching its peak during the Civil War, sheet music provided inspiration and the lifting of military morale for millions of mothers, wives, and soldiers. Above is a typical lithographed music cover published in 1862.

Edison issued the first commercial recordings, and the Automatic Phonograph Company's "nickelodeon" appeared.

During this same period another American, Emile Berliner, was experimenting with a system that used flat disks instead of cylinders. Berliner's gramophone, which was patented in November 1887, used a governor to control the speed. The advantages of the disk over the cylinder

Thomas Edison poses with his tin foil cylinder phonograph for photographer Matthew Brady, Washington, D.C., April 18, 1878.

In 1887, Emile Berliner patented the grammophone, a sound recording system which, unlike Edison's phonograph, used flat disks instead of cylinders.

were these: (*a*) The disk could be mass-produced from an etched negative master, whereas each early cylinder had to be an original; (*b*) the shellac record was harder and more durable than the wax cylinder; (*c*) the disk was more easily stored than the cylinder; (*d*) the disk produced greater volume and better quality from a simpler machine.

The last decade of the nineteenth century was a time of company warfare with everybody trying to drive everyone else out of business. Edison gained control of North American Phonograph as a part of the Edison Phonograph Company, while Berliner formed the United States Gramophone Company. The Columbia Phonograph Company also entered the business. In 1901 Eldridge Johnson formed the Victor Talking Machine Company and changed the course of recording history. Johnson made the phonograph business respectable and profitable, and soon over 10,000 dealers were selling Victor's wares.

Victor, using the Berliner-Johnson system, and Columbia, operating under Edison and Bell-Tainter patents, dominated the phonograph industry for the first 20 years of the twentieth century. Assets for Victor grew to over $30 million by 1917 with Americans buying 25 million two-sided disks (introduced by Germany's Odeon Company in 1905) a year. As prices came down, audiences increased. After an initial coolness toward the medium, famous artists turned to the phonograph as a means of expanding their audiences, and millions of their records were sold. Enrico Caruso did more than any other artist to legitimize the medium, and over the years fans rewarded him with more than $5 million, tax free, from sales of his records. The industry was worldwide as interlocking patents permitted the sale of records everywhere.

From 1905 to 1923, few significant technical changes took place in records, and only minor changes were made in the recording device. Although the speaker horn was enclosed in the cabinet of the first Victrola (1906), the scratchy quality persisted. Many musical instruments could not be used because they did not record well. Artists stood in front of a huge bell or horn and shouted their songs onto masters. It was a far cry from the concert hall. Nevertheless, in 1921, 100 million records were sold.

1924–1945

Economically, the 1920s were expected to be a boom time for the recording industry. Low-cost, reliable sets were available, and people had the money to buy them. Although developments in electronic-radio technology (microphones and speakers) led to significant improvements in the technical quality of the phonograph, the public acceptance of radio created an economic recession for the recording industry. Radio provided "live" rather than recorded music produced a better sound and, best of all, the music was free. The recording business was rapidly disintegrating. Then Western Electric patented an electrical recording process and demonstrated the system for Victor. Eldridge Johnson, however, declined to participate in a project that had anything to do with radio, the medium

that was destroying his business. Finally, in financial desperation, the
phonograph industry moved into "radio recording."

The first commercial, electrically produced recordings were marketed
by both Victor and Columbia in 1925. The new process opened an entirely
new aural dimension. The electrical recording process expanded the frequency range, could be played back louder with "blast," allowed musicians to work in a studio setup approximating the physical arrangements
of live performances, and improved the home phonograph with a dynamic
loudspeaker. That same year, the Brunswick Company marketed a low-
cost electric phonograph with speakers of brilliant quality compared to
previous mechanical horns. By 1926 whole symphonies and operas were
being recorded on albums of up to 20 disks.

Despite the technical progress, the medium continued to lose ground,
first to radio, then to talking pictures. In 1928 RCA purchased Victor and
discontinued production of record players in favor of radio receivers.
Edison had previously stopped all phonograph production in 1927. The
depression hit the recording industry harder than it did any other medium. Record sales dropped to a tenth of what they had been, and few
playback devices were marketed. In 1932 only 6 million records were sold
and 40,000 machines produced. The phonograph seemed headed for extinction.

The one bright spot in the mid-1930s was the development of the jukebox. By 1940 more than 250,000 "jukes" were using 15 million records
a year made by bands of the "swing era." Despite this public consumption
of popular music, the record business was still dominated by classical

During the Great Depression, production of records for use in jukeboxes helped somewhat to offset the dramatic drop in record sales to the general public.

(AP/Wide World Photos.)

music, limited by drained financial resources, and hindered by unimaginative marketing.

Several business changes stimulated the medium's growth. Jack Kapp and E. R. Lewis bought and reorganized U.S. Decca. They produced 35-cent records to compete with the 75-cent versions of their major competitors. By 1939 Decca was the second-ranking company (behind RCA Victor) and sold 19 million units. In 1940 RCA and Decca sold two of every three records.

Columbia, in serious financial difficulty, was purchased by CBS in December 1938. Edward Wallerstein, a former RCA executive, was hired to rebuild Columbia's fortunes. Wallerstein signed a large number of successful pop musicians and almost cornered that market. He cut the price of Columbia's classical albums to $1: overnight, sales jumped 1500%. By late 1941 a revitalized Columbia helped the industry sell 127 million disks. Radio-phonograph combinations were also selling well.

World War II destroyed all hope for the industry's immediate rebirth. Shellac, required for disk production, became unavailable, and electronics manufacturers turned to war work. And on 31 July 1942, the American Federation of Musicians (AFM), headed by James Caesar Petrillo, refused to allow its members to cut any more records. The AFM was concerned that "canned" music would cut back employment opportunities. The record companies initially refused to negotiate, but a year later economic pressure forced Decca Records to allot up to 5 cents per record sold to the AFM's funds for unemployed musicians in order to bring out the first original Broadway cast album, *Oklahoma*. In mid-1944 RCA and Columbia accepted similar terms. The AFM gains were wiped out in 1947, however, when the Taft-Hartley Act made it illegal to collect royalties in this fashion.

1946–1963 Following World War II, five major forces revolutionized the phonograph industry: (*a*) technical achievements in electromagnetic recording: (*b*) improvements in records and playback systems; (*c*) television's destruction of radio's old format; (*d*) changes in marketing procedures; (*e*) a revolution in the content of the medium.

Electrical Magnetic Recording. Electromagnetic recordings had been experimented with as early as 1889, when a Danish engineer, Vladimir Poulsen, produced a recording on steel wire. Later, paper was used; later still, plastic tape.

In July 1945 John T. Mullin, then in the Army Signal Corps, came across a sophisticated magnetic tape recorder in a Radio Frankfurt station in Bad Nauheim, Germany, where the American Armed Forces Radio Network was supervising a German staff. This *Magnetophone* was a truly superior sound system, without the background noise so typical of phonograph recordings. Mullin brought two machines and 50 rolls of tape back to the States and in May 1946 demonstrated the system to a meeting of engineers. In June 1947 Mullin and a partner were invited to show the system to Bing Crosby and the staff of his ABC radio show. Mullin was hired, Ampex duplicated and improved the machines, and the 3M Company started producing tape.

Tape recording revolutionized the record business. Real-time performances gave way to multitrack, engineered-time performances, with Capitol and Decca the first record companies to take advantage of the new system. By 1949 most major studios were using noise-free tape recordings for masters, which were then edited and transferred to disks.

The 1950s saw extensive use of reel-to-reel tapes, and technical experiments during these years led to a tape bonanza in the 1960s. Today there are three basic tape systems:

1. Reel-to-reel systems, which can be edited and have both playback and record capability. High-quality units are fairly large even in portable models.

2. Cartridge systems (1958). These are compact, have great selectivity in 8-track models, but do not usually have record capability.[2]

3. Cassette systems (1964), which are portable but cannot be easily edited. They have record capability, however, and dubs can be cheaply made on inexpensive blank tape.

The introduction of tape improved sound quality, provided detailed aural separation of instruments, allowed for the most minute editing (e.g., coughs, miscues), and led to the engineer becoming a vital force in "mixing" the final product. Modern production methods are increasingly using the direct-to-disk process, eliminating the tape-to-disk transfers. Computers and digital recording are being used with great frequency, further enhancing the quality of recorded sound.

[2] For all practical purposes, new production of prerecorded music on 8-track cartridges ceased in 1983, and manufacture of the playback systems is at a standstill. The hardware has gone the way of all obsolete electronic gear: first the basement, then the junk pile, then the collector.

(Courtesy RCA.)

RCA introduced the seven inch 45-rpm record in 1949 in order to compete with Columbia's development of the 33⅓-rpm LP.

Record and Record-Player Improvements. In 1948 Columbia introduced the microgroove 33⅓-rpm long-play (LP) record developed by Peter Goldmark. This was far superior to the 78-rpm shellac record. The 33⅓ could handle nearly 25 minutes of music per side because of its slower speed, larger size, and narrower grooves, whereas the 78 produced only 3 to 5 minutes of music. The 33⅓ records were made of plastic "biscuits" and were so resilient they were called "unbreakable."

Rather than submit to a coup by Columbia, RCA Victor in 1949 brought out its 7-inch 45-rpm records in both single and extended-play (EP) versions. The center hole was far larger than that on either the 78s or 33⅓s. This meant that the consumer needed both a larger spindle and lower speed to adapt to the 45s.

The "Battle of the Speeds" lasted 2 years, and both Columbia and RCA spent a great deal of money promoting their products. RCA produced record players for their 45s and sold them for less than cost. By 1950, when the speed war ended, record sales had dropped $50 million below the 1947 level. The consumer, uncertain as to which of the two systems would be adopted, bought neither. The companies reached a compromise that established the 33⅓ LP album as the vehicle for recording classical works and collections by pop artists; the 45-rpm record was for pop singles. By 1955, 78-rpm records were no longer in production.

During this period, significant improvements were made in the sound quality of record players, and high-fidelity recordings became possible with advances in electromagnetic recording-studio techniques. The hi-fi boom lasted nearly 10 years. Stereophonic, or multichannel, sound systems, demonstrated in 1957 and marketed in 1958, made monaural systems obsolete. An equipment boom has continued for phonograph manufacturers. Today, all LPs produced by the major companies are hi-fi stereo albums, and even the 45 is a total stereo production.

The home sound-recording unit of today may be composed of a variety of playback units including a stereo phonograph, a cassette or cartridge or reel-to-reel tape system, and an AM–FM radio, with speaker sets throughout the house. In addition, tape units have become important accessories in automobiles. The component system is now a major part of the international electronics business.

The Emergence of Television. From 1948 to 1952 television began to emerge as the dominant mass entertainment medium. Both radio and films had to adapt in order to survive economically. Once the Federal Communications Commission lifted the "freeze" on local TV station allocations in 1952, there was no holding back video broadcasting. Financial conditions forced network radio to cut back operations, and local radio stations had to develop a new source of programming. The music, news, talk, and sports format evolved as the program policy of most U.S. radio stations. Music was the dominant element in the mix. Since the recording industry is popular music, the phonograph record became the content of radio. This provided free exposure of the record industry's products to a huge, affluent young audience of potential buyers, and the boom was on. It is ironic, considering past history, that the radio and recording industries are such good "bedfellows" now.

Marketing Procedures. At the end of World War II, the majors controlled the industry and released 40 to 100 new records each week. Local dealers marked up the records about 40%. There was a "straight-line" marketing system from manufacturer to distributor to retailer to consumer. It was a tight, profitable system for everyone except those outside the system.

Soon, however, independent producers began to produce records, and they made stars of unknown performers. This development meant that small retailers were faced not only with the speed war and with pricing and stock-duplication headaches but with an increasing number of "off brands." The widening variety of musical types forced larger investments or an inadequate inventory. In addition, promotion people replaced salespeople. The promotion staff worked with radio stations, and retailers were left to their own devices.

The real crack in the majors' armor was the profit motive. The majors controlled the talent and the music, the studios and the manufacturing, as well as the distribution. They were secure, and so they rented studios to the independents. These were the only studios the new labels had available, and even though they paid high prices—it was the only game in town—it taught them the tools of the trade. In order to "cover" hits (record a song first issued by another company with your artist) of the independents, the majors each set up a subsidiary: RCA (Bluebird), Columbia (Okeh), Decca (Brunswick), and so forth.

The patterns of selling records changed in the mid-1950s as (a) discount outlets (low-margin retailers) offered significantly reduced prices on all popular records; (b) the major record producers, noting the success of small record societies, started their own record clubs; (c) rack-jobbers rented space in dime stores, drugstores, grocery stores, and anywhere else one would be likely to buy a record on impulse. All these marketing innovations hurt traditional retail sales outlets—record and department stores. But business was so brisk that the traditional dealers' complaints carried little weight with the record companies. Today, rack jobbers and national record-store chains dominate retail record sales.

The Revolution in Content. Popular music in the United States today reflects the diversity of America's "melting pot" culture. Thirty years ago, this was not the case. The four majors (RCA Victor, Columbia, Decca, and Capitol) and three emerging companies (MGM, Mercury, and London) produced essentially three kinds of music: white popular, classical, and show (theatrical). Each company had an all-powerful artist and repertoire

(A&R) person, who was in effect the company's record producer. This individual selected all the songs and all the artists to record them. Performers were *told* what they would record and when a "take" was acceptable. Each major also told their artists which potential hits on the other labels would "cover." In effect, a very small number of people controlled the music industry. It was the independent record producers who generally spearheaded new musical trends. As a result, they were responsible for many structural changes in the business. As minority musical tastes were identified as economically viable, independents found the talent to serve them.

In the early 1950s these independents created a musical form that shook the music industry to its foundations. Nowhere was the cultural gap between young and old so evident as in the controversy over the sound Cleveland disk jockey Alan Freed named rock 'n' roll. Rock has never been rock *and* roll. Grammar is not its forte.

Rock music is the only musical form that is indigenous to the electronic media. In fact, rock is the only music where the recording is the original, and the live performance is the imitation. Rock 'n' roll is a four-letter word that has been defined best by music expert Richard Penniman as *Awopbopaloobopalopbamboom*, which translated means there is no satisfactory definition of this musical form. But we can identify its characteristics.

1. Rock is a heavy *beat*.
2. Rock is *loud*. It is tactile and insulates listeners from problems.
3. Rock is *electric* music. It is plugged in and turned on.
4. Rock is traditionally *simple* (but not simpleminded).
5. Rock is *crude*, as are all four-letter words.
6. Rock is *blatant*. It is the most sexually up-front of any musical form.
7. Rock is a *rejection* of adult sensibilities, an assault on the status quo, and a sign of alienation.
8. Rock is *committed* to social change. It was and is the voice of the young during times of wars, recession and cultural upheaval.
9. Rock is *people* music. It is the most "pop" of pop cultures.
10. Rock is *young*. The young make it, buy it, use it. Every teenager is a potential star.
11. Rock is *color blind*. A major part of the civil rights movement, it desegregated the young as well as their music.
12. Rock is *unpredictable*. Who knows what will be popular tomorrow?
13. Rock is *immediate* music that depends on high turnover. Today's hit is tomorrow's "golden oldie."

14. Rock is *international* and has fans worldwide.

15. Rock is *very big business.*

Rock comes out of five traditions in American music:

1. *Rhythm and blues* (R&B) provided the horns, the black beat, and a frank approach to the sexual experience. R&B was rural music urbanized for southern blacks who migrated to northern cities. The form was influenced by jazz, boogie, and the blues. Gospel traditions of "rocking and reeling" were critical in its development. The independents were the major source of R&B records because it was "race" music to the majors. Chess, Atlantic, King, Imperial, and others cut the R&B originals, which were "whitewashed" by the majors that covered their records. But it still introduced white kids to the black R&B sound.

2. *Country and Western* (C&W) provided the first "stars," the basic instrument (the guitar), and "songs of life and pain." Jimmy Rodgers, "the father of country music," fused the blues with country. Then western swing bands took the "hillbilly" out of it. The music spoke to the lower class (now the middle class) about the traditions of poverty, a hard life, and the sadness of "sneakin' around." It held to traditional values and was slow to change.

3. *White popular ("pop") music* provided sentimentality, the "crooner" sex symbol, and industrial know-how. "Pop" was money, power, status, and respectability. It was *the* music for most Americans until the rock-'n'-roll revolution.

4. *Folk* provided the tradition of untrained writers performing their own music, the participation of the audience, and the rebellion against those in power. Folk music was "people" music, by and for them. It held that the "amateur" professional had to be close to his "roots." For years, folk had been integrated with the blues, country, and gospel traditions.

5. *Jazz* provided high-quality, trained musicianship, and improvisation and a tradition of racial integration. Jazz came upriver from rural southern America. It developed from a fusion of both black and white musical traditions and innovations that spawned "swing," "bop," "cool," and so forth.

All five forms remain integrally involved in the rock mainstream, as well as independent musical forms.

In the early 1950s, there were consistent hits that bordered on rock 'n' roll, including Johnny Ray's "Cry" (1951), Tennessee Ernie Ford's "Shotgun Boogie" (1950), Lloyd Price's "Lawdy Miss Clawdy" (1952), and the Crewcuts' "Sh-Boom" (1953). But rock did not crystallize until 1955 when one monster record, Bill Haley and the Comets' "Rock Around the Clock," sold over 15 million copies.

The first superstar of rock 'n' roll was the late Elvis Presley, a hip-swinging, greasy-looking, brilliant performer. The period from 1956 to 1958 was the "age of Elvis." He was James Dean and Marlon Brando set to music. Elvis had 14 straight million-seller 45s and was RCA's best $40,000 investment, the price they paid Sun Records for his contract. Sam Phillips, the founder of Sun Records, used that $40,000 to create "rock-abilly," and the "sale of Elvis" made it possible for him to develop Carl Perkins, Jerry Lee Lewis, and Gene Vincent.

The dynamic Elvis Presley, rock's first superstar, reigned supreme in the late 1950s.

(Photo: *Photoplay Presents.*)

The music field became racially integrated in the period from 1954 to 1960. White performers sang black music and sold it to white consumers. This later made it possible for black singers to sing black music and sell it to white consumers. Previously, blacks like Nat "King" Cole, the Ink Spots, and Lena Horne had sung white music for "white folks." Rock helped legitimize the black beat and black themes.

Elvis Presley, Jerry Lee Lewis, the Everly Brothers, and Buddy Holly sang rock that had black roots. This opened the door for blacks doing rock. Little Richard (Penniman) sold a million copies of "Tutti Frutti" and "Long Tall Sally"; Fats Domino sold 50 million records to youngsters before 1960; Larry Price did "Bony Maronie"; the Coasters and the Drifters opened the door for other stylized black groups to reach white audiences. Most important was Chuck Berry, an extraordinary writer as well as performer, whose "Maybelline" was one of the first black monster rock hits.

In the late 1950s, rock created a whole series of noncontact sports, starting with Chubby Checker's "twist," then the "monkey," "frug," "mashed potato," ad infinitum. Nobody touched anybody—the body movement was detached yet sensual. As soon as a dance was adopted by adults, it was often discarded by their children. Whether purists like it or not, rock 'n' roll has always been dance music, loud enough to cut through street, auto, and party noise and overcome the inadequacies of AM radios and inferior record players.

(Courtesy Dick Clark Productions.)

Dick Clark's "American Bandstand" helped to create many teenage idols among rock performers of the 1950s and 1960s.

The biggest fad of the early 1960s was strictly white middle-class surfing music that rejected the corporation life for the beach buggy, bikini, and surfboard. Brian Wilson and the Beach Boys made hotrods, motorcycles, and beach bums into national symbols. The teenaged pop stars of that era—Frankie Avalon, Neil Sedaka, and Paul Anka—are alive and well and living in Las Vegas. Pat Boone, who "covered" more R&B hits than anyone else, is making middle-of-the-road commercials. Ricky Nelson, who had real talent, is living off royalties.

During 1959–1960, the government investigated rock music. The record companies regularly paid disc jockeys for plugging records; this "payola" and other overt types of "hype" were stopped, but "hype" is so integral a part of the entertainment industry it is almost impossible to stop. Stopping payola did not stop rock because rock was a significant cultural force with young people.

By the 1960s rock was also an economic force, although the music establishment and rock 'n' roll were still at odds. Several song publishers attempted to bridge that gap. The Motown sound of Berry Gordy, through his talented writers and the great artists who recorded on his labels, served as a black bridge between middle-class musical taste (the music establishment) and rock-'n'-roll America. By the mid-1960s, three of every four songs recorded by Motown artists made the charts.

Pat Boone typified the white middle-class pop star of the early 1960s.

(Photo: Wagner International Photos, New York City, Courtesy Pat Boone.)

Great Motown artists like
The Supremes bridged the
gap between the music
establishment and
rock'n'roll.

(Photo: James J. Kriegsman, New York, Courtesy Motown Record Corporation.)

The white transitional team was Don Kirschner and Al Nevins of Aldon
Music, a Philadelphia-based publishing company that supplied songs to
the majors using then unknown writers such as Neil Sedaka, Carole King,
and Neil Diamond. They developed a style called the "Brill Building
Sound" that came to cover all the music of the urban east. It was, in effect,
Tin Pan Alley music for teenagers. It all culminated in the manufactured
supergroup and sound of the Monkees.

By 1963 big business had "homogenized" rock with pop music techniques and embraced the economic potential of the sound wholeheart-
edly. Teen tastes, styles, and habits were "aped" shamelessly because kids
had power in the form of money and leisure time. Rock 'n' roll manufactured songs about teen love and teen heartbreak and cars and parental
interference.

It was a business of turnover. New groups were easily recruited off the streets, schoolyards, and churches and were then reorganized, reproduced, reprogrammed, and just as easily forgotten. The music was less alive. The kids began to lose interest, and the music business went into a mild recession. Then President Kennedy was assassinated, and Don McLean sang some 10 years later, about "the day the music died."

1964–1978   This 15-year period is looked back on by many who lived it as the "golden age" of rock 'n' roll. After a mild recession the business was "born again" in 1963–1964. Two far-reaching events helped rocket the phonograph industry into the cultural and economic stratosphere:

1. Without much fanfare, the cassette recording was introduced, and, unlike 8-track machines and cartridges, it had *recording* capability. This fact had implications that are haunting the music business today.
2. The British invaded America. Today, foreigners won't let American music alone. They have staked a permanent claim on a sizable portion of the top 100.

It all began innocently enough when the Beatles broke into the charts in February 1964 and revitalized a sagging rock economy. More important, that re-energized the sound.

Although rock is an American creation, it reached fruition under the British. If the late 1950s belong to Elvis, the late 1960s belong to the Beatles.

In 1967, The Beatles revolutionized popular music with "Sgt. Pepper's Lonely Hearts Club Band," one of rock's highest artistic achievements.

(Photo: The Bettman Archive, Inc.)

This shaggy bunch of household words (John, Paul, George, and Ringo) had the top five records in America in April 1964. Every album they cut was a million seller. They were a cultural phenomenon as well as a musical phenomenon. They were artists—poets—performers. Without a doubt they influenced contemporary music more than anyone in the 1960s. Their uniqueness lay not only in the quantity of their work and its financial success; it was the quality of the Beatles' music that set them apart.

The Beatles reached one of rock's highest artistic summits in June 1967 when "Sgt. Pepper's Lonely Hearts Club Band" was released. That it would be a gold mine was a foregone conclusion, but it was the innovation, vision, beauty, and expertise that set off the musical reaction that is still with us. The Beatles' quarrels, Apple failures, lackluster *Let It Be* movie, fratricidal Klein war, breakup, and various personal problems and idiosyncracies cannot dim the contribution of "Sgt. Pepper" and the great musical cartoon, *Yellow Submarine*, that it spawned. They *are* "the once and future" Beatles.

Mick Jagger, the ultimate rock showman with the pouting satanic style, soon drove the Rolling Stones to the forefront. Their personal hassles with drugs, the law, and the Altamont concert killings somehow added to the mystique their hard-core followers loved. They became one of the best rock "touring shows" of the 1960s and 1970s.

"Tommy," the milestone recorded by The Who and rerecorded by everybody else, and then made into a movie, was the rock opera achieve-

(Photo: Movie Star News.)

Bob Dylan reflected the concern of young Americans with social conscious issues in the 1960s.

ment, along with *Jesus Christ, Superstar*, which became a show-business phenomenon that only *Hair* could approach in the late 1960s.

In the mid-1960s Bob Dylan was the most influential American pop musician. His music was socially conscious and reflected many young people's interests in peace, ecology, and race relations. Rock music is part of a cultural lifestyle. The 1970 Woodstock Music and Art Festival was a celebration of this rock–youth culture. Rock music is, in effect, rock politics, rock economics, and rock sociology.

As the 1970s broke, three deaths in rapid succession hit the industry. Jimi Hendrix choked to death on barbiturate-induced vomit while asleep. Janis Joplin died of a heroin overdose. Jim Morrison (The Doors) had a heart attack in a bathtub after a series of drunken-lewd performances that lacked professionalism and destroyed his career. It was as though rock stars, like movie stars before them, could not control their success.

The war in Vietnam and the social protest movements set in musical motion by Bob Dylan in the 1960s continued through the end of America's most unpopular war and Nixon's "Watergate" administration. In the 1970s, James Brown's support of Hubert Humphrey and the Allman Brothers concert for President Jimmy Carter have, along with other rock-politic moves, legitimized the form. In the mid-1970s the heavy metal sounds were dominated by Led Zeppelin and Bad Company. The glitter rock of Kiss and the rock theater of Alice Cooper held sway as rock became "show biz." Stevie Wonder was in command of the Grammys every time he cut an album. The "wars" were over. Young and old kids were dancing again to the reggae, salsa, and white–black, black–white disco sounds. Bruce Springsteen made the cover of *Time* and *Newsweek* as the establishment proclaimed the great white hope of rock. But Barry Manilow wore the crown, and Elton John and Bernie Taupin, a great singer–showman and his songwriter, made the million-dollar deals. Happy times were here again.

As the 1970s ended, the results of the happy times were evident. It was an era of excess for the recording business. The watershed year was 1967. Sales of phonograph records went over $1 billion for the first time; the Beatles released their "Sgt. Pepper" album; and the affluent youth market, smoldering just under the surface, burst into an open flame. It was at this time that the major record companies made their first heavy financial commitment to rock, which until then had been nurtured and then dominated by independent companies.

Also in 1967, radio programmer Tom Donahue began what has become known as progressive album-oriented rock (AOR) on FM radio in Los Angeles and San Francisco. The use of FM radio in the 1970s triggered much of the audio industry's huge growth.

This growth was characterized by economic euphoria as sales of records, FM radios, and audio hardware geometrically expanded. The majors expanded their profiles, and new record companies entered the industry.

Stevie Wonder was one of the many recording stars of the 1970s who succeeded in negotiating multi-million dollar contracts. (Courtesy Motown Record Corporation.)

As sales rose, however, competition increased, and the cost of signing performers escalated. Neil Diamond signed one of the first megabuck contracts in 1971 when he negotiated with Columbia Records a $400,000 per LP guarantee. In 1972 Elton John signed a 5-year, $8 million, 20% royalty contract with MCA. Stevie Wonder signed a $13 million deal with Motown in 1976. These costs coupled with the economic recession of 1974 were to bring several major changes in the record industry.

In the mid-1970s the music took on new overtones and seemed to fractionalize under the impetus of the specialized forms created by radio stations staking claim to a narrow range of musical tastes. In the 1950s top-40 stations were rock stations and served as an umbrella for all of what was then rock 'n' roll. But as the number of stations in each market grew, they carved out an ever-narrower definition of rock music, and rock 'n' roll fractionalized.

Rock music had been created out of rhythm and blues, country and western, folk, jazz, and white pop. Rock also has had an impact on each of its parent forms and in the 1970s spawned the following:

The Rock-'n'-Roll Dynamic.

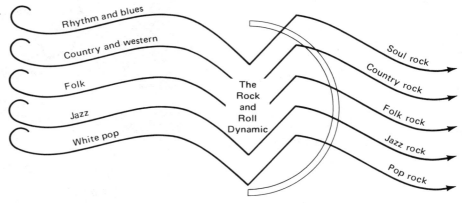

1. *Soul rock,* typified by James Brown, Joe Simon, Wilson Pickett, Al Green, and Boz Scaggs.

2. *Country rock,* typified by Kris Kristofferson, The Band, Waylon Jennings, and Jimmy Buffet.

3. *Folk rock,* typified by Donovan, Buffalo Springfield, and Gordon Lightfoot.

4. *Jazz rock,* typified by the Brothers Johnson; Chicago; Blood, Sweat, and Tears; George Benson; and the Blackbyrds.

5. *Pop rock,* typified by Barry Manilow, Elton John, Steely Dan, and David Bowie.

As a cultural force, rock 'n' roll had unified young people, but it has splintered along cultural and racial lines with crossovers common. Crossovers are often derided by purists as not really rock music.

For example, when the war in Vietnam ended, young people threw off their fatigues and started to celebrate. Nightclubs used recorded music and adapted the European discothèque to their needs. The "disco" became a gathering place for young people and then a showcase for local dancing talent. Whether self-anointed critics (and nondancers) like it or not, disco was a legitimate extension of rock music. Disco smoothed out what was then the discordant "show band" sound and made rock danceable again, as it had been in the 1950s. Latin music (salsa) was infused into it. The gay community used it as a comic assault on "macho, macho man." The roaring 1970s had arrived, and the good times were celebrated in a rebel-without-a-cause movie called *Saturday Night Fever* starring John Travolta, an upbeat teen love story about the 1950s called *Grease* (Travolta and Olivia Newton-John), and *Sgt. Pepper's Lonely Hearts Club Band* (Bee Gees, Peter Frampton, and assorted crazies). These films, masterminded by Robert Stigwood (RSO Records), were box-office hits as well as *platinum* albums.

The disco craze reached
its peak with *Saturday
Night Fever.*

(Photo: Movie Star News, Courtesy Paramount Pictures Corporation.)

In the fading light of the 1970s, hoping to keep volume expanding, major record producers began to add to their rosters of contract performers, confident that if 1 or 2 releases out of every 10 issued were successful, they could carry the rest. But volume did not increase, and growth was realized only through price increases. Sales of single records, for example, fell. Yet 1977 was a monster year, due primarily to Fleetwood Mac's 13-million-selling "Rumours" album and the *Saturday Night Fever* soundtrack. Overall, LP sales were soft and 8-tracks were dying; prerecorded cassette sales increased, however, and blank tape was doing a great business, but selling blank tape encouraged home taping.

No matter, 1978 was the biggest year yet—$4.1 billion in sales—and next year would be better yet.

In 1979, the bottom fell out. The sound recording business was to decline for 4 straight years, then stabilize in 1983.

1979 to the Present

As the 1980s began, record companies were retrenching; thousands of employees lost their jobs. Small independents went under or were swallowed up by the majors. Coupled with an 11% decrease in sales (1979), record companies were faced with high interest rates, exorbitant prices for plastic (made from petroleum), and talent contracts negotiated in better times. The 3-month billing cycle, standard in the music business, combined with rampant inflation that caused currency devaluations worldwide, also hurt.

Rock 'n' roll economics depended on lots of kids spending lots of money and time listening to lots of rebellious music. The previous generation of rockers were adults now, but they were not having enough children to support the music, and unemployment changed Dad's yelling, "Get a job!" to teenagers' pleading, "I need a job. I'm out of work." It's tough to be rebellious when times are hard. To make things worse, affluent kids taped one another's records and spent their extra money on video games.

By 1982, sales levels of prerecorded records and tapes were 150 million units below the 1978 high, a decrease of 21%. Both wholesale and retail volume was below 1981 levels. Raising retail prices to $8.98 was the industry's answer; the consumer responded by buying more blank tapes.

THE CURRENT STATE OF THE RECORDING INDUSTRY

A number of conditions exist today that are interacting and reshaping both the art and the business of music. They are (*a*) The rampant, illegal taping of copyrighted material; (*b*) the complacency of FM radio; (*c*) the rise of music video; (*d*) the loss of American direction in the new music; (*e*) another revolution in technology: computers, digital recording, synthesizers, and compact discs.

Illegal Taping

It is estimated that home duplication of music (from other tapes, records, and radio broadcasts) and the pirating of copyrighted music by organized crime reduces record and tape sales by as much as 50%. Data suggest that perhaps 75% of all tapes sold in Asia and Latin America are "pirated" copies. Upward of 80% of all blank-tape sales are used for illegal tapings; that is equivalent to 550 million lost sales. Because of the illegal tapings, the recording business is asking for a surcharge of at least a dollar on blank tapes. Legislation concerning the surcharge is now pending.

The Complacency of FM Radio

When FM radio was young and hungry, it married itself to rock music. As FM radio became profitable it became cautious and musically entrenched. Broadcasters looked at their profit-and-loss statements and ratings and stopped listening to innovative music, the life blood of rock 'n' roll. New artists and new musical styles could not get exposure. Radio sells "numbers" and "demographics" to advertisers who could not care less about rock music. Stations have narrow playlists with heavy rotation of "charted" songs within tightly formatted schedules. Airtime is not available to the new musical ideas being tried out in urban clubs, at free college concerts, and on music video. Album-oriented rock (AOR) stations were the rage in the early 1980s and smugly assumed they knew what rock music sounded like; *their* audience (white, young, male) would always listen to Led Zeppelin's "Stairway to Heaven." In the summer and fall of 1983, in spite of FM radio, some of the new music made the charts, and top-40 stations made it on the radio. The AOR and other "old" formats got trounced in the ratings. Stations made wholesale changes in music styles to play the songs of video. The same songs that audiences had phoned in to request and that had been rejected were now staples. Radio began to ape rock-'n'-roll television.

Rock music on television is not new. Both Elvis and the Beatles appeared on "The Ed Sullivan Show." "American Bandstand" featured rock 'n' roll. Even Ricky Nelson starred in "Ozzie and Harriet." There have been videotapes of rock concerts on pay cable for years, and concept video albums began with "Blondie" in the 1970s.

Music Video

But music television is different. It is more like radio with pictures, 24 hours a day.

In 1982, Warner-Amex put Music Television (MTV) on the satellite, which bounced it into cable homes. The pictures were accompanied by an FM stereo signal that could be connected to sophisticated home sound systems. By 1983 an industry study indicated that MTV was more influential in determining record purchases than all the radio stations in America. Record companies now coordinate new releases with MTV premieres.

Production costs for early music videos averaged $10,000 per cut. By 1983 the average cost had risen to the $25,000–30,000 range; Billy Joel and Paul McCartney music videos ran into the hundreds of thousands. In late 1983 John Landis directed Michael Jackson in the title cut from "Thriller" at a cost of $1 million. It was packaged with "The Making of Thriller" and premiered on MTV in December 1983. The lid was off and the rush was on.

Video promotions, at almost any cost, are cheap when compared to the cost of mounting a concert tour of a European band in the United States. And, at present, video promotions are more effective than tours in generating record sales. They even create a demand for tickets for tours that are mounted.

Originally, video production costs were absorbed by the record companies and budgeted as promotions. Today, contracts call for videos to be paid for out of joint profits, and new groups sometimes pay the entire video bill. MTV Music Television is not the only game on television. Cinemax and HBO run "Video Jukeboxes" and "Pop Spots" as filler. "Video Soul" is on the Black Entertainment Network cable feed. "Night Tracks" is on Ted Turner's superstation WTBS-TV. The "Nashville Network" plays country and western videos on cable channels throughout

America, and NBC has "Friday Night Videos" and was the first to offer token royalty payments in 1983. But record companies do not want to kill the golden goose that may lead the recording business out of the wilderness. Only BMI and ASCAP seem concerned about royalty payments at this time. MTV Music Television, is offering to pay for exclusive rights to music videos during their initial release.

Video clips had been used widely in European music and dance clubs. Because European acts had a *ready* supply of videos, they were the first to take advantage of music television. That generated immediate, widespread interest in and demand for what simply came to be called *new music*.

THE RISE OF NEW MUSIC   Some rock fans have trouble adjusting to new forms of rock music, whether disco, reggae, glitter, or electropop. Billy Joel sang it best: "It's still rock 'n' roll to me." And make no mistake: *New music* is rock music.

First, there was the mumble of punk, English working-class music. Punk sounded and looked weird, rude, negative, and nihilistic. Played by unskilled musicians, the music was roughly crafted. Sid Vicious and the Sex Pistols had an image to live down to. Punk was a costume, a switchblade, a brawl, getting busted, and an attack on establishment rock 'n' roll. Punk was to rock what rock had been to pop—scary.

Punk never really caught on in the United States, but it cleaned up its act and became *new wave*. With some middle-class values added, it was noticed and almost accepted in America, but it was not anywhere near as popular here as it was in Europe.

New music is not exactly new wave and is certainly not punk. It comes from a much better neighborhood and has manners. New music has costumes and performance values. It owes a debt to reggae for complex rhythms and phrasing, gentle complaints against oppression, and Jamaican club mixing techniques. New music is visual, romantic, danceable, European, energized, complex, jazzy, and very electronic.

Duran-Duran, Culture Club, and Dexy's Midnight Runners are prototype groups. All had European (international) followings before Americans listened in.

The English, and to a lesser extent the Australians, Canadians, and continentals, are the major innovators in new music, and their visualness lends itself to video interpretations. In 1982 and 1983 most of the successful new groups in pop music were not American. Among the leaders were Men at Work, The Human League, Spandau Ballet, A Flock of Seagulls, The Thompson Twins, Loverboy, The Eurythmics, The Alan Parsons Project, INXS, The Stray Cats, Paul Young, Bow Wow Wow, Thomas Dolby, Kajagoogoo, Ultravox, The English Beat, ABC, Joe Jackson, and U-2. Established American groups still have hits, but most of the *new* acts

The "New Music" of Culture Club lends itself to video interpretations.

are from abroad. The Police, for example, are innovative and musically flexible and seem able to anticipate the tastes of American consumers.

There is also a new black urban style of music for "break" dancing. "Break" dancing was popularized in the films *Flashdance* and *Breakin'* with a number of songs by Michael Sembello that made the charts as singles as well as an album. These films and *Beat Street* hyped the sale of 12-inch singles for "breakin' rather than fightin'."

All New music relies heavily on the newest digital, computer-based synthesizer technology for its sound.

**THE NEW
REVOLUTION IN
RECORDING
TECHNOLOGY**

The synthesizer is revolutionizing rock music. "Digital synths" are replacing guitars as the lead instrument and the percussionist is being usurped by a "drum box." Eliminated are entire string–woodwind–brass sections. New music requires *new* sounds and new colorations of old, familiar sounds.

It all began with the invention of what came to be called "the moog," a modular synthesizer developed by Robert Moog and Donald Buchla. The moog was intended for classical music and was popularized by Wendy Carlos in the film *A Clockwork Orange*. Rock innovators—the Moody Blues and Emerson, Lake, and Palmer—used it early on. Synthesized music was further developed by Kraftwerk and Tangerine Dream, and then went through "techno pop" with Gary Newman and Ultravox. Its widest popular acceptance was in disco. It is also widely used to score commercials and by Vangelis, Giorgio Moroder, and others for motion-picture sound tracks. Computer software programs became available in 1983 to use home computers as basic synthesizers, and the Korg Vocoder is close to reproducing vocals.

Now, one artist, working alone and at home, without the special acoustics of a recording studio, can create music that goes straight from the synthesizer through a computer to a digital recorder using an electrical code. The sound-to-microphone step is no longer necessary. Northeastern Digital's Synclavier is part of the new wave of instruments that actually can add harmonics to the sine wave. Precise sounds can be called up from memory and repeated ad infinitum. Timbre, vibrato, and attack can be duplicated to resemble almost any instrument. The more complex the computer, the more exact the sound that can be replicated. Synclavier has 16 tracks and will soon be able to be hooked to a printer and print

The Moog Synthesizer, developed for classical electronic music, has revolutionized the sound of rock.

(Courtesy Moog Electronics.)

out complete scores in up to 16 parts. The cost range is somewhere between $30,000 and $70,000, depending on auxiliary equipment. Even complete systems of multiple instruments costing $200,000 can pay for themselves over a short period by eliminating the cost of studio rental and studio musicians. Digital technology has revolutionized the production process.

Other innovations include the introduction of the compact disc (CD) and CD player (1983). The cost of a CD player should be under $500 by 1985, and disc costs will drop below the current $20 retail price rapidly as demand increases. Compact digital disc players scan the "pits" of a reflective computer-encoded surface through its protective cover with a laser. The light is reflected from the pits in the disc and digitally filters noise (unless the noise was on the master tape). These 4¾-inch one-sided discs have a 75-minute capacity, and since nothing touches the disc, there is no wear or surface noise. Estimated sales in 1983 were 12 million copies of 850 titles. The discs are cheaper and easier to produce than standard records. And most important, the system has absolute speed stability, very low distortion, and again, no noise. This new technology will force artists to demand even better recording and mastering of their music, which brings us full circle to the synthesizer–computer–digital recorder hookups that musicians will need to produce that quality of sound.

The music business is stable, which is a euphemistic way of saying **THE SCOPE OF** that it is a nongrowth industry at present or that the recording industry **SOUND RECORDING** is not in the steep decline that characterized 1979 to 1982. Unit sales in the mid-1980s are at levels equal to those of the mid-1970s but significantly below levels of the bonanza years 1977 to 1979. Estimates place 1983 record and tape shipments at approximately 578 million units shipped at a value of $3.8 billion. There would have been another decline

Manufacturer Unit Shipments Net after Returns (in Millions)*

Recording Medium	1973	1974	1975	1976	1977	1978	1979	1980	1981	1982	1983	Percent Change 1978– 1983
Singles	228.0	204.0	164.0	190.0	190.0	190.0	195.5	164.3	154.7	137.2	124.7	−34
LPs/EPs	280.0	276.0	257.0	273.0	344.0	341.3	318.3	322.8	295.2	243.9	209.6	−39
CDs	—	—	—	—	—	—	—	—	—	—	.8	—
Cassettes	15.0	15.3	16.2	21.8	36.9	61.3	82.8	110.2	137.0	182.3	236.8	+286
8-Tracks	91.0	96.7	94.6	106.1	127.3	133.6	104.7	86.4	48.5	14.3	6.1	−95
Total	614.0	592.0	531.8	590.9	698.2	726.2	701.1	683.7	635.4	577.7	578.0	−20

* This table illustrates the growth of sales up to 1978 and then the drop until 1983, when sales of "Thriller" (Michael Jackson/Quincy Jones) stabilized the market at mid-1970 levels. (By permission Recording Industry of America.)

in 1983 if it had not been for the "monster" record of all-time—Michael Jackson's "Thriller," which in 1983–1984 sold an estimated 30 to 35 million albums.

The industry, in effect, is healthy but not really growing. A variety of factors are contributing to this condition, but high prices, pirating and home taping, the recession, the aging of America, and a kind of dormancy in musical innovation are all important factors. Music videos have been a real shot in the arm for the music business and they continue to be the major influence on most pop music record/tape purchases. They constitute the major marketing tool of the industry in the 1980s.

Specific releases continue to decline. Only 2300 LP's are now released annually compared to nearly 4200 in 1978. That is a decrease of 45% in terms of the music selection available to consumers. It also makes it much more difficult for new groups to get an album released. Single releases on 45 rpm records have also decreased to only 2100 today compared to 2900 in 1978, which is a drop of 30%. For all practical purposes 8-tracks are no longer a factor in the market with less than 50 titles being released each year. The new compact disc releases now number 600 per year and are steadily increasing. In 1983, for the first time in sound recording history, cassettes outsold record albums, even when compact/laser discs are included in the latter group. Cassettes are the major growth area.

When the unit shipments and retail dollar volume are compared for 1978, the "platinum" year in the record business and 1983, the drastic nature of the decline of the music business becomes clearer;

1. Single unit sales are off over one-third, and despite dramatic increase in prices for 45 rpm records, the dollar volume is only up 3%.

2. Album unit sales have decreased 39% and dollar value is down by nearly a third.

Manufacturer's Dollar Value at Suggested Retail List Price (in Millions)

Recording Medium	1973	1974	1975	1976	1977	1978	1979	1980	1981	1982**	1983	Percent Change 1978–1983
Singles	190.0	194.0	211.5	245.1	245.1	260.3	275.4	269.3	256.4	283.0	268.9	+3
LPs/EPs	1246.0	1356.0	1485.0	1663.0	2195.1	2473.3	2136.0	2290.3	2341.7	1925.1	1689.5	−32
CDs	—	—	—	—	—	—	—	—	—	—	16.5	—
Cassettes	76.0	87.2	98.8	145.7	249.6	449.8	604.6	776.4	1062.8	1384.5	1811.8	+303
8-Tracks	489.0	549.2	583.0	678.2	811.0	948.0	669.4	526.4	309.0	49.0	28.2	−97
Total	2001.0	2186.4	2378.3	2732.0	3500.8	4131.4	3685.4	3862.4	3969.9	3641.6	3814.9	−8

* The inflated dollar values of sales is due totally to dramatic price increases since 1978. The only real dollar growth area since that time is in cassette sales. (By permission Recording Industry of America.)

** NOTE: 1982 figures differ slightly from previous reports owing to more accurate reporting for the direct marketing sector in 1983.

3. The major loser in terms of format is 8-track units sold (down 95%) with dollar value bottoming out at 3% of what it was in 1978. The format is economically defunct.

4. Only cassette sales have dramatically improved with unit figures up 286% and dollar volume up 303%.

5. In terms of total sales, units sold are down one-fifth and dollar volume is off 8%.

Sound recording is the only mass medium to show this type of decline. It is a very tough market, and the 1980s will only get tougher for the music industry.

Although it is sometimes hard to categorize music types because of "crossovers" from one category to another, the pie chart below gives an interesting picture of retail music sales in the mid-1980s. Rock music, although less dominant than in the late 1970s, still accounts for more than one-third of all dollar volume. When rock music is combined with country, easy listening, and black music, nearly three out of every four retail record dollars are accounted for.

The pie chart on the next page displays similar information, but in direct mail marketing percentages. These data show rock at only 30% and black music at 4%. The country and easy listening categories combined account for nearly four of every ten dollars spent in direct marketing, and that should increase as the record consumer continues to age.

In terms of a consumer profile, (1) males account for 55% of all sales; (2) whites buy 89% of all records sold; (3) the 20–34 age group accounts for 49% of the music sold; and (4) the South leads the other four regions of the country with 36% of all sales.

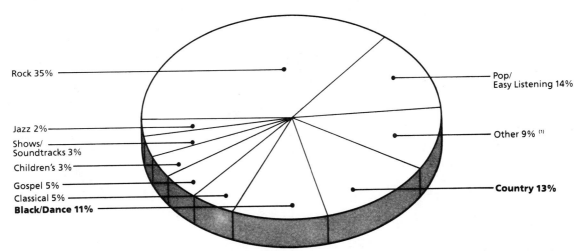

Expenditures by Music Type as a Percentage of Total Dollars Spent in Retail Sales. (By permission of Recording Industry of America.)

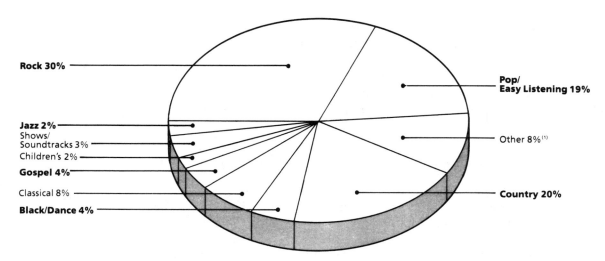

Expenditures by Music Type as a Percentage of Total Dollars Spent in Direct (Mail) Marketing Sales. (By permission Recording Industry of America.)

The Retail and Direct Marketing Consumer Profile as a Percentage of Dollars Spent Provides an Interesting Analysis of Who Is Buying What*

	Total	Rock	Country	Pop/Easy Listening	Black/Dance	Classical	Gospel	Children's	Jazz	Soundtracks/Shows
Age										
10–14	4	**7**	1	2	**5**	1	1	2	0	3
15–19	15	**26**	7	9	**18**	3	8	1	6	13
20–24	24	**32**	19	21	**26**	15	14	12	22	18
25–34	25	22	25	24	**30**	23	**32**	**53**	**35**	27
35+	32	13	**48**	**44**	21	**58**	45	32	37	39
Race										
White	89	**95**	**97**	91	50	94	87	93	77	**96**
Nonwhite	11	5	3	9	**50**	6	13	7	**23**	4
Sex										
Male	55	**63**	47	47	48	**63**	44	22	**82**	54
Female	45	37	53	53	52	37	**56**	**78**	18	46
Region										
Northeast	21	**27**	14	22	21	21	11	20	18	**26**
North Central	22	22	23	22	20	18	25	24	**26**	**27**
South	36	30	**44**	35	**45**	36	**46**	34	**42**	34
West	21	21	19	21	14	**25**	18	**22**	14	13

* This complex table should be carefully examined to determine the value of various consumer groups in the marketing of music in America. (By permission Recording Industry of America.)

The table on the opposite page provides a detailed picture of consumer preferences:

1. Age is a primary determinent in record sales. Rock and black music is dominated by the 10–24 age group. And the 35+ age group is a major force in the sale of country, easy listening, classical, and gospel music.

2. Nonwhite purchasing power is most dominant in the black music and jazz categories, but whites overwhelmingly account for sales in all categories other than black music, in which they are equal partners.

3. Males dominate rock, classical, and jazz sales. Females have a substantial edge only in the purchase of gospel and children's records.

4. The South dominates sales in *every* music category, with a substantial share of the country, black, gospel, and jazz categories.

If another monster "hit" does appear each year or the music does not rejuvenate itself or video music sales and compact disc sales don't escalate dramatically, the late 1980s could be difficult times for the music business.

Before a record can be a success, several groups must support it: (a) the creative element; (b) the business element; (c) the information-distribution element; and (d) the consumer element. No single element can create a hit or prevent one.

THE STRUCTURE AND ORGANIZATION OF SOUND RECORDING

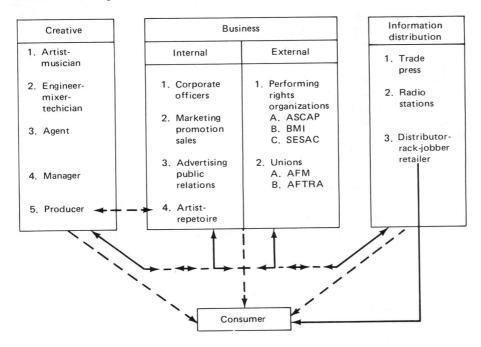

The Structure of the Music Recording Industry.

The Creative Element

The artist—musician creates the material. Many successful rock performers write as well as perform their own material. The engineer—mixer—technician manipulates the inherent qualities of the medium to create recorded music. Performers are aided, guided, and supervised by a business consultant, generally called an agent. Performers also have managers to handle details and run concert tours. Both agents and managers are paid a percentage of the performer's income, usually 10%. Artist and repertoire (A&R) people serve a similar function for production companies. The record producer often also serves an A&R function, although the task here is not to select the groups but to get them taped in a satisfactory manner.

The Business Element

There are two subcategories: internal, individuals within the record company; and external, groups outside the record company that have a significant impact on the music business.

Internal. Decisions to exploit the creative element are made by high-level corporate officers who approve the financial appropriations considered essential to the successful marketing of the record. They provide the capital and reap the greatest portion of the profits. The marketer—promoter—sales representative devises the best way to get visibility for the record. If an established star or group makes a record, there is less difficulty than if it is made by an unknown. The field-representative can promote only what his company puts out, and there is no way to force radio stations to play the company's product. Since all the company's records cannot be pushed with equal effort, the field representative must promote one unit in preference to another. The advertising and public relations staffs prepare trade announcements for radio stations, distributors, and retailers, as well as consumer advertising for the general public. Most of the effort and money is spent on trade materials. In effect, records are "pushed'' through the distributor—retailer by the trade press and airplay, rather than "pulled" through by consumer demand. The A&R person is a talent scout who seeks the next "stars" in the field. Other A&R people, not associated with established companies, act as go-betweens for the artist and the producer.

External. Publishing-rights organizations collect performance payments, which come primarily from radio and TV stations. Under the copyright law of 1976 each jukebox pays an annual tax in order to play records. The three organizations handling publishing rights are the American Society of Composers, Authors and Publishers (ASCAP), which has about 18,000 members and collects 67% of the fees; Broadcast Music, Incorporated (BMI), which has over 21,000 writers and 9500 publishers as clients and accounts for 32% of all fees; and SESAC, a small, family-owned company that does about $2 million business annually for its 200 publishers and 375 catalogues. Broadcasters normally subscribe to both ASCAP and BMI.

The two major labor unions in the recording business are the American Federation of Television and Radio Artists (AFTRA) and the American Federation of Musicians (AFM). Record companies are "closed shops" in that vocalists and musicians must join a union in order to record. Union-scale wages are set for every aspect of the business from studio sessions to club appearances to concert tours. The unions are a real power in the music business.

This area has three participants: the trade press; radio-station programmers; and distributors, rack jobbers, and retailers. The trade press serves as a general information and evaluation source. Four major publications serve this function. *Billboard* is considered the most reliable source for business and creative information. *Cashbox* and *Record World* are less important but serve the same function. *Rolling Stone* concentrates on creative evaluation and has a wide public as well as trade readership. All

The Information-Distribution Element

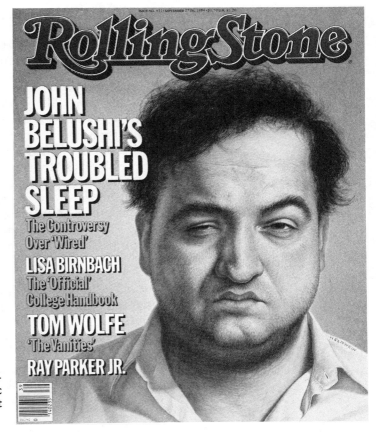

Rolling Stone concentrates on creative evaluation of the music business and has a wide public as well as trade readership. (Courtesy Straight Arrow Publishers, Inc.)

four aid in the selection process by featuring articles on what records are expected to be successful. Radio-station programmers greatly affect the sales performance of many records—if the local DJs do not play the records, the public cannot become acquainted with them, and audiences are less likely to buy them. Stations must choose a limited number of songs each week to add to their playlist. Only a handful of the 200 singles and 100 LPs received each week ever get extensive airplay, which is more valuable than any advertising. The distributors, rack jobbers, and retailers are also crucial to the whole process. If a record is not in stock, it cannot be bought. And since the life of popular music, especially singles, is short, it is crucial that the record be available immediately upon public demand.

The Consumer Element

Finally, there is the audience, the consumer of phonograph records. This individual makes the final decision as to whether a record will be a success. A million seller is, in the end, determined by the audience. The gold record presented to an artist attests to the fact that a million consumers bought a single or that 500,000 people bought an album. Platinum awards have been added for "supersellers" (2 million singles or 1 million albums).

The audience can select only from what is available. Therefore, each of the above elements serves as a gatekeeper in phonograph communication. Nevertheless, even if they all support a given record, the public can and often does prefer to buy something else.

The "Music Flow" of the Music Business

In order to understand how records get into the hands of consumers, the following flow chart is helpful. Record companies send copies of records to the trade press and radio stations for publicity and airplay. They also take out ads and get stories about artists printed and broadcast. Performers hit the road to push their recordings. These road shows or concert tours are covered by the press and stations and attended by consumers. Records are distributed by the company distribution system or general distributors to rack jobbers, who sell their units in non-record-store outlets, record-store chains, and one-stops, which service jukebox operators as well as consumers. Record clubs are another source of sales for the company.

The consumer is influenced by concerts, radio plays, jukeboxes, and the press; and then buys records from clubs, one-stops, chains, and low-margin retailers. Each year the consumer makes selective purchases from the 3600 singles and 2500 LPs released annually by the record companies.

Sound recording is a tough, competitive business where 8 of every 10 singles and 3 of every 4 albums do not make money. In the classical field 90% of the albums lose money: this field is literally subsidized by the government and foundations in their grants to orchestras. Big new hits and the work of established artists pay most of the company overhead.

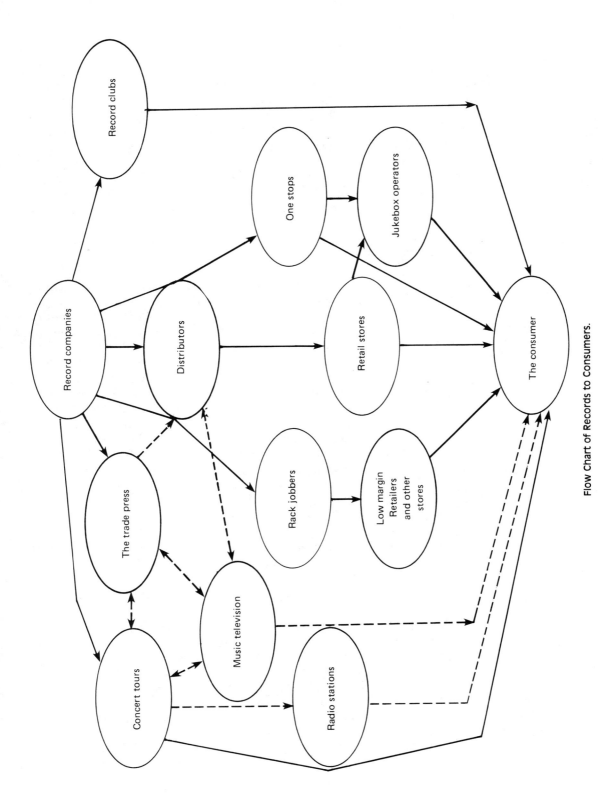

Flow Chart of Records to Consumers.

To break even, a single must sell about 50,000 copies, an album 145,000 copies. When an artist has a hit, the individual group can earn a royalty of from 5% to 15% on the list price. Songwriters get $.0275 for each sale under the 1976 copyright law. A single that sells a million copies, therefore, can earn a writer over $30,000. One measure of success is the charts of the leading hits in trade magazines such as *Billboard*, *Cashbox*, and *Record World*.

The economics of the industry work out so that the producer earns from 40% to 50% of the retail price; distributors get from 15% to 25%; the retailer gets the remaining 20–30%, depending on his markup. The rack jobber pays the record company 40–50% and the retailer a flat fee of 10–15% of total sales, which means that the jobber keeps 35–40% of every record he markets.

The individual artist or group is usually advanced money to produce an album, but that advance must also take care of touring expenses, which for groups can cost $7,000 per week. For example, say that a group gets $100,000 for an album. Production costs are roughly $50,000 for audio and $30,000 for a video clip, which leaves $20,000 to tour an average of ten weeks. If the group is new, it can expect only $1,000–3,000 a week in pay. If the album sells 100,000 copies, the group's royalty is $63,000, which the company keeps to pay back part of the advance. This leaves the group in arrears $37,000 for the advance, in debt for the tour, and in need of money to produce a second album. The company does a bit better. At $.94 per album, it earns $94,000 on album sales plus $63,000 in artist royalty for a total of $157,000, which gives it $57,000 above the advance. These facts notwithstanding, rock superstars earn from $2 million to $6 million each year from song royalties, concerts, singles, albums, promotions, and tours.

CHARACTERISTICS AND ROLES OF SOUND RECORDING

The record industry is *massive* with sales in excess of 550 million units and $7 billion annually.

Recordings are the primary content of radio, are in the process of creating music video on a grand scale, and are a continuing force in motion pictures.

The medium is international in scope. American music is heard everywhere, and English sounds are sold throughout America. The industry is more international than any other mass medium, even film.

Culturally, sound recording is highly selective. It has to be because the music is multifaceted, appealing to many specialized tastes. Pop music is dominant, with rock and soul accounting for 50% of all sales.

Traditionally a youth medium, the audience for recordings is aging. Those aged 15–24 now only account for 40% of all unit and 30% of all dollar sales, whereas they dominated sales in the 1960s and 1970s. Nevertheless, sound recordings and films still cater to the youth market more than other media.

The medium is more portable than ever. Miniaturization and excellent quality in headphones have made the Sony Walkman a real success with up to 2 hours of listening that fits in your pocket. Nearly one-third of all new cars sold are cassette equipped.

The phonograph is a high-technology, high-quality medium. New compact discs and digital recordings are a significant improvement over what were already high standards. This new technology also makes the product more durable; the content ages before the record wears out.

The sound-recording medium is a major instrument in the socialization process, especially of the young. It is dated to, danced to, touched to, and fallen in love to. But parents worry, perhaps unduly, about a decay of moral values.

The recording business remains committed to the causes of the young artists and consumers it serves. Politicians should be wary of its power.

Sound recording has the highest turnover of talent and content of any medium. Like the book, it is a storehouse of our musical heritage. It makes for easy retrieval of that cultural force.

THE BARNUM & BAILEY GREATEST SHOW ON EARTH

AND

P.T. BARNUM.

J.A. BAILEY.

IMRE KIRALFY'S "NERO"
OR THE DESTRUCTION OF ROME.

ALL TIME'S MOST STUPENDOUS, SPLENDID AND SUCCESSFUL

HISTORIC SPECTACLE

AND UNIVERSALLY PRONOUNCED IN EUROPE, THE GLORIOUS INTRODUCTION OF A NEW, ALL ECLIPSING, FABULOUSLY RESPLENDENT ERA, IN SCENIC, TERPSICHOREAN PANTOMIMIC, CHORAL & PROCESSIONAL DISPLAY, AND HEROIC, TREMENDOUS, DRAMATIC ACTION.

·· ONLY ··
OLYMPIA HIPPODROME.
MILLIONAIRE MENAGERIES.
PRODIGIOUS FEATURES.
PERFORMING CARAVANS.
100 CHARIOTS & DENS.
IMPERIAL BALLETS.
TRAINED ANIMALS.

· NEW ·
FOREIGN FAVORI
TRIPLE 100 ACT
ALL KINDS OF THRILLIN
WONDROUS MID-AIR
MONSTER ELEVATE
STUPENDOUS SPECT
GLADIATORIAL COMB

1200 PEOPLE

P.T. BARNUM
J.A. BAILEY
EQUAL OWNERS.

400 HORSES

THE USES
OF
MASS
COMMUNICATION

PART

News and Information ⎤ 21

The mass media, as we have seen, are institutions, and mass communication is a process. The produce of the institution and the process is a commodity, and we use that commodity in a variety of ways. In this section—over the next six chapters—we examine six different uses to which we put the mass media. They are: to inform, to interpret, to persuade, to educate, to entertain, and to sell.

In many ways, the news and information usage of mass media is the most important, and so we begin there. It is not the oldest function of mass media; most media were initially used for some selling or business purpose. Nor is it the most widespread; most of us use mass media primarily for entertainment. In fact, news and information in the past were often incidental uses of mass media. We spent time and money on mass media as part of our leisure activity, and if we got some news and information in the process, that was merely a side benefit.

Today, however, news and information are vital to the sustenance of a complex civilization. We turn to the news every day, not just to be entertained, but because the events that transpire and the facts that are communicated have direct consequences on our lives and the actions that we must take to survive.

News has become a commodity that sells all by itself. It sometimes does not need to be wrapped in a cloak of entertainment in order for the masses to be interested in it. But most people are still most interested in news that has some immediate reward for them, as we shall see.

One of the most consequential phenomena for the mass media of modern times is the increasing blame placed on the media for the ills of society. And it is mostly the news function that has caused the criticism. The bearer of bad news is often blamed for the news. In ancient times, the messenger who brought news about a defeat in battle was slain for the bad tidings he bore.

For the most part, the media do not cause the events that become news. They merely record them, interpret them, or express opinions about them. Other forces in society—political, economic, sociological, meteorological, or even personal—cause events to happen. Media react to those events. As human beings acquire greater control over their environment, they can also exercise greater control over communication by manipulating people, events, and environment to make news.

Of course the media are not simply passive agents manipulated by other forces. By making judgments about what is newsworthy, about what is important and unimportant, about what is true and false, reporters and editors in the mass media play a role in shaping the course of events. But no one has yet fully substantiated the precise impact of that role.

WHY DO WE NEED NEWS?

The need for information is basic to nearly all human beings. Even in primitive societies someone acts as a watchman for the tribe. The best climber is dispatched to climb the tallest tree and look out over the horizon for rain or fire, for animal food or tribal enemies. The tribe depends upon such reports for survival.

America is an information-hungry society. We need information of all kinds in order to survive in our complex world. News and information are commodities that we must have and are willing to pay for. Increasingly, the most successful mass media are those that provide the most information, not just the most entertainment.

In modern society we sometimes employ private informers, such as detectives or investigators, to supply us with information. But for the most part we depend upon mass media to keep us aware of dangers and opportunities on the horizon. We need journalists to provide a check on government and business. The journalist is, indeed, a tree climber, a person who knows how to get the broadest view of what is happening in the world in order to report the important news and information to a particular audience.

In the terminology of the journalist, news is that which an individual is willing to pay for with time or money in order to read or hear or watch. In other words, news must have some intrinsic value to the individual. News is different from information. A great deal of information about many subjects is available in the world, but information does not become news until a journalist selects it for presentation via news media.

Before information can become news, it must be made to fit the quality and criteria of news: It must be accurate, fair, balanced, and objective; and it must have a relatively high degree of news value based on such criteria as prominence, proximity, consequence, timeliness, and human interest.

The only area where the journalist's role is active rather than passive is in making judgments about what is news. Literally millions of events occur on any given day, and news media gatekeepers must determine which events are newsworthy and which are not. Selection and evaluation of events depend upon many factors, not the least of which is the nature of the group to which the journalist is reporting. We might say, then, that news is that which gatekeepers decide should go into the stream of communication on any given day, based on what the audience is willing to read, hear, or watch. Today's news may not be relevant tomorrow, and news for one person may not be news for another, because news values are relative.

RELATIVITY AND RELEVANCE

Perhaps the most dominant principle of news in America is the concept of *objectivity*. News is supposed to be a factual report of an event as it occurred, without the bias of the reporter or an attempt on the part of the journalist to make any one view more influential than another. In America, the journalist plays a nonpartisan role—taking the part of a teacher, passing on facts for their own sake, allowing the individual to draw conclusions and make interpretations. The journalist disavows the role of promoter, which is to pass on information in order to persuade or influence an audience.

ELEMENTS OF NEWS QUALITY

Objectivity is a difficult quality to measure and a difficult standard to attain. Journalists can never wholly divorce themselves from their work; their emotions and opinions are apt to be tied into their perceptions of facts and events whether they think they are or not. Moreover, no journalist ever sees the whole of any situation; and as events become more complex in our complicated world, the journalist necessarily sees a smaller portion of any set of facts.

A growing school of thought in American journalism argues against the principle of objectivity for these reasons. This "new journalism" is devoted to the idea that reporters should be more than messengers delivering a message; this concept says their reporting will be better if they openly and honestly admit their biases and clearly label their reports as their views of the situation.

In any case, the goal of any news operation is to keep people fully informed about vital events and information, knowledge of which is essential to full citizenship in a democratic society. The people have a right to know; that is a basic tenet of a free society, and news must provide the necessary factual basis for forming sound opinions. The reporter who wishes to fulfill this responsibility through objective reporting must work at it diligently.

Objectivity is enhanced by proper attribution of facts and opinions. The news reporter must attribute to an authority—an eyewitness, an official, a participant, an expert—anything that is not routine and readily verifiable knowledge.

Accuracy of reporting is another basic quality of news. Reporters must train their eyes to see and their ears to hear as accurately as possible. They must be constantly vigilant for detail and perpetually skeptical of those who would deceive, exaggerate, or hide in order to twist and distort the truth.

Finally, *balance* and *fairness* in reporting are crucial standards by which the quality of news should be judged. Telling both sides of the story is so much a part of American journalism that reporters sometimes seem unpatriotic, unwilling simply to accept the pronouncements of presidents or bureaucrats as the only statements on a matter. In war, this becomes particularly difficult for leaders to understand, as the press and news media seem bent on reporting the successes of the enemy as well as the failures of compatriots. But the journalist must be dedicated to the proposition that only from balanced reporting of both sides will the people be able to discover the truth.

CRITERIA FOR NEWS SELECTION

On what basis do journalists for the mass media make judgments about people and events that turn information into news? In mass communication, where millions of people depend upon the information that journalists decide to publish and broadcast, the decision about what is news and what is not must be made as rationally as possible. In the future, media will use computers as well as experience in making these judgments. Meanwhile, we depend upon a few standard bases of news judgment.

Timeliness

Certainly one of the most important criteria for news is its newness. We say that "nothing is as old as yesterday's newspaper," but actually the length of time for which a piece of information continues to be newsworthy depends upon the medium. For radio, a story may lose its timeliness after an hour. Television news may have a slightly longer lifetime, from an hour to a day. Daily newspaper news has a single-day lifetime; after that, the story must be rewritten with new information. Weeklies have a week, monthlies a month, and so on.

Proximity

Geographical factors are also important to news judgment. Relatively speaking, the nearer an event occurs to the people who read about it, the more newsworthy it is. The election of the governor of New York is much more important to New Yorkers than it is to those who live next door in Pennsylvania. A two-car accident killing two local people might be more significant to the audience in their community than a major earthquake in Peru taking the lives of thousands on the same day.

The more widely known the participants in an occurrence, the more newsworthy the event. If the president of the United States hits a hole-in-one on the golf course, it could be national news. If the mayor does the same, it might be news in his town. If the golf pro does it, it might make the newsletter at the country club. Actually, prominence has a snowballing effect on newsworthiness, since mass media make famous people more prominent through constant reference to them in the media.

Prominence

The consequences of an event have a direct bearing on its newsworthiness. The earthquake in Peru might be more newsworthy to the small community where the two-car accident occurred if the tremor will cause a shortage of Peruvian tin at the local factory.

Consequences

Finally, we can identify a criterion that we only vaguely refer to as human interest—matters that catch and hold our attention because of physical and emotional responses built into human beings. A number of elements provide human interest, including adventure and conflict, humor, pathos and bathos, sex, the odd and the unusual, and self-interest. A high percentage of each day's news is selected on the basis of these factors.

Human Interest

News covers a surprising range of subject matter. A national survey by the American Newspaper Publishers Association found more than 40 general categories of news in daily newspapers. The survey found that more space is devoted to sports than to international news, more space is given to crime than to cultural events and reviews, and more space is given to news of interest to men than news of interest to women.

CATEGORIES OF NEWS

Different media emphasize different categories of news. Newspapers give more coverage to news of crime and justice than do local and national television. National television gives more coverage to news of government and politics than do newspapers or local television. National television also gives more coverage to foreign affairs, whereas newspapers give more space to domestic policy. Local television gives more coverage to economic and social issues and to human interest items.

Various factors including sex, age, race, education, culture, and socioeconomic status affect the way in which we read news. For nearly everyone, however, news about accidents, disasters, and natural phenomena

AUDIENCES OF NEWS

holds intense interest. Women read less sports news than men, and men read more business news than women. Older people read more obituaries than younger people, while younger people read more entertainment and Hollywood news than older people.

Children develop an interest in news gradually; 6- to 8-year-olds look to newspapers mostly for comics. By the time they are 12 years old, children read newspapers for sports news more than comics. Interest in general news, local news, and editorials grows with age; interest in puzzles, games, and comics declines.

Children's news knowledge grows with age, too. During President Carter's administration in the late 1970s, more children aged 6 to 8 could identify TV and singing stars Donny and Marie Osmond than Jimmy Carter. Even teenagers had difficulty identifying some not uncommon elements in the news, such as inflation, the Equal Rights Amendment, and the SALT talks.

IMMEDIATE AND DELAYED REWARDS

All news in American journalism is selected by media gatekeepers because it fulfills some audience need. The basic criterion is, will it sell? Will people pay attention to it? Do they want it and need it? Wilbur Schramm, formerly a professor of communication at Stanford University, has categorized news as fulfilling either an immediate reward or a delayed reward to a felt need. The *immediate-reward* type of news provides instant satisfaction for the recipient, who laughs, cries, sympathizes, thrills, or muses. Schramm places in this category such news as "crime and corruption, accidents and disasters, sports and recreation, and social events."[1]

Delayed-reward news has an impact that does not affect the consumer until later. Such news includes information about "public affairs, economic matters, social problems, science, education, weather, and health." Often, delayed-reward news may bring an unpleasant consequence for the reader, listener, or viewer, whereas the immediate reward can bring instant gratification. Schramm concludes that most news consumers spend more time with, find more satisfaction in, and give greater attention to immediate-reward news than delayed-reward news.

CONSEQUENCES OF NEWS SELECTION

Judgments about news may constitute the most important decisions made in our society, with wide significance and deep consequences. It is important to examine the problems that have arisen in the past and that loom on the horizon of the future as a result of news selection.

First, since news decisions are consumer oriented, in order to sell media, news usually overemphasizes immediate-reward types of infor-

[1] Wilbur Schramm, *Mass Communications* (Urbana, University of Illinois Press, 1960), 438–450.

mation. Crime and violence almost always outweigh and outdraw stories of good deeds, constructive action, peaceful progress, and orderly dissent. Sex is not as large an element in news as it is in advertising, but it is nonetheless a significant factor. The aberrations of society—the odd, the unusual, the unique—are more often the subject of news than the normal.

One result can be a gloomy view of the world. Glenn T. Seaborg, a Nobel Prize-winning nuclear scientist and former chairman of the Atomic Energy Commission, warned that the last decades of the twentieth century may usher in a worldwide doomsday depression. People, he said, are so constantly reminded of evil and corruption in the world by the news media that they may sink into a hopeless morass of gloom and despair, not realizing that the world is still a beautiful place with much more good about it than bad.

Indeed, fright and hysteria can sometimes result from a small detail of news. The famous Orson Welles broadcast in 1938 brought such a reaction. The radio program, called "War of the Worlds," was a dramatization of a science-fiction story about Martians invading the Earth, told in the form of a news program, with bulletins interrupting a music show. Hadley Cantril, a psychologist who studied the event, summarized his findings in his book, *The Invasion from Mars*:

> Long before the broadcast had ended, people all over the United States were praying, crying, fleeing frantically to escape death from Martians. Some ran to rescue loved ones. Others telephoned farewells or warnings, hurried to inform neighbors, sought information from newspapers or radio stations, summoned ambulances or police cars. At least six million people heard the broadcast. At least a million of them were frightened or disturbed.[2]

As a result, the NAB code adopted a resolution forbidding dramas to be presented as news programs, yet legitimate news stories also have such an effect. A massive publicity effort by the federal government to tell people that smoking might cause lung cancer had the effect of sending thousands of smokers to their doctors for imagined ailments.

One news reader in Washington, D.C., expressed the feeling of many consumers when she wrote to the editors of the *Washington Post*:

> Isn't there such a thing as *good news* any more? Every morning after reading the newspaper (yours) I am left depressed for the rest of the day. Is it that I am too weak to cope with the cruel realities of the world or is it that *you* are too weak to deny the sensationalism that brings your paper its profit and salaries? Can you never print just *one* happy or amusing or heart-warming story on the front page? Or for that matter, on *any* page? Even the food advertisements on Thursdays are psychologically devastating, but that, in short, is not your fault—I guess none of it is. I guess, too, that you are just printing things as you see them.

[2] Hadley Cantril *The Invasion from Mars* (Princeton: Princeton University Press, 1947), 2.

It's a vicious cycle, though: the world is sick, which makes the people sick, which makes the sick people make a sicker world. If everybody gets as depressed as I do after reading or seeing the news, there's only one destiny for all of us—an insane asylum.[3]

Journalists have traditionally defended the publication of "bad" news and "unusual" information by saying, first, that people prefer to read such stories, and second, that exposing evil and corruption does more good for society than praising constructive action. But here, too, greater balance is desirable.

A second consequence of news selection is the distortion caused by the attempt to be objective and fair. The unprincipled person can tell a lie to make news and have it reported with the same weight as the honest person who tells the truth.

Perhpas the best historical example of this is the story of the late Senator Joseph McCarthy of Wisconsin, a man who used the exposure of Communists in government for his own political ends. The senator made charges, most of which he was never able to substantiate, sometimes ruining people's careers and lives. The news media would objectively report the fact that Senator McCarthy had charged Mr. A with being a Communist, and Mr. A would, if available, deny the charges. Both sides of the story were told, so the news media were giving a fair and balanced coverage of news. But the reporters could not inject their opinion that the senator was lying, and irreparable public damage was thus done to the accused.

Ultimately the truth will win out, if we believe John Milton's theory about putting truth to the test in the open marketplace of ideas. And ultimately, in the case of Senator Joseph McCarthy, it was the news media that continued to give him coverage until his distortions were so apparent that his colleagues in the Senate finally censured him.

In the end we must say that news is a two-edged sword that cuts both ways. Those who would use it properly to deceive the world will, sooner or later, be exposed by the same media that allow them expression. The consequences of news, however, are enormous, and no one should undertake to deal with news who does not want to accept the awesome responsibilities for making such decisions.

HOW NEWS DECISIONS ARE MADE

Of the millions of events that occur in the world each day, and of the thousands of people who do something interesting, who decides what goes on the front page of the newspaper or which will be the top story on the eleven o'clock TV news?

[3] Letters to the Editor, *Washington Post*, 4 July 1970.

Those decisions carry awesome responsibility. Ben Bradlee, executive editor of the *Washington Post*, says he can remember, early in his career, being "terrified" that he would make the wrong decision about what should appear on his paper's front page. "I'd heard about the editor somewhere who didn't put the first A-bomb on page one," Bradlee says, "and I was always afraid I might screw up like that someday."

The editor may have the last word, but he usually has a lot of help in reaching a decision. At most newspapers and TV stations, news decisions are made in regular conferences between editors and news directors and producers.

At the *New York Times* and the *Los Angeles Times* news conferences, the managing editor begins by conducting an informal inquiry of editors from the metropolitan, national, foreign, and financial departments. There are generally two such inquiries: an early one involving primarily assistant editors, and a later one involving just the top editors. From the two conferences, and from conversations before and between them, a consensus gradually emerges on the day's major stories, and an executive news editor sketches in the actual placement of the stories on a dummy (a layout form of design) during the second conference. The dummy is often distributed to all the major desks and bureaus of the newspaper, and the editors are encouraged to challenge it. At the *Washington Post*, the managing editor goes over the dummy at a final news conference, asking the appropriate editor to comment on each story already tentatively sketched in. The editors may suggest changes, and late-breaking events can force additional changes throughout the day.

Different editors and different publications and broadcast operations make different judgments about the news. *Time* and *Newsweek* often come up with the same cover story, perhaps because they are aiming at the same general audience, or because it is relatively easy to arrive at a consensus on the number-one national story of the week. Such consensus is much rarer from one metropolitan newspaper to the next, and even from one TV newscast to the next.

A study of the front pages of the *New York Times*, *Los Angeles Times*, and *Washington Post* reveals great differences in judgment, interest, style, scope, and tone among the papers. Only 28 times over a 155-day period did the three papers agree on the most important story of the day. On 56 days (one-third of the time) each paper had a different lead story. On 33 days (one-fifth of the time) there was not one single story that appeared on the front pages of all three papers. Only on 32 days did the three front pages have more than two stories in common.

Another study of newspapers in more than a dozen cities on 50 selected days showed an even greater diversity in front-page selection. Local stories generally dominated newspaper front pages, leaving room for only one or two, if any, national or foreign stories.

**NEWS SERVICES
AND NEWS
GATHERING**

Most news media have a network outside their local communities for gathering news. Some employ homemakers or students as part-time stringers in suburban communities or outlying towns. Some have bureaus in their state capitals or county seats to report local government news. A few large stations and publications have bureaus in New York City, primarily to report business and financial news. An increasing number of media of all sizes have correspondents or bureaus in Washington, D.C., often called the news center of the world. And the larger media have their own foreign correspondents. Most newspapers and broadcast stations, however, have as their primary purpose the processing of local news.

No one newspaper (not even the *New York Times*), no radio or TV station or network (not even NBC, CBS, or ABC) could provide worldwide coverage of news on an efficient basis. Increasingly, the news media have turned to independent news services or wire services for such coverage.

The wire services today are the world's news brokers, providing the vast bulk of national, international, and regional news for most media. Their news and information usually goes out to their subscribers by telegraph wire. In America the important services are the Associated Press and United Press International; in England it is Reuters; in France, Agence France-Presse; and in Russia, TASS, which is part of the Soviet government.

The Associated Press, started in 1848, is a cooperative, owned by the newspapers and other media that subscribe to its services. Today, AP serves more than 10,000 newspaper, magazine, TV, and radio clients around the world; more of its clients are now in broadcast than print media. An amalgam of the old Hearst International News Service, begun in 1909, and the Scripps-Howard United Press, UPI started in 1907 and has more than 7000 subscribers, worldwide.

Each of these wire services is active in more than a hundred countries around the world. Together they lease more than a million miles of telephone wire and make extensive use of radio-teletype circuits and trans-oceanic cables. Together they employ more than 12,000 full- and part-time journalists, who operate nearly 400 bureaus. They transmit nearly 10 million words a day, thousands of pictures, and hundreds of special broadcast reports.

News services provide a variety of coverage, such as a national wire, a state wire, a local wire, or a special radio wire written for broadcast. They charge their subscribers a fee based on circulation or station size. A small newspaper of 25,000 circulation may pay from $100 to $400 a week, while a large metropolitan daily might be charged as much as $6000 a week. Both AP and UPI have annual budgets in excess of $50 million.

The wire services are staffed by seasoned reporters who work out of bureaus organized much like the city staff of a daily newspaper, again with researchers, reporters, copyreaders, and editors. Nearly every state capital, all major cities, and most foreign capitals of the world have wire-service bureaus. New York City is the headquarters and houses the largest operation for both AP and UPI. By the mid-1980s about 75% of all the news most Americans read and heard was provided by Associated Press and United Press International.

The wire services provide excellent training ground for newswork. The top minimum salary at a wire-service job as of 1 June 1984—$619 a week at AP and $557 at UPI—is higher than the salaries at newspapers in many American cities. Only reporters for major newspapers have a higher top minimum.

One of the most important developments in news and information has been the increase in investigative reporting. Indeed, investigative reporters such as Robert Woodward and Carl Bernstein, the *Washington Post* team that cracked the Watergate story, have become the modern heroes of American journalism. Others, such as Don Bolles of the *Arizona Republic*, have been assassinated because of their success in uncovering inside information.

INVESTIGATIVE NEWS REPORTING

Investigative reporters make news by going beneath the surface situation to find the real cause or purpose. At times, they are almost a combination of police detective, spy, and gossip columnist. In their book *All the President's Men*, Woodward and Bernstein gave an unusual glimpse of the world of investigative reporting: wheedling secrets from confidential sources; talking their way into private homes and offices in hope of getting few facts; meeting contacts in dark parking garages for morsels of information; and building a case, piece by piece, until a larger picture was formed.

(Photo: Movie Star News, Courtesy Warner Bros., Inc.)

In the movie version of *All the President's Men*, investigative reporters Robert Woodward (Robert Redford) and Carl Bernstein (Dustin Hoffman) discuss the evidence surrounding the Watergate break-in with the editor of the Washington Post (Jason Robards).

To satisfy the journalistic need for speed and thoroughness, investigative reporting is often done best by teams of reporters. Jack Anderson, who bills himself as an investigative reporter in Washington, employs a small staff of aides who serve as researchers and investigators for his column. A number of newspapers have set up investigative teams, as have the wire services.

THE STYLE AND STRUCTURE OF PRINT NEWS

Since the purpose of news is to transmit information as efficiently as possible, it must have a style and structure that permits quick and effective communication. Language must be clear, simple, and to the point. Syntax must be direct and concise. Organization must be logical. The writing must have clarity and brevity.

The news story must be organized and written in such a way that others can work on it easily; it might be compared to a racing car with easily accessible parts for rapid repair by all mechanics at the pit stop. Copyreaders, announcers, editors, directors—all must be able to work with the news copy quickly and cooperatively.

In the newspaper, the "inverted pyramid" structure is usually used to organize the news story. Inverted-pyramid organization places the most important part of the story at the beginning, the less significant material in the middle, and the least meaningful at the end. Newspaper stories usually are not told chronologically or dramatically, for the most important things usually happen at the end of an event or a drama, not at the beginning. If we were writing fiction about a baseball game, we might start our story with a description of the weather and a discussion of the butterflies in the stomach of the pitcher. But a newspaper article will begin with the final score of the game.

This method of reporting serves two important functions. First, it gives the hurried newspaper reader the most important information immediately. Readers need not learn more about the event unless they have time or special interest. Second, it allows the editors to cut a story at the end, if there is competition for time or space (as there usually is) without losing the essential facts of the story.

Since the beginning of the story is the most important, the usual lead, or opening paragraph, is used to summarize the significant facts of the event. In the past, reporters spoke of the five *w*s and the *h*—who, what, when, where, why, and how. If these questions about each event were answered in the lead, the main points of the story would be summarized. Today there is less emphasis on the five *w*s and the *h*, and yet the basic principle remains—that the first paragraph must summarize the most important elements of any news situation.

RADIO AND TELEVISION AS NEWS MEDIA

The number of people who depend upon the broadcast media for their news has risen steadily; today, the majority of the people in the United States fall into this category.

The major broadcast networks have large news operations, with correspondents covering the world in the same way the wire services do, although not nearly so extensively. The networks concentrate their news coverage on major news centers such as Washington, D.C., New York City, Los Angeles and foreign capitals.

Local radio and TV stations have increased their news operations as well. Indeed, local news has become one of the most important functions of individual stations.

Both network and local broadcasting have been increasing the amount of time devoted to news. Although radio usually provides news only in short bursts—5 minutes on the hour—the number of radio stations has increased to more than make up for the loss of the older 15-minute newscasts. Television news has settled into a format of network news in the morning, some local news at noon, network and local news in the evening, and local news in the late evening. A recent trend that expands the news day is late-evening network news, such as ABC's "Nightline."

Ted Koppell hosts ABC's "Nightline", a program of late evening network news. (Courtesy American Broadcasting Companies, Inc.)

ELECTRONIC NEWS GATHERING

One of the most important developments in broadcast news has been the introduction of electronic news gathering, or ENG, as it is called in the trade. The use of ENG is possible because of the perfection of mini-cams—miniature hand-held TV cameras instead of motion-picture cameras and film. Minicams can be used either for videotape or for live transmission, doing away with the time-consuming problem of developing and editing movie film.

Electronic news gathering enables the TV station to send out a crew for live coverage of a news event, say a fire. The crew travels in a van that has a microwave relay dish on top of it. They use the minicam to get a video picture of the fire and maybe an interview with the fire chief or a fire victim. The relay dish on the van sends the signal directly to the TV station, and the station in turn puts the live picture on the air. The viewer at home can see the fire while it is happening and listen to the reactions of persons on the scene.

The development of ENG is greatly changing the nature of TV news. For one thing, it is expanding the TV news day. When stations were limited to the use of movie film, which involved setting up elaborate equipment, a TV station could cover events only from, say, 10:00 A.M. to 2:00 P.M. With ENG requiring a minimum of setup time and no film-development time, the news day can run from early morning to late at night. Electronic news gathering poses some new problems for broadcast journalism, too, such as the ethical problems of live coverage. When ENG reporters go on the air live, they have no editors to prepare the news for

Defense lawyer David H. Waxler, representing Joseph Vieira in the "Big Dan's" rape trial is converged on by ENG media as he leaves the Fall River, Mass. Superior Court Building during his lunch break.

(Photo by Norman A. Sylvia, AP/Wide World Photos.)

the viewers. Whatever happens live happens on the screen as well. This is the excitement but also the dnager of this new kind of news presentation.

The videotext, teletext, and viewdata systems described in Chapter 15 will also have an impact in the future on the news and information uses of mass media. But the systems that are already in place are far from providing a really new medium for news.

As David H. Weaver concludes in his book on *Videotext Journalism*, these systems do not provide much new information that is not already available from existing media. The choice and volume of news in these new systems are quite limited as compared to newspapers. Journalists working for teletext and viewdata still do very little original reporting. The news carried on these systems tends to be superficial and event oriented. The systems themselves are not dramatically new in their appeal to different senses. They have not had significant impact on other media in Britain and the Netherlands, which have the most developed programs. They are more difficult and expensive to use for casual reading than printed media are. And, where available, they are not being accepted by the public as quickly as many thought they would be.

Weaver concludes that these systems will become viable as news media only when the content itself is as journalistically sound as the content of the old news media. These systems will require the same reporting skills and editorial judgments that newspapers require.

Videotext news and information systems will soon compete with traditional media for viewer news and information needs. (Courtesy AT&T Information Systems.)

MEDIA DIFFERENCES IN NEWS

News is not treated the same by all the mass media. For one thing, communication designed to be viewed must be structured in a different way from communication designed to be heard.

In writing for the print media, an important principle to note is that the eye is apt to be attracted to the first part of the page or the story or the paragraph or the sentence; the eye then is attracted elsewhere. Thus the most important element is usually placed at the beginning. A newspaper lead would begin "Ronald Reagan has won the election, according to the latest figures."

Unlike the eye, which focuses immediately, the ear needs time to become accustomed to sound. So radio and TV news copy generally backs into a story, giving the ear time to listen for the important element of the sentence. Our lead for radio or television might begin: "According to the latest figures, Ronald Reagan has won the election."

In addition, print media have more space to develop stories in depth, whereas the broadcast media usually have time only to skim the surface of the news. Broadcast news must use fewer words and transmit fewer stories. A 15-minute newscast contains only about 1800 words and about

25 different stories. An average daily newspaper has more than 100,000 words and dozens of different news items.

In the future, media news coverage may become even further differentiated, with the media complementing one another with various kinds of coverage instead of competing for the same facts and using the same methods. The print media will no doubt increasingly stress in-depth coverage, interpretation, explanation, and analysis; the broadcast media will assume the headline and spot-news responsibilities, the extra editions, and perhaps more of the light, dramatic, and human interest elements of the news.

Analysis and Interpretation 22

During the war in Vietnam, the U.S. government would often give a daily "body count" of the North Vietnamese soldiers killed in action. The next day the news media would duly report the government's count as an objective fact. The impression left with the American people was that U.S. forces were killing more Vietnamese than they were killing Americans, and so the United States must be winning the war. It took some time for the American people to realize that this was not so. The objective reports of the facts released by the government did not alone provide all the information needed for the people to know what was going on.

It is essential to have facts, but facts often need to be interpreted. The man who climbs the highest tree and looks out over the horizon may send back an accurate and objective report, yet he may not be communicating all his tribe needs to know. A black cloud may turn out to contain locusts, not rain. A friendly-looking tribe may prove hostile. A promising supply of fruit or game may not be edible. As we saw in the preceding chapter, even the fair and objective account of an occurrence may be misleading.

During World War II it became apparent that objective news reports about the war were often influenced by Allied and Axis propaganda activities. American concern about the effects of international propaganda prompted the establishment of a high-level group to study the problems of free communication in modern society. The Commission on Freedom of the Press carefully investigated and analyzed the passive objectivity of news and concluded, among other things, that "it is no longer enough to report *the fact* truthfully. It is now necessary to report *the truth about the fact.*"

Many indications from the world around us confirm the notion that straight reporting of the facts, while essential, may not always be sufficient. At no time in American history was this better illustrated than during the years of student unrest and political protest over the war in Vietnam. Many groups practiced manipulation of the news media to serve their own political purposes. The term *media event* was coined to describe a "happening" staged to attract maximum media coverage. As dissenters became increasingly street-smart in dealing with people and savvy about what reporters and broadcasting crews looked for in a news story, they orchestrated confrontational events, demonstrations, and sit-ins in places normally considered off-limits, such as the office of a university president or the lanes of an interstate highway. These tactics usually attracted throngs of reporters, whose cameras and microphones recorded the activity and the comments of an activist spokesman.

In May 1979, members of the New Hampshire Clam-shell Alliance chained themselves together in an attempt to block delivery of a reactor vessel to a power plant site, thus creating a "media event" to publicize their anti-nuclear cause.

(Courtesy the *Concord Monitor*.)

Today such techniques are used by those who demonstrate against the manufacture and deployment of nuclear weapons and capital punishment, among other things. Since an execution can be witnessed only by those required or invited to be present, editors usually did not send many reporters or much equipment to the prison for coverage. But now that executions are preceded by vigils outside prisons, more coverage is being given to them. Antinuclear activists have also attracted more attention to the deployment of weapons by conducting themselves in a way that will ensure the interest of the media: chaining themselves to fences at weapons' depots and military installations, using their bodies as roadblocks, conducting "street theater" performances predicting disaster—all designed to force the media to discuss feelings as well as facts in a story.

Those who wish to express a particular point of view, from the right to the left, from the old to the young, can use the news function of the media to communicate their ideas. To balance the use and abuse of news, the media must also be used to fulfill the need for analysis and interpretation, to put facts into perspective, to tell what it all means, to explain, to argue, to persuade, to express expert opinion about what happened, and to provide a forum for the expression of other opinions as well.

Actually, the role of persuader, the act of molding opinion, came earlier in the historical development of media than the role of informer. Early newspapers and magazines were often more a collection of editorials and advertisements than news stories. It was not until the mid-nineteenth century that news assumed great importance in mass communication.

THE SEPARATION OF FACT AND OPINION

When news became a part of American journalism, the tradition grew that news and opinion should be communicated separately. The reporter has been taught not to editorialize, not to express ideas and opinions and feelings about what happened, but to tell simply what happened. This practice is not followed by journalists in all countries. In many European countries, journalists are expected to bring their interpretation to the news they report.

The usual practice among American newspapers is to place editorial comment and opinion on a separate editorial page, often printed toward the end of the first section of the paper, leaving the front page and first inside pages for the publication of straight news. Another practice is to label clearly interpretative analysis or comment. Often the newspaper will publish a straight news account of a major story on page one, followed by an interpretative report as a sidebar feature, either on the same page or the inside pages. An editorial might then be written, on the same day, but more often on succeeding days, telling what the newspaper management's opinion is about the occurrence.

Much criticism is frequently directed at the news media for injecting editorial remarks into the presentation of news. The political affiliation

ARTHUR OCHS SULZBERGER, *Publisher*

A. M. ROSENTHAL, *Executive Editor*
SEYMOUR TOPPING, *Managing Editor*
ARTHUR GELB, *Deputy Managing Editor*
JAMES L. GREENFIELD, *Assistant Managing Editor*
LOUIS SILVERSTEIN, *Assistant Managing Editor*

MAX FRANKEL, *Editorial Page Editor*
JACK ROSENTHAL, *Deputy Editorial Page Editor*

CHARLOTTE CURTIS, *Associate Editor*
TOM WICKER, *Associate Editor*

The New York Times

Founded in 1851

ADOLPH S. OCHS, *Publisher 1896-1935*
ARTHUR HAYS SULZBERGER, *Publisher 1935-1961*
ORVIL E. DRYFOOS, *Publisher 1961-1963*

JOHN D. POMFRET, *Exec. V.P., General Manager*
LANCE R. PRIMIS, *Sr. V.P., Advertising*
J. A. RIGGS JR., *Sr. V.P., Operations*
HOWARD BISHOW, *V.P., Advertising*
RUSSELL T. LEWIS, *V.P., Circulation*
JOHN M. O'BRIEN, *V.P., Controller*
ELISE J. ROSS, *V.P., Systems*

The Squandering of a Panacea

It's hard to read without wonder about the long series of unlikely events that enabled Alexander Fleming to discover penicillin. The folly, greed and neglect with which the priceless gift of antibiotics is now being squandered command almost equal awe.

Antibiotics are a uniquely potent defense against bacteria, but they possess a fatal weakness: If used to excess, their power fails. That's what's now happening because of doctors who overprescribe antibiotics and farmers who routinely add them to animal feed.

Many disease bacteria are now resistant to six or more different antibiotics. They can be killed by others to which they have not yet acquired resistance. But the fallback antibiotics are often more toxic and more expensive than those they replace. And there's no guarantee that there will always be new antibiotics in reserve.

Some biologists fear the day may come when 80 percent of infections are resistant to all known antibiotics.

About 40 percent of the antibiotics produced in the United States are used not to control disease but because of a strange side effect: They promote growth in farm animals. All poultry and most pigs and cattle receive low doses of antibiotics in their feed. The practice insures the widest possible spread of resistance.

With daily doses of antibiotic in the animal's feed, the resistant bacteria have an overwhelming advantage over others. The genes that confer resistance are easily transferred from one bacteria to another, even to different species.

Several European countries long ago banned medically useful antibiotics from animal feed. They feared that the resistance genes were being transferred from animal bacteria to those that infect humans. In 1977 the Food and Drug Administration followed suit, proposing to reserve penicillin and tetracyclines for combating disease, and letting farmers switch to alternatives for promoting animal growth.

But Congress has persistently thwarted the proposal, demanding one new study after another. Producers of feed antibiotics, a $250-million-a-year industry, contend that hospitals, not farms, are the main forcing grounds of resistance, and that it's mere speculation to suppose that disease bacteria that gain resistance on a farm ever in fact infect humans.

Just such a case has now been documented by the Centers for Disease Control.

Investigating an outbreak of food poisoning in Minnesota, researchers traced back the chain of transmission from the patients to a consignment of hamburger, to the supermarkets where it was sold, to the meat broker, to the farm where the beef was raised. There they found that the farmer had fed tetracycline to his herd to promote growth.

The exact frequency of traffic between the animal and human pools of bacteria is hard to assess. But it could be high. Rather than risk continued debilitation of antibiotics needed for human and animal disease, why not let farmers pay a few cents more for the available alternatives?

Congress has needlessly stalled the obvious remedy for seven years. Further delay could well earn it the landmark opprobrium of helping render penicillin completely useless.

Cigarettes in Congress

A pregnant woman who smokes cigarettes puts her fetus at risk of injury, premature birth and low birth weight. And anyone who smokes cigarettes invites lung cancer, heart disease and emphysema.

Reminding the addicted of these dangers on cigarette packages with messages that are changed on a rotating schedule would revive a warning system now largely ignored because the nonspecific messages are taken for granted.

Congress and the cigarette industry agreed last spring on a bill that would put explicit rotating warnings on cigarette packages and advertising. The warnings haven't appeared yet, however, thanks to Senator Jesse Helms, who's been trying to talk cigarette companies into promising to buy more tobacco from American growers and less from Africa and Brazil. If they won't, he threatens,

he'll block this bill and let Congress come up with an even stiffer one.

Though Mr. Helms has succeeded in getting assurances from the industry, he still refuses to release the bill from committee because he's waiting for proof that the companies have cut their money where they said they would.

With the marketing season under way, he should soon have his proof, and there's every reason to believe that he'll now let the bill move through the Senate. In the meantime, action is expected this week on a House version of the bill.

That Senator Helms should wish to protect a major industry in his state is understandable. But a responsible Congress will give first priority to protecting America's health. Let a clear expression of House support provide the final nudge for quick Senate action.

How to Grade the Schools

The Chancellor of New York City's public schools, Nathan Quinones, proposes annual report cards to evaluate his system's performance. That's a promising idea. The Chancellor has named the subjects he would grade, among which parents and the public can find the issues of greatest concern.

Our report card would carefully grade the schools in the following categories:

☐ *Dropouts.* Can the schools graduate a larger proportion of students? Reducing the 42 percent dropout rate should be the Board of Education's highest priority. It has received $22 million in state aid for the effort but is not concentrating expenditures on junior and senior high schools, where the problem is most acute.

☐ *Class Size.* Teaching is most effective in smaller classes, and the Board has received enough money from the city to hold high-school classes to 34 students and the average first-grade class to 25. Will the money be properly spent and produce the desired results?

☐ *Teacher Quality.* The Board has hired a number of new teachers this year who did not major in

education training. How well will they perform and how many will remain in a year?

☐ *Special Education.* How many of the 111,000 children classified as needing special but expensive support can be properly dealt with in regular classes? Last year, 2,000 were moved out of special programs into regular classes, an increase of 50 percent over the previous year. The total number receiving special instruction, however, continued to increase. Can more handicapped children be taught in regular classes?

☐ *Management.* How well does the Board manage its budget of nearly $4 billion, and is it restraining administrative costs?

Mr. Quinones has challenged the entire school system to upgrade its performance. If in the process he and the Board can stem the flow of dropouts and gain control of the special education program without cheating handicapped children, they'll deserve the highest marks. If they fail, New York's children will be the losers.

Letter: On the Philippines
'Unfair to President Marcos'

To the Editor:

Your Aug. 27 editorial "The Burden in Manila" is full of errors of fact. It is also grossly unfair to President Marcos:

● A majority of the more than 25 million Filipino voters gave President Marcos a new vote of confidence in the May 14 election by electing a majority of the ruling party's candidates for the National Assembly.

● The Agrava Commission, an independent body formed by the President last year to ferret out the truth in the Aquino assassination, has summoned close to 200 witnesses and had made special trips to Tokyo and Los Angeles to seek out the testimony of reluctant Filipinos and Japanese, including journalist Kiyoshi Wakamiya, who testified for more than eight hours behind closed doors in February.

● The President's self-imposed 60-day deadline in the form of a brief rest in February. In an interview with The Times's Robert Trumbull last March that he was willing to relinquish his emergency powers if the majority of the members of the National Assembly said so.

● Independent Filipino and foreign economists, including foreign correspondents, have said that the Aquino assassination only contributed to the aggravation of the current economic crisis, which has been plaguing the Philippines since its independence in 1946.

● The President never promised not to reappoint the First Lady, Mrs. Imelda Romualdez Marcos, to any post in Government. Because of her major contribution to the social amelioration of poor Filipinos, the President had deemed it fit to reappoint her to her old positions.

● In a meeting with visiting American Congressmen early this year, the President said that if the U.S. felt the rental for the bases was too heavy a burden for it the U.S. should consider

removing them from the Philippines. Even before the Agrava Commission could release its findings, The Times concluded that it would just be part of the President's unfulfilled promises. This despite the fact that independent Filipino and foreign observers have given the commission high marks for impartiality.

As for the restoration of democracy, a host of ranking American officials have cited the May 14 elections as a further step in liberalization. The latest is that of U.S. Ambassador Stephen Bosworth, who said he was "amazed at the compromises" made on the restoration of the vice presidency, considered the recent election as a "significant step" in the restoration of democratic institutions and was "impressed" by the pluralism of views in the Philippine press.

WILLY C. GAA
Consul of the Philippines
New York, Aug. 27, 1984

Letters

The Real Gains in the War on Unemployment

To the Editor:

Unemployment figures can be misleading, claims David A. Page, chairman of Regional Research, Inc. ("The Phantom Jobless," Op-Ed, Aug. 24). After reviewing his flagrant abuse of such statistics, I could not agree more.

Arguing in part from data from western Pennsylvania, eastern Ohio and West Virginia, Mr. Page asserts that the national unemployment figures reported by the Reagan Administration appear favorable only because the Administration chooses to ignore the "phantom unemployed" — those who have dropped out of the labor force. He implies that the improvement in the national unemployment rate since December 1982 can be attributed to people's disappearance from the labor force, and not to an improvement in employment.

I would like first to point out that the monthly national employment and unemployment statistics are not the product of the Reagan Administration. The statistics are prepared and reported by the Bureau of Labor Statistics under the expert guidance of its Commissioner, Dr. Janet Norwood.

The bureau is a nonpartisan organization responsible for safeguarding the integrity of some of our nation's most important economic statistics. Both Republican and Democratic leaders have repeatedly praised the bureau for its careful and objective work. Americans are fortunate that neither the concept of what constitutes unemployment nor the statistical procedures used to estimate it are manipulated for the advantage of one political party or another.

Secondly, the employment and unemployment figures reported each month by the B.L.S. simply do not support Mr. Page's argument.

Since December of 1982, the civilian unemployment rate has fallen from 10.7 percent to 7.5 percent. In these same 19 months, the number of Americans holding jobs has increased by more than six million, growing more rapidly than at any other time since World War II; the civilian labor force (both the employed and the unemployed)

has increased by approximately three million.

According to Mr. Page, the Joint Economic Committee reports that 2.5 million people have disappeared from the labor force. Yet neither I, as chairman of that committee, nor the economists on the committee staff who deal with the B.L.S. can account for Mr. Page's "phantom" figure.

It may be that in referring to the "phantom jobless" he confused changes in the labor force with changes in the number of discouraged workers (persons who state that they would like to work but are not actively looking because they believe it would be difficult to find a job).

However, it is clear that labor market conditions are improving dramatically. According to the most recent B.L.S. estimates, the number of discouraged workers fell by over half a million between the fourth quarter of 1982 and the second quarter of 1984.

Long-term unemployment is certainly a serious problem, particularly in the steel- and coal-producing region from which Mr. Page draws most of his evidence. It is true that the labor force in the region is declining. Yet even here, where the data are most supportive of his argument, Mr. Page's interpretation of the statistics appears very questionable.

He cites a decline in the labor force of 134,000 out of about five million and refers to these as the "phantom unemployed." But according to his own figures, the population in the region has declined by 2 percent in the last two years. Thus, a decline in the labor force of approximately 100,000 would be expected (even more if those who left were more likely of working age).

Unemployment is a great tragedy. Because it is such a serious issue, I cannot allow the Administration's positive record in this area to be distorted. During the past year, the unemployment rate has declined in every state — even in my own hard-hit state of Iowa, and even in the coal- and steel-producing states from which Mr. Page draws much of his data.

Under the current Administration, lower taxes and less Government regulation provide a favorable climate for private investment and job creation nationwide. The success of this approach is demonstrated by the nation's falling unemployment rate.

(Senator) ROGER W. JEPSEN
Washington, Aug. 29, 1984

One Democratic Primary Too Many

To the Editor:

On Sept. 11, voters in a number of Congressional and legislative districts in New York State will cast their ballots in the Democratic primary for Congress, state legislator and county legislator. This is the second primary in five months — in April, New York Democrats cast their ballots in the Presidential primary.

It seems to me that having two primary dates (when only one is needed) is absurd. The costs of administering Congressional primaries run into the hundreds of thousands of dollars in inspector fees, polling place rentals, equipment, voting machine technicians, etc., and our tax dollars could be better spent.

In addition, with voter participation low to begin with, having two primary dates will only discourage a healthy turnout.

Many states combine Presidential primary dates with primaries for Congress and the legislatures. The tax dollars saved as a result of not having double primaries go into services, and more people have input into the selection of their representatives.

I hope that when New York's Legislature convenes in January it will mandate that in Presidential election years the primaries for all public offices be

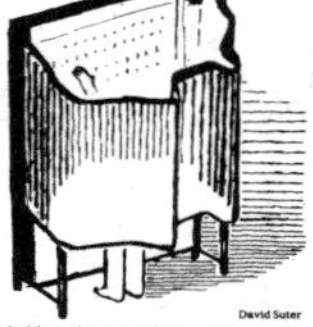

David Suter

held on the same date so that towns, cities, villages and counties will be able to save hundreds of thousands of dollars.

PAUL FEINER
Westchester County Legislator
Hastings-on-Hudson, N.Y., Sept. 3, 1984

COLA's Don't Boost Pension Buying Power

To the Editor:

J. Peter Grace's letter of Sept. 4, "American Military Pensions — Beyond Half Pay," is a deceptive presentation of the effect of cost-of-living adjustments (COLA's). Mr. Grace asserts that "military personnel with 20 years of service do not 'draw half their base pay for the rest of their lives'" and then proceeds to cite much larger figures — pension incomes corrected for inflation.

The purpose of COLA's is to maintain pensions — i.e., their purchasing power — exactly where they were to begin with. Cost-of-living adjustments do not increase the value of a pension, even if a $10,000 retirement check turns into a $1 million check because of wild inflation.

Furthermore, the Federal Government's income is also swelling with inflation, and therefore is at least in theory keeping even.

What the evidently well-to-do Mr. Grace and the other members of the President's Private Sector Survey on Cost Control have never mentioned is the terrible effect that inflation has on retirement incomes where there is no COLA.

I retired from high-school teaching in 1977. There are no cost-of-living adjustments for my pension, and there is no prospect that there will ever be. Today, my retirement check is worth approximately 35 percent less than it was in 1977.

DONALD J. QUIGLEY
Cornwall-on-Hudson, N.Y., Sept. 4, 1984

The Grapes of 'Inflation-Free Recovery'

To the Editor:

How could I have missed it? This "inflation-free recovery" you describe (editorial Sept. 4), resulting from some individually indistinguishable effects of the Carter Administration, the Federal Reserve Board and Mr. Reagan — did it happen here? Earthbound, even confined to the U.S.A. these past dozen years, I'm sure I would have noticed.

Perhaps I just don't know what you mean by "inflation-free recovery" (the old failure to communicate by virtue of using different meanings for the same term). But is the bottled-out building on the Lower East Side that cost $30,000 to buy three years ago and now costs $350,000 an example of this "inflation-free recovery"? Is the loft that three years ago could be rented for $600 a month and today goes for $2,000?

What about the half-gallon of seltzer water that just went from 69 cents to 79 cents, one day to the next — a 14.5 percent pole vault?

Is it just me, or are other people's salaries limping along behind this nonexistent inflation, the likes of 1,000 percent and 333 percent. I mean, if you can afford $250,000 for a modest one-bedroom apartment (and don't mind paying no outlandish a price), you might not have noticed that "inflation-free recovery" means astronomically expensive.

Maybe New York is atypical (could it have seceded from the U.S. while I wasn't looking?). Then perhaps it's Mayor Koch, rather than President Reagan, for whom great shouts of "Throw the bum out!" should ring from the rafters.

Such expensive rafters — better evict them both, and see how well they find the decent housing in the throes of the "inflation-free recovery."

ADRIENNE LEBAN
New York, Sept. 4, 1984

Philosophers Without Rock-of-Faith Support

To the Editor:

"The poets and philosophers," says Anthony L. Piazza in his Sept. 2 letter ("An Overdue Return to Religious Values"), "have long recognized the impossibility of constructing a culture and a civilization protective of the human condition without the rock of religious faith and values."

I wonder which philosophers Mr. Piazza has in mind.

Which of the great philosophers were even believers in God? Presumably Descartes, Leibnitz and Kant, in their own highly unorthodox ways, but surely not Hume, Schopenhauer, Nietzsche, Russell, Wittgenstein or Sartre, all of whom were self-evidently atheists. (If these names seem suspiciously "modern," one must realize that many earlier philosophers were very likely nonbelievers as well, though under extreme pressure from the state to conceal their views.)

Indeed it is in the nature of philosophy that it will not get along well with religion. Its point is to analyze and question, rather than to affirm received dogma. Religion deals with some of the same matters, but from an authoritarian viewpoint.

Schopenhauer wrote that religions thereby "... encroach on the sphere of metaphysics proper, and provoke its antagonism" and that "... such antagonism is expressed at all times, when metaphysics has not been chained up."

The philosopher who does not see this conflict might find his true calling to be that of theologian — or perhaps, as Mr. Piazza suggests, poet. And then agreement with the claim at issue here would be unremarkable: It is, after all, the theologian's business to be concerned with religion, while the poet "nothing affirmeth and therefore never lied."

ANTHONY BRUCK
Chicago, Sept. 4, 1984

Third-World Dictators Unworthy of U.S. Aid

To the Editor:

The two letters about Haiti you published on Aug. 29 illuminate serious questions of how the U.S. should deal with third-world countries. The point made in both is that the local rulers and elites do not care for their own populations and do not help in the process of economic development.

One letter writer, Dr. Joseph Bentvegna, concludes that "unless we Americans begin to address the social problems of Haiti and the third world in general intelligently, we will have many new Soviet bases to look forward to." The other, Charles Foster, says "it ought to be the task of the donor countries ... in the absence of effective national institutions, to encourage 'bottom-up' development, i.e., sponsor local self-help cooperatives and utilize private organizations for the distribution of food, fertilizer and the finance of local projects."

Both writers are motivated by the highest ideals, but what they are suggesting is a prescription for disaster. The only way such things could be done effectively is to have massive U.S. involvement in the direction and implementation of such programs: we could make them work by, in effect, taking over the country.

Americans in the "aid business" tend to be remarkably naive about the nature of the governments and elites around the world that we support liberally. We always assume that the governments have the best interests of all their citizens in mind. This is certainly not true in the bulk of the third-world countries, where various forms of dictatorship share the contributions of the U.S. taxpayers with small elites for the express purpose of staying in power and enjoying their perquisites.

It is nowhere written in our Constitution that we have to support every impotent dictator who uses his or her citizens as hostages. If we started to drop these countries, the "Soviet bases" Dr. Bentvegna fears could not materialize since the sheer number of countries would overwhelm Moscow's capacity for mischief-making.

Also, it may be time to call the bluff of many of the so-called leaders: If they believed that we were really going to pull out — not just threaten it — they might start to take a much more positive approach to development.

PETER P. ROGERS
Cambridge, Mass., Aug. 31, 1984

NYT
The New York Times Company
229 West 43d St., N.Y. 10036

Operating Groups

ARTHUR OCHS SULZBERGER, *Chairman*
SYDNEY GRUSON, *Vice Chairman*
WALTER MATTSON, *President*
CARL D. GORHAM, *Senior Vice President*
BENJAMIN HANDELMAN, *Senior Vice President*
MICHAEL E. RYAN, *Senior Vice President*
GUY T. GARRETT, *Vice President*
JOHN R. HARRISON, *Vice President*
SOLOMON B. WATSON IV, *Secretary*
DENISE K. FLETCHER, *Treasurer*

JOHN D. POMFRET, *Senior Vice President*
CHARLES B. BRAKEFIELD, *Vice President*
WILLIAM H. DAVIS, *Vice President*
JOHN R. HARRISON, *Vice President*
WILLIAM T. KERR, *Vice President*

---

of a newspaper or the bias of its staff may sometimes seem to affect its political news coverage. News magazines such as *Time*, *Newsweek*, and *U.S. News & World Report* have a particular problem because, while they conceive of their mission as a weekly "interpretation" of the news, their stories are not individually labeled as interpretation, and many readers accept these stories as unbiased news accounts. The blurring of fact and opinion in the news media has become an increasing problem, requiring more critical attention on the part of the consumer.

Radio and television also have a special problem in being used for interpretation and analysis. For many years, the FCC prohibited editorializing on the somewhat nebulous ground that broadcasting was such a powerful medium that it should not be allowed to influence opinions; it should only report facts. Happily, that situation no longer exists, but the FCC still regulates the editorial function of broadcasting, particularly through the so-called Fairness Doctrine. The Fairness Doctrine requires that when a station presents one side of a controversial issue of public importance, a reasonable opportunity must be afforded for the presentation of contrasting views. For example, when KURT in Houston, Texas, expressed the opinion that the John Birch Society engaged in "physical abuse and violence" and "local terror campaigns against oppositon figures," the FCC ruled that the station must give the society equal opportunity to express its views. Many such rulings have been made.

It is useful to examine the variety of ways in which mass media are used to provide interpretation and analysis of the world in which we live.

HOW THE MEDIA INTERPRET AND ANALYZE

Interpretative and Background Reports

An increasing emphasis is being placed on reporting that attempts to tell more about an occurrence than the fact that it happened today. Historical background and perspective are needed. Many facts need further explanation, amplification, and clarification. The news media are increasingly developing specialists among their reporting staffs, people who know as much about their subjects as the experts, and in reporting about a complex or controversial matter they can add their own expert opinions to give their audience fuller understanding of the situation.

Even the wire services, long the staunchest defenders of straight, objective news reporting, are making more use of background and interpretative reports. The Associated Press employs teams of special reporters who carry out in-depth investigations of complicated yet vital concerns and practices. They are under no deadline pressures that would force them to write a quick and superficial report of the facts. They can get behind the facts, explore the ramifications and meanings of the facts, and reveal the "truth about the facts."

Editorials   Editorials have become a standard feature of American newspapers and of some magazines as well. At times they are placed on the front page when they concern an issue that is extremely important to the publisher, but the responsible practice is to put the editorial in a box, set it in larger type, or in other ways make it appear separate from news coverage.

Generally, editorials are not bylined. They are written by writers who specialize in persuasive writing. The editorial-page staff begins each day by deciding which issues require editorial statements. Editorial staff members discuss the general treatment of these issues and, with guidance from management on crucial issues, determine the stand the newspaper will take. Others may write editorials, too, including the editors and publisher and reporters who might develop strong opinions about the news they are covering and feel compelled to make a relevant editorial judgment.

Unlike the print media, which have long enjoyed freedom of expression in America, the broadcast media have not yet unanimously embraced their right to air their opinions. A survey by the National Association of Broadcasters indicated that only slightly more than half the stations in the country (57% of radio and 56% of television) regularly broadcast editorials (following the NAB's definition of an editorial as an "on-the-air expression of the opinion of the station licensee, clearly identified as such, on a subject of public interest").

But the editorial function is growing in broadcasting. The larger stations are more apt to editorialize, which bears out the journalistic theory that the stronger the medium, the more courageously it accepts its responsibilities. Four out of 10 TV stations now put editorials on the air every day; 2.5 out of 10 radio stations do the same.

Weekly Summaries and Interpretations   Weekly news magazines, Sunday newspaper supplements, and some weekly newspapers also fulfill the need for interpretation and analysis. News magazines, particularly *Time*, *Newsweek*, and *U.S. News & World Report*, have had a major impact on interpretative journalism. They see their role as weekly summarizers and explainers, putting the news of the week into historical, political, or scientific perspective, to express the meaning in the news. *Time*, especially, has perfected the technique of *group journalism*, where facts are sent to New York City headquarters from many different reporters and many different angles on a given story. These facts are scrutinized by editors and specialists, who then put together a final summary, snythesizing, interpreting, and analyzing the facts from a broad perspective.

Most major metropolitan newspapers are now also publishing special weekly reviews for their Sunday editions; here, news for the past week in various fields—politics, education, finance, culture—is reviewed and interpreted. A few publications, in weekly newspaper format, have been started for this purpose alone, such as *Barron's*, a national weekly financial review published by Dow Jones & Company.

The editorial cartoon may be the most widely communicated interpretation or analysis. It has been a force on the editorial page in American journalism since 1754, when the first cartoon appeared in the *Pennsylvania Gazette*, accompanying an editorial written by Benjamin Franklin. It pictured a snake, cut into 13 pieces, representing the British colonies, and it was entitled "Join or Die."

Effective editorial cartoons use the art of caricature, employing a few swift lines to exaggerate a character, personality, or feature to make a point. Bill Mauldin's "G.I. Joe" came to represent the attitudes and feelings of servicemen for an entire generation, and a few strokes of the pen could communicate much meaning. Herblock's grim, five-o'clock-shadowed hydrogen bomb expressed widely shared opinions about banning nuclear warfare. The economies of time and space permitted by the editorial cartoon give it particular force for mass communication; by the same token, the editorial cartoon is often a superficial and exaggerated statement about people or issues.

Editorial Cartoons

The broadcast media have combined interpretive reporting, analysis, and even editorial comment into the documentary, one of the best vehicles for getting at the truth behind the facts. The documentary has often been a powerful force for interpretation and analysis of events that often cannot be better communicated any other way. The documentary, using historic film footage and current interviews, can provide a vehicle to review recent

Documentaries

(Drawing by Steve Sack, Courtesy the *Minneapolis Tribune*.)

A documentary, such as the thirteen part series "Vietnam: A Television History", can be a powerful force for interpretation and analysis of recent events.

(François Sully, "Vietnam: A Television History", WGBH Educational Foundation.)

history and put confusing events into clearer perspective. In 1983, PBS produced such a documentary in "Vietnam: A Television History," a thirteen-part series shown on prime time, interpreting and analyzing an event in American history that was difficult to report on objectively while it was happening.

Some interpretative programs and documentaries have been "tucked away at unwanted hours" of Sunday mornings or afternoons, the so-called Sunday ghetto of broadcasting, says William S. Small, former news executive at CBS and NBC, in his book, *To Kill a Messenger: Television News and the Real World.*

The networks use special documentaries that preempt regularly scheduled shows whenever an event of major consequence occurs—an earthquake, a space launch, a riot, or the death and funeral of a great person. Using sight and sound, television has been able to probe, capture, and communicate such events with great effectiveness. After the return of the hostages from Iran, ABC produced a powerful 3-hour documentary, narrated by Pierre Salinger. This history of the hostage situation in sight and sound and interview analyzed the events better than most printed accounts could have.

The same techniques have been used to probe, analyze, and interpret great issues. The networks have produced documentaries on race relations, drug addiction, court procedures, political campaigns and elections, espionage, island invasions, and war. Local news staffs of both radio and TV stations have used the documentary to expose local police corruption, poverty, hunger, housing, and education problems.

The documentary can have a powerful effect because it can use sounds and pictures together to move people. Small describes one of the most impressive CBS News efforts, a documentary on "Hunger in America," a moving hour of broadcasting that opened with film of a baby actually dying of starvation in front of the camera. Says Small:

> The broadcast had tremendous impact, particularly on the then Secretary of Agriculture, Orville Freeman, who bitterly attacked it and demanded equal time. He called it "shoddy journalism" that blackened the name of the Agriculture Department. Even as Freeman attacked, he was taking official steps that CBS interpreted as conceding the broadcast's main points: The Department abandoned its ceiling on food stamp programs, sharply expanded the number of counties with such programs, enlarged the quantity and variety of surplus food and sought (and won) Senate approval for an additional $200 to $300 million for food programs.[1]

In 1971 CBS's "The Selling of the Pentagon," a documentary on the public relations efforts of the military, in turn became an editorial issue. Supporters and detractors used the media to praise or attack the production. The program's format eventually caused an attempt by the House of Representatives Commerce Committee, led by Chairman Harley O. Staggers, to issue a contempt citation against CBS president Frank Stanton. Dr. Stanton refused to submit "outtakes" (film not actually used in the program) for committee analysis. The committee was concerned over whether two personal interviews shown in "The Selling of the Pentagon" were used out of context. Eventually, the issue was settled on whether Congress should become the arbiter of what is *truth* in programming. The FCC ruled that the program met all criteria under the Fairness Doctrine. Some cynics saw the criticism of the documentary as an attempt by Pentagon supporters to cloud the issue or prevent future media disclosure of military–industrial activities for fear of reprisals.

In some ways the print media counterpart to broadcast documentaries   **Crusades**
is the crusade. A newspaper might undertake a crusade for an issue on which it feels public interpretation and analysis is vital. The *Washington Star* undertook a crusade against fraudulent used-car sales practices and forced the government to improve regulations. The *Washington Post* crusaded against deceitful savings-and-loan-bank operations, which helped bring about new legislation curbing such activities. Crusades have been the hallmark of courageous journalism and often have led to media prizes.

A crusade often starts with a news story that uncovers some problem in society that the editors feel should be exposed. A reporter or a team of researchers and writers might be assigned to dig into the facts. After the

[1] William Small, *To kill a Messenger: Television News and the Real World* (New York: Hastings House, 1970), 270.

The dangers of asbestos

Discovery at WCC highlights the cancer-causing hazard

By Jean Hall
Science/Medicine Editor

Asbestos is a natural, fibrous material composed of magnesium silicates and calcium. It is fire and acid resistant, light weight and used in thousands of everyday products, such as the brake linings on our cars.

For years, it was used as an insulating and fireproofing material in homes, businesses and schools. Now, it is generally regarded as a cancer-causing health hazard.

Asbestos dust was found Thursday circulating through the air conditioning ducts of the 7-year-old Science Building at Westchester Community College in Valhalla. The building was closed Friday as a week-long effort to remove the asbestos-containing insulation material got under way.

Dr. Anita Curran, Westchester County health commissioner, said Saturday she believes there is a "99.9 percent" chance that none of the thousands of WCC students and employees who used the building will suffer any ill effects.

The bad news about asbestos first surfaced in 1935, when two physicians found what was called "asbestosis" in two of their patients. The link to cancer was definitely established in 1960 by researchers under Dr. Irving Selikoff at Mt. Sinai Hospital in New York.

Asbestosis, which is acquired through heavy exposure to asbestos particles, is a lung disease much like emphysema; its progressive damage eventually leads to asphyxiation. It could be compared to the "black lung" disease of coal miners, or the lung disease of cotton pickers who inhaled cotton dust — but unlike those particles, asbestos stays in the body.

The fibers sometimes migrate to other parts of the body, mainly the gastrointestinal tract, the ovaries, skin, liver and larynx (voice box). Fibers reaching the lining of the lungs can cause mesothelioma, a rare, but always fatal, form of cancer.

The incubation period from asbestos fiber inhalation to the appearance of disease is estimated at from four to 50 years.

According to the latest statistics available from the National Institute for Occupational Safety and Health, an estimated 58,000 to 75,000 Americans die each year from disease caused by exposure to asbestos.

In April, the federal Occupational Safety and Health Administration cut by a fourth the amount of asbestos previously allowed in workplaces. The move could cut asbestos-related deaths from 64 per 1,000 workers to between 17 per 1,000.

A tighter restriction is also being contemplated. The earlier standard was set in 1976.

Also in April, the U.S. Environmental Protection Agency reinstated standards for handling asbestos, especially in building demolitions, that had been invalidated six years earlier for technical reasons by the U.S. Supreme Court.

The dangers of asbestos first came to national public attention as a result of World War II when the steam lines and pipes of Liberty and Victory ships were insulated with the material. Some 20,000 workers contracted some form of asbestos-related disease.

One major manufacturer of the material, the Johns-Manville Corp. went bankrupt to avoid hundreds of damage claims. Another, Raybestos-Manhattan Inc., was still settling claims with workers as of last November.

Exposure to asbestos is not limited to factories, schools or buildings. An estimated 158,000 pounds of asbestos dust is emitted each year from automobile brake linings.

Dr. John H. Weisburger, vice president of the American Health Foundation and a world-renowned cancer researcher, said Sunday there are several things to emphasize about asbestos exposure.

ASBESTOS
From page one

information.

Rosell said the union plans to consult an environmental health expert today.

Students arriving for class this morning were confronted by barricades preventing them from entering the Science Building. Signs directed them to where classes were being relocated.

Edmund Ford, a 24-year-old engineering student from the Bronx, said he is aware of the the dangers of asbestos from having repaired automobile brakes. "A little asbestos can do a lot of damage," he said.

But another engineering student, Therese Caruso of Mount Vernon, said she doesn't feel threatened by the asbestos. She was more concerned about her schedule being disrupted, noting she typically spends eight to nine hours a day in the Science Building.

Hankin said Friday he had been told architectural plans for the Science Building specified that no asbestos was to be used. County health officials believe insulation for the building's air conditioning system contained asbestos.

Officials say the problem was created when insulation in one of four air conditioning units on the building's roof began to fall apart in clumps. The clumps wound up in the air conditioning system and were distributed through the building as a powder.

The insulation began falling into the air conditioning ducts after a wheel in one of the units had broken as a result of heavy rains on Sept. 3, Hankin said.

Hankin said the asbestos was being removed from all four units by the Asbestos Corp. of America, a Yonkers-based firm.

Other air conditioning units throughout the campus are to be checked, Hankin said, including those atop the Academic Arts Building, which is connected to the Science Building by a glass corridor.

The arts building has a separate air conditioning system. However, small traces of asbestos, believed to have come in from the Science Building, were found.

Staff Writers Edward Frost and Donna Greene contributed to this report.

The most important, he says, is the "tremendous" risk of lung cancer for heavy smokers who are exposed to asbestos fibers.

The American Cancer Society agrees. Asbestos workers who smoke may be 92 times more likely than the average non-smoker to develop lung cancer. For that reason, smoking has been barred since 1978 for workers at plants where asbestos is used in manufacturing.

"In the '40s," said Weisburger, "no one knew much about the hazards of asbestos. In cities where ship building went on — Charleston, S.C.; Jacksonville, Fla.; Mobile, Ala.; New Orleans and throughout the Boston and New York shipyards, large numbers were heavily exposed. Today, 40 years later, these people are suffering from all the diseases asbestos can cause.

"But, while we know the dangerous effects of heavy contamination, we don't know much about the effects of small amounts, as in a school — there is no data."

WCC president says he's certain no more asbestos will be found

By Harlan Marks
Staff Writer

The president of Westchester Community College says he is certain no more asbestos will be found at any of the Valhalla campus' 13 buildings once workers remove the cancer-causing agent that was discovered Thursday at the school's Science Building.

The building was closed Friday until the expected week-long clean-up operation is finished. Traces of asbestos were also reported in the adjacent Academic Arts building, which remains open.

College President Joseph Hankin said Sunday the entire complex, where 12,500 students attend classes each day, was thoroughly tested for asbestos in 1979, after the school's library was temporarily shut down when the substance was found in ceiling duct work.

In those 1979 tests, the Westchester County Health Department conducted visual inspections and surface-air quality testing. "We were told everything was fine," Hankin said, adding he had been "pretty well assured that there's nothing left on campus."

Construction of the Science Building was not completed until after asbestos was discovered in the library, he said.

Some faculty members who work in the Academic Arts building said Sunday they were considering refusing to enter it today.

"I think the college has to respect people's wishes not to go into the building if they feel it's not safe," Richard Rosell, president of the Westchester Community College Federation of Teachers, said Sunday.

But there were no apparent disruptions this morning, with classes in the Academic Arts building proceeding as scheduled.

Douglas Plath, an adjunct professor of psychology who was teaching a class in the Academic Arts building, said today he was not aware of the union's concern. He said he would be interested in getting more

Please see ASBESTOS
on back page of this section

The *Reporter Dispatch* conducts a crusade against asbestos. The front page story represents the paper's continuing coverage of the discovery of asbestos on a local college campus and is supplemented by an article on the dangers of the substance by the science and medicine editor. (Courtesy the *Reporter Dispatch*.)

newspaper knows the facts, it decides how it will treat the story; it might publish the material in a series of news stories or interpretative reports, sometimes following up with sidebars and features on various aspects of the problem, and finally concluding the crusade with an editorial or series of editorials in which the newspaper presents its conclusions and recommendations.

Columnists and Commentators

The media provide an opportunity for experts and specialists to analyze and interpret public problems in their fields regularly through the column, a bylined feature. Many newspapers and magazines have staff columnists who write on local or special interests. But most columnists are handled by national syndicates, to which the publications subscribe. Columnists have great latitude to handle material in their own way, with a light or heavy touch, with sarcasm, satire, or humor.

A typical newspaper publishes an amazing variety and number of columns. On an average Sunday, the *Washington Post* published about two dozen columnists, who covered a wide range of topics. Among them were four nationally syndicated political columnists representing a variety of political viewpoints: Joseph Kraft, liberal; George F. Will, conservative; David S. Broder, moderate; and Jack Anderson, investigative. A fifth, Henry Fairlie, a British journalist, wrote on international topics. The *Post* also ran a variety of columns on cultural subjects, including Sander Vanocur on television; Paul Hume on music; Joseph McLellan on records and paperback books; and Norman Eisenberg on stereo equipment.

Syndicated columnists dealt with personal problems for the *Post*: Ann Landers's advice on sex, love, marriage, and almost anything else (the modern version of the old "advice to the lovelorn" columns); Jean Mayer and Johanna Dwyer's advice on nutrition; and Timothy Johnson's advice on health. The *Post* also carried four columns on a variety of sports in

Gannett Westchester Newspapers
Monday, September 10, 1984

Advice/entertainment

Best defense against slurs is laughter

Ann Landers

Dear Readers: A few weeks ago, I printed a letter from a Mrs. Hooker who enlisted my help to restore respectability to the family name. (She was sick and tired of seeing "hooker" used in newspaper stories as a substitute for "prostitute.")

I was inundated with letters from other Hookers applauding her efforts and urging me to undertake the crusade. I also heard from a prostitute who did not like being called a hooker because it suggested that she used a hook to get customers. "Not necessary," the respondent wrote, "I'm well-known here and have not solicited in years."

My mail this week has been fascinating. Here's a sampling:

From El Paso:
Dear Ann Landers:
While I sympathize with all the decent people named Hooker, I wonder if they realize they have plenty of company. What about folks named Pratt, Fanny, Butts, Duff, Flake, Crumm, Jerke, Fink, Sapp, Nutt. I could go on forever. Believe me, the best defense is a sense of humor. —Texas Fan

Dear Texas: I agree.

Dear Ann Landers:
Our only child (24) has been married for three years. He and his wife Jane have a 2-year-old daughter whom I have only seen twice. Why? Because my husband and I both smoke and our daughter-in-law forbids smoking in their home.

I can respect that, but she refuses to come to our home. When our son comes to visit she will not let him bring the baby. He brings pictures and says, "What can I do, I have to keep peace at home."

I believe it is impossible to protect a child from the outside world with all the pollution from cars, factories and so on. Jane refuses to accept these realities.

We did not smoke in their home when Jane made her wishes known, but I refuse to be bullied in our own home. When we were there two years ago for Christmas she made my husband go outside to smoke. It was bitter cold. She then asked me to wash my hands before I held the

baby because they smelled like smoke!

She avoids all family functions and no one ever sees the baby. I can't believe my son is such a wimp. He just hangs his head and says, "I'm sorry!" We want your advice. — Sad Grandparents (Buffalo, N.Y.)

Dear Sad:
You have made it plain that you are going to continue to smoke in your own home, and that is your right. I see nothing in your letter, however, that says your son and husband cannot visit in Jane's home if you refrain from smoking.

That seems like the best solution. If you and your husband must go outside to smoke, then GO!

Dear Ann Landers:
I am seething over the letter from "Disgusted in Arizona." She is the old battleaxe who insists that her husband "chooses" to be overweight. She may be right, but I'll bet *she* is the reason. My husband

spent 14 years doing to me exactly what she is doing to him.

If "Wifey Dearest" really wants her husband to lose weight, she will: 1) Give him her unqualified support; 2) give him a sense of self-worth, self-respect and 3) get the desserts, ice cream, beer and potato chips out of the house.

In other words, if she wants to get back on his lap she must start by getting off his back. — Been There In Van Nuys

Dear Van Nuys:
You make some good points. Fatties sometimes stay fat to spite the one who is constantly nagging them to take off weight.

They find it a highly effective weapon. When the nagging stops, the weight loss begins.

Are your parents too strict? Hard to reach? Ann Landers' booklet, "Bugged By Parents? How to Get More Freedom," could help you bridge the generation gap. Send 50 cents with your request and a long, stamped, self-addressed envelope to Ann Landers, P.O. Box 11995, Chicago, Illinois 60611.

Ann Landers is one of the many columnists who appear regularly in the *Washington Post*. (Courtesy Ann Landers, News America Syndicate.)

this particular issue: two on local sports, one on motor sports, and one on outdoor sports. Sports columnists' coverages vary from day to day, taking in almost every sport imaginable.

Other columns dealt with hobbies and helpful hints, and in this particular issue there were columns on stamp and coin collecting, needlepoint, gardening, and consumer problems. Columns on humor and "just plain easy reading" were also carried. This issue of the *Post* carried Art Buchwald's "Capitol Punishment," a column of Washington satire that often has more political bite than the work of some serious writers.

The Sunday *Washington Post* contained special sections with news reports and comments, too, including a book-review section and sections on business and travel; *Parade*, a national Sunday supplement magazine; *Potomac*, a local magazine; a TV guide for the week; and 16 pages of comics in color.

Radio and television also utilize commentators who play a similar role for electronic audiences. The old format of 15-minute radio commentaries by strong personalities have vanished: individuals with strong political commitments, like Gabriel Heatter, Raymond Gram Swing, and Fulton Lewis, Jr., or persons with strong interpretative reporting talents, such as Elmer Davis, H. V. Kaltenborn, and Edward R. Murrow, are gone and have not been replaced.

Most stations now use a variety of reporters and correspondents, some of whom might comment upon and analyze local news, but often not as personalities. The networks have commentators, but they too are more likely to be reporters than persuaders—people such as CBS's Dan Rather,

NBC's Tom Brokaw and ABC's Peter Jennings. Only Mutual's Paul Harvey still falls into the category of the strong personality with definite political commitments.

Criticism and Reviews

The mass media assume a responsibility to provide critical analysis of public performances, particularly in the popular arts. Books, movies, concerts, recordings, and dramas are all public performances that need comment. Reviews help the audience find the right performance, the performer find the right audience, aiding the artist in perfecting a craft and the public in making decisions.

In the past most mass media commentaries on popular arts were reviews rather than criticisms; they were reports of what happened, and only sometimes were they critical reports. Reviewers were more likely to be news reporters who had been given the book beat, the movie beat, or the music beat. There is now a general trend on the larger newspapers, at the networks, and certainly among national magazines for these reviewers to be critics, expert and trained judges of literary, dramatic, or artistic performances, who can make authoritative evaluations.

Letters to the Editor

Finally, it is the responsibility of the mass media to provide a forum for the expression of audience opinion. This function increases in importance as the ability of the masses to communicate publicly decreases because of the rising costs of printing and broadcasting. The people who write letters to the editor do not represent a true cross section of the public, nor can the media publish or broadcast all the letters that come into their offices. As in all other phases of mass communication, selection and judgment are key elements in communicating the public's opinions.

PUBLIC ACCESS

The analysis and interpretation of information raises the issue of the right of access to the mass media by the public. Do only media analysts and interpreters have a right to comment on and pass judgment on facts and events and ideas? What right do outsiders have to express their opinions in the mass media? The mass media are privately owned institutions, but do they have an obligation to make their air time and pages available to nonowners who want to express themselves?

Public access to the mass media has become a critical issue. Some forceful pressure groups advocate open access to the media. In his book *Freedom of the Press vs. Public Access*, Benno C. Schmidt, Jr., describes some of the rights claimed by those who advocate access: the right of political candidates to advertise or appear in the media in which their opponents appear; the right of a person to respond to an attack or criticism; the right to advertise competing goods, services, or ideas in a medium that accepts advertising; or the right of anyone to have his or her views published or news covered on subjects about which the medium has carried its views or news.

Letters

Reagan should apologize

Editor, The Record:

We have just returned from a trip across country during which time the president made the remark: "My fellow Americans, I am pleased to tell you I just signed legislation which outlaws Russia forever. The bombing begins in five minutes." Everywhere we went, people couldn't believe that such an irresponsible statement could be made by a president of the United States.

An editorial in the Wichita Eagle-Beacon, Kansas, called for the president to apologize to the Soviet people, to America's friends in Europe, to the people of the United States, and especially to "the children of the future. It's not likely any of them are going to be laughing about the threat of total destruction that this generation sometimes seems determined to pass on to the next."

I would add that Congress itself should demand an apology. It would have to be legislation passed by Congress that the president would be signing. Congress has been insulted. There is still some sanity in the Congress that must cringe at the implications of such a statement.

Frankly, the whole thing is frightening. Calling the Russians an "Evil Empire" and then announcing "the bombing begins in five minutes" i not a joke; it is a warped state o mind.

In a world saturated with a pletl ora of nuclear weapons ready to g at the press of a button, Americ needs a caring and responsible pres dent in the White House. Certainl;

the present incumbent has difficulty fulfilling that charge. It all adds up to the need for a change in November.

E. WILLIAM CLARK
Ridgewood

•

Too wide a net

Editor, The Record:

There are some people, it seems, destined to ever-lasting damnations by newspapers such as The Record. Lodi Police Chief Andy Voto is one of them.

No matter who is involved in anything, so long as he has some direct, indirect, or peripheral connection to Andy Voto, Voto's name is automatically linked to the story.

A story Aug. 6 reported that Howard Clarke and another man began serving a 30-day sentence for bookmaking. The Record felt compelled to note Clarke was Andy Voto's son-in-law. The fact that Andy Voto had nothing to do with the charges against this individual did not stop your reporter from linking him to the story.

This kind of journalism reminds me of the old Daily News headlines: "Ex-Marine kills four." The fact that the person may have served only one hitch in the Marines and was discharged 20 years before made no difference. Somehow linking him to

the military made him seem so much more of a wanton killer.

The same holds true for Chief Voto. As soon as something happens, drag Andy Voto into the story and make it into something it isn't. Isn't it time you reported the significant facts of a story, and omitted insignificant, irrelevant details?

CHARLES P. SERWIN
Hackensack

Mr. Serwin is a detective in the sheriff's office.

A teacher in space

Editor, The Record:

Do I detect a note of sarcasm? Your editorial of Aug. 30 gives me the impression you feel our teachers don't deserve the recognition President Reagan is giving them with this invitation to have a teacher join the next space crew. For shame!

There may be many other professions from which to attract a crew member, but for the sake of our future adults, it is our teachers who contribute more than their share to our country's development. The selection of a teacher to be first in space is a small but truly significant attempt to acknowledge the contribution our teachers have made, do make, and will continue to make to our society.

The president is doing the right thing!

EAMON T. FENNESSY
Upper Saddle River

Audience opinion can be communicated publicly in the form of letters to the editor. (Courtesy The Bergen Record Corp., Letters reprinted with permission of the authors.)

In broadcasting, FCC regulations such as the Fairness Doctrine and formerly the equal-time provision made access a fact of life. The 1969 Red Lion ruling of the Supreme Court not only upheld the notion that broadcasters should provide reasonable opportunity for contrasting views to be heard on a subject but also supported the idea that all media have an obligation to preserve an uninhibited marketplace of ideas.

The FCC regulations on cable television, adopted in 1972, required each new cable system in the top 100 markets to keep available one access channel for the general public, educational institutions, and local government. This channel was to be available without charge at all times on a first-come, first-served nondiscriminatory basis. Live studio presentations of less than 5 minutes were to be subsidized by the cable system, but other production costs were to be paid by the user. The public-access channel caused some problems in cities where it was in use, such as New York, where the programs tended to appeal to narrow and special-interest groups such as homosexuals or transcendentalists, and the channel had trouble attracting audiences and financing.

In the late 1970s, in an effort to reduce restrictions on the growth of cable television, the FCC removed the open-access channel regulation for cable-TV systems. Now, no mass medium must provide access to outsiders to its properties. No one can walk into a radio or TV station and demand to go on the air with his or her version of the news or opinions. And no one can demand that any newspaper, magazine, or book publisher must accept his or her ideas and put them into print.

The access philosophy accepted by the FCC in the area of cable television has been suggested for other media, but it has not been implemented. Further definitions of access rights came about as a result of the most celebrated access case of the 1970s, *Miami Herald Publishing Co. v. Tornillo*. In 1972 the *Miami Herald* ran an editorial opposing the candidacy of a Florida union leader who was running for the nomination for the state house of representatives. The candidate, Pat L. Tornillo, Jr., wrote a reply, which the *Herald* refused to publish. The case ultimately reached the U.S. Supreme Court, which ruled that the newspaper did not have to publish the reply. The Court's decision in the *Miami Herald* case constituted a firm rejection of the idea that anyone has a constitutional right to force a publisher to print something against the publisher's will. The Court held that such a ruling would do greater damage to freedom of the press than access would help freedom of expression.

Nevertheless, the mass media have an obligation to encourage uninhibited public dialogue and freedom of expression for everyone. And today the mass media have voluntarily accepted this responsibility in larger measure than ever before. For example, newspapers are providing more space for letters to the editor. Some newspapers, such as the *Salt Lake City Tribune*, have a "common carrier" column for outsiders, and pay a community panel to screen the contributions. Bill Monroe, executive editor of NBC's "Meet the Press" and former Washington editor of the "Today" show, has advocated a "letters to the editor" feature for radio and TV stations as well, and a growing number of stations are moving in this direction. The popular CBS investigative news program "60 Minutes" now concludes the show each week with letters of reaction to previous shows. Other media have appointed ombudsmen to deal with reader and listener complaints. Many newspapers are giving greater visibility to their published corrections than they used to. These are all signs that mass media leaders are concerned about public access at the same time that they enjoy their essential rights to use their own franchise freely.

SYNDICATES   As news services provide for the centralized gathering and distribution of news and information, so syndicates serve as central agencies for the analysis and interpretation function for the media. More than 400 agencies sell feature and editorial material to the media, both print and electronic. Small, independent weekly and daily newspapers or radio and TV stations are the most likely customers for syndicated material.

Syndicates hire writers and commentators and market their work to individual media. Like wire services, they charge the media on the basis of circulation or size. A widely syndicated columnist like political humorist Art Buchwald can earn well over $250,000 a year through syndication.

Editor and Publisher Yearbook lists more than 2500 features that can be purchased from syndicates in the following categories: astrology, automotive, aviation, beauty, books, bridge, business–financial, cartoons and panels, chess, checkers, farming, health, history, household, maps, motion pictures, music, nature, patterns, photography, puzzles–quizzes, radio and television, religion, science, serials, short stories, special pages, sports, stamps, travel, veterans, women's pages. These are main features. Other classifications include agriculture, bedtime stories, dogs, foreign news, labor, manners, politics, questions and answers, schools, and verse.

Finally, we must ask the question, how effective are the media in fulfilling a role as interpreters and analysts in our society? Most readership studies show that more people read comic strips than editorials.

THE IMPACT OF ANALYSIS AND INTERPRETATION

In its study of the impact of broadcast editorials, the National Association of Broadcasters concluded that awareness and actual exposure to editorials are more prevalent among men, young adults, and college-educated people. The NAB's survey showed that about two-thirds of the public felt that broadcasting stations should editorialize. A large majority of those who have seen or heard editorials (83% for television, 73% for radio) remembered instances in which an editorial made them think more about a particular issue. And about half (54% for television and 47% for radio) reported that these editorials helped them make up their minds about issues.

Do editorials change minds? Probably not as much as editorial writers would like. During political campaigns, editorial endorsement of political candidates does not seem to have made a great impression on voting, according to most studies. Frank Luther Mott's analysis of the power of the press in presidential elections showed that newspapers' candidates had been beaten more frequently than they had triumphed.

On the other hand, there is much tangible evidence of the immediate impact of the mass media's analysis and interpretation, from editorials, columns, commentaries, crusades, and documentaries, including legislation passed, injustices corrected, individuals aided, tasks completed, and political victories won.

In summary, well-informed citizens, who alone can make democracy work, require news, information, analysis, and interpretation. They should get their facts, and the truth about the facts, from as wide a selection of media as possible. They should not depend upon any one radio or TV station, or any one newspaper or magazine. They should have access to as many different reporters and interpreters for any given event or issue as possible. Otherwise, they will be like the blind men who touched only one part of the elephant and interpreted it as the whole.

23

Education and Socialization

In 1982 the CBS TV network and New York University announced the end to one of TV's grand experiments in formal education, "Sunrise Semester." After 25 years, the televised college course on which some of the university's most distinguished professors reached an early-morning audience of credit and noncredit students was being canceled. The numbers told the story as CBS indicated that in 1981 only 42 of its 200 affiliated stations carried the program and only 47 students were enrolled for credit. Thus, another of TV's attempts to integrate formal education with broadcast function and design came to an undistinguished end.

With the single exception of books, media and education have had a checkered history. Both sides are apt to blame the other for everything from lack of vision to lack of money. In the case of "Sunrise Semester" the problems were familiar ones to the media–education dialogue; primarily a minimal investment in production. The most articulate teachers could not overcome this limitation. In addition, the university did not always provide the more eloquent lecturers, who in the early years gave the program much of its reputation. On camera, lectures without visual and production support (i.e., "talking heads") make for dull education. Neither the American educational system nor the American media have done much to move beyond this phase.

In an age when government and industry have embraced new technologies as a fact of communication life, the American educational system is woefully out of date. Schools have neither the resources to acquire the technology nor the teachers to train students in its use. Additionally the administration, faculty, and students have shown little inclination to fight for the "new" media.

The American educational system is primarily dependent on one mass medium—the book—whether it be the textbook, the workbook, the reader, the reference book, or the index. Teaching remains classroom and library based. The educational system, the school, the teacher, and the book have served this country well, regardless of education's current low estate. But technology, even the technology of word processing, is passing education by. That can lead to learning suicide.

The most innovative uses of the communication revolution and instructional techniques are not in the "halls of ivy" but in the "real world" of work. Advanced uses of media learning are invading the home before they are seen in school. Indeed, many secondary schools, colleges, and universities are only responding to the demands of students who come to school with advanced skills and knowledge acquired at home.

Some critics are raising the alarm that the physical school is in jeopardy unless it can reorient and redirect itself to describe future challenges rather than react to an obsolete past. But adults as well as children are involved in more than one learning mode or environment. The mass media surround us, and so it is important to understand the extent to which the media have become our tutors, both within and outside a formal educational system. No less a group than the National Council of Teachers of English (NCTE) has recognized and endorsed this point of view. A recent report from the Council's media commission stated, "We are recognizing a need to integrate all media into the teaching of English."

Media other than the printed word should be integrated into the English curriculum, the commission's report said, because "communication today demands the ability to understand, use, and control more complex symbol systems." Schools must teach "through" the new media in order to impart a complete understanding of how they function.

MEDIA AND EDUCATION

The mass media perform three major educational tasks: (a) *socialization*, the process of reinforcing or modifying cultural norms that usually occurs in the home; (b) *informal education*, which supplements the education of the individual and usually occurs outside the school; (c) *formal instruction*, the process of systematically imparting specialized information and skills in a controlled, supervised environment, which usually occurs in the school.

The extent and mix of media in each individual's learning process is different. Nevertheless, some general patterns are evident in the amounts and kinds of formal instruction, informal education, and socialization in which Americans participate. The Learning Wheel indicates that a variety of contacts determine learning. A learner's ability, energy, health, work habits, home, peers, parents, family, activities, schools, teachers, and media material all form a part of his or her educational achievement.

SOCIALIZATION

Socialization is the most important learning process. It is how we gain membership in our society. And communication is the primary means of socialization. In fact, socialization is impossible without communication. Interpersonal communication is more important than mass communication for most socialization. But to what extent are the mass media involved in acculturation? It depends on both the society and the individual, but the media impact is significant and is becoming more so.

It is obvious that infants acquire much of their behavior patterns from the family and the immediate environment. Child psychologists tell us that children's concepts of themselves in relation to others are well established before they can even talk; their social values are well on the way to being established before they have sufficient social experiences to have any rational perceptions of radio or television. And children usually experience considerable formal instruction before they can read newspapers, magazines, and books. For young children, however, even those

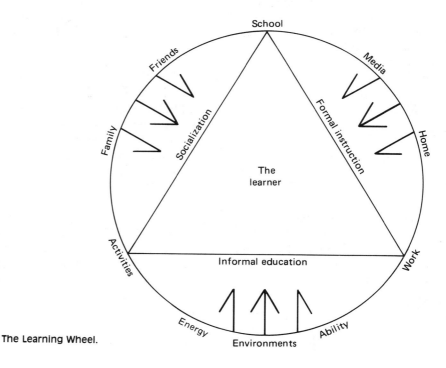

The Learning Wheel.

The Great Wall of China is part of the historic path traveled by "Sesame Street's" Big Bird (Carroll Spiney) and friends on an NBC TV special.

(AP/Wide World Photos.)

under 2 years of age, media, especially television, have a powerful effect on the socialization process. "Mr. Rogers' Neighborhood" and "Sesame Street," for example, have demonstrated impact on preschool children, not simply in learning to count to 10, but in developing concepts such as friendship and emotions. The use of Sesame Street characters such as Big Bird, Oscar the Grouch, Bert and Ernie, and the Cookie Monster to teach, to socialize, and even to sell has become an established fact of media life for young children.

As we continue a personal inventory of the media socialization process, it becomes even clearer. Did you go to church last Sunday? What are you wearing? Where do you go on dates? What records, books, magazines do you buy? What movies or television do you watch? To which radio station do you listen? Are the answers the same ones your parents or grandparents would have given?

To the last question, your answer is probably no. You have been socialized by your peers and the media as well as by your parents. And, often, your peers and the media do not agree with your parents. There is a definite mix of interpersonal and media socialization.

For young people, the electronic media are truly significant in modifying attitudes about lifestyles. Radio, television, film, and sound recordings also affect other age groups. The print media assume greater impact as age, education, and income rise. If the media pick up an issue (e.g., the rights of minorities or women), resocialization can be slowly accomplished. The length of time required for the modification to occur depends on the complexity and importance of the issue, as well as the exposure given the issue in the mass media.

It is useful to view socialization as consisting of different sorts of learning, some of which are more affected by mass media than others. Gerhart D. Wiebe, former dean of the School of Public Communication at Boston University, has sharpened the definition of socialization by breaking the communication process into three zones in a continuum. He refers to these as directive media messages, maintenance media messages, and restorative media messages.[1]

Directive messages command, exhort, instruct, persuade, and urge in the direction of learning and new understanding. They must, says Wiebe, come from authoritative figures and call for substantial and conscious intellectual effort by the learner. Most studies show that messages that intend to direct performance or change behavior do not succeed unless they tie in to a structured, face-to-face, teacher–pupil relationship. Since the mass media cannot provide this relationship, they are not important bearers of directive messages. They may supplement and enrich the direct learning process, but they cannot replace it. In classrooms from kindergarten to college, teachers have a direct relationship to students, one that cannot be replaced by books, TV sets, or computerized learning machines. As Weibe says, "The printed Bible has not made the church obsolete nor has it reduced the role of the clergy."

Maintenance messages tell us what to do in the everyday business of living. They tell us where we can find food, what dangers we should avoid, when we should pay our taxes, how we can get a driver's license, who we should regard as friend or foe. Such messages call for relatively little conscious intellectual effort. Here the mass media play an extensive role through the communication of new information, analysis, interpretation,

[1]Gerhart D. Wiebe, "The Social Effects of Broadcasting," in *Mass Culture Revisited*, ed. Bernard Rosenberg and David Manning White (Princeton, NJ: D. Van Nostrand, 1971), pp. 154–168.

persuasion, and sales promotion. Wiebe maintains, however, that three conditions must exist before communication messages will have an impact on maintaining social norms: (a) The audience must be predisposed to react along the lines indicated in the message; (b) social provisions must exist for facilitating such action; (c) the message itself must have audience appeal.

Restorative messages renew and refresh the human capacity for productive social relationships. Restorative messages include fantasies, which allow us to escape the realities of life; humor, which allows us to relieve the tensions of the day; and drama and violence, which can provide catharsis for frustrations and anxieties. Here the mass media play perhaps their most important role in the socialization process, not only in the dramas of pulp novels and soap operas, but also in escapist TV serials and televised sports events and the violence of news.

All mass media provide content that is neither socialization nor formal instruction. *National Geographic* specials on public television; the "Schoolhouse Rock," "Multiplication Rock," and "Grammar Rock" episodes in ABC-TV's Saturday morning lineups; recordings of children's literature; and a variety of other content are used for learning purposes in both the home and school. Perhaps the most visible and successful examples of informal education are "Sesame Street," produced by the Children's Television Workshop, and "Mr. Rogers' Neighborhood."

Research in the area of informal education is limited, but all of us have learned about sharks, whales, seals, and other creatures of the sea from the televised programs of Jacques Cousteau. We have learned about the

INFORMAL EDUCATION

(Courtesy Metromedia Producers Corporation.)

Captain Jacques Cousteau and his son, director–underwater photographer, Philippe, travel to Mexico for "The Sea Birds of Isabela" on "The Undersea World of Jacques Cousteau."

world we live in from books and magazines. Informally, we educate ourselves about food, wines, travel, and art from all media. In effect, our informal education occurs before, during, and after our school years. It is the means by which we stay intellectually and emotionally alive.

Motion pictures and television in recent years, especially, have become our history educators with a series of docudramas on Killer Gary Gilmore ("The Executioner's Song"), the Civil War ("The Blue and the Gray"), the life of Gandhi (*Gandhi*), and the career of actress Joan Crawford (*Mommie Dearest*). In addition the media teach us about World War II ("The Winds of War"), the Russian Revolution and the life of John Reed (*Reds*), revolution in South America (*Missing*), the lives of British Olympic runners (*Chariots of Fire*) and the life of George Washington ("George Washington").

The list of recent specials on network television reads like the index of a history book—George Washington, Christopher Columbus, Charles DeGaulle, Michelangelo, Montezuma, Napoleon, Clarence Darrow, Pope John Paul II.

It's no accident. After the mini-series on the Civil War, "The Blue and the Gray," scored well in ratings, network officials felt audiences would respond to other historical subjects. "The American public likes to be taken into the landscapes of the past," said Marian Brayton, vice president—dramatic specials for CBS Entertainment. "After 'The Blue and the Gray' was well received, we wanted to do something else in American history." A quick check found that not much had been done on the Revolutionary War. "We thought if we could tell a deeply personal story about Washington, if we could show him as a man—living, breathing flesh—we thought the public would respond."[2]

The CBS's lineup of historical specials especially improved its reputation among educators, church officials, and others who are often critical of network programming. For example, the New York Archdiocese worked with CBS on "Pope John Paul II." The church officials were very cooperative and supportive of the project, and the archdiocese even encouraged Catholic churches in New York to run items in their Sunday bulletins alerting parishioners that the movie would be broadcast on Easter.

Many educators hope that these TV specials will encourage children to investigate the subjects further with a trip to the local library. Through its TV reading program CBS sent out a teaching guide and classroom materials, including a list of suggested sources to be used in conjunction with "George Washington." Either through its "Read More about It" program or the extensive "CBS Television Reading Program," Joanne Brokaw, vice president of CBS/Broadcast Group's educational and community services department, rides herd over a department that has provided millions of copies of teacher and student guides and book lists for several years

---

[2] *USA Today*, March 3, 1984, p. 12.

(Photo: Movie Star News, Courtesy Warner Bros., Inc.)

Docudramas like *Chariots of Fire* represent the media in the area of informal education.

now. Though some critics tend to view such network public service programs with disdain, believing it's merely a ploy to take the heat off TV, Mrs. Brokaw disagrees. "We operate from as pure an educational posture as possible," she says. "No one in the network ever tells us what to do and that allows us to maintain our credibility."[3]

CBS/Broadcast Group generates about four student–teacher TV reading programs every year. Additionally, the "Read More about It" program, which CBS runs in conjunction with the Library of Congress, provides reading lists for a greater number of network programs through the year. In the 1981–1982 TV season, for example, CBS provided reading lists for a diversity of programs ranging from "A Charlie Brown Celebration" to "Skokie" and "Bill" to "The Magic of David Copperfield."

Perhaps most important educational series have been the exciting, well-made explorations of science, including "The Ascent of Man," "The Body in Question," "Connections," and "Cosmos." These TV series evaluate the cultural impact and the future implications of our uses of technology. "Civilisation," "Alistair Cooke's America," and "Nova" are other examples of media contributions to general learning.

[3] *Ibid.*

Dr. Carl Sagan uses a giant model of the solar system to explain why the orbits of the planets are stable on "Cosmos," the Public Television series devoted to astronomy and space exploration in the broadest human context.

(Photo by Edwardo Castaneda, Courtesy Scott Meredith, Inc.)

Informal education is a critical educational force in the United States. It is the "high" culture of the electronic and print media. It has cultural impact and broadens the intellectual horizons of those who choose to use this content.

FORMAL INSTRUCTION

In the United States classroom instruction involves the more than 54% of our population that enrolls in formal instruction in nursery schools, kindergartens, elementary schools through senior high schools, 4-year colleges and universities, junior and community colleges, professional schools, vocational and technical schools, correspondence schools, and continuing education. Over 70 million children and adults attend school every day. They are taught by over 2 million teachers. Another 11 million students go to colleges and universities.

BOOKS IN INSTRUCTION

The most influential medium in formal instruction is the book, which also plays an important role in socialization and informal education. Books are successful largely because they adapt so well to the individual needs and habits of the students who use them.

Three crucial elements interact in the classroom: the student, the book, and the teacher. In many situations the book is the central reference point for both students and teachers. For example, books may be the only common, shared intellectual experience most white middle-income teachers have with black low-income pupils in ghetto schools.

A specialized form of the book has evolved in the school environment. The textbook, by definition, is a book prepared specifically for classroom use; it provides an exposition of one subject area and serves as the content core of a given class. Several other kinds of books are specifically designed for the classroom; these include teacher editions of the text, consumable workbooks (the student writes directly in the book) used in conjunction with the text, standardized tests to evaluate student performance on the text, and manuals and trade books used to supplement and reinforce textbooks. The paperback, a softbound, less expensive form of trade book, is used for a variety of classroom purposes, largely in higher education. Two kinds of textbooks are of primary importance: Authored books focus on a special topic within the general subject area; and edited books provide a general survey of materials written by a large number of specialists in their field of expertise.

Before a textbook gets into the hands of elementary school children, it must pass through the hands of a series of gatekeepers. No book format has more levels of gatekeeping than the grade school text.

1. The book must be selected and printed by a publisher, who either solicits someone to write it or accepts a manuscript submitted by the authors.
2. The book must be adopted by both the state and local school boards; competition here is intense because adoptions are crucial economically. Unfortunately, some boards exercise their power not only to modify the style of textbooks but to censor content as well.
3. The book must be chosen by the total school faculty, although some individual teachers have some degree of latitude in the use of supplementary material.

The selection process is similar at the secondary school level, but professional organizations such as the National Council of Teachers of English exert considerable influence. At most universities the individual teacher makes the book selections. This has led to a procedure in which salesmen contact professors not only to sell books but to procure future manuscripts. Many college bookstores are little more than clearinghouses for course materials, but the more progressive stores serve a critical role by carrying an extensive stock beyond course demands.

Although most of the publicity goes to best-sellers, much of the income in the publishing industry comes from the sale of textbooks and reference works. If you consider all the educational possibilities of books, more than 60% of all book sales are education related. In terms of textbooks sold to a particular audience, approximately 50% are sold to college students, 30% to elementary schools, and 20% to high schools. Textbooks cost Americans more than $3 billion annually and account for almost one-third of all book sales.

One of the major problems for textbook publishers is that elementary and secondary school enrollments are dropping. There are 10–15% fewer students in the 1980s than in the 1970s. College enrollments are also beginning to decline, which means that more schools are competing for fewer students in a time of severe cost increases.

Textbooks have a relatively low profit margin and are expensive to market. It costs well over $1 million to launch a new elementary school series. For the individual high school text, preparatory costs can run as high as $250,000; for one college text, $100,000. To compound the problem, many textbooks have life spans of only 3 to 5 years before revisions are necessary.

Paperback editions and resales help hold down costs somewhat, but that is relative to the inflationary spiral educational institutions and students now face. In the mid-1980s the average college student faces a book bill of more than $100 a semester.

Societies have created a separate institution just to house their books. Libraries provide long-term storage and easy retrieval of information. In order to make efficient use of the information stored in the library, a new class of books has been developed. Reference books, despite their limited numbers, account for 8% of book revenue each year. This group includes general references, indexes, annuals, encyclopedias, handbooks, and other subcategories. The reference book is crucial to the retrieval of data from large, complex library systems.

The book is a useful learning device because it is compact, portable, low in cost, and reusable; it does not require special equipment to use; it does not disrupt nonusers; it provides individualized learning experiences as people set their own rate of learning; it has easy reference capacity. And the reader can reread portions of a book that were not mastered at first reading.

Without doubt, the book is the best medium for many kinds of classroom instruction. Its inherent characteristics, and the schools' predisposition to exploit them, make the book an important information source in the classroom, library, and bookstore. Books are important for providing insights into a variety of activities and skills.

Books, as a particular combination and structure of words on paper, are in transition as new technology has its impact on this oldest medium, particularly in education. Increasingly, the most economical way of moving, storing, and displaying words is electronically rather than on paper. As Ithiel de Sola Pool observed in his article "The Culture of Electronic Print": "Virtually all handling of text . . . and also publishing, will be done within computers. . . .Printing the text onto paper will be for the convenience of the reader alone." Storage of books is also being revolutionized by the computer and the concept of the library is changing. As de Sola Pool indicates in the same article, "The videodisc may be the most promising storage technology. Over 100,000 books can be stored on an optical-digital disc pack of six discs. At $51,000 a pack, the cost of storing a book would be 40 cents. One hundred disc packs, or the total contents of the library of Congress, would cost $5 million and would fit into a medium sized room."[4]

Just as important to the emerging electronic book is the method of publishing. Traditionally, the book is a fixed unit in which certain ideas exist. Electronic publishing can alter this concept as a group of authors, such as the authors of this text, can write and edit on computer networks. Hiebert can type some comments at a terminal and give access to Ungurait and Bohn on the network. As each author modifies, edits, and expands the content, the text changes from day to day. In turn, the teacher in the classroom would use the text in new ways. This text would be on-line, and like many teachers of mass communication, the teacher might like to make modifications in the text. The student could do the same modifications, and so reading would become an interactive dialogue with the teacher and the authors. The notes that many students make in the margins could become part of the text and part of a growing dialogue.

The *Standard Periodical Directory* lists more than 62,000 titles of periodicals other than newspapers. The education system uses a wide variety of these magazines and other serials, but two kinds of periodicals are more important than the others: the 5000 or more scholarly journals, which print the latest research and other information in a given field; and the 20,000 or more trade journals, which offer the latest information about the application of new research.

MAGAZINES IN INSTRUCTION

These two kinds of magazines provide important learning tools, especially at the university level. As a field expands, the number of scholarly and trade journals proliferates as well. For example, almost 2000 periodicals deal with education, about 1000 cover library science, and more than 500 deal with media and media-related activities. It is almost impossible to stay abreast of the information in these fields, and so special reference services, which cover a given area, have emerged. For example, *Topicator* is a periodical guide to a select group of magazines that deal with radio and television.

The magazine plays a minor role in the primary grades of public schools because few magazines of the quality of *Highlights* are published for elementary pupils. Publishers find that subscribers outgrow their material rapidly, and it is too expensive to resell their product to each generation. Also, many classes of advertising are not considered suitable for children's

---

[4] Ithiel De Sola Pool, "The Culture of Electronic Print," *Daedalus*, Vol. III, No. 4, Fall, 1982, pp. 17–32.

fare. Most school libraries fill the void by subscribing to general adult periodicals like *National Geographic, Popular Science,* and *Popular Mechanics,* which are used by children. Since few school libraries can afford to bind back issues, these periodicals are usually used for recreation rather than instruction or research, however. Even in high school, when term papers become part of the assignment, most students who want to search periodical literature must use the public library.

Thus, students making the transition from high school to college sometimes have difficulty adjusting to the increased emphasis placed on the magazine. Although the book is easier to find and use than the magazine, a large library's periodical collection can and should expand the amount of data available.

Magazines, even more than books, will see their use in education revolutionized. Since scholarly journals are published more frequently than books, and since their purpose is to communicate the results of ongoing contemporary research, electronic publishing is more compatible with their structure and function than with the structure and function of books. Rather than subscribe to a journal, a teacher will have on-line access to a data base that will "publish" information in forms unique to each individual. The whole concept of information input, storage, and delivery is changing rapidly, and although books, magazines, and newspapers will not die, their methods of publication will change how they are used, especially in formal education.

NEWSPAPERS IN INSTRUCTION

Although the newspaper is heavily used in the socialization of society, especially for the communication of maintenance and restorative messages, it is the least used mass medium in formal instruction. Newspaper organizations are increasing their efforts to have newspapers used in classrooms, but barring a few exceptions, such as *My Weekly Reader,* newspapers are not widely used.

Curiously, newspaper organizations increasingly think of themselves as educational institutions rather than merely businesses. The editorial staff of the daily newspaper is essentially in the business of developing and communicating knowledge, researching facts, and packaging them for their audience. Some newspapers approach this task with the same seriousness that universities bring to the development of knowledge, allowing their staffs sufficient time, freedom, and security to pursue knowledge; and even providing a sort of tenure and sabbatical leave system for expert writers and specialists on the staff.

Without a doubt, newspapers provide a wide variety of information necessary for carrying out day-to-day living, as well as an increasing number of facts and ideas to round out a well-informed citizen. Newspapers have also become source materials for some academic disciplines, particularly the social sciences.

Here, too, although few people would predict the newspaper's death, new technologies are changing its form and function. Especially important are the distribution systems known as videotext and teletext. Transmitted over television frequencies or phone–cable TV lines, teletext is a one-way system that continuously transmits information from which viewers–students can select news and information. Videotext is a two-way system allowing services such as at-home shopping and electronic mail. Teletext, especially, has major implications for newspapers, especially in any formal educational system.

Before analyzing electronic media, it is important to understand that despite the potential educational impact of television, film, radio, and the phonograph in classroom instruction, there is little use of electronic media, compared with print media use, in most classrooms.

Six major issues have had a negative impact on the use of electronic media in schools:

1. Society's general attitude is that electronic media are for entertainment, not education.
2. Teachers often are print oriented and have little free time to develop the skills and attitudes necessary to use electronic media in the classroom.
3. The decision to use electronic media in schools is often made at the administrative level and forced on teachers, who resent this imposition.

ELECTRONIC MEDIA IN INSTRUCTION

(Courtesy Control Data Corporation.)

Learning skills on an interactive computer terminal.

4. Most of the materials available do not exploit the inherent qualities of electronic media.

5. Electronic media are expensive unless they are used for a large number of students.

6. The "software" (content) of electronic media is a threefold problem: (a) The traditional suppliers of materials have not moved vigorously to provide it; (b) local "in-house" materials do not reach the production standards children have become accustomed to in commercial radio-TV films; (c) the content ages rapidly and is difficult to maintain professionally and economically.

Judith Murphy and Ronald Gross observe in *Learning by Television*:

> Education is slow to accept innovation. It is a widely accepted fact that, on the average, an educational innovation takes fifty years to trickle down to the mass of schools and colleges. Earlier technological tools of communication, with obvious implications for learning, have not to this day become an intrinsic part of education. Films, radio, recordings, etc., play little more than token roles in instruction. Acclaimed in their day as TV is today, these devices have for the most part never been used with any real imagination.[5]

The book is the *essential* classroom tool. If electronic media are to find a place in the current education structure, that place will more than likely be as a supplement to the teacher and the book.

Sound Recording

Recordings are seldom used in classroom instruction. Some tapes and records are made in music-appreciation classes, but few if any teachers have been able to obtain sophisticated, stereo-equipped, acoustically satisfactory learning environments. About the only significant contribution in this field are aural books for the blind.

Foreign-language teachers have been able to develop expensive language laboratories to handle rote learning of pronunciation (a Berlitz approach). Audiotutorial systems based on programmed instruction are a bright area for the future. This process uses cartridge and cassette tapes, sometimes with auxiliary slides or film strips, for individualized instruction.

Radio

Using phonograph music for the bulk of its content, radio serves a significant role in socialization. Yet the general-education function of radio in the United States is expensive and fairly ineffective. For a number of years, some of the more than roughly 1100 public radio stations served as little more than classical jukeboxes for an elite audience within the total society. National Public Radio, formed in 1969 and government and

---

[5] Judith Murphy and Ronald Gross, *Learning by Television* (New York: Fund for the Advancement of Education, 1966), 11.

foundation subsidized, is attempting to change the educational-radio service. Attempts have been made to use educational radio as a means of formal instruction, but despite its potential, radio is not involved in classroom instruction.

Film is used extensively in socialization; along with radio and the phonograph, it is a crucial molder of youth culture. Film is used in limited amounts in formal instruction. Unfortunately many films supplied by audiovisual centers are either commercial films from television, which require modification of the course content in order to be used successfully, or poor-quality films designed for specific classes. When the commercial film is used, often little attempt is made to integrate it into the course. Student reaction to films in class is that screenings mean a day off from learning. Many specially developed, low-budget films are poorly produced. They become adverse experiences, which reinforce both the teachers' and students' negative attitudes about electronic instruction.

Film

Future movies in the classroom will probably take the form of the super 8-mm, cartridge, single-concept film. The function of such films is to teach one idea or operation in a few minutes. The film can be repeated until the student has mastered the body of information. The equipment is fairly inexpensive, and once the cartridge is assembled, the loading and unloading of the projector can be handled by the student without difficulty. But there is a problem with "software." The ready-made cartridge films are few in number, and many are poorly made. Even more significant are the new technologies of videodisc and videocassette. The cost and flexibility of these video systems, especially when they are linked to the computer in an interactive mode, will ultimately make the single-concept film obsolete.

Film may have had more impact on classrooms than any other electronic medium, yet the impact is still minimal. If film is to become a significant part of classroom instruction, motion pictures must be integrated into the total curriculum and cease to be used as vicarious experiences and classroom entertainment.

Television is the medium that contributes most to the socialization of Americans because it is the medium used by more people more of the time. Both commercial and public stations and networks contribute significantly to general education.

Television

In 1952 the Federal Communications Commission set aside 242 (later increased to 309) station allocations for educational television (ETV). This was done in spite of considerable indifference toward the idea on the part of most educators. Four years later, fewer than 30 ETV stations were in operation. Educational institutions were not willing to invest the capital necessary to build the facilities. Thanks to an investment of more than $100 million by the Ford Foundation and extensive federal grants, roughly

260 public television (PTV) stations are now on the air. Sixty percent, unfortunately, use the less-desirable UHF channels. Despite tremendous dollar investments plus extensive interconnection, ratings successes have been few in number, although in recent years the track record is improving as the result of federal funding of the Corporation for Public Broadcasting (CPB). Most public stations are on the level of paupers compared with commercial stations and their resources, and federal support has been reduced.

To date, there have been two truly superior achievements of American educational television: the Children's Television Workshop's "Sesame Street" and "The Electric Company." Despite some carping from special interests in the school community, both series remain the best educational programs yet produced. The two series use the unusual approach that learning can be pleasurable. These programs succeed because they use flashy, commercial TV techniques to "enterteach" youngsters.

A similar but more recent example of "enterteaching" is occurring with rock videos. "For many years, people around the world have used music as a means of teaching their children language acquisition," says J. Michael Bell, whose ColorSounds program uses current chart-toppers to teach such things as phonics, grammar, spelling, and reading comprehension.

Students using Bell's ColorSounds system watch rock videos while the lyrics appear at the bottom of the screen. Different vowel sounds, parts of speech, and grammatical structures stand out from the rest of the words with an identifying color—say, green for adverbs. The students are also provided with lyric sheets and crayons so they can practice and be tested on what they've learned using a similar color-coding system.

Records may be used in place of the ColorSounds videos. Supplementary materials—all based on the music—include crossword puzzles, various drills, computer games, and a 20,000-circulation monthly magazine that contains interviews with the rock stars. The basic system costs as little as $30 per class per year.

The music used by ColorSounds is carefully screened for vocabulary, grammar, diction and suitability. It covers a wide spectrum of rock, pop, country and soul—and such performers as Alabama, Donna Summer, Genesis, Diana Ross, The Stray Cats, Kool & The Gang, David Bowie, and Culture Club.

Classroom use of television or instructional television (ITV) has been less than a complete success, especially when money spent and successful results are compared. Most of the research literature indicates that tele-lessons are no more effective than other methods of teaching.

Two generalizations become evident after a review of the research literature: Most ITV materials are developed without adequate consideration of learning theory and the inherent qualities of the medium; and the experimental situation has been unable to assess the complex nature of TV learning. Most studies examine *how much* was learned, and a few assess user attitudes, but longitudinal studies over periods of time have not been made. At present the educational uses of television are limited.

Although educational researchers have spent millions of dollars of government money, few of their findings have been put to use by administrators and teachers, even at the institutions that did the research.

> Most important is the point, rarely made, that the major—possibly only major—practical attempts made to use TV as a teaching tool have not come from conventional innovators in education (that is, from schools of education, administrator's groups, educational specialists' organizations or even the general public). Neither . . . have teachers . . . or students shown much spontaneous impetus in demanding TV. . . .[6]

In effect, the single major reason for the condition of educational content in television is lack of funding. "The situation can be summed up in the fact that in a country where we spend almost $14 per capita each year for commercial television, we spend less than 70 cents on public television. . . ."[7]

As we pointed out at the beginning of the chapter, the major reason for the demise of "Sunrise Semester" was money: money to create, money to produce, money to distribute, and money to promote. An even more ambitious experiment in televised learning also met an untimely death in 1982, the University of Mid-America's American Open University.

The open-university concept was inspired by the British Open University started in 1971 with government financing; the expertise of the British Broadcasting Corporation; and a large, full-time faculty. The instructors not only develop radio and TV programs and extensive textbooks for home study but also run a system of remote-control homework and examinations with the help of computers and tutors.

The British program has reached hundreds of thousands. In 1981 it admitted 21,000 new degree-seeking students. In its first 10 years, it has had a graduation rate of nearly 60%, more than 10 percentage points higher than America's on-campus colleges.

In 1979 the American Open University began to conduct in-depth feasibility studies and obtained the approval of the University of Mid-America trustees for plans to establish a nationwide, independent degree-granting institution of higher learning. Preparations included surveying existing correspondence courses, telecourses, and computer-aided instruction; hiring a staff with academic expertise; and assembling two sets of advisory faculties, one in the arts and sciences and one in business. Rejection of further financing by the National Institute of Education

[6] George N. Gordon, *Classroom Television* (New York: Hastings House, 1970), 3.
[7] George W. Tressel, Donald P. Buckelew, John T. Suchy, and Patricia L. Brown, *The Future of Educational Telecommunication* (Lexington, MA: D. C. Heath, 1975), 3.

dashed all hopes for further operations. However, through funding by the Annenberg Foundation new life has been breathed into the telecourse concept.

In 1984 an estimated 100,000 tuition-paying students tuned into PBS telecourses—college-credit instruction on topics ranging from history to computers to money management. As Dee Brock, director of PBS Adult Learning Service notes, "the telecourse student is very goal-oriented, very motivated. Eighty percent are working toward a bachelor degree, taking the courses to move ahead faster or to make a career change." Further information indicates that the average off-campus television student is a high school graduate, working, with 60% holding full-time jobs outside the home, 25% working part-time and the rest handicapped or working inside the home, over the age of 25, with the bulk 30–35 years old, and lower middle class or middle class.[8]

An example of the new telecourse is *The New Literacy: An Introduction to Computers,* a 26-segment telecourse offered for college credit. The $1.2 million series was produced by the Corporation for Community College Television and is telecast by PBS stations across the country.

The New Literacy was the first show to be broadcast from among several funded by the Annenberg School of Communications and administered by the Corporation for Public Broadcasting. The Annenberg School and the CPB are partners in a 15-year, $150 million program to create innovative, college-level courses with an emphasis on new ways of using telecommunications.

Each year, the program distributes $10 million in funds. *The New Literacy* received $550,000 during 1981, the project's first year. The balance of the production money came from the series' producer, the text publisher and a number of college districts.

Interactive video has become the latest "buzz word" in media instruction. The possibilities for branching, collecting data, using computer-generated text and graphics and creating individual personalized message systems makes this linkage between computer and video technology one of the most flexible mediated systems of instruction in use today.

As Diane Gayeski, a professor of Ithaca College, points out: "One of the simplest, but most powerful, techniques using the random accessibility of video segments is showing people what they're interested in. This can be done by providing a menu in print, through computer generation, or in the tape or disc itself, by which a participant can select a topic."[9]

One segment in a demonstration tape Gayeski produced for Panasonic's Interactive Video Training System works like a data bank; the section allows the student to learn how to use various reference tools (a dictionary,

[8] *The New York Times,* July 27, 1982, p. 23.
[9] Diane Gayeski and David Williams, "Interactive Video—Accessible and Intelligent," *E-ITV,* June, 1984, pp. 31–32.

a thesaurus, industrial reference manuals, Zip Code directory, etc.). Using a menu, the user can go immediately to an explanation of just what he or she needs to learn about.

The difference between random access video and traditional linear video is like the difference between a book and scroll. With a book or random access device, you can locate just the "page" or "chapter" you want without "scrolling" through the whole program.

Training and information can be provided by the branching capabilities of interactive video. By asking questions, it can be determined whether or not a trainee has grasped an important concept. If not, remedial segments can be shown that correct misunderstandings. People who understand particular concepts quickly can speed through a program without being bogged down in more explanation than they need.

Systems which allow for multiple branching can "diagnose" a learner's particular misconceptions, and address them with specific feedback. Rather than merely showing a segment over and over until the correct response is given (perhaps by elimination), such programs can present the information in different terms, or clarify the confusion indicated by the response. Many computer-based programs can keep track of patterns of responses, and branch to a specific style or level of explanation accordingly.

Other systems include printout or record-keeping options, allowing the teacher to see exactly how students responded and how long it took them to respond. This record keeping provides useful information about the user's progress, as well as the program itself. Such hard copy can become a part of a student's record for documentation of skills learned or concepts mastered.

Interactive video can increase the effectiveness of testing and assessment—allowing for immediate scoring and/or feedback, and supplementary instruction, if necessary, as part of the test. Instead of being limited to print or diagrams to present test items, video can present dramatized scenes, moving parts, and realistic sounds adding to the scope and face-validity of the assessment. Using one tape-based system, you can even hook up a camera and microphone and record trainees' responses to questions.

Of course, at the leading edge of the new technologies and their use in the classroom is the computer. The following excerpt from an article by James Traub illustrates both the potential and the problems of computer-assisted instruction.[10]

In the beat-up, flattened slum where the Brooklyn Dodgers' Ebbets Field used to stand, in a virtually all-black junior high school named after Jackie Robinson, four adolescents sit before the precise screens of microcomputers.

[10] *Ibid*

Sondra Kennedy plays a Pac-Man-type game in which she must "eat" verbs and leave nouns alone. Sheldon Brutus runs through a math program, and then a game that requires the player to zap the names of animals but not of plants.

An otherwise unremarkable scene glimpsed last June—except that these were not whiz kids but "slow" kids, the kind who seem to go through school in a daze. Delano Dubinson, their teacher, says something truly special happened. Sondra, who once rarely came to class, improved her reading and math scores by at least two grades in a single year. Sheldon successfully completed New York University's summer computing program. Both kids are now moving full-speed through high school.

None of Dubinson's students has advanced less than a full year in math, and most have gone further. "And it's not just the math," says Dubinson delightedly. "They'll improve their math, but what's even more important, they gain confidence. They're succeeding at something for the first time. And it makes them better in everything they do."[11]

The transformation of schools by technology, for good or ill, however, remains a long way off. As Marc Tucker, who is conducting a study on the use of information technology in education, remarks, "Society and schools and most students are not about to change. But it's easy to get smoke in your eyes."

The smoke of high expectations, in fact, has obscured the vision of educational reformers throughout this century. The educational-theory section of the library is a graveyard of would-be assaults on orthodoxy: *Teaching Machines*, for example, and *Individualizing Instruction* and *The Guided Design Approach*. Educational technology seems to constitute yet another entertaining diversion from the intractable problems of public education.

But the usual cynicism may not be justified at this time. The microcomputer will soon be a major household appliance, and it will not be banished from the schools, which already own more than 130,000 of them. The new forms of television appearing in the classroom—cable (especially two-way cable) and videocassette recorders—already are ubiquitous. The videodisc also has profound educational possibilities, if only a flickering existence now. The question is not, ultimately, whether the new technology will be deployed; it is whether the door that separates the dedicated and imaginative teachers, the brilliant psychologists, the human philosophers, and the creative software designers from the world of misuse, indifference, suspicion, and hostility will be unlocked.

There are serious problems in education, and the new technologies of mass media alone cannot solve them. If the technologies are intelligently developed and used by teachers and learners, however, the education process can most certainly be improved.

[11] James Traub, "*Why Johnny Can't Program*," *Channels*, Vol. 3, No. 4, November/December 1983, pp. 32–35.

Public Relations and Persuasion 24

In Bethesda, Maryland, a government official at the National Institutes of Health approves a news release that will be sent out
to the mass media announcing a new discovery in cancer research. In
New Brunswick, New Jersey, a corporation officer at Johnson & Johnson
calls a press conference to tell reporters about a new, tamperproof con-
tainer for Tylenol. In Dallas, Texas, at the national headquarters of the
Boy Scouts of America, an audiovisual specialist puts the finishing
touches on a 30-second filmed public service announcement that will be
sent out to TV stations encouraging community support for the scouting
movement.

All over the country, day in and day out, thousands of people are engaged in the business of shaping messages for the mass media that will
further their cause, whatever it might be. The media, as we have seen,
are used to inform, interpret, and educate. But they are also used to promote causes, to persuade others to act or believe or accept or understand.

It is important to make a distinction at this point between information
and education, on the one hand, and persuasion and propaganda on the
other. Education is the communication of facts, ideas, and concepts for
their own sake, because they have an intrinsic value to the receiver of the
message. Teachers should be interested in passing information on to stu-

dents, regardless of how students use that information. News media reporters and editors, in providing news, information, interpretation, and analyses for their audiences, should inform their readers, listeners, and viewers, without regard to how that information is used. Teachers and journalists should attempt to provide a balanced, fair, objective, and accurate presentation of the facts, from which receivers can make up their own minds and take their own action.

Propaganda, on the other hand, is the communication of facts, ideas, opinions, and concepts, not for their intrinsic merit or for the sake of the audience, but for the benefit of the communicator, to further the communicator's purposes, whatever they might be. Propaganda has had many definitions; the word comes from the Latin *propagare*, meaning the gardener's practice of pinning fresh roots into the earth in order to reproduce new plants. The Roman Catholic church took this meaning when it established its College of Propaganda in 1622, considering its mission one of propagating the Christian religion.

Most specialists accept the definition of propaganda given by the Institute for Propaganda Analysis in the 1930s and inspired by Harold Lasswell: "Propaganda is the expression of opinions or actions carried out deliberately by individuals or groups for predetermined ends through psychological manipulation."

Any attempt to persuade another person is propagandistic, whereas any attempt to inform is educational. Of course, propaganda contains a good deal of information, and there is much persuasion in education. People's minds are changed by both education and propaganda; the difference between the two often lies in the purpose of the communicator.

THE RIGHT TO PERSUADE

Human beings are more often persuaders than teachers. Most of us communicate only when we want someone to do something for us. Early in life, babies communicate to get their diapers changed or have someone bring food or warmth. Most private communication is purposive. In most democratic societies it is a basic right of individuals to express themselves freely so that they can get others to serve their needs or believe in their ideas.

Not only do we each have a right to our point of view, but we each have a *different* point of view. As we have seen earlier in this book, we are all conditioned by different cultural, psychological, physical, and informational frames of reference. As the world grows more populated and more complicated, the variety of points of view multiplies and the difficulty in achieving agreement on the truth increases.

THE ROLE OF PUBLIC RELATIONS

Because it is increasingly difficult to get one's point of view expressed in a mass society, experts and specialists have come into existence to aid that process. In fact, a profession has developed to provide counsel on communication between parties with differing perceptions, languages, and cultures. That profession has become known as public relations.

Public relations professionals are experts in relating one public to another through communication. The techniques of public relations provide ways to adjust relationships between individuals and groups with different points of view, expecially when those differences can lead to misunderstanding, disagreement, or even hostility.

Public relations professionals are interpreters or translators. They must take the viewpoint of one group and restructure it or translate it so it can be understood by another group. Newspaper editor Walter Lippmann commented on this new phenomenon in American society in his book *Public Opinion*.[1] He wrote:

> The development of the publicity man is a clear sign that the facts of modern life do not spontaneously take a shape in which they can be known. They must be given a shape by somebody, and since in the daily routine reporters cannot give a shape to facts, and since there is little disinterested organization of intelligence, the need for some formulation is being met by the interested parties.

Public relations is a profession devoted to getting others to see the world as one sees it. Public relations systematizes the persuasive efforts of individuals and organizations because access to mass media requires expert techniques and knowledge. Public relations is necessary because in a democratic society it is essential to win public acceptance, for nothing can succeed without the approval of the people.

The public relations person is an advocate of an idea or point of view, much as an attorney is an advocate for a client. Public relations practitioners have a right and responsibility to defend their client's point of view before the court of public opinion as much as attorneys have a right and obligation to defend their client's actions before a court of law.

In this book we are primarily concerned with the media or communication functions of public relations. But public communication is only one part of the work of public relations, just as courtroom activity is only one part of the role of a lawyer; and in both professions, the public work may be the smaller role. Public relations professionals also spend time on counsel and advice, helping guide the client in ways that will be acceptable to public opinion.

DEFINING PUBLIC RELATIONS

Public relations is a difficult term because it has been often misused. In 1976 Rex Harlow, a social scientist and public relations practitioner, used a survey of professionals in the field to devise the following definition:

[1] New York: Macmillan, 1922.

Public relations is a distinctive management function which helps establish and maintain mutual lines of communication, understanding, acceptance, and cooperation between an organization and its publics; involves the management of problems of public opinion; defines and emphasizes the responsibility of management to serve the public interest; helps management keep abreast of and effectively use change, serving as an early warning system to help anticipate trends; and uses research and sound and ethical communication techniques as its principal tools.[2]

Organizationally, public relations is perhaps best conceived as the total public-communication effort of an operation, the overall umbrella under which would come advertising, marketing, promotion, publicity, employee communication, community relations, press relations, public affairs, and other such functions, including public relations counseling. Of course, not all organizations follow this formula.

Advertising, for our purposes, should be defined as a very specific kind of communication effort, one that is based on purchasing time or space in the communication media in order to send out a message. Institutional advertising, which promotes the total institution rather than individual products, plays an important role in public relations.

Publicity should be defined in specific terms as free time or space in the communication media to send out a message. In order to get free space in the newspaper, for example, the message must contain some element of news or human interest. To get free time on radio, the message must contain some element of news or human interest, or some element of public service, because of a long history of FCC requirements for radio–TV stations.

The main difference between advertising and publicity is that, since the message sender pays for the time or space in advertising, he or she has more control over what is said. In publicity, since the message is free, the final shaping of it is left in the hands of the media gatekeepers. Of the two, publicity may be more effective, however, because it carries the tacit endorsement of the media.

Promotion means the use of both advertising and publicity over an extended time to communicate a specific point. We speak of "promotional campaigns," implying that a longer time period is involved over which message senders wage efforts to get their views into the public consciousness.

Public, for our purposes here, has two meanings. There is, of course, a general public, meaning all the human beings in the universe. But more often we use the term to mean some specific public, such as American citizens, or more specifically, employees, stockholders, customers, and so forth.

[2] Rex Harlow, "Building a Public Relations Definition," *Public Relations Review*, Vol. 2, No. 4, Winter 1976, pp. 34–42.

Public relations as a process consists of three basic parts: management, communication, and publics. Management involves administration dealing with public opinion, and evaluating effectiveness. Communication includes six primary methods: person-to-person, publicity, printed materials, audiovisual materials, advertising, and special events. Finally, the process requires knowledge of the publics—and of course these publics vary from case to case.

Public relations should best be conceived as a circular process. It starts with a problem or a case; then efforts to define the problem and determine solutions; then development of the themes, ideas, and facts that need to be communicated; then choice of appropriate methods to communicate in order to reach the appropriate publics to achieve the desired results, which then must be evaluated through feedback to determine the extent to which the problem was solved.

THE PUBLIC RELATIONS PROCESS

Today most large business concerns, corporations, associations, and institutions with in-house public relations activities have a person in charge of these activities at a high level in the organization, often equivalent to that of a vice-president. This person's job is to help the organi-

THE ORGANIZATION OF PUBLIC RELATIONS

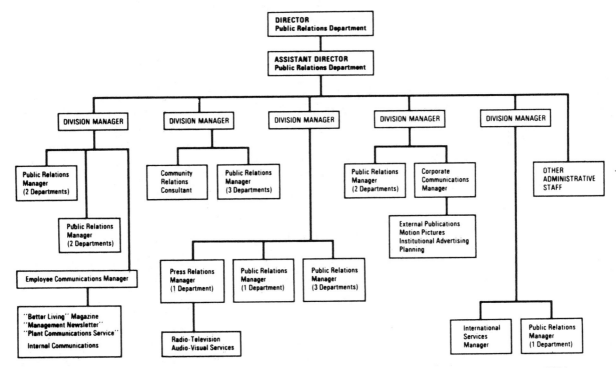

A Typical Public Relations Department in a Large Multinational Corporation. (Source: IPRA Exhibition London, 1978.)

zation with its communication, making use of the mass media whenever possible. Communication with and between employees is an essential element, of course, and so the person in charge of public relations often has a staff of people who specialize in internal communication, producing employee newspapers, magazines, or other house organs. Public relations directors are also concerned with the owners or principals of their organizations, for whom they may produce stockholders' reports or an annual report. The larger the organization, the more publics they must deal with, and the more they need specialists on their staffs to deal with those publics or the special media needed to communicate with them.

Perhaps most important, the public relations executive is concerned with the public at large: the customer, consumer, voter, and the persons who make up "public" opinion. Reaching this audience means using publicity, institutional advertising (which seeks to promote the institution rather than its by-products), promotional materials, and special events to establish communication channels to the mass public. Here public relations makes its greatest use of mass media.

To use the media, public relations experts must put the intended message into terms acceptable to the media—that is, they must make the message newsworthy, compellingly vital for human interest, or of public service for the broadcast media. The public relations person puts messages in the form of news releases, public service announcements, or other means to get communications into the media.

The other side of public relations is the external public relations counsel. Counseling firms, like legal firms, exist to provide independent advice and counsel on public relations problems for clients. Some of these firms undertake the entire public relations effort of their clients, producing their internal communications as well as providing direction for achieving their overall public image.

We have discussed here mostly the public communication aspects of public relations, the "outbound" communication. But there is also a very large "inbound" communication aspect, where the public relations practitioner is concerned with public attitudes, opinions, and conceptions, and it is a large job to report these to the client. This part of the task involves analysis of the media as well as analysis of public opinion, through polls, surveys, and other measurement instruments.

**THE GROWTH OF
PUBLIC RELATIONS**

J. A. C. Brown, in his *Techniques of Persuasion*, shows how the development of the printing press enhanced people's ability to persuade others. The first printed books, Bibles and missals, were used not only to win souls but to reform and revolutionize the church. Printed tracts were used to persuade Europeans to migrate to the New World. Early newspapers quickly became organs of propaganda for economic, religious, and political causes, persuading people of the New World to break with the old, to revolt, and to adopt a democratic form of government. When the mass magazine appeared in America in the late nineteenth century, it was quickly put to use to persuade readers of the ills of society.

The forerunner of the modern public relations practitioner was the individual who worked as a press agent, publicity stunt man, and promoter. His job was to get information about his clients into the newspaper. He promoted ideas, gimmicks, schemes, gadgets from the assembly line, land-speculation deals, theater personalities, and carnival freaks. Press agents were men like P. T. Barnum, the circus entrepreneur who made Tom Thumb and Jenny Lind, "the Swedish Nightingale," into the sensations of the nineteenth century; and Buffalo Bill, who made a hero out of the ruffians of the West.

The first professional public relations man was Ivy Lee, a former *New York Times* and *New York Journal* reporter. He opened a publicity firm in 1904, which was involved not simply in promoting his clients but in guiding their total public communication. He saw an analogy between the court of law and the role of public opinion, and saw himself as a new kind of lawyer, one who would represent his client before the court of public opinion by counseling the client on its public communication. He saw his job as one of "adjusting relationships between clients and their publics"; he spoke of "public relationships," and so the phrase "public relations" came into use.

Ivy Lee counseled such important men and groups in America as John D. Rockefeller, the Pennsylvania Railroad, Standard Oil, Bethlehem Steel, Chrysler, the American Red Cross, Harvard, and Princeton.

P.T. Barnum's talent as a promoter made Tom Thumb one of the sensations of the nineteenth century. (Photo: Brown Brothers.)

(Photo courtesy Communication Research Associates, Inc.)

Public relations pioneer Ivy Lee oversaw the total public communications of clients such as John D. Rockefeller and Standard Oil.

Before long, many others were engaged in similar practice. During World War I, the U. S. government officially recognized, for the first time, that it had to organize persuasive efforts in its behalf in winning the war. It had to use communication to advocate its position before the American public and the world. President Woodrow Wilson employed a Colorado newspaper editor, George Creel, to head a Committee on Public Information. Creel's committee advertised, publicized, and promoted America's role in the war.

Although Creel's committee was disbanded after the war, America's increasing role in international affairs led to the realization that the nation needed to defend itself before the world court of public opinion, to express its national views to the other countries of the world. Nothing of this sort was done, however, until World War II had been declared. The government then established an Office of War Information, headed by Elmer Davis, a radio news commentator.

After World War II, the Office of War Information evolved into the United States Information Agency, the official public relations organization for the U.S. government in its relationships with other nations and foreign people.

Between World Wars I and II, private public relations firms multiplied and grew to maturity in the United States. Chief among these who pioneered in the maturation of public relations during this period was Edward Bernays, a nephew of Sigmund Freud, Bernays attempted to take public relations out of the realm of art and make it systematic and scientific.

Systematic and scientific persuasion required accurate measurement of public opinion. In the 1930s and 1940s the practice of public opinion polling emerged, pioneered by such men as George Gallup, a former journalism professor, and Elmo Roper, a social scientist. Polling not only provided a mechanism for the media to obtain feedback from their messages but also became a necessary adjunct to communication efforts of those who used the media to persuade the public .

In the 1950s and 1960s, public relations professionals turned increasingly to social and behavioral scientists to help measure public attitudes and test the effects of different ideas and messages on public opinion. Yet most public relations activities in the 1970s still centered on communication efforts and utilized basic communication skills, using the mass media to send messages to persuade millions.

THE SCOPE OF PUBLIC RELATIONS   Englishman J. A. R. Pimlott said in his *Public Relations and American Democracy*:

> Public relations is not a peculiarly American Phenomenon, but it has nowhere flourished as in the United States. Nowhere else is it so widely prac-

ticed, so lucrative, so pretentious, so respectable and disreputable, so widely suspected and so extravagantly extolled.[3]

By the mid-1980s more than 100,000 people were directly engaged in public relations in the United States. Several hundred independent public relations consulting firms provide advice and counsel to clients. Most of these are headquartered in New York City, often with branch offices in the other large American and foreign cities. But almost every sizable organization in America has its own public relations representative, whether business corporation, labor union, political party, educational institution, or religious group; show-business personalities and other influential public figures also utilize the services of such representatives. Governments, too, at local and national levels, employ public relations experts to help get government facts and opinions expressed in the mass media, since in American society the government does not own the mass media.

The Public Relations Society of America (PRSA), an association of about 12,000 professional members, maintains a program of accrediting public relations practitioners through a series of written and oral examinations on the body of public relations theory and practice. Another organization, the International Association of Business Communicators (IABC), also with about 12,000 members, represents those people who work in communication within organizations. Both organizations maintain a code of ethical and professional standards. Such programs have increased professionalism in the field.

DIRECT MAIL

Some tools of communication that are used extensively in public relations but are not dealt with elsewhere in this textbook are direct mail and graphic materials.

The personal letter can be used as a form of advertising for persuasive communication. Direct mail is based on sending a message through the postal system to a mailing list of potential readers who have something in common. The gathering of such mailing lists has itself become a big business, and one can rent or buy the list of names from a mailing-list company to reach almost any desired audience.

In the past, direct-mail letters have been printed and sent out to anonymous recipients; today, with sophisticated computer capability and the development of the word processor and printer, letters can be individually addressed, with individual messages inserted at key points in the letter. Also, the letter can be signed, with pen and ink, by a signature machine that can produce an exact copy of an original handwritten signature. Letters from the president, congressmen, or political, governmental, or busi-

---

[3] J. A. R. Pimlott, *Public Relations and American Democracy* (Princeton: Princeton University Press, 1951), 3.

This direct mail brochure
will be sent out to a mailing list of potential textbook buyers in the com-
munications field.

EXPERTS
EXPERTS
EXPERTS

EXPERTS
IN ACTION
Inside Public Relations

Bill Cantor

Edited by Chester Burger

Experts in Action offers the most insightful and
knowledgeable examination of public relations
available to date. This firsthand authoritative por-
trait of the real world of public relations, brings
together the thought and advice of some of the
world's foremost practitioners.

Part I defines what public relations is and what it
should do; Part II tells what tools and techniques
public relations people use to successfully conduct their business; Part III thoroughly discusses
how public relations is managed; Part IV deals
with staffing; Part V examines the direction in
which public relations work is going; and in the
final section Bill Cantor offers public affairs job
guidelines including an extremely helpful index of
job descriptions, and an authoritative glossary
of public relations terms.

YOU CAN LEARN HOW THE BEST IN THE
PUBLIC RELATIONS BUSINESS HAVE
ACHIEVED AND CONTINUE TO ACHIEVE
SUCCESS. Turn this page to see whose exper-
tise you'll be sharing by reading *Experts in
Action,* then fill in and mail the enclosed
order card.

Longman Series in Public Communications

ness officials are now often handled in this manner, with thousands of
letters sent to individuals; they appear to be personal letters but in fact
are mass-produced by machine.

A typical congressman's office, having received a heavy volume of mail
on a political issue, might program into the computer half a dozen stock
replies; each incoming letter is simply marked for one of those responses.
Names and addresses and any variations can be inserted in the program;

the computers automatically do the rest, even signing the congressman's name.

Printed matter other than books and periodical publications is also expanding. Again, these are not new media, but they are being put to new use. They include tracts, leaflets, flyers, pamphlets, brochures, and booklets. Their proper distribution has always been a problem; the government alone produces many thousands of such printed materials each year, ranging from booklets on legislative actions to leaflets on rat control in inner-city slums. But in the past, many of these have remained on literature racks in public post offices or stored in government warehouses. The use of direct-mail techniques to distribute these reading materials to appropriate mailing lists has vastly increased their utility.

Thus, direct mail has become a new mass medium, capable of reaching millions of people with direct messages more personally and more intimately than newspapers, magazines, books, or electronic media can do the job.

GRAPHIC MATERIALS

The volume of other printed materials is increasing so rapidly that mention should be made here of the nonperiodic graphic media as well.

Use of display graphics, one of the oldest forms of communication, is increasing. Earlier societies used bulletin boards and wall posters for information and persuasion. Many countries, particularly China and Russia, still use wall newspapers and posters, as well as outdoor radios and TV sets, to inform and exhort their citizens. In America, posters have experienced a rebirth and revitalization; poster publishing companies have come into existence to produce eye-catching posters in volume for decoration and information. Billboards have been a fixture in graphic display for as long as America has had highways and automobiles. Equally ubiquitous but even more effective, according to research findings, are exterior and interior car cards on streetcars, subways, and buses. Even the automobile bumper sticker carries a message, often political, and so can matchbook covers and even restaurant menus.

The National Institute of Mental Health, a U.S. government agency fighting drug use among young people, decided to tell its message about the abuses of drugs, not through the traditional media, but through new display graphics. As a result, it produced brilliant posters for the bedroom as well as the classroom, eye-catching billboards, striking car cards, bumper stickers, and even clever matchbook covers. These media carried a message to many people who might not otherwise have been reached.

PUBLIC RELATIONS AND POLITICS

Nowhere is public relations more important than in American politics. Politicians are most often persuaders of public opinion, and increasingly they employ the mass media to influence the electorate. They often use

The American Cancer Society uses poster graphics to communicate information on cigarette smoking and health.

WHY START A LIFE UNDER A CLOUD?

Smoking is harmful to your baby's health. Quit for both of you. For help call your American Cancer Society.

AMERICAN CANCER SOCIETY

(Courtesy the American Cancer Society.)

the techniques of public relations, and they sometimes hire professional public relations firms to help them win election to public office and guide their relationship with constituents.

The process of legislation itself requires publicity and promotion through the mass media. Bills that cannot capture the attention of the public through mass communication rarely reach the floor of Congress or state legislatures. Former Senator Joseph Tydings of Maryland expressed a growing sentiment when he charged that congressmen who could win media publicity were more likely to get their bills signed into law than those who were ignored by the press.

Extensive use of public relations has also been made in the process of electing public officials. Consultants who specialize in political persuasion have tried to make election campaigning more sophisticated, systematic, and scientific. They use survey research and polling to determine voter interests, to gauge the popularity of issues, and to test the public image of their candidates. They use computers to analyze the research and aid in targeting the audience for the candidate's message. They advise the candidate, on the basis of research data, on the platforms to adopt and the personality aspects to emphasize or conceal. And they prepare the messages—through speeches, TV commercials, press conferences, news releases, and such—to reach the voter.

Interestingly, these new techniques of political persuasion can make the election process more democratic. Politicians can take their candidacy directly to the people through the mass media, particularly through television. They can bypass the traditional party structure, the political boss, and backroom politics. The public can be brought more directly into political decision making.

Unfortunately, however, the new public relations techniques in electioneering require money and a new kind of talent. The costs are high for public relations advice, polling, computers, advertising, perparation, and media time and space. More than $400 million was spent on such electioneering in the 1972 presidential campaign. But expenses were far less in 1976, 1980, and 1984, as a result of federal laws limiting the amount of money that can be contributed to and spent on a political campaign. For a time in the 1960s and early 1970s, much concern was expressed that the "new politics" of public relations campaigning through mass media would result in only very wealthy candidates being able to run for political office. But the election of Jimmy Carter, a farmer of relatively modest wealth from rural Georgia, proved that the new campaign reform laws were working and dispelled many fears.

A new kind of political talent is often required, too. Politicians who use media—particularly television—to reach the voter must have a certain charisma. They must be able to captivate the audience through media. For example, Jimmy Carter used a low-key, common-folks' approach to television that did not feel out of place or unwelcome in millions of American homes. Ronald Reagan, on the other hand, has spent most of his professional life in front of the cameras as an actor. Few could argue that he has not used his acting skills to exercise political leadership through the persuasive mechanism of mass media.

In the Carter–Reagan debate in 1980, Carter was the more authoritarian, more aggressive of the two men. He tried hard to seem decisive and presidential, qualities his critics felt were often lacking during his administration. Reagan appeared softer, easier, less aggressive. He seemed to know and use the medium better than Carter did. A telephone survey conducted by ABC immediately after the debate showed that more than two-thirds of the people who responded felt that Reagan had won the debate. Later, election analysts often agreed that the Carter–Reagan debate was a crucial factor in Reagan's victory.

In sum, the new politics requires a thorough understanding and effective use of mass media. The public relations adviser who can help a political candidate win elections will increasingly be part of the American political scene.

GOVERNMENT AND NONPROFIT PUBLIC RELATIONS

Although public relations is often viewed in terms of corporate and business interests, most areas of our society use public relations as a way of maintaining and adjusting relationships with their various publics, including local, state, and federal governments, hospitals, schools, religious organizations, the arts, the sciences, and even the mass media themselves. The federal government increasingly uses public relations people and techniques. By the mid-1980s more than 10,000 federal government employees were directly involved in the practice of public communication.

America has a long-standing tradition that government should not be directly involved with public communication. The government does not own or publish any daily newspapers or own and operate any radio or TV stations in the United States. The philosophy has been that government should not use media to propagandize citizens in a free society. Rather the media should be privately owned and unrestricted so they can report the activities of government and keep the bureaucracy from growing too powerful.

Nevertheless, it has become increasingly clear that even the government in a free society must communicate vital information to the public and must be sensitive to the attitudes and opinions of the people. So government employs public relations practitioners, both to counsel government on its public relations and to inform people through the media, by using press releases, press conferences, media events, films, brochures, magazines, newsletters, and any other means that would prove effective.

At the federal level, government has not permitted the use of the term "public relations" because some politicians and legislators in Congress still feel that government should not be engaged in "propaganda" and that only elected officials should be in direct contact with the public. The executive and judicial branches should only carry out the laws created by Congress; they should not be responsive to their publics. So the public relations function in the executive branch of the federal government is called "public information," and public information personnel are supposed to "inform the public," not persuade the public.

The same attitude does not apply to our international communication efforts. Congress long ago recognized that America must communicate its policies and point of view to other nations. After World War II, Congress set up the United States Information Agency to inform and persuade the people of the world about America. The Voice of America is the broadcasting station of the United States to the rest of the world, but the VOA cannot be heard in America because of our tradition of keeping the government out of direct communication with its citizens.

RIGHTS IN CONFLICT

Unfortunately, not all that is sent to the mass media from public relations offices is legitimate news or genuine human interest material. Much of it is puffery, self-promotion, or a coverup of damaging facts. One cannot blame the public relations person for putting the client's best foot forward. That is not only a natural human tendency; it is a human right. We cannot expect the public relations practitioner to have the objective judgment about his or her message that the journalist should have.

Even more unfortuantely, however, journalists often fail in their role as objective judges of the competing messages of various vested interests. Too often, the public relations professional's news release provides an easy way out for reporters or editors. It gives them a story for which they do not have to do extensive interviewing and research. The lazy journalist, the hurried journalist, the untrained journalist too often fall victim to the messages of public relations.

How much of today's news starts in a public relations office? No authoritative answer has been given to that question. Obviously, the answer depends upon the medium. Newspapers and news broadcast offices that maintain large, well-trained, and well-paid staffs are less likely to depend upon the messages of outsiders than are small, economically weak, and marginal news operations. Some studies of some media have shown that more than 50% of the editorial matter originated in press releases or promotional material.

Clearly, two rights are involved and are sometimes in conflict here. One is the right of individuals or groups to express their point of view and tell their version of the truth. The other is the right to know, the right of individuals and groups to have access to accurate information about any subject of immediate concern. When these two rights are in conflict, it is difficult to know which has supremacy over the other. Perhaps the best that can be done in a democratic society is to maintain a balance between the two; the tension resulting from the effort to maintain such a balance should help preserve a healthy society.

THE FUTURE

Without doubt, the role of public relations will grow more important in the late 1980s and beyond. As the population of the world grows and as the size of the planet shrinks (with supersonic jets and instantaneous global electronic communication), the relationships among people will become more crucial.

Communication, indeed, is essential to world peace. Understanding is essential to satisfactory relationships. Increasingly, more people in the world will need expert advice and counsel on how they can make themselves understood, or how they can change their ways to make themselves acceptable. This can be, and should be, the work of public relations, making use of mass media for human persuasion, through two-way communication, to achieve consensus and accord.

Advertising and Sales ▢ **25**

Consider the products we buy and use: toothpaste, automobiles, diet drinks, cigarettes, clothing, hardware, appliances, beer, tires, deodorants, watches, toys, typewriters, paper products, cosmetics, patent medicines, waterbeds, and so on ad infinitum. Why does the consumer spend money on these items? There must be some perceived physical or social value that assists the buyer to distinguish among brands when there is a great deal of similarity. Advertising is a major part of the answer to these and other questions regarding the economic decisions of consumers in the United States.

Advertising creativity depends on the ability of the advertiser to develop advertisements that encourage the consumer to respond positively by purchasing advertised products. With the ever-increasing political, social, and economic pressures of our complex mass society, creative advertisers need to do more than exercise creative freedom. They must constantly improve media plans, research skills, and marketing approaches. The competition for consumer attention is growing more fierce, and the truly creative advertising campaign must assist the consumer to handle this information implosion. The target audience must *comprehend* as well as read, *hear* as well as listen, and *see* as well as watch a given ad, if the ad is to be a creative sales tool.

The creative advertisement revolves around consumer needs and the ability of a given product to satisfy those needs. Consumers are not some unthinking mass; they are individual, thinking beings making economic decisions. The few intellectuals who sneer at advertising as some sort of drivel are as foolish as the rare advertiser–communicator who believes that he can consistently mislead the public. David Ogilvy, in *Confessions of an Advertising Man*, argues most persuasively for intelligent, creative advertising when he states "The consumer isn't a moron; she is your wife."

THE GROWTH OF ADVERTISING

The ancient world was filled with the calls of street criers hawking their wares or praising the goods of their employers. The crier was aided by hand-lettered, carved, chiseled signs and by guild emblems that identified the seller and encouraged the buyer. Not until the seventeenth century, however, did advertising find a truly efficient means of information dissemination—the mass media. And by the eighteenth century England had established a tax designed to discourage advertising and protect the ignorant from being cheated.

In the second half of the nineteenth century, with the rise of mass production, mass consumption, and new mass media systems, advertising grew to the extent that specialized functions were assigned to separate advertising organizations. In the early twentieth century advertising became an integral part of the economic facts of life in the United States. A truth-in-advertising statute was drafted by *Printer's Ink* and adopted by nearly every state in the union.

After World War II, advertising and the demand for consumer goods and services reached phenomenal proportions. The 1950s and 1960s saw increases in advertising expenditures of approximately 400% in 20 years. With the emergence of television, advertisers had an efficient new sales tool and possibly the most dynamic advertising medium of all time.

In the 1970s new technological achievements had their impact on advertising. The computer radically overhauled many facets of the business. The expectation is that new techniques, new media campaigns, and new message construction, coupled with the anticipated population growth, will continue that unequaled advertising boom during the 1980s.

Advertising's increasing importance in the economy since the turn of the century can be easily demonstrated by noting that billings have grown from about $500,000 in 1900 to nearly $30 billion today. Significantly, most of that growth has occurred since World War II. Advertising now accounts for approximately 2% of the gross national product (GNP).

Demands for time and space to sell goods are now generating new media vehicles because the availability of time and space in traditional advertising media cannot keep up with demand. Some media ad costs have gotten so high that only the industrial giants can compete. Advertising demand undoubtedly will help satellite and cable programming in the

An eighteenth century street vender hawking his wares. (Drawing: New York Public Library Picture Collection.)

1980s in much the same way that it gave renewed energy to specialized magazines in the 1970s. Advertising remains a "boom" industry in America's confusing economic picture.

In the past the overwhelming concern of American industry has been production. Since World War II, however, distribution—getting goods and services to the public—has become the dominant consideration of many consumer-oriented companies. One of the critical components of the marketing mix, or plan, is advertising.

In order for a message to be classified as advertising, it must have the following characteristics: (a) A medium must be used to transmit the message; (b) money must be paid by the advertiser to the medium for carrying the message; (c) the message must be directed at more than one person, preferably a large number of potential consumers; (d) the message must identify the goods–services and/or the sender of the message. These characteristics make advertising a different business communication from personal selling, sales promotion, publicity, or public relations.

Advertising supports commercial broadcasting entirely and pays for over half the costs of newspapers and magazines. In turn, consumers pay for this advertising when they buy the goods and services advertised. But rarely, if ever, is a consumer decision based solely on an advertisement. Consumers are affected by price, by their needs, by their familiarity with the product, by previous satisfaction, by packaging, by product availability, and by myriad other factors. Advertising can help create awareness of the product, a favorable attitude toward the product, and action in regard to buying the product.

Advertising decision making is based on many forces, within and outside the client's organization, based on the marketing program. They include (a) distribution, pricing, and the number of brands a company sells (b) the amount of personal selling involved; (c) the nature of the product, its competition, the demand for it, and the type of consumer who uses it; (d) the budget available. You must remember, as advertisers do, that advertising is only *one* part of the total marketing mix.

The basic advertising convictions of most large advertisers in the United States are these:

1. *The advertiser's chief role is selling the consumer.* Ads emphasize the distinctive qualities of the product and reflect the overall cultural values of the society.

2. *Advertising creates new markets.* Ads suggest new uses for old products and new products to solve old problems. Competition has created new technologies and made better products available in the marketplace.

3. *Advertising lowers costs to consumers.* Ads increase sales, and per unit production costs decrease because of this. The per unit savings far exceed the cost of the advertising, which the consumer eventually pays.

4. *Advertising spurs continual product improvement.* Ads cannot "resell" poor products, and the competition will overwhelm those products that do not become "new and improved."

5. *Advertising forces competition.* Ads are necessary in today's marketplace, where price and quality are essentials in the marketing mix. The sales-distribution system is incomplete without advertising.

6. *Advertising and scientific research work hand in glove on a vast and amazingly productive scale.* Ads help the consumer profit from inventions by speeding up the diffusion of innovation process.

Many individuals have very strong attitudes about advertising as a result of some ad campaigns and the "pop literature" concerning the power and influence of the advertising industry. Advertising is neither the devil incarnate nor the savior of our economic system.

ADVERTISING CONTROLS

In order to protect the consumer and counteract public criticism of advertising, a variety of controls have evolved. These controls over advertising come from three major sources: governmental regulation, industry codes of self-regulation, and public pressure groups seeking specific changes from one or both of the above groups.

Governmental Regulation

The primary force in governmental regulation of advertising is the Federal Trade Commission (FTC), which was set up under the Federal Trade Commission Act of 1914 and bolstered by the Wheeler-Lee amendments of 1938. Since that time a variety of laws have increased the FTC's role. Each new law has, in effect, been a compromise between the forces seeking stringent governmental controls and the industry, which feels any additional legislation is unnecessary. This kind of compromise is characteristic of our society, which is in a constant state of flux.

Although the Federal Communications Act of 1934 and subsequent broadcast legislation have never given the commission direct control over advertisers, the FCC can and does exert some influence over radio and TV stations in advertising matters. In the case of cigarette ads, the commission had no jurisdiction over the tobacco companies. However, this agency forced the radio and TV stations, which it licenses, to refuse to accept cigarette advertising after 1 January 1971, but allowed them to accept ads for cigars and pipe tobacco.

In the end, however, it is the FTC that serves as the major federal watchdog over advertising practices. Most of the current laws and proposed legislation deal with seven basic problem areas:

1. Copyright laws protect expressions of advertising ideas from being exploited by anyone other than the creator or his agents.

2. The Lanham Trade Mark Act (1947) protects use of distinctive product names, identifying symbols, and advertising exclusively by the creator and his agents.

3. An individual's "right of privacy" is protected since the advertiser must obtain written permission for any use of a person's name or his endorsement in an advertisement.

4. A lottery is an illegal interstate activity and is also outlawed in many states. Advertising contests must not contain all of these three elements: prize, consideration, and chance. If they do, they are defined as lotteries and are subject to gambling laws.

5. Obscenity and bad taste are difficult to identify because the morals of this country are in a constant state of flux. What is acceptable today would have been obscene ten years ago. Some ads in *Playboy* could be thought in bad taste by some people if seen in the context of media like *Boy's Life*.

6. Truth in advertising is generally agreed to be an absolutely essential item of an advertisement. An exact definition of truth is hard to come by, however. The FTC attacks untruths in advertising because they are "unfair methods of competition."

7. Libel or defamation (the intent to harm a person's reputation) is a legally punishable offense, and advertisers take every precaution against it.

Most of the cases handled by the Federal Trade Commission originate with a business competitor or a consumer. Some cases originate from studies initiated by the FTC or another agency. After investigation a formal complaint may be issued; the advertiser is given an opportunity to respond in a hearing. If the advertiser is found guilty, a cease-and-desist order is issued, forcing the advertiser to end the practice.

Besides the FTC and FCC, the U.S. Postal Service, Food and Drug Administration, Alcohol Tax Unit, Patent Office, and Securities and Exchange Commission exert pressures, if not actual control, over advertising at the federal level.

Industry Regulation

Public and governmental outcries over excessive amounts of advertising, special-product advertising (liquor), labeling, and other problems have led the industry to devise self-regulations to avoid the passage of new, more stringent laws.

Industry self-regulation of advertising practices comes from three sources: advertisers, advertising agencies, and media. Although this form of regulation is not legally binding, it is effective because internal pressures are applied by the industry on offenders.

Advertisers. Self-regulation occurs on both the local-retailer and national-manufacturer levels. Retailers have organized Better Business Bureaus to investigate consumers' and competitors' advertising complaints before legal action becomes necessary. There are approximately 100 local bureaus associated with the National Better Business Bureau, which developed a "Fair Practice Code for Advertising and Selling." In addition, "The Advertising Code of American Business" has been adopted by both the Advertising Federation of America and the Association of National Advertisers.

Agency. Self-regulation functions here under the auspices of the American Association of Advertising Agencies. The "4As" endorses "The Advertising Code of American Businesses." This code's major concerns are truthfulness, responsibility, decency, and accuracy.

The Committee on Improvement of Advertising Content of the American Association of Advertising Agencies seeks to evaluate offensive ads and recommends changes in that campaign to its agency. The advertisers individually or through trade associations police advertising practices.

Media. The media also review advertising and regulate the kinds of products and appeals that appear for public consumption. The stronger a given newspaper, magazine, radio, or TV station becomes financially, the less likely it is to permit marginally acceptable ads. The fleeting quality of the broadcast media makes radio and TV ads more difficult to review, but the National Association of Broadcasters has established a "code" for advertising and other member activities. Unfortunately, not all stations subscribe to the code.

The general purpose of self-regulation is twofold: It helps protect the public from false advertising; and it heads off further governmental restriction of advertising.

Public Pressure Groups

The individual's major form of advertising control—the refusal to buy the offending product—could be the most effective ad control, but generally it is not because this form of protest is not organized.

The consumer's major success has been in group protests and information campaigns such as the Consumers Union, which publishes *Consumer Report*. Occasionally, crusaders arise to take up the consumer's cause. Under the leadership of Ralph Nader, an increasingly successful group of dedicated people has committed itself to consumer protection.

THE STRUCTURE OF THE ADVERTISING INDUSTRY

Four distinct industrial groups are involved in the process of advertising communication: (a) the advertiser or company that produces and/or sells the goods or services being advertised; (b) the advertising agency that represents the advertiser and creates advertisements; (c) the media representative who has three essential duties—to sell a given medium in preference to another, to sell a given market area in preference to another, and to sell one basic media unit in preference to another; (d) the medium that carries the advertisement.

In most cases the local advertiser deals directly with the local media. Ads are usually prepared in one of three ways. First, the local merchant's advertising department can design them. That is the case for most large department stores such as Marshall Field & Company in Chicago, which has an outstanding advertising department. Second, the local merchant can use advertisements provided by the national manufacturer of the goods he sells. Third, the medium can prepare the ad for the advertiser as a part of the total media service. In all these circumstances there is considerable interaction between the advertiser and the medium.

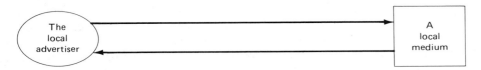

Advertisers that use agencies to represent them seldom deal directly with the media. In this situation the agency, the company's advertising expert, prepared ads for, and recommends media to, the advertiser. If the advertiser approves, the agency then deals with the newspapers, magazines, or broadcasting stations involved in that ad campaign. In this case the agency initiates the action with both the advertiser and the medium.

At another level of complexity, the media may also have advertising representatives. In these instances the agency devises an advertising campaign and secures the advertisers' approval. Then the agency contacts the media representative, who makes the necessary arrangements with the media. Under this interaction pattern, the media and advertisers are still farther removed from one another, since the major negotiations are conducted between the advertising agency and the media representative.

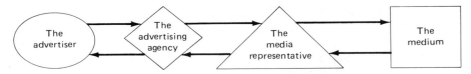

As the advertising industry has grown more complex, advertising agencies and media reps have become extremely important communication partners of advertisers and media in the sales communication process.

Each of the above components of the advertising business has an impact on the amounts and kinds of goods and services Americans purchase.

ADVERTISING CLASSIFICATIONS

Advertiser-communicators have developed labeling systems to clarify advertising processes. The four basic ways of classifying advertising are by type of advertiser; by audience; by message—content, placement, and approach; and by medium. These classification systems are important because they identify the who, what, where, when, and how in relation to advertisers' expenditures and media earnings.

Type of Advertiser

The two major categories of advertisers are general and retail. The *general advertiser* is usually a national or regional producer or distributor of a limited number of product classes. The company does not normally sell directly to the consumer. Most general advertisers' campaigns are developed and executed by an advertising agency. Some corporations that produce competing brands in the same product class utilize the services of several agencies. Most general advertisers have come to use television heavily but also invest large sums in supplementary advertising in magazines, radio, and newspapers.

The *retail advertiser* by contrast, is normally a local or limited regional operation that traditionally does not retain an advertising agency. The retailer's ads are prepared or supplied by (a) the retailer's advertising department; (b) the media in which the ads are placed, or (c) the general advertiser whose products the retailer merchandises. The retail advertiser depends most heavily on local newspapers and radio stations.

Most retail and general advertisers maintain continuing ad campaigns to obtain the positive, cumulative effects of repetitive advertising. The most pressing concern of the retailer is immediate sales from specific ads, whereas the general advertiser is more concerned with the long-range effects and future sales of the total advertising campaign. The retailer must reach the consumer seeking immediate gratification of a specific need. The general advertiser is seeking to lay a foundation for purchasing decisions when the consumer need arises.

In terms of advertiser classification that has an impact on advertising style, consider supermarket ads. Unquestionably, the overall style of food retailers is essentially the same: large local newspaper pages with multiple product lines, departments, sales, specials, coupons, and so on. The consumer *shops* the ad as well as the store. This format is valuable to both shopper and seller. Interestingly, attempts to transfer this technique to fast-talking, flash-cutting radio and TV ads are less successful. In today's food market, and with today's prices, most consumers want to comparison-shop very deliberately.

The personality of the consumer often becomes involved with the personality and use and function of the product. The advertiser must know his "place" in the market and then convince the consumers that they need to shop in that intellectual, emotional, and physical "place"—*the retail outlet*. Store loyalty is more important than brand loyalty for supermarkets and similar advertisers.

Type of Audience

Two groups to whom advertisers seek to sell their goods and services are other businesses and consumers. Advertisers who seek industrial buyers, including other manufacturers, distributors, and retailers, are involved in *business advertising*. Most business advertising appears in the industry or trade press and in specialized direct-mail campaigns. Advertisers who seek individuals or individual home units are involved in mass, *consumer advertising*. Consumer advertising uses all the available media to varying degrees, depending on the specific thrust of the ad campaign.

The target audiences of business and consumer advertising make significantly different demands on the advertiser, especially regarding the media plan and the number of buyers available. The business advertiser sells goods and services that are in turn converted into consumer goods and services. The advertiser of consumer goods is selling items to be used directly by the people that buy them.

Advertising can benefit the consumer in a variety of ways:

1. Advertising is an important source of *information* if the consumer uses the data intelligently.
2. It saves *time*, and in today's world it can save energy. Let your eyes and ears do the driving, as your fingers do the walking.
3. It eventually improves *quality* because it encourages competition.
4. It can lower per-unit cost for products when it increases sales volume.

The sophistication of audience research has gone beyond demographics and now includes psychographic profiles of the likes, dislikes, and personality traits of the consumer. Advertising messages are beginning to reflect these preferences and tastes as well as initiate them.

Type of Message

The content, placement, and approach of advertisements are important because they designate the intent of the advertising communication.

The content of an advertising message may be institutional or product oriented. *Institutional* ads refer to messages that develop the *image* of the advertiser. Institutional messages do not seek the immediate sale of specific products but attempt to create a positive attitude of goodwill in the mind of the public toward that advertiser. Institutional advertising may also seek to correct a negative corporate image; align the company with specific national goals; or, more recently, place the company in the vanguard on a specific social issue, such as race relations. Many industries pool individual, corporate, and financial resources to improve the general

Why do we buy this space?

For more than 12 years now, we've been addressing Americans with weekly messages in principal print media. We've argued, cajoled, thundered, pleaded, reasoned and poked fun. In return, we've been reviled, revered, held up as a model and put down as a sorry example.

Why does Mobil choose to expose itself to these weekly judgments in the court of public opinion? Why do we keep it up now that the energy crisis and the urgent need to address energy issues have eased, at least for the present?

Our answer is that business needs voices in the media, the same way labor unions, consumers, and other groups in our society do. Our nation functions best when economic and other concerns of the people are subjected to rigorous debate. When our messages add to the spectrum of facts and opinion available to the public, even if the decisions are contrary to our preferences, then the effort and cost are worthwhile.

Think back to some of the issues in which we have contributed to the debate.

• Excessive government regulation—it's now widely recognized that Washington meddling, however well intentioned, carries a price tag that the consumer pays.

• The folly of price controls—so clear now that prices of gasoline and other fuels are coming down, now that the marketplace has been relieved of most of its artificial restraints.

• The need for balance between maintaining jobs and production and maintaining a pristine environment—a non-issue, we argued, if there's common sense and compromise on both sides, a view that's now increasingly recognized in Washington.

Over the years, we've won some and lost some, and battled to a draw on other issues we've championed, such as building more nuclear power plants and improving public transportation. We've supported presidents we thought were right in their policies and questioned Democrats and Republicans alike when we thought their policies were counterproductive.

In the process we've had excitement, been congratulated and castigated, made mistakes, and won and lost some battles. But we've enjoyed it. While a large company may seem terribly impersonal to the average person, it's made up of people with feelings, people who care like everybody else. So even when we plug a quality TV program we sponsor on public television, we feel right about spending the company's money to build audience for the show, just as we feel good as citizens to throw the support of our messages to causes we believe in, like the Mobil Grand Prix, in which young athletes prepare for this year's Olympics. Or recognition for the positive role retired people continue to play in our society.

We still continue to speak on a wide array of topics, even though there's no immediate energy crisis to kick around anymore. Because we don't want to be like the mother-in-law who comes to visit only when she has problems and matters to complain about. We think a continuous presence in this space makes sense for us. And we hope, on your part, you find us informative occasionally, or entertaining, or at least infuriating. But never boring. After all, you did read this far, didn't you?

Mobil®

image of industry as a whole. In effect, this advertising message serves a function generally assigned to public relations. However, it is hoped that the long-range effect of institutional ads may lead to future sales by creating this positive image.

Product advertising seeks to generate sales of a specific commodity. The sales may occur immediately or at a later date when the consumer needs to replace or replenish a specific item. In terms of total dollar volume spent, product advertising overwhelmingly exceeds institutional advertising.

The *placement* category identifies the advertiser placing the message in a given medium. There are three designations of type of ad placement: national, spot, and local. National advertising refers to ads placed by general advertisers in national media (e.g., broadcast networks, magazines). Spot (or national spot) advertising identifies ads placed in local media by general advertisers. Local advertising specifies messages that retailers place in local media.

When the Oldsmobile Division of General Motors advertises on the NBC radio network, that is national advertising. When Oldsmobile places an ad direct with WSB-TV, an Atlanta TV station, that is spot advertising. When a Milwaukee Oldsmobile dealer buys space in the *Milwaukee Journal*, that is local advertising.

In terms of TV income, national advertising accounts for nearly 45% of every TV dollar; spot uses 38% and local 17%. For radio income, local advertising accounts for 68%, spot 29%, and national only 3%.

A hybrid has emerged in this category: cooperative (co-op) advertising. Co-op refers to ads placed in local media by general advertisers and their retail outlets in combination. They share the costs and reap the benefits of the lower local-media rates.

The *content* approach is another way of analyzing advertising messages. Advertisements may be *direct* and demand immediate action: "Sale, Today Only!" "Buy Now and Save!" The *indirect* approach is a "soft sell." It seeks action but is calmer and more reserved: it may use whimsy, humor, and informality in its approach. "Now" is replaced by "soon" or "at your convenience" or "when the need arises."

Both approaches are effective, and when handled by experts, neither content approach is insensitive or offensive. But the indirect approach seems to be growing more dominant as time goes by.

The message of the 1980s in clothing seems to be sex. Who would ever have thought that the working man's canvas pants (blue jeans) would be sold in semi-nude, sexual innuendo ads in which the message is "panted"? But the "designer-jean wars" of the 1980s manage to do it in style. And it seems that the more controversial the ad, the more sensuous the headline, the more titillating the photograph—the better the sales. The message to the consumer has always been price, satisfaction, image, identification, packaging—and the "bottom line" in today's jean ads emphasizes all those message attributes.

To be successful advertisements must (a) *create awareness* of the goods—services well enough to have them considered as an option; (b) *associate positive aspects* of product with the consumer's need (the *unique selling points* must be emphasized); (c) *emotionally involve* consumers and make them identify with and desire the product; (d) *produce action* that influences the potential consumer to become a *buyer* and eventually a committed heavy user.

Type of Medium   This classification system helps assess the relative strengths of the various media. Radio and television account for practically all advertising revenue for electronic media, although a small amount is spent for consumer advertising in motion-picture theaters. Five media account for most of the revenue earned by print advertisers; newspapers, magazines, billboards, transit, and direct mail.

Every company's media plan begins with an analysis of alternate classes of media. There is no universal rule as to which medium is best because each medium has advantages and drawbacks. More important, marketing objectives for most products require an advertising campaign that requires a "media mix" to provide the greatest degree of flexibility.

The medium remains a substitute for "the real thing" in advertising. The real thing, of course, is personal selling; what politicians call "pressing the flesh." All the TV ads for the Chrysler "K" car and all the newspaper layouts ballyhooing the mileage estimates and rebates only get the potential buyer into the showroom. It is the salesperson's personal selling skills and the point-of-purchasing advertising tools that clinch that sale. But in an ever-increasing number of product categories, the medium is replacing the salesclerk to a degree. The catalogue showroom is a retailing fact of life, and in the near future the video display terminal in the home may replace that catalogue. Shop-by-television could eliminate personal selling altogether.

The media mix is essential to the success of an advertising campaign. Too often, beginners emphasize the more glamorous and expensive ad media and lose the impact that direct mail, outdoor, transit, specialty items, and point-of-purchase advertising can have.

Remember that media strategy emerges from and does not normally determine general marketing, advertising, brand, and creative strategy. The media mix involves (a) selecting the medium (radio); (b) selecting media vehicles (stations and networks); (c) scheduling chosen media (the number of spots, when they are run, and in what pattern they are run).

The overall media strategy is structured around (a) marketing and sales objectives; (b) creative style; (c) target-audience coverage; (d) budget constraints; (e) cost efficiencies; (f) timing and seasonality of consumption; (g) competition strategy; and (h) availability of media time and space.

The media element of the advertising mix is perhaps the most scientific aspect of the total process. It is quantifiable, and evaluation is rigorous.

The emphasis on and use of advertising by a company determines its place in the corporate structure.

1. The advertising department can report directly to the head of the company. This format gives advertising its strongest corporate role on an equal footing with other departments.

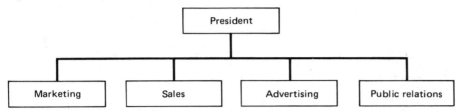

2. The advertising department can be a part of the marketing area. This pattern is very common and emphasizes the importances of all three subelements to the marketing function.

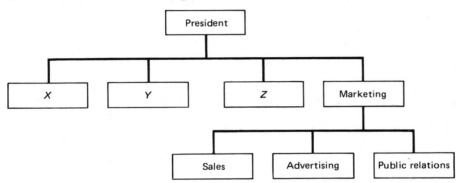

3. The advertising department can report to the sales manager. This structure is dominant in corporations where personal selling is an essential, and advertising supports that effort through distributors and retailers.

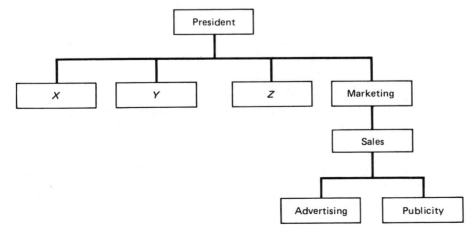

4. Today's conglomerates and those companies with franchise operations may use a hybrid where (*a*) there are two levels of advertising decisions (national and local) within the corporate structure; (*b*) each division or brand has its own decision-making apparatus.

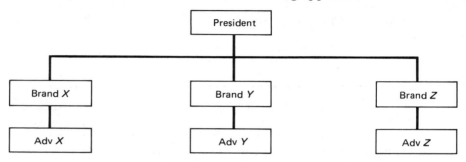

The preceding format ensures creative independence and allows for specificity in ad development.

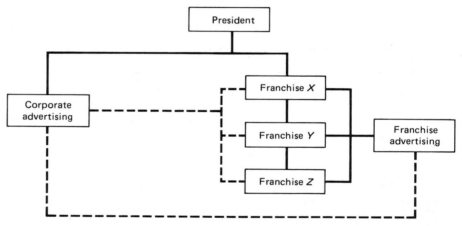

The above pattern creates two layers of cooperating advertising with the corporate advertising creating national awareness and coordinating regional and local cooperation and with franchise advertising generating immediate sales and based on price and convenience.

Within the advertising department, internal organization is usually based on market, brand, function, or medium. The advertiser's ad department has to interface with the media, with media representatives, and most important, with the advertising agency. The overriding consideration of the ad manager is to function effectively within the constraints of the advertising budget.

Perhaps the most important decision an advertising department makes or advises the parent company to make is the selection of an advertising agency. A number of important considerations are involved:

1. The cost of creative talent is high; a good advertising agency can attract it and then spread the cost across a number of clients.

2. Media decisions are complex and specialized. Ad agencies are trained and equipped to deal with these problems.

3. Agencies over the long haul can offer insights into the marketing and sales and publicity and public relations areas for little or no additional cost.

4. A good ad agency has close and good ties to suppliers (talent agencies, producers, specialty houses).

5. The most important element an agency can offer is an additional voice that tends to be relatively uninfluenced by corporate politics.

6. The hows and whys of selecting a specific agency involve the following questions; Do we need an agency? Do we like a particular agency's work? Will we work well with their people, their business style, their work patterns? Which of the "top" people in the agency will actually work on our account? Has the agency had experience with our type of goods and services, and do they now have a client in our product class or industry segment? Will we be a big or small account in the agency, and is size of billings an issue in determining the servicing of our account? How wide are their specialized services, and how much do they cost? Where is the agency located? How long has it been in business? How big is it? How financially sound is it? What is its reputation among other agencies and with *former* clients? How much turnover is there in *key* personnel?

In the long run, the smooth functioning of an advertiser–agency relationship is based on (*a*) mutual trust and respect; (*b*) open communication in all areas at all times; (*c*) more than one contact person at both ends; (*d*) clear-cut objectives and expectations; (*e*) correcting areas of disagreement quickly and positively.

Remember, the selection and retention of an agency is a million-dollar decision for a major corporation. It costs about that much to change agencies if they do not make a good selection the first time.

THE NATIONAL ADVERTISER

Advertising is only one element in a company's overall marketing plan and functions in relation to publicity, public relations, promotion, and sales considerations, which involve

1. Introducing new services, hard goods (e.g., autos, furniture), soft goods (e.g., clothes, draperies), and package goods (e.g., ready-to-eat cereals, soaps).
2. Building brand loyalty for established lines.
3. Rejuvenating older product lines with refurbished contents and images.

4. Modifying overall consumer attitudes of the company and its goods and services.

Besides advertising, the corporation must plan, package, price, promote, distribute, service, display, and work with franchisees and retailers. A general advertiser normally has national, regional, and local campaigns all going at the same time, which have to be coordinated. An advertiser will conduct industrial campaigns to gain business clients and consumer advertising while running trade advertising to bolster its image in its peer group and with the government, which is not unlike institutional ads for the general public.

Sales can be increased with sample distribution, pricing, couponing, contests with rewards, premiums, trade shows, public exhibitions, and tours and plant promotions, in conjunction with ad campaigns.

THE NATIONAL ADVERTISING AGENCY

Of the approximately 550 advertising agencies in the United States, fewer than 100 bill more than $25 million with the media. Yet it is the larger national entities that dominate and lead the field creatively and economically. Therefore, they, like the national accounts they serve, are worth special attention.

Agency Structure

Most agencies are organized around the major services they provide their clients. The figure below illustrates the four major functions of an advertising agency. Agencies are in business to solve their clients' prob-

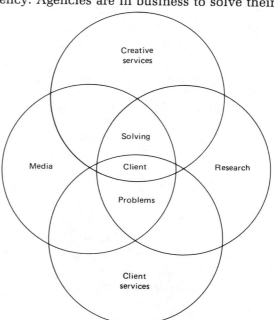

The Four Major Functions of Advertising Agencies: (1) Creative Services, (2) Media, (3) Client Services, and (4) Research. These interactive services are designed to help the advertiser solve problems, sell goods and services, and improve the corporate image.

lems around essentially four areas: creative, media, client services, and research. In addition, a large agency must perform its own administrative tasks. The organization of a typical large agency has four major divisions:

1. An administrative unit to handle the day-to-day business details and corporate public relations.
2. A client services unit manned by account personnel to deal with client needs and interface directly with the advertiser as liaison officers.
3. A marketing unit, which handles media decisions, sales promotion, and media research.
4. A creative unit, which is the heart of every agency because it is here that print and electronics campaigns are designed, tested, and executed.

Notice that the research function reports to both the creative and marketing units.

To better serve client needs and make sure that all four services interrelate, most agencies work under some sort of committee structure. For example, the Leo Burnett Agency relies on committee action at all levels and has a team concept that provides for intense consultation among corporate groups.

Because this agency services a limited number of accounts (approximately 30) this team approach is very dynamic and successful. Not only does it serve the client but it also trains new employees by allowing them to work closely with more experienced personnel in all areas.

Creative Services

The process of creative decision making has one goal in advertising: *to help the client*, usually in the form of selling goods and services. Objectivity, avoidance of quick decisions to support cute or clever ideas, and simplicity are essential. Three basic considerations ultimately affect an ad:

1. What to put in it (copy, art, research, service, and mechanical).
2. Where to put it (media and research).
3. How to extend its results at point of sale (research and merchandising).[1]

Ads need to be simple, attractive so as to catch the eye and ear, pleasurable, and memorable. Above all else, the ad should sell the client's goods and services.

When an ad is being designed, many questions are asked:

1. Is this a good, simple idea?

---

[1] Leo Burnett memorandum, "What, Where, and How of Advertising," 9 April 1940.

2. Will the reader–listener–viewer be left with the idea? What will they remember from the ad?

3. Is this a good technique for presenting the idea?

4. How will the audience feel about the product and advertiser? (Most consumers want to do business with people they like!)

5. Is the presentation talking to the right people—people who will buy the product?[2]

The product, the ideas, and the ads have to come from writers, artists, art directors, musical talent, and other creative specialists in art, copy, and production. These creators must be able to conceptualize as well as write or draw or storyboard. The development of ideas is the most valuable contribution a creative individual can offer an agency. The members of the creative team must understand and appreciate every aspect of creative activity as well as their own specialty because the words of the writer must "jibe" with the visuals of the artist and the "music" of the arranger.

Creative ads depend on a select number of considerations in creative development.

Source. Who is the loneliest man in town? *The Maytag repairman.* Who sends you to the store to buy Starkist? *Charlie the Tuna.* Other product spokespersons are the *Jolly Green Giant,* the *Pillsbury doughboy,* the *Kee-*

[2] Interview with Dick Stanwood, Chicago, December 1976.

The Keebler elves are effective spokespersons for the line of packaged baked goods they advertise.

(Courtesy the Keebler Company.)

bler elves, and the ladies in the laundry room who use Cheer. Whether real or created, their attractiveness adds power to an advertisement.

Message. "Weekends were Made for Michelob." "Fly the Friendly Skies of United," "You're in Good Hands with Allstate," and "Take the Nestea Plunge" are phrases that focus the message, develop conclusions, and state the product's case. They are central in developing the brand image. The most difficult lesson for advertising students to learn is that they need to create messages that sell. If the messages are *also* witty and clever, all well and good, but selling is the important issue.

Production. The quality and style of an ad depends on the creative talents of those who produce it. The artists, copyeditors, cartoonists, and others make good ideas work.

Copy strategy varies by product conditions; in general, however, new brands seek to create awareness and promote a first purchase, whereas established brands seek to create unique images to expand their market share. The overall objectives of the marketing plan must guide creative work. Copy can (a) characterize a product by creating an image; (b) provide a description of the type and quality of functions it performs; and (c) serve as a physical description of the product. But ads must at some point increase sales by providing reminders that the product is available and that it has multiple uses, many of which are new or can be used in new situations. The recruitment of new consumers and increased rate of consumption by current users are the two major ways to increase market share.

Client Service

For the general public, the account executive may be the most commonly recognized role in the agency business. He or she is both the liaison and the policymaker, who interprets client needs for the agency and presents agency solutions to the client. Client-service personnel are in the middle and are a key force in the planning, coordination, and evaluation of the total ad campaign. Account group personnel are generalists among the specialists who populate the agency business.

Client-service personnel deal with a wide variety of client advertising departments, but five traditional approaches are common:

1. The client's advertising department may be organized by media. Under this arrangement, the advertiser has a television-and-radio manager, a newspaper manager, and an outdoor manager. The emphasis of specialization in this case is based on the unique characteristics of each medium.

2. The department may be organized by product. At Procter & Gamble, each of the company's brands has a complete team to service it, which leads to strong competition between teams as well as with other manufacturers.

3. The advertising director may have assistants for the South, Northeast, Midwest, and West. This geographical pattern of organization works well with companies that produce regional products or use specialized channels of distribution.

4. Some companies base their advertising operations on the kinds of users who buy their products and therefore have a farm manager, an industrial manager, an institutional manager, and a consumer manager.

5. The functional approach is used by many companies. This arrangement has an art manager, a copywriting manager, a media manager, and a production manager.

The client-service department of the agency is literally a part of the marketing staff of the advertiser. The account executive often has a counterpart in the advertiser's organization known as a brand manager, and they are the working contacts or partners or links in the agency–advertiser relationship.

Every advertising campaign should be developed around a set of specific objectives, which serve as operational directives for lower-level management to follow in developing the campaign and as a basis for evaluating the results. Sales, product recognition, public attitudes, share of market, brand loyalty, and other goals are logical objectives or goals of advertising campaigns.

Client service is, in effect, involved in everybody else's business. It is the account group's responsibility to bring to bear all of the resources of the agency to solve the client's problems intelligently and efficiently.

Media Services   The buying of "space" and "time" has value only if it reaches the client's prospective consumers. The selection and buying of media is a highly complex operation that is increasingly research based. Time and space buyers must be evermore "on target" because the placement of ads has taken on new intensity as ad costs skyrocket.

Advertisers seek out target audiences who use or are likely to buy their products. Advertising research seeks to specify the characteristics of the target audience, to identify the basic media units that reach the target audience most efficiently, and to develop advertisements that persuade that target audience to purchase the product being marketed.

Consumers must work to sort out the thousands of product advertisements that compete for their attention, time, and money. It is estimated that Americans see or hear more than 1500 ads each day, and as consumers they have created psychological mechanisms that filter out those advertising communications that are of no value to them and have become increasingly aware of products for which they have an immediate need. That is why advertisers must ensure that their ads reach more of the right people and are better communications than those of the competition.

Media research asks eight critical questions about target audiences.

1. Who are our potential customers in terms of demography?
2. Are there geographic differences in consumption? How much of the budget should be allocated to each market?
3. Are there seasonal differences in consumption? Should advertising weight vary across the year, or should it be level?
4. What are competitive brands doing in terms of budget size and advertising strategy?
5. How do the consumers' demographic characteristics relate to their exposure to the various media?
6. Does the product's sales message lend itself to a particular medium?
7. Is exposure in one medium more valuable than in another in terms of impact on brand preference?
8. In terms of cost per thousand persons in the desired target group exposed to the advertising, which media vehicles are the most efficient?[3]

Every media plan seeks to enhance the advertising and marketing objectives. A media mix is built to maximize the advertiser's dollars and ensure that each medium makes unique contributions.

Television. In television, cost to the advertiser is based on audience size and characteristics, production–distribution costs, and advertiser demand, which has accelerated dramatically. This increase in demand has increased prices paid by national advertisers. Local TV advertising is sold by commercial units to local advertisers and by audience units (Gross Rating Points) to national advertisers through local stations' media representatives. Most network advertising plans today are packages or scatter plans, which provide a series of spots spread over a variety of shows at a group price. Full or partial sponsorship of programs and specials is relatively rare because of costs, risks, and demand. The 30-second commercial dominates; it was the child of necessity when costs and demand for spots required a change in the 60-second format. The transition began with advertisers "piggybacking" spots (combining two shorter commercials in a 60-second slot). The 30-second commercial delivers about 75% of the recall of a 60-second spot. The national advertiser is very dependent on network television and the high cost and lack of availability of network commercial times is generating considerable interest in the development of "fourth TV network" alternatives. High network costs have also increased interest in other advertising media by traditional heavy users of television.

---

[3] *Training Manual for the Media Department* (Chicago: Leo Burnett, 1970), 1–6.

Radio. Radio is classified in the same way as television, but the medium is used in significantly different ways. Radio tends to supplement the media plans of most local advertisers, whose major focus is on newspapers and on national advertisers who emphasize television. Radio dayparts and program formats are key factors in audience size and composition, and because of this, radio audience selectivity has become an advantage to the advertiser with a specialized target audience.

Magazines. Magazines are generally classified by content, lifestyle of consumer, trade, and farm periodicals. The trend is toward greater selectivity in audiences, rather than general readership. This has proved to be an excellent development for the advertiser with a narrowly defined target audience that can be provided at a low cost per thousand readers. Regional runs of magazines have increased flexibility for smaller national advertisers, as well as larger local advertisers. Ads can now be run in some periodicals on the basis of Zip-code references. Sales reps for magazines sell all advertisers at rates that decrease as advertising volume increases. Size of ad, position in the magazine, use of color, and number of copies in the run all have an impact on the cost.

Newspapers. Newspapers are the backbone of retail advertising. This is the largest ad medium in the United States because it offers good geographical flexibility for advertisers seeking general audiences. National advertisers pay higher rates than do local advertisers, and this has led to co-op advertising, where the national advertiser pays most of the cost. Because the ad is placed by the local advertiser, the lower local rate is paid. Costs of advertising are based on rate systems that go down as annual ad volume goes up. Size of ad, type of reproduction, use of color, and position have an impact on newspaper ad costs. Both national and local Sunday supplements are valuable and offer superior reproduction and environment. However, as in magazines, newspaper readership rather than circulation is a true measure of the medium's value. Like magazines, newspapers have *primary readership*, those who purchase the newspaper, and *pass-along readership*, where use is based on casual availability, but readers do not have enough interest to buy. In-home versus out-of-home readership also is important because the out-of-home reader is generally a short-term user and the advertiser must depend on repeated exposure for impact.

Direct Mail. Direct mail is the second-largest medium by dollar volume in the United States and is very selective, based on personalized messages sent to names on specific lists. It is expensive but successful. It can include letters, stuffers, cards, brochures, and anything else that will fit in an envelope. Many companies now include ads with their monthly billing statements; this is an excellent advertising format, which cuts postal costs because the bill has to be sent anyway.

Outdoor. Outdoor ads take essentially two forms, the 24-sheet billboard and the painted spectacular (always lighted and sometimes animated). Boards have a life span of 1–6 months on the average. Outdoor ads are not selective, have to be bought locally, and usually carry reminder messages. This is an excellent supplementary medium for ads that do not rely on extensive copy.

Other Formats. Other ad formats include car cards, displays at airports and sporting arenas, matchbooks, sky writing, shoppers' specials, sound trucks, and anything else from ballpoint pens to T-shirts. Media plans attempt to reach the greatest number of prospects, as often as possible, to meet marketing objectives within tight fiscal controls.

Billboards function particularly well as reminder ads that do not rely on extensive copy. (Photo by Brendan Beirne.)

Research Services

Traditionally, creative research is an in-house operation, whereas media research is supplied by outside sources that survey print and electronic media audiences. The numbers in media research are important and have an impact on agency decisions. Agencies vary in the amount of research effort they support, but there is a trend to decision making based on supportable facts, rather than the old "seat of the pants" approach. However, suspicion of the "numbers crowd" remains in some areas of the advertising business. The research department is primarily involved in three activities: (a) evaluating creative ideas and copy in the research workshop to identify and articulate problems early on so that they can be corrected before huge dollar investments are involved; (b) developing of new up-front marketing research and development funded out of profits and not the client's budget; and (c) evaluating government, private, or consumer research that might have an impact on client products.

26 | Entertainment and Art

For most Americans, the day is filled with work—work that is often boring, exasperating, and exhausting and that can be tension and anxiety producing as well. When the workday ends, most of us need to relax and enjoy our free time. Entertainment in the mass media is the prime means to that end.

The mass media also serve as the primary source of what some have come to call *popular culture*, which is, as we shall see, the chosen art of the people. This "pop art" is used to shrug off the world of work and refresh us so that we can return to, and cope with, the labor ahead.

Entertainment and art in the media, although much abused by self-appointed social critics, may well be the most important service the mass media provide many Americans, especially the young, the undereducated, the poor, the elderly, and minorities.

THE NATURE OF MEDIART

If art is the application of skills in various modes or expression with the intent to please, involve, and arouse consumers, then the products of these doers can be referred to as art. Media artists use machines as tools, as extensions of their minds and hands to produce content of skill and imagination. This is *mediart*, and its quality depends on the combined skills of all the artists involved because mass communication is a collaborative art.

As in other arts, there are no exact rules in mediart or in its evaluation. The shared perceptions that determine what is "good" in the "good art" in television, film, records, books, magazines keep changing. Taste in mediart content changes by discarding established values and once again adopting values previously discarded. Taste in mediart, then, is *learned*, and *mediartists* do the teaching.

Mediartists are also bound up with audiences; the rise in audience expectations requires a requisite improvement in the content that artists display in the media. The customer has affected artists throughout history. Demand for an artist's product is one measure of artistic success. Audiences, like the other facts of a mediartist's life (e.g., training, media availability, cost), have an impact on the quality and kind of content produced.

Consider the impact of the computer-driven camera on special effects. *Star Wars, E.T., Indiana Jones and the Temple of Doom*, and *Star Trek III: The Search for Spock, Close Encounters of the Third Kind*, among others, have raised the understanding and taste of the audience to technical levels that are an order of magnitude leap from 10 years ago. A whole genre of films depend upon a miniaturization process that has created a new kind of "futuristic naturalism." Artists in this field must meet or challenge these audience expectations in their next work.

Everyone knows something about mediart because it is an important fiber in our everyday cloth of life. "We know what we like and we like what we know." Audiences respond to a variety of content in ways different from critics. Many feel that something is wrong with mediart if it needs to be explained to audiences. But audiences learn to appreciate better mediart by exposure to it. Goethe argued that critics need to con-

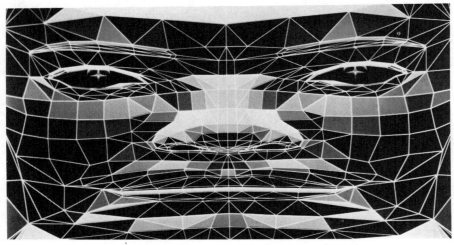

(Photo: New York Public Library at Lincoln Center, Courtesy Walt Disney Productions.)

The movie *Tron* employed state-of-the-art computer graphic techniques to create the kind of sophisticated special effects modern audiences have come to expect.

sider (*a*) what is the artist attempting to do? (*b*) did he do it? (*c*) was it worth doing? Audiences need to understand (*a*) how a work is created; (*b*) how to see or hear it; (*c*) how to interpret it; and (*d*) how to let it affect them in ways they want to be affected.

There is almost always a difference in mediart between what was the artist's intention and what is the audience's perception. The artist's craftsmanship and skill are a part of mediart but do not guarantee high quality. The audience must join in leaps of the imagination with the artist so that meaning can be shared.

THE MIX OF ART AND ENTERTAINMENT IN MEDIA

In every culture, much of what came to be considered as art began as entertainment. New movements in art emerged out of a rejection or modification of the art that came before it.

It always takes a period of time before any new art is accepted. New art forms are often enjoyed by audiences long before they are recognized by critics. So it is with the content of mass communication.

Not all mass media entertainment is art, but even the content that has artistic merit takes time to be recognized. Consider the Italian Renaissance and the dramatic literature that period produced. It is not the stilted im-

Commedia dell' arte, denegrated as vulgar amusement during the Italian Renaissance, later gained sufficient artistic respectability to provide subject matter for French Rococo painter Antoine Watteau. (*Italian Comedians*; Antoine Watteau (1684–1721); National Gallery of Art, Washington; Samuel H. Kress Collection 1946.)

itations of classical tragedies produced by the *literati* (the cultural elite of the day) that is remembered. We celebrate the low, vulgar, knockabout comedies of the streets, the *commedia dell'arte*, as the dramatic legacy from that time. Who can predict with certainty what will be remembered as the *high art* of the twentieth century? Yet it is safe to assume that some of it, perhaps much of it, will come from the ranks of what is now entertainment in the mass media. Perhaps JR from *Dallas* or Indiana Jones or James Bond or the "crazies" that inhabited *Saturday Night Live* will become the dramatic characters of our time.

In the marketplace of popular entertainment and art, two forces are in tension: the demand for content and creative potential.

The Demand for Content

The economic and physical need to fill the time and space of the mass media is very real. Enormous quantities of content produced at equally enormous costs are the facts of life in mass communication. Although quality and quantity are not theoretically impossible to produce in tandem, the timetable producers set for themselves makes it a difficult feat to accomplish.

Creative Potential

All media artists wish to create the best work they can under the time limitations of the media. No director, novelist, editor, or designer sets out to produce a failure, or worse, trash. Creative people believe in their projects, but sometimes these storytellers, dancers, artists, or actors falter along the way in the execution of their vision. Every generation is blessed with only a limited number of significant artists, let alone a genius like a Shakespeare or a Mozart or a Nijinsky or a Van Gogh. If we are realistic in our expectations, the quality of mass media entertainment and art far exceeds that which we could possibly predict.

Two elements have a significant impact on the demand for quality product and the creative ability to produce it: time and audience taste.

Time

As mentioned, time refers both to the amount of content that must be produced to fill the schedule and the hours allotted to accomplish this task. Time also relates to the years it takes to recognize and truly appreciate the merit of a work of art produced as popular entertainment. Traditionally, entertainment is thought of as a diversion of the moment, whereas art is considered to be an expression of lasting beauty. Since media content is evaluated immediately upon (and sometimes before) public exhibition, it cannot be expected that critics will be able to evaluate the critical value of a film after one or even multiple screenings. It takes time to make a *Citizen Kane*, and it takes time to reflect on its beauty. Many films that were undervalued by contemporaries are revered much later as objects of lasting beauty. The films of Charlie Chaplin and Buster Keaton are prime examples. Only recently has the status of these men been elevated from media clown to film artist.

Audience Taste   The evaluation of media content as entertainment or art depends upon the acquired taste of audience and critic alike. Perceptions of the value of both art and artist vary by region and tradition and prior experiences with the style in question. For example, Jerry Lewis is a popular entertainer in the United States; in Paris, however, he is regarded as an artist, as the equal of Chaplin. Tastes change; in total honesty, the mass media have improved some cultural standards over the past century as well as expanding audiences for works of art. More and better novels, plays, films, short stories, graphic art, and music are being produced as a result of their widespread distribution via mass communication. The level of audience taste is higher for more people than ever before. And the mass media are contributors to that cultural phenomenon.

THE PLACE OF ENTERTAINMENT AND MEDIART IN SOCIETY

Popular art is in effect folk art aimed at a mass audience. It is a product of current technology. Tradition and originality are caught up in the speed of the times, and qualitative evaluation is difficult. Several basic conclusions can be offered, however.

1. Entertainment has long been the basis for art, and mediart does emerge from mass entertainment.
2. Mediart exists to be enjoyed by the largest possible audience because we live in a mass society.

Jerry Lewis, here as *The Nutty Professor*, is revered today by many Parisians as a major comic artist.

(Photo: Movie Star News, Courtesy Paramount Studios.)

3. To enjoy mediart fully, audiences need to learn to understand it.

4. Mediart exists for audiences as well as artists and critics, and educated audiences should be and are sought.

5. There are various audiences for various media; it should not be necessary for every medium to provide every form of mediart at every cultural level. Trained audiences will find what's *good*.

6. Artists have always needed patrons, and the patrons of mediart-ists are big business and big audiences.

7. There will always be tension between mediartists and media audiences. The greater the originality, the greater the tension; but this tension leads audiences to "better" preferences in future selection of media content.

8. Mediart is what you "like," and you learn to like it. Media appreciation can be learned, although it is difficult because audiences are so close to it, and, as always, there are levels of enjoyment.

Value judgments in mediart come from the paying customer. What we are willing to pay for now will determine the quality of media entertainment and art that the mass media will provide in the future. The advance of culture depends on the education of the public.

The content of mass media will improve to meet the challenges the audience provides. Over the long haul both the media and their audiences have benefited; not in every case, but enough to keep us going on.

Always bear in mind, nearly all mediart is immersed in entertainment. The TV play, film, recorded music, novel, or magazine is designed to entertain; but art through the ages has served this purpose. Michelangelo's *David* is entertainment; Aristophanes' *The Birds* is entertainment; Beethoven's *Ninth Symphony* is entertainment. All had audiences of various levels of skill in understanding, but all these works of art, like mediart, were created to entertain.

Considerable debate has taken place over the value and effects of mass media entertainment—art on our culture and society. Cultural anthropologists, sociologists, and critics have tended to group cultural artifacts into three categories, and these have been given various terms. Van Wyck Brooks coined the phrases "highbrow, middlebrow, and lowbrow" to describe these categories.

LEVELS OF MEDIART

Highbrow, or high culture, is composed of cultural artifacts that can be appreciated only by an educated and intellectual elite. Examples might include Shakespearean plays, T. S. Eliot's poetry, Beethoven sonatas, Matisse paintings, the *Economist*, *Daedalus*, and Ingmar Bergman movies.

Middlebrow culture has pretensions of being refined and intellectual but also has wider human appeal. Examples might include *Horizon* magazine, the *Washington Post*, plays by Neil Simon, paintings by Modigliani, the poetry of Ogden Nash, and novels by Norman Mailer.

Lowbrow culture consists of those artifacts that have massive appeal to the largest possible audience, an appeal that is usually visceral rather than cerebral, emotional rather than rational, crass rather than aesthetic. Examples might include soap operas, TV situation comedies, confession magazines, lovelorn newspaper columns, sex–violence movies, and pulp novels.

There is in this analysis an elitism that verges on snobbery. It seems more reasonable to adopt a method of analysis that is more objective and a classification based on (a) the medium used; (b) the techniques used; (c) the function of the content; and (d) the success of the content.

Originality and tradition are in conflict in many works. *Barry Lyndon*, a brilliant film by Stanley Kubrick, based on a minor novel by William Makepeace Thackeray, goes against the grain of Kubrick's traditional films; and his originality was misunderstood by his movie audience. The beauty, elegance, and grace of *Barry Lyndon* are a joy. The photography, sets, music, and acting are remarkable. But audiences were less responsive to the film because it lacked the story, the liveliness, and the hype of *2001: A Space Odyssey* or *A Clockwork Orange*. Mass audience rejection or acceptance of a film is not necessarily the measure of its worth. Beauty can be learned over time or, in some cases, realized instantly.

Interestingly, Kubrick turned back to a popular genre, the horror film, for *The Shining*. But this film depended less on shock treatments and the

Stanley Kubrick's film *The Shining* (based on the Stephen King novel) is an artistic depiction of a man (Jack Nicholson) sliding into insanity. It may well stand with Alfred Hitchcock's *Psycho* as a masterpiece of the horror genre in the years to come.

(Photo: Museum of Modern Art/Film Stills Archive, Courtesy Warner Bros., Inc.)

standard hype of this film genre and instead offered an intense study of a character, played by Jack Nicholson, crumbling into insanity. High art for the lowbrow brought some grumbling from horror fans in need of their fix of stock scares. Perhaps Stanley Kubrick was ahead of his audience. Nonetheless, movies are made for a "now" box office and not for tomorrow's critical credos.

If we use highbrow, middlebrow, and lowbrow over a period of time to measure film as a medium, its techniques, function, and success, the motion pictures have moved from lowbrow in the 1890s to middlebrow in the 1940s to highbrow in the 1980s. The interaction of the mediartist, the mass medium and its techniques, and the audience create the film's worth.

Once again the quality of the mediart produced depends on the interaction of the artist with the audience, using the tools and techniques of the medium. The audience must be an active participant. Great artists improve the tastes of audiences, but not all producers of media content are great artists. This dichotomy leads to both intense criticism and defense of mass culture.

On one side of the debate are those who argue that the purveyors of entertainment—art through the mass media are little more than panderers, catering to the lowest common denominator in the mass audience. These critics maintain that most mass media entertainment has a degrading effect on our culture. The mass media, these critics say, by emphasizing that which is popular and salable, ruin standards of style and taste, leading to a "cultural democracy" where "the good, the true, and the beautiful" are decided by the vote in the marketplace of mass media rather than by sensitive, refined and knowledgeable authorities. Some critics take the position that "the only antidote to mass culture is high culture, that high culture means art and learning, and that these goods are potentially accessible to every person not suffering from severe brain damage."

Criticism of Mass Culture

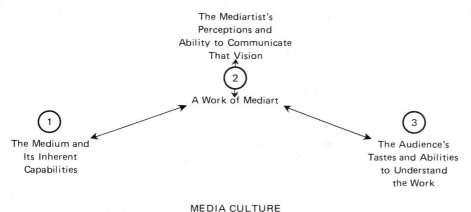

The Mediartist's
Perceptions and
Ability to Communicate
That Vision

2

A Work of Mediart

1

The Medium and
Its Inherent
Capabilities

3

The Audience's
Tastes and Abilities
to Understand
the Work

MEDIA CULTURE

This model suggests that media art exists in a cultural framework and depends upon: (1) the medium and its inherent capabilities; (2) the media artist's perceptions and ability to communicate his perceptions; and (3) the audience's tastes and their ability to appreciate the artist's work. All three elements work in concert; technology, artist and audience.

Popular culture, or popular arts, might best be called "current culture," or "current arts." These arts have massive audiences and therefore are rejected out of hand by some critics. The popular arts are designed to entertain and, one hopes, to earn large returns on the dollar investment. Popular culture is big business and therefore suspect, yet artists have always had patrons and tried to sell their work. The popular arts are democratic rather than elitist arts.

Traditionally, art criticism has been based on the value judgments of others trained in that art form. Today's media critics tend not to be trained artists in film, music, or television, but people trained in English or journalism. Many of these "pop critics" have an inordinate impact on art forms in which they were not trained.

In Defense of Mass Culture

The crass statement of the mass culture position is that of the media entrepreneur who says, "Give the fools what they want. If people will pay for comic books but not poetry, give them comics. If the audience demands burlesque and will not attend tragedy, give them Gypsy Rose Lee and not Lady Macbeth." Most media owners are, first and foremost, businessmen who must sell a product to as many customers as are necessary to make a profit.

But there is an intellectual side to this argument, and it is that the content of the mass media is important to the overall soothing and comforting of an anxious and complex society. The mass media of necessity make news, information, and education digestible. Most people do not read comic books or watch situation comedies all day long. Even for those who do, their attention to the mass media helps involve them in other uses of media, which is culturally beneficial.

Mass and Class as Interdependent

A similar but perhaps more meaningful argument in defense of mass culture maintains that both good and bad exist in "class" culture and in mass culture, and that class and mass do not only coexist in a society but also enrich and enliven one another. There are pretentious elements of class culture, just as there are products of genuine quality that emerge from mass culture.

Because these art forms enliven and enrich one another, it is as important for students to study the popular arts as it is for them to give serious attention to sculpture, sonnets, and sonatas. This broadening of the critical perspective to include mass culture also has a potentially beneficial effect on classical studies.

"Class" products and artifacts that reach a mass audience through the mass media—Jacques Cousteau's TV documentaries, James Reston's newspaper columns, or Stanley Kubrick's films—prove that a growing number of people have a taste for quality at a price they can afford. By the same token, mass-produced or mass-communicated culture that acquires unexpected quality—Charlie Chaplin's little tramp, Red Smith's sports columns, the Beatles' rock recordings, or Rod Serling's "Twilight Zone" TV series—prove that what moves the masses often has genuine and long-lasting quality.

Three aspects are relevant to an understanding of the importance of entertainment and art in the mass media. They are (a) leisure, or free time from work or duty; (b) play, or nondirected, random, spontaneous amusement; (c) recreation, or diverting pastime for relaxation and rejuvenation. Both art and entertainment are a combination of the mental, emotional and physical acts that occur during leisure time in the form of play for enlightening and recreational purposes.

THE INTERACTION OF LEISURE, ENTERTAINMENT, AND ART

In order for artists to write, direct, and perform in plays, movies, TV series, operas, concerts, records, and the like, they need "free time" to be creative. It is difficult, if not impossible, to work all day at a job and then come home and be creative. Psychologist B. F. Skinner suggests that leisure time is a prerequisite for the emergence of art both for its creation and enjoyment. This does not mean that everyone who has time will use it to create art or that consumers will use their free time to enjoy that art. But without freedom from care or want, art is an unaffordable luxury.

Leisure and Art

Time to enjoy life or relax and prepare for the next work period is essential. Entertainment, whether self-produced or supplied by the mass media, requires leisure time. Think about the difference in your TV viewing at school during exam week versus winter break back home. During vacation, you have time to spend watching television. Only when you have it can you spend it.

Leisure and Entertainment

A large segment of the media audience uses music, film, television, novels, and magazine reading to meet their need for art; this art literally improves the quality of life in our intense, crowded, increasingly urbanized society. Art brings "beauty" to humankind.

Traditionally, the leisured class was composed of the wealthy and well-educated elite who were expected to use their freedom from work to refine the culture and to use their money to encourage artists to improve life. For the rest of society, limited leisure was earned by working; often "leisure" time had to be used to prepare for future labors. Art has flourished under these conditions, as did entertainments in previous periods of history—the Renaissance, for example.

The New Leisured Class

The modern world has forced us to change our attitudes toward leisure. Machines have taken over much of our heavy labor, shortening our workweek and leaving us with more free time. In 1900 the average workweek was 6 days, 72 hours; by 1950 it had been reduced to 5 days, 44 hours; by 1970 less than 40 hours a week was average; today the 4-day workweek is becoming increasingly popular. One observer computed that the average worker in 1970 had 2750 hours of "free" time each year—time not spent at work, sleep, eating, or commuting. A large portion of those 2750 hours was spent with attention focused on the media and the art and entertainment they provide. Consider the average weekday of 8 work hours, 8 sleep hours, 2 personal needs hours, and 2 household-activity hours; that leaves 4 leisure hours a weekday, plus most of the weekend, for recreation.

In addition, life expectancy is increasing; the later adult years, which do not usually include a job, must be made worth living. The development of a leisure ethic could imbue individuals with confidence to use spare time. Leisure has worth in learning, self-expression, and personal well-being. A major challenge in this society has become what to do in free time. For too many Americans, free time has become a plague.

Mass Media and Play

Americans formerly had difficulty coping with play because our society was work oriented. Those who followed the work ethic praised labor and achievement and condemned play and idleness. Play was considered worthwhile only when it was evaluated as the *work* of children. Entertainment and nonessential art were often suspect because they occupied time that could be better spent at work. For many Americans, work was the real business of life; the periods between labors were times of guilt. Much criticism of the mass media has been inspired by this work ethic, prompting the feeling that if readers or listeners or viewers are not being informed, enlightened, persuaded, or educated, their time is being wasted.

Mass Media and Recreation

Today we recognize that recreation is vital to personal happiness and self-development. The human being needs to be restored and rejuvenated through diversion and relaxation. The pressures of society, the pace of modern life, the intensity of competition, and the anxieties caused by increasing change and mobility have made recreation more important than ever.

Much mass media fare has been designed specifically to provide recreation. Television situation comedies, newspaper lovelorn columns, romantic movies, comic strips, magazine features, radio DJ chatter, and the publishing bonanza of the "romance novels" of Rosemary Rogers (*Sweet Savage Love*) and Kathleen Wido (*Shanna*) and others have often been criticized by segments of the intellectual community, but they have an important recreational function. They provide emotional escape, create fantasy, and allow for the physical catharsis necessary to the renewal of the human spirit.

Audiences and Entertainment–Art

Americans are part of mass media audiences because they have free time. They spend this leisure both actively (e.g., hobbies, sports) as physical participants and passively (e.g., reading, listening, viewing) as emotional participants. The physical activity shakes out the body's kinks and is good for health. Passive entertainments replenish us emotionally, physically, intellectually, and spiritually. Both kinds are necessary.

Away from work, mental play is just as important as physical play. All of one and none of the other is unhealthy. The dumb jock is no better or worse off than the weakling aesthete.

Recreation in the media environment is valuable because audiences are offered many kinds of entertainment and art. These audiences make conscious choices among various entertainments of varying levels of artistry. This choice is based on (*a*) what audiences have learned to like; (*b*) what their immediate physical, emotional, and intellectual conditions are; (*c*) what is available for the time and money they have to spend. The mass media provide both entertainment and art.

ENTERTAINMENT, THE OVERLAID FUNCTION

Entertainment is an important element in almost all aspects of mass media. Artists, writers, journalists, teachers, and preachers have long known the value of drama, humor, entertainment, and art in the process of creating, reporting, educating, and promoting. We might speak of entertainment as an "overlaid" use of mass media because it is an aspect of almost all media content.

In fact, entertainment is vital because audiences are available to the media; they have leisure, which they use for play. In effect, we seek recreation in our use of news, analysis, education, propaganda, and advertising. When this process reaches its zenith, we call it an art.

Edward R. Murrow was an information artist. The editorial cartoons of Ernie Pyle are artistic analyses. Education is an art in its own right; but "Cosmos" and "The Ascent of Man" and "Civilisation" and "Alistair Cook's America" are, if nothing else, artful. The propaganda films of Leni Riefenstahl (*Triumph of the Will, Olympiad*) are works of art. Advertising may be the most expressive communication art in this area of consumption.

News as Entertainment

Newspapers and news magazines often try to make the news as entertaining as possible. The layout of the page is designed to make information attractive and palatable. News content is often intermingled with humorous features, amusing sidebars, diverting human interest stories, and clever fillers.

Sometimes news provides unexpected entertainment. One of the most interesting moments in news entertainment came during the NBC-TV broadcast of the 1964 Rupublican convention when John Chancellor was carried off the convention floor in semi-arrest. As he was being taken away, he signed off with, "This is John Chancellor, somewhere in custody." It was news, and it said something about that convention; but it was also entertaining.

In preparation for the 1983–1984 TV season, the three major networks returned to the single-anchorman format for their evening news programs.

"News star" Tom Brokaw, anchorman of NBC News, reports from the 1984 Democratic National Convention in San Francisco. (Photo courtesy of The National Broadcasting Company, Inc.)

That decision was based in large part on research that indicated that most viewers preferred the sole source so that there would be no confusion about who was really in charge of the news. Tom Brokaw (NBC), Peter Jennings (ABC), and Dan Rather (CBS) are "in the know." They are "news stars"—for as long as their ratings say they are. They have the charm and poise and style of movie actors of the highest rank. They are consummate entertainers as well as competent newsmen.

On local stations it is sometimes difficult to determine where the "happy talk" ends and the news begins. The set is crowded with chatty and charming news, weather, and sports personalities. As Bloody Mary sings in *South Pacific*, "Happy talk, keep talkin' happy talk. . . ." On sports pages in newspapers across America the "coverage" of local sports favorites reads as much like public relations as it does news. And it is certainly entertaining. Especially when the home team defeats their "bitterest" rival.

There is considerable disagreement in the journalism fraternity as to whether sports coverage is newsworthy, but there is no question as to Howard Cosell's entertainment quotient—even when he tells it like it is.

Often publications or productions designed primarily to be entertaining also provide news and information. "Roots," the widely viewed TV miniseries, attempted to provide information about the history and struggle of Afro-Americans; and it was informational and entertaining. *The Godfather* and *The Godfather, Part II* entertained, but they also informed the audiences about underworld operations. Even the comic book provides certain information for many young readers.

Much analysis contains entertainment. Editorial cartoons take positions on issues, analyze and interpret events, but also entertain audiences. The humor in such cartoons helps attract the reader's attention and becomes important in the analysis of the problems involved.

Both the Wright and Kagle cartoons are humorous analyses of two very serious issues. Wright comments on the radical changes that may occur in our environment as a result of burning coal, oil, and other carbon-dioxide-producing energy sources. Kagle comments on the "invasion" of Grenada by the United States in October 1983, to "liberate it from the grasp of Cuban expansionist policies." He uses the military tradition of awarding campaign ribbons as the vehicle for his analysis. Political cartoons have always entertained as they editorialized about the serious news events of the day.

The *Peanuts* comic strips, paperback books, TV specials, and feature motion pictures are all blatant, unadulterated, good-natured fun. For many fans, *Peanuts* is the ultimate entertainment, and Charlie Brown is a child's version of Everyman. The philosophy of Charles Schulz (creator of *Peanuts*) is that a comic strip that does not say something is valueless. Schulz analyzes, interprets, and editorializes as he entertains.

Entertainment is an ingredient essential to persuasion and propaganda. One must attract and hold public attention in order to persuade, and entertainment is often more effective than information in winning over an audience. Sometimes the most subtle propaganda is that which contains the least haranguing and most entertainment, for example a military concert to promote the Pentagon, or the programming of the Voice of America to promote U.S. interests.

(Drawing by Don Wright, Copyright © 1983 The Miami News.)

(Drawing by Mike Keefe, Copyright © News Group Chicago, Inc. Courtesy of News America Syndicate.)

During World War II, Hollywood was actively en-
gaged in making films
that presented a one-
sided view of the war and
the reasons for it. By contrast, Hollywood made
only one pro-Vietnam film
during that war, *The
Green Berets* starring
John Wayne.

(Photo: Movie Star News, Courtesy Warner Brothers, Inc.)

During World War II, hundreds of feature films supporting the war effort were made, such as *Across the Pacific, Bataan, Guadalcanal Diary, Lifeboat, Master Race, Mrs. Miniver*, and *They Were Expendable*. In each of these films the enemy was depicted as evil and dehumanized; Americans and their allies, by contrast, were pure, tough, and right. Interestingly, few major films were made in direct support of America's military involvement in Vietnam. An exception was *The Green Berets*, which was entertainment that propagandized in a World War II fashion. The film was not very popular, suggesting that factors other than entertainment are involved in effective propaganda. In the late 1970s, however, American artist-propagandists released a series of antiwar films set in the Vietnam period: *The Boys in Company C, Coming Home, The Deer Hunter*, and *Apocalypse Now*. The successful persuasion came in the form of entertainment years after the war was over. It was as if the war needed to be purged from America's soul.

Advertising as Entertainment

The primary purpose of advertising is to sell products, but to make sales requires audience attention. Entertainment is one way to get that attention; entertaining ads also sell. One of the best ad campaigns was the Volkswagen series. They were good advertisements because they helped sell VW "bugs" and "rabbits." The same ads were good entertainment because they were interesting, diverting, and amusing. Another campaign entertainingly sold the Miller Brewing Company's Lite beer by placing retired athletes in comic settings to argue about the ad campaign's two major selling points: that the beer is "less filling" and "tastes great." The Florida Department of Commerce produced an award-winning ad that sought to attract motion-picture production to that state by taking a humorous look at the famous sign *Hollywood*. Advertising makes more overt use of entertainment variables than any other mass communication function other than entertainment itself. The entertaining advertisement is a way of life in ad media throughout the world.

Hollywood weather
without Hollywood overhead.

California's weather is great for location shooting. So is Florida's. In fact, in Florida, you can produce as good a film as you could in Hollywood or New York. On a much better budget.

You don't pay a premium for more and longer days of good shooting light.

You don't pay more for the nation's third-largest pool of acting talent. Or for experienced, professional technicians or state-of-the-art equipment, facilities, or services.

You don't pay extra travel, shipping, and per diems to get to locations like jungles, plains, deserts, cities, seashores, New England village greens — just about everything except snow-capped mountains.

And you don't waste time and money coping with hassles and red tape, because those are about the only things we don't have here.

Call us for all the help you need in planning your next location shoot:

scouting, information on crews, equipment, facilities, you name it.

You'll bring back New York or Hollywood film in the can. On a Florida budget.

Ben Harris, Charlie Porretto or Ray Quinn, Motion Picture and Television Bureau, Suite WV4-1, Collins Building, Tallahassee, Florida 32301.

(904) 487-1100

(Courtesy Florida Department of Commerce, Motion Picture and Television Bureau.)

The Department of Commerce of the State of Florida sought to advertise its merits for location work on feature films. The approach taken plays off the easily recognizable sign high above Los Angeles in the Hollywood Hills.

ABC's "Grammar Rock" employs entertaining graphics to teach reading skills to children.

(Courtesy American Broadcasting Companies, Inc.)

Education as Entertainment

"Sesame Street" is an educational TV program that is also highly entertaining. The series was designed to teach preschoolers basic skills that would be helpful when they entered kindergarten and first grade. In order to maintain attention, the program uses the most interesting qualities and techniques of film and television. For example, highly sophisticated TV commercial styles are used to teach the alphabet and numbers in ABC's "Multiplication Rock" and "Grammar Rock" inserts in their Saturday morning lineup.

Films like *The Rocky Horror Picture Show, Sixteen Candles, Risky Business,* and *Spinal Tap* and MTV Music Television or radio programming of rock music, are elements in the socialization of young people. Both media are primarily concerned with entertainment but play an educational role as well.

Textbooks are designed to hold the child's attention as they teach reading skills. Much English instruction in the United States is designed to teach youngsters to appreciate entertaining literature. Television, too, can combine entertainment with socialization. "Phyllis," "Rhoda," "The Mary Tyler Moore Show," "Maude," "Three's Company," and "One Day at a Time" were TV shows designed primarily to entertain audiences, but they also taught us something about the changing roles and status of women in American society and the problems they face, problems that were very different when "I Love Lucy," "My Friend Irma," and "Our Miss Brooks" were popular.

In the early television series "I Remember Mama", actress Peggy Wood's portrayal of the mother of a Norwegian immigrant family emphasised the traditional role of women as the center of the domestic household. (Photo: New York Public Library Picture Collection.)

Each medium has technical, cultural, and economic limitations that determine how much and what kinds of entertainment it can provide. Some media are essentially purveyors of mass culture and others of elite culture. The media and the audiences tend to be selective and seek each other out.

SPECIFIC MEDIA ROLES IN ENTERTAINMENT

More than 80 million American households are equipped with at least one TV set that is used an average of more than 6.5 hours per day. Watching television has become one of our major leisure-time activities. People seem to want to use television to be diverted, interested, amused, and entertained. This does *not* mean that television provides no service to specialized audiences. It does mean that mass culture dominates commercial TV content.

Television

Commercial television provides an array of escapist entertainment. It has been called a "vast wasteland" of programming determined by a "cultural vote" through ratings that are accurate only within specific statistical limits. Network television provides filmed dramas and videotaped variety shows in prime time (8:00–11:00 p.m. EST). Daytime television consists of situation comedies, soap operas, and quiz shows. Local stations provide little more than a news block and syndicated series that were previously on the networks. To many critics, the total impact of television seems to have been designed primarily to be a massive pop-culture machine catering to the entertainment needs of its audiences.

Unlike the pages in a book, the cuts in a record album, or the footage of a film, broadcast media cannot increase the hours in a day. Television entertainment is time-bound. In addition, television is a limited natural resource—only a specific number of channels are available. Our society seems to have charted a course to television, and that course is entertainment. But not all TV content is popular, mass culture. Significant progress is being made to provide outstanding cultural experiences such as "Bill," "The Bunker," "Masterpiece Theatre," "The Shakespeare Plays," and "Playing for Time," and the coverage of conventions, elections, inaugurations, and the Olympics.

The Motion Picture

Unlike the situation in television, anyone willing to spend enough money can make a film, and with the technical advances being made in 16-mm production equipment, the cost is coming down. The days of mass production of theatrical films are over. The U.S. film industry produces fewer than 200 films a year. The masses who used to flock to movie houses now stay at home to watch television. Because of this loss of its general audience, the film medium has begun to turn to specialized entertainment films, which seem to come in topical waves, for minority audiences. Films try to provide content that is not available on television.

America is in the midst of a period of rapid social change. Motion pictures often reflect this state of affairs. Major trends in entertainment and social values are being exploited: (a) The market for films has become youth oriented because some two-thirds of all movie tickets are bought by people under 30; (b) the presentation of content has become much more explicit, especially in terms of violence and sex; (c) the spectacle and large-budget disaster, horror, and science-fiction cycles have emerged.

These three characteristics exist because young people seem to prefer frank, explicit, and fright-oriented films. With the replacement of the old movie code by the new rating system, greater artistic freedom has been afforded filmmakers. As a result, we have low-budget "nudies," sadistic motorcycle-gang films, and horror flicks. But this same freedom has also produced some outstanding films. The violence in the statements of Sam Peckinpah in *The Wild Bunch*, Francis Ford Coppola in both *Godfathers*, and William Friedkin in *The French Connection* is integral to the manhood of the dying breed of the wild bunch and their place in history, to the insidiousness of organized crime, and to the nature of police work and what it does to men. The sex and nudity in Federico Fellini's *Casanova*, Bob Fosse's *All That Jazz*, and John Schlesinger's *Midnight Cowboy* are valid in the human dramas they present.

Of all the electronic media, the motion picture seems to serve specialized tastes most satisfactorily. It has been discarded by most general audiences, and criteria to evaluate films have been institutionalized. Nevertheless, although film is the most socially conscious of all the electronic media, it is still primarily an entertainment medium.

These two media are closely linked in the entertainment function because recorded music constitutes the bulk of most radio stations' programming. A wide range of musical tastes is served, but most markets are dominated by a top-40 or rock-music station.

The Phonograph and the Radio

The phonograph has great flexibility and provides almost any kind of music desired. Although classical music does not dominate, classical records continue to be produced, and most university towns and metropolitan areas are served by at least one FM classical "jukebox." The primary cultural thrust of these media, however, is to provide music for specialized audiences.

Of all the mass media, newspapers provide the greatest amount of information and perhaps the smallest amount of pure entertainment. But mass entertainment is an essential part of the daily newspaper fare. The *Washington Post*, for example, which prides itself on being the equal of the *New York Times* as a national newspaper, for years published the largest number of comic strips of any newspaper in the country. It claimed that those comics helped build its circulation to make it the largest newspaper in the nation's capital. Almost every newspaper publishes comics and cartoons, as well as features and human interest stories, to entertain as well as inform and instruct.

Print Media

Magazines are able to provide a more specialized form of entertainment for special audiences. The comic book itself is a form of entertainment for a specific type of reader. The range of such entertainment in magazine form stretches as far as the imagination will allow, from the most mundane (such as comic books and titillating sex–violence magazines), to esoteric journals on jazz, poetry, folk art, and classical drama.

Books also seem on the surface to be a primary medium for an elite audience, useful more for education and art than entertainment. But books have informational and entertainment uses as well. The paperback revolution has brought the book to the economic level of mass audiences, which has allowed books to be used for popular entertainment ranging from best-selling gothic romances to such entertainment as *The Joy of Sex*.

In effect, entertainment is the "overlay" function of every mass medium. It is the reason many people are willing to be informed, editorialized, persuaded, educated, and advertised to by the mass media.

PERSPECTIVES OF MASS COMMUNICATION

PART **5**

Ethics and Responsibility 27

Perhaps no recent media event has done more to focus the general public's attention on the issue of media ethics than the movie *Absence of Malice*. In this film the narrow distinction between accuracy and truth in reporting is dramatically illustrated through the actions of the reporter played by Sally Field. In presenting the facts about how and why a person accused of a crime could not have been involved, she causes the death of one of the people concerned in the story. Accuracy in this case was perhaps unnecessary to telling the truth. All the facts of the story did not need to be reported.

Another example, and a more frightening one because it is not fictional, is reported in *Media Ethics* by Christians, Rotzoll, and Fackler. In 1976, the editors of the *Dallas Times Herald* chose to publish a story identifying a man as a Soviet spy, even when the individual told the editors such a disclosure would leave him no choice but suicide. The man killed himself the day the story appeared.

As the authors indicate, the people at the paper made these critical choices: (*a*) to investigate and write the story; (*b*) to publish it as originally scheduled; and (*c*) to ignore a man's suicide threat. The choices reflect

In *Absence of Malice*, Sally Field stars as a zealous newspaper reporter, eager to get her story.

(Photo: Movie Star News. Courtesy Columbia Pictures.)

an attitude that should be cause for concern to any student of mass communication. The first choice revolved around the public's *need* to know versus the public's *desire* to know. The choice to publish on schedule despite the man's appeal is little better than the wartime cry "damn the torpedoes, full speed ahead." As the authors in *Media Ethics* point out, the story was clearly one that could keep. It was newsworthy, but the criterion of timeliness was not an inherent part of the story. The third choice—to ignore the man's suicide threat—involves not simple media ethics but basic human ethics. Again, as the authors note, the failure of the editors to alert anyone to the problem, to make any attempt to prevent the suicide, is "remarkable." The paper violated a basic moral principle that says, not only should we not cause harm, but we should prevent harm when doing so does not subject us to a risk of comparable harm.[1]

In a third recent media event, two cameramen from a local TV station filmed a man setting himself on fire. The cameramen made no attempt to prevent the act. The desire to provide film for the late-night newscast overrode basic moral principles.

In all these examples, the public's "right to know" became confused with the media's "right to publish" and with individuals' rights as human beings. These rights, as well as several others, are at the heart of what we call media ethics.

[1] Clifford G. Christians, Kim B. Rotzoll, and Mark Fackler, *Media Ethics* (Longman: New York & London, 1983), pp. 114–117.

Ethics is one of the current buzzwords making the rounds, not only in television stations and newspaper decision meetings, but in corporate boardrooms, courtrooms, and doctors' offices. The right to live is a critical issue for the medical profession; so is the right to a fair trial for the legal profession, the right to publish for the media, and the right to make a profit for business and industry. Business ethics, especially, has become a hot issue in recent years. Over the last decade, most major companies have put together written codes of ethics ranging from single page "statements of principles" to publications such as Citicorp's 62-page booklet *Ethical Standards and Conflict of Interest Policy.* The "bottom line" here is that most people now believe that corporations should be concerned about something in addition to making money; they have responsibilites to wider publics than their shareholders.

It is precisely the issue of responsibility around which ethics in contemporary society, and for our analysis, media ethics, revolves. Despite the current publicity and concern over media ethics, the issue is not new. As modern mass media evolved in the late nineteenth and early twentieth centuries, issues of ethics and responsibility were discussed and debated. Not until a social responsibility theory of the press was identified, however, was a consistent effort made to understand the role of the press in broad ethical and moral terms. The social responsibility theory, developed out of post–World War II inquiry, postulated that absolute freedom for the press was no longer possible.

SOCIAL RESPONSIBILITY AND MEDIA

In an environment where freedom is considered paramount, where the First Amendment is carved like a shield of armor and broadcast at every opportunity, words such as *accountability* and *responsibility* are often not understood or even heard. Increasingly, however, they are "watch words" for today's media. The regulation of media, especially broadcasting, has decreased in recent years, and so the need for ethical and moral responsibility in media has become especially important.

Consider the following recent events involving radio station KTTL-FM in Dodge City, Kansas. Broadcasts by two self-styled preachers created a wave of controversy and criticism around the station. With such remarks as "if the Jews even fool around with us . . . every rabbi in Los Angeles will die within 24 hours" and "blacks and browns are the enemy," these two brought into sharp relief the issues of First Amendment rights and broadcast regulation. On the one side was Charles Ferris, a former FCC chairman, who stated: "You can't take the license away because of what they said. Some things are very distasteful or offensive but you have to be patient with the remedy. It's the price you pay to protect First Amendment rights."[2] On the other side were those who claimed that the programs'

---

[2] Merrill Brown, "KTTL's License to Malign," *Channels,* Vol. 4, No. 1, March/April, 1984, pp. 15–16.

statements were irresponsible calls for violence—the equivalent of a person shouting "Fire!" in a crowded theater—and were therefore unprotected by the First Amendment. On the surface, the issue involved the legal apparatus surrounding a radio license challenge. But, the deeper issue involves the sense of social responsibility (or lack of it) on the part of the owners of KTTL. The regulatory apparatus of the FCC is of little concern here. Whether a radio station is operating in the "public interest, convenience or necessity" is at the heart of the crisis.

ETHICS AND TECHNOLOGY

As new technologies explode into reality, old rules concerning such fundamental issues as censorship, privacy, the right to know, and the right to a fair trial are being questioned and often challenged successfully. Interactive cable television as developed by Warner-Amex in Columbus, Ohio—the system known as Qube—revealed tremendous potential for viewer feedback and participation in everything from choosing a certain ending to a dramatic program to expressing opinions and even "voting" on major issues affecting the community. The technology cuts two ways, however, and its potential for invading the privacy of homes equipped with Qube was real and potentially dangerous. The expansion of this wired model to satellite distribution of content raises even more questions. Visions of George Orwell's 1984 begin dancing in the heads of responsible media professionals and educators.

Technology itself has no inherent value. The values, the ethical dimensions of the machinery, lie in the choices made in using it. In medicine the technology that allows victims of kidney failure to continue to live through dialysis treatment is in itself neither good nor evil. But the ethical questions regarding who should receive such treatment and who should pay for it involve choices, value decisions. Similarly, lightweight and unobtrusive cameras are reshaping traditional attitudes toward televising courtroom proceedings. The recent example of "gavel to gavel" TV coverage of the New Bedford, Massachusetts trial of six men on gang-raping charges aroused great controversy. Controversial, too, is the televising of the execution of criminals. Ted Koppel, the ABC journalist, favors televising executions because, in his opinion, TV viewers have witnessed plenty of evil and can stomach a little more. This kind of thinking misses the point; it confuses and obscures the concept of social responsibility, of ethics, of a basic morality in such a decision.

In all these illustrations the technical ability to *achieve* communication conflicts with both the social responsibility and the legal right of the communicator to *publish* the content. These three ingredients—technology, regulation, and social responsibility—are at the heart of many ethical issues in mass media today. As technology becomes more and more "user friendly" and regulations become more difficult to enforce and interpret (three of every four libel cases in which the jury found in favor of the

John Codeiro testifies before television cameras in Bristol County Court (Fall River, Ma., March 19, 1984) explaining where he and others were during the alleged rape that took place at Big Dan's bar in New Bedford.

defendant and "against" the press have in recent years been overturned in appeal), the critical issue in maintaining a basic sense of social responsibility in mass media becomes the personal professional responsibility of the men and women who work the system, from corporate board chairpersons to editors to reporters and camerapersons.

CODES OF CONDUCT

One way of looking at this issue in greater detail is to differentiate among *professional* ethics, *institutional* ethics, and *personal* ethics; that is, among formal codes of conduct and vaguely developed and often equally vaguely articulated institutional and personal value systems and morality. Three areas of media content are affected by these areas of ethics: news, advertising, and entertainment. Formal institutionalized codes of conduct are most often found in news and advertising.

Institutional

Before examining several of the formal codes more carefully, we should examine the gray area that lies between formal codes of conduct and individual morality. This is the informal ethical system that operates in most media institutions by the "raised eyebrow" or "consensus of upper management." This *institutional* ethical system is most often associated with gatekeepers and involves both personal and professional values. For example, in many major-city newspapers ombudsmen exist to investigate and recommend action on ethical issues involving news stories and reporting procedures. These individuals do not operate from a fixed code of conduct but apply personal, professional, and institutional "codes" to specific situations. Charles Seib, a former *Washington Post* ombudsman, has urged that in training future journalists more attention be given to "basic matters, personal integrity, the making of ethical judgments." The ombudsman often acts as the bridge between personal, professional, and institutional ethics and attempts to apply all three standards to individual issues.

The three major TV networks all have departments of broadcast standards. (We discussed the gatekeeping function of these units in Chapter 7.) The key here is that few, if any, of these network units have written codes. Yet they are not run on the whim or fancy of the person in charge. Rather, the ethical system is an agreed-upon set of values that combines personal, professional, and institutional values. For example, in 1984 the *New York Post* banned all advertising of pornographic films, burlesque houses, and topless bars from its pages. This decision was made by a "consensus at an upper management level" at the paper. This "consensus," in effect, is an institutional ethical system at work. The following article in the *Ithaca Journal* illustrates yet another attempt to develop and implement institutional ethics. Having no code or doctrine to regulate fairness comparable to the one that currently exists in broadcasting, newspapers have in recent years developed a wide variety of systems and procedures related to issues of ethics and social responsibility. Here the *Journal* is primarily concerned with "reinforcing the perception that we are concerned with accuracy and fairness."

Accuracy and fairness are two cornerstones of any successful newspaper.

A newspaper can be dynamic and profitable, but if it fails to meet high standards of accuracy and fairness consistently, then it is failing its mission.

Accuracy is more than spelling someone's name correctly. It's a reporter taking the time to doublecheck the spelling of Cascadilla; it's an editor taking the time to make sure the mayor is 41 years old; it's the publisher taking the time to reinforce the notion that we are best when we are accurate.

Fairness is more than giving both sides in a debate the chance to present a point of view: It's a reporter making sure that the presentation of all sides is not skewed by personal opinions; it's an editor making sure that diverse opinions are offered to the readers and that all angles have been given adequate consideration; it's a publisher making sure that all aspects of a community are given consideration and that biases toward businesses and minorities are shelved.

With this in mind, the *Journal* is introducing a means of measuring our accuracy and fairness as we report the news.

Lacking a better name, I'll call it an "accuracy check."

I will be sending these one-page questionnaires to residents of the Eastern Finger Lakes whose names appear in the *Journal*.

A coach in Watkins Glen might receive one after he is quoted in a basketball story; a Dryden funeral director might get one in connection with a funeral he handled; the subject of a feature article might find one in the mail.

The reason for this "accuracy check" is twofold:
—To reinforce the perception that we are concerned about accuracy and fairness.
—To give reporters and editors an idea of what their readers think of the job being done every day on the second floor at 123 W. State Street.[3]

In distinct contrast to the rather gray area of *institutional* ethics is the system of codes and, in some cases, regulations that forms the environment of *professional* ethics. Most of these codes relate to news, for historically the press has been the least controlled of any mass communication institution in the United States. Two of the most respected codes are those of the Society of Professional Journalists, Sigma Delta Chi (SAT/SDC), and the Radio/Television News Directors Association (RTNDA). The SPJ/SDX code essentially preaches social responsibility. The code covers six areas:

Professional

1. *Responsibility* emphasizes both the public's right to know and the public-trust mission of mass media.
2. *Freedom of the press* stresses the right and responsibility of the media to question and challenge society's institutions, particularly government.
3. *Ethics* addresses personal "lifestyle" issues, such as moonlighting, as well as areas of news judgment, such as protecting the confidentiality of news sources.
4. The section on *accuracy and objectivity* looks at the concept of truth and attempts to draw the line between news and opinion.
5. *Fair play* discusses in a more technical way such issues as invasion of privacy, correcting errors, and the right to reply.
6. The *pledge* section simply indicates that compliance with the code is voluntary, signified by a pledge charging journalists to "ensure and prevent violations of these standards."

The RTNDA code addresses many of the same issues but applies them specifically to broadcast news. The RTNDA Code of Broadcast News Ethics contains 10 articles and covers such areas as rights of privacy, confidentiality of sources, fair trial, and conflict of interest. Other codes, such as the Code of Ethics of the American Society of Newspaper Editors and the Code of Professional Standards of the Public Relations Society of America, emphasize many of the same basic issues.

One form of media content that has developed a relatively elaborate and systematic code of conduct is advertising. Self-regulation in advertising has existed for most of the present century. For example, in 1924 the American Association of Advertising Agencies asked its members to cooperate with a creative code that set forth some ground rules for ethical

---

[3] *Ithaca Journal*, July 14, 1983, p. 5.

CREATIVE CODE

American Association of Advertising Agencies

The members of the American Association of Advertising Agencies recognize:

1. That advertising bears a dual responsibility in the American economic system and way of life.

To the public it is a primary way of knowing about the goods and services which are the products of American free enterprise, goods and services which can be freely chosen to suit the desires and needs of the individual. The public is entitled to expect that advertising will be reliable in content and honest in presentation.

To the advertiser it is a primary way of persuading people to buy his goods or services, within the framework of a highly competitive economic system. He is entitled to regard advertising as a dynamic means of building his business and his profits.

2. That advertising enjoys a particularly intimate relationship to the American family. It enters the home as an integral part of television and radio programs, to speak to the individual and often to the entire family. It shares the pages of favorite newspapers and magazines. It presents itself to travelers and to readers of the daily mails. In all these forms, it bears a special responsibility to respect the tastes and self-interest of the public.

3. That advertising is directed to sizable groups or to the public at large, which is made up of many interests and many tastes. As is the case with all public enterprises, ranging from sports to education and even to religion, it is almost impossible to speak without finding someone in disagreement. Nonetheless, advertising people recognize their obligation to operate within the traditional American limitations: to serve the interests of the majority and to respect the rights of the minority.

Therefore we, the members of the American Association of Advertising Agencies, in addition to supporting and obeying the laws and legal regulations pertaining to advertising, undertake to extend and broaden the application of high ethical standards. Specifically, we will not knowingly produce advertising which contains:

a. False or misleading statements or exaggerations, visual or verbal.

b. Testimonials which do not reflect the real choice of a competent witness.

c. Price claims which are misleading.

d. Comparisons which unfairly disparage a competitive product or service.

e. Claims insufficiently supported, or which distort the true meaning or practicable application of statements made by professional or scientific authority.

f. Statements, suggestions or pictures offensive to public decency.

We recognize that there are areas which are subject to honestly different interpretations and judgment. Taste is subjective and may even vary from time to time as well as from individual to individual. Frequency of seeing or hearing advertising messages will necessarily vary greatly from person to person.

However, we agree not to recommend to an advertiser and to discourage the use of advertising which is in poor or questionable taste or which is deliberately irritating through content, presentation or excessive repetition.

Clear and willful violations of this Code shall be referred to the Board of Directors of the American Association of Advertising Agencies for appropriate action, including possible annulment of membership as provided in Article IV, Section 5, of the Constitution and By-Laws.

Conscientious adherence to the letter and the spirit of this Code will strengthen advertising and the free enterprise system of which it is part.   *Adopted April 26, 1962*

Endorsed by

Advertising Association of the West, Advertising Federation of America, Agricultural Publishers Association, Associated Business Publications, Association of Industrial Advertisers, Association of National Advertisers, Magazine Publishers Association, National Business Publications, Newspaper Advertising Executives Association, Radio Code Review Board (National Association of Broadcasters), Station Representatives Association, TV Code Review Board (NAB)

Codes represent the collective moral and ethical sensibilities of members of a profession. (Courtesy the American Association of Advertising Agencies.)

behavior. The code was a detailed instrument that articulated both a philosophy of advertising and comments on specific practices. It was segmented into areas dealing with a particular community, product, or medium. In 1971 this segmentation changed, and with the creation of the National Advertising Review Board (NARB) the chief advertising organizations formed the most comprehensive self-regulation system ever established in advertising.

The NARB is concerned primarily with deceptive advertising and is one branch of the National Advertising Review Council. The National Advertising Division of the Council of Better Business Bureaus employs a full-time professional staff that works to resolve advertising-practice complaints in a private and personal way. If this procedure does not work, then the "case" is given to the NARB, which reviews the information and then communicates with the advertiser. If the advertiser still does not correct the deceptive material, the issue is referred to an appropriate government agency, such as the Federal Trade Commission, the Securities and Exchange Commission, or the U.S. Postal Service.

Easily the most comprehensive and systematic self-regulatory system is that used by motion pictures. Developed out of a long-established "code," the current system is known primarily by the rating classifications G, PG, R, and X assigned to American motion pictures. The ratings are made by the Classification and Rating Administration (CARA) in accordance with a vaguely developed set of criteria that considers "among others as deemed appropriate the treatment of theme, language, violence, nudity and sex." (We discussed CARA in terms of its role as a gatekeeper in Chapter 7.) It is also important to understand CARA as the formal embodiment of certain moral values and ethical principles. These principles and values are not set in stone, however.

Perhaps the best example of the principles and values by which the system works is found in the appeals process where a particular CARA rating is defended or attacked. Here the personal value systems of the seven people who sit on the CARA board are more clearly illuminated. What ultimately emanates from such a process is the lack of rules. As one CARA board member stated: "Rules make decision easy but they rob it of wisdom." The member went on to say further, in defending a PG rating for a movie using an infamous four-letter word, "I wanted us not to have an easy time, but to be wise. I wanted our rating system to be wise, not rigid. . . . I urged upon you only *one* commanding rule: the rule of reason." The point here is that the bedrock of any professional value—ethical system, be it a code or council, is a sense of individual *and* collective wisdom and reason.

The authority of the NARB, CARA, and other codes to "regulate" conduct and content is almost negligible. With virtually every professional code, council, or statement of principles, the authority is almost exclusively moral. Codes cannot stop content, impose fines, boycott advertisers, or remove people from their jobs. What codes do is bring the judgment of one's professional peers to bear on a particular case or issue. Ultimately the codes represent the collective moral and ethical sensibilities of members of a profession—be it news, advertising, or entertainment. The success of a code depends on individual and institutional *acceptance* of the moral–ethical principles on which the code is based and *compliance* with the specific credos formulated in the code. This agreement in principle makes self-regulation possible. The demise of the National Association of Broadcasters Radio and Television Codes occurred because fewer than one-third of broadcast stations subscribed to their code. The code was unenforceable, yes; but that is true of almost every media code. It was the lack of professional consensus and agreement, coupled with increasing deregulation of broadcasters, that made these codes inappropriate and meaningless. The following comment from *Time* magazine illustrates the problem.

> If the news is covered as badly as much of the public thinks it is, why doesn't the press clean its own house? Where is its professional responsibility? The difficulty begins with that word professional. Medicine and law, being professions, can expel or censure wrongdoers, even though fraternal coziness makes such action rare. Journalism has no admission standards. A plumber or a hairdresser must pass a test to get a license, but no journalist does, on the grounds that licensing would be abhorrent to the idea of a free and robust press. . . .
>
> The inability of the press to get together to reform itself is more than arrogance and orneriness. The need for a diverse press makes for strange and incompatible bedfellows. The sleazy *Hustler* magazine may have a legal right to exist, but few in the press consider its publisher a colleague. Yet most members of the press feel that editorial independence, which tolerates the worst of journalism, is essential to producing the best. Salant acknowledges that the American press is "better than it had ever been before." If so, this improvement has two causes. One is the standards many editors and publishers set for themselves, vying to earn one another's informed esteem; this is the true professionalism in what is not a profession. The second is the constant prodding of a dissatisfied public, demanding a press that is accurate, fair and responsible. That prodding goes on.[4]

Ultimately, then, *institutional* ethics and *professional* ethics are grounded in *personal* ethics. This finally becomes the point at which all ethical systems arrive and media ethical systems are no exception. The following column by the *Chicago Tribune* columnist Bob Greene graphically and dramatically illustrates this position.

---

[4] Robert McCloskey, "Journalism Under Fire," *Time* 122, December 12, 1983, pp. 76–93.

I may have blown this one. I don't think so, but I have enough doubts that I'm not sure. I think I'd like your opinion on it.

In Chicago, there is a very prominent businessman who has gained great wealth largely on the strength of patronage by Jewish customers. The man is not Jewish.

I received a copy of a personal letter the man wrote. He and his wife were engaged in a dispute with a dry-cleaning store; the couple charged that the store had ruined one of the woman's garments and had refused to pay for it. The owner of the dry-cleaning store was Jewish. In the letter, the gentile businessman—who depends on Jews for much of his income—called the dry-cleaning store owner a "kike."

I telephoned the dry-cleaning store. The manager told me that he was not at fault. He said he had tried to reach a settlement with the businessman, and then the letter had arrived. So I called the businessman.

"That's right, I called the man a kike," he told me. "He is a kike. There's a difference between a Jew and a kike."

When I asked him what the difference was, he said: "The low-class Jew is a kike. The immoral Jew is a kike. Everyone knows that."

"The man who runs that dry-cleaning store proved himself to be a kike by the way he did business with us, and he proved himself to be even more of a kike by showing that letter to you."

The man readily admitted to me that he did a high percentage of his business with Jewish customers. But he told me he was confident those customers would not resent his attitude.

"They won't be offended. Even a Jew knows that a low-class Jew is a kike. I have always referred to the immoral, low-class Jew as a kike."

He said to me:

"You're not Jewish, are you?"

I told him that indeed I was.

"Well, are you offended?" he said.

I said that "kike" was probably the ugliest name you could call a Jew; I couldn't imagine anyone, including any of his Jewish customers, who wouldn't be offended.

He seemed surprised. "Anyone who says I am anti-Semitic is an absolute liar," he said. "I do 90 percent of my business with Jews, and 90 percent of my friends are Jews." He said that he had always used the term "kike" and that he thought it was a perfectly acceptable way to refer to a "bad jew."

I asked him what he called "bad Protestants."

"I never knew there was a name you called bad Protestants," he said.

That ended our conversation. He called back a little later. "I feel like Patton, at the end of that movie," he said. "Remember, he had slapped the soldier? And at the end of the movie he said, 'I wish I had kissed him instead of slapped him.'"

So I had a strong column, which I wrote. I intended to run it in my home paper, the *Chicago Tribune*. The peg was perfect: Here was a man who made his living off Jews, who readily admitted he used the word "kike." I moved the column, naming the man, and the page proofs came up. There it was, ready to be seen by all the people who read the *Tribune* every day.

And I killed it.

I requested that my editors yank it out of the paper. My column did not appear the next day.

My reason was this:

The man is a bigot. He has a foul mouth, an ugly temper and a nasty streak of prejudice.

However, the more I thought about it, the more I was unsure whether his bigotry ought to be exposed to the more than a million people who read the *Tribune*. If some guy on the street says something that ugly, you don't print it, because it's not news. If Chicago Mayor Jane Byrne says it (not that she would), you print it, because she's a public figure.

This guy fell somewhere in between. I knew what the reaction would be if the column appeared. His business would be damaged, and damaged badly. The whole public image of his company would change. For the rest of his life, he would be known not as a successful businessman, but as a Jew-hater. (I know he said he didn't hate Jews, but when you starting writing letters calling people "kikes" and then try to defend it, you are pretty well branded.)

So why didn't I just run the column? Five years ago I might have just thrown it in there and watched the reaction. But now . . . the man seemed stupid and naive, but I wasn't sure that the punishment of the mass-distributed column was worth the crime of his ignorant remarks. There are a lot of bigots out there; by picking him out, I wasn't sure what I was accomplishing. Proving that such bigotry exists? I think we all know that.

I have given a lot of thought in recent months to the press as bully. We have grown so powerful; on the surface the column would have appeared to be exposing a wrong, but the *Chicago Tribune* is so much bigger than this one ugly-spirited businessman . . . should the full weight of the *Tribune* really be brought down on him because of his muddled attitude?

Many people I respect greatly, including a number of my editors, urged me to run the column. In a way, there was unintentional humor to the situation: Here was a columnist trying to kill a controversial column he had written, and his bosses trying to persuade him to go ahead and run it. The exact opposite of the way things are alleged to be. (As a matter of fact, a Jewish man who works in the *Tribune's* composing room saw the column in proofs and then saw the paper come out without the column. He called me to ask me why my bosses had killed the column, and seemed skeptical when I told him that they hadn't; I had.)

Anyway . . . I decided that the column would not run. But a week later, I'm still thinking about it. I honestly don't know if I did the correct thing or not—and that's the purpose of today's column. You and I have this regular interchange, through the paper. I'd be grateful to hear your opinion.[5]

Here, Greene points out forcefully and clearly that his ethical system had made the difference. His personal sense of social responsibility had killed the story.

[5] Bob Green in *The Chicago Tribune*, May 17, 1982, p. 47.

Media communicators, especially journalists like Bob Greene, face such decisions daily. Each situation is unique, and yet in practical terms the ethical issues faced by individual media communicators seem to fall into six major categories: (a) conflict of interest; (b) truth–accuracy; (c) unnamed sources–disclosure; (d) payola, gifts, and business pressure; (e) privacy; and (f) social justice–responsibility.

Conflict of interest is, simply put, an issue of divided loyalty. The conflict usually occurs as a result of multiple employment or personal friendships. If a broadcast journalist works part-time for a local bank, and the bank is the subject of an investigation, conflict occurs. Can the journalist perform the task of properly investigating and reporting the story and still be employed by the bank? Even if the bank applies no pressure to "close down" the story, the reporter still faces a personal ethical dilemma. To whom does he or she owe loyalty? Even more serious is the misuse of information based on multiple employment.

CONFLICT OF INTEREST

In covering business news, the *Wall Street Journal* frequently publishes stories about the misuse of inside information in stock purchases. Recently the paper revealed that it had found such a case in its own newsroom. It disclosed that one of its reporters had acknowledged leaking upcoming items from the influential "Heard on the Street" column, which features stock tips, to investors. The reporter, one of the column's two principal writers, admitted the leaks to the Securities and Exchange Commission, which had been investigating evidence that a group of traders made illicit profits after receiving the information. The reporter subsequently was fired.

The *Wall Street Journal* noted that in a policy designed to prevent such cases, new employees are expected to sign a $3\frac{1}{2}$-page conflict-of-interest statement. The paper's managing editor said the case left the paper with "a collective sense of shock, outrage and betrayal."

Many journalists take the issue of conflict of interest so seriously that they will not broadcast or act as a spokesperson for a commercial product. The late Frank McGee, when he anchored NBC's "Today Show," was adamant in his refusal even to introduce commercials on the air. He felt his role as a journalist placed him in a position of public trust and acceptance, and he would be trading on that reputation if he were to sell a product.

Personal friendships obviously can interfere with a journalist's role. The concept of an adversarial role for a free press is grounded in the absence of conflict of interest. It would have been difficult for Roger Mudd of NBC to have interviewed then presidential candidates Edward Kennedy (1980) and Gary Hart (1984) in a tough, inquiring manner had he been close personal friends with either man. Mudd, or any reporter, does not have to *dislike* an interviewee in order to be an effective adversary. Adversary does not imply enemy. Nevertheless, as adversaries, Mudd and other reporters represent the public. Their role is to fairly question a person on behalf of the public. This is the public-trust role all journalists should live by.

TRUTH AND ACCURACY

Truth and accuracy are perhaps the two hottest words in a reporter's lexicon. Almost all ethical codes begin with the need of reporters to tell the truth under all conditions. This may seem like a simple task; but truth in today's society is often not without major ambiguities. Truth is not simply collecting all the facts or not lying. Outright deceit rarely occurs in newswriting; deception is always a temptation, especially in the news-gathering process. A typical situation involves reporters posing as employees of a particular organization or as consumers in order to get a story. Misrepresentation in this sense is usually viewed as harmless and in many cases necessary. Too often, however, misrepresentation is used as an easy way to obtain a story rather than take the more difficult path of informed consent.

Perhaps the most ambiguous aspect of the truth issue is equating truth with facts. A small daily newspaper, the *Ithaca Journal*, found itself in an ethical dilemma in reporting the death of a local man in a car accident. Commenting on the death, which was caused in part by the young man's state of sobriety, the *Journal* also reported that this young man had been involved in a DWI (driving while intoxicated) accident two years previously and had caused the death of his passenger. Many people in the community were angry about the reporting; they felt the newspaper was insensitive to the man's family by "digging up" past history that, in their opinion, was not relevant to the story. The *Journal* defended its story by stating that the young man's previous accident was part of a pattern of behavior that shed light on his death. Here is clearly a case when reporting the facts and telling the truth are not necessarily the same thing. There are no easy answers to the ethical dilemmas posed by questions of truth and accuracy. What is important is that reporters, editors, and publishers be aware of the need to make difficult decisions and moral judgments. Objectivity is not a shield to hide behind and does not excuse the newsperson from exercising his or her value system. Walter Lippmann in *Public Opinion* articulated this issue by defining news as fragments of information that come to a reporter's attention, while explicit and established standards guide the pursuit of truth.

SOURCES OF INFORMATION

Unnamed sources, the disclosure of sources, or both, have in recent years been the subject of intense and often sensationalized controversy. The dilemma is a classic one. When personal ethics conflict with the law, is it wrong to follow one's ethics? The distinction lies between what is legally permitted and what is ethically correct. In refusing to disclose a source a reporter is clearly breaking the law. Nevertheless, by naming the source after having given one's word not to do so, a reporter is also unethical. As John Merrill and S. Jack Odell argue in their book *Philosophy and Journalism*, for the most part the law of the land reflects the ethical code of that land. But it does not have to, and sometimes it does not.

As the authors indicate, this fact can easily be grasped if one considers what so often happens after a revolution and the seizing of political power by those outside the establishment. Either the revolutionaries change the existing laws, altering some and dropping others so as to guarantee what they conceive to be the basic ethical rights of each person, or the laws are changed to fit the political objectives of those seizing power at the expense of certain individuals or groups. The former alternative is evidenced by the American and French revolutions; the latter alternative, by the Nazis seizing power in Germany.

Injustices can be rectified only as long as people are willing to break existing laws for the sake of ethical principles. The continuance of the community depends upon it. The upshot of these considerations is that a reporter's refusal to divulge sources, even when it means incarceration, can in general be justified and even applauded.[6]

Therefore, no set of exact rules can be formulated that will always tell the reporter what to do. One can only hope to educate and sensitize reporters to ethical issues and trust in their ability and willingness to address these issues intelligently, forcefully, and ethically. As the authors of *Media Ethics* point out:

> Most news operations have developed specific guidelines to help prevent chaos and abuse. Certain conventions also hold journalistic practice together. It is typically assumed that all information must be verified by two or three sources before it can be printed. Most codes of ethics and company policies insist on attribution and specific identification whenever possible. A few news operations allow reporters to keep sources totally secret, but a majority openly involve editors as judges of the data's validity. The rules also include accurate quotation marks, correction of errors, and an account of the context. However, even with these safeguards, a responsible press must continually agonize over its treatment of sources in order to prevent lapses.[7]

PAYOLA, GIFTS, AND BUSINESS PRESSURE

In distinct contrast to the much publicized and controversial issue of disclosure is the "back of the house" problem of accepting gifts. As Tony Mauro of Gannett News Service said: "The problem is not new. Walk into any newsroom, find an employee with graying hair, buy him a couple of drinks and you will hear stories about the old days when reporters who

[6] John C. Merrill and S. Jack Odell, *Philosophy and Journalism* (Longman: New York & London, 1983), p. 99.

[7] Clifford G. Christians, et al. *Media Ethics* (Longman: New York & London, 1983), p. 71.

boosted their friends were rewarded with a bottle of J&B . . . at Christmas. One crusty editor I know lives by this rule: 'Never accept a gift you can't consume in 24 hours.'"[8] Unfortunately, this attitude toward gifts makes the issue less controversial and problematic for many journalists. Most media communicators would agree that overt "under the table" practices, such as the payola scandal involving disc jockeys, require ethical surveillance and legal regulation. The more subtle practices—a restaurant critic accepting free meals, a travel editor accepting free trips, or a business editor sitting on a corporate board—are considered ethical gray areas. Yet if a reader expects objective information and independent opinion from a restaurant critic or travel editor, this expectation can easily be compromised by free meals or lodging. As the American Society of Newspaper Editors states: "Journalism must avoid impropriety and the appearance of impropriety . . . conflict of interest or the appearance of conflict. They should neither accept anything nor pursue any activity that might compromise or seem to compromise their integrity." The line between proper and improper conduct in this arena is a thin one. As Tony Mauro reported:

> *Washington Post* financial writer John Berry was at a meeting more than a year ago when a New York investment analyst walked up to him and said, "Thank you."
>
> Some months earlier, it turned out, a story by Berry appearing in the *Post* had helped the analyst earn $10 million for some investors.
>
> The analyst, who had arranged to have an early edition of the *Post* delivered to his home in New York every day, found a story by Berry predicting a shift in Federal Reserve Board policy. It confirmed the analyst's suspicions, and he acted swiftly and profitably, before the rest of the investment community had a chance to react.
>
> Berry himself never profited from the story.
>
> But his editor, Frank Swoboda, tells the anecdote to illustrate the kind of power reporters could wield with the information they obtain while gathering the news.
>
> "In this instance, the story was already printed, but suppose the reporter had called the broker the day before it was in the paper," said Swoboda. "He could have demanded a 10 percent cut for the information," and made himself a millionaire.
>
> In 1979, stock in Smith Kline Corp. fell sharply the day before the highly influential *New England Journal of Medicine* published an article critical of the company's popular anti-ulcer medicine, Tagamet. At that time, medical writers and anyone else willing to pay first-class postage could obtain the journal several days in advance of its general publication.
>
> After the Tagamet incident, editors at the journal took a look at the first-class mailing list and found dozens of Wall Street analysts and others besides reporters who would not otherwise be reading a technically medical journal. "It made us feel uncomfortable," recalled editor Dr. Arnold Relman. As a

---

[8] Tony Mauro, "Shooting Ourselves in the Foot," *USA Today*, April 5, 1984, p. 10a.

result, the magazine has limited the advance mailing to bona fide medical writers who agree to abide by an embargo on advance publication.

The new policy places an even higher premium on ethical behavior by reporters, since they are now the only ones who get the journal in advance. Relman said he has detected no stock manipulation problems since their new policy, but he acknowledges that "if reporters are unethical and they want to cheat, there's no way we can stop them. We can't prevent leaks. We're not the CIA."[9]

Once again, as with most personal ethical issues faced by today's journalists, the bottom line is individual integrity. No set of rules or code of ethics can prevent conflict of interest, accepting gifts, or business pressure. It is up to the individual media communicator to set personal standards for behavior.

Another ethical issue that often ends up in a journalistic "twilight zone" is the issue of privacy. There have been great gains in the legal definition of privacy in recent years, and they focus on these areas: (a) intrusion upon seclusion or solitude; (b) publicity that puts an individual in a false light; (c) public disclosure of embarrassing private affairs; and (d) use of an individual's name or likeness for personal gain. An interesting twist on the last issue is the privacy rights of deceased persons. A computer firm has been sued for using the likeness of the late silent film star Charlie Chaplin to sell its product. Other companies have used W. C. Fields and Laurel and Hardy clones to sell everything from windshield wipers to wine.

THE PRIVACY ISSUE

The critical theme in the privacy issue is the public's "right to know" versus the individual's right of privacy. For example, a Montana newspaper recently lost its bid to force the state's board of regents to open meetings during which state-college presidents are evaluated. The *Missoulian*, a daily newspaper in Missoula, where the University of Montana is located, claimed that the policy of barring the press and public from such sessions violated a state open-meeting law. But the Montana Supreme Court upheld a lower court's finding that the college presidents' right to privacy outweighed the public's interest in attending the sessions. The justices noted "that alternately opening and closing the evaluation as sensitive private matters came up was burdensome and impractical" and that "frank employee evaluations are an essential part" of sound university management.

Despite the increasing number of court decisions, legal definitions of privacy, as with most ethical issues, are an inadequate foundation for journalistic behavior. As Christians et al. state in *Media Ethics*:

[9] *Ibid*

Merely following the letter of the law—presuming that can even be reasonably determined—certainly is not sufficient. There are several reasons why establishing an ethics of privacy that goes beyond the law is important in the gathering and distribution of news.

First, the law that conscientiously seeks to protect individual privacy excludes public officials. In general, the courts have upheld that political personalities cease to be purely private persons and First Amendment values take precedence over privacy considerations. In recent years, court decisions have given the media extraordinary latitude in reporting on public persons.

Second, the press has been given great latitude in defining newsworthiness. People who are catapulted into the public eye by events are generally classed by privacy law along with elected officials. In nearly all important cases, the American courts have accepted the media's definition.

Third, legal efforts assume many debatable questions about the relationship between self and society. Professor Thomas Emerson's summary is commonly accepted:

> The concept of a right to privacy attempts to draw a line between the individual and the collective, between self and society. It seeks to assure the individual a zone in which to be an individual, not a member of the community. In that zone he can think his own thoughts, have his own secrets, live his own life, reveal only what he wants to the outside world. The right of privacy, in short, establishes an area excluded from the collective life, not governed by the rules of collective living.

Shortcuts and easy answers arise from boxing off these two dimensions. Glib appeals to "the public's right to know" are a common way to cheapen the richness of the private/public relationship.

Therefore, sensitive journalists who struggle personally with these issues in terms of real people lay on themselves more demands than the technically legal. They realize that ethically sound conclusions can emerge only when various privacy situations are faced in all their complexities.[10]

**SOCIAL JUSTICE—
RESPONSIBILITY**

Ultimately, then, the ethical issues faced by contemporary journalists are difficult ones not easily resolved by subscribing to a code of ethics or adhering to some law. The critical ingredient becomes the individual journalist's sense of values, his or her own concept of social responsibility. It should be noted also that these issues are confronted and analyzed by virtually all media people, not only national columnists or major-city newspapers, and that they do not always deal with issues of national importance. The column by Joe Junod of the *Ithaca Journal* illustrates that ethical issues are an everyday fact of life for media communicators.

CENSORSHIP

Individual communicators are not the only ones involved in media ethics. The media also face generic issues that, although ultimately articulated on a personal level, are larger and more symptomatic of the system itself.

[10] Clifford G. Christians et al., *Media Ethics* (Longman: New York & London, 1983), pp. 110–111.

When the comics aren't so funny

By JOE JUNOD
Journal Managing Editor

A popular part of most newspapers (excepting The Wall Street Journal and The New York Times) is its comics.

It's often said that comics are the most popular part of a newspaper, that they provide the best diversion from the day's events, which quite often are not funny.

Comic strips are plentiful. There are dozens of them available for purchase.

Not all comic strips, however, are always funny. There are times when a strip, such as Beetle Bailey, goes beyond what I consider the mark of good taste and fairness.

We keep an eye on the comic strips we run in The Journal, reading them for content and taste before they get into the paper.

Printed here is an example of one Beetle Bailey strip that I did not publish — until today, and now only as an example of what I would call a cheap shot to about half the population of this country.

This strip, and others, sometimes portray women are objects of lust or scorn. The strip Nancy also edges into this category on occasion, usually when Sluggo makes some comment about "women drivers," or somesuch.

By withholding certain comic strips, some people will accuse me of censorship, of being selective to suit my own tastes and biases.

I would argue that the job of being an editor is a process of being selective, choosing this picture over that one, writing a headline in one manner instead of another.

An editor has two jobs: Deciding what readers want to read and what they ought to read. I don't think they ought to read comic strips such as the one published here.

If you have a problem with this approach, try this: In place of the word woman, or the image woman, substitute the derogatory expression for a black person. Do that, and then decide if you would run the comic strip referring to a black in that manner.

I don't think that comic strips which treat women as sex objects, as stupid, or as objects of scorn are worth publishing. Since The Journal buys the rights to publication — most strips cost about $7 a week at this newspaper — I believe we also buy the rights to edit them.

Holding an individual up to ridicule is not a function of this newspaper.

In addition, I don't believe that such strips are beneficial as object lessons for children. If we are concerned that our children are not being exposed to a sufficient number of responsible adults, do we ag-gravate the situation by teaching them that half the population of America is dumb, or that they should be valued for the shape of their body? This newspaper endeavors to avoid passing such myths and stereotypes. Eyeballing the comic strips is one way we do this.

We are considering some changes in our comic strip selection. If you have an opinion about what strips should be dropped, or added, or about the process I described above, reach for the pen and paper, or the telephone.

Perhaps no media issue is of greater concern and has as long and richly debated a history as censorship. The word itself almost immediately raises the collective temperature of the mass media. Here, too, long legal battles have been fought over the years. Similar to the conflict between the public's right to know and the individual's right of privacy, the censorship battle has centered on the right of freedom of the press versus the constraints and responsibility such freedom requires. Chief Justice Holmes expressed it most simply when he said freedom of speech does not extend to allowing the cry of "Fire!" in a crowded theater. The paradox was eloquently expressed 30 years later by William Hocking of the Hutchins Commission on Freedom of the Press:

> Are . . . thoughts all equally worthy of protection? Are there no ideas unfit for expression, insane, obscene, destructive? Are all hypotheses on the same level, each one, however vile or silly, to be taken with the same mock reverence because some academic jackass brings it forth? Is non-censorship so great a virtue that it can denounce all censorship as lacking in human liberality?[11]

[11] *Ibid*, p. 285.

Particularly troublesome is censorship in education. Perhaps because education has few powerful interest groups, perhaps because it is localized, perhaps because, ironically, it receives so little media attention, the issues are at times clouded. Whatever the reason, nowhere in American society can censorship be more counterproductive than in education. Yet education remains particularly vulnerable to pressure groups when it is a question of the availability of literature and other learning materials.

The incidence of censorship is growing. Its presence was felt almost twice as often in the 1970s as in the preceding decade. With the increasing power of small groups in the population who use the mass media to gain exposure, and with the recent militant position of conservative elements, attempts to impose censorship may double again in the 1980s.

Librarians bear the brunt of these attacks because of their position in the community and in education as "supervisors of information." They run the information store. Teachers are vulnerable to "open, public retribution" for using certain materials in class. Interestingly, the lowest incidence of censorship is in the South and Southwest; the highest incidence is in New England and in the nation's capital, Washington, D.C. More than half of all censorship attempts are successful.

As our culture becomes more combative, attempts at censorship are likely to increase. The tragedy of this fact lies in three areas:

1. The merits of the case aside, the kinds of materials available to students decrease. The users suffer.
2. The institution involved is painted into a corner; that is, it must lose support from *some* segments of the community.
3. The teacher or librarian or media specialist involved is subjected to personal pressure and at times abuse. In some cases, the individual becomes "gun shy" and begins to make choices that are unnecessarily narrow.

In numbers of objections, books are attacked most often; and about one in four attacks concerns textbooks. Of the books attacked by would-be censors, *Catcher in the Rye* by J. D. Salinger is cited more often than any other work. *Catch-22* by Joseph Heller is another favorite target.

Two major areas of concern are (a) racial materials, with criticism arising from groups and individuals objecting to racism as well as radicalism; and (b) sexual references, which always draw fire from segments of the population, especially when the references occur in films, plays, and books.

Textbook censorship can occur at many levels. The pressure that surfaces in schools is normally addressed toward respected literary works by such writers as John Steinbeck, Ernest Hemingway, and Aldous Huxley. The public library that tends to offer a broad selection of popular works is another target; it is often pressured to remove works of lesser literary merit or works dealing with controversial issues.

Does a community, a society, have the right or responsibility to police media materials? There are no simple answers. To say yes in some cases (dealing with children?) and no in others (adults?) may be close to the facts of life in this society, but another question arises: When does a person become an adult?

A larger problem lies in the suppression of ideas. This should not be tolerated in a democratic society, but tragically it is in some situations. Ultimately, in a democracy, too little censorship is undeniably better than too much.

The interpretation of censorship in contemporary society is, of course, centered in First Amendment law. A major distinction is made between print and broadcast media in the application of this law. For print media, the First Amendment declares boldly that no government—federal, state, or local—can interfere with the right of a publisher to print whatever information he or she cares to put on paper. Of course, certain economic and labor regulations apply to print media, but in general print media are free from repressive government controls. Broadcasting, on the other hand, is regulated by the federal government to the point of broadcasters being required to hold a license in order to communicate on radio or television. The basic licensing structure of broadcasting, established in 1927, has led to a wide variety of other controls, several of them directly affecting the content of radio and television. These controls received their strongest court endorsement in the *Red Lion* decision of 1969 in which the Supreme Court ruled that the standard of the Fairness Doctrine, which requires broadcasters to balance their public affairs programming and to provide air time to persons or points of view that the broadcaster might otherwise ignore, was constitutional.

MEDIA AND THE FIRST AMENDMENT

In applying a different First Amendment standard to broadcasting from the one that covers print media the Court stated: "Differences in the characteristics of news media justify differences in the First Amendment standards applied to them." The differences noted are grounded in the physical characteristics of broadcasting, primarily the scarcity of spectrum space, which prevents anyone who wants to from going on the air. Therefore, as William Read points out in his article "The First Amendment Meets the Information Society":

> At the heart of the distinction drawn by the U.S. Supreme Court between the press and broadcasting is the belief that "the broadcast media pose unique and special problems not present in the traditional free speech case." What the Court finds to be "special" is the technological nature of the medium. Because broadcast frequencies are finite (and thus for reasons of efficient use must be allocated), the Court concluded in *Red Lion* that "it is idle to posit an unabridgeable First Amendment right to broadcast comparable to the right of every individual to speak, write or publish."

The upshot of all this is clear: The technological underpinnings of *Red Lion* are eroding as the technological distinctions among media blur. To cling to spectrum scarcity as a rationale for a divergent legal approach to broadcasting is no longer viable. Indeed it is risky. For as newspapers and magazines more and more come to rely on satellites and other regulated communications technologies the danger exists that they will be drawn into the regulatory web.

The conclusion to be drawn from the foregoing is simply this: The rationale for a divergent, two-track legal approach for mass media has eroded. Once seemingly clear distinctions between print and broadcasting are no longer clear; "blur" is fast becoming an appropriate word. The question then is whether, in an information society, both media should be placed under the print standard or under the broadcast standard? Or, perhaps, a standard yet to be developed?[12]

DEREGULATION AND BROADCAST MEDIA

The broadcast media are increasingly unable to escape behind FCC rules and regulations and are faced with the full impact of a social responsibility ethic that places them on a par with the print media. Whether the issues are the "big brother" role of television, checkbook journalism, violence on television or in films, or media stereotyping, the bottom line again becomes a sense of media responsibility, media ethics, and media values.

The issue of checkbook journalism, in particular, has generated controversy not only within the print and broadcast media but, more interestingly, between them. In 1984 CBS reportedly paid $500,000 for an interview with former President Richard Nixon. The payment raised the issue of checkbook journalism and what some journalists considered a bigger question: Was CBS News abdicating its editorial control—a former Nixon White House aide conducted the interview—and letting Nixon, in effect, produce his own program? The purchase was severely criticized by the *New York Times* and the *Los Angeles Times*, which in turn were accused of a "double standard" by former CBS News President Van Gordon Sauter. As Sauter stated in commenting on the newspapers' purchases of memoirs by Nixon and Jimmy Carter:

> There is nothing inherently wrong about the *New York Times* or *Los Angeles Times* publishing subjective judgments about the motivation or skills or shortcomings of CBS News, its executives or its journalists. But when will those newspapers, or any other, render the same subjective judgments about, say, the *Washington Post*, or *USA Today*, or the *Daily News*, or the (Los Angeles) *Herald-Examiner*? Do not the editorial merits, or lack of them, of these communicators deserve the same scrutiny, the same subjective judgment, passed with such regularity on broadcast journalists?[13]

[12] William Read, "The First Amendment Meets the Information Society," in *Telecommunications*, ed. by Jerry L. Salvaggio (Longman: New York & London, 1983), pp. 95–96.
[13] *Broadcasting*, March 19, 1984, p. 48.

Whatever the specific issues—checkbook journalism, stereotyping, violence, deceptive advertising, conflict of interest, etc.—ethical conduct in mass communication ultimately depends on the personal integrity of the individual communicator. As Muriel Reis, vice-president of WNEW-TV in New York City, stated in a commentary on nonfiction programming:

> In reality programming, production techniques should be used for one purpose only—to clarify and enlighten, not to confuse, to obfuscate or deceive. If production techniques remove the program from the sphere of reality, then something is wrong.
>
> How does a broadcaster deal with these added responsibilities? And who should be responsible? Clearly, a general manager or a program director cannot be everywhere at all times. My recommendation is, from the general manager down, to develop an awareness of the responsibilities and of the problems that can arise. This awareness should be instilled among those directly responsible for production. Producers cannot be required to solve problems, but they should be able to recognize them. Management must also be aware that staffs change; there can be a well-educated staff one day and novices the next. Indoctrination into programming responsibilities must be an ongoing process.
>
> To insure the all-important integrity of reality programming, management must be ever-vigilant. Program directors should insure that their producers and staff understand the principles upon which their programming responsibilities are based. Setting forth lists of specific do's and don't's may appear to some to be the answer, but it can be a dangerous trap. Because it is impossible to anticipate all contingencies, relying on specific rules can provide false security. The key is for the principles and standards of honest and credible programming to be thoroughly understood at all levels. If reality programming is both accurate and honest, not only are legal problems avoided, but credibility insured. And unless there is credibility, no program will succeed.[14]

MEDIA FREEDOM

The theme running through this chapter is one of freedom. Freedom of media and freedom for media. Media must be free from inhibiting external controls in order to protect and correct society. Nevertheless, media freedom carries with it the responsibility of self-regulation and self-correction. As *USA Today* editorialized in a debate on media ethics,

> Journalism is a high calling. The First Amendment to the Constitution makes the news media free to serve democracy, inform the public, promote debate and scrutinize and criticize the conduct of public officials. Some have described these rights and responsibilities of the news media as a "watchdog" role. But who watches the watchdog?
>
> Crooked lawyers can be disbarred, unethical doctors can lose their licenses, dishonest brokers can be banned from trading. While journalistic societies have codes of conduct, they have no power to enforce standards

[14] *Broadcasting*, October 15, 1983, p. 15.

or punish members. That can't change if the press is to remain free. But the press must not be corrupt.

The news media have a special responsibility to assure that those who report and edit the news never use their power for personal gain for themselves or their friends.

That's why every news-gathering organization must enforce its own rules to protect its credibility. Unethical journalists must be fired. Those who violate laws must be prosecuted.

The news media are more aware than ever of the need to provide internal regulations to protect against journalistic conflicts of interest. Any case of abuse is one too many. But self-regulation is the answer. Any other "solution" would offend the constitutional guarantee of press liberty.

Journalists insist that they have a professional duty to disclose "the truth"—however ugly—in other institutions and individuals. But those who are unwilling to face the sometimes ugly truth about their own business will fail the public. Worse, they fail themselves.[15]

[15] *USA Today,* April 5, 1984, p. 10a.

Mass Media and Society $\boxed{}$ **28**

America is a very different place today from what it was in the 1780s or 1880s, or even a decade ago. Our values, mores, customs, habits, lifestyles, dress, tastes, economic and political ideas, and even our religious traditions are all changing continually. Change is one of the chief characteristics of our age. For tens of thousands of years, human beings did not change as much as they have in the past hundred years.

The mass media have often been blamed for changes in our society, especially those that have been disagreeable. We tend to charge the mass media with making us more violent, more prone to criminal acts, more sexually permissive, more irreverent, and more apathetic. If we accuse the media for those changes, we should also credit the media for making us more socially and economically equal, less racist and sexist, more participatory in political affairs, more entertained, and more informed.

The question remains: To what extent have the mass media caused social and cultural developments, and to what extent have they simply reflected those changes? The answer to that question, as we saw in the chapter on the effects of mass media, is exceedingly complex. From a historical perspective, however, there would certainly appear to be close relationships between media and social–cultural–political–economic–religious movements.

HISTORICAL PERSPECTIVES

Harold A. Innis, a Canadian economic historian, was a pioneer in examining the effects of media on human activity. He was concerned primarily with the study of different currencies that various societies used, from bartering to beads and shells to coins to printed money. He came to the conclusion that the currency used by a society influenced the nature of its commercial activity and its daily lifestyle. He found that the printing of money had an important impact on the economics and politics of a society, and he thus posed the proposition that "Western civilization has been profoundly influenced by different media of communication."[1]

The most influential communication development prior to the twentieth century occurred in 1450: Gutenberg's invention of movable type, which made mass-production printing possible. One of the first books to be printed was the Bible. Before the invention of the printing press, only the privileged few had hand-copied Bibles. In fact, a Bible was so rare and precious that it was usually kept locked in the inner sanctums of churches and monasteries, and access to it was limited to those of high priestly rank. Those who had access to a Bible had great power to interpret the word of God for their own benefit.

The printing of the Bible changed the power of the church and brought

[1] Harold A. Junis, *Empire and Communications* (Toronto: University of Toronto Press, 1972), 14.

An exceptionally prolific writer, Martin Luther exploited the technology of printing to mass communicate his revolutionary religious ideas. (Etching: New York Public Library Picture Collection.)

about a religious revolution. A Catholic priest, Martin Luther, who was born in Germany 30 years after the invention of the printing press, ultimately declared that his conscience was more important to him than was the pope in Rome, and thus he started the Reformation and the Protestant religion.

Luther felt that all persons should be able to read the word of God for themselves and conduct themselves according to their own consciences, not according to the dictates of a priesthood. He translated the Bible from Latin into vernacular German (virtually inventing the German language in the process). When laymen could read the Scriptures, priests could be challenged in their role as mediators between the laity and God. Martin Luther understood the impact of the printed word, and he devoted much of his life to using it for his purposes. He was the most prolific serious writer in history; one edition of his works exceeds 100 volumes.

George Will, writing in 1983 on the five-hundredth anniversary of Luther's birth, called him "the first great life bound up with mass communication. . . . Luther showed how the tangible (a new technology, printing) can shape the intangible (the idea of an institutional church)."[2] Certainly, the Christian religion has never been the same since the invention of movable type.

Other revolutionary movements, in politics, economics, and science, came from the printed word. The printed word made possible the rise of science by allowing facts and observations to be gathered and shared so that new and more valid conclusions could be drawn about the universe. Books could carry the message that the world was round, not flat. Less than 50 years after the invention of printing, Columbus set sail across the Atlantic and did not fall off the edge of the earth. One can easily conjecture that without the printed word, the New World would not have been discovered.

The printed word also made possible the transfer of economic and commercial information necessary to the conduct of business. A new mercantile class arose, armed with information, to challenge the monopolies of the landed aristocracy. Out of the mercantile class came the middle class, which profoundly changed the economics and politics of Western civilization.

The printed word also brought about the political revolution that replaced monarchical and authoritarian governments with democracy and libertarianism. The printed word gave citizens access to information, and armed with the power of information, they could demand that governments serve their needs rather than the needs of the governors. These new revolutionary political ideas, culminating in the French and American revolutions, probably had their most succinct expression in the Declaration of Independence, which Thomas Jefferson penned to justify the

[2] George Will, "Luther's Quest," *Washington Post*, Nov. 10, 1983, p. A21.

[Vol. IX.] [Numb 429]

THE
INDEPENDENT CHRONICLE.
AND
THE
UNIVERSAL ADVERTISER.

THURSDAY, NOVEMBER 7, 1776.

MASSACHUSETTS-STATE:
POWARS AND WILLIS,

BOSTON: PRINTED BY
Opposite the NEW Court-House.

From the PENNSYLVANIA JOURNAL, Octo. 9.

The CONSTITUTION, of the COMMON-WEALTH of PENNSYLVANIA, as established by the GENERAL CONVENTION, elected for that purpose, and held at PHILADELPHIA, July 15th, 1776, and continued by adjournments to September 28, 1776.

WHEREAS all government ought to be instituted and supported for the security and protection of the community as such, and to enable the individuals who compose it to enjoy their natural rights, and the other blessings which the author of existence has bestowed upon man; and whenever these great ends of government are not obtained, the people have a right by common consent, to change it, and take such measures as to them may appear necessary to promote their safety and happiness. AND WHEREAS the inhabitants of this Common-Wealth have, in consideration of protection only, heretofore acknowledged allegiance to the King of Great Britain, and the said King has not only withdrawn that protection, but commenced and still continues to carry on, with unabated vengeance, a most cruel and unjust war against them, employing therein not only the troops of Great Britain, but foreign mercenaries, savages, and slaves, for the avowed purpose of reducing them to a total and abject submission to the despotic domination of the British Parliament, with many other acts of tyranny, (more fully set forth in the declaration of Congress) whereby all allegiance and fealty to the said King and his successors are dissolved and at an end, and all power and authority derived from him ceased in these Colonies. AND WHEREAS it is absolutely necessary for the welfare and safety of the inhabitants of said Colonies, that they be henceforth free and independent States, and that just, permanent, and proper Forms of Government exist in every part of them, derived from, and founded on the authority of the people only, agreeable to the directions of the honorable American Congress. WE, the representatives of the Freemen of Pennsylvania, in General Convention met, for the express purpose of framing such a Government, consulting the goodness of the great Governor of the Universe (who alone knows to what degree of earthly happiness mankind may attain by perfecting the arts of Government) in permitting the people of this State, by common consent, and without violence, deliberately to form for themselves such just rules as they shall think best for governing their future society; and being fully convinced that it is our indispensable duty to establish such original principles of Government as will best promote the general happiness of the people of this State and their posterity, and provide for future improvements, without partiality for, or prejudice against any particular class, sect, or denomination of men whatever, DO, by virtue of the authority vested in us by our constituents, ordain, declare, and establish the following Declaration of Rights and Frame of Government, to be THE CONSTITUTION of this Common-Wealth, and to remain in force therein forever, unaltered, except in such articles as shall hereafter on experience be found to require improvement, and which shall by the same authority of the people, fairly delegated as in this Frame of Government directs, be amended or improved for the more effectual obtaining and securing THE GREAT END AND DESIGN OF ALL GOVERNMENT, herein before mentioned.

CHAPTER I.

A DECLARATION of the Rights of the Inhabitants of the State of PENNSYLVANIA.

I. THAT all men are born equally free and independent, and have certain natural, inherent and unalienable rights, amongst which are the enjoying and defending life and liberty, acquiring, possessing and protecting property, and pursuing and obtaining happiness and safety.

II. That all men have a natural and unalienable right to worship Almighty GOD, according to the dictates of their own consciences and understanding: And that no man ought or of right can be compelled to attend any religious worship, or erect or support any place of worship, or maintain any ministry, contrary to, or against, his own free will and consent: Nor can any man, who acknowledges the being of a GOD, be justly deprived or abridged of any civil right as a citizen, on account of his religious sentiments or peculiar mode of religious worship. And that no authority can or ought to be vested in, or assumed by, any power whatever, that shall in any case interfere with, or in any manner controul, the right of conscience in the free exercise of religious worship.

III. That the people of this State have the sole, exclusive and inherent right of governing and regulating the internal police of the same.

IV. That all power being originally inherent in, and consequently derived from, the People, therefore all officers of Government, whether legislative or executive, are their trustees and servants, and at all times accountable to them.

V. That Government is, or ought to be, instituted for the common benefit, protection and security of the people, nation or community; and not for the particular emolument or advantage of any single man, family or set of men who are a part only of that community. And that the community hath an indubitable, unalienable and indefeasible right to reform, alter or abolish Government in such manner as shall be by that community judged most conducive to the public weal.

VI. That those who are employed in the legislative and executive business of the State may be restrained from oppression, the people have a right, at such periods as they may think proper, to reduce their public officers to a private station, and supply the vacancies by certain and regular elections.

VII. That all elections ought to be free; and that all free men having a sufficient evident common interest with, and attachment to the community, have a right to elect officers, or be elected into office.

VIII. That every member of society hath a right to be protected in the enjoyment of life, liberty and property, and therefore is bound to contribute his proportion towards the expence of that protection, and yield his personal service, when necessary, or an equivalent thereto: But no part of a man's property can be justly taken from him, or applied to public uses, without his own consent, or that of his legal representatives: Nor can any man who is conscientiously scrupulous of bearing arms, be justly compelled thereto, if he will pay such equivalent: Nor are the people bound by any laws, but such as they have in like manner assented to, for their common good.

IX. That in all prosecutions for criminal offences, a man hath a right to be heard by himself and his council, to demand the cause and nature of his accusation, to be confronted with the witnesses, to call for evidence in his favour, and a speedy public trial, by an impartial jury of the country, without the unanimous consent he cannot be found guilty. Nor can he be compelled to give evidence against himself: Nor can any man be justly deprived of his liberty, except by the laws of the land or the judgment of his peers.

X. That the people have a right to hold themselves, their houses, papers and possessions free from search or seizure, and therefore warrants without oaths or affirmations first made, affording a sufficient foundation for them, and whereby any officer or messenger may be commanded or required to search suspected places, or to seize any person or persons, his or their property, not particularly described, are contrary to that right, and ought not to be granted.

XI. That in all controversies respecting property and in suits between man and man, the parties have a right to trial by jury, which ought to be held sacred.

XII. That the people have a right to freedom of speech, and of writing and publishing their sentiments, therefore the freedom of the press ought not to be restrained.

XIII. That the people have a right to bear arms for the defence of themselves and the State; and as standing armies, in time of peace, are dangerous to liberty, they ought not to be kept up: And that the military should be kept under strict subordination to, and governed by, the civil power.

XIV. That a frequent recurrence to the fundamental principles, and a firm adherence to justice, moderation, temperance, industry, and frugality, are absolutely necessary to preserve the blessings of liberty, and keep a Government free: The people ought therefore to pay particular attention to these points, in the choice of officers and representatives, and have a right to exact a due and constant regard to them, from their legislators and magistrates in the making and executing such laws as are necessary for the good Government of the State.

XV. That all men have a natural inherent right to emigrate from one State to another that will receive them, or to form a new State in vacant countries, or in such countries as they can purchase, whenever they think that thereby they may promote their own happiness.

XVI. That the people have a right to assemble together, to consult for their common good, to instruct their representatives, and to apply to the legislature for redress of grievances, by address, petition or remonstrance.

CHAPTER II.

PLAN or FRAME of GOVERNMENT.

Section 1. THE Common-Wealth or State of Pennsylvania shall be governed hereafter by an Assembly of the Representatives of the Freemen of the same, and the President and Council, in manner and form following—

Sect. 2. The supreme legislative power shall be vested in a House of Representatives of the Freemen of the Common-Wealth or State of Pennsylvania.

Sect. 3. The supreme executive power shall be vested in a President and Council.

Sect. 4. Courts of Justice shall be established in the city of Philadelphia and in every county of this State.

Sect. 5. The Freemen of this Common-Wealth and their sons shall be trained and armed for its defence, under such regulations, restrictions and exceptions as the General Assembly shall by law direct, preserving always to the people the right of chusing their Colonel and all commissioned officers under that rank in such manner and as often as by the said laws shall be directed.

Sect. 6. Every freeman of the full age of twenty-one years, having resided in this State for the space of one whole year next before the day of election for Representatives, and paid public taxes during that time, shall enjoy the right of an elector: Provided always, that sons of freeholders of the age of twenty-one years shall be entitled to vote although they have not paid taxes.

Sect. 7. The House of Representatives of the Freemen of this Common-Wealth shall consist of persons most noted for wisdom and virtue, to be chosen by the Freemen of every city and county of this Common-Wealth respectively. And no person shall be elected unless he has resided in the city or county for which he shall be chosen, two years immediately before the said election; nor shall any member while he continues such, hold any other office except in the militia.

Sect. 8. No person shall be capable of being elected a member to serve in the House of Representatives of the Freemen of this Common-Wealth more than four years in seven.

Sect. 9. The members of the House of Representatives shall be chosen annually by ballot by the freemen of the Common-Wealth, on the second Tuesday

In the events that led up to the Revolutionary War, newspaper media played a critical role in consolidating Colonial opinion behind the need and desire to establish an independent American nation. (New York Public Library Picture Collection.)

withdrawal of the thirteen colonies from the control of the British monarchy.

Indeed, without mass media, America as we know it would not exist. It was the printed word—broadside and pamphlet—that induced masses of Europeans to emigrate to the New World. Without colonial weekly newspapers, as Arthur M. Schlesinger, Jr., argues in his *Prelude to Independence*, the war against the British Crown would probably not have been fought or, if fought, would probably not have been successful. He quotes David Ramsey: "In establishing American Independence, the pen and the press had a merit equal to that of the sword."[3]

From the founding of the country to the present day, mass media have played an important role in nearly all the important events of the nation. Antislavery publications like *Uncle Tom's Cabin* did much to foment the Civil War, as did the newspaper editorials of Horace Greeley and James Gordon Bennett. William Randolph Hearst's sensational headlines helped spark the Spanish-American War. Crusading newspaper and magazine reporters and editors at the turn of the century—the so-called muckrakers—brought much-needed political reform and social legislation to America.

In the twentieth century electronic media added their impact to the printed word, and mass media became big business. In October 1969 George Gerbner, dean of the Annenberg School of Communication at the University of Pennsylvania, stated in testimony before the National Commission on the Causes and Prevention of Violence:

> In only two decades of massive national existence television has transformed the political life of the nation, has changed the daily habits of our people, has molded the style of the generation, made overnight global phenomena out of local happenings, redirected the flow of information and values from traditional channels into centralized networks reaching into every home. In other words, it has profoundly affected what we call the process of socialization, the process by which members of our species become human.

MEDIA AND THE THREE STAGES OF MAN

One of Harold Innis's students was Marshall McLuhan, a scholar of English literature who was much influenced by Innis's ideas about the impact of media on culture and society. McLuhan startled and inspired the intellectual world of the mid-twentieth century with his ideas that media are more important than the messages they carry. The "medium is the message," he declared, and that single phrase reshaped much of our thinking about the impact of mass communication.

McLuhan meant that the medium shapes the message and the audience because it alters the way in which messages are perceived by audiences.

[3] Arthur M. Schlesinger, *Prelude to Independence* [a study of Colonial American newspapers] (New York: Alfred Knopf, 1957), 13.

The dominant medium of any society shapes the thought processes of that society and molds its culture. McLuhan suggested that human history can be divided into three great stages, each caused by the dominant medium of the time.

In the first stage, the pre-alphabet, prewritten language age, people lived in acoustic space. They knew only what they could hear and see in their immediate environment. Their world was small and tribal, governed by the group's emotions of the moment, a world of mystery and communal participation. Even today, in the few primitive societies that remain on earth, where there is no written or mass communication, the inhabitants live in a culture of good and evil spirits rather than laws, of feeling and emotion rather than ideas and information.

The second great stage was marked by the development of an alphabet, forcing people to think in logical terms. The development of writing as the dominant mode of communication made people think in a linear, connected, and continuous fashion. One could think for oneself, become an individual separate from the tribe, develop a rational universe, governed by laws based on logic, and a logical pattern of thought that could lead to science, invention, technology, an industrial society, the assembly line and mass production.

The third great stage, according to McLuhan, came with the development of the electric media, starting with the telegraph in the nineteenth century. The electric media changed the linear way of thinking, making the aural and tactile senses important again in the perception of messages. High-speed information, sent far distances by means of electronic waves, are changing our sense of time and space, reasoned McLuhan.

This third stage could be the most revolutionary. The electronic media may well be changing not only our perceptions but our thought patterns, our lifestyles, our values, and even the way we govern ourselves. With electronic media, for example, we can slow down or speed up reality and thus change our perceptions of what is taking place. We can slow down the process of a drop of water falling into a glass and observe the spire of water that rises as a result, with a small ball on the top. That scene would never be observable to the naked eye. The electronic media can give us "instant replay," allowing us to observe a football play, for example, from many different angles, in slow motion or fast motion, allowing us to see things that we never knew about.

In fact, football is a good example of a sport that is uniquely suited to color television. And baseball is a sport uniquely suited to printed newspapers. Baseball is a linear sport; one thing happens at a time; The pitcher winds up and then throws the ball; the batter swings, hits the ball, runs to first base, then to second, third, and home, all in a logical and rational sequence. Baseball is a perfect newspaper sport because it can be written about in a logical, linear manner, even with a "line score" that denotes the progress of the game in a sequential manner. Football, on the other hand, is more explosive than linear. Literally dozens of things happen at once. Each of the 22 men on the playing field has his own assignment on any given play. It would be impossible to do football complete justice by writing about it in the old-fashioned newspaper style. Television, on the other hand, can use a variety of cameras to capture the explosion of action, with instant replay, from different angles, reverse angles, zooms, stills, and slow motion. Baseball might have been America's national sport during its newspaper days of the mid-nineteenth to the mid-twientieth century, but in the age of television, football seems much more appropriate as a national passion.

Television seems to be involved in many changes that have occurred in our society in the last decades of the twentieth century. Some examples would be civil rights, women's rights, sexual rights, government, politics, and even war.

CIVIL RIGHTS AND MASS MEDIA

If you are white, compare your feelings about blacks with those of your parents and grandparents. If you are black, how does your self-concept differ from that of your parents and grandparents? The TV spectacle "Roots" opened the eyes of many white Americans and encouraged black Americans to take pride in their African heritage. "Roots" was light-years away from the slave images in *Birth of a Nation* and *Gone with the Wind*. Film and other mass media reflect the times in which they are made as much as the historical period they cover. Media are both agents of change and reflections of what society wants to believe at a particular time. Political–economic groups who control the media can also control the images on the screen.

The past three decades have been a "30 years' war" for civil rights, and mass media have been major weapons. Events in the news and entertainment media have become the conscience of America. Covert discrimination may continue in our society; lynchings, segregated public facilities, and attacks on peaceful demonstrators are gone because the media exposed them.

Television was the major news instrument used by black Americans to carry their grievances to the American body politic. Events—parades, speeches, protests, sit-ins, marches, freedom rides—were staged for the media and the white power structure.

A blossoming TV news industry was ready to bring dramatic events into 8 of every 10 American homes when a black woman, Rosa Parks, refused to surrender her seat on a Montgomery, Alabama, bus to a white man. The Montgomery bus boycott was one of the first successful mass challenges to public segregation. It also produced a black leader for the news media, especially for television. The Reverend Martin Luther King, Jr., was a master propagandist. His low-key, reasoned, Gandhi-inspired approach to nonviolent protest was perfect for the news. Television helped make Dr. King a symbol of change.

Civil rights marchers, led by Dr. Martin Luther King, Jr., waving at right center with his wife to the right, move on to the capitol at Montgomery, Alabama (March 25, 1965). To the left of King is Dr. Ralph Bunche, another Nobel Peace Prize winner. (AP/Wide World Photos.)

Because the media often deal in stereotypes and power symbols, Martin Luther King was essential as a symbol for black progress in a white society. Only Dr. King's objection to this country's Vietnam policy (before it became popular to object) cast a negative shadow on his media standing as a symbol of the need for black progress.

Because civil rights protests were covered by the media, the federal government as well as the people of America was moved to action in the 1960s. A protest is worthless unless the people and the power structure know that it is happening. The "freedom rides" of the Congress of Racial equality (CORE); the marches of the Southern Christian Leadership Conferences (SCLC); the manifestos, posturings, and programs of the Black Panthers; the urban riots in Harlem, Watts, Newark, and Detroit—mass media highlighted them and pressured politicians to act.

Murdered whites and blacks, and ultimately the murdered Dr. King, became martyrs under the glare of television. The violence of riots and the senseless stupidity of beatings and killings were given full media treatment. The civil rights movement was a media movement; and because of news coverage, civil rights legislation was passed. The media could focus society's attention on events and make visible the cancer of a racist society.

The entertainment industry (sound recording, motion pictures, and television) was also involved. The blatant racism of *The Wooing and Wed-*

Lou Gossett's portrayal of a tough army drill sargeant in *An Officer and a Gentleman* earned him an Academy Award for Best Actor in a Supporting Role. (Photo: Movie Star News, Courtesy Paramount Pictures.)

ding *of a Coon*, the "Sambo" and "Rastus" series, *The Nigger,* and *The Birth of a Nation* were supplanted in the 1920s and 1930s by black "fools" and "mammys." The tragedy of such great talents as Stepin Fetchit, Willie Best, and Mantan Moreland was not that they played buffoons but that these were the only roles available to them and the only blacks that movie audiences saw. With a few notable exceptions (e.g., *Hallelujah, Heart in Dixie, Green Pastures,* and *Cabin in the Sky),* the screen was lily white. Few white Americans knew that a black B-film industry was flourishing under the talents of Oscar Micheaux and other independents throughout the 1940s.

The watershed year for black images in white media was 1949, when four problem films were released: *Home of the Brave, Lost Boundaries, Pinky,* and *Intruder in the Dust.* This last film is notable as the first Hollywood portrayal of an independent black man. In the 1950s one black star, Sidney Poitier, saved dozens of whites and emerged as a visible hero and improved white impressions of blacks. He is the first and only black to win an Academy Award for best actor (in *Lilies of the Field).* By the mid-1960s, the "age of Poitier" had paved the way for a number of black talents, including Lou Gossett who won an Academy Award for Best Supporting Actor in *An Officer and a Gentleman.*

An economically viable black urban audience made it possible for "black exploitation" films to emerge. The superbad heros of *Shaft*, *Superfly*, and *The Legend of Nigger Charlie* were important because black talent was providing black entertainment for black audiences. The 1970s produced a number of quality films—*Sounder*, *Lady Sings the Blues*, *Conrack*, *Claudine*, *Mahogany*, *The Wiz*, *Blue Collar*—some of which centered on black living conditions in America, by both black and white directors.

A TV breathrough came in 1965. After a virtual "whiteout" since the early 1950s, Bill Cosby starred in "I Spy." Cosby proved that black stars could attract high ratings, and he won two Emmy awards doing it. Many TV shows have featured black characters; and such shows as "Sanford and Son" and "The Jeffersons" point to the acceptance of a black style on television. "Julia," an often maligned series that starred Diahann Carroll, was important because it offered the example of a black professional woman making it in a white man's world. "The A Team," one of the most successful TV shows, features a black character, Mr. T, who has become an international star. Also, Nell in "Gimme a Break" symbolized the emerging black identity on television.

In the late 1970s "Roots" and "Roots II" validated early breakthroughs. The public acceptance of "Roots" was evidenced by the highest ratings ever achieved by any program to that time. The combined miniseries dealt with many issues that just a few years earlier would have been impossible.

The key in both motion pictures and television was the presence of blacks in the shows and their acceptance by white audiences in a wide variety of roles. Blacks were no longer invisible. They lived and breathed and were heroes and villains. It was not a revolution, but it was a step forward; and the entertainment media were a part of the process of change.

Black ownership of broadcasting stations started to increase in the 1970s, and black radio has become a viable instrument in the advertising marketplace. In addition, special-interest magazines such as *Ebony*, *Essence*, *Black Enterprise*, and *Players* have continued to serve black readers. More job opportunities in all phases of the communication industry have also opened for blacks.

Perhaps in no other medium does black artistic input dominate as it does in the recording industry. Traditionally the entertainment entry point for blacks, records made by blacks now reach most white home audiences. In the 1980s, Michael Jackson, a black singer, has emerged as one of the most successful recording artists in history.

In all media, the fact that blacks appear as part of "the system" is a major change of the past 20 years. Tokenism still exists in mass media, but affirmative action is becoming a reality.

Without mass media, the progress made in civil rights may still have occurred, but not with the speed and impact that it did. Mass media have access to, and influence on, the power elites of this society. The media have challenged the old saw that you cannot legislate cultural change. Mass media have not done it on their own, but attitudes and behaviors have changed on racial issues because of what all of us read, heard, and saw in the media.

Mass media are in the process of overhauling their presentation of women in America. It is fruitless to argue over whether mass media changed society's attitudes toward women or whether a changed society modified the media's portrayal of women. The best approach may be to accept the fact that a vital interaction took place. Most assuredly, a relationship exists between how men and women view themselves and one another and what media culture holds up as role models. **WOMEN'S RIGHTS**

For the most part, the women's movement has made better use of print media than it has of electronic media. Women have had easier access to print, print costs are lower and offer a wider range of media vehicles, and more women are trained to write than are trained to use radio–television–film. Books and magazines have been by far the most successful information and propaganda instruments of feminists.

Simone de Beauvoir's *The Second Sex*, Betty Freidan's *The Feminine Mystique*, Kate Millett's *Sexual Politics*, magazines such as *Ms.* and *Working Woman*, and myraid other media vehicles were involved in observing, redefining, and advocating new roles for women in society. Even such traditional magazines as *Cosmopolitan*, *Redbook*, and *Woman's Day* have moved in new directions. Counterproposals to women's liberation ideas have also been mounted in the print media, most notably *The Total Woman*, which advocates a more conservative approach to male-female relationships.

The news media have assisted and resisted women's groups when staged events and other protests have occurred. By any measure, women's rights events are covered more sparingly and less enthusiastically than were civil rights stories in the 1960s. This is in part because the women's movement is (a) *decentralized*, which makes it difficult for journalists to cover several groups that often seem to be at ideological odds; (b) *localized*, made up of essentially independent local groups so that the news media cannot always identify important issues; (c) *nonhierarchical*, which does not give media a leader to focus on; (d) *nonritualized*, so that mass media sometimes cover events that make "poor news," such as conferences, women's studies, and women's centers; and (e) *internally opposed*, with some women's groups in public opposition to the goals of the movement, for example, passage of the Equal Rights Amendment.

The most significant progress in electronic journalism has been the increasing numbers and responsibilities of newswomen. The cumulative effect of daily TV appearances by Barbara Walters, Catherine Mackin, Carol Simpson, Connie Chung, Nina Totenberg, and Jane Pauley on the

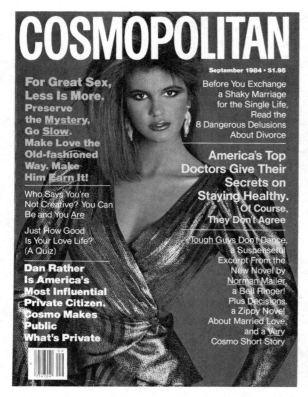

Even traditional women's magazines such as *Cosmopolitan* have been influenced by the expanding role of women in society and have evolved to reflect a more modern outlook. (Courtesy *Cosmopolitan,* The Hearst Corporation.)

Democratic Presidential Candidate Walter Mondale solicits campaign support at the National Organization for Women Convention (Miami, Florida, June 30, 1984). Mondale's choice of Geraldine Ferraro as Vice Presidential running mate did much to engratiate him with progressive women's groups.

The repeated television appearances of newswomen like Connie Chung have significantly affected the attitudes of men and women viewers on a wide range of issues.

(Photo courtesy of the National Broadcasting Company, Inc.)

news has been important in consciousness raising, and affects the attitudes of men as well as women on a wide range of issues.

Some of the better TV series in the early 1980s included "Kate and Allie," and the cancelled series "Cagney and Lacey," which a viewer letter-writing campaign succeeded in reinstating. These independent, bright women were a far cry from the earlier stereotypes of TV women in "I Love Lucy," "My Friend Irma," and "Father Knows Best." The new TV women could take care of themselves, and if they had to, could handle the bad guys in "Police Woman," the first successful adventure series with a woman (Angie Dickinson) in the title role. One of the biggest hits on television, now in syndication, "Charlie's Angels," stars rough-and-tumble beauties catered to by an affable male backup who is constantly in need of their help. This show's basis is sex, but it does present a new-for-television stereotype of women.

Even daytime soap operas and the TV commercials that sponsor them have changed their appeal for the stay-at-homes. The "soaps" are now peopled with career women involved in the business and professional worlds. Commercials project an image of women as attractive, childless, and wage earning, with male friends and husbands who are "liberated" as well as good-looking. Even if the TV characterizations of women have not come of age, signs of change exist. Women on television "have come a long way, baby."

In the motion-picture and sound-recording industries the opportunity to express opinions corresponds with the ability to sell tickets and records. No woman at present can patch the success of Barbra Streisand, an accomplished singer and actress who was also the executive producer of the rock remake of *A Star is Born*. Her dominance of that film and her performance of "The Woman in the Moon" is a political message as powerful as Helen Reddy's "I Am Woman." These songs may have had more cultural impact than the amateur "librock" bands of the 1960s because Streisand and Reddy reach audiences outside the women's movement. In the early 1980s, Streisand expanded her roles, becoming actress, composer, director, and producer of *Yentl*, a widely successful Hollywood film.

The very late 1970s and early 1980s saw the rebirth of "women's movies." The significant difference was that the women's roles included new stereotypes and themes that are traditionally the province of male stars. The films of Jane Fonda, including *Klute*, *Julia*, *The Electric Cowboy*, *9 to 5*, *Coming Home*, and *On Golden Pond*, displayed a broad range of heroines, many of whom deviated from older Hollywood types. Many strong roles—*Norma Rae* (Sally Field), *Coal Miner's Daughter* (Sissy Spacek), "The Women's Room" (Lee Remick), "Playing for Time" (Vanessa Redgrave), *Turning Point* (Anne Bancroft and Shirley McLaine), *Terms of Endearment* (Shirley MacLaine and Debra Winger) among others—offered feature films and TV films with fine women's parts.

The interpersonal group process has been central to the development of issues and platforms of the women's movement. For most women, the key means of dissemination in mass media was print. Although the electronic media as a whole have been less supportive of women's crusade for equality than they were in the quest of black Americans for civil rights, media images and media opportunities for women are growing at a rapid rate.

SEXUAL RIGHTS   The sexual revolution that has taken place in our society in the past 30 years was begun, as it was in the women's movement, not by the massive electronic media, but by the more specialized print media. But in both cases, and in the case of civil rights as well, the electronic media no doubt changed human perceptions of civil rights, women, and sex, to make possible the acceptance of the radical ideas espoused by the more specialized print media.

The sexual revolution really started with writers of books for very narrow and specialized audiences. Those notions of sexual freedom finally found their way into men's magazines that reached a national audience in *Playboy* magazine, started in the mid-1950s. The "Playboy philosophy" of sexual permissiveness and frank sexual pleasure had considerable influence on other magazines and books, but it did not creep into mass media such as newspapers, radio, television, or publicly shown motion pictures until a decade or two later. Even in the mid-1980s, the mass media—prime-time television, metropolitan newspapers, national news magazines—shy away from nudity and obscene language.

But these media have made a steady progression toward more sexual explicitness. In 1972 ABC produced a prime-time drama called "That Certain Summer," which examined a homosexual relationship. Yet it was not until 1980 that a sitcom, "Love, Sidney," could deal with homosexuality with some ease. In 1974 "A Case of Rape" was the first major TV drama to investigate that crime from a woman's point of view. It was not until October 1983 that a network soap opera, "All My Children," used a continuing character who was clearly lesbian. In 1983 NBC produced "Princess Daisy," a tentative look at a brother–sister sexual relationship. And in 1984, ABC produced a 2-hour drama, "Something about Amelia," which was the first frank and honest treatment on national prime-time television of an incestuous father–daughter relationship.

The gay rights movement has been largely confined to specialized print media. There are now newspapers and magazines that cater to gays. But most daily newspapers and national TV programs still treat the subject as an aberration in society, not as normal behavior. The film industry has produced some feature films with gay central characters—*Suddenly Last Summer, The Fox, The Boys in the Band, Reflections in a Golden Eye,*

The television treatment of an incestuous father–daughter relationship in "Something About Amelia" (1984) is evidence of the media's continuing progress in dealing frankly with sexual subject matter. (Photo courtesy the Leonard Goldberg Company.)

Fleeing a gang of assassins, and unaware that his companion is a man in woman's clothing, Walter (Gianrico Tondinelli) registers for a hotel room for himself and Albin (Michel Serrault) in *La Cage Aux Folles II*. (Photo: Movie Star News, Courtesy United Artists.)

Fortune and Men's Eyes, *The Ritz*, and *Outrageous*. But in most TV shows only a very infrequent episode alludes to "the problem." With the exception of "That Certain Summer," television has not concerned itself with the gay issue in any significant drama. A sizable portion of the specialized erotic film industry, however, does exploit this sexual preference in films produced for urban markets.

One of the major motion-picture hits of the 1970s was *La Cage Aux Folles*, a comedy about an aging gay couple. It was a major box-office success attracting largely "straight" audiences. It was so popular that *La Cage Aux Folles II* continued the gay escapades at movie houses around the world. The point was not that gay characters were everywhere on the screen, but that when the issue of homosexuality was presented, it no longer created a sensation. It was just a part of the media scene.

Perhaps no other current media issue carries the emotional impact for audiences as does the issue of gay rights. With increasing numbers of activists, the gay rights issue is bound to receive increasing coverage in mass media. Unlike resistance to civil rights and the women's movement, which is subtle and diffuse, open resistance to gay rights is a reality.

WAR AND POLITICS   Electronic communication has certainly changed the nature of both war and politics since the mid-twentieth century. War has now become a media event, covered in color video from helicopters as if it were a movie in the making.

Before the age of radio and television, coverage of warfare by the news media was limited to the printed word, which could be more controlled and was less vivid about the realities of war. Prior to the war in Vietnam, the U.S. government maintained wartime security measures over news dispatches that were sent from the front lines, and all news copy went through a government military review, a form of wartime censorship. Reports sent from the war front on this basis were usually carefully guarded and subdued, and as a result news readers never received the full gruesome details of war.

The war in Vietnam, however, was never officially declared as a war, so there were no official censorship procedures. In addition, TV networks had pressed very hard for free coverage of the war, and politicians needed television to deal with the American people. As a consequence, the war in Vietnam was the first to be reported, often live and in living color, without any government restraints on the coverage. For the first time, the American people could really see the gory details of war, and the government could not hide the futility of its efforts.

Without a doubt, TV coverage played a role in turning American opinion against the war in Vietnam, to such an extent that the government ultimately had to withdraw from the battle. Indeed, it may never again be possible to have a war such as the one in Vietnam as long as television is permitted to cover it freely and fully. So the nature of war will be changed as a result.

When Great Britain went to war with Argentina over ownership of the Falkland Islands in 1982, Prime Minister Margaret Thatcher kept the British news media away from the war zone, and so the battle could not be covered live. The British government reasoned that it would be easier to win the war without the "prying" press providing coverage that might stir up negative public opinion.

President Reagan followed the same procedure when the United States sent military forces onto the island of Grenada in 1983 to prevent Communists from gaining a stronghold in the Caribbean. American news media were not allowed to go ashore with the troops to cover the action, as the press had done in all previous wars. The White House felt it could bring the conflict to a speedier conclusion without the interference of journalists.

The British and the American governments succeeded in keeping the press out of those two engagements because they were short. If they had been long, drawn-out battles, the media and the public would no doubt have insisted on full coverage. The lessons that have been learned from all this, it seems, is that war can succeed if it amounts to quick skirmishes away from the limelight of media coverage. And wars of the future might be like that.

The electronic age has also spawned another kind of war—terrorism— where the terrorist strikes in order to gain national or international publicity for political purposes. The taking of American hostages in Iran was an example of terrorist action motivated by the interest in achieving worldwide publicity for Iran's anger at the United States. Individual terrorist acts, aimed at getting electronic coverage, have become all too common in the electronic age. An American military officer is kidnapped in Italy, not for financial ransom, but for political publicity. A radical hijacks an airplane full of civilian passengers, not to get a free ride to his destination, but to get reporters to give some coverage to his point of view. An elderly gentleman fills a van full of dynamite and drives it up to the Washington Monument, threatening to blow it up, not for some irrational or insane motive, but because he wants to warn the world of nuclear war.

As we saw in the chapter on public relations, the mass media have also changed the nature of American politics. In his book *Channels of Power*, Austin Ranney, former president of the American Political Science Association, examines the impact of television on American politics. Television does not necessarily depict reality, he writes, but TV's reality has become "the reality in politics." Television has reshaped American political culture, he says, weakening political parties, strengthening political candidates who have media charisma, weakening the presidency because the president is in the constant glare of TV's cameras, and strengthening the bureaucracy because it can hide from the publicity spotlight.[4]

The rise of investigative reporting, coupled with the impact of television, has made it more and more difficult for the government to behave in a manner that can be shown on television to be detrimental to the public interest. It is harder for the government to get away with graft and corruption, and it is also harder to establish policies that are not acceptable to the majority.

The most important example in recent years, of course, was the Watergate scandal. Two newspaper reporters, Carl Bernstein and Robert Woodward, will go down in history for their role in uncovering Richard Nixon's coverup of illegal activities in the White House. But the *Washington Post* did not bring about Nixon's resignation. Its reports of the Watergate affair brought the information to the attention of Congress, which, through its televised hearings, brought the scandal to the world. And Richard Nixon, certainly not the first American president to commit questionable or even illegal acts in office, became the first ever to resign.

---

[4] Austin Ranney, *Channels of Power* (New York: Basic Books, 1983).

MASS MEDIA AND   At the beginning of this chapter we raised a question about the role of
PUBLIC POLICY   mass media in social, political, economic, and cultural developments. It
seems clear that the mass media play an important role, even if we cannot
yet scientifically prove a cause-and-effect relationship. The power and
influence of mass media have made many individuals and groups cry out
for a new public policy of greater government control. The question of
mass media and public policy will be one of the most interesting and
pertinent debates of the last half of the 1980s.

There are results of this discussion will have far-reaching implications for
our children and grandchildren, for freedom, for democracy, and for the
quality of life. What we decide now about our mass media and public
policy may one day be as important to society as the decisions made 200
years ago by the founding fathers. The readers of this book will no doubt
be important in making those decisions.

There are many lessons that can come from the study of mass media
that you are now concluding. But perhaps the most important is this: We,
you and I, still control the mass media in our society. We make the final
determination about what we want to read, view, or hear. And as long as
there are options, then we can make a free choice. We must learn to use
those choices well. The mass communication industry is still only what
we allow it to be. It can and does influence us, but by making choices in
the open marketplace of media, we can determine which of the media
will succeed by serving us well, and which will fail. Increasingly, however, our society will have to be educated about mass media in order to
make the right choices.

The great British writer, H. G. Wells, put it aptly when he said: "History
is becoming more and more a race between education and catastrophe."
Perhaps of all the things we need to study to avoid that catastrophe, mass
media have become most important.

Your Future in Mass Communication 29

Most introductory mass media textbooks, including the previous edition of this one, incorporate chapters on the future of mass media and careers in mass communication. These two chapters are logical ways to conclude an introductory study of mass communication; yet, in reflecting on the content of the chapters it is clear that careers *in* and the future *of* mass communication are closely intertwined. Essentially, your career in mass communication *is* the future, and the future represents *your* career. Subsequently, we have chosen to integrate these two areas and, in attempting to glimpse into mass media's future, to provide some insights into your future as well.

John Naisbitt, in his best-selling book *Megatrends*, identifies 10 megatrends that he believes are reshaping our society and the world. The most important of these—in fact, the other nine are consequences of the first—is that we are in a "megashift" from an industrial to an information-based society. Naisbitt points out that currently only 13% of the U.S. work force is employed in manufacturing, whereas more than 60% either produces or processes information. As a result, one of the major consequences of this megatrend is Naisbitt's "megatrend 5," which posits the idea that our centralized structures are crumbling and that we are becoming increasingly decentralized in everything from manufacturing to political power to national policies to mass media. Naisbitt says that, today, people can start an information business with a telephone and a typewriter or computer terminal. This decentralization trend will affect our mass media as well. For example, the national TV networks, according to Naisbitt, will become the *Life, Look,* and *Saturday Evening Post* of the future as specialized cable television and local programming proliferate. As a result, your career possibilities in mass communication will be altered and expanded. The time of simply moving from one closed system (college–university) to another (network–station–newspaper) is fast coming to an end. Your career(s) in mass communication will require a more individual entrepreneurial approach, which in turn will require a more individual and broadly based educational foundation. In this sense, you must clearly be *educated for success* as well as *trained for access.* You must not only *acquire* certain skills and knowledge, you must *inquire* about the world in which you will be a part.

CAREERS AND EDUCATION

Therefore, before surveying the brave new world of communication and your particular future in it, it is necessary to look at your preparation for this future from an admittedly philosophical point of view. Just as we will not attempt, in true "megatrend style," to provide a nuts-and-bolts view of the future of mass communication, we will also try not to outline specific courses or plans of study for your consideration. Rather, you should consider the following as a megatrend approach to communication education that attempts to *describe* rather than *proscribe* an approach to career preparation.

For many people, a career in communication is a fantasy come true. Visions of big cars, big houses, and big bank accounts dominate many students' perceptions and ideas about working in the media.

This road to success is paved with stories of starlets being discovered in drugstore soda fountains, college sophomores having a script from their writing class accepted by "Hill Street Blues," and rookie reporters breaking another Watergate story. Unfortunately, the reality of a communication career differs significantly from the illusion created by the "immediate success" myth that is so prevalent today, as illustrated by this actual position announcement.

	ANNOUNCER/ENGINEER
Job Description:	Read commercials, play records, tapes, cart-tridges; operate audio console and announce musical selections. Part-Time, Regular – 20 hours/week.
Job Requirements:	Restricted Radiotelephone Operator Permit (FCC required). High school education or equi-valnt, some communication course work de-sired. Audition and broadcast experience re-quired. Audio production skills. Knowledge of FCC rules and regulations. Must be available nights, weekends and holidays.
Hiring Range:	$9,492 – $11,500 (annualized)

Further evidence of the financial realities of a communications career is found in the latest RTNDA survey of weekly news salaries.

Highlights of the survey:
■ A station's highest paid reporter made 4% more than a year earlier. The median for 1983 was $365 weekly in television, $250 in radio.
■ TV news director's salaries showed a median of $225 a week, up 6%; for radio news directors the typical figure was $275, unchanged from 1982.
■ Not surprisingly, TV anchors fared best on payday with a median $600 a week in mid-1983, 11% more then a year earlier. However, in the top 25 markets that median was $1,255. Also, "star pay" in radio news was much less than television: The median for the highest paid newscaster/anchor at radio stations was $275, 6% above 1982.

Weekly news salaries in 1983 and percentage increase

	Television				Radio			
	Median	Up	Mean	Up	Median	Up	Mean	Up
Staff low	$225	10%	$237	6%	$225	7%	$253	10%
Cameramen	265	2	301	1	NA	NA	NA	NA
News producer	340	NA	361	NA	NA	NA	NA	NA
Top producer	385	NA	412	NA	NA	NA	NA	NA
Reporters	300	NA	352	NA	224	NA	258	NA
Top reporter	365	4	448	12	250	4	288	7
Anchors	450	NA	564	NA	250	NA	296	NA
Top anchor	600	11	809	15	275	6	331	6
News director	600	6	675	13	275	0	336	3

Understanding this reality begins with education.

Communication education has a responsibility to provide job-related tools and skills that allow graduates to enter professional communication fields successfully with a minimum of retraining or reeducation by employers. However, communication education cannot simply be a farm system for the broadcaster, film producer, or newspaper publisher. It also has the responsibility to educate students for success, to prepare them for change and growth in their lives and careers.

In this sense, communication education must develop professionals who understand both the internal and external rewards of a career in communication. Too often, aspiring communication professionals have their vision of a career clouded by much-publicized external-reward factors such as a *Time* magazine profile of Dan Rather as the "$8 million man." If they read the article closely, however, they will find that the internal satisfaction of doing the best job possible, of still being "turned on" by the process of reporting the news, is also a strong ingredient in Dan Rather's success.

While job-related skills are important, the communication major must be exposed to and incorporate other necessary components of an education, the most significant being ideas, attitudes, and values. Nothing changes as quickly as technology; to learn equipment and not ideas is fatal. And it is not enough simply to learn ideas without developing attitudes and values. Too often, students learn only data when, ultimately, the career skills most necessary to success—the ability to conceptualize data, to make conclusions about concepts, and finally to form judgments—are left to some vague form of osmosis. The goal of a professional communication education should be to develop the whole person; to provide the skills necessary for effective job performance, but also to educate students in the broader tradition of becoming media professionals. Communication education's responsibility is to facilitate the process of self-discovery in which students understand and incorporate not only data but also attitudes and values regarding their careers and lives. The quote below illustrates the potential trap of technology and reinforces the importance of the educated communicator.

Students reply to this message that "it's scary out there" and that they need all the tools and skills employers demand. However, it's always been scary "out there." It was scary in the 1930s, when thousands of the best college graduates could aspire to nothing higher than a day shift at the post office or teaching elementary school; it was scary in the war years, when leaving college meant that someone might soon be shooting at you.

"This instrument can teach, it can illuminate; yes, and it can even inspire. But it can do so only to the extent that humans are determined to use it to those ends.

Otherwise it is merely lights and wires in a box." Edward R. Murrow

One way of looking at this process of self-discovery can be found in *Zen and the Art of Motorcycle Maintenance* by Robert Pirsig. In the book Pirsig talks a great deal about form and essence in life. Motorcycles, according to Pirsig, can be talked about in terms of immediate appearance but also discussed in terms of their underlying essence. We discuss the hows, whats, and whens of motorcycles, but too often we fail to discuss the whys. Pirsig's concept of form and essence is very applicable when you look at other forms of technology, especially in mass communication. We can easily become terrorized by the forms of technology. Opening up the hood of a car can be a psychologically damaging experience. The wires, tubes, knobs, and plugs can be totally confusing. But if you understand the essence of an engine, any engine, you can often get to the heart of the problem.

This is especially true when we consider mass communication as it exists today. What is happening in mass communication right now is a technological revolution not experienced since television came into being 40 years ago.

The new technology of mass communication is awesome, and the technological changes imploding on us are truly staggering. We are faced with the prospect not only of increased cable saturation and capacity but we also must learn to cope with satellites, videodiscs, video cassettes, computer-interactive video, two-way television, and talk-back. If we get caught up in the technology, in the forms of technology, we are going to be in the same bind as the person fixing a particular motorcycle—learning one form of motorcycle and then, 3 months later, when another form of motorcycle appears, being totally confused.

New technology is opening up new ways of looking at mass communication. It is altering and changing our methods of interacting with mass media, and unless we understand the essence of what technology is all about, unless we understand its origins and basic functions and not just the forms themselves, we will encounter significant problems.

It is a matter of form and essence, of understanding mass communication as process and not just performance. Mass communication involves performance, to be sure. Nevertheless, performance is only the tip of the iceberg, and unless we understand the process—the essence of mass communication—we aren't really going to understand the forms of technology that make this communication possible.

The essence of communication education, therefore, involves understanding that the new technologies are not simply new forms of communication; rather, they are changing the ways we interact with mass media. The essence of this change is that we are no longer simply passive consumers of whatever media give us—we are becoming active participants in media distribution, media exhibition, and even media production. Not only do we have more choices in terms of the selection of cable, videodiscs, and video cassettes, but we are interacting in different ways with these media. We talk back to them; we program them ourselves.

Newspapers do not rely exclusively on typewriters anymore. Glue pots are gone; editors are discarding their blue pencils. Instead, reporters type on video terminals, and that information is processed directly into typesetting machines so that the *Chicago Tribune*, for example, publishes basically a 24-hour edition: a rotating, evolving, continuing newspaper. The computer also changes the concept of what reporters do. They are no longer simply writers, translators of information upon which an editor passes judgment. Reporters are now involved in the judgment process because they make decisions on what information to enter into their terminals. What this means is that reporters who have not been trained to make news judgments are going to have problems.

All of this reinforces the understanding of mass communication as a process. It implies the idea of a progression of skills in communication education toward the goal of being able to make judgments; ultimately going beyond the "Ugh!" and "Wow!" response to life.

Communication education, therefore, must provide ITS—immediately transferable skills—but it also has the obligation to provide LAM—a liberal arts mentality. Certain journalism professionals are fond of saying that they don't really need journalism majors but prefer liberal arts majors such as English or history students. Many of these people are not being completely honest. These professionals do not want liberal arts majors. They want people who have immediately transferable skills (ITS) so that they do not have to retrain them in the tools and skills and styles their newspapers run by—but they *also* want people who have a liberal arts mentality (LAM). In other words, they would like a Bob Woodward and Carl Bernstein who can type 120 words a minute, take accurate notes, and make instant judgments.

Communication education, therefore, must go beyond training people for access, must go beyond training people for the forms that mass communication may take at the *Washington Post* or *Time* or NBC. It must provide people with the means to educate themselves for success, to develop a liberal arts mentality that takes them beyond specific entrance-level jobs and allows them to grow and change and develop into successful communication professionals.

SUCCESS AND CAREERS

How, then, do we define success? There are forms and essence to success as well. Dan Rather is successful, but too often we simply define his success by the salary he makes. A young communication graduate was quoted after he had just signed a $200,000 contract with a national network that "the money I am getting says they respect me. It also says that I deserve that respect." How naive. The money means very little to the network, where people are essentially commodities to be bought. In the whole sense of situational success, this person happened to be at a time and place where he was needed and therefore was worth $200,000. Money

JOHN DARLING by Armstrong & Batiuk

AND SO FOR SOMEONE PLANNING TO GO INTO COMMUNICATIONS, IT REQUIRES NOT ONLY A SOLID BACKGROUND IN JOURNALISM, BUT AN UNDERSTANDING OF THE VARIOUS TECHNICAL ASPECTS OF THE MEDIUM!

IN CLOSING I THINK THAT TELEVISION CAN PROVIDE A CHALLENGING, SATISFYING AND REWARDING CAREER! ARE THERE ANY QUESTIONS?

IS THE MONEY ANY GOOD?

(Copyright © News Group Chicago, Inc. Courtesy of News America Syndicate.)

is a form of success, but money does not imply respect. If respect is what you are looking for in terms of success, you have to go beyond money.

We wonder why $100,000-a-year advertising executives all of a sudden quit to run maple-syrup farms in Vermont. Well, perhaps they are going through a midlife crisis. What's a midlife crisis all about? Whether you're male or female, it means reevaluating the concepts and forms of success that you have achieved so far in your life, and saying, "Where am I?" or "What does that form mean?" or "I've got a big office, a title on the door, a Bigelow on the floor, but what does that particular form mean to me?" Unless the form translates itself into something more elemental, into, "Yes, I am pleased with what I am doing" or "I am happy where I am," that success doesn't mean much.

If you read Studs Terkel's book *Working*, you will find very good examples of people who have achieved a sense of harmony, who have achieved the essence of success in their lives whether they are waitresses or steel factory workers or advertising executives. In mass communication we often take the external forms of success as a measure of internal evaluation, a measure of where we are in life; and so it's one car, two cars, a Porsche, a Mercedes, and on and on it goes.

But what of the essence of success? How do you measure success? You're not an *A*, *B*, *C*, or *D*; you're not a 9 or 10. Those marks are simply measures of a specific task—your ability to memorize facts for a test or your ability to keep your hair and your body in shape. But such abilities no more define you than I suspect the word *conservative* defines Ronald Reagan. Success is self-defining; you assimilate it, you accumulate it, you reject what you feel is not an accurate measure. If an accurate measure for you is two cars or a big house, that's fine. But don't limit your definition of success by measuring your life and self-respect in terms of the money you are getting, regardless of what you have to do to get it.

The forms of success, accomplishment, and position are many. The essence of your communication career is how you feel about yourself and

COMMUNICATION AND CAREERS

how you measure and evaluate yourself against your own internal standards of success.

Now that we have explored some of the more philosophical foundations of communication education and careers, let us examine some of the forms these careers are developing in the mid-1980s.

The *New York Times* reported at the start of the decade that the 1980s would be "heady times for communication-related industries." They pointed out that the public's increasing need for information coupled with the emergence of new technological tools to transmit information would result in more career opportunities in communication.

It seems clear that the *Times* was correct in its assessment of the situation. Career opportunities in communication are expanding rapidly, but the directions these opportunities are taking are increasingly nontraditional. To be sure, there are jobs for newspaper reporters, radio announcers, and film directors. These traditional sources of communication employment have limited growth potential, however,. It is in corporate and industrial communication, cable programming, interactive video instruction, advertising, and public relations that the real growth in communication employment is occurring.

As new and existing media are capable of transmitting more and more information, the need to decode, organize, and communicate this information in a wide variety of occupations has become critical. Art museums, for example, can no longer afford simply to exist in a physical sense. A building by itself is not going to deliver the kinds of messages museum directors want the public to hear. Museums have found it necessary to communicate an emotional and intellectual presence that transcends architecture professionals. The role of public relations in creating and maintaining a certain image for museums and such related artistic clusters as symphony orchestras and opera and ballet companies has become essential for success, and in many cases, for survival.

This is but one example of the expanding careers that are available to communication majors. There are few common points of reference for many of these positions except that they all require people who can communicate with professional skill. They require the ability to analyze, organize, write, speak, and use media effectively. However, there are a few trends that indicate future directions for mass communication, and these trends may guide you in your search for both the form and essence of a career.

FUTURE TRENDS

In general, we prefer personal communication to mass communication. We want to see and touch when we communicate. We want messages that are personal, that are directed to us as individuals, that come from communicators who understand our personal needs. Our spending on personal communication through the mail and over the telephone is increasing at a faster rate than our spending on mass communication.

One reason for the increase in personalized communication is the growing need for special information. As our world becomes more complex, we must use more specialists, each providing more and more information about a narrower and narrower field of expertise. The mass media predominantly provide general information for a general audience, and so we are turning increasingly to specialized media. The new technologies are making it possible to produce personalized and specialized messages on a mass basis.

In Arthur Smith's study of newspapers in the 1980s, *Goodbye Gutenberg*, he shows that the changing production technology will make the newspaper a much more personal medium. He predicts that by 1990 newspaper publishers will find their readers looking to new systems for specialist and semispecialist offerings. One way or another, Smith writes, the traditional mass audience for newspapers will break up. Selection, not "passive acceptance," will slice the market into smaller and smaller bits.

Alvin Toffler, author of *Future Shock* and *The Third Wave*, predicts that the 1980s will see the emergence of a new kind of consumer, a new kind of marketplace, and a new system of mass media to connect the two. He describes a de-massified world where ideas, media, and advertising are dismantled from a mass orientation into segments, regions, and localities. New technology, he predicts, will make small production runs profitable, while the greatly shortened distribution channels will make locally produced products price competitive and eventually cheaper than nationally distributed products, especially as energy costs climb.

Toffler says this will bring about the end of the national advertising campaign. The United States has already moved part of the way from a national marketplace; what we have is a collection of regional economies that are increasingly disparate. In fact, each is as large now as the national economy was 30 to 40 years ago.

Even smaller, more discrete, target audiences are being assembled. In the case of the housewife, a combination of cable television, supermarket scanners and computers can be used by information gathering firms to identify her viewing and buying habits. The information can be stored and interpreted, analyzed by the computer, then distributed to whomever is willing to pay for it—marketing executives, politicians, etc.

One of these information gathering services is Information Resources, Inc., which tracks the buying and viewing habits of 15,000 women in six small U.S. cities. The women are volunteers who allow microcomputers to be attached to their television sets and who shop at markets specially equipped with scanning devices to record purchases. With the data they collect the IRI company claims that they can predict with 95% accuracy what products will sell successfully and which ads will be most effective. Its clients include such companies as General Foods, Campbell's Soup, and Quaker Oats. IRI also tells television advertisers which programs their buyers watch. On 11 February 1983, IRI found that 46% of the Heinz ketchup buyers watched the fifth installment of the TV movie, *Winds of*

War. Chairman John Malec said, "Imagine the millions of dollars to be saved through the efficiency of advertising to the right audience." He thinks the revolution has just begun, that the different demographic segments can someday be identified. And when a commercial television break comes on, the high income group could be sent a high-income type ad and the low income group a low-income type ad.

The Computer The main technological component in the future of mass communication is the computer. The computer is essential to the revolution that is enveloping mass communication. The first computer, built in 1951, had about the same power as your pocket calculator, and it cost millions. Today's computers are far more powerful, much smaller and more compact, and cost pennies by comparison.

Newspapers have already been revolutionized by computers and electronics, and this trend will continue. As we saw in earlier chapters, most newspapers now use computers to automate many of the functions of composition and printing and to store and retrieve material for editorial and advertising content. Most newspapers have already moved away from the use of typewriters to produce written copy. Instead, reporters prepare their copy on a video display terminal that has a keyboard similar to a typewriter and a video screen similar to a TV set. The words appear on a screen instead of on paper. The words can be changed and edited on the screen by an editor. And when they are in final form, the words can be transmitted to and stored in the computer; the computer can automatically set the words in type, in any type size, typeface, and line length desired.

Newspapers will soon turn to computers and electronics to deliver the paper as well as process the news and publish it. Several systems are already perfected and should be in wide use within a decade.

Specialization and personalization are especially important to the future of magazines and books. Like newspapers, magazines and books will turn increasingly to computers and electronic transmission to produce content and distribute it to targeted audiences.

Magazines have already become specialized, as we saw in an earlier chapter. Using computers and demographics, they can target not only the individual magazine but advertising and editorial content within the magazine; this trend will continue into the 1990s. Twenty years ago, for example, you might have read *Time* or *Newsweek* for a variety of general news, such as sports, science, politics, and art. But as you grew in your profession, let's say science, these magazines could not provide specific enough science information, and so you subscribed to a more specialized magazine, let's say *Science.* As you became even more specialized, you added additional specialized magazines and journals to your subscription list. Now you've got *Time, Science,* and *Biological Sciences.* Then you added the *Journal of Microbiology,* later the *Quarterly on Lasers in Microbiology,* and finally the newsletter *Purple Lasers in Microbiology.*

That's typical of the way magazines have specialized. But now magazines can also put specialized information under the same title. Your subscription of *Time* already has regionalized advertising, and in the future, it may have personalized ads. That is, your copy of *Time* may have more ads for scientific products than your neighbor's copy. He's more interested in sports, and so his copy will have more sports ads. And of course that can apply to editorial content as well.

Books are becoming more personalized, too. Information stored on microfilm and microfiche can be retrieved by computer and assembled, a hard copy made and bound together in a folder, and you have a customized book. Information stored in a computer, without microfiche and microfilm, can be custom assembled in an infinite variety of configurations, and when printed out in hard copy and bound together, it can form a personalized book.

Libraries welcome these developments as it allows them to save storage space. The Library of Congress is starting to put texts and periodicals on 12-inch discs, which are indestructible and can be used by many people at the same time. Some predict that in the near future all materials will be computerized at time of publication.

Publishers are using the new technology with more efficient composition and printing processes to enable them to produce books in small quantities for a highly specialized audience and still make a profit. Some publishers are having authors set their own books in type by doing the original writing on a video display terminal or word-processing machine, producing a tape rather than sheets of paper. The tape is then used to generate the composition for the camera-ready copy needed to make the plates for printing. This allows the publisher considerable economic leeway to produce limited editions at a profit. It is estimated that two-fifths of all published authors use computers or word processors instead of typewriters, including former President Carter who wrote *Keeping Faith* on one.

Home computers started coming on the market in 1977, and by 1981 half a million had been sold. By 1982 home computers were selling at the rate of 40,000 to 50,000 a month, at prices ranging from $50 to $2000 or more for a viable machine and accessories. Soon, computers may be used by audiences of mass media almost as much as by communicators. Indeed, computers will allow audiences to become part of the communication process, participating in the organization of messages to fit their own needs.

The combination of home computer, television, and telephone is turning households into communication centers. This development is spurred in part by the increasing rise of energy costs. Many people will stay at home for work and education. Alvin Toffler described the future as the era of the "electronic cottage." And the electronic cottage of the late 1980s and 1990s will be quite different from the homes with TV sets in the 1970s.

In the new electronic cottage we will turn to mass media, not so much for entertainment as for information, education, and work. For rest and relaxation, we may well prefer to get away from video screens and computers. We may turn increasingly to real people and real participation for our entertainment. Toffler predicts that the now-booming home entertainment business of mass media may well go bust in the postindustrial age. "In fact," he says, "entertainment may turn out to be the least important aspect of the TV screen. People will be raging to get out of their houses."

John Naisbett calls this reaction the "high-tech, high-touch" syndrome. As we deal more and more with machines and technology on the job, he says, we want to turn more and more to the personal touch off the job. The rise of computers has been accompanied by a rise in human interaction groups; the rise of televised sports has been accompanied by great increases in jogging, tennis, racquetball, Little League, and hundreds of other rapidly growing popular participatory activities.

The Information Age   Perhaps the most critical trend for the future is the so-called information age. Technology is offering society more information and communication resources than ever before. The resources are so pervasive and their effect so powerful that, according to many media scholars, we are quickly moving into this age. Wilson Dizard, in his book *The Coming Information Age*, says that the United States is the first nation to complete the three-stage shift from an agricultural society to an industrial one to a society whose new patterns are only now emerging. As Dizard points out, the one characteristic of this new age that stands out above all others is the emphasis on the production, storage, and distribution of information.

A report commissioned by the National Science Foundation in 1983 speculates that by the end of this century electronic information technology will have transformed Americans' home, business, manufacturing, school, family, and political life. The report suggests that one-way and two-way home information systems, called teletext and videotext, will penetrate deeply into daily life, with an effect on society as profound as those of the automobile and commercial television earlier in this century.

The report stresses what it calls "transformative effects" of the new technology, the largely unintended and unanticipated social side effects. "Television, for example, was developed to provide entertainment for mass audiences but the extent of its social and psychological side effects on children and adults was never planned for," the report says. "The mass-produced automobile has impacted on city design, allocation of recreation time, environmental policy, and the design of hospital emergency room facilities." Such effects, it adds, were likely to become apparent in home and family life, in the consumer marketplace, in the business office, and in politics.

Widespread penetration of the technology, according to the report, would mean, among other things, these developments: The home will double as a place of employment, with men and women conducting much of their work at the computer terminal. This will affect both the architecture and location of the home. It will also blur the distinction between places of residence and places of business, with uncertain effects on zoning, travel patterns, and neighborhoods.

Home-based shopping will permit consumers to control manufacturing directly, ordering exactly what they need for "production on demand."

There will be a shift away from conventional workplace and school socialization. Friends, peer groups, and alliances will be determined electronically, creating classes of people based on interests and skills rather than age and social class.

A new profession of information "brokers" and "managers" will emerge, serving as "gatekeepers," monitoring politicians and corporations and selectively releasing information to interested parties.

With the home becoming a communications center around which the lives of families will increasingly revolve, the family structure, interrelationships outside the home, living patterns, the physical environment, and social, cultural, and commercial institutions—in short, society as we know it—will be revolutionized. Closer knit families reminiscent of preindustrial farm families, when mobility and social contacts and activities were limited, may evolve, along with the tension such close interaction can bring. It could also lead to the extinction of that time-honored method of getting out of the house for teenagers—going to the movies, and with the increase of businesses operated from the home by computer and telecommunication connections, bring back the cottage industry society of the eighteenth century, doubling the amount of time husband and wife spend together in a lifetime! Such changes in society have tremendous implications for the relationship between sexes, traditional male–female roles, and the community as a whole. The building of mass transit systems, sports complexes, malls, office buildings, conference centers, schools, libraries, and places of worship will naturally be affected by their degree of displacement by this window on the world—the home communications center—and will have to be redesigned accordingly.

"I believe totally that man's lifestyle will change because of the new wired society," said Michael Dann, a former commercial television programmer and a leading television consultant. He was referring specifically to cable, but could just as easily have been referring to any one of the technological "wonders" that populate and are beginning to dominate our society.

Dann, the developer of the Qube system for Warner Communications, predicts that in the America of the 1990s cable television will offer up to 220 different channels of services and entertainment, catering to individual needs and tastes such as bridge, dieting, education, computer games, and religion. Most homes will not only have cable but videodisc or videotape playback machines, plus several television sets with screens ranging from a few inches to several feet. Instead of routine trips to do routine errands, electronic catalogues will allow the consumer to order food, information, clothing, books, conduct banking and business, even vote from the privacy and comfort of the home via cable and telephone lines hooked up to computers that function much like big office industrial units. They have keyboards and display numerical and verbal information on the television screen. Video teleconferencing which ties several office locations together electronically in order to have a business meeting can also include the participant from the home, by using the phone lines or cable wires to patch in a particular communications network. In addition, a personal computer in the den of the user can send and receive electronic mail and connect with his or her company's central data files and office systems directly. From these sources enough information can be retrieved to compile and produce graphics, spread sheets, and reports, freeing an individual from unnecessary time spent in travel and office overhead, saving the company money.[1]

1984 and Beyond

It seems, then, that the future of mass media may be considerably different from the present, and if so, these changes will certainly affect our way of life. The major use of mass media will shift to information and education. If that is the case, the importance of mass communicators will grow, for they will be called upon in ever-growing numbers to gather, process, and make judgments about the data that will be put into the storage banks for personal and specialized use.

The mass media of the future can offer far greater access to information than is available today. And if we have more information at our fingertips, we will be able to make more personal choices about the alternatives in our lives and about our lifestyles. The greater the array from which we can choose, the freer we will be as human beings.

Thus, if the mass media keep moving in the direction of increased choice and personalization, we can be optimistic about the future. Instead of turning us into mass robots manipulated by the big brothers of George Orwell's *1984*, the mass media can become the instruments that enable each individual human being to live a free, full, and rich personal life as he or she desires. That is the goal of a free and good society.

The directions that new technology takes may also create problems and concerns, however. The awesome technology that George Orwell wrote about in 1948 has passed from fantasy into reality. "Big Brother" is as much a possibility as individual freedom, and it is clear that we cannot simply accept technology as passive and neutral. Technology by itself cannot create tyranny, but it can be used by people to serve it. As Peter C. T. Ellsworth, an Orwellian scholar, notes in *Channels* magazine:

---

[1] Peter and Sandra Klinge, *Mass Media: Past, Present, Future* (West Publishing, 1983), 412–413.

Young computer buffs succeed in gaining access to the strategic nuclear weapons system of the U.S. Department of Defense in the motion picture *War Games*.

It is simply not enough to dismiss Orwell's vision as an overly feverish nightmare. Information is power, and keeping power from evil, greedy, or stupid people is one of the enduring problems of political thought. Unless we can be sure that we have strict safeguards against misuse of the new communications technologies, our doubts will lead at best to the climate of fear and distrust described in *Nineteen Eighty-Four*. At worst, our fears could quite easily be realized.[2]

Another consideration of the new technologies is security. Who knows who is listening out there? As private telecommunications executives well know, networks of all types can be tapped.

Like the movie *WarGames*, where kids tap into military computers, it happened for real in 1983. Inspired by the movie, a group of young people made a computer raid on a nuclear weapons laboratory before the government stepped in. One 21-year-old participant said it was really easy to do; it didn't take too much intelligence. James Breen, public affairs officer for the Los Alamos National Laboratory confirmed the raid from home computers which gained access to other computers, via a local TELENET telephone number.

While the new technology allows for greater accuracy in marketing to target audiences at the risk of loss of privacy, it also allows for greater

---

[2] Peter C. T. Ellsworth, "The Menace of the Machine," *Channels* Vol. 3, No. 3, September/ October, 1983, pp. 67–72.

efficiency in government at the cost of the nation's security. Instead of President Reagan or his staff sending a written message to a Cabinet member by messenger through the streets of the Capital, they sent it at the speed of light by a computer located 431 miles away in Columbus, Ohio. The use of this new electronic mail system, called Executive Data Link, connects 200 officials—some of the most influential people in Washington.

One of the implications of this new mobility and versatility is that the environment for decision making will change. How, when, where, with whom, and within what time frame a decision is made can tremendously influence the course of events.

This interconnecting system is only in its initial phase, with the upgrading of automatic data processing and telecommunications on a government-wide basis the end objective. The goal raises once again the question of privacy to individuals, as well as possible breaches of security when highly confidential material is some day sent through an electronic network which, with the proper expertise, can be tapped into. David Burnham writes in the *New York Times*:

> The potential hazard of unifying the computerized data bases of the major Federal agencies has long worried civil liberties advocates and was a factor in the enactment in 1974 of the Privacy Protection Act. Some Congressional experts, too, are worried about making it easier for agencies to compare information about individuals whose data are contained in different Government computers. They fear that such matching might, for example, be used to track political opponents or that information from tax returns, provided by taxpayers in the belief that it would be used only for tax purposes, might be used for unrelated matters.[3]

In addition to Orwellian concerns about technology and tyranny, other media scholars have been concerned with the problems of technology and communication. James W. Carey, Dean of the College of Communications at the University of Illinois, in an essay for the *Chronicle of Higher Education*, wrote:

> There is an old saw . . . that improvements in communication make communication more difficult. Nowhere is the contradiction felt with more force than in the growth of a worldwide linked system of communication through cable, computer and satellite.
> While we live with this technological marvel of communication and organized intelligence and information, we also live with deep fissures and fractures, with active conflicts and unintelligibility that are as great as ever— or greater. It seems as if the ability to convert knowledge into forms that can

---

[3] *The New York Times*, September 23, 1983, p. 38.

be transmitted and utilized by highly technological systems dries up the interpretive capacity to understand other people. The technical system, for all its power, is in many ways superficial and creates problems with mutual understanding: the ability to grasp an argument, listen to people who speak with foreign accents, and interpret complex cultures that are not one's own.[4]

Ultimately, the future of mass communication, of our society, and of the world depends on the people who live and work in it. The future is no more and no less than the sum of the individual futures of all of us. In mass communication, the future depends on those who are reading this book. It is your future, your career, that will ultimately determine the media's future. Serve that future well.

[4] James W. Carey, "Point of View," *The Chronicle of Higher Education*, April 17, 1984, p. 71.

30 Research Materials and A Selected Bibliography

This section is designed to provide a survey of materials used in the preparation of this book and sources of information for additional study in mass communication. Rather than offer nothing more than a standard bibliographic list, an attempt has been made to annotate major works, describe important periodicals, and provide a list of organizations involved in various phases of mass communication operations.

It is difficult to produce an up-to-date bibliography in a field that is changing as rapidly as mass communication. Therefore, this section is designed primarily to provide major sources useful for the student interested in independent study.

MATERIALS FOR USE IN THE STUDY OF MASS COMMUNICATION

This section attempts to provide a variety of sources of information for research in mass communication. It is designed to assist the beginner and in no way purports to be *the* final word in research possibilities.

Four divisions have been established to help speed up the source-selection process: (1) general reference materials, (2) organizations involved in mass communication activities, (3) a selected bibliography of periodicals, and (4) a selected bibliography of books. The bibliographies of periodicals and books are divided according to medium (books, newspapers, magazines, television, radio, motion pictures, recordings, cross media), and the area of advertising/public relations.

Part of the beginner's horror of research derives from a lack of knowledge concerning where to start. The teacher can ease the situation by identifying materials paramount to the successful completion of the project. If that information is not forthcoming, start with the available encyclopedias and almanacs and the library's card catalogue (subject headings) and then turn to this list.

General Reference Materials

Ayer Directory of Newspapers, Magazines, and Trade Publication (One Bala Avenue, Bala Cynwyd, PA 19004) published by William Luedke for N. W. Ayer and Sons of New York on an annual basis provides excellent information on print media.

Books in Print is published by R. R. Bowker Co., 1180 Avenue of the Americas, New York, NY 10036, on an annual basis. This source, available in libraries and bookstores of most educational institutions, annually lists all available books from 1600 publishers by author and title. The *Subject Guide to Books in Print* is also produced annually by R. R. Bowker and is the subject index to *BIP*. It uses the subject headings and cross references established by the Library of Congress. *Paperbound Books in Print*, another Bowker publication, is divided into three sections: (1) subject, (2) author, and (3) title, to facilitate access to paperbacks.

Broadcasting Yearbook (Broadcasting Publications, Inc., 1735 DeSales Street, N. W. Washington, DC 20036) is *the* sourcebook for the broadcast industry.

Business Periodical Index (H. W. Wilson, New York) provides a cumulative index of approximately 170 advertising, communication, marketing, public relations, and other business periodicals.

Dissertation Abstracts (University Microfilms, 300 North Zeeb Road, Ann Arbor, MI 48106) lists all dissertations written in the field of journalism, mass communication, and speech. Copies of dissertations of interest can be ordered by writing the company. Prices are listed for a copy of each citation.

Editor and Publisher (575 Lexington Avenue, New York, NY 10022) provides statistical data on the newspaper industry.

Encyclopedia of Associations (Gale Research Co., Book Tower, Detroit, MI 48226) is an annual directory listing national and international organizations by category of interest.

Facts on File (460 Park Avenue South) New York, NY 10016, provides a biweekly digest of events and is an excellent source for historical research.

Federal Communications Commission Orders, Opinions, Rules, and Statutes (Pike and Fisher, 1735 DeSales Street, N.W., Washington, DC 20036) is an expensive but invaluable source for research in broadcast law. It provides a complete set of *all* legal decisions made by the FCC, case by case.

Film Literature Index (R. R. Bowker Co., New York) is an annual cumulative index to the international literature of film.

International Literary Market Place (R. R. Bowker Co., New York) is a general, annual analysis of publishing internationally.

International Motion Picture Almanac (Quigley Publishing Co., 159 West 53 Street, New York, NY 10019) is an annual industry review with a great deal of data and information.

New York Times Index (New York Times Company, 229 West 43 Street, New York, NY 10036) provides a cumulative index to all articles printed in that newspaper.

Public Affairs Information Service (11 West 40 Street, New York, NY 10018) provides a cumulative index to government-oriented periodicals.

Readers Guide to Periodical Literature (H. W. Wilson, New York) is the largest cumulative index of general-interest magazines.

Standard Periodical Directory. Annual edited by Leon Garry for the Oxbridge Publishing Company (150 East 52 Street, New York, NY 10022) provides excellent data on all periodicals.

The Standard Rate and Data Service (5201 Old Orchard Road, Skokie, IL 60077) publishes directories for media advertising rates plus marketing data. Libraries can obtain the following volumes by writing SRDS: *Business Publications Rates and Data; Canadian Advertising Rates and Data; Daily Newspaper Rates and Data; Direct Mail Rates and Data; Network* (TV and Radio) *Rates and Data; Outdoor Advertising Circulation Rates and Data; Spot Radio Rates and Data; Spot Television Rates and Data; Transit Advertising Rates and Data;* and *Weekly Newspaper Rates and Data.*

Television Almanac (Quigley Publishing Co., 159 West 53 Street, New York, NY 10019) is an annual review of the television industry.

Television Factbook (Television Digest, Inc., 1836 Jefferson Avenue, N.W., Washington, DC 20035) is a major trade reference for the broadcasting industry and is published annually.

Topicator (Thompson Bureau, 5395 South Miller Street, Littleton, CO 80120) is a cumulative index of magazines in the advertising and broadcasting trade press.

Organizations Involved in Mass Communication Activities

There are times during research when standard printed sources do not provide needed information, and the student may want to turn to professional or educational organizations for assistance. Most groups are willing to help if the *specific* question asked does not require excessive work on their part. It is extremely important that persons seeking information be very clear as to what they are requesting.

The Academy of Motion Picture Arts and Sciences (8949 Wilshire Boulevard, Beverly Hills, CA 90211) is the organization that each year presents awards known as the "Oscar" for meritorious achievement in various areas of film work. It also maintains a 12,500-volume library.

The A. C. Nielsen Company (Nielsen Plaza, Northbrook, IL 60062) is a major marketing and audience-research organization. It provides industry measurements of local and national television audiences. Nielsen will furnish assistance upon request and supply special publications regarding broadcasting research.

Action for Children's Television (46 Austin Street, Newtonville, MA 02160) is a consumer action group designed to encourage and support quality programming for children. Maintains resource library.

The Advertising Research Foundation (3 East 54 Street, New York, NY 10022) is designed to further scientific advertising and marketing research to improve the content of advertisements and media plans. It maintains a library of over 2100 volumes.

The American Association of Advertising Agencies (200 Park Avenue, New York, NY 10017) is an association that promotes the interests of agency owners.

The American Broadcasting Company (1330 Avenue of the Americas, New York, NY 10019) is one of the three major TV networks and provides four network-radio services to affiliated stations.

The American Federation of Television and Radio Artists (1350 Avenue of the Americas, New York, NY 10019) is the major union representing broadcast performers.

The American Film Institute (John F. Kennedy Center for the Performing Arts, Washington, DC 20566) is an important data source for researchers in film.

The American Marketing Association (222 South Riverside Plaza, Chicago, IL 60606) is a very helpful organization of marketing and market-research for students of the mass media.

The American Newspaper Publishers Association (11600 Sunrise Valley Drive, Reston, VA 22091) is an organization representing newspaper management. It maintains a library of over 5000 volumes.

The American Society of Magazine Editors (575 Lexington Avenue, New York, NY 10022) is an important source of data about current trends in that medium.

American Women in Radio and Television, Inc. (1321 Connecticut Avenue, N.W., Washington, DC 20036) is a source of employment statistics in the broadcasting field.

The Arbitron Co. (1350 Avenue of the Americas, New York, NY 10019) provides measurement of local radio and television audiences. Special reports and copies of its research are available upon request.

The Association of American Publishers (One Park Avenue, New York, NY 10016) speaks for all aspects of the publishing industry.

The Association of National Advertisers (155 East 44 Street, New York, NY 10017) is an organization of regional and national manufacturers (general advertisers) concerned with company, rather than agency, problems.

The Association of Motion Picture and Television Producers (8480 Beverly Boulevard, Hollywood, CA 90048) is a source of film and television industry statistics.

The Broadcast Pioneers (320 West 57 Street, New York, NY 10019) contains the important Broadcast Industry Reference Center for historical research.

The Broadcast Rating Council (420 Lexington Avenue, Room 2347, New York, NY 10017) is able to provide information on ratings procedures and current policy.

The Columbia Broadcasting System, Inc. (51 West 52 Street, New York, NY 10019) is a national television and radio network and is most helpful in answering academic inquiries.

The Comics Magazine Association of America (60 East 42 Street, New York, NY 10017) is the self-regulation agency of the comic book industry.

The Corporation for Public Broadcasting (1111 16 Street, N.W., Washington, DC 20036) is a major source of programming for educational radio and TV stations and is funded by the federal government.

The Federal Communications Commission (1919 M Street, N.W., Washington, DC 20554) is the federal regulatory agency of broadcasting and is most helpful in providing specific data for researchers. Most of the FCC's reports and other publications are available through the Government Printing Office at a nominal charge.

The Foundation for Public Relations Research and Education (845 Third Avenue, New York, NY 10022) sponsors and distributes basic research in that field.

International Advertising Association (475 Fifth Avenue, New York, NY 10017) is an organization of international advertisers. It maintains a library of periodicals and reference works.

The International Radio and Television Society (420 Lexington Avenue, New York, NY 10017) is an organization of broadcast executives that conducts student/faculty conferences and awards summer internships.

The Magazine Publishers Association (575 Lexington Avenue, New York, NY 10022) is an organization representing magazine management.

The Motion Picture Association of America (1600 Eye Street, N.W., Washington, DC 20036) is one of the best sources of information on the American film industry.

The National Academy of Television Arts and Sciences (110 West 57 Street, New York, NY 10019) serves to promote improvements in television programming and awards the "Emmy" each year for meritorious achievement.

National Academy of Recording Arts and Sciences (444 Riverside Drive, Burbank, CA 91505) serves to promote improvement in the recording field and awards the "Grammy" each year for recording excellence.

The National Association of Broadcasters (1771 N Street, N.W., Washington, DC 20036) is an organization representing commercial broadcasters in the United States. It is a powerful group and provides extensive information upon specific request.

The National Association of Theater Owners (1500 Broadway, New York, NY 10036) is concerned with chain and local movie-theater operations.

The National Broadcasting Company (NBC) (30 Rockefeller Plaza, New York, NY 10022), a subsidiary of RCA, is one of the three major networks and can assist with research.

The National CATV Association (918 16 Street, N.W., Washington, DC 20006) is an organization that promotes the interests of community-antenna operations in the United States.

The National Newspaper Association (1627 K Street, N.W., Suite 400, Washington, DC 20006) is an organization of publishers and has source materials available to researchers.

The National Newspaper Publishers Association (770 National Press Building, Washington, DC 20045) is an organization of blacks involved in journalism.

National Public Radio (2025 M Street, N.W., Washington, DC 20036) is the network organization for public radio.

The National Radio Broadcasters Association (1705 DeSales Street, N.W., Number 500, Washington, DC 20036) is a good source of general information on radio.

The Newspaper Comics Council (260 Madison Avenue, New York, NY 10016) deals with the problems of newspaper comic strips. It maintains a library and information center.

The Newspaper Information Service (American Newspaper Publishers Association, Sunrise Valley Drive, Reston, VA 22070) is the public relations service of the newspaper industry and is very helpful to researchers.

The Office of Communication of the United Church of Christ (289 Park Avenue South, New York, NY 10010) is one of the most active religious organizations in the field of mass communication, especially broadcasting. This organization is extremely helpful to beginning students in the mass media.

The Public Relations Society of America (845 Third Avenue, New York, NY 10022) is a professional association of public relations practitioners.

The Publishers Information Bureau (575 Lexington Avenue, New York, NY 10022) provides data on magazines for consumers and the public as well as researchers.

The Radio Advertising Bureau (488 Lexington Avenue, New York, NY 10017) is involved in research as to the effectiveness of radio in ad campaigns.

Radio Free Europe (1201 Connecticut Avenue, N.W., Washington, DC 20036) is a broadcasting service beamed into Eastern Europe.

The Radio Information Office (1771 N Street N.W., Washington, DC 20036) is a good source of local radio data.

The Radio-Television News Directors Association (1735 DeSales Street, N.W., Washington, DC 20036) is an organization of broadcast news directors.

Recording Industry Association of America (1633 Broadway, New York, NY 10019) represents companies that manufacture records. Awards gold and platinum records for top-selling songs.

The Television Bureau of Advertising (1345 Avenue of the Americas, New York, NY 10019) provides excellent service for students analyzing TV programming and advertising.

The Television Information Office (745 Fifth Avenue, New York, NY 10022) is sponsored by local television stations and is a good source of TV data.

A Selected Bibliography of Periodicals

This list of magazines has been developed as a selected core for a library used for research in mass communication. Only those magazines primarily concerned with the media or media-related activities have been included. It is assumed that standard consumer and general-interest magazines are available.

Advertising/Public relations

Advertising Age. Crain Communications, Inc. 740 North Rush Street, Chicago, IL 60611.
Advertising Techniques. A.D.A. Publishing Co., Inc., 10 East 39 Street, New York, NY 10016.
Ad Week. A/S/M Communications, 230 Park Avenue, New York, NY 10017.
Journal of Advertising Research. Advertising Research Foundation, 3 East 54 Street, New York, NY 16022.
Journal of Marketing. American Marketing Association, 222 South Riverside Plaza, Chicago, IL 60606.
Journal of Marketing Research. American Marketing Association, 222 Riverside Plaza, Chicago, IL 60606.
Marketing Communications. Joel Harnett, Publisher, 475 Park Avenue South, New York, NY 10016
Marketing; Media Decisions. Decisions Publications, Inc., 342 Madison Avenue, New York, NY 10017.
Marketing Times. Donald Horton, Publisher, 380 Lexington Avenue, New York, NY 10017.
Public Relations Journal. 845 Third Avenue, New York, NY 10022.
Public Relations News. 127 East 80 Street, New York, NY 10021.
Public Relations Quarterly. 44 West Market Street, New York, NY 12572.
Public Relations Review. Communications Research Associates, Inc. 7338 Baltimore Boulevard, College Park, MD 20740.
Publicist. Public Relations Aids, Inc., 221 Park Avenue South, New York, NY 10003.

Books

Book Production Industry. 425 Huehl Road, Building 11B, Box 368, Northbrook, IL 60662.
Publishers Weekly. R. R. Bowker Co., 1180 Avenue of the Americas, New York, NY 10036.
Writer's Digest. F. W. Publishing Corp., 9933 Alliance Road, Cincinnati, OH 45242.

Cross Media/General

Alternative Media. Alternative Press Syndicate, Box 775, New York, NY 10010.
Audio-Visual Communications. 475 Park Avenue South, New York, NY 10016.
Communications Research. Sage Publications, Inc., 275 South Beverly Drive, Beverly Hills, CA 90212.
Journal of Communication. Annenberg School Press, University of Pennsylvania, 3620 Walnut Street C5, Philadelphia, PA 19104.
Media Law Reporter. The Bureau of National Affairs, Inc., 251 25 Street, N.W., Washington, DC 20037.
Public Opinion Quarterly. Columbia University Press, Columbia University, New York, NY 10027.
Variety. 154 West 46 Street, New York, NY 10036.

Magazines

Folio: The Magazine for Magazine Management. Charles Tannen, Publisher, 125 Elm Street, P.O. Box 697, New Canaan, CT 06840.
Media Industry Newsletter. 75 East 55 Street, Suite 201, New York, NY 10022.
Writer. 8 Arlington Street, Boston, MA 02116.

Motion Pictures

Action. Directors Guild of America, 7950 Sunset Boulevard, Los Angeles, CA 90046.
American Cinematographer. P.O. Box 2230, Hollywood, CA 90028.

American Film. American Film Institute, John F. Kennedy Center for the Performing Arts, Washington, DC 20566.

Film Comment. 140 West 65 Street, New York, NY 10023.

Films in Review. Film News Co., 250 West 57 Street, Suite 1527, New York, NY 10021.

Journal of Popular Film and Television. Bowling Green State University, Bowling Green, OH 43403.

Millimeter. 12 East 46 Street, New York, NY 10017.

Take One. Unicorn Publishing Corp., Box 1778 Montreal, Quebec H3B 3L3, Canada.

Newspapers

ASNE Bulletin. American Society of Newspaper Editors, Box 551, 1350 Sullivan Trail, Easton, PA 18042.

Columbia Journalism Review. Columbia University, 700 Journalism Building, New York, NY 10027.

Editor and Publisher. 575 Lexington Avenue, New York, NY 10022.

Fourth Estate. Box 3184 Station C Ottawa, Ontario K1X 4J4, Canada.

Journalism Educator. American Society of Journalism School Administration, Department of Journalism, University of Minnesota, Minneapolis, MN 55455.

Journalism Quarterly. Association for Education in Journalism, 111 Murphy Hall, University of Minnesota, Minneapolis, MN 55455.

Masthead. National Conference of Editorial Writers, P.O. Box 34928, Washington, DC 20034.

Quill. 35 East Wacker Drive, Chicago, IL 60601.

Recordings

Billboard. 9000 Sunset Boulevard, Los Angeles, CA 90069.

Cashbox. 1775 Broadway, New York, NY 10019.

High Fidelity. ABC Leisure Magazines, Inc., Great Barrington, MA 62130.

Rolling Stone. Straight Arrow Publishers, 745 Fifth Avenue, New York, NY 10022.

Television-Radio

Access. National Citizen Committee for Broadcasting, 1028 Connecticut Avenue, N.W., Suite 525, Washington, DC 20036.

ACT News. ACT, 46 Austin Street, Newtonville, MA 02160.

Broadcasting. 1735 DeSales Street, N.W., Washington, DC 20036.

CATV Magazine. Communications Publications Corp, 1900 West Yale, Englewood, CO 80110.

Channels of Communications. Media Commentary Council, Box 2001, Mahopac, NY 10541

Educational & Industrial Television. 51 Sugar Hollow Road, Danbury, CT 06810.

Public Telecommunications Review. NAEB, 1346 Connecticut Avenue, N.W., Suite 1101, Washington, DC 20036.

RTNDA Communicator. 1735 DeSales Street, N.W., Washington, DC 20036.

Satellite Communications. 3900 South Wadsworth Boulevard, Suite 560, Denver, CO 80235.

Television Digest. 1836 Jefferson Place, N.W., Washington, DC 20036.

Television International Magazine. P.O. Box 2430, Hollywood, CA 90028.

Television/Radio Age. Television Editorial Corporation, 666 Fifth Avenue, New York, NY 10017.

TV Communications. Communications Publishing Corp., 1900 West Yale, Englewood, CO 80110.

TV Guide. Triangle Publications, Inc., Radnor, PA 19088.

A Selected Bibliography of Books

The books in the following list have been selected to provide the student with a useful survey of materials available in the field of mass communication. Obviously this list will not contain all the materials necessary for every study undertaken, but if the bibliographies in each of the books listed are carefully examined, the student will be well on the way with his or her literature search.

Advertising/Public Relations

Adler, Richard P., et al. *The Effects of Television Advertising on Children.* Lexington, MA: Lexington Books, 1980. An extensive review of current research along with recommendations for further studies; a revision and update of a 1977 U.S. government report.

Aronoff, Craig E. and Baskin, Otis W. *Public Relations: The Profession and the Practice.* St. Paul, MN: West Publishing Company, 1983.

Bernays, Edward L. *Biography of an Idea: Memoirs of a Public Relations Counsel.* New York: Simon and Schuster, 1965.

Burnett, John J. *Promotion Management: A Strategic Approach.* St. Paul, MN: West Publishing Co., 1984.

Cantor, Bill. *Experts in Action: Inside Public Relations.* New York: Longman Inc., 1984.

Cutlip, Scott M. and Center, Allen H. *Effective Public Relations, Revised Fifth Edition.* Englewood Cliffs, NJ: Prentice-Hall Inc., 1982.

Grunig, James E. and Hunt, Todd. *Managing Public Relations.* New York: Holt, Rinehart and Winston, 1984.

Heighton, Elizabeth J., and Cunningham, Don R. *Advertising in the Broadcast Media.* Belmont, CA: Wadsworth, 1976.

Herpel, George L. and Slack, Steve. *Specialty Advertising: New Dimensions in Creative Marketing.* Irving, TX: Specialty Advertising Association International, 1983.

Hiebert, Ray Eldon. *Courtier to the Crowd.* Ames, IA: Iowa State University Press, 1966.

Kleppner, Otto. *Advertising Procedure.* 7th ed. Englewood Cliffs, NJ: Prentice-Hall, 1979.

Newsom, Doug and Scott, Alan. *This is PR: The Realities of Public Relations,* 2nd ed. Belmont, CA: Wadsworth, 1981.

Norris, James S. *Public Relations.* Englewood Cliffs, NJ: Prentice-Hall, 1984.

Weaver, Clark J. *Broadcast Copywriting as Process: A Practical Approach to Copywriting for radio and television.* New York: Longman Inc., 1984.

Witek, John. *Response Television: Combat Advertising of the 1980s.* Chicago, IL: Crain Books, 1981.

Wright, John W. *The Commercial Connection: Advertising and the American Mass Media.* New York: Dell/Delta Books, 1979.

Books

Dessauer, John P. *Book Publishing: What It Is, What It Does.* New York: Bowker, 1974.

Petersen, Clarence, *The Bantam Story: Thirty Years of Paperback Publishing,* 2nd ed. New York: Bantam, 1975.

Mott, Frank Luther. *Golden Multitudes: The Story of Best Sellers in the United States.* New York: Macmillan, 1947.

Cross Media/General

Agee, Warren K. *Mass Media in a Free Society.* Lawrence, KS: University of Kansas Press, 1969.

Bagdikian, Ben H. *The Information Machines: Their Impact on Men and the Media.* New York: Harper & Row, 1971.

Barber, James David. *The Pulse of Politics: Electing Presidents in the Media Age.* New York: Norton, 1980.

Barrett, Marvin. *Rich News, Poor News: The Alfred I. duPont-Columbia University Survey of Broadcast Journalism.* New York: Crowell, 1978.

Blakely, Robert J. *To Serve the Public Interest: Educational Broadcasting in the United States.* Syracuse, NY: Syracuse University Press, 1979.

Braestrup, Peter. *Big Story: How the American Press and Television Reported and Interpreted the Crisis of Tet 1968 in Vietnam and Washington.* Boulder, CO: Westview, 1977.

Chafee, Zechariah. *Government and Mass Communication.* 2 vols. Chicago: University of Chicago Press, 1947.

Cherry, Colin. *On Human Communication.* Cambridge, Ma: MIT Press, 1978.

Compaine, Benjamin M. *Who Owns the Media? Concentration of Ownership in the Mass Communications Industry.* New York: Harmony Books, 1979.

Czitrom, Daniel J. *Media and the American Mind: From Morse to McLuhan.* Chapel Hill, NC: University of North Carolina Press, 1982.

DeFleur, Melvin L. and Ball-Rokeach, Sandra. *Theories of Mass Communication,* 4th ed. New York: Longman Inc., 1982.

Ewen, Stuart and Ewen, Elizabeth. *Channels of Desire: Mass Images and the Shaping of American Consciousness.* New York: McGraw-Hill Book Company, 1982.

Gayeski, Diane M. *Corporate and Instructional Video.* Englewood Cliffs, NJ: Prentice-Hall, 1983.

Geraci, Philip C. *Photo-Journalism: New Images in Visual Communication,* 3rd ed. Dubuque, IA: Kendall/Hunt Publishing Co., 1984.

Gurevitch, Michael, Bennett, Tony, Curran, James, and Woollacott, Janet. *Culture, Society and the Media.* New York: Methuen, 1982.

Halberstam, David. *The Powers That Be.* New York: Knopf, 1979.

Hall, Edward T. *The Silent Language.* Garden City, NY: Doubleday, 1959.

Haight, Timothy R. *Journalism Trends: Aspen Institute Guide to Print and Electronic Journalism Statistics.* New York: Praeger, 1981.

Helm, Lewis, Hiebert, Ray Eldon, et al., *Informing the People: A Public Affairs Handbook.* New York: Longman, 1981.

Innis, Harold A. *The Bias of Communication.* Toronto, Canada: University of Toronto Press, 1951.

Lawery, Shearon and DeFleur, Melvin L. *Milestones in Mass Communication Research: Media Effects.* New York: Longman, 1983.

Lippmann, Walter. *Public Opinion.* New York: Free Press, 1965.

McLuhan, Marshall. *The Medium Is the Message.* New York: Bantam, 1967.

McLuhan, Marshall. *Understanding Media: The Extensions of Man.* New York: McGraw-Hill, 1964.

McQuail, Denis. *Towards a Sociology of Mass Communication.* London, England: Collier-Macmillan, 1969.

Rivers, William L., Schramm, Wilbur, and Christians, Clifford G. *Responsibility in Mass Communication,* 3rd ed. New York: Harper & Row, 1980.

Rubin, Bernard, ed. *Questioning Media Ethics.* New York: Praeger, 1978.

Schwartz, Tony. *Media: The Second God.* New York: Random House, 1981.

Siebert, Fred S., Peterson, Theodore, and Schramm, Wilbur. *Four Theories of the Press.* Urbana, IL: University of Illinois Press, 1956.

Stein, Jay W. *Mass Media, Education, and a Better Society.* Chicago: Nelson-Hall, 1979.

Tan, Alexis S. *Mass Communication Theories and Research.* Columbus, Ohio: Grid Publishing Inc., 1981.

Tuchman, Gaye, Daniels, Arlene Kaplan, and Benet, James, eds. *Hearth and Home: Images of Women in the Mass Media.* New York: Oxford University Press, 1978.

Wilhoit, G. Cleveland, and deBock, Harold, eds. *Mass Communication Review Yearbook.* Vol. 1. Beverly Hills, CA: Sage, 1980.

Wright, Charles R. *Mass Communication: A Sociological Perspective,* 2nd ed. New York: Random House, 1975.

Ethics

Christians, Clifford G., Rotzoll, Kim B., and Fackler, Mark. *Media Ethics: Cases and Moral Reasoning.* New York: Longman, 1983.

Goodwin, H. Eugene. *Groping for Ethics in Journalism.* Ames, IA: Iowa State University Press, 1983.

Merrill, John C. and Odell, S. Jack. *Philosophy and Journalism.* New York: Longman, 1983.

Thayer, Lee, ed. *Ethics, Morality and the Media.* New York: Hastings House, 1980.

Future of Mass Communication

Cornish, Edward. *Communications Tomorrow: The Coming of the Information Society.* Bethesda, MD: World Future Society, 1982.

Didsbury, Howard F. Jr. *Communications and the Future: Prospects Promises, and Problems.* Bethesda, MD: World Future Society, 1982.

Dizard, Wilson P. Jr. *The Coming Information Age: An Overview of Technology, Economics, and Politics.* New York: Longman, 1982.

Ganley, Oswald and Ganley, Gladys. *To Inform or to Control: The New Communications Network.* New York: McGraw-Hill, 1982.

Haigh, Robert W., Gerbner, George, and Byrne, Richard B. *Communications in the Twenty-First Century.* New York: Wiley, 1981.

Williams, Frederick. *The New Communications.* Belmont, CA: Wadsworth, 1984.

International Mass Communication

Gerbner, George and Siefert, Marsha. *World Communications: A Handbook.* New York: Longman, 1984.

Hamelink, Cees J. *Cultural Autonomy in Global Communications: Planning National Information Policy.* New York: Longman, 1983.

Howkins, John. *Mass Communication in China.* New York: Longman, 1982.

MacBride, Sean. *Many Voices, One World: Towards a New, More Just and More Efficient World Information and Communication Order.* Paris: UNESCO, 1980.

Martin, L. John and Chaudhary, Anju Grover. *Comparative Mass Media Systems.* New York: Longman, 1983.

Merrill, John C. *Global Journalism.* New York: Longman, 1983.

Magazines

Anderson, Elliott, and Kinzie, Mary. *The Little Magazine in America: A Modern History.* Yonkers, NY: Pushcart Press, 1978.

Ford, James L. C. *Magazines for the Millions.* Carbondale, IL: Southern Illinois University Press, 1970.

Mott, Frank Luther. *A History of American Magazines.* Cambridge, MA: Harvard University Press, 1957.

Peterson, Theodore. *Magazines in the Twentieth Century.* Urbana, IL: University of Illinois Press, 1964.

Taft, William H. *American Magazines for the 1980s.* New York: Hastings House, Publishers, 1982.

Tebbel, John. *The American Magazine: A Compact History.* New York: Hawthorn, 1969.

Motion Pictures

Balio, Tino, ed. *The American Film Industry.* Madison, WI: University of Wisconsin Press, 1976.

Bobker, Lee R. *Elements of Film.* 2nd ed. New York: Harcourt, 1976.

Bohn, Thomas and Stromgren, Richard. *Light and Shadows: A History of Motion Pictures.* 2nd ed. Palo Alto, CA: Mayfield Publishing, 1978.

Cook, David. *A History of Narrative Film.* New York: Norton, 1981.

Ellis, Jack, Derry, Charles, and Kern, Sharon. *The Film Book Bibliography, 1940–1975.* Metuchen, NJ: Scarecrow Press, 1979.

Ellis, Jack C. *A History of Film.* Englewood Cliffs, NJ: Prentice-Hall, 1979.

Gianetti, Louis D. *Understanding Movies.* 2nd ed. Englewood Cliffs, NJ: Prentice-Hall, 1976.

Guback, Thomas H. *International Film Industry.* Bloomington, IN: Indiana University Press, 1969.

Haskell, Molly. *From Reverence to Rape: The Treatment of Women in the Movies.* New York: Holt, Rinehart and Winston, 1972.

Jacobs, Lewis. *The Documentary Tradition.* 2nd ed. New York: Norton, 1979.

Jowett, Garth, and Linton, James M. *Movies as Mass Communication.* Beverly Hills, CA, and London, England: Sage, 1980.

Mast, Gerald. *A Short History of the Movies,* 3rd ed. Indianapolis: Bobbs-Merrill, 1981.

Monaco, James. *American Film Now: The People, Power, Money, Movies.* New York: Oxford University Press, 1979.

Perkins, V. F. *Film as Film.* New York: Pelican/Penguin, 1972.

Rosenthal, Alan. *The Documentary Conscience: A Casebook in Film Making.* Berkeley: University of California Press, 1979.

Rotha, Paul, Road, Sinclair, and Griffith, Richard. *Documentary Film.* New York: Hastings House, 1963.

Schumach, Murray. *The Face on the Cutting Room Floor: The Story of Movie and Television Censorship.* 2nd ed. New York: Morrow, 1979.

Sklar, Robert. *Movie Made America.* New York: Random House, 1975.

Stephenson, Ralph, and Debrix, J. R. *The Cinema as Art.* London, England: Penguin, 1969.

Newspapers

Bernstein, Carl, and Woodward, Bob. *All The President's Men.* New York: Simon and Schuster, 1974.

Chalmers, David Mark. *The Social and Political Ideas of the Muckrakers.* Secaucas, NJ: Citadel, 1964.

Compaine, Benjamin M. *The Newspaper Industry in the 1980s.* White Plains, NY: Knowledge Industry Publications, 1980.

Emery, Edwin. *The Press and America.* Englewood Cliffs, NJ: Prentice-Hall, 1972.

Merrill, John C., and Fisher, Harold A. *The World's Greatest Dailies.* New York: Hastings House, 1980.

Mott, Frank Luther. *American Journalism.* New York: Macmillan, 1964.

Schudson, Michael. *Discovering the News: A Social History of American Newspapers.* New York: Basic Books, 1978.

Smith, Anthony. *Goodbye Gutenberg: The Newspaper Revolution of the 1980's.* New York and Oxford, England: Oxford University Press, 1980.

Recordings

Denisoff, R. Serge. *Solid Gold: The Popular Record Industry.* New Brunswick, NJ: Transaction Press, 1974.

Gillett, Charlie. *The Sound of the City.* New York: Outerbridge & Dienstfrey, 1972.

Mattfeld, Julius. *Variety Music Calvacade.* Englewood Cliffs, NJ: Prentice-Hall, 1962.

Murrell, Joseph. *The Book of Golden Discs.* London: Barrie & Jenkins, 1978.

Pichaske, David. *A Generation in Motion: Popular Music and Culture in the Sixties.* New York: Schirmer Book/Macmillan, 1979.

Regulation

Ashley, Paul P. *Say it Safely: Legal Limits in Publishing, Radio, and Television.* 5th ed. Seattle: University of Washington Press, 1976.

Brenner, Daniel L. and Rivers, William L. *Free but Regulated: Conflicting Traditions in Media Law.* Ames, IA: Iowa State University Press, 1982.

Chamberlin, Bill F. and Brown, Charlene J. *The First Amendment Reconsidered: New Perspectives on the Meaning of Freedom of Speech and Press.* New York: Longman, 1982.

Denniston, Lyle W. *The Reporter and the Law: Techniques of Covering the Courts.* New York: Hastings House, 1980.

Foley, John, Lobdell, Robert C., and Trounson, Robert. *The Media and the Law.* Los Angeles: Times Mirror Press, 1977.

Lofton, John, *The Press as Guardian of the First Amendment.* Columbia, SC: University of South Carolina Press, 1980.

Pember, Don R. *Mass Media Law.* Dubuque, IA: William C. Brown, 1977.

Television

Adler, Richard P. *Understanding Television: Essays on Television as a Social and Cultural Force.* New York: Praeger, 1981.

Arlen, Michael J. *Thirty Seconds.* New York: Farrar, Straus and Giroux, 1980.

Arlen, Michael J. *The View from Highway 1.* New York: Ballantine, 1977.

Baldwin, Thomas F. and McVoy, D. Stevens. *Cable Communication.* Englewood Cliffs, NJ: Prentice-Hall, Inc., 1983.

Barrett, Marvin, and Sklar, Zachary. *The 7th duPont-Columbia Survey of Broadcast Journalism.* New York: Lippincott and Cromwell, 1980.

Barnouw, Erik. *A History of Broadcasting in the United States.* 3 vols. New York: Oxford University Press, 1966, 1968, 1970.

Barnouw, Enk. *The Sponsor: Notes on a Modern Potentate.* New York: Oxford University Press, 1978.

Barnouw, Erik. *Tube of Plenty: The Evolution of American Television.* New York: Oxford University Press, 1975.

Bleum, A. William. *Documentary in American Television.* New York: Hastings House, 1964.

Blakely, Robert J. *To Serve the Public Interest: Educational Broadcasting in the United States.* Syracuse, NY: Syracuse University Press, 1979.

Brooks, Tim, and Marsh, Earle. *Complete Directory of Prime-Time Network TV Shows.* New York: Ballantine Books, 1979.

Brown, Les. *Les Brown's Encyclopedia of Television.* New York: Zoetrope, 1982.

Cantor, Muriel G. *Prime-Time Television: Content and Control.* Beverly Hills, CA: Sage, 1980.

Charren, Peggy and Sandler, Martin. *Changing Channels: Living (sensibly) with Television.* Reading, MA: Addison-Wesley, 1983.

Comstock, George. *Television in America.* Beverly Hills, CA: Sage, 1980.

Comstock, George, et al. *Television and Human Behavior.* New York: Columbia University Press, 1978.

Diamant, Lincoln, ed. *The Broadcast Communications Dictionary.* 2nd ed. New York: Hastings House, 1978.

Eastman, Susan Tyler, Head, Sydney W., and Klein, Lewis. *Broadcast Programming: Strategies for Winning Television and Radio Audiences.* Belmont, CA: Wadsworth, 1981.

Epstein, Edward Jay. *News from Nowhere: Television and the News.* New York: Random House, 1973.

Esslin, Martin. *The Age of Television.* San Francisco: Freeman, 1982.

Fiske, John, and Hartley, John. *Reading Television.* New York: Methuen, 1979.

Gans, Herbert J. *Deciding What's News: A Study of CBS and NBC News, Newsweek and Time.* New York: Pantheon, 1979.

Gross, Lynne Schafer. *The New Television Technologies*. Dubuque, IA: Wm. C. Brown, 1983.

Gitlin, Todd. *Inside Prime Time*. New York: Pantheon, 1983.

Goethals, Gregor T. *The TV Ritual: Worship at the Video Alter*. Boston: Beacon Press, 1981.

Himmelstein, Harold. *On the Small Screen: New Directions in Television and Video Criticism*. New York: Praeger, 1981.

Levinson, Richard and Link, William. *Stay Tuned: An Inside Look at the Making of Prime-Time Television*. New York: St. Martin's Press, 1981.

Lichty, Lawrence W., and Topping, Malachi C., eds. *American Broadcasting: A Source Book on the History of Radio and Television*. New York: Hastings House, 1975.

MacDonald, J. Fred. *Don't touch that Dial! Radio Programming in American Life, 1920-1960*. Chicago: Nelson-Hall, 1979.

Linsky, Martin, *Television and the Presidential Elections*. Lexington, MA: Lexington Books, 1983.

Marc, David. *Demographic Vistas: Television in American Culture*. Philadelphia, PA: University of Pennsylvania Press, 1984.

McGinniss, Joe. *The Selling of the President, 1968*. New York: Trident, 1969.

McNeil, Alex. *Total Television: A Comprehensive Guide to Programming from 1948 to 1980*. New York: Penguin, 1980.

Newcomb, Horace and Alley, Robert S. *The Producer's Medium: Conversations with Creators of American TV*. New York: Oxford University Press, 1983.

Newcomb, Horace, ed. *Television: The Critical View*. New York: Oxford University Press, 1979.

Noble, Grant. *Children in Front of the Small Screen*. Beverly Hills, CA: Sage, 1975.

Paley, William S. *As It Happened: A Memoir*. Garden City, NY: Doubleday, 1979.

Powers, Ron. *The Newscasters*. New York: St. Martin's, 1977.

Quaal, Ward, and Brown, James A. *Broadcast Management: Radio, Television*, 2nd ed. New York: Hastings House, 1975.

Quinlan, Sterling. *Inside ABC: American Broadcasting Company's Rise to Power*. New York: Hastings House, 1979.

Routt, Edd, McGrath, James B., and Weiss, Frederic A. *The Radio Format Conundrum*. New York: Hastings House, 1979.

Saldich, Anne Rawley. *Electronic Democracy: Television's Impact on the American Political Process*. New York: Praeger, 1979.

Shanks, Bob. *The Cool Fire: How to Make it in Television*. New York: Norton, 1976.

Schiller, Don, et al. *CATV Program Origination and Production*. Blue Ridge Summit, PA: TAB Books, 1979.

Sterling, Christopher, and Kittross, John. *Stay Tuned: A Concise History of American Broadcasting*. Belmont, CA: Wadsworth, 1978.

Tuchman, Gaye. *Making News: A Study of the Construction of Reality*. New York: Free Press, 1978.

Wood, Donald, and Wylie, Donald G. *Educational Telecommunications*. Belmont, CA: Wadsworth, 1977.

Turow, Joseph. *Entertainment, Education and the Hard Sell: Three Decades of Network Children's Television*. New York: Praeger, 1981.

Whetmore, Edward Jay. *The Magic Medium: An Introduction to Radio in America*. Belmont, CA: Wadsworth, 1982.